単元パターン別問題集 2025

過去問でやりたいところを連続して演習できる

共通テスト対策
新！虎の巻

JN116664

共通テスト過去問＋センター問題

☞無料質問ができる 'とらサポ' 付き

英語

共通テスト過去問	令和 6 年
共通テスト過去問	令和 5 年
共通テスト過去問	令和 4 年
共通テスト過去問	令和 3 年
共通テスト過去問	令和 3 年 追試
共通テスト試行問題	平成 30 年
共通テスト試行問題	平成 29 年
センター過去問	
令和 2 年～平成 25 年	

単元ごとに
再編集

【リーディング対策】
過去問をテーマ (パターン) 別に練習！
出題形式・時間配分に慣れるぞ！

[テーマ]
① ビジュアル
② 事実・意見
③ 体験
④ データ
⑤ ヒストリー
⑥ 物語・手紙・メール・日記
⑦ 論理的文章

漫画でわかる！
新！虎の巻活用方法！

共通テスト・国公立・中堅私立対策

共通テスト対策 新！虎の巻

共通テスト過去問＋センター問題

A　You are studying about Brazil in the international club at your senior high shool. Your teacher asked you to do research on food in Brazil. You find a Brazilian cookbook and read about fruits used to make desserts.

Popular Brazilian Fruits	
Cupuaçu	**Jabuticaba**
· Smells and tastes like chocolate · Great for desserts, such as cakes, and with yogurt · Brazilians love the chocolate-flavored juice of this fruit.	· Looks like a grape · Eat them within three days of picking for a sweet flavor. · After they get sour, use them for making jams, jellies, and cakes.
Pitanga	**Buriti**
· Comes in two varieties, red and green · Use the sweet red one for making cakes. · The sour green one is only for jams and jellies.	· Orange inside, similar to a peach or a mango · Tastes very sweet, melts in your mouth · Best for ice cream, cakes, and jams

問1　Both *cupuaçu* and *buriti* can be used to make ⬚1⬚ .

① a cake　　② chocolate

③ ice cream　　④ yogurt

問2　If you want to make a sour cake, the best fruit to use is ⬚2⬚ .

① *buriti*　　② *cupuaçu*

③ *jabuticaba*　　④ *pitanga*

B   You are looking at the website for the City Zoo in Toronto, Canada and you find an interesting contest announcement. You are thinking about entering the contest.

Contest!
Name a Baby Giraffe
Let's welcome our newest animal to the City Zoo!

A healthy baby giraffe was born on May 26 at the City Zoo.
He's already walking and running around!
He weighs 66 kg and is 180 cm tall.
Your mission is to help his parents, Billy and Noelle, pick a name for their baby.

How to Enter

◆ Click on the link here to submit your idea for his name and follow the directions.
→ **Enter Here**

◆ Names are accepted starting at 12:00 a.m. on June 1 until 11:59 p.m. on June 7.

◆ Watch the baby giraffe on the live web camera to help you get ideas.
→ **Live web Camera**

◆ Each submission is $5. All money will go towards feeding the growing baby giraffe.

Contest Schedule

June 8	The zoo staff will choose five finalists from all the entries. These names will be posted on the zoo's website by 5:00 p.m.
June 9	How will the parents decide on the winning name? Click on the live stream link between 11:00 a.m. and 12:00 p.m. to find out! → **Live Stream** Check our website for the winning name after 12:00 p.m.

Prizes

All five contest finalists will receive free one-day zoo passes valid until the end of July.
The one who submitted the winning name will also get a special photo of the baby giraffe with his family, as well as a private Night Safari Tour!

問1   You can enter this contest between ☐ 3 ☐.

① May 26 and May 31   ② June 1 and June 7

③ June 8 and June 9   ④ June 10 and July 31

問2   When submitting your idea for the baby giraffe's name, you must ☐ 4 ☐.

① buy a day pass   ② pay the submission fee

③ spend five dollars at the City Zoo   ④ watch the giraffe through the website

問3   If the name you submitted is included among the live finalists, you will ☐ 5 ☐.

① get free entry to the zoo for a day   ② have free access to the live website

③ meet and feed the baby giraffe   ④ take a picture with the giraffe's family

A　You have invited your friend Shelley to join you on your family's overnight camping trip. She has sent a text message to your mobile phone asking some questions.

問1　Shelley asks you if she needs to bring　|　1　|　.

① a blanket　　　　② a jacket

③ sleeping bags　　④ walking shoes

問2　You expect Shelley to　|　2　| tomorrow morning.

① call you as soon as she is ready　　② come to see you at the campsite

③ pick you up in front of your house　　④ wait for you outside her house

B   You have received a flyer for an English speech contest from your teacher, and you want to apply.

The 7th Youth Leader Speech Contest

The Youth Leader Society will hold its annual speech contest. Our goal is to help young Japanese people develop communication and leadership skills.

This year's competition has three stages. Our judges will select the winners of each stage. To take part in the Grand Final, you must successfully pass all three stages.

The Grand Final

Place: Centennial Hall

Date: January 8, 2022

Topic: *Today's Youth, Tomorrow's Leaders*

GRAND PRIZE

The winner can attend
The Leadership Workshop
in Wellington, New Zealand
in March 2022.

Contest information:

Stages	Things to Upload	Details	2021 Deadlines & Dates
Stage 1	A brief outline	Number of words: 150-200	Upload by 5 p.m. on August 12
Stage 2	Video of you giving your speech	Time: 7-8 minutes	Upload by 5 p.m. on September 19
Stage 3		Local Contests: Winners will be announced and go on to the Grand Final.	Held on November 21

Grand Final Grading Information

Content	Gestures & Performance	Voice & Eye Contact	Slides	Answering Questions from Judges
50%	**5 %**	**5 %**	**10%**	**30%**

➤   You must upload your materials online. All dates and times are Japan Standard Time (JST).

➤   You can check the results of Stage 1 and 2 on the website five days after the deadline for each stage.

For more details and an application form, click *here*.

問1 To take part in the first stage, you should upload a ⬛ 3 ⬛ .

① completed speech script   ② set of slides for the speech

③ summary of your speech   ④ video of yourself speaking

問2   From which date can you check the result of the second stage? ⬛ 4 ⬛

① September 14   ② September 19   ③ September 24   ④ September 29

問3   To get a high score in the Grand Final, you should pay most attention to your content and ⬛ 5 ⬛ .

① expressions and gestures   ② responses to the judges

③ visual materials   ④ voice control

A Your dormitory roommate Julie has sent a text message to your mobile phone with a request.

> Help!!!
> Last night I saved my history homework on a USB memory stick. I was going to print it in the university library this afternoon, but I forgot to bring the USB with me. I need to give a copy to my teacher by 4 p.m. today. Can you bring my USB to the library? I think it's on top of my history book on my desk. I don't need the book, just the USB. ♡

> Sorry Julie, I couldn't find it. The history book was there, but there was no USB memory stick. I looked for it everywhere, even under your desk. Are you sure you don't have it with you? I'll bring your laptop computer with me, just in case.

> You were right! I did have it. It was at the bottom of my bag. What a relief!
> Thanks anyway. ☺

問1　What was Julie's request? ☐1

① To bring her USB memory stick　② To hand in her history homework

③ To lend her a USB memory stick　④ To print out her history homework

問2　How will you reply to Julie's second text message? ☐2

① Don't worry. You'll find it.　② I'm really glad to hear that.

③ Look in your bag again.　④ You must be disappointed.

B   Your favorite musician will have a concert tour in Japan, and you are thinking of joining the fan club. You visit the official fan club website.

TYLER QUICK FAN CLUB

Being a member of the **TYLER QUICK (TQ)** fan club is so much fun! You can keep up with the latest news, and take part in many exciting fan club member events. All new members will receive our New Member's Pack. It contains a membership card, a free signed poster, and a copy of **TQ**'s third album **Speeding Up**. The New Member's Pack will be delivered to your home, and will arrive a week or so after you join the fan club.

TQ is loved all around the world. You can join from any country, and you can use the membership card for one year. The **TQ** fan club has three types of membership: Pacer, Speeder, and Zoomer.

Please choose from the membership options below.

What you get (♬)	Membership Options		
	Pacer ($20)	Speeder ($40)	Zoomer ($60)
Regular emails and online magazine password	♬	♬	♬
Early information on concert tour dates	♬	♬	♬
TQ's weekly video messages	♬	♬	♬
Monthly picture postcards		♬	♬
TQ fan club calendar		♬	♬
Invitations to special signing events			♬
20% off concert tickets			♬

◇ Join before May 10 and receive a $10 discount on your membership fee!

◇ There is a $4 delivery fee for every New Member's Pack.

◇ At the end of your 1st year, you can either renew or upgrade at a 50% discount.

Whether you are a Pacer, a Speeder, or a Zoomer, you will love being a member of the **TQ** fan club. For more information, or to join, click _here_.

問1   A New Member's Pack ☐ 3 .

①   includes TQ's first album   ②   is delivered on May 10

③   requires a $10 delivery fee   ④   takes about seven days to arrive

問2   What will you get if you become a new Pacer member? ☐ 4 .

①   Discount concert tickets and a calendar   ②   Regular emails and signing event invitations

③   Tour information and postcards every month   ④   Video messages and access to online magazines

問3   After being a fan club member for one year, you can ☐ 5 .

①   become a Zoomer for a $50 fee   ②   get a New Member's Pack for $4

③   renew your membership at half price   ④   upgrade your membership for free

A You are a member of the English club. You are going to have a farewell party for one of the members, Yasmin from Malaysia. You have received a note from Amelia, an Assistant Language Teacher (ALT) and the club advisor.

Dear members of the English club,

It's about time we decide when to have the English club farewell party for Yasmin. She's leaving Japan on December 15, so the club members should meet sometime next week. Can you ask Yasmin which day is convenient for her to come to the party and let me know? When the day is fixed, I'll help you by planning a few nice surprises. Also, is it all right if I invite other students? I know some students from the tennis team who want to take part because they really had a good time playing tennis with her over the past six months.

Best wishes,
Amelia

問1 The teacher wants you to ask Yasmin ☐1☐ .

① what she would like to eat at the party   ② when she can attend the party

③ where she would like to have the party   ④ who she would like to invite to the party

問2 The teacher would also like to invite ☐2☐ .

① a few students who don't belong to the English club

② all the members of the English club and the tennis team

③ some of Yasmin's other English teachers

④ students who want to study abroad in Malaysia

B   You visited your town's English website and found an interesting notice.

Call for Participants: Sister-City Youth Meeting
"Learning to Live Together"

Our town's three sister cities in Germany, Senegal, and Mexico will each send ten young people between the ages of 15 and 18 to our town next March. There will be an eight-day youth meeting called "Learning to Live Together." It will be our guests' first visit to Japan.

We are looking for people to participate: we need a host team of 30 students from our town's high schools, 30 home-stay families for the visiting young people, and 20 staff members to manage the event.

Program Schedule

March 20	Orientation, Welcome party
March 21	Sightseeing in small four-country mixed groups
March 22	Two presentations on traditional dance: (1) Senegalese students, (2) Japanese students
March 23	Two presentations on traditional food: (1) Mexican students, (2) Japanese students
March 24	Two presentations on traditional clothing: (1) German students, (2) Japanese students
March 25	Sightseeing in small four-country mixed groups
March 26	Free time with host families
March 27	Farewell party

● Parties and presentations will be held at the Community Center.

● The meeting language will be English. Our visitors are non-native speakers of English, but they have basic English-language skills.

To register, click **here** before 5 p.m. December 20.

▶▶ International Affairs Division of the Town Hall

問1   The purpose of this notice is to find people from the host town to ⎡ 3 ⎤ .

①   decide the schedule of activities   ②   take part in the event

③   visit all of the sister cities   ④   write a report about the meeting

問2   During the meeting the students are going to ⎡ 4 ⎤ .

①   have discussions about global issues   ②   make presentations on their own cultures

③   spend most of their time sightseeing   ④   visit local high schools to teach languages

問3   The meeting will be a good communication opportunity because all of the students will ⎡ 5 ⎤ .

①   be divided into different age groups   ②   have Japanese and English lessons

③   speak with one another in English   ④   stay with families from the three sister cities

A   You are planning to go to an amusement park in Hong Kong．You are looking at its webpage.

Blue Stone Hong Kong

BLUE STONE AMUSEMENT PARK

TOP > Crowd Calendar   🔍 [＿＿＿＿＿＿＿]   English | Chinese

This webpage will help you find the best dates to visit Blue Stone Amusement Park.

What's New

A new show titled "Pirates' Adventure" will start on November 13.

Crowd Calender

On the following calendar, you can see the opening and closing times, and the crowd levels. The percentage in each box is an estimate of the number of people expected to be in the park. The maximum, 100%, is shown by the face icon. The percentage is calculated automatically based on advance ticket sales and past data.

On the days with the face icon, entrance to the park will be difficult. Visitors without an advance ticket may have to wait at the entrance gate for a long time. Advance tickets are only available online one week ahead.

By clicking each date on the calendar, you can see detailed information about the average waiting time for each attraction.

Crowd Calendar for November(information updated daily)						
Monday	Tuesday	Wednesday	Thursday	Friday	Saturday	Sunday
5	**6**	**7**	**8**	**9**	**10**	**11**
55%	65%	70%	70%	85%	90%	😖
9:00-17:00	9:00-19:00	9:00-19:00	9:00-19:00	9:00-21:00	9:00-21:00	9:00-21:00
12	**13**	**14**	**15**	**16**	**17**	**18**
55%	😖	😖	90%	85%	😖	90%
9:00-16:00	9:00-21:00	9:00-21:00	9:00-21:00	9:00-21:00	9:00-21:00	9:00-21:00

問1   If you go to the park on November 13 without an advance ticket, at the entrance gate you will probably [1] .

① go straight in   ② have to pay 55% more to enter

③ have to show your parking ticket   ④ stand in a long line

問2   When you click the dates on the calendar, you will find information about [2] .

① how long visitors have to wait for the attractions

② the cost of the advance tickets for the attractions

③ the food and drinks at various park restaurants

④ where visitors can park their cars at Blue Stone

B   You are visiting a Japanese university during its open campus day. You have found a poster about an interesting event.

The Holiday Planning Research Club   **HPRC**

Open Campus Event

HPRC Meeting for High School Students

What is the HPRC?
One of the greatest parts of university life is the lovely long holiday breaks. The Holiday Planning Research Club (HPRC) is run by Japanese and international students. Our club welcomes students from all years and from every department. Our purpose is to help each other make interesting holiday plans.

Date ： Saturday, October 27 from 2:00 until 3:30 p.m.
Place ： The Independent Learning Center
Event ： Four students will tell you about their own recent experiences during their vacations. See the table below for outlines of the presentations.

Speaker	Description	Location
1. Mary MacDonald Department of Agriculture	＊Did hard work in rice and vegetable fields ＊No cost to live with a host family	A farm in Ishikawa Prefecture
2. Fumihiro Shimazu Department of Japanese Language and Culture	＊Prepared teaching materials for a Japanese language teacher ＊Paid his own airfare and insurance	A primary school in Cambodia
3. Risa Nishiura Department of Tourism	＊Assisted foreign chefs with cooking and translation ＊Good pay	A Spanish restaurant in Tokyo
4. Hiroki Kobayashi Department of Education	＊ Taught judo ＊ Free airfare and room	A junior Olympic training camp in Bulgaria

Message for University Students

Join Us as a Speaker at the December HPRC Meeting!
You have a total of 12 minutes. Your talk, in English, should be about 8 minutes. Please prepare slides with photos. After each talk, there is a 4-minute question period and the audience usually asks lots of questions. You can get more information on our website (http://www.hprc-student.net/).

問1   The HPRC is organized and led by ⬚3⬚ .

① NGO staff   ② students   ③ teachers   ④ university staff

問2   You can learn from each of the four speakers about ⬚4⬚ .

① interesting courses in different departments of the university

② low-cost trips to other countries in the world

③ outside-of-class experiences during university breaks

④ volunteer work with children in developing countries

問3   At the December meeting, the HPRC speakers should ⬚5⬚ .

① be ready to answer questions   ② put their speech scripts on the website

③ speak in English and Japanese   ④ talk for about 20 minutes

B　あとにあるフリーマーケットの出店申請の説明を読み，次の問い（問1〜4）の 37 〜 40 に入れる

のに最も適当なものを，それぞれ下の①〜④のうちから一つずつ選べ。

問1　Fran will sell her handmade jewelry on both days. She needs only a small space. How much will it cost ?
37

① 　$ 14 ② 　$ 16 ③ 　$ 18 ④ 　$ 20

問2　Pat wants to sell some big household items, including a refrigerator, so she needs an outdoor space. What
offer can she take advantage of ?　 38

① 　Free assistance in setting up her tent

② 　Full cash refund due to cancelation

③ 　Selection of the location of her space

④ 　Use of a large truck free of charge

問3　Mark makes herbal soaps and candles. He has chosen an indoor space. Which of the following will he be
allowed to do ?　 39

① 　Choose a space close to the sink to get water easily

② 　Have a bowl of water for customers to try his soaps

③ 　Keep his pet hamsters in a cage at his booth

④ 　Let his customers light some sample candles

問4　Which of the following is true about this flea market ?　 40

① 　People are discouraged from selling items they created.

② 　People can throw away anything in the same trash can.

③ 　The organizers choose applicants who apply for both days.

④ 　The organizers provide information about schedule updates.

Greenly Fall Flea Market

We are now accepting applications for the Fall Flea Market at Greenly Sports Center ! Please
bring your used and/or handmade goods. We have only a limited number of spaces and accept
applications in order of arrival, so email your application soon. We are a pet-friendly market, but
if you are planning to bring your pet, you must apply for an outdoor space. For outdoor spaces,
the organizers will help set up tents for no extra charge. Trucks are available for additional fees
if you need to transport your goods.

	Saturday, October 3rd (13:00 – 17:00)	Sunday, October 4th (10:00 – 15:00)
Indoor space (2 × 2 meters)	$ 8	$ 10
Outdoor space (4 × 4 meters)	$ 9	$ 11

▶　Water is available for indoor spaces.

▶　If you apply for both Saturday and Sunday, you'll get a $ 2 discount each day.

Keep in Mind

1. Location of the spaces is decided by the organizers. No requests or changes are possible.

2. Any changes in opening and closing times are announced two days in advance.

3. If you cancel your application, 80% of all fees will be refunded.

4. Garbage must be separated and put into the appropriate garbage cans at the end of each day.

5. Fires and open flames are prohibited.

B　あとの，ある地域の城に関する案内を読み，次の問い（**問1〜4**）の　37　〜　40　に入れるのに最も適当なものを，それぞれ下の①〜④のうちから一つずつ選べ。

問1　What is a common characteristic of all four castles ?　37

①　Amount of damage

②　Displays of pictures and weapons

③　Histories of more than 500 years

④　Purposes of construction

問2　Three guitar club members from Grandlefolk University want to give a concert one afternoon in April. Which castle are they most likely to choose ?　38

①　Crestvale Castle　　②　Holmsted Castle　　③　King's Castle　　④　Rosebush Castle

問3　Teachers at one school want to take their students to Grandlefolk one Saturday in May. The purpose is to expand the students' knowledge of the area's history by visiting castles and listening to explanations from the castle staff. Which two castles are the teachers most likely to select ?　39

①　Crestvale Castle and Holmsted Castle

②　Crestvale Castle and King's Castle

③　Rosebush Castle and Holmsted Castle

④　Rosebush Castle and King's Castle

問4　A mother, father, and their two children, ages 4 and 8, will visit one of the castles in Grandlefolk for one day in September and want to see fine arts. How much will it cost ?　40

①　€14　　②　€17　　③　€20　　④　€25

Castles in Grandlefolk

Crestvale Castle

This ruined 13th-century castle, built to defend the northern border of Grandlefolk, is currently being studied by researchers. During the open season, except on Sundays, guides explain what the research is revealing about local history.

Holmsted Castle

Holmsted Castle, built in the 12th century to protect the southern border area, fell into ruin in the 16th century. At the entrance, signboards explain its history. This castle's open spaces are suitable for performances.

King's Castle

Dating back to the 11th century, King's Castle is one of the grandest in the country. Its large collection of paintings and furniture provide a look at the area's past. Guides are available every day.

Rosebush Castle

Though called a castle, this perfectly preserved 15th-century building was constructed purely as a family home. From Mondays to Fridays, guides tell the story of the family's history and explain their collection of modern sculptures. Some of its rooms are available for public events.

	Opening Times		Daily Admission	
	Months	Hours	Adults	Children (5-16 years old) *
Crestvale Castle	April–October	10:00–16:00	€3	€1
Holmsted Castle	April–September	10:00–17:00	€5	€2
King's Castle	April–November	10:00–18:00	€7	€3
Rosebush Castle	April–July	9:00–12:00	€10	€5

＊ Children under 5 years old are admitted free of charge.

B　次の料理教室に関する広告を読み，次の問い（**問1～4**）の 37 ～ 40 に入れるのに最も適当なもの を，それぞれ下の①～④のうちから一つずつ選べ。

問1　What inspired Ralph Bearison to start Papa Bear Cooking School ?　37
①　He knew his family and friends were jealous of his cooking skills.
②　He knew that fathers were not interested enough in cooking.
③　He wanted to give fathers opportunities to become professional cooks.
④　He wanted to teach fathers to cook quick, delicious, and healthy meals.

問2　Tony is going to participate in the French Course and use the discount coupon provided. He will also buy an apron-and-towel set from the school. How much will he pay in total ?　38
①　$ 270　②　$ 275　③　$ 285　④　$ 300

問3　Ed hopes to expand the variety of food he can cook for his family. He has no free time on weekends or mornings. Which cooking course would he most likely take ?　39
①　Chinese　②　Italian　③　Japanese　④　Sunday Family Breakfast

問4　The advertisement suggests that 40 .
①　12-year-old children can participate in the Sunday course at no cost
②　Cooking Courses for Fathers will last longer than three months
③　Papa Bear Cooking School requires students to bring ingredients to classes
④　students at Papa Bear Cooking School can eat the food they cook

---

Papa Bear Cooking School :
Cooking Courses for Fathers

Papa Bear Cooking School was established in 1992 by Ralph Bearison. He recognized that many fathers liked to cook but often didn't have enough time to prepare meals.
He hoped to share his interest in cooking meals in a short time that would taste good and be good for their families. At Papa Bear Cooking School, you can learn to create a variety of meals under the guidance of professional cooks, making you the envy of your family and friends. The following cooking courses start in the first week of May.

Cooking Course	Day	Time	Course Fee
Italian	Tuesday	10 : 00–12 : 00	$ 150
French	Wednesday	9 : 00–12 : 00	$ 250
Japanese	Thursday	15 : 00–18 : 00	$ 250
Chinese	Saturday	17 : 00–19 : 00	$ 200
Sunday Family Breakfast*	Sunday	8 : 00–10 : 00	$ 150

* Children aged 10 to 15 are welcome to join their fathers in the Sunday Family Breakfast Course for $ 100 per child.

▶　All courses are 10 weeks long.
▶　Fees include all ingredients.
▶　Cooking knives, silverware, such as forks and spoons, and plates will be provided by the school.

What to Bring
▶　An apron and towels（You can rent an apron-and-towel set for $ 6 per week or purchase a new set at our store for $ 50.）
▶　An empty stomach !

Check out our Papa Bear Cooking School website for details of our facilities and other cooking courses.

10% Off
Course Fee
Papa Bear
Cooking School

第1回目   第2回目

／3題   ／3題

H 29 4

B　次のビデオ制作コンテストに関するウェブサイトを読み，次の問い（**問1～3**）の　39　～　41　に入れるのに最も適当なものを，それぞれ下の①～④のうちから一つずつ選べ。

問1　The purpose of the IAYP Video Clip Competition is to provide　39　.

①　a place to meet new friends of the same age

②　an airplane ticket to Australia to create a video clip

③　instructions to create a video clip on a computer

④　opportunities for young people to exhibit their works

問2　Members of a high school baseball team will submit a four-minute video clip about their bonds with players from a sister school abroad. Under which category should the video clip be entered ?　40

①　Category A　　②　Category B　　③　Category C　　④　Category D

問3　Which of the following meets the submission requirements for this competition ?　41

①　A nine-minute mystery drama featuring a young Japanese detective

②　A six-minute video clip showing students practicing for a rugby game

③　A three-minute video clip that won third prize at a local film festival

④　A three-minute video clip uploaded to this website on October 30, 2017

Video Clip Competition: Call for Entries

　　The International Association of Young Producers （IAYP） is proud to open its annual Video Clip Competition again this year. This is a great way to share your creations with a wide audience. Anyone aged 25 and under can participate. The IAYP invites submissions in the following four categories :

	Theme	Maximum length
Category A	A topic related to a team sport	3 minutes
Category B	An idea connected to friendship	5 minutes
Category C	A social problem based on a true story	5 minutes
Category D	A mystery with a dramatic ending	7 minutes

　　The deadline is 11 : 59 pm, October 31, 2017 （Japan Standard Time）. The three best clips in each category will be selected by a committee of famous video creators and posted on this website in December. One overall grand champion will be awarded a ticket to the next IAYP Conference in Sydney, Australia. So, don't miss this chance ! Get out your video camera and start filming !

Follow these steps:

▶　Shoot a video and edit it on a computer to an appropriate length for the category you choose.

▶　Click here to enter your details and upload your video clip.

Rules and conditions:

▶　Each person or group can choose only one category.

▶　Only clips sent before the deadline will be accepted.

▶　Clips must be original and submitted to a competition for the first time.

ビジュアル

目標 **5**分　　H 28　④　　　　　　　　　　　　　　　　　／3題　　／3題

B　次の美術館に関するウェブサイトを読み，次の問い（**問1〜3**）の　39　〜　41　に入れるのに最も適当なものを，それぞれ下の①〜④のうちから一つずつ選べ。

問1　Kazuko, a 19-year-old shop assistant, wants to participate in a museum activity but is only free on weekday evenings.　Which activity will she most likely choose ?　39

①　Comprehensive tour　　②　Drawing class　　③　Photography workshop　　④　Short tour

問2　A retired couple and their 6-year-old grandchild wish to participate together in a weekday afternoon activity.　Which activity will they most likely choose and how much will they pay in total ?　40

①　Comprehensive tour, $20　　　　　　　②　Comprehensive tour, $40

③　Short tour, $20　　　　　　　　　　　④　Short tour, $28

問3　Which of the following is true according to the website ?　41

①　Advance booking is not necessary for "Art Talks."

②　Comprehensive tours are held every day.

③　The admission fee is not included in the fees of tours.

④　There are lectures given by amateur artists.

Octagon Museum of Art ☼ M A

Octagon Museum of Art (OMA) offers exhibitions and programs featuring contemporary art such as paintings, sculptures, and photographs.　Established in 1972 by the Octagon Foundation, it has a vast collection with many permanent exhibits, and also offers special exhibits, lectures by professional artists and critics, classes for school children, and tours guided by specialists.

Admission Fee: $5/person　(Children 6 and under — **free**)

Program Fees:

Short tour (90 minutes)	Adult (18+)	$10	Twice daily 9 am & 2 pm
	Student (7-17)	$8	
	Child (6 and under)	free	
Comprehensive tour (3 hours)	Adult (18+)	$20	Tuesday & Saturday 10 am
	Student (7-17)	$15	
	Child (6 and under)	free	
Drawing class (90 minutes)	Adult (18+)	$15	Monday, 7 pm
	Student (7-17)	$8	Wednesday, 4 pm
	Child (6 and under)	free	Wednesday, 10 am
Photography workshop (2 hours)	Adult (18+)	$17	Sunday, 7 pm
	Student (7-17)	$12	Sunday, 10 am

Notes:

　– The fees for tours, classes, and workshops include the admission fee.

　– Sign up　here　at least a week in advance for tours, classes, and workshops.

　– We also offer "Art Talks," where invited guest speakers talk to adult audiences in OMA Hall every other Saturday.　No reservation or additional fee is required.　For this month's schedule, click　here　.

B　下のキャンプ場に関するウェブサイトを読み，次の問い（**問1～3**）の 39 ～ 41 に入れるのに最も
適当なものを，それぞれ下の①～④のうちから一つずつ選べ。

問1　A man who likes water activities is looking at the website.　Which are the campgrounds he is most likely
to be interested in ?　 39

①　Apricot and Maple Campgrounds　　　②　Maple and Orange Campgrounds
③　Orange and Stonehill Campgrounds　　④　Stonehill and Apricot Campgrounds

問2　Two people are making plans to stay in Green National Park for nine nights.　They want to enjoy nature,
but they need a power supply to use their computers.　How much will they have to pay per night for the site
they are likely to choose ?　 40

①　$20　　②　$24　　③　$32　　④　$96

問3　A family of four is planning a four-day camping trip with their dog.　Their budget for a camp site is under
100 dollars for three nights.　Their main interests for the trip are barbecuing and bicycle riding in the
national park.　Which campground is this family most likely to choose ?　 41

①　Apricot　　②　Maple　　③　Orange　　④　Stonehill

Green National Park Campground Guide

The campgrounds in Green National Park are open from April 1 to November 30.

Apricot Campground

Walking trails from this campground lead you to the top of Green Mountain.
Enjoy the fantastic view from the top.　You can also enjoy cycling on the bike
trails in the woods.

Maple Campground

Maple Campground has direct access to Green River.　Have fun doing such
activities as fishing, boating, and swimming.　You can also enjoy a campfire by
the river.

Orange Campground

This campground is on Orange Lake, and offers a comfortable outdoor
experience.　Water skiing is popular on the lake.　Other activities include
fishing, swimming, and bird-watching.

Stonehill Campground

A pine tree forest surrounds Stonehill Campground.　The giant
pine trees are impressive.　You can see a lot of wild animals while
riding a bicycle or hiking through the forest.

Campground Information

Camp-ground	Site Type (available spaces)	Site Rate/ night	Max. People	Max. Stay	Facilities	Restrictions
Apricot	Tents (15)	$20	4	15 nights	BG	—
Maple	Tents (20)	$24	5	12 nights	BG　PG	—
Orange	Deluxe Cabins (5)	$96	7	7 nights	K　E　HS	No pets
Stonehill	Standard Cabins (10)	$32	6	14 nights	E　HS	No fireworks

Site Rate＝Rate per site (up to the maximum number of people); Max.＝Maximum
K Kitchen, E Electricity, BG Barbecue Grill, HS Hot Shower,
PG Playground

B　下のマラソン大会の申込みに関するウェブサイトを読み，次の問い（問1～3）の 39 ～ 41 に入れるのに最も適当なものを，それぞれ下の①～④のうちから一つずつ選べ。

問1　Which of the following statements is **NOT** true about applying ? 39

① You must apply during the month of August.

② You must be at least 16 years old when you apply.

③ You must enter your application via the Internet.

④ You must submit no more than one application.

問2　A 70-year-old woman living in Lakeville who competed in the 26th marathon will have to pay 40 to participate.

① $10　② $15　③ $25　④ $30

問3　According to the website, which of the following is true ? 41

① You can pay the application and entry fees in cash.

② You have to make all inquiries by phone.

③ You must check online to see if you are accepted.

④ You will have eight hours to finish the race.

The 28th LAKEVILLE MARATHON
February 26, 2015

APPLICATION

➢ Period: August 1 - August 31, 2014 (NO late applications will be accepted.)
➢ Anyone 16 or older on the day of the race may apply for entry.
➢ Online applications only.
➢ One application per person. Multiple applications will be automatically rejected.
➢ Reporting any false personal information will result in elimination.

SELECTION

➢ Unfortunately, due to the size of Lakeville Sports Field, not all applications can be accepted. The 15,000 runners will be determined by lottery.
➢ Applicants will receive their acceptance or rejection letter in mid-October.

PAYMENT

➢ Online credit card payments only.
➢ The application fee cannot be returned. NO exceptions.
➢ The entry fee will be charged only to those selected by lottery.

Category	Application fee*	Entry fee**
Minor (16 or 17)	$15	$25
Adult (18 to 64)	$15	$50
Senior (65 or over)	$15	$15

*No application fee if you live in Lakeville!
**$5 discount if you entered either of the last two Lakeville Marathons!

RACE DAY

➢ Check-in: Opens at 7:00. All participants must present a photo ID (for example, driver's license or passport) and their acceptance letter on the day of the race.
➢ Race schedule: Starts at 8:00/Finishes at 16:00 (Runners who fail to finish by the designated time must stop running.)

For inquiries, contact: marathondesk@lkve.com

CLICK HERE TO APPLY

B　下の写真スタジオの広告を読み, 次の問い (問 1 ～ 3) の　38　～　40　に入れるのに最も適当なものを, それぞれ下の①～④のうちから一つずつ選べ。

問1　Which is true about the studio's services?　38

①　Customers must arrive an hour before the session.

②　Frames come in three different colors.

③　Photographs will be delivered within three business days.

④　Someone on the staff can help customers look great.

問2　How much can non-club members save when they use the Fantastic Package Plan instead of buying the same products individually?　39

①　$20.　　②　$30.　　③　$40.　　④　$50.

問3　Which of the following statements is true?　40

①　As many as five pictures can be included in a Multi-image sheet.

②　Club members need to pay a $40 membership fee every year.

③　Customers can receive a 20th anniversary discount until December 31.

④　You must have a Fantastic Club membership to receive a free gift.

Fantastic Photo Studio

Specializing in Family Portraits

You'll love our elegant traditional photos as well as our more contemporary styles.

Our Services

- Our stylist can help with hair and make-up. You'll look fantastic!
- You can choose the style of your photos: full color, black & white, or sepia.
- Your photo session will take just an hour.
- Your photos will be ready for pickup within 3 business days, guaranteed!

Call us today at 555-456-0721 to schedule an appointment.

Basic Portrait Types (Frames: $20 each)

Single-image sheet			Multi-image sheet
$40	$20	$5	$50
Large	Medium	Wallet-size	Any combination of 2 to 5 photos

Special Offers

$200 Fantastic Package Plan includes:

- 1 Large, 2 Medium, and 8 Wallet-size Single-image sheets
- 2 Multi-image sheets of your choice
- 1 frame for Large Single-image sheet

Fantastic Club Membership

Join the club for just $40, and receive a 20% discount on all our products and services, including the Fantastic Package Plan, for 2 years.

Anniversary Special

Help us celebrate Fantastic Photo Studio's 20th anniversary! Receive a free gift when you have a photo session with us before December 31.

A   You are on a *Future Leader* summer programme, which is taking place on a university campus in the UK. You are reading the information about the library so that you can do your coursework.

Abermouth University Library
Open from 8 am to 9 pm
2022 Handout

Library Card: Your student ID card is also your library card and photocopy card. It is in your welcome pack.

Borrowing Books
You can borrow a maximum of eight books at one time for seven days. To check books out, go to the Information Desk, which is on the first floor. If books are not returned by the due date, you will not be allowed to borrow library books again for three days from the day the books are returned.

Using Computers
Computers with Internet connections are in the Computer Workstations by the main entrance on the first floor. Students may bring their own laptop computers and tablets into the library, but may use them only in the Study Area on the second floor. Students are asked to work quietly, and also not to reserve seats for friends.

Library Orientations
On Tuesdays at 10 am, 20-minute library orientations are held in the Reading Room on the third floor. Talk to the Information Desk staff for details.

Comments from Past Students
● The library orientation was really good. The materials were great, too!

● The Study Area can get really crowded. Get there as early as possible to get a seat!

● The Wi-Fi inside the library is quite slow, but the one at the coffee shop next door is good. By the way, you cannot bring any drinks into the library.

● The staff at the Information Desk answered all my questions. Go there if you need any help!

● On the ground floor there are some TVs for watching the library's videos. When watching videos, you need to use your own earphones or headphones. Next to the TVs there are photocopiers.

問1   ⬚6⬚ are two things you can do at the library.
    A：bring in coffee from the coffee shop   B：save seats for others in the Study Area
    C：use the photocopiers on the second floor   D：use your ID to make photocopies
    E：use your laptop in the Study Area
    ① A and B   ② A and C   ③ B and E   ④ C and D   ⑤ D and E

問2   You are at the main entrance of the library and want to go to the orientation．You need to ⬚7⬚．
    ① go down one floor   ② go up one floor   ③ go up two floors   ④ stay on the same floor

問3   ⬚8⬚ near the main entrance to the library.
    ① The Computer Workstation are   ② The Reading Room is
    ③ The Study Area is   ④ The TVs are

問4   If you borrowed three books on 2 August and returned them on 10 August，you could ⬚9⬚．
    ① borrow eight more books on 10 August   ② borrow seven more books on 10 August
    ③ not borrow any more books before 13 August   ④ not borrow any more books before 17 August

問5   One **fact** stated by a previous student is that ⬚10⬚．
    ① headphones or earphones are necessary when watching videos
    ② the library is open until 9 pm
    ③ the library orientation handouts are wonderful
    ④ the Study Area is often empty

B   You are the editor of a school English paper. David, an exchange student from the UK, has written an article for the paper.

Do you like animals? The UK is known as a nation of animal-lovers; two in five UK homes have pets. This is lower than in the US, where more than half of homes have pets. However, Australia has the highest percentage of homes with pets!

Why is this so? Results of a survey done in Australia give us some answers.

Pet owners mention the following advantages of living with pets:
→   The love, happiness, and friendship pets give (90%);
→   The feeling of having another family member (over 60% of dog and cat owners);
→   The happy times pets bring. Most owners spend 3-4 hours with their 'fur babies' every day and around half of all dog and cat owners let their pets sleep with them!

One disadvantage is that pets have to be cared for when owners go away. It may be difficult to organise care for them; 25% of owners take their pets on holidays or road trips.

These results suggest that keeping pets is a good thing. On the other hand, since coming to Japan, I have seen other problems such as space, time, and cost. Still, I know people here who are content living in small flats with pets. Recently, I heard that little pigs are becoming popular as pets in Japan. Some people take their pig (s) for a walk, which must be fun, but I wonder how easy it is to keep pigs inside homes.

問1   In terms of the ratios for homes with pets, which shows the countries' ranking from **highest to lowest**? 11
①   Australia — the UK — the US   ②   Australia — the US — the UK
③   The UK — Australia — the US   ④   The UK — the US — Australia
⑤   The US — Australia — the UK   ⑥   The US — the UK — Australia

問2   According to David's report, one advantage of having pets is that 12 .
①   you can save money   ②   you can sleep longer
③   you will become popular   ④   your life can be more enjoyable

問3   The statement that best reflects one finding from the survey is 13 .
①   'I feel uncomfortable when I watch TV with my cat.'
②   'I spend about three hours with my pet every day.'
③   'Most pets like going on car trips.'
④   'Pets need a room of their own.'

問4   Which best summarises David's opinions about having pets in Japan? 14
①   It is not troublesome to keep pets.   ②   People might stop keeping pets.
③   Pet owners have more family members.   ④   Some people are happy to keep pets inside their homes.

問5   Which is the most suitable title for the article? 15
①   Does Your Pet Sleep on Your Bed?   ②   What Does Keeping Pets Give Us?
③   What Pet Do You Have?   ④   Why Not Keep a Pet Pig?

A You are reading the results of a survey about single-use and reusable bottles that your classmates answered as part of an environmental campaign in the UK.

Question 1: How many single-use bottled drinks do you purchase per week?

Number of bottles	Number of students	Weekly subtotal
0	2	0
1	2	2
2	2	4
3	3	9
4	4	16
5	9	45
6	0	0
7	7	49
Total	29	125

Question 2: Do you have your own reusable bottle?

Summary of responses	Number of students	Percent of students
Yes, I do.	3	10.3
Yes, but I don't use it.	14	48.3
No, I don't.	12	41.4
Total	29	100.0

Question 3: If you don't use a reusable bottle, what are your reasons?

Summary of responses	Number of students
It takes too much time to wash reusable bottles.	24
I think single-use bottles are more convenient.	17
Many flavoured drinks are available in single-use bottles.	14
Buying a single-use bottle doesn't cost much.	10
I can buy drinks from vending machines at school.	7
I feel reusable bottles are too heavy.	4
My home has dozens of single-use bottles.	3
Single-use bottled water can be stored unopened for a long time.	2
(Other reasons)	4

問1　The results of Question 1 show that ☐ 6 ☐.
① each student buys fewer than four single-use bottles a week on average
② many students buy fewer than two bottles a week
③ more than half the students buy at least five bottles a week
④ the students buy more than 125 bottles a week

問2　The results of Question 2 show that more than half the students ☐ 7 ☐.
① don't have their own reusable bottle　② have their own reusable bottle
③ have their own reusable bottle but don't use it　④ use their own reusable bottle

問3　One **opinion** expressed by your classmates in Question 3 is that ⬚8⬚.
① some students have a stock of single-use bottles at home
② there are vending machines for buying drinks at school
③ washing reusable bottles takes a lot of time
④ water in unopened single-use bottles lasts a long time

問4　One **fact** stated by your classmates in Question 3 is that single-use bottles are ⬚9⬚.
① available to buy at school　② convenient to use
③ light enough to carry around　④ not too expensive to buy

問5　What is the most likely reason why your classmates do not use reusable bottles? ⬚10⬚.
① There are many single-use bottled drinks stored at home.
② There is less variety of drinks available.
③ They are expensive for your classmates.
④ They are troublesome to deal with.

B　You need to decide what classes to take in a summer programme in the UK, so you are reading course information and a former student's comment about the course.

COMMUNICATION AND INTERCULTURAL STUDIES

Dr Christopher Bennet

bennet. christopher@ire-u.ac.uk

Call: 020-9876-1234

Office Hours: by appointment only

3-31 August 2021

Tuesday & Friday

1.00 pm-2.30pm

9 classes-1 credit

Course description: We will be studying different cultures and learning how to communicate with people from different cultures. In this course, students will need to present their ideas for dealing with intercultural issues.

Goals: After this course you should be able to :
− understand human relations among different cultures
− present solutions for different intercultural problems
− express your opinions through discussion and presentations

Textbook: Smith, S. (2019). *Intercultural studies*. New York: DNC Inc.

Evaluation: 60% overall required to pass
− two presentations: 90% (45% each)
− participation: 10%

Course-takers' evaluations (87 reviewers)　　　★★★★☆ (Average: 4.89)

Comment

☺Take this class! Chris is a great teacher. He is very smart and kind. The course is a little challenging but easy enough to pass. You will learn a lot about differences in culture. My advice would be to participate in every class. It really helped me make good presentations.

問1　What will you do in this course? ☐ 11
  ① Discuss various topics about culture
  ② Visit many different countries
  ③ Watch a film about human relations
  ④ Write a final report about culture

問2　This class is aimed at students who ☐ 12 .
  ① are interested in intercultural issues
  ② can give good presentations
  ③ like sightseeing in the UK
  ④ need to learn to speak English

問3　One **fact** about Dr Bennet is that ☐ 13 .
  ① he has good teaching skills
  ② he is a nice instructor
  ③ he is in charge of this course
  ④ he makes the course challenging

問4　One **opinion** expressed about the class is that ☐ 14 .
  ① it is not so difficult to get a credit
  ② most students are satisfied with the course
  ③ participation is part of the final grade
  ④ students have classes twice a week

問5　What do you have to do to pass this course? ☐ 15
  ① Come to every class and join the discussuions
  ② Find an intercultural issue and discuss a solution
  ③ Give good presentations about intercultural issues
  ④ Make an office appointment with Dr Bennet

A　As the student in charge of a UK school festival band competition, you are examining all of the scores and the comments from three judges to understand and explain the rankings.

Judges' final average scores				
Band names ＼ Qualities	Performance (5.0)	Singing (5.0)	Song originality (5.0)	Total (15.0)
Green Forest	3.9	4.6	5.0	13.5
Silent Hill	4.9	4.4	4.2	13.5
Mountain Pear	3.9	4.9	4.7	13.5
Thousand Ants	(did not perform)			

Judges' individual comments	
Mr Hobbs	Silent Hill are great performers and they really seemed connected with the audience. Mountain Pear's singing was great. I loved Green Forest's original song. It was amazing!
Ms Leigh	Silent Hill gave a great performance. It was incredible how the audience responded to their music. I really think that Silent Hill will become popular! Mountain Pear have great voices, but they were not exciting on stage. Green Forest performed a fantastic new song, but I think they need to practice more.
Ms Wells	Green Forest have a new song. I loved it! I think it could be a big hit!

Judges' shared evaluation (summarised by Mr Hobbs)

　　Each band's total score is the same, but each band is very different. Ms Leigh and I agreed that performance is the most important quality for a band. Ms Wells also agreed. Therefore, first place is easily determined.

　　To decide between second and third places, Ms Wells suggested that song originality should be more important than good singing. Ms Leigh and I agreed on this opinion.

問1　Based on the judges' final average scores, which band sang the best?　| 6 |

　① Green Forest　② Mountain Pear　③ Silent Hill　④ Thousand Ants

問2　Which judge gave both positive and critical comments?　| 7 |

　① Mr Hobbs　② Ms Leigh　③ Ms Wells　④ None of them

問3　One <u>fact</u> from the judges' individual comments is that　| 8 |　.

　① all the judges praised Green Forest's song　② Green Forest need to practice more

　③ Mountain Pear can sing very well　④ Silent Hill have a promising future

事実・意見

問4　One **opinion** from the judges' comments and shared evaluation is that ⬚9⬚ .

① each evaluated band received the same total score

② Ms Wells' suggestion about originality was agreed on

③ Silent Hill really connected with the audience

④ the judges' comments determined the rankings

問5　Which of the following is the final ranking based on the judges' shared evaluation? ⬚10⬚

	1st	2nd	3rd
①	Green Forest	Mountain Pear	Silent Hill
②	Green Forest	Silent Hill	Mountain Pear
③	Mountain Pear	Green Forest	Silent Hill
④	Mountain Pear	Silent Hill	Green Forest
⑤	Silent Hill	Green Forest	Mountain Pear
⑥	Silent Hill	Mountain Pear	Green Forest

B　You've heard about a change in school policy at the school in the UK where you are now studying as an exchange student. You are reading the discussions about the policy in an online forum.

New School Policy ＜Posted on 21 September 2020＞
To: P. E. Berger
From: K. Roberts

Dear Dr Berger,

　On behalf of all students, welcome to St Mark's School. We heard that you are the first Head Teacher with a business background, so we hope your experience will help our school.

　　I would like to express one concern about the change you are proposing to the after-school activity schedule. I realise that saving energy is important and from now it will be getting darker earlier. Is this why you have made the schedule an hour and a half shorter? Students at St Mark's School take both their studies and their after-school activities very seriously. A number of students have told me that they want to stay at school until 6.00 pm as they have always done. Therefore, I would like to ask you to think again about this sudden change in policy.

Regards,
Ken Roberts
Head Student

Re: New School Policy ＜Posted on 22 September 2020＞
To: K. Roberts
From: P. E. Berger

Dear Ken,

　　Many thanks for your kind post. You've expressed some important concerns, especially about the energy costs and student opinions on school activities.

　　The new policy has nothing to do with saving energy. The decision was made based on a 2019 police report. The report showed that our city has become less safe due to a 5% increase in serious crimes. I would like to protect our students, so I would like them to return home before it gets dark.

Yours,
Dr P. E. Berger
Head Teacher

問1　Ken thinks the new policy 　11　 .

　① can make students study more

　② may improve school safety

　③ should be introduced immediately

　④ will reduce after-school activity time

問2　One **fact** stated in Ken's forum post is that 　12　 .

　① more discussion is needed about the policy

　② the Head Teacher's experience is improving the school

　③ the school should think about students' activities

　④ there are students who do not welcome the new policy

問3　Who thinks the aim of the policy is to save energy? 　13　

　① Dr Berger　　　② Ken　　　③ The city　　　④ The police

問4　Dr Berger is basing his new policy on the **fact** that 　14　 .

　① going home early is important

　② safety in the city has decreased

　③ the school has to save electricity

　④ the students need protection

問5　What would you research to help Ken oppose the new policy? 　15　

　① The crime rate and its relation to the local area

　② The energy budget and electricity costs of the school

　③ The length of school activity time versus the budget

　④ The study hours for students who do after-school activities

A You are a member of the cooking club at school, and you want to make something different. On a website, you found a recipe for a dish that looks good.

EASY OVEN RECIPES
Here is one of the top 10 oven-baked dishes as rated on our website. You will find this dish healthy and satisfying.

Meat and Potato Pie

Ingredients (serves about 4)

A　1 onion　　　　　　　　2 carrots　　　　　　　　500g minced beef
　　🥄 × 2 flour　　　　　🥄 × 1 tomato paste　　🥄 × 1 Worcestershire sauce
　　🥄 × 1 vegetable oil　📦 × 2 soup stock　　　salt & pepper

B　3 boiled potatoes　　　40g butter

C　sliced cheese

Instructions

Step 1: Make **A**
1. Cut the vegetables into small pieces, heat the oil, and cook for 5 minutes.
2. Add the meat and cook until it changes color.
3. Add the flour and stir for 2 minutes.
4. Add the soup stock, Worcestershire sauce, and tomato paste. Cook for about 30 minutes.
5. Season with salt and pepper.

Step 2: Make **B**
1. Meanwhile, cut the potatoes into thin slices.
2. Heat the pan and melt the butter. Add the potatoes and cook for 3 minutes.

Step 3: Put **A**, **B**, and **C** together, and bake
1. Heat the oven to 200℃.
2. Put **A** into a baking dish, cover it with **B**, and top with **C**.
3. Bake for 10 minutes. Serve hot.

Enjoy!

REVIEW & COMMENTS

cooking@master　*January 15, 2018 at 15:14*
This is really delicious! Perfect on a snowy day.

Seaside Kitchen　*February 3, 2018 at 10:03*
My children love this dish. It's not at all difficult to make, and I have made it so many times for my kids.

問1 This recipe would be good if you want to ☐6☐ .
① cook chicken for lunch　　② eat something sweet
③ enjoy a hot dish on a cold day　　④ prepare a quick meal without using heat

問2 If you follow the instructions, the dish should be ready to eat in about ☐7☐ .
① half an hour　② one hour　③ twenty minutes　④ two to three hours

問3 Someone who does not like raw carrots may eat this dish because ☐8☐ .
① carrots are not used　　② many kinds of spices are used
③ the carrots are cooked　　④ the carrots are very fresh

問4 According to the website, one **fact** (not an opinion) about this recipe is that it is ☐9☐ .
① highly ranked on the website　　② made for vegetarians
③ perfect for taking to parties　　④ very delicious

問5 According to the website, one **opinion** (not a fact) about this recipe is that ☐10☐ .
① a parent made this dish many times　② it is easy to cook
③ it is fun to cook with friends　　④ the recipe was created by a famous cook

B　Your English teacher gave you an article to help you prepare for the debate in the next class. A part of this article with one of the comments is shown below.

No Mobile Phones in French Schools

By Tracey Wolfe, Paris
11 DECEMBER 2017 • 4:07PM

The French government will prohibit students from using mobile phones in schools from September, 2018. Students will be allowed to bring their phones to school, but not allowed to use them at any time in school without special permission. This rule will apply to all students in the country's primary and middle schools.

Jean-Michel Blanquer, the French education minister, stated, "These days the students don't play at break time anymore. They are just all in front of their smartphones and from an educational point of view, that's a problem." He also said, "Phones may be needed in cases of emergency, but their use has to be somehow controlled."

However, not all parents are happy with this rule. Several parents said, "One must live with the times. It doesn't make sense to force children to have the same childhood that we had." Moreover, other parents added, "Who will collect the phones, and where will they be stored? How will they be returned to the owners? If all schools had to provide lockers for children to store their phones, a huge amount of money and space would be needed."

21 Comments

Newest

Daniel McCarthy 19 December 2017 • 6:11PM

Well done, France! School isn't just trying to get students to learn how to calculate things. There are a lot of other things they should learn in school. Young people need to develop social skills such as how to get along with other people.

問1　According to the rule explained in the article, students in primary and middle schools in France won't be allowed to ⬚11⬚ .
① ask their parents to pay for their mobile phones
② bring their mobile phones to school
③ have their own mobile phones until after graduation
④ use their mobile phones at school except for special cases

問2　Your team will support the debate topic, "Mobile phone use in school should be limited." In the article, one **opinion** (not a fact) helpful for your team is that ⬚12⬚ .
① it is necessary for students to be focused on studying during class
② students should play with their friends between classes
③ the government will introduce a new rule about phone use at school
④ using mobile phones too long may damage students' eyes

問3　The other team will oppose the debate topic. In the article, one **opinion** (not a fact) helpful for that team is that ☐13☐.

① it is better to teach students how to control their mobile phone use

② students should use their mobile phones for daily communication

③ the cost of storing students' mobile phones would be too high

④ the rule will be applied to all students at the country's primary and middle schools

問4　In the 3rd paragraph of the article, "One must live with the times" means that people should ☐14☐.

① change their lifestyles according to when they live

② live in their own ways regardless of popular trends

③ remember their childhood memories

④ try not to be late for school

問5　According to his comment, Daniel McCarthy ☐15☐ the rule stated in the article.

① has no particular opinion about

② partly agrees with

③ strongly agrees with

④ strongly disagrees with

A You are traveling abroad and trying to find places to eat on the Internet.

The following are reviews of some restaurants written by people who have visited them.

Shiro's Ramen

★★★★☆　　by Boots (3 weeks ago)

Best choice: *cha-shu* noodles.　Cheap, crowded & lots of noise.　Very casual. Felt rushed while eating.　Open 5 p.m. ～ 6 a.m.

Annie's Kitchen

★★★☆☆　　by Carrie (2 weeks ago)

Was in the mood for variety, and Annie's Kitchen did NOT disappoint.　The menu is 13 wonderful pages long with food from around the world.　Actually, I spent 25 minutes just reading the menu. Unfortunately, the service was very slow.　The chef's meal-of-the-day was great, but prices are a little high for this casual style of restaurant.

Johnny's Hutt

★★★☆☆　　by Mason (2 days ago)

The perfect choice when you want to eat a lot.　But you might need to wait for a bit.

★★★★★　　by Roosevelt (5 days ago)

For a steak fan, this is the best！　The chef prepares steak dishes to suit any customer's taste.　My favorite was the Cowboy Plate—perfect!

★☆☆☆☆　　by Ken-chan (2 weeks ago)

Sadly, below average, so won't be going back again.　The steak was cooked too long!　The fish dishes were also disappointing.

問1　You would most likely visit Shiro's Ramen when you ☐6☐ .
① are looking for a quiet place to have a conversation　② have an empty stomach at midnight
③ need to have a formal meal　④ want to have a casual lunch

問2　You would most likely visit Annie's Kitchen when you ☐7☐ .
① feel like eating outdoors　② have lots of free time
③ must have a quick breakfast　④ want to have cheap dishes

問3　The opinions about Johnny's Hutt were all ☐8☐ .
① different　② favorable　③ negative　④ neutral

問4　Based on the reviews, which of the following are facts, not personal opinions?（You may choose more than one option.）☐9☐
① Annie's Kitchen offers dishes from many countries.
② Johnny's Hutt is less crowded than Shiro's Ramen.
③ Johnny's Hutt serves some fish dishes.
④ The chef at Johnny's Hutt is good at his job.
⑤ The chef's meal-of-the-day is the best at Annie's Kitchen.
⑥ The menu at Annie's Kitchen is wonderful.

B　You are going to have a debate about students working part-time. In order to prepare for the debate, your group is reading the article below.

Students and Part-Time Jobs

According to a recent survey, about 70% of Japanese high school and university students have worked part-time. The survey also reports that students have part-time jobs because they need money for going out with their friends, buying clothes, and helping their families financially. Even with such common reasons, we should consider the following question: Is it good or bad for students to work part-time?

Some people believe that students learn several things from working part-time. They come to understand the importance and difficulty of working as well as the value of money. Moreover, they learn how to get along with people. Students can improve their communication skills and gain confidence.

Others think that there are negative points about students working part-time. First, it may harm their studies. Students who work too hard are so tired during class that they might receive poor grades in school. Second, it seems difficult for students to balance work and school. This could cause stress. Third, students may develop negative views of work itself by working too much. They may become less motivated to work hard after graduation.

What do you think? In my view, part-time work is not always bad for students. My point is that students shouldn't do too much part-time work. Research suggests that if students work part-time over 20 hours a week, they will probably have some of the negative experiences mentioned above.

問1　In the survey mentioned in the article, the students were asked, " | 10 | "
　① Have you ever worked part-time abroad?
　② How much money per week do you make working part-time?
　③ What kind of part-time jobs would be good for you?
　④ Why do you work part-time?

問2　Your group wants to collect opinions **supporting** students working part-time. One such opinion in the article is that students | 11 | .
　① can become good communicators　　　　② mostly have worked part-time
　③ will have a better chance of getting a full-time job　④ will learn how to dress appropriately

問3　Your group wants to collect opinions **opposing** students working part-time. One such opinion in the article is that students | 12 | .
　① cannot be helpful in the workplace　　　② might perform poorly in class
　③ should spend more time with their family　④ work part-time to buy what they want

問4　If students work over 20 hours a week, they may | 13 | .
　① begin to feel they need a well-paid job　　② continue to work hard at part-time jobs
　③ lose interest in working hard after leaving school　④ want to be independent of their families

問5　The writer of this article | 14 | students working part-time.
　① does not have any particular opinion about　② partly agrees with
　③ strongly agrees with　　　　　　　④ strongly disagrees with

以下の文章は，映画紹介サイトに投稿されたある日本映画についての感想である。文章を読み，次の問い（**問 1〜5**）の ▢41 〜 ▢45 に入れるのに最も適当なものを，それぞれ下の①〜④のうちから一つずつ選べ。

"Tomo and Aki"（2005）Japan

Satoko from Osaka, Japan

Rating：★★★★☆

I finally watched the DVD of "Tomo and Aki," the award-winning film based on the famous book by Yukio Kodama.　I love this book and have read it many times.　Kodama's detailed descriptions of life in Japan's countryside are amazing, and the story is both funny and touching.　Tomo and Aki, a young urban couple, move to a rural village but struggle with their strange new life.　I avoided the movie for a long time because I thought it could never be as good as the book.　While I was right in some ways, the movie was still very enjoyable to watch.

While the small village in the movie is realistic, I never quite felt like I was there as I did when reading Kodama's words.　The actor playing Tomo, a shy and ordinary character in the book, looks too confident and handsome for the role.　On the other hand, the actress who plays Aki is very believable, perfectly showing emotions such as joy, frustration, and sorrow.　Aki really regrets their move.　Throughout the first half of the movie, she tries to maintain at least one small part of her city lifestyle by often wearing high heels and perfect makeup around the village.　In the powerful conclusion of the movie, she gives birth to twins, which helps her to let go of the past completely and become truly content with her life in the village.　One interesting point is the appearance of Jun Daichi, only 15 years old then, playing a supporting role as a boy from a neighboring village.　I am a big fan of this actor, who became famous for his later work but already shows his talent for acting in this small part.

Although I was extremely familiar with the book, watching the movie increased my appreciation of the original story.　Anyone who loves the book can still enjoy this movie, and if you love the movie, go read the book too !

Joe from Buffalo, NY, USA

Rating：★★★★★

My Japanese friend took me to the Asian Film Festival yesterday to see "Tomo and Aki." I usually avoid foreign language movies as I find it difficult to read the subtitles and pay attention to the scenes at the same time. However, this movie was so fascinating and delightful that I soon forgot I was reading the dialogue.　The story describes a young woman who moves to the countryside with her husband when he tries to escape his busy life in the city.　The best part of the movie is how it shows the interesting and unique life in Japan's countryside.　The camera work and soundtrack also add to the experience and fit nicely with the lively atmosphere of the film.　I was fascinated and entertained throughout the entire two hours.

The opening scene immediately grabbed my attention with a huge frog jumping in front of Aki, the main female character, and her screaming voice echoing into the surrounding mountains.　Actually, I was very impressed with the actress's performance as she transforms herself from a fashion store salesclerk into a successful farmer.　The actress is also a talented comedian, particularly in the scenes where she is trying to manage a vegetable garden while battling insects, rainstorms, and lots of mud.

Among the many older village people, who are usually staring curiously at the young couple, there are some truly amusing and unique characters.　My favorite was an old woman, a legend in the village, who eventually becomes a good friend of the couple.　In a memorable scene towards the end of the movie, the old woman teaches Aki how to cook wild mushrooms while telling strange traditional folk stories from the village.

Overall, I really liked this movie.　The story is entertaining and the acting is great, but best of all, you can really see a different side of Japanese culture in the movie.　I highly recommend this film!

問1　After watching the movie, Satoko thought that it [41] .
　① accurately showed the life of Yukio Kodama　② gave her a feeling of being in the village
　③ made her like the book even more　④ should be avoided by the fans of the book

問2　Before watching the movie, Joe expected that it would be [42] .
　① a valuable cultural experience　② different from the original book
　③ great because it was famous　④ hard for him to follow the story

問3　Both Satoko and Joe praise [43] .
　① the performance of the main actor　② the performance of the main actress
　③ the quality of the camera work　④ the quality of the original book

問4　According to the reviews, the theme of the story can be best described as [44] .
　① a character's adaptation to a new life
　② a historically accurate description of old village life
　③ the changing roles of women in modern society
　④ the importance of sharing cultural traditions

問5　Which of the following shows the order of the scenes as they appear in the movie? [45]
　① (B)→(C)→(D)→(A)　② (B)→(D)→(C)→(A)　③ (D)→(A)→(B)→(C)　④ (D)→(B)→(A)→(C)

(A) 　(B) 　(C) 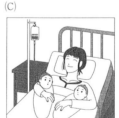　(D)

A You are interested in how Japanese culture is represented in other countries. You are reading a young UK blogger's post.

Emily Sampson
Monday, 5 July, 8.00 pm

On the first two Sundays in July every year, there is an intercultural event in Winsfield called A Slice of Japan. I had a chance to go there yesterday. It is definitely worth visiting! There were many authentic food stands called *yatai*, hands-on activities, and some great performances. The *yatai* served green-tea ice cream, *takoyaki*, and *yakitori*. I tried green-tea ice cream and *takoyaki*. The *takoyaki* was especially delicious. You should try some!

I saw three performances. One of them was a *rakugo* comedy given in English. Some people were laughing, but somehow I didn't find it funny. It may be because I don't know much about Japanese culture. For me, the other two, the *taiko* and the *koto*, were the highlights. The *taiko* were powerful, and the *koto* was relaxing.

I attended a workshop and a cultural experience, which were fun. In the workshop, I learnt how to make *onigiri*. Although the shape of the one I made was a little odd, it tasted good. The *nagashi-somen* experience was really interesting! It involved trying to catch cooked noodles with chopsticks as they slid down a bamboo water slide. It was very difficult to catch them.

If you want to experience a slice of Japan, this festival is for you! I took a picture of the flyer. Check it out.

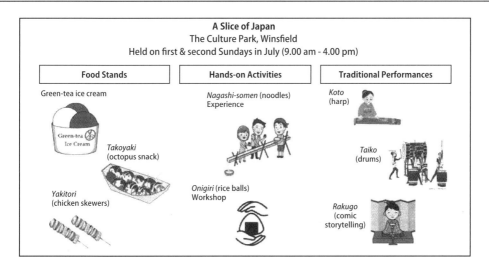

A Slice of Japan
The Culture Park, Winsfield
Held on first & second Sundays in July (9.00 am - 4.00 pm)

Food Stands	**Hands-on Activities**	**Traditional Performances**

Green-tea ice cream

Green-tea Ice Cream

Takoyaki (octopus snack)

Yakitori (chicken skewers)

Nagashi-somen (noodles) Experience

Onigiri (rice balls) Workshop

Koto (harp)

Taiko (drums)

Rakugo (comic storytelling)

問1 In Emily's blog, you read that she 　16　 .
① enjoyed Japanese traditional music ② learnt how to play Japanese drums
③ made a water slide from bamboo ④ was able to try all the *yatai* foods

問2 Emily was most likely 　17　 when she was listening to the *rakugo* comedy.
① confused ② convinced ③ excited ④ relaxed

B You enjoy outdoor sports and have found an interesting story in a mountain climbing magazine.

Attempting the Three Peaks Challenge

By John Highland

Last September, a team of 12 of us, 10 climbers and two minibus drivers, participated in the Three Peaks Challenge, which is well known for its difficulty among climbers in Britain. The goal is to climb the highest mountain in Scotland (Ben Nevis), in England (Scafell Pike), and in Wales (Snowdon) within 24 hours, including approximately 10 hours of driving between the mountains. To prepare for this, we trained on and off for several months and planned the route carefully. Our challenge would start at the foot of Ben Nevis and finish at the foot of Snowdon.

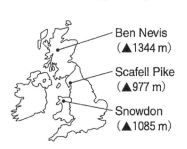

Ben Nevis
(▲1344 m)

Scafell Pike
(▲977 m)

Snowdon
(▲1085 m)

We began our first climb at six o'clock on a beautiful autumn morning. Thanks to our training, we reached the summit in under three hours. On the way down, however, I realised I had dropped my phone. Fortunately, I found it with the help of the team, but we lost 15 minutes.

We reached our next destination, Scafell Pike, early that evening. After six hours of rest in the minibus, we started our second climb full of energy. As it got darker, though, we had to slow down. It took four-and-a-half hours to complete Scafell Pike. Again, it took longer than planned, and time was running out. However, because the traffic was light, we were right on schedule when we started our final climb. Now we felt more confident we could complete the challenge within the time limit.

Unfortunately, soon after we started the final climb, it began to rain heavily and we had to slow down again. It was slippery and very difficult to see ahead. At 4.30 am, we realised that we could no longer finish in 24 hours. Nevertheless, we were still determined to climb the final mountain. The rain got heavier and heavier, and two members of the team decided to return to the minibus. Exhausted and miserable, the rest of us were also ready to go back down, but then the sky cleared, and we saw that we were really close to the top of the mountain. Suddenly, we were no longer tired. Even though we weren't successful with the time challenge, we were successful with the climb challenge. We had done it. What a feeling that was!

問1 Put the following events (①~④) into the order they happened.

| 18 | → | 19 | → | 20 | → | 21 |

① All members reached the top of the highest mountain in Scotland.
② Some members gave up climbing Snowdon.
③ The group travelled by minibus to Wales.
④ The team members helped to find the writer's phone.

問2 What was the reason for being behind schedule when they completed Scafell Pike? 22

① It took longer than planned to reach the top of Ben Nevis.
② It was difficult to make good progress in the dark.
③ The climbers took a rest in order to save energy.
④ The team had to wait until the conditions improved.

問3 From this story, you learnt that the writer 23 .

① didn't feel a sense of satisfaction   ② reached the top of all three mountains
③ successfully completed the time challenge   ④ was the second driver of the minibus

A　Your British friend, Jan, visited a new amusement park and posted a blog about her experience.

Sunny Mountain Park: A Great Place to Visit
Posted by Jan at 9.37 pm on 15 September 2020

Sunny Mountain Park finally opened last month! It's a big amusement park with many exciting attractions, including a huge roller coaster (see the map). I had a fantastic time there with my friends last week.

We couldn't wait to try the roller coaster, but first we took the train round the park to get an idea of its layout. From the train, we saw the Picnic Zone and thought it would be a good place to have lunch. However, it was already very crowded, so we decided to go to the Food Court instead. Before lunch, we went to the Discovery Zone. It was well worth the wait to experience the scientific attractions there. In the afternoon, we enjoyed several rides near Mountain Station. Of course, we tried the roller coaster, and we weren't disappointed. On our way back to the Discovery Zone to enjoy more attractions, we took a short break at a rest stop. There, we got a lovely view over the lake to the castle. We ended up at the Shopping Zone, where we bought souvenirs for our friends and family.

Sunny Mountain Park is amazing! Our first visit certainly won't be our last.

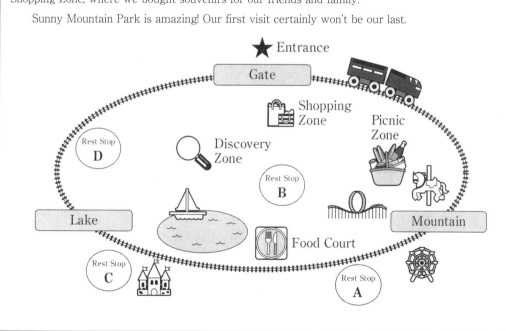

問1　From Jan's post, you learn that ⎡16⎤.

① Jan skipped going to the Shopping Zone for gifts

② Jan waited for a while to enjoy the scientific attractions

③ the Food Court was more crowded than the Picnic Zone

④ the roller coaster did not meet Jan's expectations

問2　At which rest stop did Jan and her friends take a break in the afternoon? ⎡17⎤

① Rest Stop **A**　② Rest Stop **B**　③ Rest Stop **C**　④ Rest Stop **D**

B Your friend in the UK introduced her favourite musician to you. Wanting to learn more, you found the following article in a music magazine.

Dave Starr, a Living Legend

At one time, Black Swan were the biggest rock band in the UK, and their dynamic leader Dave Starr played a large part in that achievement. Still performing as a solo singer, Dave's incredible talent has inspired generations of young musicians.

When he was a little boy, Dave was always singing and playing with toy instruments. He was never happier than when he was playing his toy drum. At age seven, he was given his first real drum set, and by 10, he could play well. By 14, he had also mastered the guitar. When he was still a high school student, he became a member of The Bluebirds, playing rhythm guitar. To get experience, The Bluebirds played for free at school events and in community centres. The band built up a small circle of passionate fans.

Dave's big break came when, on his 18th birthday, he was asked to become the drummer for Black Swan. In just two years, the band's shows were selling out at large concert halls. It came as a shock, therefore, when the lead vocalist quit to spend more time with his family. However, Dave jumped at the chance to take over as lead singer even though it meant he could no longer play his favourite instrument.

In the following years, Black Swan became increasingly successful, topping the music charts and gaining even more fans. Dave became the principal song writer, and was proud of his contribution to the band. However, with the addition of a keyboard player, the music gradually changed direction. Dave became frustrated, and he and the lead guitarist decided to leave and start a new group. Unfortunately, Dave's new band failed to reach Black Swan's level of success, and stayed together for only 18 months.

問1　Put the following events (①~④) into the order in which they happened.

$$\boxed{18} \rightarrow \boxed{19} \rightarrow \boxed{20} \rightarrow \boxed{21}$$

① Dave became a solo artist.   ② Dave gave up playing the drums.

③ Dave joined a band as the guitarist.   ④ Dave reached the peak of his career.

問2　Dave became the lead singer of Black Swan because $\boxed{22}$.

① he preferred singing to playing the drums

② he wanted to change the band's musical direction

③ the other band members wanted more success

④ the previous singer left for personal reasons

問3　From this story, you learn that $\boxed{23}$.

① Black Swan contributed to changing the direction of rock music

② Black Swan's goods sold very well at concert halls

③ Dave displayed a talent for music from an early age

④ Dave went solo as he was frustrated with the lead guitarist

A　You are planning to stay at a hotel in the UK. You found useful information in the Q&A section of a travel advice website.

I'm considering staying at the Hollytree Hotel in Castleton in March 2021. Would you recommend this hotel, and is it easy to get there from Buxton Airport?　　　　　　　　　(Liz)

Answer

- -

Yes, I strongly recommend the Hollytree. I've stayed there twice. It's inexpensive, and the service is brilliant! There's also a wonderful free breakfast. (Click *here* for access information.)

Let me tell you my own experience of getting there.

On my first visit, I used the underground, which is cheap and convenient. Trains run every five minutes. From the airport, I took the Red Line to Mossfield. Transferring to the Orange Line for Victoria should normally take about seven minutes, but the directions weren't clear and I needed an extra five minutes. From Victoria, it was a ten-minute bus ride to the hotel.

The second time, I took the express bus to Victoria, so I didn't have to worry about transferring. At Victoria, I found a notice saying there would be roadworks until summer 2021. Now it takes three times as long as usual to get to the hotel by city bus, although buses run every ten minutes. It's possible to walk, but I took the bus as the weather was bad.

Enjoy your stay!　　　　　　　　　　　　　　　　　　　　　　　　　　　　　　　　(Alex)

問1　From Alex's answer, you learn that Alex 　16　 .

①　appreciates the convenient location of the hotel

②　got lost in Victoria Station on his first visit to Castleton

③　thinks that the hotel is good value for money

④　used the same route from the airport both times

問2　You are departing on public transport from the airport at 2.00 pm on 15 March 2021. What is the fastest way to get to the hotel? 　17　

①　By express bus and city bus

②　By express bus and on foot

③　By underground and city bus

④　By underground and on foot

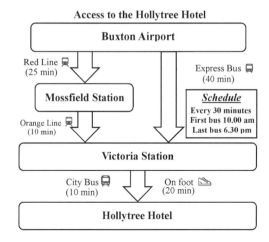

Access to the Hollytree Hotel

B　Your classmate showed you the following message in your school's newsletter, written by an exchange student from the UK.

Volunteers Wanted!

Hello, everyone. I'm Sarah King, an exchange student from London. I'd like to share something important with you today.

You may have heard of the Sakura International Centre. It provides valuable opportunities for Japanese and foreign residents to get to know each other. Popular events such as cooking classes and karaoke contests are held every month. However, there is a serious problem. The building is getting old, and requires expensive repairs. To help raise funds to maintain the centre, many volunteers are needed.

I learnt about the problem a few months ago. While shopping in town, I saw some people taking part in a fund-raising campaign. I spoke to the leader of the campaign, Katy, who explained the situation. She thanked me when I donated some money. She told me that they had asked the town mayor for financial assistance, but their request had been rejected. They had no choice but to start fund-raising.

Last month, I attended a lecture on art at the centre. Again, I saw people trying to raise money, and I decided to help. They were happy when I joined them in asking passers-by for donations. We tried hard, but there were too few of us to collect much money. With a tearful face, Katy told me that they wouldn't be able to use the building much longer. I felt the need to do something more. Then, the idea came to me that other students might be willing to help. Katy was delighted to hear this.

Now, I'm asking you to join me in the fund-raising campaign to help the Sakura International Centre. Please email me today! As an exchange student, my time in Japan is limited, but I want to make the most of it. By working together, we can really make a difference.

Class 3 A
Sarah King (sarahk@sakura-h.ed.jp)
セーラ・キング

問1　Put the following events (①～④) into the order in which they happened.

| 18 | → | 19 | → | 20 | → | 21 |

① Sarah attended a centre event.　　② Sarah donated money to the centre.

③ Sarah made a suggestion to Katy.　　④ The campaigners asked the mayor for help.

問2　From Sarah's message, you learn that the Sakura International Centre [22].

① gives financial aid to international residents　　② offers opportunities to develop friendships

③ publishes newsletters for the community　　④ sends exchange students to the UK

問3　You have decided to help with the campaign after reading Sarah's message. What should you do first?
[23]

① Advertise the events at the centre.　　② Contact Sarah for further information.

③ Organise volunteer activities at school.　　④ Start a new fund-raising campaign.

A　You found the following story in a blog written by a female exchange student in your school.

School Festival

Sunday, September 15

　　I went with my friend Takuya to his high school festival. I hadn't been to a Japanese school festival before. We first tried the ghost house. It was well-made, using projectors and a good sound system to create a frightening atmosphere.

　　Then we watched a dance show performed by students. They were cool and danced well. It's a pity that the weather was bad. If it had been sunny, they could have danced outside. At lunch time, we ate Hawaiian pancakes, Thai curry, and Mexican tacos at the food stalls. They were all good, but the Italian pizza had already sold out by the time we found the pizza stall.

　　In the afternoon, we participated in a karaoke competition together as both of us love singing. Surprisingly, we almost won, which was amazing as there were 20 entries in the competition. We were really happy that many people liked our performance. We also enjoyed the digital paintings and short movies students made.

　　I can't believe that students organized and prepared this big event by themselves. The school festival was pretty impressive.

問1　At the school festival, 　16　 .

　① most food at the stalls was sold out before lunch time

　② the dance show was held inside due to poor weather

　③ the ghost house was run without electronic devices

　④ the karaoke competition was held in the morning

問2　You learned that the writer of this blog 　17　 .

　① enjoyed the ghost tour, the dance show, and the teachers' art works

　② sang in the karaoke competition and won third prize

　③ tried different dishes and took second place in the karaoke contest

　④ was pleased with her dancing and her short movie about the festival

B　You found the following story in a study-abroad magazine.

Flowers and Their Hidden Meanings

Naoko Maeyama（Teaching Assistant）

　　Giving flowers is definitely a nice thing to do. However, when you are in a foreign country, you should be aware of cultural differences.

　　Deborah, who was at our school in Japan for a three-week language program, was nervous at first because there were no students from Canada, her home country. But she soon made many friends and was having a great time inside and outside the classroom. One day she heard that her Japanese teacher, Mr. Hayashi, was in the hospital after falling down some stairs at the station. She was really surprised and upset, and wanted to see him as soon as possible. Deborah decided to go to the hospital with her classmates and brought a red begonia in a flower pot to make her teacher happy. When they entered the hospital room, he welcomed them with a big smile. However, his expression suddenly changed when Deborah gave the red flower to him. Deborah was a little puzzled, but she didn't ask the reason because she didn't want to trouble him.

　　Later, in her elementary Japanese and with the help of a dictionary, Deborah told me about her visit to the hospital, and how her teacher's expression changed when she gave him the begonia. Deborah said, "It's my favorite flower because red is the color of passion. I thought my teacher, who was always passionate about teaching, would surely love it, too."

　　Unfortunately, flowers growing in a pot are something we shouldn't take to a hospital in Japan. This is because a plant in a pot has roots, and so it cannot be moved easily. In Japanese culture some people associate these facts with remaining in the hospital. Soon after Deborah heard the hidden meaning of the potted begonia, she visited Mr. Hayashi again to apologize.

問 1　According to the story, Deborah's feelings changed in the following order: ☐18☐ .

　　① nervous → confused → happy → shocked → sorry
　　② nervous → confused → sorry → shocked → happy
　　③ nervous → happy → shocked → confused → sorry
　　④ nervous → happy → sorry → shocked → confused
　　⑤ nervous → shocked → happy → sorry → confused
　　⑥ nervous → sorry → confused → happy → shocked

問 2　The gift Deborah chose was not appropriate in Japan because it may imply ☐19☐ .

　　① a long stay　　② congratulations　　③ growing anger　　④ passion for living

問 3　From this story, you learned that Deborah ☐20☐ .

　　① chose a begonia for her teacher because she learned the meanings of several flowers in her class
　　② not only practiced her Japanese but also learned about Japanese culture because of a begonia
　　③ visited the hospital with her teaching assistant to see her teacher and enjoyed chatting
　　④ was given an explanation about the begonia by Mr. Hayashi and learned its hidden meaning

A　You want to visit a country called Vegetonia and you found the following blog.

My Spring Holiday on Tomatly Island

Sunday, March 23

　　I went with my family to a country named Vegetonia to visit Tomatly Island, which is located to the southwest of the main island of Vegetonia. The fastest way to get to Tomatly is to take an airplane from Poteno, but we took a ferry because it was much cheaper. It started to rain when we got to the island, so we visited an art museum and a castle. Then, we enjoyed a hot spring bath. In the evening, our dinner was delicious. Everything was so fresh!

　　Luckily, the next morning was sunny. We rented bicycles and had fun cycling along the coast. After that, we went fishing on the beach but we didn't catch anything. Oh well, maybe next time! In the evening, we saw a beautiful sunset and later on, lots of stars.

　　On the last day, we took a private taxi tour and the driver took us to many interesting places around the island. She also told us a lot about the nature and culture of the island. We had a great holiday, and as a result, I've become more interested in the beauty and culture of small islands.

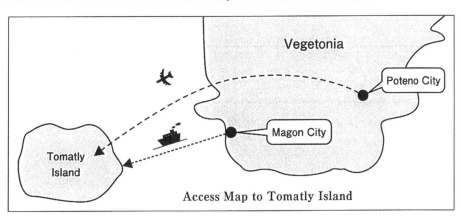

Access Map to Tomatly Island

問 1　The family went to Tomatly Island from ⬚15⬚ .

① Magon by air

② Magon by sea

③ Poteno by air

④ Poteno by sea

問 2　From this blog, you learned that ⬚16⬚ .

① the best month to visit Tomatly Island would be March because it is less crowded

② there are still some things you can enjoy on the island even if the weather is bad

③ you can enjoy various outdoor activities and local food at reasonable prices

④ you can join a bus tour around the island that explains the island's nature and culture

B You found the following story written by a salesperson in a newspaper.

March of the Machines

Nick Rightfield

After graduating from university in Toronto, I started working for a trading company. This means I have to live and work in various cities. My first post was in New York, a city famous for its office buildings, stores, and nightlife. In my free time, I loved to walk around and search for stores selling interesting items. Even into the night, I would wander from store to store.

Then after two years, I moved to Tokyo. My first impression of Tokyo was that it is a busy city very similar to New York. However, on the first day when I took a night-time walk down the streets of Shinjuku, I noticed a difference. Among the crowds of workers and shoppers, I found rows of brightly-lit vending machines giving off a candy-colored light. In New York, most vending machines are located in office buildings or subway stations. But I never imagined lines of vending machines—standing like soldiers on almost every street—selling coffee, juice, and even noodles 24 hours a day.

As I stood in Shinjuku, I thought about Vancouver, where I was born and raised. To me it was a great city, but having experienced city life in New York and Tokyo, I have to admit how little I knew back in Vancouver. As I was thinking about my life so far, it began to rain. I was about to run to a convenience store when I noticed an umbrella vending machine. Saved! Then I thought perhaps as technology improves, we will be able to buy everything from machines. Will vending machines replace convenience stores? Will machines replace salespeople like me? I didn't sleep well that night. Was it jet lag or something else?

問1 The writer moved from place to place in the following order: ⬚17⬚ .

① Toronto → New York → Tokyo → Vancouver

② Toronto → Vancouver → New York → Tokyo

③ Vancouver → New York → Tokyo → Toronto

④ Vancouver → Toronto → New York → Tokyo

問2 The writer says that ⬚18⬚ .

① life in New York is more comfortable than life in Tokyo

② life in Tokyo is less interesting than life in New York

③ the location of vending machines in New York and Tokyo differs

④ the same goods are sold in vending machines in New York and Tokyo

問3 While the writer was in Tokyo, he ⬚19⬚ .

① began to think about selling vending machines

② realized Vancouver was better because it was his hometown

③ started to regret moving from city to city

④ suddenly worried about the future of his job

次の文章を読み，下の問い（**問1〜5**）の　41　〜　45　に入れるのに最も適当なものを，それぞれ下の①〜④のうちから一つずつ選べ。

A couple of weeks ago, I was hiking with my dog on a mountain when something unexpected happened and I lost sight of him. I looked and looked but couldn't find him. He had been with me for so long that it was like I was missing part of my soul.

Ever since that day, I had a strange feeling. It was beyond sadness—a feeling that I didn't quite understand, as if something were pulling me to go back to the mountain. So every chance I got, I grabbed my backpack to see if the mountain could offer me some sense of relief.

One sunny morning, I stood at the foot of the mountain. Something felt different this day. "Please forgive me," I said out loud. "I'll find you !" I took a deep breath and began my journey with this mysterious pull growing stronger. After making my way along paths I thought I knew well, I realized I was somehow in an unfamiliar place. I panicked a little, lost my footing, and slipped. From out of nowhere, an elderly man came running towards me and helped me up.

Looking at his gentle, smiling face, I felt a sense of ease. The old man said he was looking for a way to the top of the mountain, so we decided to climb together.

Soon the path began to feel familiar again. We talked about many things, including my dog. I told him that he was a German shepherd. When he was younger, he served briefly as a police dog but had to stop due to an injury. The man let out a laugh saying he had been a police officer for a short time, but he quit. He didn't say why. Later, he spent a long time as a bodyguard. He also had German roots. We laughed at these similarities.

Before we knew it, we reached a large open area and took a break. I told the man what had happened to my dog. "He had a tiny bell on his collar to scare away bears. We came to this very spot and saw a bear. It was looking back at us. I should have held my dog because, sensing danger, he chased after the bear. I couldn't find him after that. I should have been more careful."

As I was telling the story, the man's expression changed. "It wasn't your fault. Your dog just wanted to keep you safe," he said. "I'm sure Tomo would want to tell you this. Also, thank you for not giving up."

Tomo is my dog's name. Did I tell him this ? The old man's comment <u>rang in the air</u>.

Before I could ask anything, the man proposed we hurry to get to the top of the mountain. I was planning to do this with my dog a few weeks ago. After two more hours of hiking, we reached the peak. I set down my backpack and we sat taking in the magnificent view. The old man looked at me and said, "Mountains offer truly magical experiences."

I looked around for a place to rest. I guess I was pretty tired, because I fell asleep right away. When I woke up, I noticed that the old man had disappeared. I waited, but he never returned.

Suddenly, in the sunlight, something caught my eye. I walked over and saw a small metal tag beside my backpack. It was the same silver name tag that my parents originally gave to my dog. *Tomo* it said.

It was then that I heard a familiar noise behind me. It was the ringing of a tiny bell. I turned around. What I saw caused so many emotions to rush over me.

After a while on the mountaintop, I attached the name tag to my old friend and carefully made my way home with the mountain's gift beside me. My soul felt very much complete.

問1　The author kept returning to the mountain because [41] .

   ① she felt an urge she couldn't explain

   ② she planned to meet the elderly man

   ③ she thought she could practice magic

   ④ she wanted to find out about the bear

問2　Which of the following happened first on the author's most recent trip ?　[42]

   ① She arrived at a large open area.

   ② She climbed to the mountaintop.

   ③ She saw a bear running away.

   ④ She was assisted by an old man.

問3　What similarity between the author's dog and the old man was talked about ?　[43]

   ① They experienced workplace injuries.

   ② They recently lost close family friends.

   ③ They were acquaintances of the author.

   ④ They worked to help protect the public.

問4　Which of the following is closest to the meaning of the underlined phrase rang in the air as used in the text ?

   [44]

   ① brought happiness

   ② left an impression

   ③ made a loud noise

   ④ seemed offensive

問5　How did the author's feelings change over the course of the last hiking experience ?　[45]

   ① She was depressed and then became sadder.

   ② She was determined and then became comforted.

   ③ She was hopeful but then became homesick.

   ④ She was miserable but then became entertained.

次の文章を読み，下の問い（**問1～5**）の　41　～　45　に入れるのに最も適当なものを，それぞれ下の①～④のうちから一つずつ選べ。

"Christine, come and help me in the garden. I want to plant all of the seeds today." My father was calling to me. "I'm busy," I said. My father loves his garden, but at that time I didn't understand why working in the dirt excited him so much.

By the end of April, his plants had come up in neat rows, and he put wooden stakes marked with the name of the vegetable on each row. Unfortunately, in early May, my father was seriously injured in an accident. He was in the hospital for about two months and during that time he often asked me about his garden. Even after he came home, he had to stay in bed for a while. My mother had several business trips so she couldn't take care of the garden. I didn't want my father to worry, so without being asked, I said that I would take care of his garden until he recovered. I assumed that the little plants would continue to grow as long as they had water, and luckily it rained fairly often so I didn't think much about the garden.

One Saturday morning in July, my father said to me, "Christine, I think that the vegetables should be about ready to be picked. Let's have a salad today !" I took a bowl and went out to the garden. I looked at the leaf lettuce and was upset to see that many of the leaves had been half eaten. There were hundreds of bugs all over them ! I tried to get them off, but there were just too many. I looked at the carrots next, but they didn't look healthy. I pulled up a carrot, but it was tiny and looked like something had taken small bites from it.

I panicked for a moment, but then thought of a good idea. I got my wallet, quietly went out the door, and rode my bicycle to the nearest store to buy some vegetables. I went back home and cut them up to make a salad for my father.

When I gave it to him, he said, "Oh, Christine, what a beautiful salad ! I can't believe the carrots are this big already. The lettuce is so crisp and delicious. You must be taking very good care of my garden." My father looked happy, but I felt a little bit guilty.

I went back to the kitchen and was cleaning up when my mother came home from her most recent business trip. She saw the bag from the supermarket. I was embarrassed when she looked at me. So, I confessed, "Dad wanted a salad, but the garden was a disaster. I didn't want to disappoint him so I went to the store." She laughed but promised to make time to help me in the garden, and we worked hard for the next few weeks. We made a mixture of water with chopped-up fresh hot peppers and then sprayed it on the vegetables. I thought this was a great idea because the spray is not harmful to humans or animals, or even the bugs. They simply don't like the spicy water. The bug-free vegetables grew quickly, and finally I was able to pick some.

I carefully made a salad and took it to my father. He looked at it with a hint of a smile. "Christine, the carrots are smaller in this salad, but they taste better." I realized that he had known all along about my shopping trip. I smiled back at him.

Now, I better understand how putting a lot of effort into caring for something can help you appreciate the results more, however small they may be. Perhaps this was one of the reasons for my father's love of gardening.

In a few days he'll be back in the garden. I'll be right beside him helping him in any way I can.

問1 Christine originally said she would do the gardening because she [41] .

① knew it was important to her father

② wanted to improve her gardening skills

③ was asked by her father to do it

④ was interested in growing vegetables

問2 Which of the following was a problem in the garden ? [42]

① Animals often dug in the garden.

② Insects ate the lettuce and carrots.

③ The plants were given too much water.

④ The vegetables were marked incorrectly.

問3 Christine could secretly make the salad from store-bought vegetables because [43] .

① her father couldn't see the garden's progress

② her father was in the hospital at that time

③ her mother helped her to buy the vegetables

④ her mother helped her to make a spray

問4 Which of the following is closest to the meaning of the underlined word bug-free ? [44]

① All bugs have been killed.

② Bugs can do what they like.

③ No bugs can be found.

④ The bugs don't cost any money.

問5 What did Christine learn through her experience of gardening ? [45]

① Always prepare for a rainy day.

② Don't be disappointed by bugs.

③ Hard work can be rewarding.

④ Working alone produces results.

You are a new student at Robinson University in the US. You are reading the blogs of two students, Len and Cindy, to find out where you can buy things for your apartment.

New to Robinson University?
Posted by Len at 4:51 p.m. on August 4, 2021

　Getting ready for college? Do you need some home appliances or electronics, but don't want to spend too much money? There's a great store close to the university called Second Hand. It sells used goods such as televisions, vacuum cleaners, and microwaves. A lot of students like to buy and sell their things at the store. Here are some items that are on sale now. Most of them are priced very reasonably, but stock is limited, so hurry!

Second Hand *Sale for New Students!*

Television
2016 model
50 in.
$250

Vacuum Cleaner
2017 model
W 9 in. x L 14 in. x H 12 in.
$30

Rice Cooker
2018 model
W 11 in. x D 14 in. x H 8 in.
$40

Microwave
2019 model
1.1 cu. ft. 900 watts
$85

Kettle
2018 model
1ℓ
$5

https://secondhand.web

　Purchasing used goods is eco-friendly. Plus, by buying from Second Hand you'll be supporting a local business. The owner is actually a graduate of Robinson University!

Welcome to Robinson University!

Posted by Cindy at 11:21 a.m. on August 5, 2021

Are you starting at Robinson University soon? You may be preparing to buy some household appliances or electronics for your new life.

You're going to be here for four years, so buy your goods new! In my first year, I bought all of my appliances at a shop selling used goods near the university because they were cheaper than brand-new ones. However, some of them stopped working after just one month, and they did not have warranties. I had to replace them quickly and could not shop around, so I just bought everything from one big chain store. I wish I had been able to compare the prices at two or more shops beforehand.

The website called save4unistu.com is very useful for comparing the prices of items from different stores before you go shopping. The following table compares current prices for the most popular new items form three big stores.

Item	Cut Price	Great Buy	Value Saver
Rice Cooker (W 11 in. x D 14 in. x H 8 in.)	$115	$120	$125
Television (50 in.)	$300	$295	$305
Kettle (1ℓ)	$15	$18	$20
Microwave (1.1 cu. ft. 900 watts)	$88	$90	$95
Vacuum Cleaner (W 9 in. x L 14 in. x H 12 in.)	$33	$35	$38

https://save4unistu.com

Note that warranties are available for all items. So, if anything stops working, replacing it will be straightforward. Value Saver provides one-year warranties on all household goods for free. If the item is over $300, the warranty is extended by four years. Great But provides one-year warranties on all household goods, and students with proof of enrollment at a school get 10% off the prices listed on the table above. Warranties at Cut Price are not provided for free. You have to pay $10 per item for a five-year warranty.

Things go fast! Don't wait or you'll miss out!

問1　Len recommends buying used goods because ⬚24⬚ .

①　it will help the university

②　most of the items are good for the environment

③　they are affordable for students

④　you can find what you need in a hurry

問2　Cindy suggests buying ⬚25⬚ .

①　from a single big chain store because it saves time

②　from the website because it offers the best prices

③　new items that have warranties for replacement

④　used items because they are much cheaper than new items

問3　Both Len and Cindy recommend that you [26] .

① buy from the store near your university　② buy your appliances as soon as you can

③ choose a shop offering a student discount　④ choose the items with warranties

問4　If you want to buy new appliances at the best possible prices, you should [27] .

① access the URL in Cindy's post　② access the URL in Len's post

③ contact one big chain store　④ contact shops close to the campus

問5　You have decided to buy a microwave from [28] because it is the cheapest. You have also decided to buy a television from [29] because it is the cheapest with a five-year warranty. (Choose one for each box from options ①〜④.)

① Cut Price　② Great Buy　③ Second Hand　④ Value Saver

You are preparing a presentation on tourism in Japan. You emailed date about visitors to Japan in 2018 to your classmates, Hannah and Rick. Based on their responses, you draft a presentation outline.

The data:

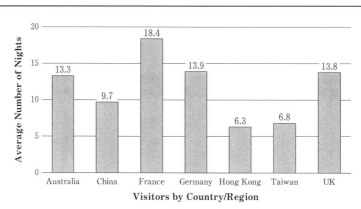

Figure 1. Length of stay in Japan.

（国土交通省観光庁による平成30年統計資料の一部を参考に作成）

Table1

Average Amount of Money Spent While Visiting Japan

Visitors by country/region	Food	Entertainment	Shopping
Australia	58,878	16,171	32,688
China	39,984	7,998	112,104
France	56,933	7,358	32,472
Germany	47,536	5,974	25,250
Hong Kong	36,887	5,063	50,287
Taiwan	28,190	5,059	45,441
UK	56,050	8,341	22,641

（yen per person）

（国土交通省観光庁による平成30年統計資料の一部を参考に作成）

The responses to your email:

Hi,

Thanks for your email! That's interesting data. I know that the number of international visitors to Japan increased previously, but I never paid attention to their length of stay. I assume that visitors from Asia come for shorter stays since they can go back and forth easily.

Also, the table shows that Asian visitors, overall, tend to spend more on shopping compared to visitors from Europe and Australia. I guess this is probably because gift-giving in Asian cultures is really important, and they want to buy gifts for friends and family. For example, I have seen many Asian tourists shopping around Ginza, Harajuku, and Akihabara. Perhaps they don't have to spend so much money on accommodations, so they can spend more on shopping. I'd like to talk about this.

However, I've heard that visitors from Asia are now becoming interested in doing some other things instead of shopping. We may see some changes in this kind of data in the near future!

Best,
Hannah
P. S. This message is going to Rick, too.

Hi,
Thanks for sending your data! This will help us prepare for our presentation!

I notice from the data that Australians spend the most on entertainment. I'll present on this.

Also, the other day, on Japanese TV, I saw a program about Australian people enjoying winter sports in Hokkaido. I wonder how much they spend. I'll look for more information. If you find any, please let me know. This could be good for a future project.

In addition, I agree with Hannah that there seems to be a big difference in the length of stay depending on the country or region the visitor is from.

What about you? Do you want to talk about what Hannah found in relation to the spending habits? I think this is very interesting.

All the best,
Rick
P. S. This message is going to Hannah, too.

The presentation draft:

Presentation Title: _____ 24 _____

Presenter	**Topic**
Hannah:	25
Rick:	26
me:	Relation to the length of stay

Example comparison:

People from 27 stay just over half the time in Japan compared to people from 28 , but spend slightly more money on entertainment.

Themes for Future Research: _____ 29 _____

問 1　Which is the best for ☐24☐ ?

① Money Spent on Winter Holidays in Hokkaido

② Shopping Budgets of International Tourists in Tokyo

③ Spending Habits of International Visitors in Japan

④ The Increase of Spending on Entertainment in Japan

問 2　Which is the best for ☐25☐ ?

① Activities of Australian visitors in Japan　② Asian visitors' food costs in Japan

③ Gift-giving habits in European cultures　④ Patterns in spending by visitors from Asia

問 3　Which is the best for ☐26☐ ?

① Australian tourists' interest in entertainment　② Chinese spending habits in Tokyo

③ TV programs about Hokkaido in Australia　④ Various experiences Asians enjoy in Japan

問 4　You agree with Rick's suggestion and look at the data. Choose the best for ☐27☐ and ☐28☐ .

① Australia　② China　③ France　④ Taiwan

問 5　Which is the best combination for ☐29☐ ?

A : Australians' budgets for winter sports in Japan

B : Future changes in the number of international visitors to Tokyo

C : Popular food for international visitors to Hokkaido

D : What Asian visitors in Japan will spend money on in the future

① A, B　② A, C　③ A, D　④ B, C　⑤ B, D　⑥ C, D

Your English teacher, Emma, has asked you and your classmate, Natsuki, to help her plan the day's schedule for hosting students from your sister school. You're reading the email exchanges between Natsuki and Emma so that you can draft the schedule.

Hi Emma,

We have some ideas and questions about the schedule for the day out with our 12 guests next month. As you told us, the students from both schools are supposed to give presentations in our assembly hall from 10:00 a.m. So, I've been looking at the attached timetable. Will they arrive at Azuma Station at 9:39 a.m. and then take a taxi to the school?

We have also been discussing the afternoon activities. How about seeing something related to science? We have two ideas, but if you need a third, please let me know.

Have you heard about the special exhibition that is on at Westside Aquarium next month? It's about a new food supplement made from sea plankton. We think it would be a good choice. Since it's popular, the best time to visit will be when it is least busy. I'm attaching the graph I found on the aquarium's homepage.

Eastside Botanical Garden, together with our local university, has been developing an interesting way of producing electricity from plants. Luckily, the professor in charge will give a short talk about it on that day in the early afternoon! Why don't we go?

Everyone will want to get some souvenirs, won't they? I think West Mall, next to Hibari Station, would be best, but we don't want to carry them around with us all day.

Finally, every visitor to Azuma should see the town's symbol, the statue in Azuma Memorial Park next to our school, but we can't work out a good schedule. Also, could you tell us what the plan is for lunch?

Yours,
Natsuki

Hi Natsuki,

Thank you for your email! You've been working hard. In answer to your question, they'll arrive at the station at 9:20 a.m. and then catch the school bus.

The two main afternoon locations, the aquarium and botanical garden, are good ideas because both schools place emphasis on science education, and the purpose of this program is to improve the scientific knowledge of the students. However, it would be wise to have a third suggestion just in case.

Let's get souvenirs at the end of the day. We can take the bus to the mall arriving there at 5:00 p.m. This will allow almost an hour for shopping and our guests can still be back at the hotel by 6:30 p.m. for dinner, as the hotel is only a few minutes' walk from Kaede Station.

About lunch, the school cafeteria will provide boxed lunches. We can eat under the statue you mentioned. If it rains, let's eat inside.

Thank you so much for your suggestions. Could you two make a draft for the schedule?

Best,
Emma

Attached timetable:

Train Timetable

Kaede—Hibari—Azuma

Stations	Train No.			
	108	109	110	111
Kaede	8:28	8:43	9:02	9:16
Hibari	8:50	9:05	9:24	9:38
Azuma	9:05	9:20	9:39	9:53

Stations	Train No.			
	238	239	240	241
Azuma	17:25	17:45	18:00	18:15
Hibari	17:40	18:00	18:15	18:30
Kaede	18:02	18:22	18:37	18:52

Attached graph:

Number of Visitors to Westside Aquarium

問1　The guests from the sister school will arrive on the number ☐24☐ train and catch the number ☐25☐ train back to their hotel.

① 109　② 110　③ 111　④ 238　⑤ 239　⑥ 240

問2　Which best completes the draft schedule? ☐26☐

A：The aquarium　　B：The botanical garden　　C：The mall　　D：The school

① D→A→B→C　② D→B→A→C　③ D→B→C→A　④ D→C→A→B

問3　Unless it rains, the guests will eat lunch in the ☐27☐ .

① botanical garden　　② park next to the school

③ park next to the station　　④ school garden

問4　The guests will **not** get around ☐28☐ on that day.

① by bus　② by taxi　③ by train　④ on foot

問5　As a third option, which would be the most suitable for your program? ☐29☐

① Hibari Amusement Park　　② Hibari Art Museum

③ Hibari Castle　　④ Hibari Space Center

You are doing research on students' reading habits. You found two articles.

Reading Habits Among Students　　　　　　　　　　　　　　by David Moore

July, 2010

　　Reading for pleasure is reading just for fun rather than for your school assignment or work. There is strong evidence linking reading for enjoyment and educational outcomes. Research has shown that students who read daily for pleasure perform better on tests than those who do not. Researchers have also found that reading for fun, even a little every day, is actually more beneficial than just spending many hours reading for studying and gathering information. Furthermore, frequent reading for fun, regardless of whether reading paper or digital books, is strongly related with improvements in literacy.

　　According to an international study, in 2009, two-thirds of 15-year-old students read for enjoyment on a daily basis. The graph shows the percentage of students who read for enjoyment in six countries. Reading habits differed across the countries, and there was a significant gender gap in reading in some countries.

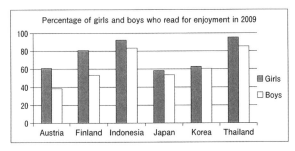

Percentage of girls and boys who read for enjoyment in 2009

　　In many countries, the percentage of students who read for enjoyment daily had decreased since the previous study in 2000. Back in 2000, on average, 77% of girls and 60% of boys read for enjoyment. By 2009, these percentages had dropped to 74% and 54%, respectively.

　　In my opinion, many students today do not know what books they should read. They say that they have no favorite genres or series. That's why the percentage of students who read for pleasure daily has been decreasing. Parents and teachers should help students find interesting books in order to make reading for pleasure a daily routine.

Opinion on "Reading Habits Among Students"　　　　　　　　　by Y. T.

August, 2010

　　As a school librarian, I have worked in many different countries. I was a little sad to learn that fewer students around the world read for enjoyment daily than before. According to David Moore's article, approximately 60% of female students in my home country reported they read for enjoyment, and the gender gap is about 20%. I find this disappointing.

　　More students need to know the benefits of reading. As David Moore mentioned, reading for pleasure has good effects on students' academic skills. Students who regularly read many books get better scores in reading, mathematics, and logical problem solving. Also, reading for enjoyment has positive effects on students' mental health. Research has shown a strong relationship between reading for fun regularly and lower levels of stress and depression.

　　Regardless of these benefits, students generally do not spend enough time reading. Our daily lives are now filled with screen-based entertainment. Students spend a lot of time playing video games, using social media, and watching television. I think students should reduce their time in front of screens and should read books every day even for a short time. Forming a reading habit in childhood is said to be associated with later reading proficiency. School libraries are good places for students to find numerous resources.

問1　Neither David Moore nor the librarian mentions ☐21☐ .

① gender differences in reading habits　② problems connected with reading digital books

③ the change in reading habits among students　④ the importance of reading regularly in childhood

問2　The librarian is from ☐22☐ .

① Austria　② Finland　③ Japan　④ Korea

問3　According to the articles, reading for pleasure has good effects on students' ☐23☐ . (<u>You may choose</u>
<u>more than one option.</u>)

① choice of career　② educational success

③ mental well-being　④ views of social media

問4　David Moore states that students ☐24☐ , and the librarian states that they ☐25☐ . (Choose a different
option for each box.)

① are busier than ever before　② cannot decide what books to read

③ choose similar books as their parents　④ enjoy playing with electronic devices

⑤ get useful information from TV

問5　Based on the information from both articles, you are going to write a report for homework. The best title
for your report would be " ☐26☐ ."

① Like It or Not, Reading Classic Novels is Important

② Make Reading for Entertainment a Part of Your Daily Life

③ Pleasure Reading is Becoming Popular in Different Countries

④ School Libraries: Great Resources for Doing School Projects

In class, everyone wrote a report based on the two graphs below. You will now read the reports written by Ami and Greg.

A survey was given to people between the ages of 13 and 29. To answer the question in Graph 2, the participants were able to choose more than one reason.

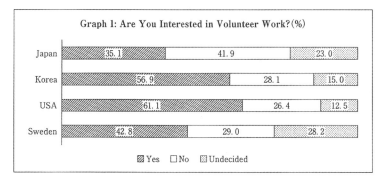

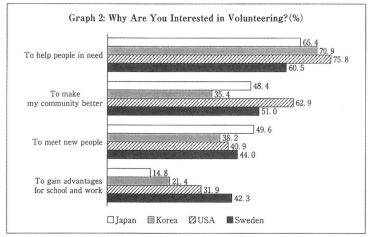

Ami Kitamura

 I was surprised when I saw Graph 1 because the percentage of Japanese participants who are interested in volunteering was higher than I had expected. As far as I know, none of my friends are doing any volunteer activities. So, I think we should motivate students in Japan to do more volunteering.

 In order to do that, it's important to consider the merits of doing volunteer work. According to Graph 2, 65.4% of Japanese participants said they are interested in volunteering because they want to help people in need. Also, the percentage of Japanese participants who chose "To meet new people" was the highest among the four countries.

 I think more Japanese students should learn about the benefits of volunteering. Thus, for the school festival I plan to make a poster that says, "You can help people in need and make new friends at the same time!" I hope many students will see it and become more interested in volunteer work.

Greg Taylor

In the USA, volunteering is common, so I was not surprised that it has the highest percentage of people who are interested in volunteer work. Graph 2 shows that a lot of American participants answered they are interested in volunteer work because they want to help people in need. I think this reason is important because students would feel a sense of achievement by helping people.

However, I was shocked to see that only 35.1% of Japanese participants are interested in volunteer work. I thought it would be more common in Japan. According to the information in Graph 2, only a few participants in Japan recognize the advantages for school and work. I recently heard Japanese universities and companies now put more value on volunteer experience than before. If more students understand these advantages, I think their interest in volunteering will increase.

Students should do volunteer work for the following two reasons. First, helping people in need will give students a feeling of accomplishment. Second, volunteering will also provide them with advantages for their future career. Therefore, I will compose a newsletter about these two benefits of doing volunteer work, and distribute it to students at school.

問1 　20　 felt that the percentage of Japanese participants who were interested in volunteer work was lower than expected.

① Ami 　② Both Ami and Greg 　③ Greg 　④ Neither Ami nor Greg

問2 　Both Ami and Greg say that Japanese students should 　21　.

① discuss the benefits of volunteer work with students from other countries

② focus on studying and then consider doing volunteer work after graduating

③ know that doing volunteer work has good effects on those who do it

④ realize that volunteer work is becoming popular in other countries

問3 　Neither Ami nor Greg mentioned " 　22　 " in their reports.

① To gain advantages for school and work 　　② To help people in need

③ To make my community better 　　④ To meet new people

問4 　In their reports, Ami says she will 〔 a 〕 and Greg says he will 〔 b 〕. 　23　

① a. give a survey 　b. make a speech 　② a. give a survey 　b. write a newsletter

③ a. make a poster 　b. make a speech 　④ a. make a poster 　b. write a newsletter

問5 　You found four articles on the Internet. Based on the titles below, the most useful article for both Ami's and Greg's plans would be " 　24　 ".

① Differences between Volunteer Work and Community Service

② How to Make Friends while Volunteering Abroad

③ Supporting People in Need through Volunteer Work

④ Volunteer Experiences and Your Future Career

A 次の文章はある説明文の一部である。この文章を読み，下の問い（**問1～4**）の 33 ～ 36 に入れるのに最も適当なものを，それぞれ下の①～④のうちから一つずつ選べ。

　　Sports coaches and players are interested in how training programs can be designed to enhance performance. The order of practice potentially facilitates learning outcomes without increasing the amount of practice. A study was conducted to examine how different training schedules influence throwing performance.

　　In this study, elementary school students threw a tennis ball at a target laid on the floor. They threw the ball from three throwing locations at distances of 3, 4, and 5 meters from the target. The target consisted of the center (20 cm wide) and nine larger outer rings. They served as zones to indicate the accuracy of the throws. If the ball landed in the center of the target, 100 points were given. If the ball landed in one of the outer zones, 90, 80, 70, 60, 50, 40, 30, 20, or 10 points were recorded accordingly. If the ball landed outside of the target, no points were given. If the ball landed on a line separating two zones, the higher score was awarded.

　　The students were assigned to one of three practice groups : Blocked, Random, or Combined. All students were instructed to use an overarm throwing motion to try to hit the center of the target with the ball. On the first day of this study, they each completed a total of 81 practice throws. Students in the Blocked group threw 27 times from one of the three throwing locations, followed by 27 throws from the next location, and ended practice with 27 throws from the final location. In the Random group, each student threw the ball 81 times in the order of throwing locations that the researchers had specified. No more than two consecutive throws were allowed from the same location for this group. In the Combined group, the students started with a blocked schedule and gradually shifted to a random schedule. On the next day, all students completed a performance test of 12 throws.

　　Results showed that during the practice of 81 throws, the Blocked group performed worse than the other two groups. Performance test scores were also analyzed. The Combined group showed the best performance among the three groups, followed by the Random group and then by the Blocked group. It is still uncertain if similar results can be obtained for adults in training programs for other throwing actions, such as those seen in bowling, baseball, and basketball. This will be addressed in the following section.

(Esmaeel Saemi 他（2012） *Practicing Along the Contextual Interference Continuum: A Comparison of Three Practice Schedules in an Elementary Physical Education Setting* の一部を参考に作成)

問1　What is the total score achieved by the five throws in this figure ? 33

① 200

② 210

③ 220

④ 230

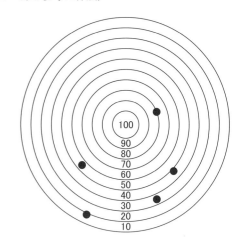

問2　Which of the following statements is true about the experiment？　34

① Eighty-one throws were made from the same initial throwing location in the Blocked group.

② The distance from the target remained unchanged during the entire experiment for the Combined group.

③ The set of throws from the same location involved various ways of throwing for the Combined group.

④ Throwing three or more times in a row from the same location was against the rules for the Random group.

問3　Which of the following statements is true about the results？　35

① The Blocked group had the best score both during practice and on the performance test.

② The Blocked group showed the worst score among the three groups on the performance test.

③ The Combined group showed lower accuracy than the Random group on the performance test.

④ The Random group had the lowest accuracy both during practice and on the performance test.

問4　What will most likely be discussed next in this report？　36

① Mental imagery training of underhand throws　② Observation of younger students' movements

③ Overarm throws with eyes closed　④ Various kinds of throwing motions

A　次の文章はある説明文の一部である。この文章と表を読み，下の問い（**問1〜4**）の　33　〜　36　に入れるのに最も適当なものを，それぞれ下の①〜④のうちから一つずつ選べ。

Art may reflect the ways people lived. Researchers have discussed how art portrays clothing and social settings. One study was conducted to determine if this idea could be extended to paintings featuring family meals. The results of this study might help illustrate why certain kinds of foods were painted.

The researchers examined 140 paintings of family meals painted from the years 1500 to 2000. These came from five countries : the United States, France, Germany, Italy, and the Netherlands. The researchers examined each painting for the presence of 91 foods, with absence coded as 0 and presence coded as 1. For example, when one or more onions appeared in a painting, the researchers coded it as 1. Then they calculated the percentage of the paintings from these countries that included each food.

Table 1 shows the percentage of paintings with selected foods. The researchers discussed several findings. First, some paintings from these countries included foods the researchers had expected. Shellfish were most common in the Netherlands' (Dutch) paintings, which was anticipated as nearly half of its border touches the sea. Second, some paintings did not include foods the researchers had expected. Shellfish and fish each appeared in less than 12% of the paintings from the United States, France, and Italy although large portions of these countries border oceans or seas. Chicken, a common food, seldom appeared in the paintings. Third, some paintings included foods the researchers had not expected. For example, among German paintings, 20% of them included shellfish although only 6% of the country touches the sea. Also, lemons were most common in paintings from the Netherlands, even though they do not grow there naturally.

Table 1

The Frequency of Selected Foods Shown in Paintings by Percentage

Item	USA	France	Germany	Italy	The Netherlands
Apples	41. 67	35. 29	25. 00	36. 00	8. 11
Bread	29. 17	29. 41	40. 00	40. 00	62. 16
Cheese	12. 50	5. 88	5. 00	24. 00	13. 51
Chicken	0. 00	0. 00	0. 00	4. 00	2. 70
Fish	0. 00	11. 76	10. 00	4. 00	13. 51
Lemons	29. 17	20. 59	30. 00	16. 00	51. 35
Onions	0. 00	0. 00	5. 00	20. 00	0. 00
Shellfish	4. 17	11. 11	20. 00	4. 00	56. 76

Comparing these results with previous research, the researchers concluded that food art does not necessarily portray actual life. The researchers offered some explanations for this. One explanation is that artists painted some foods to express their interest in the larger world. Another is that painters wanted to show their technique by painting more challenging foods. For example, the complexity of a lemon's surface and interior might explain its popularity, especially among Dutch artists. As other interpretations are possible, it is necessary to examine the paintings from different perspectives. These are the period in which the paintings were completed and the cultural associations of foods. Both issues will be taken up in the following sections.

(Brian Wansink 他（2016）　*Food Art Does Not Reflect Reality : A Quantitative Content Analysis of Meals in Popular Paintings* の一部を参考に作成)

問1 For the category "Apples" in this research, a painting with two whole apples and one apple cut in half would be labeled as ☐33☐ .

    ① 0   ② 1   ③ 2   ④ 3

問2 According to Table 1, the paintings from ☐34☐ .

    ① France included apples at a lower percentage than the German ones

    ② France included cheese at a higher percentage than the Dutch ones

    ③ Italy included bread at a lower percentage than the American ones

    ④ Italy included onions at a higher percentage than the German ones

問3 According to the passage and Table 1, ☐35☐ .

    ① chicken frequently appeared in the American paintings because people there often ate chicken

    ② fish appeared in less than one tenth of the Italian paintings though much of Italy lies next to seas

    ③ lemons appeared in more than half of the Dutch paintings as they are native to the Netherlands

    ④ shellfish appeared in half of the paintings from each of the five countries because they touch seas

問4 According to the passage, foods in these paintings can ☐36☐ .

    ① demonstrate the painters' knowledge of history

    ② display the painters' desire to stay in their countries

    ③ indicate the painters' artistic skills and abilities

    ④ reflect the painters' love of their local foods

A　次の文章はある説明文の一部である。この文章とグラフを読み，下の問い（**問1〜4**）の　33　〜　36　に入れるのに最も適当なものを，それぞれ下の①〜④のうちから一つずつ選べ。

Color is an important feature considered by consumers when shopping for various products. Marketing companies need to identify the colors that can create an intention to purchase and a desired atmosphere in retail stores. However, it is not easy to anticipate which colors will be popular for individual items, because consumers have different preferences depending on product types. Through the research reported here, we can deepen our understanding of the influence of color on consumers.

In this study, researchers surveyed German consumers to obtain information on whether the participants thought color was important when shopping, how much they were influenced by color when buying various products, and what emotions and associations were related to various colors. First, the researchers examined the data and found that color was indeed important for the participants when shopping, with 68% of them mentioning color as a determining factor when choosing the product they intended to purchase.

Next, the researchers investigated whether the degree of importance consumers put on color varied depending on the products purchased. Figure 1 shows six everyday products and the percentages of the participants who placed high importance on color when purchasing those products. The top two products were both those worn by the participants, and the three lowest were all electronic devices. A total of 36.4% of the participants placed importance on color for cellphones. This was the highest among the electronic products, but only slightly more than half of that for bags, which appeared one rank above.

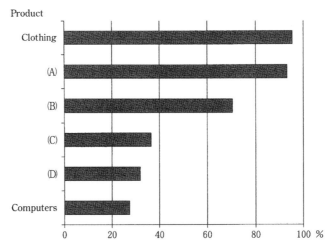

Figure 1. The percentages of the participants who placed high importance on color when purchasing six everyday products.

Third, the researchers looked at the participants' perceptions of and associations with colors. The results showed that red had various meanings: love, danger, anger, and power. Green produced a relationship with nature, good luck, and health. Furthermore, the color white was associated with balance, health, and calm. Results showed each color had several different meanings.

The findings summarized in the above passage explained how colors influenced German consumers. However, this influence may vary from country to country. In this globalized world, it has become easier to market products internationally, partly due to the increased use of the Internet. Therefore, it is necessary to consider the importance consumers in other parts of the world place on color in their choices of products. The next part of this passage will examine this topic.

(Okan Akcay (2013) *Product Color Choice and Meanings of Color : A Case of Germany* の一部を参考に作成)

問1　The passage mentions that it is difficult to understand which colors consumers like better because $\boxed{33}$.

① color preferences differ from generation to generation

② consumers' favorite colors vary for different products

③ product marketers choose the most popular colors

④ various products are purchased by consumers when shopping

問2　In Figure 1, which of the following do (A), (B), (C), and (D) refer to ?　$\boxed{34}$

① (A) Bags (B) Footwear (C) Cellphones (D) Music players

② (A) Bags (B) Footwear (C) Music players (D) Cellphones

③ (A) Footwear (B) Bags (C) Cellphones (D) Music players

④ (A) Footwear (B) Bags (C) Music players (D) Cellphones

問3　Which of the following statements is correct according to the passage ?　$\boxed{35}$

① German businesses consider green to represent passion to consumers.

② German consumers perceive one color as containing multiple images.

③ German people appear to prefer green clothing to red clothing.

④ German producers choose one color for products after observing their sales.

問4　What topic is most likely to follow the last paragraph ?　$\boxed{36}$

① The effects of globalization on color choices in international business

② The importance of marketing electronic devices in other countries

③ The influence of the Internet on product choices in international business

④ The significance of color for the consumers in other countries

目標
10分　H 29　④

A　次の文章はある説明文の一部である。この文章と図を読み，下の問い（問1〜4）の 35 〜 38 に入れるのに最も適当なものを，それぞれ下の①〜④のうちから一つずつ選べ。

Physical activity in your childhood, such as playing sports and exercising, can greatly benefit your health when you are older. Therefore, it is important to promote physical activity in childhood for one's good health. The schoolyard is one place where children and adolescents can be encouraged to take part in physical activity. Thus, knowing how schoolyards are used by students may give us some helpful ideas to promote their physical activity.

A study was conducted at four schools in Denmark in order to investigate how much different types of schoolyard areas were used and whether students were active or passive in those areas. In the study, schoolyard areas were classified and defined by their primary characteristics. *Grass* represented playing fields and natural green lawn areas, often used for soccer, but without any marked lines or goals. *Multi-court* referred to fenced areas on various surface, like artificial grass and rubber, designed for tennis and other such ball games. *Natural* represented areas with, for example, bushes, trees, and natural stones. *Playground* represented areas with play equipment, such as swings and slides on safe surfaces like sand. *Solid Surface* described the areas with the hardest surfaces, like concrete. These areas were identified by flat open spaces, often having numerous markings painted for games and benches set in different places.

Using GPS devices and other instruments, the researchers measured the lengths of time the students spent in the different schoolyard areas as well as the degrees of their physical activity. Figure 1 displays the average amounts of time spent per day in each area for All students and those averages divided into Children（aged 12 and under）and Adolescents（aged 13 and over）. Solid Surface was clearly the area in which All students spent most of their time, followed by Multi-court then Grass. Natural and Playground showed similar averages for All students, with the average for All students in Playground being just over two minutes.

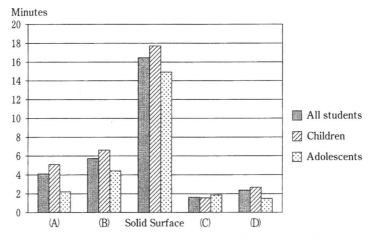

Figure 1. Average times spent in each area by All students, Children, and Adolescents.

Furthermore, the study revealed differences between the average amounts of time spent in schoolyards by Children and Adolescents. In comparison with Adolescents, Children spent more time in all schoolyard areas except for Natural areas. The greater amount of time spent by Children might be explained by the fact that, according to the regulations at all four schools, Children could not leave the schoolyard during lunch time, but Adolescents could when they wanted to.

When looking at the degree of physical activity, researchers discovered differences among the schoolyard areas. Students were most active in Grass and Playground areas. On the other hand, students were quite passive in Solid Surface areas, with Adolescents spending only 7% of their time there being physically active.

The findings of this study show the importance of investigating the potential of various environments and features in schoolyards. To promote students' health, it is also beneficial to observe how varieties of games Children and Adolescents play affect the length of time spent taking part in physical activity. Let us now take a look at these relationships.

(Henriette Bondo Andersen 他 (2015) *Objectively Measured Differences in Physical Activity in Five Types of Schoolyard Area* を参考に作成)

問1　According to the passage, what is the difference between Multi-court and Solid Surface ?　| 35 |
　　① Unlike Multi-court, Solid Surface contains artificial grass for younger students to play on.
　　② Unlike Multi-court, Solid Surface does not contain boundaries marked for students' games.
　　③ Unlike Solid Surface, Multi-court has a relatively soft surface made of various materials.
　　④ Unlike Solid Surface, Multi-court is not surrounded by anything, which makes it easy to access.

問2　In Figure 1, which of the following do (A), (B), (C), and (D) refer to ?　| 36 |
　　① (A) Grass　　　(B) Multi-court　　(C) Natural　　　(D) Playground
　　② (A) Grass　　　(B) Multi-court　　(C) Playground　(D) Natural
　　③ (A) Multi-court　(B) Grass　　　(C) Natural　　　(D) Playground
　　④ (A) Multi-court　(B) Grass　　　(C) Playground　(D) Natural

問3　The main purpose of this passage is to | 37 | .
　　① discuss the benefits of being physically active at school in childhood
　　② give advice to increase the number of physically active adolescents
　　③ introduce schools that encourage students to play on grassed areas
　　④ show that types of schoolyards affect students' behavior there

問4　What topic is most likely to follow the last paragraph ?　| 38 |
　　① The benefits of studying various school environments for different activities
　　② The connections between types of games and lengths of time being active
　　③ The influence of the schoolyard environment on Adolescents' physical activity
　　④ The way schoolyard surfaces affect the time spent doing physical activity

A　次の文章はある説明文の一部である。この文章とグラフを読み，下の問い（問1〜4）の 35 〜 38 に入れるのに最も適当なものを，それぞれ下の①〜④のうちから一つずつ選べ。

US consumers have benefited from an increased volume and variety of fresh-fruit imports, particularly since the 1990s. The fruit and vegetable section in today's grocery store often has dozens of different fresh fruits on display all year around, which come from all corners of the globe as additions to domestic fresh fruit.

The rapid growth of fresh-fruit imports has affected many aspects of the US fresh-fruit market. For example, while oranges are the US's leading domestically grown fruit, the volume of US orange imports has grown steadily since the 1990s, with occasional sudden increases when the US crop experienced freezing weather（see Figure 1）.

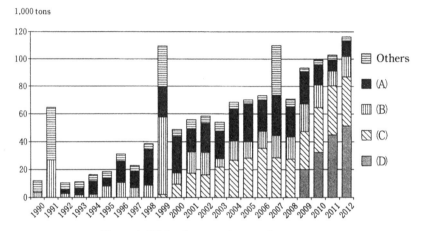

Figure 1. US fresh-orange imports by country.

The US domestic market receives orange imports from various countries and regions. Among the major suppliers, Mexico is a longtime source. However, due to the strong US demand for fresh oranges throughout the year, the Southern Hemisphere countries have also become major suppliers, especially during the summer months when domestic navel oranges are not available. Australia was the first such country, starting in the early 1990s after it obtained permission from the US government to export its navel oranges there. Australia was followed by South Africa in the late 1990s, and most recently by Chile as well.

In the US, two main types of oranges are produced domestically : "navel oranges" and "Valencia oranges." Navel oranges — virtually without seeds, with flesh that separates easily and is firm rather than watery — are the most popular oranges for eating fresh. The navel orange share of US production of fresh-market oranges was 76 percent during the years 2010-2012. In comparison, Valencia oranges — with thin skins, containing occasional seeds, and with juicy and sweet flesh — accounted for 24 percent during the same period. As the US's top supplier of fresh-market oranges, California produced 87 percent of fresh-market navel oranges and more than 81 percent of fresh-market Valencia oranges.

The main harvest period for domestic fresh-market oranges is from November through May, a time when California's navel oranges are in season. However, the amount of oranges produced and shipped domestically falls significantly from June through October. In earlier years, when fresh-orange imports still accounted for only a small portion of domestic use, Valencia oranges were a popular variety when navel oranges were out of season. As seen in Figure 2, however, navel orange imports from the Southern Hemisphere countries have come to dominate the US in the summer season.

Because of seasonal production patterns, the majority of Mexico's oranges arrive in the US market from

December through June, when US supplies are relatively high. In contrast, the season for imports from the Southern Hemisphere countries is mainly from July through October, when US supplies are relatively low. This trend is similar to that seen with many other fruits as well.

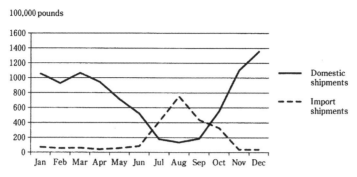

Figure 2. Seasonal relationship between imported and domestic oranges (2010-2012 average).

(Sophia Wu Huang（2013）*Imports Contribute to Year-Round Fresh Fruit Availability* を参考に作成)

問1　In Figure 1, which of the following do (A), (B), (C) and (D) refer to ? ☐35

①	(A) Australia	(B) Chile	(C) Mexico	(D) South Africa
②	(A) Australia	(B) Mexico	(C) South Africa	(D) Chile
③	(A) South Africa	(B) Chile	(C) Australia	(D) Mexico
④	(A) South Africa	(B) Mexico	(C) Australia	(D) Chile

問2　According to the passage, which of the following correctly describes one difference between navel oranges and Valencia oranges ? ☐36

① Navel oranges contain fewer seeds than Valencia oranges do.

② Navel oranges contain more juice than Valencia oranges do.

③ Valencia oranges are more popular than navel oranges in the winter.

④ Valencia oranges are more suitable for eating fresh than navel oranges.

問3　What is the main purpose of this passage ? ☐37

① To account for the seasonal changes in the US production of oranges

② To explain the differences between navel oranges and Valencia oranges

③ To illustrate the relation between US production and imports of oranges

④ To improve the quality of the navel oranges produced in the US

問4　What topic is most likely to follow the last paragraph ? ☐38

① Export rates of other fruits from the US to the Southern Hemisphere

② Statistics showing the seasonal changes in imports of other fruits

③ The shipping methods of navel oranges from the Southern Hemisphere

④ The variety of fruits commonly grown in the US and Mexico

A 以下の文章はある説明文の一部である。この文章とグラフを読み，次の問い（**問1〜4**）の 35 〜 38 に入れるのに最も適当なものを，それぞれ下の①〜④のうちから一つずつ選べ。

Social Networking Services （SNS）, online services that allow users to communicate with others, are used by a growing number of young people to keep in touch with friends and family. However, this rise in the use of SNS by young people has been accompanied by increasing anxiety among parents and teachers. They are concerned about whether young users are prepared for the risks that come with using SNS, including privacy issues and unwelcome contact.

A 2011 survey asked Australian parents, students, and teachers about their perceptions of the degree of risk when using SNS ─ specifically, whether they felt it to be "safe," "a little risky," "very risky," or "risky but what everyone does." Figure 1 shows that over a quarter of students chose "safe," in other words, that they felt SNS use was without risk. In addition, 19.6% of students reported that, though they knew the dangers, they still used SNS because that is "what everyone does." In contrast with the students' responses, their parents and teachers were more cautious about the risk associated with SNS use, with teachers slightly more likely to see high risk.

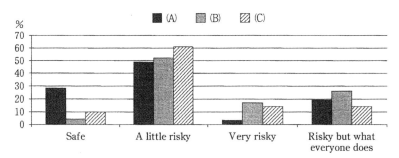

Figure 1. Perceptions of SNS risk by parents, students, and teachers.

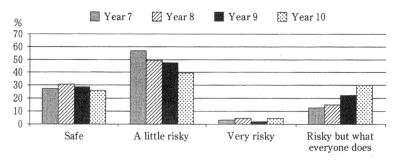

Figure 2. Perceptions of SNS risk by student year level.

Interestingly, not all students had the same perception of risk. Figure 2 shows a comparison between students by year ─ "Year 7" refers to first-year junior high school students and "Year 10" refers to first-year high school students. While the percentage of students who responded that SNS usage is "safe" was almost the same regardless of year, there was a drop by year in the percentage of students who chose "a little risky," and a rise in those who chose "risky but what everyone does."

Furthermore, the study asked students about information security.   It found that students from years 7 to 10 were increasingly cautious about privacy, becoming more careful by year about who could see their personal information online.   Because Year 7 students, in addition to being the least cautious about information security, also tended to see SNS use as either "safe" or only "a little risky," they were believed to be at the greatest risk.

The study then examined whether adults were discussing SNS risks with young people.   However, the results here were not clear.   While the study found that over 91% of parents and 68% of teachers said they discuss SNS issues with students, almost half of the students （46.1%） responded they do not talk with their parents, and almost three-quarters of the students （74.6%） responded that they do not talk with teachers. There are several possible explanations for this gap.

(Melissa de Zwart 他 （2011） *Teenagers, Legal Risks & Social Networking Sites* を参考に作成)

問 1　In Figure 1, which of the following do (A), (B), and (C) refer to ?　[35]
　① (A) Parents　(B) Students　(C) Teachers　② (A) Parents　(B) Teachers　(C) Students
　③ (A) Students　(B) Parents　(C) Teachers　④ (A) Students　(B) Teachers　(C) Parents

問 2　Which of the following is mentioned as one of the reasons that Year 7 students are thought to have the highest risk ?　[36]
　① They are the least careful about security when using SNS.
　② They are the least likely to think SNS is "safe."
　③ They are the most likely to think SNS is "very risky."
　④ They are the most likely to use SNS to contact friends.

問 3　The main purpose of this passage is to [37] .
　① describe the various dangers of using SNS　② discuss differences in awareness of SNS risk
　③ explain why students are using SNS more　④ suggest solutions for the problems with SNS

問 4　What topic might follow the last paragraph ?　[38]
　① Examples of the different risks students face in using SNS
　② Reasons for the different responses from students and adults
　③ Trends in how students and adults use the Internet
　④ Ways to reduce the number of younger students using SNS

A　以下の文章はある報告書の一部である。この文章とグラフを読み，次の問い（問1～4）の ┌ 35 ┐ ～ ┌ 38 ┐ に入れるのに最も適当なものを，それぞれ下の①～④のうちから一つずつ選べ。

Magnet and Sticky : A Study on State-to-State Migration in the US

Some people live their whole lives near their places of birth, while others move elsewhere.　A study conducted by the Pew Research Center looked into the state-to-state moving patterns of Americans.　The study examined each state to determine how many of their adult citizens have moved there from other states.　States with high percentages of these residents are called "magnet" states in the report.　The study also investigated what percent of adults born in each state are still living there.　States high in these numbers are called "sticky" states.　The study found that some states were both magnet and sticky, while others were neither.　There were also states that were only magnet or only sticky.

Figures 1 and 2 show how selected states rank on magnet and sticky scales, respectively.　Florida is a good example of a state that ranks high on both.　Seventy percent of its current adult population was born in another state ; at the same time, 66% of adults born in Florida are still living there.　On the other hand, West Virginia is neither magnet （only 27%） nor particularly sticky（49%）.　In other words, it has few newcomers, and relatively few West Virginians stay there.　Michigan is a typical example of a state which is highly sticky, but very low magnet.　In contrast, Alaska, which ranks near the top of the magnet scale, is the least sticky of all states.

Three other extreme examples also appear in Figures 1 and 2.　The first is Nevada, where the high proportion of adult residents born out of state makes this state America's top magnet.　New York is at the opposite end of the magnet scale, even though it is attractive to immigrants from other nations.　The third extreme example is Texas, at the opposite end of the sticky scale from Alaska.　Although it is a fairly weak magnet, Texas is the nation's stickiest state.

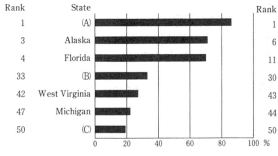

Figure 1. Magnet scale (selected states).

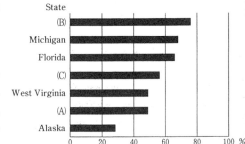

Figure 2. Sticky scale (selected states).

The study went on to explore the reasons why "movers" leave their home states and "stayers" remain.　As for movers, there is no single factor that influences their decisions to move to other states.　The most common reason they gave for moving is to seek job or business opportunities.　Others report moving for personal reasons: family ties, the desire to live in a good community for their children, or retirement.

（Pew Research Center（2008）*American Mobility* を参考に作成）

問1　If a state is magnet, ___35___ .

① few adults born there have stayed

② few adults living there were born elsewhere

③ many adults born there have stayed

④ many adults living there were born elsewhere

問2　Which three states are represented in Figures 1 and 2 as (A), (B), and (C) ?　___36___

① (A)　Nevada　　　(B)　New York　　　(C)　Texas

② (A)　Nevada　　　(B)　Texas　　　　(C)　New York

③ (A)　New York　　(B)　Nevada　　　(C)　Texas

④ (A)　New York　　(B)　Texas　　　　(C)　Nevada

問3　The main purpose of this passage is to ___37___ .

① describe various patterns in American migration

② explain why some states are less popular than others

③ list states with a high ratio of adults who were born there

④ report how the Pew Research Center collected data

問4　What topic might follow the last paragraph ?　___38___

① Reasons why some Americans stay in their home states.

② States that attract immigrants from other countries.

③ Types of occupations movers look for in other states.

④ Ways to raise children in a magnet state community.

A 以下の文章と表を読み，次の問い（**問1～3**）に対する答えとして　35　～　37　に入れるのに最も適当なものを，それぞれ次の①～④のうちから一つずつ選べ。

The World Health Organization (WHO) has published a report on the availability and distribution of human health resources around the world. *The World Health Report 2006* analyzes factors affecting countries' health care environments. The data collected reveal a range of situations and have helped WHO propose a long-term action plan for improving health care offered in every country.

One of the key factors contributing to a country's health care conditions is its numbers of health care workers. The report estimates the shortage of these professionals at an alarming 4.3 million worldwide. It further points out that the shortage is most severe in the poorest nations, especially those located south of the Sahara Desert which are faced with high rates of disease. As Table 1 shows, Senegal and Ghana, for example, have very low numbers of doctors and nurses per 10,000 people.

Surprisingly, perhaps, countries such as Russia and Cuba actually have higher proportions of medical professionals than some richer countries. The systems for qualifying health care workers do differ from country to country. Still, these two countries clearly give priority to ensuring that there are sufficient numbers of professionals.

Another important factor is a country's health care spending, shown in Table 1 as a percentage of its gross domestic product (GDP), or the total value of all its goods and services. Despite their lower proportions of doctors, countries such as the USA, Sweden, and France spend much more on health care, both as a percentage of GDP and as an actual amount, than Russia and Cuba.

With these factors and other conditions in mind, WHO has proposed solutions to the global shortage of health care workers. Areas of particular concern include war-torn countries such as Somalia and Afghanistan. Countries and organizations have provided financial aid in the past. Because money donated has not always led to more spending in health care, however, the report recommends a 10-year plan to help countries build sustainable training systems. International cooperation is vital to WHO's proposal ; countries at risk must be able to rely on the support of various global partners. Japan, the UK, and other countries are expected to give assistance including medical knowledge. Perhaps WHO's vision of "universal access to health care" can become a reality.

Table 1
Health Care Indicators by Country

Country	Doctors per 10,000 people*	Nurses per 10,000 people*	Health care spending (2003)	
			% of GDP	Actual amount spent per person (US $)
Senegal	0.6	3.2	5.1	29
(A)	1.5	9.2	4.5	16
Afghanistan	1.9	2.2	6.5	11
Japan	19.8	77.9	7.9	2662
(B)	25.6	93.7	15.2	5711
Sweden	32.8	102.4	9.4	3149
France	33.7	72.4	10.1	2981
(C)	42.5	80.5	5.6	167
Cuba	59.1	74.4	7.3	211

*Data collected at different times between 2000-2005.
(WHO (2006) *The World Health Report 2006* を参考に作成)

問1 Which of the following combinations represents the three countries (A), (B), and (C) in Table 1? ⬚35

① (A) Ghana (B) Somalia (C) Russia

② (A) Ghana (B) the USA (C) Russia

③ (A) Russia (B) Somalia (C) the USA

④ (A) Russia (B) the USA (C) Ghana

問2 According to the report, which two aspects influence a country's health care situation most? ⬚36

① Sustainable training systems and health care spending.

② Sustainable training systems and money donated.

③ The numbers of health care workers and health care spending.

④ The numbers of health care workers and money donated.

問3 Which of the following statements is **NOT** true? ⬚37

① The lack of health care workers worldwide is reported to be around 4.3 million.

② The proportion of doctors and nurses is higher in Sweden than in Japan.

③ WHO's report includes an action plan to help countries with poor health care systems.

④ WHO's report proposes sending more doctors and nurses to poorer countries.

In your English class, you will give a presentation about a great inventor. You found the following article and prepared notes for your presentation.

Who invented television? It is not an easy question to answer. In the early years of the 20th century, there was something called a mechanical television system, but it was not a success. Inventors were also competing to develop an electronic television system, which later became the basis of what we have today. In the US, there was a battle over the patent for the electronic television system, which attracted people's attention because it was between a young man and a giant corporation. This patent would give the inventor the official right to be the only person to develop, use, or sell the system.

Farnsworth in 1939

Philo Taylor Farnsworth was born in a log cabin in Utah in 1906. His family did not have electricity until he was 12 years old, and he was excited to find a generator—a machine that produces electricity—when they moved into a new home. He was very interested in mechanical and electrical technology, reading any information he could find on the subject. He would often repair the old generator and even changed his mother's hand-powered washing machine into an electricity-powered one.

One day, while working in his father's potato field, he looked behind him and saw all the straight parallel rows of soil that he had made. Suddenly, it occurred to him that it might be possible to create an electronic image on a screen using parallel lines, just like the rows in the field. In 1922, during the spring semester of his first year at high school, he presented this idea to his chemistry teacher, Justin Tolman, and asked for advice about his concept of an electronic television system. With sketches and diagrams on blackboards, he showed the teacher how it might be accomplished, and Tolman encouraged him to develop his ideas.

On September 7, 1927, Farnsworth succeeded in sending his first electronic image. In the following years, he further improved the system so that it could successfully broadcast live images. The US government gave him a patent for this system in 1930.

However, Farnsworth was not the only one working on such a system. A giant company, RCA (Radio Corporation of America), also saw a bright future for television and did not want to miss the opportunity. They recruited Vladimir Zworykin, who had already worked on an electronic television system and had earned a patent as early as 1923. Yet, in 1931, they offered Farnsworth a large sum of money to sell them his patent as his system was superior to that of Zworykin's. He refused this offer, which started a patent war between Farnsworth and RCA.

The company took legal action against Farnsworth, claiming that Zworykin's 1923 patent had priority even though he had never made a working version of his system. Farnsworth lost the first two rounds of the court case. However, in the final round, the teacher who had copied Farnsworth's blackboard drawings gave evidence that Farnsworth did have the idea of an electronic television system at least a year before Zworykin's patent was issued. In 1934, a judge approved Farnsworth's patent claim on the strength of handwritten notes made by his old high school teacher, Tolman.

Farnsworth died in 1971 at the age of 64. He held about 300 US and foreign patents, mostly in radio and television, and in 1999, *TIME* magazine included Farnsworth in *Time 100: The Most Important People of the*

Century. In an interview after his death, Farnsworth's wife Pem recalled Neil Armstrong's moon landing being broadcast. Watching the television with her, Farnsworth had said, "Pem, this has made it all worthwhile." His story will always be tied to his teenage dream of sending moving pictures through the air and those blackboard drawings at his high school.

Your presentation notes:

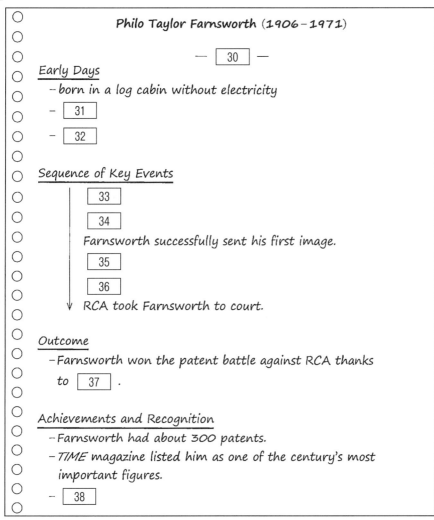

Philo Taylor Farnsworth (1906 – 1971)

— 30 —

Early Days
 – born in a log cabin without electricity
 – 31
 – 32

Sequence of Key Events
 33
 34
 Farnsworth successfully sent his first image.
 35
 36
 RCA took Farnsworth to court.

Outcome
 – Farnsworth won the patent battle against RCA thanks to 37 .

Achievements and Recognition
 – Farnsworth had about 300 patents.
 – *TIME* magazine listed him as one of the century's most important figures.
 – 38

問1 Which is the best subtitle for your presentation? 30
 ① A Young Inventor Against a Giant Company
 ② From High School Teacher to Successful Inventor
 ③ Never-Ending Passion for Generating Electricity
 ④ The Future of Electronic Television

問2 Choose the best two options for 31 and 32 to complete Early Days. (The order does not matter.)
 ① bought a generator to provide his family with electricity
 ② built a log cabin that had electricity with the help of his father
 ③ enjoyed reading books on every subject in school
 ④ fixed and improved household equipment for his family
 ⑤ got the idea for an electronic television system while working in field

問3　Choose **four** out of the five events　(①〜⑤) in the order they happened to complete Sequence of Key Events.

| 33 | → | 34 | → | 35 | → | 36 |

① Farnsworth rejected RCA's offer.

② Farnsworth shared his idea with his high school teacher.

③ RCA won the first stage of the battle.

④ The US government gave Farnsworth the patent.

⑤ Zworykin was granted a patent for his television system.

問4　Choose the best option for 37 to complete Outcome.

① the acceptance of his rival's technological inferiority

② the financial assistance provided by Tolman

③ the sketches his teacher had kept for many years

④ the withdrawal of RCA from the battle

問5　Choose the best option for 38 to complete Achievements and Recognition.

① He and his wife were given an award for their work with RCA.

② He appeared on TV when Armstrong's first moon landing was broadcast.

③ His invention has enabled us to watch historic events live.

④ Many teenagers have followed their dreams after watching him on TV.

目標
14分

You are going to give a talk on a person you would like to have interviewed if they were still alive. Read the following passage about the person you have chosen and complete your notes.

Vivian Maier

This is the story of an American street photographer who kept her passion for taking pictures secret until her death. She lived her life as a caregiver, and if it had not been for the sale of her belongings at an auction house, her incredible work might never have been discovered.

It was 2007. A Chicago auction house was selling off the belongings of an old woman named Vivian Maier. She had stopped paying storage fees, and so the company decided to sell her things. Her belongings—mainly old photographs and negatives—were sold to three buyers: Maloof, Slattery, and Prow.

Slattery thought Vivian's work was interesting so he published her photographs on a photo-sharing website in July 2008. The photographs received little attention. Then, in October, Maloof linked his blog to his selection of Vivian's photographs, and right away, thousands of people were viewing them. Maloof had found Vivian Maier's name with the prints, but he was unable to discover anything about her. Then an Internet search led him to a 2009 newspaper article about her death. Maloof used this information to discover more about Vivian's life, and it was the combination of Vivian's mysterious life story and her photographs that grabbed everyone's attention.

Details of Vivian's life are limited for two reasons. First, since no one had interviewed her while she was alive, no one knew why she took so many photographs. Second, it is clear from interviews with the family she worked for that Vivian was a very private person. She had few friends. Besides, she had kept her hobby a secret.

"film negative"

"printed image"

Vivian was born in 1926 in the United States to an Austrian father and a French mother. The marriage was not a happy one, and it seems her mother and father lived apart for several years. During her childhood Vivian frequently moved between the US and France, sometimes living in France, and sometimes in the US. For a while, Vivian and her mother lived in New York with Jeanne Bertrand, a successful photographer. It is believed that Vivian became interested in photography as a young adult, as her first photos were taken in France in the late 1940s using a very simple camera. She returned to New York in 1951, and in 1956 she moved to Chicago to work as a caregiver for the Gensburg family. This job gave her more free time for taking photographs.

In 1952, at the age of 26, she purchased her first 6 × 6 camera, and it was with this that most of her photographs of life on the streets of Chicago were taken. For over 30 years she took photos of children, the elderly, the rich, and the poor. Some people were not even aware that their picture was being taken. She also took a number of self-portraits. Some were reflections of herself in a shop window. Others were of her own shadow. Vivian continued to document Chicago life until the early 1970s, when she changed to a new style of photography.

An international award-winning documentary film called *Finding Vivian Maier* brought interest in her work to a wider audience. The film led to exhibitions in Europe and the US. To choose the photographs that best represent her style, those in charge of the exhibitions have tried to answer the question, "What would Vivian Maier have printed?" In order to answer this question, they used her notes, the photos she actually did print, and information about her preferences as reported by the Gensburgs. Vivian was much more interested in capturing moments rather than the outcome. So, one could say the mystery behind Vivian's work remains largely "undeveloped."

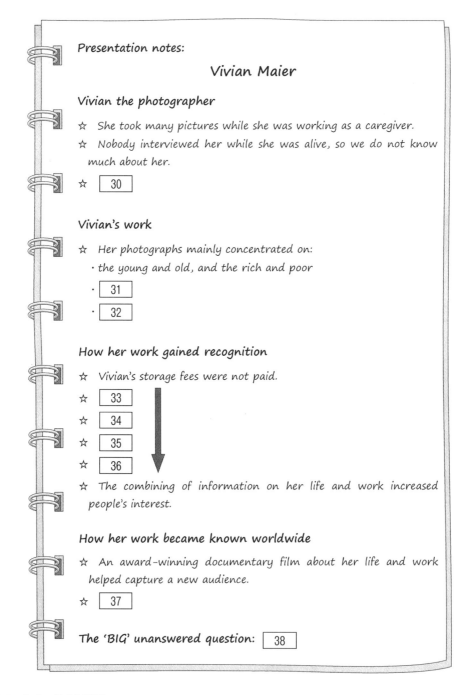

Presentation notes:

Vivian Maier

Vivian the photographer

☆ She took many pictures while she was working as a caregiver.
☆ Nobody interviewed her while she was alive, so we do not know much about her.
☆ [30]

Vivian's work

☆ Her photographs mainly concentrated on:
· the young and old, and the rich and poor
· [31]
· [32]

How her work gained recognition

☆ Vivian's storage fees were not paid.
☆ [33]
☆ [34]
☆ [35]
☆ [36]
☆ The combining of information on her life and work increased people's interest.

How her work became known worldwide

☆ An award-winning documentary film about her life and work helped capture a new audience.
☆ [37]

The 'BIG' unanswered question: [38]

問1 Choose the best statement for ⬚30⬚ .

① Her work remained undiscovered until it was sold at auction.

② She is thought to have become attracted to photography in her thirties.

③ She took her camera wherever she went and showed her pictures to others.

④ The majority of her photos were taken in New York.

問2 Choose the two best items for ⬚31⬚ and ⬚32⬚ . (The order does not matter.)

① documentary-style pictures

② industrial landscapes

③ natural landscapes

④ pictures of herself

⑤ shop windows

問3 Put the following events into the order in which they happened. ⬚33⬚ ~ ⬚36⬚

① A buyer linked his blog to some of her pictures.

② A report on Vivian's death was published in a newspaper.

③ An auction company started selling her old photographs and negatives.

④ Her work was published on the Internet.

問4 Choose the best statement for ⬚37⬚ .

① Exhibitions of her work have been held in different parts of the world.

② Her photography book featuring street scenes won an award.

③ She left detailed instructions on how her photographs should be treated.

④ The children of Vivian's employers provided their photographs.

問5 Choose the best question for ⬚38⬚ .

① "What type of camera did she use for taking photos?"

② "Where did she keep all her negatives and prints?"

③ "Why did she leave New York to become a caregiver?"

④ "Why did she take so many photos without showing them anyone?"

Using an international news report, you are going to take part in an English oral presentation contest. Read the following news story from France in preparation for your talk.

Five years ago, Mrs. Sabine Rouas lost her horse. She had spent 20 years with the horse before he died of old age. At that time, she felt that she could never own another horse. Out of loneliness, she spent hours watching cows on a nearby milk farm. Then, one day, she asked the farmer if she could help look after them.

The farmer agreed, and Sabine started work. She quickly developed a friendship with one of the cows. As the cow was pregnant, she spent more time with it than with the others. After the cow's baby was born, the baby started following Sabine around. Unfortunately, the farmer wasn't interested in keeping a bull—a male cow—on a milk farm. The farmer planned to sell the baby bull, which he called Three-oh-nine (309), to a meat market. Sabine decided she wasn't going to let that happen, so she asked the farmer if she could buy him and his mother. The farmer agreed, and she bought them. Sabine then started taking 309 for walks to town. About nine months later, when at last she had permission to move the animals, they moved to Sabine's farm.

Soon after, Sabine was offered a pony. At first, she wasn't sure if she wanted to have him, but the memory of her horse was no longer painful, so she accepted the pony and named him Leon. She then decided to return to her old hobby and started training him for show jumping. Three-oh-nine, who she had renamed Aston, spent most of his time with Leon, and the two became really close friends. However, Sabine had not expected Aston to pay close attention to her training routine with Leon, nor had she expected Aston to pick up some tricks. The young bull quickly mastered walking, galloping, stopping, going backwards, and turning around on command. He responded to Sabine's voice just like a horse. And despite weighing 1,300 kg, it took him just 18 months to learn how to leap over one-meter-high horse jumps with Sabine on his back. Aston might never have learned those things without having watched Leon. Moreover, Aston understood distance and could adjust his steps before a jump. He also noticed his faults and corrected them without any help from Sabine. That's something only the very best Olympic-standard horses can do.

Now Sabine and Aston go to weekend fairs and horse shows around Europe to show off his skills. Sabine says, "We get a good reaction. Mostly, people are really surprised, and at first, they can be a bit scared because he's big—much bigger than a horse. Most people don't like to get too close to bulls with horns. But once they see his real nature, and see him performing, they often say, 'Oh he's really quite beautiful.' "

"Look!" And Sabine shows a photo of Aston on her smartphone. She then continues, "When Aston was very young, I used to take him out for walks on a lead, like a dog, so that he would get used to humans. Maybe that's why he doesn't mind people. Because he is so calm, children, in particular, really like watching him and getting a chance to be close to him."

Over the last few years, news of the massive show-jumping bull has spread rapidly; now, Aston is a major attraction with a growing number of online followers. Aston and Sabine sometimes need to travel 200 or 300 kilometers away from home, which means they have to stay overnight. Aston has to sleep in a horse box, which isn't really big enough for him.

"He doesn't like it. I have to sleep with him in the box," says Sabine. "But you know, when he wakes up and changes position, he is very careful not to crush me. He really is very gentle. He sometimes gets lonely, and he doesn't like being away from Leon for too long; but other than that, he's very happy."

Your Presentation Slides

30

Central High School
English Presentation Contest

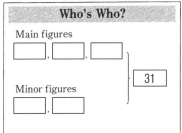

Who's Who?

Main figures

☐ , ☐ , ☐

Minor figures

☐ , ☐

31

Pre-fame Storyline

Sabine's horse dies.
↓
32
↓
33
↓
34
↓
35
↓
Aston and Sabine start going to shows.

Aston's Abilities

Aston can:
· learn by simply watching Leon's training.
· walk, gallop, and stop when Sabine tells him to.
· understand distance and adjust his steps.
· 36 .
· 37 .

Aston Now

Aston today:
· is a show-jumping bull.
· travels to fairs and events with Sabine.
· 38 .

問1　Which is the best title for your presentation? 30
　　① Animal-lover Saves the Life of a Pony
　　② Aston's Summer Show-jumping Tour
　　③ Meet Aston, the Bull who Behaves Like a Horse
　　④ The Relationship Between a Farmer and a Cow

問2　Which is the best combination for the **Who's Who?** slide? 31

	Main figures	Minor figures
①	309, Aston, the farmer	Sabine, the pony
②	Aston, Aston's mother, Sabine	309, the farmer
③	Aston, Leon, the farmer	Aston's mother, Sabine
④	Aston, Sabine, the pony	Aston's mother, the farmer

問3　Choose the four events in the order they happened to complete the **Pre-fame Storyline** slide. 32 ～ 35
　　① Aston learns to jump.
　　② Sabine and Aston travel hundreds of kilometers together.
　　③ Sabine buys 309 and his mother.
　　④ Sabine goes to work on her neighbor's farm.
　　⑤ Sabine takes 309 for walks.

問4　Choose the two best items for the **Aston's Abilities** slide. (The order does not matter.) 36 · 37
　　① correct his mistakes by himself
　　② jump side-by-side with the pony
　　③ jump with a rider on his back
　　④ pick up tricks faster than a horse
　　⑤ pose for photographs

問5　Complete the **Aston Now** slide with the most appropriate item. 38
　　① has an increasing number of fans　　② has made Sabine very wealthy
　　③ is so famous that he no longer frightens people　　④ spends most nights of the year in a horse trailer

Your group is preparing a poster presentation entitled "The Person Who Revolutionized American Journalism," using information from the magazine article below.

Benjamin Day, a printer from New England, changed American journalism forever when he started a New York City newspaper, *The Sun*. Benjamin Day was born in Springfield, Massachusetts, on April 10, 1810. He worked for a printer as a teenager, and at the age of 20 he began working in print shops and newspaper offices in New York. In 1831, when he had saved enough money, he started his own printing business, which began to struggle when the city was hit by a cholera epidemic the following year. In an attempt to prevent his business from going under, Day decided to start a newspaper.

In 1833, there were 650 weekly and 65 daily American newspapers, with average sales of around 1,200. Although there were cheap newspapers in other parts of the country, in New York a newspaper usually cost as much as six cents. Day believed that many working-class people were able to read newspapers, but chose not to buy them because they did not address their interests and were too expensive. On September 3, 1833, Day launched *The Sun* with a copy costing just one cent. The introduction of the "penny press," as cheap newspapers became known, was an important milestone in American journalism history.

Day's newspaper articles were different from those of other newspapers at the time. Instead of reporting on politics and reviews of books or the theater, *The Sun* focused on people's everyday lives. It was the first newspaper to report personal events and crimes. It led to a paradigm shift in American journalism, with newspapers becoming an important part of the community and the lives of the readers. Day also came up with another novel idea: newsboys selling the newspaper on street corners. People wouldn't even have to step into a shop to buy a paper.

The combination of a newspaper that was cheap as well as being easily available was successful, and soon Day was making a good living publishing *The Sun*. Within six months, *The Sun*'s circulation reached 5,000, and after a year, it had risen to 10,000. By 1835, sales of *The Sun* had reached 19,000, more than any of the other daily papers at that time. Over the next few years, about a dozen new penny papers were established, beginning a new era of newspaper competition. The success of *The Sun* encouraged other journalists to publish newspapers at a lower price. By the time of the Civil War, the standard price of a New York City newspaper had fallen to just two cents.

Despite his success, after about five years of operating *The Sun*, Day lost interest in the daily work of publishing a newspaper. In 1838, he sold *The Sun* to his brother-in-law, Moses Yale Beach, for $40,000, and the newspaper continued to publish for many years. After selling the paper, Day moved into other business areas, including the publication of magazines, but by the 1860s he was basically retired. He lived quietly until his death on December 21, 1889. Although he had been involved in the American newspaper business for a relatively short time, Day is remembered as a revolutionary figure who showed that newspapers could appeal to a mass audience.

The Person Who Revolutionized American Journalism

■ The Life of Benjamin Day

Period	Events
1810s	Day spent his childhood in Springfield
1820s	27
1830s and beyond	28 ↓ 29 ↓ 30 ↓ 31

Benjamin Day

■ About *The Sun*

▶ Day launched *The Sun* on September 3, 1833.
▶ This newspaper was highly successful for the following reasons: 32 .

■ A Shift in U.S. Journalism: A New Model

▶ The motto of *The Sun* was " 33 ".
▶ *The Sun* changed American journalism and society in number of ways: 34 .

問 1　Members of your group listed important events in Day's life. Put the events into the boxes 27 ~ 31 in the order that they happened.

① Day created other publications
② Day established a printing company
③ Day gained experience as a printer in his local area
④ Day started a newspaper business
⑤ Day's business was threatened by a deadly disease

問 2　Choose the best statement (s) to complete the poster. (**You may choose more than one option.**) 32

① Day focused on improving the literacy levels of the working class.
② Day introduced a new way of distributing newspapers.
③ Day realized the potential demand for an affordable newspaper.
④ Day reported political affairs in a way that way easy to understand.
⑤ Day supplied a large number of newspapers to every household.
⑥ Day understood what kind of articles would attract readers.

問 3　Which of the following was most likely to have been *The Sun*'s motto? 33

① Nothing is more valuable than politics
② The daily diary of the American Dream
③ *The Sun:* It shines for all
④ Top people take *The Sun*

問 4　Choose the best statement (s) to complete the poster. (**You may choose more than one option.**) 34

① Information became widely available to ordinary people.
② Journalists became more conscious of political concerns.
③ Journalists started to write more on topics of interest to the community.
④ Newspapers became less popular with middle-class readers.
⑤ Newspapers replaced schools in providing literacy education.
⑥ The role of newspapers became much more important than before.

A　You are the editor of your school newspaper. You have been asked to provide comments on an article about origami written by an American student named Mary.

Origami

［1］　Many people in Japan have childhood memories of origami, where square sheets of paper are transformed into beautiful shapes such as animals and flowers. Origami has been enjoyed widely by people of all ages for centuries

［2］　A recent event reminded us that origami is viewed as a traditional Japanese art form overseas. When President Barack Obama visited Hiroshima in 2016, he made four origami paper cranes neatly. He then presented them to Hiroshima City. This was seen as a symbol of his commitment to friendship between the two countries and to world peace.

［3］　Two positive influences of origami can be seen in care for the elderly and rehabilitation. Origami requires the precise coordination of fingers as well as intense concentration to fold the paper into certain shapes. It is thought to slow the progression of memory loss associated with such medical problems as Alzheimer's disease. It is also believed that origami helps keep motor skills and increases brain activity, which aid a person recovering from injuries. For these reasons, both inside and outside Japan, there are many elderly care and rehabilitation programs in which origami is used.

［4］　Children also benefit from origami. It fosters creativity and artistic sense while allowing them to have fun. This has resulted in a large number of associations—both domestic and international—regularly holding events for young children such as origami competitions and exhibits. Isn't it surprising that many organizations that are active in these areas can be found overseas?

［5］　　A　Furthermore, origami paper folding technology has promising applications in medicine. 　B　In 2016, an international team of researchers developed a tiny paper-thin robot that can be used for medical treatment. The robot, made of material from pigs, is folded like origami paper and covered with a capsule made of ice. When the capsule is swallowed by a patient and reaches the patient's stomach, the capsule melts, and the robot unfolds as it absorbs water from the surrounding area. 　C　After this, the robot is controlled from outside of the body to perform an operation. When the task is complete, the robot moves out of the body naturally. 　D

［6］　As seen in the examples above, origami is no longer merely a traditional Japanese art from that many of us experienced as a leisure activity in childhood. In fact, it is a powerful agent that can bring positive change to the lives of all generations worldwide. While the appreciation of its beauty is likely to continue for generations to come, nowadays origami has come to influence various other aspects of our lives.

問1　Mary's article mainly discusses 　25　 .

① the greater importance of origami in medicine than in other fields

② the invention of new types of origami in many foreign countries

③ the major role origami plays in promoting world peace and cooperation

④ the use of origami for cultural, medical, and educational purposes

問2　Mary's intention in Paragraphs [3] and [4] is probably to ☐26☐ .

① describe the history of origami's development outside Japan

② discuss the difficulties of using origami for treating diseases

③ express concerns about using origami for rehabilitation, elderly care, and education

④ introduce some contributions of origami to the lives of people of different ages

問3　You found additional information related to this topic and want to suggest that Mary add the sentence below to her article. Where would the sentence best fit among the four locations marked ☐A☐ , ☐B☐ , ☐C☐ , and ☐D☐ in Paragraph [5]? ☐27☐

The developers of the robot say that this technology can be used, for instance, to remove a small battery from the stomach of a child who has accidentally swallowed it.

① ☐A☐　② ☐B☐　③ ☐C☐　④ ☐D☐

B　You are preparing for a presentation about the characteristics of spices. You have found an article about black and white pepper. You are going to read the article and take notes.

Black and White Pepper

[Part 1]　Some recent studies have increased our understanding of the role of spices in helping us live longer. There are a variety of spices in the world, but most likely you are familiar with two of them, black and white pepper. Black and white pepper both come from the fruit of the same pepper plant. However, they are processed differently. Black pepper is made from the unripe fruit of the pepper plant. Each piece of fruit looks like a small green ball, just 3 to 6 millimeters across. The harvested fruit turns black when it is dried under the sun. Each piece of dried fruit is called a *peppercorn*. The color of the powdered black pepper comes from the skin of the peppercorn. On the other hand, to get white pepper, the pepper fruit is harvested when it is cherry-red. The skin of the fruit is removed before sun-drying. The color of the seed inside the pepper fruit is white. This is how white peppercorns are processed. Because the skin is very thin, the size of black and white peppercorns is similar. White pepper is usually more expensive than black because there are more steps in processing it.

[Part 2]　Where does the flavor of pepper come from? The sharp spicy taste is caused by a natural compound called *piperine*. Not only the seed but also the outer layer of the peppercorn contains lots of piperine. Therefore, some people say black pepper tastes hotter than white. Black pepper also contains many other substances that make its taste more complex. The unique flavor of black pepper produced by the mixed substances goes well with many kinds of dishes. White pepper's flavor is often regarded as more refined than that of black pepper, but it is too weak to bring out the flavor of meat dishes such as steak. Thanks to its color, white pepper is often used in light-colored dishes. Mashed potatoes, white sauce, and white fish may look better when they are spiced with white pepper.

[Part 3]　Historically, people have used pepper as a folk medicine. For instance, it was a popular remedy for coughs and colds. The health effect of pepper is partly caused by piperine. Like vitamin C, piperine is a potent antioxidant. This means that, by eating foods including this compound, we may prevent harmful chemical reactions. Furthermore, recent studies have found the pepper reduces the impact of some types of illnesses. All spices that include piperine have this effect on a person's body. Both black and white pepper have the same health benefits.

Complete the notes by filling in ☐28 to ☐33 .

```
┌─────────────────────────────────────────────────────────┐
│                         Notes                            │
│   Outline:                                               │
│       Part 1:  _____ 28 _____        │
│                                                          │
│       Part 2:  _____ 29 _____        │
│                                                          │
│       Part 3:  _____ 30 _____        │
│                                                          │
│   Table: Comparing Black and White Pepper                │
│   ┌──────────────────────┬──────────────────────────┐   │
│   │    Common points      │      Differences          │   │
│   ├──────────────────────┼──────────────────────────┤   │
│   │                       │                          │   │
│   │         31            │           32             │   │
│   │                       │                          │   │
│   └──────────────────────┴──────────────────────────┘   │
│                                                          │
│   Main points:  _____ 33 _____       │
│                                                          │
└─────────────────────────────────────────────────────────┘
```

問1   The best headings for Parts 1, 2, and 3 are ☐28 , ☐29 , and ☐30 , respectively. (You may use an option only once.)

① The characteristics of pepper as a spice

② The effects of pepper on health

③ The place of origin of black and white pepper

④ The production of black and white pepper

問2   Among the following, the common points and differences described in the article are ☐31 and ☐32 , respectively. (You may choose more than one option for each box.)

① the amount of vitamin C   ② the effect on illnesses   ③ the flavor

④ the plant   ⑤ the price   ⑥ the removal of the skin

問3   This article mainly discusses ☐33 .

① the advantages and disadvantages of using black and white pepper compared to other spices

② the reason why people started to make black and white pepper, and why they have lost popularity

③ the reason why white pepper is better than black pepper, and why it is better for us

④ the similarities and differences between white and black pepper, and also the health benefits of both

次の文章を読み，あとの問い（**A・B**）に答えよ。なお，文章の左にある⑴～⑹はパラグラフ（段落）の番号を表している。

⑴　Vending machines are so common in Japan that you can find one almost anywhere you go. Some of these machines sell train or meal tickets, and others sell snacks or drinks. They are especially useful for people who want to get something quickly and conveniently.

⑵　While vending machines are found throughout the country today, they were not originally developed in Japan. It is generally believed that the first one was constructed by a Greek mathematics teacher about 2,200 years ago. This machine sold special water used in prayers at temples. People who wanted to purchase the water put in a coin, which hit a metal lever attached to a string. Then, the weight of the coin let a specific amount of water pour out until the coin fell off. This ensured that people received an equal portion of the special water.

⑶　About 1,000 years ago, a vending machine that sold pencils was developed in China. Later, in the 1700s, coin-operated tobacco boxes appeared in English bars. When people wanted the product sold by one of these boxes, they inserted a coin and turned a lever. The product then dropped down for the customer to pick up. However, it was not until the 1880s that vending machines spread around the world. In 1883, an English inventor created one that sold postcards and paper. This became popular, and soon vending machines selling paper, stamps, and other goods appeared in many countries. In 1904, vending machines came into service in Japan. In 1926, technology had advanced and machines could be set to sell products with different prices. After that, a wider variety of products were sold. When this happened, the vending machine industry expanded rapidly.

⑷　The greatest problem faced by the global vending machine industry in its expansion was not the use of coins; it was paper money. This was a challenge as it proved easy for dishonest individuals to make money that could fool machines. This forced the vending machine industry to establish better detection methods and was one reason countries took steps to develop money that was difficult to counterfeit. Now, vending machines have become technologically advanced, not only to prevent problems with cash but also to accept credit cards and more recent forms of electronic payment.

⑸　It is in Japan that vending machines have become most popular. Currently, Japan has more than 4.2 million vending machines, with about 55% of them selling beverages such as tea, coffee, and juice. One of the main reasons Japan has become the vending machine capital of the world is its overall level of safety. Unlike many places, where vending machines must be monitored to prevent theft, they can be placed virtually anywhere in Japan. This extraordinary degree of public safety is considered amazing by visitors, as well as the range of products available. Tourists often take pictures of machines that sell unexpected products like bananas, fresh eggs, and bags of rice. It is understandable that visitors see them as one aspect particular to Japanese culture.

⑹　Given the popularity and usefulness of vending machines, it is unlikely that they will disappear anytime in the near future. They provide a place where various goods can be sold without the need for a sales clerk. The next time you want to purchase a hot drink on a cold day, remember that, in Japan at least, there is probably a vending machine just around the next corner.

A 次の問い（問1～5）の 46 ～ 50 に入れるのに最も適当なものを，それぞれ下の①～④のうちから一つずつ選べ。

問1 According to paragraph (2), what was the first vending machine capable of doing ? 46
  ① Allowing people to acquire a fixed amount of liquid from it
  ② Offering books of ancient Greek mathematical principles
  ③ Permitting visitors to enter temples when they wanted to pray
  ④ Providing a regular income to the person who created it

問2 According to paragraph (3), which of the following statements about vending machines is true ? 47
  ① An English inventor's vending machine sold goods at various prices.
  ② Sales by vending machines increased when high value coins appeared.
  ③ Vending machine technology was found in Asia many centuries ago.
  ④ Vending machines were common in the world by the 18th century.

問3 Which of the following is closest to the meaning of the underlined word counterfeit in paragraph (4) ? 48
  ① accept illegal exchanges
  ② create unauthorized imitations
  ③ restrict unapproved technology
  ④ withdraw unnecessary support

問4 According to paragraph (5), what is true about vending machines in Japan ? 49
  ① Foreign tourists hesitate to make purchases from them.
  ② Over three quarters of them sell a variety of drinks.
  ③ The highly safe products sold in them attract customers.
  ④ The variety of items makes them unique in the world.

問5 What would be the best title for this passage ? 50
  ① The Cultural Benefits of Vending Machines in Japanese Society
  ② The Development of Vending Machines From Historical Perspectives
  ③ The Economic Impact of Vending Machines by International Comparison
  ④ The Globalization of Vending Machines Through Modern Technology

B 次の表は，本文のパラグラフ（段落）の構成と内容をまとめたものである。 51 ～ 54 に入れるのに最も適当なものを，下の①～④のうちから一つずつ選び，表を完成させよ。ただし，同じものを繰り返し選んではいけない。

Paragraph	Content
(1)	Introduction
(2)	51
(3)	52
(4)	53
(5)	54
(6)	Conclusion

  ① A certain factor that has allowed vending machines to exist widely in one country
  ② Creation of one vending machine and a description of how the device was used
  ③ Difficulties in building vending machines after introducing a different form of money
  ④ Types of vending machine goods sold at different locations in the past

ヒストリー

次の文章を読み，あとの問い（**A**・**B**）に答えよ。なお，文章の左にある(1)〜(6)はパラグラフ（段落）の番号を表している。

(1) Opera is an art form that celebrates the human voice at its highest level of expression. No other art form creates excitement and moves the heart in the way that opera does, especially when performed by a great singer. Such singers are trained to present some of the greatest and most challenging music that has ever been composed for the human voice.

(2) Opera is an important part of the Western classical music tradition. It uses music, words, and actions to bring a dramatic story to life. Opera started in Italy at the end of the 16th century and later became popular throughout Europe. Over the years, it has responded to various musical and theatrical developments around the world and continues to do so. In recent decades, much wider audiences have been introduced to opera through modern recording technology. Some singers have become celebrities thanks to performing on radio, on television, and in the cinema.

(3) However, in recent years, opera has been facing serious challenges. The causes of some of these are beyond its control. One current challenge to opera is economic. The current world economic slowdown has meant that less money is available for cultural institutions and artists. This shortage of money raises the broader question of how much should be paid to support opera singers and other artists. Society seems to accept the large salaries paid to business managers and the multi-million-dollar contracts given to sports athletes. But what about opera singers? Somehow, people have the idea that artists can be creative only if they suffer in poverty, but this is unrealistic: If artists, including opera singers, lack the support they need, valuable talent is wasted.

(4) Not only the shortage of money, but also the way money is managed in the opera world has led to hardships. Principal singers are generally paid performance fees once they complete a show. They typically receive nothing during the many weeks of rehearsal before a show starts. To prepare for a role, they must pay the costs of lessons and coaching sessions. If they become ill or cancel their performance, they lose their performance fee. The insecurity of this system puts the future of opera at risk.

(5) Another problem faced by opera is how to meet the demands of audiences who are influenced by popular entertainment. Pop singers are often judged as much on the basis of how they look as how they sound. Therefore, opera singers, performing to audiences influenced by this popular culture, are now expected to be "models who sing." These demands may be unrealistic and possibly harmful. Opera singers simply cannot make a sound big enough to fill a large theater or concert hall without a microphone if their body weight is too low. Emphasizing physical appearance over singing ability may cause audiences to miss out on the human voice at its best.

(6) There are no easy solutions to opera's problems and there are many different opinions about the value of opera. However, every year many young people register for music courses with hopes and dreams of developing their talents in this special art form. The fact that opera has survived many obstacles and continues to attract the rising generation demonstrates that it remains a respected art form full of value.

A　次の問い（問1〜5）の 47 〜 51 に入れるのに最も適当なものを，それぞれ下の①〜④のうちから一つずつ選べ。

問1　Which of these statements is true according to paragraph (2) ? 47

   ① Opera develops by adapting to new conditions.

   ② Opera fans thank celebrities for performing.

   ③ Opera singers avoid singing on TV and in films.

   ④ Opera singers' life stories are dramatic.

問2　In paragraph (3), what is another way of asking the question "But what about opera singers ?" 48

   ① How do opera singers prepare ?

   ② How should we use opera singers ?

   ③ What are opera singers worth ?

   ④ What sums do opera singers pay ?

問3　According to paragraphs (3) and (4), which statement is true ? 49

   ① Opera singers are financially unstable.

   ② Opera singers ask only the wealthy to attend.

   ③ Opera singers get paid before the show.

   ④ Opera singers perform better if they are poor.

問4　Which statement best expresses the author's opinion in paragraph (5) ? 50

   ① Audiences know best how opera should be performed.

   ② Microphones should be used to make opera more enjoyable.

   ③ Opera singers' voices should be valued more than their looks.

   ④ Popular culture has had a positive influence on opera.

問5　What would be the best title for this passage ? 51

   ① How to Make Money in Opera

   ② Opera as a Part of Popular Culture

   ③ The Difficulties Facing Opera

   ④ The Historical Context of Opera

B　次の表は，本文のパラグラフ（段落）ごとの内容をまとめたものである。 52 〜 55 に入れるのに最も適当なものを，下の①〜④のうちから一つずつ選び，表を完成させよ。ただし，同じものを繰り返し選んではいけない。

Paragraph	Content
(1)	Introducing opera
(2)	52
(3)	53
(4)	54
(5)	55
(6)	Prospects for opera

   ① Effect of world finance on opera   ② Impact of popular culture on opera

   ③ Opera from the past to the present   ④ Problems in money management

目標
15分

／ 10題　　／ 10題

次の文章を読み，あとの問い（**A・B**）に答えよ。なお，文章の左にある⑴〜⑹は段落の番号を表している。

⑴　Dance is one of the oldest forms of art, and it is seen in every culture and performed for a variety of purposes. In modern society, dance is widely recognized as a form of entertainment : many people enjoy dancing for fun or watching their favorite artists dance on stage or screen.　It can also be a form of sport : there are dance competitions of various types.　In addition to these obvious functions, however, there are other more complex roles dance can play in a society.

⑵　Sometimes dance serves to help teach social rules to young members of a community.　A kind of dance called the minuet is a good example.　The minuet originated in France and by the 18th century had become popular among the European elite.　In Britain, debutantes, or upper-class women about to make their entrance into adult society by attending their first dance, were strictly trained for their first minuet.　They usually danced it before a crowd of people who would critically observe their movements and behavior.　This dance taught them how to behave like a member of high society.　One writer, in fact, called the minuet one of the best schools of manners ever invented.

⑶　Dance has also been used to make sure that adults follow the rules of their community.　An example comes from research conducted in the mid-1900s on dances performed after hunts by the Mbuti Pygmies, an ethnic group living in parts of Central Africa.　Suppose something had gone wrong in the hunt.　For example, an opportunity to catch an animal was missed because someone neglected to perform their role of hitting the ground to drive the animal towards the hunters.　Later, a dancer would act out the event to show the wrong action and perhaps embarrass that person.　It is easy to imagine that this would discourage behavior that could ruin a future hunt.

⑷　In some cultures, dance can be a way of displaying power.　For instance, there is another report from the mid-1900s describing how the Maring people of New Guinea would hold dances to show their military strength and recruit allies for possible battles.　Although battles often occurred after these dances, it is also said that these dances could contribute to peaceful solutions among enemy groups.　Through the dances, a group's size and strength would become obvious to potential opponents, and this could help avoid a fight.

⑸　Through dance, groups can also exhibit their traditions and, thus, increase their prestige.　An example of this is the world-famous Trinidad Carnival in Trinidad and Tobago, a Caribbean island country that was once a European colony.　The roots of this event can be traced to the late 1700s, when the European colonists held a carnival, dancing in elaborate costumes.　People of African origin, many of whom came to the island as slaves, were mostly excluded.　After slavery ended in 1838, they started to participate fully and changed the character of the carnival.　In their dances, they acted out scenes from the slavery period and displayed their own traditions.　Their performances were a way for them to show past injustices and to earn recognition for their customs.

⑹　The roles of dance discussed here, maintaining traditions and demonstrating group strength or cultural richness, have one shared effect : they unite members of a group.　Dance is not just an artistic expression but a way for groups to strengthen their shared identity.　Though it may not be apparent, this effect may also apply to us.　For example, there might be dances unique to our local regions that we participate in.　Why do we take part in such activities and how did these dances originate?　Considering the role of dance in our lives can lead to interesting discoveries about the history or values of our own society.

A 次の問い（問1〜5）の 46 〜 50 に入れるのに最も適当なものを，それぞれ下の①〜④のうちから一つずつ選べ。

問1 In paragraph (2), the topic of debutantes is introduced to provide an example of 46 .

① how long it took young people to learn the minuet

② the kind of schools that the European elite attended

③ the role women played when dancing the minuet

④ young people learning how to act properly

問2 According to paragraph (3), the Mbuti Pygmies 47 .

① disciplined careless hunters through dance   ② handed down customs and traditions through dance

③ made lazy members dance after a day's hunt   ④ performed culturally desirable behavior by dance

問3 Paragraph (4) suggests that dance could discourage 48 among the Maring people.

① military recruiting   ② peace-making   ③ physical conflict   ④ power display

問4 Paragraph (5) mentions 49 .

① how the Trinidad Carnival was transformed

② when the Caribbean area was first colonized

③ where the African dance tradition started

④ why the Europeans started the Trinidad Carnival

問5 The main idea of this passage is that 50 .

① dance can bring us together and also help us understand society

② dance plays a significant role in educating upper-class people

③ the primary purpose of dance is entertainment and exercise

④ understanding the history of dance is important

B 次の表は，本文の段落と内容をまとめたものである。 51 〜 55 に入れるのに最も適当なものを，下の①〜⑤のうちから一つずつ選び，表を完成させよ。ただし，同じものを繰り返し選んではいけない。

Paragraph	Content
(1)	Typical roles of dance today
(2)	51
(3)	52
(4)	53
(5)	54
(6)	55

① Dance for passing down appropriate cultural behavior

② How dance improves a group's status

③ The common function of dance and its significance

④ The demonstration of group force through dance

⑤ Using dance to point out unfavorable actions

目標
10分

H 30　⑤　　　　　　　　　　　　　　　　　　　　　　　／5題　　　／5題

次の日誌の抜粋を読み，あとの問い（**問1～5**）の　41　～　45　に入れるのに最も適当なものを，それぞれ下の①～④のうちから一つずつ選べ。

Selections From the Exploration Journal for Planet X

<u>DAY 1</u>　　Our mission of scientific discovery continues, and there is something exciting to report.　We may have finally found a planet capable of supporting life.　The nearby planets were either too hot or too dry to support life, but this planet seems to be different.　Its surface is mostly a blue liquid, though it is spotted with some green and brown parts, and some kind of white substance seems to be moving around the planet.

<u>DAY 4</u>　　Now we are orbiting the planet.　It seems that our assumption was correct !　There are a few mechanical devices circling around it and their designs are rather complex.　They were certainly made by some kind of intelligent beings.　Are these machines part of a monitoring system ?　Have they signaled our approach ?　There doesn't seem to be any threat, so we have decided to ignore them and get closer to the planet.　I hope that their inventors are friendly.

<u>DAY 8</u>　　Unlike our planet, which is totally covered with the precious liquid that sustains us, the green and brown parts of this planet are too dry to support life.　The blue part is mostly H_2O in a liquid state. Although it is liquid, it is not quite the same as the liquid on our home planet.　Still, we might be able to find life here.　At least, according to our equipment, there seems to be something alive down there.　We are ready to start direct observation and will soon dive in.　I'm so excited that I won't be able to sleep tonight !

<u>DAY 9</u>　　We succeeded in entering this unexplored liquid safely.　The scenery around us was very similar to that of our planet, with soft plants gently waving back and forth.　We also noticed a variety of thin swimming creatures.　How exciting !　We have found life on this planet !　However, we cannot see any creatures capable of producing an advanced civilization.　Without arms, these swimming creatures wouldn't be able to build complex machines even if they were smart.　Are the leaders of this planet hiding from us ? Do they have <u>reservations</u> about meeting us ?　Is that why they use those flying objects to check out space ? Hopefully, we will be able to find some answers.

<u>DAY 12</u>　　We found a big object lying on the bottom.　Its long body looked somewhat like our spaceship. It sat silently looking very old and damaged.　Apparently, it isn't being used anymore.　Maybe it is a part of the remains of this planet's ancient civilization.

<u>DAY 19</u>　　Since we started our dive, we have seen many more unusual creatures.　We were especially surprised to find one that looked very similar to us.　The upper part of its body was round and soft.　Underneath that were two large eyes and several long arms.　It escaped quickly, leaving a cloud of black substance.　We don't know if it is the most intelligent life on this planet, but our expectations for new discoveries continue to grow.

DAY 39   This part of our investigation will soon come to an end.   We have found more remains and abandoned objects like the one we found earlier, but there have been no signs of the creatures who made them.   Perhaps the leaders of this planet have died out.   Anyway, we found life on this planet, which is a very big discovery.   We must leave this planet for now, but we will certainly come back someday to continue our research.   We will return home with amazing reports.

DAY 40   We silently floated up to the surface and then into the air.   Just as we were leaving the planet, we saw a lot of strange creatures on the dry areas.   What a shock !   We, creatures living in liquid, had never imagined creatures like them !   Floating safely in our ship's liquid, we realized that our common sense had led us to the wrong conclusion.

問1   What was the purpose of the explorers' journey ? $\boxed{41}$
   ① To assist intelligent creatures on the planet
   ② To invade a planet and expand their colonies
   ③ To search for life outside their home planet
   ④ To test the performance of their new spaceship

問2   When the explorers were observing the planet from space, they imagined that the intelligent creatures on it would $\boxed{42}$.
   ① be aggressive toward others
   ② have advanced technology
   ③ have no interest in space
   ④ no longer live there

問3   The word reservations as used in DAY 9 is closest in meaning to $\boxed{43}$.
   ① appointments   ② concerns   ③ expectations   ④ protections

問4   Which of the following best describes the author of the journal ? $\boxed{44}$
   ① A being whose shape resembles an octopus
   ② A human scientist exploring other planets
   ③ A space creature which looks like a human
   ④ An intelligent flat animal with no arms

問5   The explorers incorrectly assumed that all intelligent creatures would $\boxed{45}$.
   ① be less creative than their species
   ② have advanced to the land
   ③ live in some kind of liquid
   ④ understand their language

物語・手紙・メール・日記

次の物語を読み，あとの問い（問1～5）の　42　～　46　に入れるのに最も適当なものを，それぞれ下の
①～④のうちから一つずつ選べ。

Ahhhhhhhhhhh !

With a big yawn I woke up.　What a fresh morning !　I felt very sharp, much sharper than usual.　I was able to hear the singing of birds more clearly than ever before.　I noticed the smell of coffee coming up from downstairs.　I stretched out my arms in front of myself and raised my back ; it felt so good.　I sat up straight, licked my hand, and started to clean my face with it . . .　Huh ? . . . Something was strange.　Why was I licking my hand with my tongue ?　Why was my body covered with fur ?　I tried to say something, but the sound that came out of my mouth was . . . "Meow."

It was certainly my bedroom that I was in.　It was certainly my bed that I was sitting on.　Everything was as usual except that . . . I seemed to have changed into a different creature.　I was so surprised that I couldn't move.　I couldn't do anything.　I wondered — would I have to spend the rest of my life as an animal ?　I began to feel afraid . . . But after a few moments those feelings passed.　So, with a wave of my tail, I started to explore my surroundings.　A cat's mind is said to be changeable like that.

As I went down the stairs, the smell of coffee grew stronger and I could tell what was for breakfast. Maybe the senses of a cat are sharper than those of a human.　When I got to the dining room, what I saw almost stopped my heart.　It was *me* !　The human *I* was sitting at the dining table !　I couldn't take my eyes off *myself*.

The human *I* was absorbed in a smartphone, maybe writing responses to friends' messages or playing an online game.　Bending *my* head down toward the phone, *I* was sitting with rounded shoulders and a curved back.　*I* looked very uncomfortable.

I sometimes took a little bite of toast, but it appeared that *I* was not noticing any taste in *my* mouth. Actually, the taste of toast in my memory was vague.　I couldn't remember what else had been served for breakfast recently, either.　The human *I* was just mindlessly putting in *my* mouth anything that was on the plate while handling the phone.　*I* was so focused on the text messages or games that *I* took little interest in what was happening around *me*.　In fact, *my* face had no expression on it at all.

"Yuji, you never study these days.　Are you ready for your final exams ?　You're making me a little bit worried," said Mom.

"Mmm," said *I*.　A sign of frustration briefly appeared on *my* face, but it disappeared in an instant.　*My* face was again as expressionless as it had been before.

"I don't like this guy," I thought.　But this guy was me.　I couldn't deny it.　For the first time, I realized how I really looked to other people.

Then, as *I* started to leave the table, our eyes met.　"Wow !　Mom, look !　There's a cat in the dining room !"

I didn't know why, but I was running.　I felt I had to escape.　Running up the stairs, I found the window in my room was open.　I jumped !　I had a strange feeling.　The world suddenly seemed to have shifted.　I felt my body falling down and . . .

Bump !

I was awake, lying on the floor of my room.　I slowly sat up and looked around.　Everything looked like it usually did.　I looked at my hands.　I was relieved to see they were no longer covered with fur.　I stood up and, with a yawn, extended my arms above my head to stretch my back.　Without thinking, as was my usual habit in the morning, I started to walk to my desk where my smartphone had completed charging and. . . I stopped.

After pausing for a moment, I turned around and went downstairs for breakfast.

問1　When Yuji realized that he had turned into a cat, he first felt ☐42☐ .

　　① astonished　　② embarrassed　　③ excited　　④ satisfied

問2　When Yuji's mother spoke to him, he was annoyed because ☐43☐ .

　　① he wanted to please her

　　② her words disturbed him

　　③ his mouth was full of food

　　④ she interrupted his studies

問3　The cat thought, "I don't like this guy," because Yuji ☐44☐ .

　　① could not recall the taste of food he had eaten at breakfast

　　② tried to hide his efforts to study for the final exams

　　③ was making fun of his mother's concern for his future

　　④ was not showing respect for people or things around him

問4　At the end of the story, Yuji did not pick up his smartphone because he ☐45☐ .

　　① decided it was time to improve his attitude

　　② realized that it was not yet fully charged

　　③ wanted to stick to his old priorities

　　④ was afraid of being scolded by his mother

問5　What is the theme of this story ? ☐46☐

　　① Cats have much better senses than humans.

　　② Observing yourself can lead to self-change.

　　③ People using smartphones look strange.

　　④ Unbelievable things can happen in dreams.

次の物語を読み，あとの問い（問1〜5）の ▢42 〜 ▢46 に入れるのに最も適当なものを，それぞれ下の①〜④のうちから一つずつ選べ。

"No one thought I would amount to much," Uncle John said, as he stood in the kitchen, showing me how he put together an award-winning four-course dinner. I had just graduated from university, and this dinner was his gift to me. It felt great to have a well-known chef cooking for me. On top of this, I was excited because in a few days he was going to compete in *The Big-Time Cook Off*, a nationwide TV cooking contest.

When Uncle John was young, his family lived in the countryside. His mother taught at a local school, but when John was 10, she had to quit to take care of her elderly mother. Until then, his father had been kind and had had enough time to play with John and his two younger sisters. But as bills kept piling up, the family got into trouble. John's father finally had to take a job in a city far away, so he could only come home on the weekends.

Gradually, because of his busy work schedule, John's father began looking tired whenever he came home. To tell the truth, he had changed from being good-humored to being in a bad mood all the time. When he was home, he just wanted to rest. He often scolded John for small things. Wanting to be accepted by his father, John tried to do his best but never felt he was good enough. Eventually, he started avoiding his father. He began hanging out at the shopping mall with friends, sometimes skipping his classes. Little by little John's grades got worse. His parents and teachers were worried about his future.

One Sunday morning, while John's mom was out taking care of her own mother, his father was napping in the TV room. John's sisters were hungry, so John started to cook something for them. He was not sure how to cook, but he did not want to bother his father.

Suddenly, the kitchen door opened, and his father was standing there. "Dad, I'm sorry if I woke you up. Chelsea and Jessica are hungry, and I was trying to cook them some eggs." His dad looked at him seriously for a moment. "Eggs? Eggs aren't good for lunch on a beautiful Sunday like today. Let's grill some steaks in the backyard." "Are you sure? You must be tired." "It's OK. I like cooking. It reminds me of my college days when I worked part-time as a cook. I'll show you how to prepare delicious steaks."

To John's surprise, his father became energetic when he started cooking. He took John aside and explained to him in detail that cooking was, in a way, like a science project. "You need to measure the ingredients precisely and know which items go together. If you master this, you can provide pleasure for a great many people." John felt close to his father for the first time in a long time. From then on, John spent more time at home. He started cooking for his family regularly, and then later for his friends at college. John always felt happy when he cooked, and this happiness spilled over into other areas of his life.

Uncle John worked his way through college with jobs in restaurants, and eventually he became a chef at a famous restaurant. He really liked the job and worked hard developing his own special techniques. He was finally able to open his own restaurant serving his unique style of food. He won several awards and cooked for the rich and famous.

This brings us back to the contest. Uncle John and I were excited about his being selected. Yet, he shared something really touching with me there in the kitchen. "You know, Mike," Uncle John said, "I'm thrilled to be able to go on TV as part of *The Big-Time Cook Off*. But what makes me the happiest is to stand here with you, one of the people I care about, and talk — just you and me. It's exactly like what my dad did for me one fine day in summer, so many years ago.　And that made all the difference in my life."

問1　At the beginning of the story, Uncle John was ☐42☐ .

　　① cooking for *The Big-Time Cook Off*

　　② making a special meal for Mike

　　③ training Mike for the contest

　　④ trying to improve his recipes

問2　Uncle John's father began working in the city because ☐43☐ .

　　① he was tired of living in the countryside

　　② it was easier to spend time with his family

　　③ the family needed more money for living

　　④ Uncle John's mother had become sick

問3　Why were Uncle John's parents and teachers worried about his future ? ☐44☐

　　① He just wanted to rest at home.

　　② He lost interest in studying.

　　③ He stopped avoiding his father.

　　④ He was no longer good-humored.

問4　What helped to change Uncle John's life the most ? ☐45☐

　　① Eating an award-winning dinner with his friends

　　② Entering cooking contests such as *The Big-Time Cook Off*

　　③ Making a connection with his father through cooking

　　④ Spending time talking with Mike in the kitchen

問5　What does Uncle John find most rewarding ? ☐46☐

　　① Developing unique four-course dinners for famous people

　　② Having meaningful relationships with people close to him

　　③ Making people happy through cooking on TV shows

　　④ Serving many people delicious meals in his restaurant

以下の文章は，Anna の父親が担任の岡本先生に宛てて送ったメールと，岡本先生からの返信である。これらを読み，あとの問い（問1～5）の 42 ～ 46 に入れるのに最も適当なものを，それぞれ下の①～④のうちから一つずつ選べ。

From：Jeff Whitmore < JeffW@×××××.com >
To：Kenji Okamoto < okamoto@×××××.com >
Date：January 10, 2015
Subject：Request for advice

Dear Mr. Okamoto,

My name is Jeff Whitmore, and my daughter, Anna, is one of your students.　As you know, we just moved back to Japan six months ago after living in Chicago for three years.　Although she had attended schools in Japan before we went to Chicago, it's Anna's first year at a Japanese junior high school.　My wife and I are a little worried about her, and we're hoping that it would be okay to ask you for advice.

She's getting good grades and likes her classes and teachers.　In particular, she has a penchant for numbers and loves her math class.　She often talks about your fun English class, too.　However, after almost half a year, it doesn't seem like she's made any friends.　Last week, she said that she usually reads by herself during breaks between classes while other girls are hanging out and chatting.　Anna also mentioned that she walks to school alone every day.　This is very different from how she was in the US.

I understand that it can take time to make friends at a new school, but I still have concerns that she may be a bit isolated.　I think it would be better for her to develop a group of good friends as soon as possible.　Even just one close friend would be a good first step.　I've never contacted one of my daughter's homeroom teachers before and hope that I'm not bothering you.　I just thought that you might know more about her life at school.　If you have any ideas about how she can make more personal connections, I would be happy to hear them.

Sincerely,
Jeff Whitmore

From：Kenji Okamoto < okamoto@×××××.com >
To：Jeff Whitmore < JeffW@×××××.com >
Date：January 11, 2015
Subject：Re：Request for advice

Dear Mr. Whitmore,

It's always nice to hear from a parent of one of my students, and I'll be happy to help you if I can.　I've talked with Anna one-on-one on several occasions and find her to be a delightful person who is confident and friendly.　Actually, I'm surprised to hear about your concerns as she seems to get along well with other students in the class. Probably, she'll soon form close friendships, but I do have a few ideas for you to consider that may help her do this.

First, our school has many different clubs that offer good environments for developing friendships.　I know that she enjoys music, so perhaps she would like to join the chorus.　If she prefers sports, we have a volleyball club, a soccer club, and even a karate club.　Also, I'm currently organizing a new English club. We will meet once a week to talk and to enjoy music and movies in English.　If Anna joins or even takes a leadership role, she can connect with other students who have a shared interest — English. I know of one Japanese student from another class who has spent time in New Zealand and is planning to participate. They may find a lot in common.

Another approach is to create social situations where she can be the center of attention. Anna told me you often had barbecue parties in your garden in the US. If it's possible, you could have an American-style barbecue party and invite some of the students in her class. I'm sure it would be an exciting experience for them. Possibly, Anna would be more herself at home and they would get to know her better.

From my experience, I honestly think you have nothing to worry about and feel confident she will establish friendships sooner or later on her own. But, if you feel that any of my ideas will help, please let me know, and we can consider the next step.

Best regards,
Kenji Okamoto

問1　What was Anna probably like at her school in Chicago ?　42

① She liked to be alone in the classroom.

② She showed off her Japanese ability.

③ She spent a lot of time with friends.

④ She was jealous of the other students.

問2　The phrase has a penchant for in the second paragraph of Mr. Whitmore's email is closest in meaning to 43 .

① is collecting　②　is exchanging　③　is fond of　④　is unsure about

問3　Which of the following statements is true according to the information in the email messages ?　44

① Anna does not talk about her school life with her parents at home.

② Anna prefers her Japanese language class to her English class.

③ Mr. Whitmore is concerned about Anna's academic performance.

④ This is the first email message Mr. Whitmore has sent Mr. Okamoto.

問4　Unlike Mr. Whitmore, Mr. Okamoto thinks that Anna 45 .

① is isolated from other students in her class

② spends a lot of time reading in school

③ will have trouble getting good grades

④ will make friends without any special help

問5　Which of the following is **NOT** one of Mr. Okamoto's suggestions for Mr. Whitmore ?　46

① Have Anna join a sports or music club.

② Invite Anna's classmates to an event.

③ Let Anna participate in the English club.

④ Take Anna on a trip to New Zealand.

目標 10分

H 26　⑤

目標 10分

H 26　⑤

第1回目　　　第2回目

／5題　　　／5題

スペイン人画家の Salvador には，日本生まれの Chitose という孫がいる。Chitose はかつて，Salvador に絵の
レッスンを受けていた。以下の文章は，Salvador の日記と，Chitose が彼に宛てた手紙である。文章を読み，
次の問い（問1〜5）の　42　〜　46　に入れるのに最も適当なものを，それぞれ下の①〜④のうちから一
つずつ選べ。

Salvador's Diary
March 30, 2012

Our last lesson was a disaster.　Chitose and I had a huge fight.　She arrived at the studio smiling and said,
"Look Grandpa, I painted this portrait of you."　The man in the portrait had a lot of hair, stood straight, looked
young, and smiled.　She might be talented enough to attend an art college in France, but she has a big weakness
as an artist.　When she paints a person, too often she paints an idealized image rather than the real person.　I
had been explaining this point to her for several months, but she just wouldn't listen.　I got a little angry and
said to her, "This is not me, and you are not a real artist."　She got angry too and said she didn't care because
she didn't need me as a teacher anymore.　I then showed her the portrait I had painted as her farewell gift and
said, "This is the real you !"　She took one look at it, said, "No, it isn't !" and left.

I gave the portrait of Chitose to her parents thinking they would appreciate it.　I had done the portrait a couple
of months before Chitose started changing her style, and I think it shows the high school student I taught for
two years.　When I painted it, she still had her natural curly hair, not her straight perm.　She was not wearing
all the accessories she has now, including the ring-shaped earrings she loves.　She also never wore makeup
then.　This was a Chitose with a fantastic future who knew she was still an amateur artist.　I understand that
she is getting older and wants to act and look more like an adult.　However, she seems to think that being an
adult means that you stop listening to others.　She will never become a great artist if she stops learning.

A Letter to Salvador
March 25, 2013

Dear Grandpa Sal,

I know this is late but I wanted to say that I am sorry for what happened the last time we met.　In our last
lesson, I didn't listen to you because I thought that you still saw me as a kid.　I looked at how you painted me in
the portrait and this confirmed my belief.　I was so hurt that I just left without taking your gift.

You don't know this, but Mom secretly put the portrait into one of my suitcases when I left home for France.
When I found it, I was still upset so I hid it in my closet.　I didn't think about the portrait for a while, but　I
rediscovered it by chance a couple of months ago.　Looking at it, I saw a Chitose who was willing to listen in
order to improve her art.　I realized that the Chitose I'd become was different.　She wanted to prove to
everyone that she was an adult and had stopped listening to others.　Until then, I'd been really struggling in my
art classes, but after I realized my weakness, I started learning again and my art got much better.　You will
always be my teacher, Grandpa.

I remember the portrait I showed you in our last lesson.　You didn't like it and told me to paint you as I saw you.
What you taught me that day makes sense to me now.　I should paint things as they actually are and then their
true beauty will shine.

I've painted a portrait of us and am sending you a photo of it. It actually won first prize in my city's young artists competition. As you can see, I've painted myself like you did, as Chitose the high school student with a lot of potential. I've also painted you as I really see you. Your wrinkles are proof of your wisdom. The cane shows your will to overcome your physical challenges. Your bent back shows that you have poured all your strength into what you love the most : your art and me. Thank you, Grandpa.

Love,
Chitose

問1　Salvador wanted Chitose to [42] .
①　appreciate things for how they are
②　dress more like an artist
③　find another art teacher
④　paint young-looking people

問2　In the last lesson, Chitose didn't accept the portrait because she believed her [43] .
①　family would appreciate it more than she would
②　family would not like her style
③　grandfather did not respect her as an adult
④　grandfather was not a very good artist

問3　Which of the following is true ? [44]
①　Chitose gave the portrait made by Salvador to her parents.
②　Chitose painted the new portrait before writing the letter.
③　It took Salvador two years to make Chitose's portrait.
④　Salvador painted the portrait after Chitose changed her appearance.

問4　What is the most likely reason for the improvement in Chitose's art ? [45]
①　She learned a lot from entering the competition.
②　She started to be open to other people's ideas again.
③　She stopped wearing makeup and earrings.
④　She tried to influence other adults' opinions.

問5　Which of the following pictures best matches the description of the portrait in the photo Chitose sent to her grandfather ? [46]

①　　　　　　②　　　　　　③　　　　　　④

A   Your study group is learning about "how time of day affects people." You have found an article you want to share. Complete the summary notes for your next meeting.

When Does the Day Begin for You?

When asked "Are you a morning person?" some reply "No, I'm a night owl." Such people can concentrate and create at night. At the other end of the clock, a well-known proverb claims: "The early bird catches the worm," which means that waking early is the way to get food, win prizes, and reach goals. The lark is a morning singer, so early birds, the opposite of *owls*, are *larks*. Creatures active during the day are "diurnal" and those emerging at night are "nocturnal."

Yet another proverb states: "Early to bed, early to rise makes a man healthy, wealthy, and wise." *Larks* may jump out of bed and welcome the morning with a big breakfast, while *owls* hit the snooze button, getting ready at the last minute, usually without breakfast. They may have fewer meals, but they eat late in the day. Not exercising after meals can cause weight gain. Perhaps *larks* are healthier. *Owls* must work or learn on the *lark* schedule. Most schooling occurs before 4:00 p.m. , so young *larks* may perform certain tasks better. Business deals made early in the day may make some *larks* wealthier.

What makes one person a *lark* and another an *owl*? One theory suggests preference for day or night has to do with time of birth. In 2010, Cleveland State University researchers found evidence that not only does a person's internal clock start at the moment of birth, but that those born at night might have lifelong challenges performing during daytime hours. Usually, their world experience begins with darkness. Since traditional study time and office work happen in daylight, we assume that day begins in the morning. People asleep are not first in line, and might miss chances.

Does everyone follow the system of beginning days in the morning? The Jewish people, an approximately 6,000-year-old religious group, believe a day is measured from sundown until the following sundown-from eve to eve. Christians continue this tradition with Christmas Eve. The Chinese use their system of 12 animals not only to mark years, but to separate each two-hour period of the day. The hour of the rat, the first period, is from 11:00 p.m. to 1:00 a.m. Chinese culture also begins the day at night. In other words, ancient customs support how *owls* view time.

Research indicates *owls* are smarter and more creative. So, perhaps *larks* are not always wiser! That is to say, *larks* win "healthy" and sometimes "wealthy," but they may lose "wise." In an early report, Richard D. Roberts and Patrick C. Kyllonen state that *owls* tend to be more intelligent. A later, comprehensive study by Franzis Preckel, for which Roberts was one of the co-authors, came to the same conclusion. It is not all good news for *owls*, though. Not only can schoolwork be a challenge, but they may miss daytime career opportunities and are more likely to enjoy the bad habits of "nightlife," playing at night while *larks* sleep. Nightlife tends to be expensive. A University of Barcelona study suggests *larks* are precise, seek perfection, and feel little stress. *Owls* seek new adventures and exciting leisure activities, yet they often have trouble relaxing.

Can people change? While the results are not all in, studies of young adults seem to say no, we are hard-wired. So, as young people grow and acquire more freedom, they end up returning to their *lark* or *owl* nature. However, concerns arise that this categorization may not fit everyone. In addition to time of birth possibly being an indication, a report published in *Nature Communications* suggests that DNA may also affect our habits concerning time. Other works focus on changes occurring in some people due to aging or illness. New research in this area appears all the time. A study of university students in Russia suggests that there are six types, so *owls* and *larks* may not be the only birds around!

Your summary notes:

When Does the Day Begin for You?

Vocabulary

Definition of <u>diurnal</u>: ⬚39

⇔ opposite: nocturnal

The Main Points

- Not all of us fit easily into the common daytime schedule, but we are forced to follow it, especially when we are children.
- Some studies indicate that the most active time for each of us is part of our nature.
- Basically, ⬚40 .
- Perspectives keep changing with new research.

Interesting Details

- The Jewish and Christian religions, as well as Chinese time division, are referred to in the article in order to ⬚41 .
- Some studies show that ⬚42 may set a person's internal clock and may be the explanation for differences in intelligence and ⬚43 .

問1　Choose the best option for ⬚39 .

① achieves goals quickly　② likes keeping pet birds

③ lively in the daytime　④ skillful in finding food

問2　Choose the best option for ⬚40 .

① a more flexible time and performance schedule will be developed in the future

② enjoying social activities in the morning becomes more important as we age

③ it might be hard for us to change what time of day we perform best

④ living on the *owl* schedule will eventually lead to social and financial benefits

問3　Choose the best option for ⬚41 .

① explain that certain societies have long believed that a day begins at night

② indicate that nocturnal people were more religious in the past

③ say that people have long thought they miss chances due to morning laziness

④ support the idea that *owls* must go to work or school on the *lark* schedule

問4　Choose the best options for ⬚42 and ⬚43 .

① amount of sleep　② appearance　③ behavior

④ cultural background　⑤ religious beliefs　⑥ time of birth

B You are in a student group preparing a poster for a scientific presentation contest with the theme "What we should know in order to protect the environment." You have been using the following passage to create the poster.

Recycling Plastic
—What You Need to Know—

The world is full of various types of plastic. Look around, and you will see dozens of plastic items. Look closer and you will notice a recycling symbol on them. In Japan, you might have seen the first symbol in Figure 1 below, but the United States and Europe have a more detailed classification. These recycling symbols look like a triangle of chasing pointers, or sometimes a simple triangle with a number from one to seven inside. This system was started in 1988 by the Society of the Plastics Industry in the US, but since 2008 it has been administered by an international standards organization, ASTM (American Society for Testing and Materials) International. Recycling symbols provide important data about the chemical composition of plastic used and its recyclability. However, a plastic recycling symbol on an object does not always mean that the item can be recycled. It only shows what type of plastic it is made from and that it might be recyclable.

Figure 1. Plastic recycling symbols

So, what do these numbers mean? One group (numbers 2, 4, and 5) is considered to be safe for the human body, while the other group (numbers 1, 3, 6, and 7) could be problematic in certain circumstances. Let us look at the safer group first.

High-density Polyethylene is a recycle-type 2 plastic and is commonly called HDPE. It is non-toxic and can be used in the human body for heart valves and artificial joints. It is strong and can be used at temperatures as low as −40℃ and as high as 100℃ . HDPE can be reused without any harm and is also suitable for beer-bottle cases, milk jugs, chairs, and toys. Type 2 products can be recycled several times. Type 4 products are made from Low-density Polyethylene (LDPE). They are safe to use and are flexible. LDPE is used for squeezable bottles, and bread wrapping. Currently, very little Type 4 plastic is recycled. Polypropylene (PP), a Type 5 material, is the second-most widely produced plastic in the world. It is light, non-stretching, and has a high resistance to impact, heat, and freezing. It is suitable for furniture, food containers, and polymer banknotes such as the Australian dollar. Only 3% of Type 5 is recycled.

Now let us look at the second group, Types 1, 3, 6, and 7. These are more challenging because of the chemicals they contain or the difficulty in recycling them. Recycle-type 1 plastic is commonly known as PETE (Polyethylene Terephthalate), and is used mainly in food and beverage containers. PETE containers — or PET as it is often written in Japan — should only be used once as they are difficult to clean thoroughly. Also, they should not be heated above 70℃ as this can cause some containers to soften and change shape. Uncontaminated PETE is easy to recycle and can be made into new containers, clothes, or carpets, but if PETE is contaminated with Polyvinyl Chloride(PVC), it can make it unrecyclable. PVC, Type 3, is thought to be one of the least recyclable plastics known. It should only be disposed of by professionals and never set fire to at home or in the garden. Type 3 plastic is found in shower curtains, pipes, and flooring. Type 6, Polystyrene(PS) or Styrofoam as it is often called, is hard to recycle and catches fire easily. However, it is cheap to produce and lightweight. It is used for disposable drinking cups, instant noodle containers, and other food packaging. Type 7 plastics (acrylics, nylons, and polycarbonates) are difficult to recycle. Type 7 plastics are often used in the manufacture of vehicle parts such as seats, dashboards, and bumpers.

Currently, only about 20% of plastic is recycled, and approximately 55% ends up in a landfill. Therefore, knowledge about different types of plastic could help reduce waste and contribute to an increased awareness of the environment.

Your presentation poster draft:

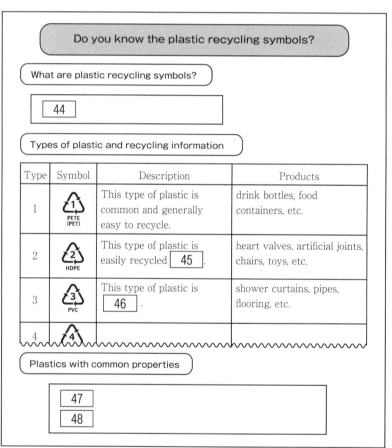

問1 Under the first poster heading, your group wants to introduce the plastic recycling symbols as explained in the passage. Which of the following is the most appropriate? 44

① They are symbols that rank the recyclability of plastics and other related problems.

② They provide information on the chemical make-up and recycling options of the plastic.

③ They tell the user which standards organization gave them certificates for general use.

④ They were introduced by ASTM and developed by the Society of the Plastics Industry.

問2　You have been asked to write descriptions of Type 2 and Type 3 plastics. Choose the best options for
　　　45 　and　46 　.

Type 2　45

① and commonly known as a single-use plastic　　② and used at a wide range of temperatures

③ but harmful to humans　　④ but unsuitable for drink containers

Type 3　46

① difficult to recycle and should not be burned in the yard

② flammable; however, it is soft and cheap to produce

③ known to be a non-toxic product

④ well known for being easily recyclable

問3　You are making statements about some plastics which share common properties. According to the article,
　　　which two of the following are appropriate? (The order does not matter.)　47 　・　48

① Boiling water (100℃) can be served in Type 1 and Type 6 plastic containers.

② It is easy to recycle products with Type 1, 2, and 3 logos.

③ Products with the symbols 1, 2, 4, 5, and 6 are suitable for food or drink containers.

④ Products with Type 5 and Type 6 markings are light in weight.

⑤ Type 4 and 5 plastics are heat resistant and are widely recycled.

⑥ Type 6 and 7 plastics are easy to recycle and environmentally friendly.

A You are an exchange student in the United States and you have joined the school's drama club. You are reading an American online arts magazine article to get some ideas to help improve the club.

Recent Changes at the Royal Shakespeare Company

By John Smith

Feb. 20, 2020

We are all different. While most people recognize that the world is made up of a wide variety of people, diversity—showing and accepting our differences—is often not reflected in performing arts organizations. For this reason, there is an increasing demand for movies and plays to better represent people from various backgrounds as well as those with disabilities. Arts Council England, in response to this demand, is encouraging all publicly funded arts organizations to make improvements in this area. One theater company responding positively is the Royal Shakespeare Company (RSC), which is one of the most influential theater companies in the world.

Based in Stratford-upon-Avon in the UK, the RSC produces plays by William Shakespeare and a number of other famous authors. These days, the RSC is focused on diversity in an attempt to represent all of UK society accurately. It works hard to balance the ethnic and social backgrounds, the genders, and the physical abilities of both performers and staff when hiring.

During the summer 2019 season, the RSC put on three of Shakespeare's comedies: *As You Like It, The Taming of the Shrew*, and *Measure for Measure*. Actors from all over the country were employed, forming a 27-member cast, reflecting the diverse ethnic, geographical, and cultural population of the UK today. To achieve gender balance for the entire season, half of all roles were given to male actors and half to female actors. The cast included three actors with disabilities (currently referred to as "differently-abled" actors) —one visually-impaired, one hearing-impaired, and one in a wheelchair.

Changes went beyond the hiring policy. The RSC actually rewrote parts of the plays to encourage the audience to reflect on male/female power relationships. For example, female and male roles were reversed. In *The Taming of the Shrew*, the role of "the daughter" in the original was transformed into "the son" and played by a male actor. In the same play, a male servant character was rewritten as a female servant. That role was played by Amy Trigg, a female actor who uses a wheelchair. Trigg said that she was excited to play the role and believed that the RSC's changes would have a large impact on other performing arts organizations. Excited by all the diversity, other members of the RSC expressed the same hope—that more arts organizations would be encouraged to follow in the RSC's footsteps.

The RSC's decision to reflect diversity in the summer 2019 season can be seen as a new model for arts organizations hoping to make their organizations inclusive. While there are some who are reluctant to accept diversity in classic plays, others welcome it with open arms. Although certain challenges remain, the RSC has earned its reputation as the face of progress.

論理的文章

問 1　According to the article, the RSC [39] in the summer 2019 season.

① gave job opportunities to famous actors

② hired three differently-abled performers

③ looked for plays that included 27 characters

④ put on plays by Shakespeare and other authors

問 2　The author of this article most likely mentions Amy Trigg because she [40].

① performed well in one of the plays presented by the RSC

② struggled to be selected as a member of the RSC

③ was a good example of the RSC's efforts to be inclusive

④ was a role model for the members of the RSC

問 3　You are summarizing this article for other club members. Which of the following options best completes your summary?

[Summary]

The Royal Shakespeare Company (RSC) in the UK is making efforts to reflect the population of UK society in its productions. In order to achieve this, it has started to employ a balance of female and male actors and staff with a variety of backgrounds and abilities. It has also made changes to its plays. Consequently, the RSC has [41].

① attracted many talented actors from all over the world

② completed the 2019 season without any objections

③ contributed to matching social expectations with actions

④ earned its reputation as a conservative theater company

問 4　Your drama club agrees with the RSC's ideas. Based on these ideas, your drama club might [42].

① perform plays written by new international authors

② present classic plays with the original story

③ raise funds to buy wheelchairs for local people

④ remove gender stereotypes from its performances

B You are one of a group of students making a poster presentation for a wellness fair at City Hall. Your group's title is *Promoting Better Oral Health in the Community*. You have been using the following passage to create the poster.

Oral Health: Looking into the Mirror

In recent years, governments around the world have been working to raise awareness about oral health. While many people have heard that brushing their teeth multiple times per day is a good habit, they most likely have not considered all the reasons why this is crucial. Simply stated, teeth are important. Teeth are required to pronounce words accurately. In fact, poor oral health can actually make it difficult to speak. An even more basic necessity is being able to chew well. Chewing breaks food down and makes it easier for the body to digest it. Proper chewing is also linked to the enjoyment of food. The average person has experienced the frustration of not being able to chew on one side after a dental procedure. A person with weak teeth may experience this disappointment all the time. In other words, oral health impacts people's quality of life.

While the basic functions of teeth are clear, many people do not realize that the mouth provides a mirror for the body. Research shows that good oral health is a clear sign of good general health. People with poor oral health are more likely to develop serious physical diseases. Ignoring recommended daily oral health routines can have negative effects on those already suffering from diseases. Conversely, practicing good oral health may even prevent disease. A strong, healthy body is often a reflection of a clean, well-maintained mouth.

Maintaining good oral health is a lifelong mission. The Finnish and US governments recommend that parents take their infants to the dentist before the baby turns one year old. Finland actually sends parents notices. New Zealand offers free dental treatment to everyone up to age 18. The Japanese government promotes an 8020 (Eighty-Twenty) Campaign. As people age, they can lose teeth for various reasons. The goal of the campaign is still to have at least 20 teeth in the mouth on one's 80th birthday.

Taking a closer look at Japan, the Ministry of Health, Labour and Welfare has been analyzing survey data on the number of remaining teeth in seniors for many years. One researcher divided the oldest participants into four age groups: A (70-74), B (75-79), C (80-84), and D (85 +). In each survey, with the exception of 1993, the percentages of people with at least 20 teeth were in A-B-C-D order from high to low. Between 1993 and 1999, however, Group A improved only about six percentage points, while the increase for B was slightly higher. In 1993, 25.5% in Group A had at least 20 teeth, but by 2016 the Group D percentage was actually 0.2 percentage points higher than Group A's initial figure. Group B increased steadily at first, but went up dramatically between 2005 and 2011. Thanks to better awareness, every group has improved significantly over the years.

Dentists have long recommended brushing after meals. People actively seeking excellent oral health may brush several times per day. Most brush their teeth before they go to sleep and then again at some time the following morning. Dentists also believe it is important to floss daily, using a special type of string to remove substances from between teeth. Another prevention method is for a dentist to seal the teeth using a plastic gel (sealant) that hardens around the tooth surface and prevents damage. Sealant is gaining popularity especially for use with children. This only takes one coating and prevents an amazing 80% of common dental problems.

Visiting the dentist annually or more frequently is key. As dental treatment sometimes causes pain, there are those who actively avoid seeing a dentist. However, it is important that people start viewing their dentist as an important ally who can, literally, make them smile throughout their lives.

Your presentation poster:

Promoting Better Oral Health in the Community

1. Importance of Teeth

A. Crucial to speak properly
B. Necessary to break down food
C. Helpful to enjoy food
D. Needed to make a good impression
E. Essential for good quality of life

2. 44

Finland & the US: Recommendations for treatment before age 1

New Zealand: Free treatment for youth

Japan: 8020 (Eighty-Twenty) Campaign (see Figure 1)

45

Figure 1. The percentage of people with at least 20 teeth.

3. Helpful Advice

46

47

問1 Under the first poster heading, your group wants to express the importance of teeth as explained in the passage. Everyone agrees that one suggestion does not fit well. Which of the following should you **not** include? 43

① A ② B ③ C ④ D ⑤ E

問2 You have been asked to write the second heading for the poster. Which of the following is the most appropriate? 44

① National 8020 Programs Targeting Youth
② National Advertisements for Better Dental Treatment
③ National Efforts to Encourage Oral Care
④ National Systems Inviting Infants to the Dentist

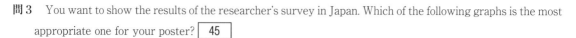

問 3　You want to show the results of the researcher's survey in Japan. Which of the following graphs is the most appropriate one for your poster? 45

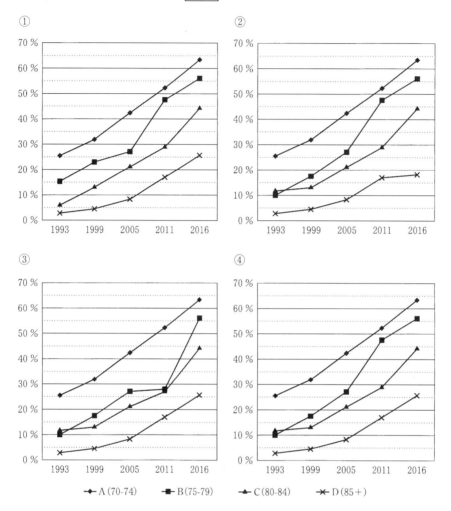

問 4　Under the last poster heading, you want to add specific advice based on the passage. Which two of the following statements should you use? (The order does not matter.) 46 ・ 47

① Brush your teeth before you eat breakfast.

② Check your teeth in the mirror every day.

③ Make at least one visit to the dentist a year.

④ Put plastic gel on your teeth frequently.

⑤ Use dental floss between your teeth daily.

A　You are working on a class project about safety in sports and found the following article. You are reading it and making a poster to present your findings to your classmates.

Making Ice Hockey Safer

Ice hockey is a team sport enjoyed by a wide variety of people around the world. The object of the sport is to move a hard rubber disk called a "puck" into the other team's net with a hockey stick. Two teams with six players on each team engage in this fast-paced sport on a hard and slippery ice rink. Players may reach a speed of 30 kilometers per hour sending the puck into the air. At this pace, both the players and the puck can be a cause of serious danger.

The speed of the sport and the slippery surface of the ice rink make it easy for players to fall down or bump into each other resulting in a variety of injuries. In an attempt to protect players, equipment such as helmets, gloves, and pads for the shoulders, elbows, and legs, has been introduced over the years. Despite these efforts, ice hockey has a high rate of concussions.

A concussion is an injury to the brain that affects the way it functions; it is caused by either direct or indirect impact to the head, face, neck, or elsewhere and can sometimes cause temporary loss of consciousness. In less serious cases, for a short time, players may be unable to walk straight or see clearly, or they may experience ringing in the ears. Some believe they just have a slight headache and do not realize they have injured their brains.

In addition to not realizing the seriousness of the injury, players tend to worry about what their coach will think. In the past, coaches preferred tough players who played in spite of the pain. In other words, while it would seem logical for an injured player to stop playing after getting hurt, many did not. Recently, however, it has been found that concussions can have serious effects that last a lifetime. People with a history of concussion may have trouble concentrating or sleeping. Moreover, they may suffer from psychological problems such as depression and mood changes. In some cases, players may develop smell and taste disorders.

The National Hockey League (NHL), consisting of teams in Canada and the United States, has been making stricter rules and guidelines to deal with concussions. For example, in 2001, the NHL introduced the wearing of visors—pieces of clear plastic attached to the helmet that protect the face. At first, it was optional and many players chose not to wear them. Since 2013, however, it has been required. In addition, in 2004, the NHL began to give more severe penalties, such as suspensions and fines, to players who hit another player in the head deliberately.

The NHL also introduced a concussion spotters system in 2015. In this system, NHL officials with access to live streaming and video replay watch for visible indications of concussion during each game. At first, two concussion spotters, who had no medical training, monitored the game in the arena. The following year, one to four concussion spotters with medical training were added. They monitored each game from the League's head office in New York. If a spotter thinks that a player has suffered a concussion, the player is removed from the game and is taken to a "quiet room" for an examination by a medical doctor. The player is not allowed to return to the game until the doctor gives permission.

The NHL has made much progress in making ice hockey a safer sport. As more is learned about the causes and effects of concussions, the NHL will surely take further measures to ensure player safety. Better safety might lead to an increase in the number of ice hockey players and fans.

Making Ice Hockey Safer

What is ice hockey?

· Players score by putting a "puck" in the other team's net

· Six players on each team

· Sport played on ice at a high speed

Main Problem: A High Rate of Concussions

Definition of a concussion

An injury to the brain that affects the way it functions

Effects

Short-term	Long-term
· Loss of consciousness	· Problems with concentration
· Difficulty walking straight	· [40]
· [39]	· Psychological problems
· Ringing in the ears	· Smell and taste disorders

Solutions

National Hockey League (NHL)

· Requires helmets with visors

· Gives severe penalties to dangerous players

· Has introduced concussion spotters to [41]

Summary

Ice hockey players have a high risk of suffering from concussions.
Therefore, the NHL has [42] .

問1　Choose the best option for [39] on your poster.
　　① Aggressive behavior　② Difficulty thinking　③ Personality changes　④ Unclear vision

問2　Choose the best option for [40] on your poster.
　　① Loss of eyesight　② Memory problems　③ Sleep disorders　④ Unsteady walking

問3　Choose the best option for [41] on your poster.
　　① allow players to return to the game
　　② examine players who have a concussion
　　③ fine players who cause concussions
　　④ identify players showing signs of a concussion

問4　Choose the best option for [42] on your poster.
　　① been expecting the players to become tougher
　　② been implementing new rules and guidelines
　　③ given medical training to coaches
　　④ made wearing of visors optional

B　You are studying nutrition in health class. You are going to read the following passage from a textbook to learn more about various sweeteners.

Cake, candy, soft drinks—most of us love sweet things. In fact, young people say "Sweet!" to mean something is "good" in English. When we think of sweetness, we imagine ordinary white sugar from sugar cane or sugar beet plants. Scientific discoveries, however, have changed the world of sweeteners. We can now extract sugars from many other plants. The most obvious example is corn. Corn is abundant, inexpensive, and easy to process. High fructose corn syrup（HFCS）is about 1.2 times sweeter than regular sugar, but quite high in calories. Taking science one step further, over the past 70 years scientists have developed a wide variety of artificial sweeteners.

A recent US National Health and Nutrition Examination Survey concluded that 14.6% of the average American's energy intake is from "added sugar," which refers to sugar that is not derived from whole foods. A banana, for example, is a whole food, while a cookie contains added sugar. More than half of added sugar calories are from sweetened drinks and desserts. Lots of added sugar can have negative effects on our bodies, including excessive weight gain and other health problems. For this reason, many choose low-calorie substitutes for drinks, snacks, and desserts.

Natural alternatives to white sugar include brown sugar, honey, and maple syrup, but they also tend to be high in calories. Consequently, alternative "low-calorie sweeteners"（LCSs）, mostly artificial chemical combinations, have become popular. The most common LCSs today are aspartame, Ace-K, stevia, and sucralose. Not all LCSs are artificial—stevia comes from plant leaves.

Alternative sweeteners can be hard to use in cooking because some cannot be heated and most are far sweeter than white sugar. Aspartame and Ace-K are 200 times sweeter than sugar. Stevia is 300 times sweeter, and sucralose has twice the sweetness of stevia. Some new sweeteners are even more intense. A Japanese company recently developed "Advantame," which is 20,000 times sweeter than sugar. Only a tiny amount of this substance is required to sweeten something.

When choosing sweeteners, it is important to consider health issues. Making desserts with lots of white sugar, for example, results in high-calorie dishes that could lead to weight gain. There are those who prefer LCSs for this very reason. Apart from calories, however, some research links consuming artificial LCSs with various other health concerns. Some LCSs contain strong chemicals suspected of causing cancer, while others have been shown to affect memory and brain development, so they can be dangerous, especially for young children, pregnant women, and the elderly. There are a few relatively natural alternative sweeteners, like xylitol and sorbitol, which are low in calories. Unfortunately, these move through the body extremely slowly, so consuming large amounts can cause stomach trouble.

When people want something sweet, even with all the information, it is difficult for them to decide whether to stick to common higher calorie sweeteners like sugar or to use LCSs. Many varieties of gum and candy today contain one or more artificial sweeteners; nonetheless, some people who would not put artificial sweeteners in hot drinks may still buy such items. Individuals need to weigh the options and then choose the sweeteners that best suit their needs and circumstances.

問1 You learn that modern science has changed the world of sweeteners by $\boxed{43}$.

① discovering new, sweeter white sugar types

② measuring the energy intake of Americans

③ providing a variety of new options

④ using many newly-developed plants from the environment

問2 You are summarizing the information you have just studied. How should the table be finished? $\boxed{44}$

Sweetness	Sweetener
high	Advantame
	(A)
	(B)
	(C)
low	(D)

① （A） Stevia （B） Sucralose
（C） Ace-K, Aspartame （D） HFCS

② （A） Stevia （B） Sucralose
（C） HFCS （D） Ace-K, Aspartame

③ （A） Sucralose （B） Stevia
（C） Ace-K, Aspartame （D） HFCS

④ （A） Sucralose （B） Stevia
（C） HFCS （D） Ace-K, Aspartame

問3 According to the article you read, which of the following are true? (Choose two options. The order does not matter.) $\boxed{45}$ ・ $\boxed{46}$

① Alternative sweeteners have been proven to cause weight gain.

② Americans get 14.6% of their energy from alternative sweeteners.

③ It is possible to get alternative sweeteners from plants.

④ Most artificial sweeteners are easy to cook with.

⑤ Sweeteners like xylitol and sorbitol are not digested quickly.

問4 To describe the author's position, which of the following is most appropriate? $\boxed{47}$

① The author argues against the use of artificial sweeteners in drinks and desserts.

② The author believes artificial sweeteners have successfully replaced traditional ones.

③ The author states that it is important to invent much sweeter products for future use.

④ The author suggests people focus on choosing sweeteners that make sense for them.

A　You are preparing for a group presentation on gender and career development for your class. You have found the article below.

Can Female Pilots Solve Asia's Pilot Crisis?

[1]　　With the rapid growth of airline travel in Asia, the shortage of airline pilots is becoming an issue of serious concern. Statistics show that the number of passengers flying in Asia is currently increasing by about 100,000,000 a year. If this trend continues, 226,000 new pilots will be required in this region over the next two decades. To fill all of these jobs, airlines will need to hire more women, who currently account for 3% of all pilots worldwide, and only 1% in Asian countries such as Japan and Singapore. To find so many new pilots, factors that explain such a low number of female pilots must be examined, and possible solutions have to be sought.

[2]　　One potential obstacle for women to become pilots might be the stereotype that has long existed in many societies: women are not well-suited for this job. This seems to arise partly from the view that boys tend to excel in mechanics and are stronger physically than girls. A recent study showed that young women have a tendency to avoid professions in which they have little prospect of succeeding. Therefore, this gender stereotype might discourage women from even trying. It may explain why at the Malaysia Flying Academy, for instance, women often account for no more than 10% of all trainees enrolled.

[3]　　Yet another issue involves safety. People may be concerned about the safety of aircraft flown by female pilots, but their concerns are not supported by data. For example, a previous analysis of large pilot databases conducted in the United States showed no meaningful difference in accident rates between male and female pilots. Instead, the study found that other factors such as a pilot's age and flight experience better predicted whether that person is likely to be involved in an accident.

[4]　　Despite the expectation that male pilots have better flight skills, it may be that male and female pilots just have skills which give them different advantages in the job. On the one hand, male pilots often have an easier time learning how to fly than do female pilots. The controls in a cockpit are often easier to reach or use for a larger person. Men tend to be larger, on average, than women. In fact, females are less likely than men to meet the minimum height requirements that most countries have. On the other hand, as noted by a Japanese female airline captain, female pilots appear to be better at facilitating communication among crew members.

[5]　　When young passengers see a woman flying their plane, they come to accept female pilots as a natural phenomenon. Today's female pilots are good role models for breaking down stereotypical views and traditional practices, such as the need to stay home with their families. Offering flexible work arrangements, as has already been done by Vietnam Airlines, may help increase the number of female pilots and encourage them to stay in the profession.

[6]　　It seems that men and women can work equally well as airline pilots. A strong message must be sent to younger generations about this point in order to eliminate the unfounded belief that airline pilots should be men.

問1　According to the article, the author calls the current situation in Asia a crisis because ⬚35⬚ .

① many more male airline pilots are quitting their jobs than before

② the accident rates are increasing among both male and female pilots

③ the number of female pilots has not changed much for the last few decades

④ the number of future pilots needed will be much larger than at present

問2　According to the article, there is little difference between men and women in ⬚36⬚ .

① how easily they learn to operate airplanes

② how likely they are to be involved in accidents

③ how much time they can spend on work

④ how people perceive their suitability for the job

問3　In Paragraph［4］, the author most likely mentions a Japanese female airline captain in order to give an example of ⬚37⬚ .

① a contribution female pilots could make to the workplace

② a female pilot who has excellent skills to fly a plane

③ a problem in the current system for training airline pilots

④ an airline employee who has made rare achievements

問4　Which of the following statements best summarizes the article? ⬚38⬚

① Despite negative views toward female pilots, they can be as successful as male pilots.

② Due to financial problems the percentage of female students in a pilot academy in Asia is too small.

③ In the future many countries worldwide may have to start hiring more female pilots like Asian countries.

④ There is little concern about increasing female pilots in the future because major obstacles for them have been removed.

B You are studying about world ecological problems. You are going to read the following article to understand what has happened in Yellowstone National Park.

Yellowstone National Park, located in the northern United States, became the world's first national park in 1872. One of the major attractions of this 2.2-million-acre park is the large variety of animals. Some people say that Yellowstone is the best place in the world to see wolves. As of December 2016, there were at least 108 wolves and 11 packs (social families) in the park. By the 1940s, however, wolves had almost disappeared from Yellowstone National Park. Today, these wolves are back and doing well. Why have they returned?

The wolves' numbers had declined by the 1920s through hunting, which was not regulated by the government. Ranchers on large farms raising cattle, horses, and sheep did not like wolves because they killed their animals. When the wolves were on the point of being wiped out by hunting, another problem arose—the elk herds increased in number. Elk, a large species of deer, are the wolves' principal source of food in the winter. The elk populations grew so large that they upset the balance of the local ecosystem by eating many plants. People may like to see elk, but scientists were worried about the damage caused by the overly large population.

To solve this problem, the U.S. government announced their intention to release young wolves brought from Canada. It was hoped that the wolves would hunt the elk and help bring down the population. However, because many ranchers were against bringing back wolves, it took about 20 years for the government and the ranchers to agree on a plan. In 1974, a team was appointed to oversee the reintroduction of wolves. The government published official recovery plans in 1982, 1985, and finally in 1987. After a long period of research, an official environmental impact statement was issued and 31 wolves were released into Yellowstone from 1995 to 1996.

This project to reduce the number of elk was a great success. By 2006, the estimated wolf population in Yellowstone National Park was more than 100. Furthermore, observers believe that the wolves have been responsible for a decline in the elk population from nearly 20,000 to less than 10,000 during the first 10 years following their introduction. As a result, a lot of plants have started to grow back. The hunting of wolves is even allowed again because of the risk from wolves to ranchers' animals. While hunting wolves because they are perceived as a threat may seem like an obvious solution, it may cause new problems. As a study published in 2014 suggested, hunting wolves might increase the frequency of wolves killing ranchers' animals. If the leader of a wolf pack is killed, the pack may break up. Smaller packs or individual wolves may then attack ranchers' animals. Therefore, there is now a restriction on how many wolves can be hunted. Such measures are important for long-term management of wolf populations.

問1 The decline of wolves in Yellowstone National Park in the early 1900s resulted in [39] .

① a decrease in the number of hunters, which was good for the wolves

② a decrease in the number of ranchers, which reduced the human population

③ an increase in the number of elk, which damaged the local ecosystem

④ an increase in the number of trees and plants, which helped elk to hide

問2 Out of the following four graphs, which illustrates the situation the best? 40

① ②

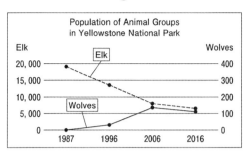

③ ④

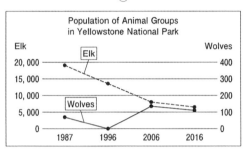

問3 According to the article, which two of the following tell us about the current situation in the park?
(**Choose two options**. The order does not matter.) 41 ・ 42

① More travelers are visiting the park than thirty years ago.

② One species was saved but another has become extinct instead.

③ People have started hunting wolves around this area again.

④ The park has both wolves and elk, as well as rich vegetation.

⑤ There is a new rule to reduce the elk population in the park.

問4 The best title for this article is 43 .

① A Decrease in the Number of Ranchers' Animals

② Addressing Problems With Nature's Balance

③ Nature Conservation Around the World

④ Releasing Elk in National Parks

You are writing a review of the story, "Oscar's Camp Canyon Experience," in class.

Oscar's Camp Cayon Experience

Twelve-year-old Oscar has just finished a wonderful week at Camp Canyon. He had the time of his life—making new friends, developing new skills, and discovering a love for science among many other things. And Oscar learned an important lesson: Sometimes, when faced with a difficult situation, it's best just to let it go. He learned, too, that things are not always what they seem.

Camp Canyon is a summer camp for boys and girls from eight to sixteen. In the U.S., there are many kinds of camps. Often, kids focus on particular skills or learn values from religious books and traditions. Camp Canyon, though, is different. Its main aim is for the kids to discover for themselves how to deal with difficult situations using ideas based on the importance of communication and mutual respect. During their week at the camp, the kids develop their powers of judgment and sense of right and wrong—all while having fun swimming, playing games, and doing hands-on science and nature projects.

This was Oscar's second summer at Camp Canyon, and he enjoyed showing newcomers around. On the first day, he introduced himself to Dylan, a boy of his age attending the camp for the first time. Oscar spent a lot of time helping Dylan get used to his new circumstances, and they quickly became close friends. They both enjoyed playing video games and climbing trees, and at the camp they discovered a shared love of Gaga Ball, a form of dodgeball. Oscar and Dylan played Gaga Ball until they were exhausted, throwing the ball at the other kids and screaming with laughter. Afterward, sitting on their bunk beds, they would talk for hours about their home and school lives, and how much they were enjoying Camp Canyon.

One of the other campers was a boy named Christopher. Initially, Christopher seemed like a well-behaved, fun-loving boy. Oscar couldn't wait to get to know him. However, it wasn't long before Christopher's behavior started to change. He didn't bother to make his bed. He left games and other belongings lying around on the floor. He was inconsiderate and self-centered. And he was mean, as Oscar and Dylan soon found out.

"Dylan didn't brush his teeth. And he's smelly! He didn't take a shower today," shouted Christopher at breakfast, making sure all the other kids could hear.

Oscar and Dylan were shocked to hear Christopher's comments. Oscar had always tried his hardest to make everyone feel welcome. Christopher seemed to take great delight in saying things that upset the other two boys. He even pushed in front of Oscar when they were lining up for lunch. He just laughed when Oscar angrily protested.

Oscar consulted the camp counselor about their problems with Christopher. She gave Christopher a strong warning, but, if anything, his behavior got worse. The other kids just kept out of his way, determined not to let anything spoil their fun activities at camp.

One of these activities was a discussion session with a science teacher. Although Oscar had shown little interest in science at school, this was something he really enjoyed at the camp. The kids talked with the teacher, growing increasingly excited with each new scientific fact they discovered. Oscar was particularly fascinated to learn about reflected light and how we see certain colors. A red object, for example, absorbs every color of the rainbow, but reflects only red light to our eyes.

"So," Oscar reported breathlessly to Dylan, "a red object is actually every color EXCEPT red—which is reflected! Isn't that amazing? I just love science!" Things, he had come to realize, are not always what they seem.

The campers also discussed ethics and the rules that would be best for the group as they experienced their week together. Whenever there was a disagreement, they stopped to consider what might be the right or wrong thing to do according to each situation. In this way, they learned to function together as a harmonious group.

Through these discussions, Oscar learned that there is not always an obvious solution to a problem. Sometimes, as with the case of Christopher's bad behavior, the answer might just be to let it go. Oscar realized that getting upset wasn't going to change anything, and that the best way to resolve the situation without drama would be walk away from it. He and Dylan stayed calm, and stopped reacting to Christopher's insults. This seemd to work. Soon, Christopher lost interest in bothering the boys.

The end of the week came far too quickly for Oscar. His memories of the camp were still fresh when, a few days after returning home, he received a postcard from Christopher.

> Dear Oscar,
>
> I'm really sorry for the way I behaved at camp. You and Dylan seemed to be having so much fun! I felt left out, because I'm not very good at sports. Later, when you stopped paying attention to my bad behavior, I realized how silly I was being. I wanted to apologize then, but was too embarrassed. Are you going to the camp again next year? I'll be there, and I hope we can be friends!
>
> So long,
> Christopher

Yes, thought Oscar, when he had recovered from his surprise, with Christopher, he had been right to let it go. Putting down the postcard, he remembered something else he had learned at camp: Sometimes, things are not what they seem.

Complete the review by filling in ⬚34⬚ to ⬚38⬚ .

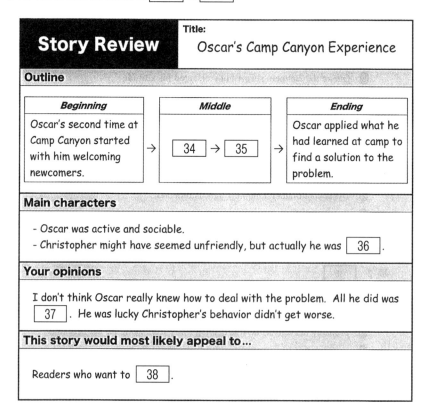

Story Review Title: Oscar's Camp Canyon Experience

Outline

Beginning	Middle	Ending
Oscar's second time at Camp Canyon started with him welcoming newcomers.	→ ⬚34⬚ → ⬚35⬚ →	Oscar applied what he had learned at camp to find a solution to the problem.

Main characters

- Oscar was active and sociable.
- Christopher might have seemed unfriendly, but actually he was ⬚36⬚ .

Your opinions

I don't think Oscar really knew how to deal with the problem. All he did was ⬚37⬚ . He was lucky Christopher's behavior didn't get worse.

This story would most likely appeal to...

Readers who want to ⬚38⬚ .

問1　(a)　[34]

① All the camp participants quickly became good friends.

② Most campers stopped enjoying the fun activities.

③ One of the campers surprisingly changed his attitude.

④ The camp counselor managed to solve a serious problem.

　(b)　[35]

① Christopher continued to behave very badly.

② Dylan could understand how light is reflected.

③ Oscar played a leading role in group discussions.

④ The counselor reconsidered her viewpoint.

問2　[36]

① just unhappy because he was unable to take part in all the activities

② probably nervous as he was staying away from home for the first time

③ smarter than most campers since he tried to hide his honest opinions

④ thoughtful enough to have brought games to share with his friends

問3　[37]

① avoid a difficult situation　　② discuss ethics and rules

③ embarrass the others　　④ try to be even friendlier

問4　[38]

① get detailed information about summer outdoor activities

② read a moving story about kids' success in various sports

③ remember their own childhood experiences with friends

④ understand the relationship between children and adults

次の文章を読み，あとの問い（A・B）に答えよ。なお，文章の左にある(1)〜(6)はパラグラフ（段落）の番号を表している。

(1)　From quiet paths by a stream in a forest to busy roads running through a city, people have created various forms of routes in different places.　These now exist all around us, and their use is <u>imperative</u> for societies.　These routes have enabled people to move, transport things, and send information from one place to another quickly and safely.　Throughout history, they have been important in our daily lives.

(2)　Early routes were often formed naturally on land.　They gradually developed over long periods of time while people traveled them on foot or horseback.　A significant turning point in their history arrived when the first wheeled carts appeared in ancient times.　Once this happened, people recognized the importance of well-maintained routes.　Therefore, towns, cities, and entire countries improved them in order to prosper.　As a result, life became more convenient, communities grew, economies evolved, and cultures expanded.　The importance of land routes increased further, especially after the appearance of automobiles.

(3)　People have established routes on water, too.　Rivers and canals have served as effective routes for people to move around and carry things.　For instance, in the old Japanese city of Edo, water routes were used for the transportation of agricultural products, seafood, and wood, which supported the city's life and economy.　People have also opened routes across the sea.　The seaways, which developed based on winds, waves, water depths, and coastline geography, were critical for the navigation of ships, particularly in the days when they moved mainly by wind power.　Using these sea routes, people could travel great distances and go to places they had not previously been able to reach.　A number of important sea routes emerged, leading to the exchange of natural resources, products, and ideas.　This, in turn, helped cities and towns thrive.

(4)　People have gone on to open routes in the sky as well.　Since the invention of the airplane, these routes have made it possible for people to travel long distances easily.　They found the best routes by considering conditions such as winds and air currents.　Eventually, people became able to travel safely and comfortably high in the sky, and going vast distances only took a small amount of time.　In fact, people used to need more than one month to travel to Europe from Japan by ship, whereas today they can travel between them in a single day by airplane.　Owing to the establishment of these sky routes, a great number of people now travel around the world for sightseeing, visiting friends, and doing business.

(5)　Today, we have a new type of route, the Internet, which specializes in the electronic exchange of information.　By using this worldwide route, people can easily obtain information that once was available mainly from books and face-to-face communication.　They can also instantly send messages to large numbers of people all at once.　According to one study, more than 3.5 billion people, which is about half of the global population, have access to this electronic route today.　As technology advances, more and more people will take advantage of this route to gather information and communicate.

(6)　As long as there have been people, there have been routes to connect them.　These have contributed not only to the movement of people, things, and information, but also to the development of our communities, economies, and cultures.　Routes have played significant roles in the development and prosperity of humankind.　Currently unknown routes will surely take us even further in the future.

A 次の問い（問1〜5）の 46 〜 50 に入れるのに最も適当なものを，それぞれ下の①〜④のうちから一つずつ選べ。

問1 Which of the following is closest to the meaning of the underlined word imperative in paragraph (1) ?
46
① accidental ② essential ③ industrial ④ traditional

問2 According to paragraph (2), which of the following statements is true ? 47
① Early routes were created by people who traveled by wheeled carts.
② People's first routes on land followed the growth of towns and cities.
③ The development of land routes led to progress in many areas of society.
④ The improvement of routes resulted in the invention of the automobile.

問3 Why is the example of Edo introduced in paragraph (3) ? 48
① To describe the difficulty of creating routes on the water
② To emphasize the fact that it was an important city
③ To explain the use of water routes to move along the coastlines
④ To illustrate the important roles of water routes for cities

問4 What does paragraph (5) tell us about routes ? 49
① Routes can be thought of as existing invisibly in the world.
② Routes that move information can be regarded as dangerous.
③ The fundamental functions of routes are declining.
④ The importance of different kinds of routes is the same.

問5 What is the main point of this article ? 50
① Humankind first created various types of convenient routes on land.
② Improvements in transportation have come at great cost.
③ Technology has interfered with opening up routes around the world.
④ The advancement of humanity was aided by the development of routes.

B 次の表は，本文のパラグラフ（段落）の構成と内容をまとめたものである。 51 〜 54 に入れるのに最も適当なものを，下の①〜④のうちから一つずつ選び，表を完成させよ。ただし，同じものを繰り返し選んではいけない。

Paragraph	Content
(1)	Introduction
(2)	51
(3)	52
(4)	53
(5)	54
(6)	Conclusion

① Creation of roads used by people, animals, and vehicles
② Developing ways for people to fly from place to place
③ Establishment of global paths for information transfer
④ Opening of lanes for ships to travel and transport things

次の文章を読み，あとの問い（A・B）に答えよ。なお，文章の左にある⑴～⑹はパラグラフ（段落）の番号を表している。

⑴　History teaches us that technology and associated discoveries have changed how we understand the world. Many technological devices provide additional range and power to our natural capacities, such as our five senses. Among these devices, many enable us to see things that we cannot see with the naked eye. This change from invisible to visible has led to tremendous growth in our comprehension of the world and has strongly influenced our ways of thinking.

⑵　In the 17th century, a scientist noticed that by holding two lenses together in a certain way he could make an object appear larger. He used this technique to construct the first simple telescope. Using these <u>archaic</u> telescopes, early scientists were able to describe the surface of the Moon in detail and to see that Jupiter had at least four such satellites. Since that time, people have developed various devices that expand our range of sight, thus revealing facts about the universe that lies beyond the Earth. The telescope continues to offer us new views concerning things beyond our immediate reach.

⑶　Later, the microscope was developed using principles similar to the telescope. The microscope allows us to study objects we normally cannot see because they are too small. Looking through a microscope opened up an entirely new world to scientists. Before the invention of the microscope, they couldn't see the structures of human tissues or cells in plants and animals. When they saw these things, they became aware that some things that they had thought were whole and could not be divided, actually consisted of smaller components. These were only visible with the assistance of microscopes. Today, electron microscopes allow us to investigate even smaller items, such as molecules. These advances have altered our concepts regarding the composition of things in the world.

⑷　The invention of the camera also made the invisible world visible. In the world, everything is changing. Some things change faster than we can see. The camera is a tool that gives us the power to freeze change at different points in time. Series of pictures have revealed how birds move in flight and athletes run. The camera can also help us see changes that are so gradual that we usually don't notice them. For example, by comparing photos of the same scene taken months or years apart, we can gain insights into how societies change. There are many other ways besides these in which the camera has changed our perceptions of the world.

⑸　In the late 19th century, machines that used the newly discovered X-rays revolutionized the way in which we looked at things. Rather than seeing only the surface of an object, we gained the ability to look into it or through it, bringing the inner elements of many things into our range of view. This capability proved practical in the workplace, useful in laboratories and museums, and instructive in universities. One of the most important applications was in medicine. Doctors often had difficulty diagnosing illnesses or finding problems inside the body. X-rays allowed them to look into their patients, identify where there were problems, and cure them. This use of X-rays brought new understandings and methods for diagnosis and treatment.

⑹　Different technological devices have made it possible to observe things that we could not see with the naked eye. This has significantly altered our understandings of the world around us. Each technological advance changes us in unpredictable ways, and each discovery increases our knowledge about the world. Just as the devices mentioned above have done, new devices will continue to impact our lives and change our ways of thinking in the future.

A 次の問い（問1〜5）の 46 〜 50 に入れるのに最も適当なものを，それぞれ下の①〜④のうちから一つずつ選べ。

問1 Which of the following is closest to the meaning of <u>archaic</u> as used in paragraph (2)？ 46

① advanced

② contemporary

③ ordinary

④ primitive

問2 According to paragraph (3), what did people learn by using microscopes？ 47

① Cells were too small to be seen with microscopes.

② Materials were made up of smaller things.

③ Molecules were the smallest components.

④ Sets of lenses decreased the size of items.

問3 According to paragraph (4), what do cameras enable us to do？ 48

① To capture moments in time accurately

② To compare rapid social changes

③ To make invisible things move faster

④ To predict what will happen

問4 According to paragraph (5), how are X-rays used？ 49

① To find the locations of problems in the body

② To improve visibility of objects' surfaces

③ To learn when paintings were created

④ To test the quality of chemical compounds

問5 What is the main idea of this passage？ 50

① Applications of two lenses can improve people's sight.

② Development of technology affects our ways of thinking.

③ People need to be aware of the dangers of technology.

④ Technology plays a vital role in changing our five senses.

B 次の表は，本文のパラグラフ（段落）の構成と内容をまとめたものである。 51 〜 54 に入れるのに最も適当なものを，下の①〜④のうちから一つずつ選び，表を完成させよ。ただし，同じものを繰り返し選んではいけない。

Paragraph	Content
(1)	Introduction
(2)	51
(3)	52
(4)	53
(5)	54
(6)	Conclusion

① Examining the interiors of things

② Exploring the universe of small things

③ Looking at instants during a series of changes

④ The use of lenses to look out into space

次の文章を読み，あとの問い（**A・B**）に答えよ。なお，文章の左にある(1)～(6)はパラグラフ（段落）の番号を表している。

(1)　For most people, their friendships are a valuable and important part of who they are.　Psychologists have pointed out that well-established friendships lead us to a better understanding of ourselves.　They have also noted that we might face conflicts not only with acquaintances but even with our good friends, which could result in ends to some of our friendships.　Fortunately, even when such conflicts occur, it is possible to find ways to maintain or save the friendships.

(2)　One way to help save a friendship in trouble is to keep in touch.　When we think a friend has done something that hurt our feelings, our first response may be to cut off contact.　However, it may be better to <u>swallow our pride</u> and avoid doing that.　For example, Mary watched her friend Susan's children every week until Susan finished night school and graduated.　But after that, Mary did not hear from Susan for several months.　So, she felt that Susan had been just using her.　She decided not to talk to her any more.　In the end, however, Mary forced herself to ignore her own feelings and told Susan about her disappointment.　Susan immediately apologized and told her that she had been just trying to catch up with things after completing her studies.　Susan would never have known there was a problem if Mary had not mentioned it.　Not cutting off contact, even when we may be angry, is very important for maintaining good relationships.

(3)　Another way to help a friendship is to see things from our friend's point of view.　For example, Mark was very upset at his good friend, Kate, because she had not visited him in the hospital.　Later, he learned from Kate's friend that she had been afraid of hospitals ever since she had been hospitalized as a little girl for a serious illness. Mark then understood why Kate hadn't come and, instead of being angry, he felt sympathy for her.

(4)　An important part of dealing with friendships is to recognize and accept that they can change as our needs and lifestyles evolve.　For example, we may have a good friend in high school, but once we graduate, move to a different city for work or study, or get married, we may see that friend less frequently and our feelings may change. In other words, sometimes a close friendship may alter in nature.　We should keep in mind that we may still be friends but not in the same way as before.

(5)　How do people keep friendships for a long time ?　In one study, researchers interviewed many people who had been friends for a long time in order to find out the secret.　They found that those people kept small misunderstandings from growing into large disputes which might cause their friendships to end.　By taking their friends' viewpoints and not being afraid to express their honest feelings, those who were interviewed were able to keep something minor from growing into a major argument.

(6)　We all know that friendships are precious, but we also understand that friendships are not always stable.　The challenge in maintaining friendships is keeping the connections strong during the ups and downs that happen in all relationships.　When things are going well, we enjoy our friendships.　If things go bad, we should remember the points above.　Sometimes we can get the relationship back on track, but at other times we should accept and appreciate that relationships can change.　However, regardless of the states of our friendships, they will continue to be an important part of our lives.

A 次の問い（問1〜5）の 47 〜 51 に入れるのに最も適当なものを，それぞれ下の①〜④のうちから一つずつ選べ。

問1 According to paragraph (1), what do psychologists say about friendships ? 47

① They are frequently compared to one's possessions.

② They are impossible to fix when they become unstable.

③ They can lead us to have conflicts with our acquaintances.

④ They help us know about ourselves but can have problems.

問2 Which of the following is closest to the meaning of swallow our pride in paragraph (2) ? 48

① Give our thanks to someone

② Hold back our feelings

③ Realize that problems happen

④ Stop seeing someone

問3 According to paragraph (5), research found it is important to 49 .

① hesitate to express one's true feelings

② ignore misunderstandings and disputes

③ put up with problems whenever one can

④ solve problems while they are small

問4 According to paragraph (6), what is difficult about maintaining friendships ? 50

① Finding new and interesting friends

② Knowing when to change relationships

③ Seeing if friends have problems

④ Staying close during bad times

問5 What would be the best title for this passage ? 51

① Advice for Friendships That Will Last

② Defending Yourself and Your Friends

③ Strength as the Key to Friendships

④ The Changing Nature of Friendships

B 次の表は，本文のパラグラフ（段落）ごとの内容をまとめたものである。 52 〜 55 に入れるのに最も適当なものを，下の①〜④のうちから一つずつ選び，表を完成させよ。ただし，同じものを繰り返し選んではいけない。

Paragraph	Content
(1)	The realization that friendships are important
(2)	52
(3)	53
(4)	54
(5)	55
(6)	What is important to keep in mind

① A report about the results of a study on long-term friendships

② The importance of looking at a situation from our friend's perspective

③ The significance of understanding that friendships undergo transformations

④ The value of staying in contact and interacting with your friends

次の文章を読み，あとの問い（**A・B**）に答えよ。なお，文章の左にある(1)〜(6)は段落の番号を表している。

Catching Bees and Counting Fish : How "Citizen Science" Works

(1)　It's a sunny afternoon here in Texas, and my wife Barbara is at the park again, counting and recording the number of eggs laid by monarch butterflies.　After collecting her data, she'll share it with the professional scientist who recruited her.　In another state, our friend Antonio listens for frogs by visiting 12 different sites, four times a year.　He has been submitting his findings to scientists for almost 20 years now.　And on the other side of the country, our niece Emily is catching native bees, putting tiny tags on them, and handing in weekly reports to the biology department at a local university.　Nobody is paying Barbara, Antonio, or Emily for their efforts, but all three consider themselves lucky to be "citizen scientists."

(2)　When volunteers participate as assistants in activities like these, they are engaging in citizen science, a valuable research technique that invites the public to assist in gathering information.　Some of them are science teachers or students, but most are simply amateurs who enjoy spending time in nature.　They also take pride in aiding scientists and indirectly helping to protect the environment.　The movement they are involved in is not a new one.　In fact, its roots go back over a hundred years.　One of the earliest projects of this type is the Christmas Bird Count, started by the National Audubon Society in 1900.　However, citizen science projects are burgeoning more than ever : over 60 of them were mentioned at a meeting of the Ecological Society of America not long ago.

(3)　In formal studies, professional scientists and other experts need to maintain the highest possible standards.　For research to be accepted as valid, it must not only be thorough, but also objective and accurate.　Some might argue that citizen scientists cannot maintain the necessary attention to detail, or that amateurs will misunderstand the context of the investigation and make mistakes when collecting and organizing information.　In other words, can citizen science be considered truly reliable ?

(4)　Two recent studies show that it can.　The first focused on volunteer knowledge and skills.　In this study, a scientist asked volunteers to identify types of crabs along the Atlantic coast of the US.　He found that almost all adult volunteers could perform the task and even third graders in elementary school had an 80% success rate.　The second study compared professional and nonprofessional methods.　Following a strict traditional procedure, a group of 12 scuba divers identified 106 species of fish in the Caribbean.　Using a procedure designed by professionals to be more relaxed and enjoyable for volunteers, a second group of 12 divers spent the same amount of time in the same waters.　Surprisingly, the second method was even more successful : this group identified a total of 137 species.　Results like these suggest that research assisted by amateurs can be trusted when scientists organize it.

(5)　The best citizen science projects are win-win situations.　On the one hand, the scientific community gains access to far more data than they would otherwise have, while spending less money.　On the other hand, citizen science is good for the general public : it gets people out into the natural world and involved in scientific processes.　Additionally, when people take part in a well-designed study that includes training to use equipment, collect data, and share their findings, they have the satisfaction of learning about new ideas and technologies.

(6)　I find it encouraging that the list of scientific studies using citizen scientists is quickly getting longer.　Still, we're just beginning to realize the potential of citizen science.　More scientists need to recognize how much volunteers can contribute to professional research.　As I see it, it's time for us to expand the old, conservative view of "science *for* people" to include a more democratic one of "science *by* people."

A 次の問い（問1〜5）の 47 〜 51 に入れるのに最も適当なものを，それぞれ下の①〜④のうちから一つずつ選べ。

問1 The citizen scientists in Paragraph (1) 47 .

① compare their data with that of other volunteers　② earn some money for the information they gather

③ monitor the life cycles of insects in laboratories　④ report on their results or activities to professionals

問2 The word burgeoning in Paragraph (2) is closest in meaning to 48 .

① causing arguments　② increasing rapidly

③ losing popularity　④ receiving awards

問3 Why does the author emphasize an 80% success rate in Paragraph (4) ? 49

① To contrast negatively with the adults' success rate

② To demonstrate the high quality of the overall results

③ To emphasize how many types of crabs there are

④ To reveal the elementary students' lack of skills

問4 What personal view is expressed in Paragraph (6) ? 50

① Eventually, scientific knowledge will come mainly from amateurs.

② Not enough scientists appreciate the advantages of citizen science.

③ The recent shift toward relying on volunteer data is disappointing.

④ Too many studies using citizen science are now being conducted.

問5 What is the author's main message in this article ? 51

① Citizen science benefits volunteers, professionals, and society.

② Scientific research should be left in the hands of specialists.

③ There is a long history of volunteers identifying fish species.

④ Traditional science has been replaced by citizen science.

B 次の表は，本文の段落構成と内容をまとめたものである。 52 〜 55 に入れるのに最も適当なものを，下の①〜④のうちから一つずつ選び，表を完成させよ。ただし，同じものを繰り返し選んではいけない。

Paragraph	Content
(1)	Introduction : Author's personal examples
(2)	52
(3)	53
(4)	54
(5)	55
(6)	Conclusion : Author's hope for the future

① Concerns : Volunteer skills and knowledge　② Evidence : Successful volunteer efforts

③ Explanation : Definition and history　④ Opinion : Merits for everyone involved

次の文章を読み，あとの問い（A・B）に答えよ。なお，文章の左にある(1)～(6)は段落の番号を表している。

Listening Convenience and Sound Quality : Is There Another Priority ?

(1)　In 1877, Thomas Edison invented the phonograph, a new device that could record and play back sound. For the first time, people could enjoy the musical performance of a full orchestra in the convenience of their own homes. A few years later, Bell Laboratories developed a new phonograph that offered better sound quality; voices and instruments sounded clearer and more true-to-life. These early products represent two major focuses in the development of audio technology — making listening easier and improving the sound quality of the music we hear. The advances over the years have been significant in both areas, but it is important not to let the music itself get lost in all the technology.

(2)　Although the phonograph made listening to music much more convenient, it was just the beginning. The introduction of the car radio in the 1920s meant that music could be enjoyed on the road as well. Interest in portable audio really started to take off in the 1980s with the development of personal music players that allowed listeners to enjoy music through headphones while walking outside. These days, we are able to carry around hundreds of albums on small digital players and listen to them with tiny earphones.

(3)　Another factor affecting our enjoyment of music is its sound quality. In the 1950s, the term "high fidelity", or "hi-fi" for short, was commonly used by companies to advertise recordings and audio equipment providing the highest possible quality of sound reproduction. Fidelity, meaning truthfulness, refers to recording and reproducing music that is as close as possible to the original performance. Ideally, if we listen to a recorded symphony with our eyes closed, we feel as if we were in a concert hall. Technological advances since the 1950s have resulted in modern recording techniques and playback equipment that allow listeners to come very close to the goals of high fidelity.

(4)　Walking into an electronics store today, consumers are faced with an amazing variety of audio technology. Someone looking for a portable system can choose from hundreds of different earphones, headphones, and digital players that come in a range of colors, shapes, and sizes. For audiophiles—music fans who see high fidelity as a priority—a different section of the store features a range of large speakers and heavy components, such as CD players and amplifiers, that often come at high prices. Faced with all this technology and so many choices, music fans often spend a great deal of time researching and making decisions about the right equipment fot their listening needs.

(5)　Even after the equipment is bought, the advances in audio technology sometimes continue to take consumers' attention away from the music itself. The convenience of portable systems lets people listen to music while doing something else, like jogging in the park or commuting to work. In these settings, music may be partly lost in background noise, making it hard for the listener to concentrate on it. In another case, audiophiles may spend a considerable amount of time and energy testing and adjusting their combination of components to achieve the highest standard of fidelity.

(6)　With so much technology available, actually listening to music can sometimes feel like a secondary issue. We are lucky to be able to take our favorite recordings with us on the train to work, but if we listen to music while our attention is focused elsewhere, we miss much of its power. Likewise, although it is good to have access to high-quality equipment, if we worry too much about achieving perfect fidelity, technology itself comes between us and the music. Music is an amazing and powerful art form, and perhaps what is most important is to make time to sit and appreciate what we hear. Thanks to the genius of Edison and other inventors, the beauty of music is now more accessible than ever. It's up to us to stop and truly listen.

A 次の問い（問1～5）の 47 ～ 51 に入れるのに最も適当なものを，それぞれ下の①～④のうちから一つずつ選べ。

問1 According to paragraph (1), Bell Laboratories' phonograph could 47 than Thomas Edison's.

① be built more quickly and cheaply
② be operated with less difficulty
③ play more musical instruments
④ reproduce sound more realistically

問2 In paragraph (3), the author suggests that today's best audio equipment 48 .

① almost recreates the sound quality of a live concert
② is used to play live music in the best concert halls
③ makes recordings sound better than original performances
④ reproduces great performances from the 1950s

問3 According to paragraph (4), audiophiles are people who 49 .

① care deeply about the quality of music reproduction
② perform in symphonies in good concert halls
③ prefer live concerts to recorded performances
④ work at shops that sell the best audio equipment

問4 Based on paragraph (5), which of the following is true ? 50

① Background noise often helps people concentrate on music.
② Portable audio systems tend to create background noise.
③ Setting up a hi-fi system can take a great amount of effort.
④ The busier people are, the more they appreciate music.

問5 The author's main point in paragraph (6) is that 51 .

① audiophiles tend to enjoy listening to music on portable devices
② convenience is an important factor in buying audio equipment
③ music is the primary consideration, regardless of technology
④ portable equipment will likely replace high-fidelity equipment

B 次の表は，本文の段落と内容をまとめたものである。 52 ～ 55 に入れるのに最も適当なものを，下の①～④のうちから一つずつ選び，表を完成させよ。ただし，同じものを繰り返し選んではいけない。

Paragraph	Content
(1)	Two goals of audio technology
(2)	52
(3)	The idea of high fidelity
(4)	53
(5)	54
(6)	55

① Advances in music listening convenience
② Concerns about the focus of music listeners
③ The value of giving music your full attention
④ The wide selection of audio products for sale

1 文法・語法

解答 158p，解説 240p

第1回目　　　　第2回目

目標 **7** 分

H 22 ②

／ 10 題　　／ 10 題

A　次の問い（問1〜10）の ⎡8⎤ 〜 ⎡17⎤ に入れるのに最も適当なものを，それぞれ下の①〜④のうちから一つずつ選べ。

問1　"Have you handed in the English assignment ?"

　　"No, but I'm halfway ⎡8⎤ it."

　① across　　　② around　　　③ over　　　④ through

問2　I have to get my commuter pass renewed because it ⎡9⎤ tomorrow.

　① activates　　② conceives　　③ expires　　④ interferes

問3　Is it possible for you to postpone today's meeting ⎡10⎤ next Wednesday ?

　① by　　　② in　　　③ on　　　④ until

問4　I was talked ⎡11⎤ buying a big car by my sister.

　① about　　　② away from　　③ out of　　④ to

問5　If I hadn't broken up with Hannah last month, I ⎡12⎤ going out with her for two years.

　① had been　　② have been　　③ will have been　④ would have been

問6　The puppy at the rescue center looked happy to have been ⎡13⎤ by the little girl.

　① choice　　　② choose　　　③ chose　　　④ chosen

問7　"Why did Jack quit his job ?"

　　"He wanted to ⎡14⎤ his dream of opening his own café."

　① come true　　② increase　　③ make sure　　④ realize

問8　In my school, when a ⎡15⎤ teacher is absent, another teacher teaches the class instead.

　① common　　② different　　③ regular　　④ retired

問9　"Going through all the steps to adjust the brightness of my computer screen is a real nuisance."

　　"Well, why don't you do it the easy way ?　Just press this key.　That's the ⎡16⎤ ."

　① shortcut　　② shortened　　③ shorthand　　④ shortsighted

問10　After many years of war, the country has lost much of its power. ⎡17⎤ , its influence should not be underestimated.

　① Even so　　② Even though　　③ So　　　④ Thus

目標 **7** 分

H 23 ②

A 次の問い（問1〜10）の ⎡8⎤ 〜 ⎡17⎤ に入れるのに最も適当なものを，それぞれ下の①〜④のうちから一つずつ選べ。

問1 Dad, if my grades improve by the end of the term, would you mind ⎡8⎤ my allowance ?

① raising　　② rising　　③ to raise　　④ to rise

問2 "I've been ⎡9⎤ on weight recently."

"You should exercise more and eat better."

① carrying　　② increasing　　③ putting　　④ reducing

問3 Kenji told me his trip to London was wonderful.　I wish I ⎡10⎤ in that program.

① had participated　　② have participated　　③ participate　　④ will participate

問4 The houses look like rows of tiny cardboard boxes when you look out of the window of a plane in ⎡11⎤.

① flight　　② flowing　　③ flown　　④ flyer

問5 The fans waited outside the door in the hope ⎡12⎤ catching sight of the movie star.

① for　　② of　　③ to　　④ with

問6 At our local health clinic, the doctor will only see you by ⎡13⎤.

① appointment　　② approval　　③ reputation　　④ resolution

問7 Some people find ⎡14⎤ difficult to economize on mobile phone costs even when times are hard.

① everything　　② it　　③ that　　④ things

問8 I've finished writing my application.　Who am I ⎡15⎤ to give it to ?

① announced　　② applied　　③ pointed　　④ supposed

問9 All the children in the family will ⎡16⎤ for the New Year's holidays.

① crowd　　② form　　③ gather　　④ set

問10 My brother loves baseball.　He's an enthusiastic, ⎡17⎤ not a gifted, player.

① as　　② if　　③ or　　④ so

A　次の問い（問1〜10）の　8　〜　17　に入れるのに最も適当なものを，それぞれ下の①〜④のうちから一つずつ選べ。

問1　Some companies have　8　a new policy of using English as the official in-house language.

① absorbed　　　　② accompanied　　③ adopted　　　　④ appointed

問2　Could you show me how to make my mobile phone ring differently,　9　who's calling me?

① depending on　　② in spite of　　③ on behalf of　　④ relying on

問3　Ms. Bell is stuck in a traffic jam.　The important meeting will have finished by the time she　10　.

① arrives　　　　② may arrive　　③ will arrive　　④ will have arrived

問4　We had the microwave, the toaster and the heater all　11　at the same time, and the circuit breaker switched off.

① in　　　　　　② on　　　　　　③ up　　　　　　④ with

問5　Mr. Brown looked over the cliff and found he was standing at the edge of a　12　drop.

① circular　　　　② cubic　　　　③ horizontal　　④ vertical

問6　You can apply for this overseas program on the　13　that you have a letter of recommendation from your teacher.

① condition　　　② limitation　　③ requirement　　④ treatment

問7　"I heard Daiki's sisters are twins.　Have you met them?"

　　"No, I haven't met　14　of them yet."

① each　　　　　② either　　　　③ every　　　　④ neither

問8　You should not let your personal emotions　15　in the way of making that important decision.

① stand　　　　　② standing　　　③ to be stood　　④ to stand

問9　"Which girl is Shiori?"

　　"The one　16　had a chat with a moment ago."

① I　　　　　　② myself　　　　③ that　　　　④ who

問10　After he joined the travel agency, he worked hard to improve his English in order to carry　17　his duties more effectively.

① away　　　　　② back　　　　　③ off　　　　　④ out

目標 **7**分

H 25 ②

A　次の問い（問1～10）の　8　～　17　に入れるのに最も適当なものを，それぞれ下の①～④のうちから一つずつ選べ。

問1　I understand　8　of our students are working part-time in the evening to pay their school expenses.

①　almost　　　　②　any　　　　③　anyone　　　　④　most

問2　Of the seven people here now, one is from China, three are from the US, and　9　from France.

①　other　　　　②　others　　　　③　the other　　　　④　the others

問3　My brother　10　have been very popular when he was a high school student.　He still gets lots of New Year's cards from his former classmates.

①　must　　　　②　ought to　　　　③　should　　　　④　would

問4　Eric's friends, Minoru and Sachiko, will be here at seven this evening.　He　11　doing his homework by then.

①　has been finished　　②　has finished　　③　will have finished　　④　would finish

問5　Our family doctor suggested that our son　12　a complete medical checkup every year.

①　get　　　　②　getting　　　　③　is getting　　　　④　to get

問6　Japan　13　of four large islands and many small islands.

①　consists　　　　②　contains　　　　③　forms　　　　④　organizes

問7　Did you have a chance to meet your grandfather　14　the winter vacation?

①　during　　　　②　inside　　　　③　on　　　　④　while

問8　I don't enjoy going to Tokyo.　It's hard for me to put　15　all the crowds.

①　away　　　　②　on　　　　③　up to　　　　④　up with

問9　When my younger brother and I were children, my mother often asked me to keep　16　him so he wouldn't get lost.

①　an eye on　　②　away from　　③　back from　　④　in time with

問10　I was offered a good position with a generous salary, but I decided to turn it　17　because I wanted to stay near my family.

①　around　　　　②　down　　　　③　out　　　　④　over

A　次の問い（問1～10）の 8 ～ 17 に入れるのに最も適当なものを，それぞれ下の①～④のうちから一つずつ選べ。ただし， 15 ～ 17 については，（ A ）と（ B ）に入れるのに最も適当な組合せを選べ。

問1　When I looked out of the window last night, I saw a cat 8 into my neighbor's yard.
① is sneaked　② sneaking　③ sneaks　④ to sneak

問2　Ever since they first met at the sports festival, Pat and Pam 9 each other.
① are emailing　② emailed　③ have been emailing　④ will email

問3　My mother asked me 10 we should go out for lunch or eat at home.
① that　② what　③ whether　④ which

問4　My wife wanted to have our son 11 dinner for us, but I ordered a pizza instead.
① cook　② cooked　③ cooks　④ to cook

問5　I took it for 12 that we were free to use the school gym on Saturdays.
① demanded　② granted　③ natural　④ truthful

問6　Could you 13 me who is planning Dan's birthday party?
① say to　② talk to　③ teach　④ tell

問7　We were shocked when the cashier added 14 the bill and the total was 20,000 yen.
① at　② from　③ off　④ up

問8　The （ A ） of treatment at the hospital is much lower for （ B ） who have health insurance. 15
① A：cost　B：them　② A：cost　B：those
③ A：fare　B：them　④ A：fare　B：those

問9　Even though I （ A ） spent two years in the US, I've never （ B ） to the Grand Canyon.　Maybe I'll go next year. 16
① A：ever　B：been　② A：ever　B：visited
③ A：once　B：been　④ A：once　B：visited

問10　My mother is trying very hard to （ A ） ends meet, （ B ） she never lets me buy anything unnecessary. 17
① A：get　B：but　② A：get　B：so
③ A：make　B：but　④ A：make　B：so

A 次の問い（問1～10）の 8 ～ 17 に入れるのに最も適当なものを，それぞれ下の①～④のうちから一つずつ選べ。ただし， 15 ～ 17 については，（ A ）と（ B ）に入れるのに最も適当な組合せを選べ。

問1 Did you make your grandfather angry again ? You should 8 that.
① know better than ② know less than ③ make do with ④ make up with

問2 Scott went to the police station because he 9 .
① caused his computer stolen ② got stolen his computer
③ had his computer stolen ④ was stolen his computer

問3 Last winter was rather unusual 10 that very little snow fell in northern Japan.
① about ② by ③ in ④ on

問4 My granddaughter has started a career as a singer, but I really 11 an actress as well in the future.
① hope she became ② hope she will become
③ wish she became ④ wish she will become

問5 I was fast asleep, so I didn't hear the car accident that 12 at 2 a.m. this morning.
① happened ② happens ③ was happened ④ would happen

問6 I always walk my dog along the beach, 13 the sea view.
① being enjoyed ② enjoy ③ enjoying ④ with enjoying

問7 Mt. Fuji stands impressively 14 the blue sky.
① against ② among ③ behind ④ by

問8 Sorry. We talked about it just now, but （ A ） did you say （ B ）? 15
① A：how B：the best solution ② A：how B：was the best solution
③ A：what B：the best solution ④ A：what B：the best solution was

問9 The Internet has become （ A ） powerful a tool （ B ） people living anywhere can access any educational resource. 16
① A：so B：but ② A：so B：that
③ A：such B：but ④ A：such B：that

問10 The manager said his team （ A ） win the soccer league and they actually did （ B ） season. 17
① A：will B：next ② A：will B：the next
③ A：would B：next ④ A：would B：the next

目標 7分

A　次の問い（問1〜10）の　8　〜　17　に入れるのに最も適当なものを，それぞれ下の①〜④のうちから一つずつ選べ。ただし，　15　〜　17　については，（　A　）と（　B　）に入れるのに最も適当な組合せを選べ。

問1　The train　8　when I reached the platform, so I didn't have to wait in the cold.

①　had already arrived　　　　　　　②　has already arrived

③　previously arrived　　　　　　　④　previously arrives

問2　　9　Tokyo has a relatively small land area, it has a huge population.

①　Although　　　　②　But　　　　③　Despite　　　　④　However

問3　Children　10　by bilingual parents may naturally learn two languages.

①　bringing up　　②　brought up　　③　have brought up　　④　were brought up

問4　My sister was not a serious high school student, and　11　.

①　either I was　　②　either was I　　③　neither I was　　④　neither was I

問5　Before the movie begins, please　12　your mobile phone is switched off.

①　keep　　　　②　make sure　　　　③　never fail　　　　④　remind

問6　We have made good progress, so we are already　13　schedule.

①　ahead of　　②　apart from　　③　far from　　④　out of

問7　Thanks to their　14　comments after my presentation, I felt very relieved.

①　friendly　　②　nicely　　③　properly　　④　warmly

問8　（　A　）you've completed this required class, you（　B　）be able to graduate.　15

①　A：If　　　B：won't　　　　　　②　A：Unless　B：would

③　A：Until　B：won't　　　　　　④　A：While　B：would

問9　Wood（　A　）be used as the main fuel, but nowadays fossil fuels（　B　）widely.　16

①　A：used to　　　B：are used　　　　②　A：used to　　　B：have been used

③　A：was used to　B：are used　　　　④　A：was used to　B：have been used

問10　（　A　）so considerate（　B　）him to come and see his grandmother in the hospital every day.　17

①　A：He is　B：for　　　　　　　②　A：He is　B：of

③　A：It is　B：for　　　　　　　④　A：It is　B：of

文法・語法

目標 **7** 分　H 29 ②

第1回目　　　　第2回目

／10題　　／10題

A　次の問い（問1～10）の ⬛8 ～ ⬛17 に入れるのに最も適当なものを，それぞれ下の①～④のうちから一つずつ選べ。ただし， ⬛15 ～ ⬛17 については，（　A　）と（　B　）に入れるのに最も適当な組合せを選べ。

問1　Today, in science class, I learned that salt water doesn't freeze ⬛8 0℃.
①　at　　　　　　②　in　　　　　　③　on　　　　　　④　with

問2　Many experts think that we need to create more job opportunities for ⬛9 .
①　a young　　　②　the young　　③　young　　　　④　younger

問3　The leaves in my neighborhood have recently ⬛10 yellow.
①　come　　　　②　developed　　③　led　　　　　　④　turned

問4　I think eating at home is often ⬛11 more economical than eating at a restaurant.
①　far　　　　　②　high　　　　　③　too　　　　　　④　very

問5　⬛12 as the leading actor in the film, Ramesh soon became a star.
①　Choosing　　②　Having been chosen　③　Having chosen　④　To choose

問6　Please give me ⬛13 information you get as soon as possible.
①　as if　　　　②　even if　　　　③　whatever　　　④　whenever

問7　The typhoon suddenly became weaker, ⬛14 was good news for the village.
①　it　　　　　　②　that　　　　　③　what　　　　　④　which

問8　He （　A　）his umbrella （　B　）in the door by accident when he boarded the rush hour train. ⬛15
①　A：got　　B：caught　　　　　　②　A：got　　B：to catch
③　A：made　B：caught　　　　　　④　A：made　B：to catch

問9　（　A　）in this class is as kind （　B　）Abbie. She always helps people who are in trouble. ⬛16
①　A：Anybody　　B：as　　　　　②　A：Anybody　　B：than
③　A：Nobody　　B：as　　　　　④　A：Nobody　　B：than

問10　Angelina （　A　）me whether I （　B　）enjoyed the festival last Saturday. ⬛17
①　A：asked　B：had　　　　　　②　A：asked　B：have
③　A：said to　B：had　　　　　④　A：said to　B：have

共通テスト虎の巻【英語編】　145

目標 **7** 分　　H 30 ②　　　　　　　　　　　　　　　／ 10 題　　／ 10 題

A　次の問い（問1〜10）の　8　〜　17　に入れるのに最も適当なものを，それぞれ下の①〜④のうちから一つずつ選べ。ただし，　15　〜　17　については，（　A　）と（　B　）に入れるのに最も適当な組合せを選べ。

問1　Jeff didn't accept the job offer because of the　8　salary.

① cheap　　　　② inexpensive　　　③ low　　　　④ weak

問2　Brenda went　9　to get something to drink.

① at downstairs　② downstairs　　③ the downstairs　④ to downstairs

問3　After I injured my elbow, I had to quit　10　for my school's badminton team.

① playing　　　② to be playing　　③ to have played　④ to play

問4　It's　11　my understanding why he decided to buy such an old car.

① against　　　② behind　　　　③ beneath　　　④ beyond

問5　Nicole　12　novels for about seven years when she won the national novel contest.

① had been writing　② has been writing　③ has written　④ is writing

問6　Our boss was sick at home, so we did　13　we thought was needed to finish the project.

① how　　　　② that　　　　　③ what　　　　④ which

問7　14　I didn't notice it, but there was a huge spider in the bathroom.

① At first　　② Beginning　　③ Besides　　④ Firstly

問8　Rafael（　A　）a pair of swallows（　B　）a nest in the tree in front of the house.　15

① A：looked　B：making　　　　② A：looked　B：to make

③ A：saw　　B：making　　　　④ A：saw　　B：to make

問9　It（　A　）be long（　B　）the plum blossoms come out. They may even bloom this coming weekend.　16

① A：should　　B：before　　　② A：should　　B：enough

③ A：shouldn't　B：before　　　④ A：shouldn't　B：enough

問10　Melissa said she（　A　）rather go snowboarding next weekend（　B　）go ice-skating.　17

① A：could　B：than　　　　② A：could　B：to

③ A：would　B：than　　　　④ A：would　B：to

A 次の問い（問1〜10）の 8 〜 17 に入れるのに最も適当なものを，それぞれ下の①〜④のうちから一つずつ選べ。ただし， 15 〜 17 については，（ **A** ）と（ **B** ）に入れるのに最も適当な組合せを選べ。

問1　Casey was getting worried because the bus going to the airport was clearly 8 schedule.

① after　　　　② behind　　　　③ late　　　　④ slow

問2　If you are in a hurry, you should call Double Quick Taxi because they usually come in 9 time.

① any　　　　② few　　　　③ no　　　　④ some

問3　After 10 dropping the expensive glass vase, James decided not to touch any other objects in the store.

① almost　　　　② at most　　　　③ most　　　　④ mostly

問4　We should make the changes to the document quickly as we are 11 out of time.

① going　　　　② running　　　　③ spending　　　　④ wasting

問5　It was impossible to 12 everyone's demands about the new project.

① carry　　　　② complete　　　　③ hold　　　　④ meet

問6　Write a list of everything you need for the camping trip. 13 , you might forget to buy some things.

① As a result　　　② In addition　　　③ Otherwise　　　④ Therefore

問7　Text messaging has become a common 14 of communication between individuals.

① mean　　　　② meaning　　　　③ means　　　　④ meant

問8　I was （ **A** ） when I watched the completely （ **B** ） ending of the movie. 15

① **A**：shocked　　**B**：surprised　　② **A**：shocked　　**B**：surprising

③ **A**：shocking　　**B**：surprised　　④ **A**：shocking　　**B**：surprising

問9　（ **A** ） is no （ **B** ） the increase in traffic on this highway during holidays. 16

① **A**：It　　**B**：avoid　　　② **A**：It　　**B**：avoiding

③ **A**：There　　**B**：avoid　　④ **A**：There　　**B**：avoiding

問10　The police officer asked the witness （ **A** ） the situation as （ **B** ） as possible. 17

① **A**：describing　　**B**：accurate　　② **A**：describing　　**B**：accurately

③ **A**：to describe　　**B**：accurate　　④ **A**：to describe　　**B**：accurately

R2 ②　　　　　　　　　　　　　　　　　　　　　　　　　／10題　　／10題

A　次の問い（問1〜10）の　8　〜　17　に入れるのに最も適当なものを，それぞれ下の①〜④のうちから一つずつ選べ。ただし，　15　〜　17　については，（　A　）と（　B　）に入れるのに最も適当な組合せを選べ。

問1　Due to the rain, our performance in the game was　8　from perfect.

　　① apart　　　　　　② different　　　　　③ far　　　　　　④ free

問2　Emergency doors can be found at　9　ends of this hallway.

　　① both　　　　　　② each　　　　　　　③ either　　　　　④ neither

問3　My plans for studying abroad depend on　10　I can get a scholarship.

　　① that　　　　　　② what　　　　　　　③ whether　　　　④ which

問4　Noriko can speak Swahili and　11　can Marco.

　　① also　　　　　　② as　　　　　　　　③ so　　　　　　　④ that

問5　To say you will go jogging every day is one thing, but to do it is　12　.

　　① another　　　　　② one another　　　　③ the other　　　④ the others

問6　Our boss is a hard worker, but can be difficult to get　13　.

　　① along with　　　② around to　　　　　③ away with　　　④ down to

問7　When Ayano came to my house,　14　happened that nobody was at home.

　　① it　　　　　　　② something　　　　　③ there　　　　　④ what

問8　We'll be able to get home on time as（　A　）as the roads are（　B　）.　15

　　① A：far　　B：blocked　　　　　　　② A：far　　B：clear

　　③ A：long　　B：blocked　　　　　　④ A：long　　B：clear

問9　I know you said you weren't going to the sports festival, but it is an important event, so please（　A　）it a（　B　）thought.　16

　　① A：give　　　　B：first　　　　② A：give　　　　B：second

　　③ A：take　　　　B：first　　　　④ A：take　　　　B：second

問10　I didn't recognize（　A　）of the guests（　B　）the two sitting in the back row.　17

　　① A：any　　B：except for　　　　② A：any　　B：rather than

　　③ A：either　　B：except for　　　④ A：either　　B：rather than

目標
各**5**分

第1回目　　　第2回目

H 22 2　　　　　　　　　　　　　　　　　　　　　　　　　　／3題　　／3題

C　次の問い（**問1〜3**）において，それぞれ下の語句を並べかえて空所を補い，文を完成させよ。解答は 21 〜 26 に入れるものの番号のみを答えよ。ただし，文頭に置かれる語句も小文字で与えられている。

問1　Something you wrote in an email upset your friend.　You could ask what had upset her by saying :

Could you ＿＿＿ 21 ＿＿＿ ＿＿＿ 22 ＿＿＿ with my email ?

①　made　②　me　③　so upset　④　tell　⑤　what　⑥　you

問2　You borrowed 800 yen from your friend for lunch yesterday.　When you pay the money back, you could say :

This is ＿＿＿ 23 ＿＿＿ ＿＿＿ 24 ＿＿＿ lunch.

①　for　②　I　③　owe　④　the 800 yen　⑤　yesterday's　⑥　you

問3　"＿＿＿ 25 ＿＿＿ ＿＿＿ 26 ＿＿＿ for your vacation ?　I thought you weren't sure."

"I decided yesterday."

①　decide　②　did　③　going　④　when　⑤　where　⑥　you　⑦　you're

H 23 2　　　　　　　　　　　　　　　　　　　　　　　　　　／3題　　／3題

C　次の問い（**問1〜3**）において，それぞれ下の語句を並べかえて空所を補い，文を完成させよ。解答は 21 〜 26 に入れるものの番号のみを答えよ。

問1　Thank you very much for ＿＿＿ 21 ＿＿＿ ＿＿＿ 22 ＿＿＿ when I bought my car.

①　advice　②　gave　③　great　④　me　⑤　the　⑥　you

問2　"What's up with Jack ? He seems so happy."

"He applied for a new job, and ＿＿＿ 23 ＿＿＿ ＿＿＿ 24 ＿＿＿ an interview."

①　called　②　company　③　for　④　him　⑤　in　⑥　the

問3　Doing a homestay with a family in another country ＿＿＿ 25 ＿＿＿ ＿＿＿ 26 ＿＿＿ skills.

①　communication　②　develop　③　help　④　would　⑤　you　⑥　your

H 24 2　　　　　　　　　　　　　　　　　　　　　　　　　　／3題　　／3題

C　次の問い（**問1〜3**）において，それぞれ下の語句を並べかえて空所を補い，文を完成させよ。解答は 21 〜 26 に入れるものの番号のみを答えよ。

問1　"Did you install that computer software you bought last week?"

"Yes. And ＿＿＿ 21 ＿＿＿ ＿＿＿ 22 ＿＿＿ use."

①　easy　②　finding　③　I'm　④　it　⑤　to

問2　The entertainer was happily ＿＿＿ 23 ＿＿＿ ＿＿＿ 24 ＿＿＿ up in the air.

①　arms　②　her　③　raised　④　singing　⑤　with

問3　Because he came down with the flu, ＿＿＿ 25 ＿＿＿ ＿＿＿ 26 ＿＿＿ for a week.

①　forced　②　he　③　stay at home　④　to　⑤　was

H 25　2

／3題　　／3題

C　次の問い（問1～3）において，それぞれ下の語句を並べかえて空所を補い，最も適当な文を完成させよ。解答は　21　～　26　に入れるものの番号のみを答えよ。

問1　My friend, who can play basketball very well, practices ＿＿＿　21　＿＿＿　22　＿＿＿.
① as　② as often　③ do　④ I　⑤ three times

問2　Mary：What are some of the reasons for your successful career?

Toshio：Mainly, I ＿＿＿　23　＿＿＿　24　＿＿＿ my uncle.　He was the one who would always help me when I was in trouble.
① am　② I　③ owe　④ to　⑤ what

問3　Kevin：What's the legal driving age in your country ?

Mie：In Japan, when people become eighteen, they ＿＿＿　25　＿＿＿　26　＿＿＿ a driver's license.
① are　② enough　③ get　④ old　⑤ to

H 26　2

／3題　　／3題

C　次の問い（問1～3）において，それぞれ下の①～⑥の語を並べかえて空所を補い，最も適当な文を完成させよ。解答は　21　～　26　に入れるものの番号のみを答えよ。

問1　Dan：How did your health check go ?

Mike：Not bad, but the doctor ＿＿＿　21　＿＿＿　22　＿＿＿.
① advised　② exercise　③ get　④ me　⑤ regular　⑥ to

問2　Ken：Do you think your parents will let you study abroad ?

Peg：I'm not sure, but I ＿＿＿　23　＿＿＿　24　＿＿＿ it.
① can　② hope　③ I　④ into　⑤ talk　⑥ them

問3　Kazuki：Penny, I have to work late tonight, and I may not get back until 10 p.m.

Penny：It'll rain tonight.　Don't ＿＿＿　25　＿＿＿　26　＿＿＿ an umbrella.
① caught　② get　③ in　④ rain　⑤ the　⑥ without

H 27　2

／3題　　／3題

B　次の問い（問1～3）において，それぞれ下の①～⑥の語句を並べかえて空所を補い，最も適当な文を完成させよ。解答は　18　～　23　に入れるものの番号のみを答えよ。

問1　Yuki：Have we met before ?　You look very familiar to me.

Anne：I don't think so.　If we had met, ＿＿＿　18　＿＿＿　19　＿＿＿ sure !
① for　② have　③ I　④ recognized　⑤ would　⑥ you

問2　Customer：Could I extend the rental period for the car ?

Agent：Yes, but ＿＿＿　20　＿＿＿　21　＿＿＿ $50 for each additional day.
① an extra fee　② be　③ charged　④ of　⑤ will　⑥ you

問3　Reiko：Shall we cook tonight, or order some Chinese food ?

Kyoko：Let's order Chinese ＿＿＿　22　＿＿＿　23　＿＿＿.
① because　② cooking　③ feeling　④ I'm　⑤ to start　⑥ too tired

語句整序

H 28 ②　　　　　　　　　　　　　　　　　　　　　　　　　　　／3題　　　／3題

B　次の問い（**問1～3**）において，それぞれ下の①～⑥の語句を並べかえて空所を補い，最も適当な文を完成
させよ。解答は　18　～　23　に入れるものの番号のみを答えよ。

問1　Hotel clerk： Good evening, Mr. and Mrs. Gomez.　How can I help you ?

　　　　Mrs. Gomez： Well, ＿＿＿ 18 ＿＿＿ ＿＿＿ 19 ＿＿＿ us how to get to the theater.

　　①　could　　②　if　　③　tell　　④　we're　　⑤　wondering　　⑥　you

問2　　　　　Student： Excuse me.　I'd like to know what we will be discussing in next week's seminar.

　　　　Professor： I haven't decided yet, so ＿＿＿ 20 ＿＿＿ ＿＿＿ 21 ＿＿＿ email.

　　①　by　　②　let　　③　me　　④　send　　⑤　the details　　⑥　you

問3　Interviewer： How did you change after becoming the head of such a large company ?

　　　　President： I ＿＿＿ 22 ＿＿＿ ＿＿＿ 23 ＿＿＿ my time more effectively.

　　①　came to　②　manage　③　need　④　realize　⑤　the　　⑥　to

H 29 ②　　　　　　　　　　　　　　　　　　　　　　　　　　　／3題　　　／3題

B　次の問い（**問1～3**）において，それぞれ下の①～⑥の語句を並べかえて空所を補い，最も適当な文を完成
させよ。解答は　18　～　23　に入れるものの番号のみを答えよ。

問1　Keita： You have so many things in your room.

　　　　Cindy： I know. Actually, ＿＿＿ 18 ＿＿＿ ＿＿＿ 19 ＿＿＿ it neat and clean.

　　①　difficult　②　find　　③　I　　④　it　　⑤　keep　⑥　to

問2　　Ted： Professor Jones suggested that I rewrite this essay.

　　　　Jack： Oh, well, ＿＿＿ 20 ＿＿＿ ＿＿＿ 21 ＿＿＿ , but I'm sure you'll get a higher grade
　　　　　　　on it.

　　①　a few　②　cost　　③　hours　　④　it　　⑤　may　⑥　you

問3　Rita： Daniel and I have to go home now.

　　　　Father： Oh, ＿＿＿ 22 ＿＿＿ ＿＿＿ 23 ＿＿＿ usual ? I thought you were going to stay
　　　　　　　for dinner.

　　①　are　　②　earlier　　③　how come　④　leaving　⑤　than　⑥　you

H 30 ②　　　　　　　　　　　　　　　　　　　　　　　　　　　／3題　　　／3題

B　次の問い（**問1～3**）において，それぞれ下の①～⑥の語句を並べかえて空所を補い，最も適当な文を完成
させよ。解答は　18　～　23　に入れるものの番号のみを答えよ。

問1　Student： What are we going to do with the Australian students after they arrive ?

　　　　Teacher： The first night, we'll have a barbecue by the river so that you all ＿＿＿ 18 ＿＿＿ ＿＿＿
　　　　　　　 19 ＿＿＿ quickly.

　　①　can　　②　each　　③　get　　④　know　　⑤　other　　⑥　to

問2　Bridget： How was your basketball season last year ?

　　　　Toshi： I ＿＿＿ 20 ＿＿＿ ＿＿＿ 21 ＿＿＿ .

　　①　highest　②　on　　③　scorer　④　the second　⑤　the team　⑥　was

問3　Evan： I want to buy my first computer, but I don't know which one I should get.

　　　　Sam： Don't worry. Electronic stores always have experts available to give advice ＿＿＿ 22 ＿＿＿
　　　　　　　 ＿＿＿ ＿＿＿ 23 ＿＿＿ using computers.

　　①　aren't　②　familiar　③　those　④　to　　⑤　who　⑥　with

H 31 ②　　　　　　　　　　　　　　　　　　　　　　　　　／3題　　　／3題

B　次の問い（問1～3）において，それぞれ下の①～⑥の語句を並べかえて空所を補い，最も適当な文を完成させよ。解答は　18　～　23　に入れるものの番号のみを答えよ。

問1　Yukio： Did you hear that a new entrance ID system will be introduced next month ?

Lucas： Really ? Do we need it ? I ＿＿＿＿ 18 ＿＿＿＿ ＿＿＿＿ 19 ＿＿＿＿ to replace the current system.

①　cost　　　　　　　②　how　　　　　　　③　it

④　much　　　　　　⑤　will　　　　　　　⑥　wonder

問2　David： What's the plan for your trip to England ?

Saki： I'll spend the first few days in London and then be in Cambridge ＿＿＿＿ 20 ＿＿＿＿ ＿＿＿＿ 21 ＿＿＿＿ .

①　for　　　　　　　②　my　　　　　　　③　of

④　rest　　　　　　　⑤　stay　　　　　　　⑥　the

問3　Junko： The party we went to last night was very noisy. My throat is still sore from speaking loudly the whole time.

Ronald： Yeah. It can sometimes ＿＿＿＿ 22 ＿＿＿＿ ＿＿＿＿ 23 ＿＿＿＿ in such a crowded place.

①　be　　　　　　　②　difficult　　　　　③　heard

④　make　　　　　　⑤　to　　　　　　　⑥　yourself

R 2 ②　　　　　　　　　　　　　　　　　　　　　　　　　／3題　　　／3題

B　次の問い（問1～3）において，それぞれ下の①～⑥の語句を並べかえて空所を補い，最も適当な文を完成させよ。解答は　18　～　23　に入れるものの番号のみを答えよ。

問1　Tony： Those decorations in the hall look great, don't they ?　I'm glad we finished on time.

Mei： Yes, thank you so much.　Without your help, the preparations ＿＿＿＿ 18 ＿＿＿＿ ＿＿＿＿ 19 ＿＿＿＿ all the guests arrive this afternoon.

①　been　　　　　　②　by　　　　　　　③　completed

④　have　　　　　　⑤　the time　　　　　⑥　would not

問2　Ichiro： Mr.Smith has two daughters in school now, right ?

Natasha： Actually, he has three, the ＿＿＿＿ 20 ＿＿＿＿ ＿＿＿＿ 21 ＿＿＿＿ London.　I don't think you've met her yet.

①　in　　　　　　　②　is studying　　　　③　music

④　of　　　　　　　⑤　whom　　　　　　⑥　youngest

問3　Peter： It might rain this weekend, so I wonder if we should still have the class barbecue in the park.

Hikaru： Yeah, we have to decide now whether to hold it ＿＿＿＿ 22 ＿＿＿＿ ＿＿＿＿ 23 ＿＿＿＿ until some day next week.　We should have thought about the chance of rain.

①　as　　　　　　　②　it　　　　　　　③　off

④　or　　　　　　　⑤　planned　　　　　⑥　put

語句整序

〈ビジュアル〉

年度	解答番号	正解	配点	第1回目得点	第2回目得点
R4 ①A	1	①	2	日付／	日付／
	2	③	2		
R4 ①B	3	②	2		
	4	②	2		
	5	①	2	／10	／10
R3(追試)①A	1	①	2	日付／	日付／
	2	④	2		
R3(追試)①B	3	③	2		
	4	③	2		
	5	②	2	／10	／10
R3(本試)①A	1	①	2	日付／	日付／
	2	②	2		
R3(本試)①B	3	④	2		
	4	④	2		
	5	③	2	／10	／10
H30(新課程2回)①A	1	②	2	日付／	日付／
	2	①	2		
H30(新課程2回)①B	3	②	2		
	4	②	2		
	5	③	2	／10	／10
H29(新課程1回)①A	1	④	2	日付／	日付／
	2	①	2		
H29(新課程1回)①B	3	②	2		
	4	③	2		
	5	①	2	／10	／10
R2 ④B	37	①	5	日付／	日付／
	38	①	5		
	39	②	5		
	40	④	5	／20	／20
H31 ④B	37	③	5	日付／	日付／
	38	②	5		
	39	②	5		
	40	②	5	／20	／20
H30 ④B	37	④	5	日付／	日付／
	38	②	5		
	39	③	5		
	40	④	5	／20	／20
H29 ④B	39	④	5	日付／	日付／
	40	②	5		
	41	④	5	／15	／15

年度	解答番号	正解	配点	第1回目得点	第2回目得点
H28 ④B	39	②	5	日付／	日付／
	40	③	5		
	41	①	5	／15	／15
H27 ④B	39	②	5	日付／	日付／
	40	③	5		
	41	①	5	／15	／15
H26 ④B	39	②	5	日付／	日付／
	40	①	5		
	41	④	5	／15	／15
H25 ④B	38	④	5	日付／	日付／
	39	③	5		
	40	①	5	／15	／15

〈事実・意見〉

	解答番号	正解	配点	第1回目得点	第2回目得点
R4 ②A	6	⑤	2	日付／	日付／
	7	③	2		
	8	①	2		
	9	③	2		
	10	①	2		
R4 ②B	11	②	2		
	12	④	2		
	13	②	2		
	14	④	2		
	15	②	2	／20	／20
R3(追試)②A	6	③	2	日付／	日付／
	7	②	2		
	8	③	2		
	9	①	2		
	10	④	2		
R3(追試)②B	11	①	2		
	12	①	2		
	13	③	2		
	14	①	2		
	15	③	2	／20	／20
R3(本試)②A	6	②	2	日付／	日付／
	7	②	2		
	8	①	2		
	9	③	2		
	10	⑤	2		
R3(本試)②B	11	④	2		
	12	④	2		
	13	②	2		
	14	②	2		
	15	①	2	／20	／20

(注)　1　－（ハイフン）でつながれた正解は，順序を問わない。
　　　2　＊は，全部正解の場合のみ点を与える。
　　　3　＊1は，過不足なくマークしている場合のみ正解とする。
　　　4　＊2は，全部を正しくマークしている場合のみ正解とする。
　　　5　＊3は，解答番号31と32の両方をそれぞれ過不足なくマークしている場合のみ正解とする。

年度	解答番号	正　解	配点	第1回目得点	第2回目得点
H30 (試行調査2回) ②A	6	③	2	日付／	日付／
	7	②	2		
	8	③	2		
	9	①	2		
	10	②	2		
H30 (試行調査2回) ②B	11	④	2		
	12	②	2		
	13	③	2		
	14	①	2		
	15	③	2	／20	／20
H29 (試行調査1回) ②A	6	②	2	日付／	日付／
	7	②	2		
	8	①	2		
	9	①, ③ [*1]	4		
H29 (試行調査1回) ②B	10	④	2		
	11	①	2		
	12	②	2		
	13	②	2		
	14	②	2	／20	／20
H25 ⑤	41	③	6	日付／	日付／
	42	④	6		
	43	②	6		
	44	①	6		
	45	④	6	／30	／30

〈体験〉

年度	解答番号	正　解	配点	第1回目得点	第2回目得点
R4 ③A	16	①	3	日付／	日付／
	17	①	3		
R4 ③B	18	①	3*		
	19	④			
	20	③			
	21	②			
	22	②	3		
	23	②	3	／15	／15
R3 (追試) ③A	16	②	3	日付／	日付／
	17	②	3		
R3 (追試) ③B	18	③	3*		
	19	②			
	20	④			
	21	①			
	22	④	3		
	23	③	3	／15	／15

年度	解答番号	正　解	配点	第1回目得点	第2回目得点
R3 (本試) ③A	16	③	3	日付／	日付／
	17	②	3		
R3 (本試) ③B	18	④	3*		
	19	②			
	20	①			
	21	③			
	22	②	3		
	23	②	3	／15	／15
H30 (試行調査2回) ③A	16	②	2	日付／	日付／
	17	③	2		
H30 (試行調査2回) ③B	18	③	2		
	19	①	2		
	20	②	2	／10	／10
H29 (試行調査1回) ③A	15	②	2	日付／	日付／
	16	②	2		
H29 (試行調査1回) ③B	17	④	2		
	18	③	2		
	19	④	2	／10	／10
R2 ⑤	41	①	6	日付／	日付／
	42	④	6		
	43	④	6		
	44	②	6		
	45	②	6	／30	／30
H31 ⑤	41	①	6	日付／	日付／
	42	②	6		
	43	①	6		
	44	③	6		
	45	③	6	／30	／30

〈データ〉

年度	解答番号	正　解	配点	第1回目得点	第2回目得点
R4 ④	24	③	3	日付／	日付／
	25	③	3		
	26	②	3		
	27	①	3		
	28	②	2		
	29	④	2	／16	／16
R3 (追試) ④	24	③	3	日付／	日付／
	25	④	3		
	26	①	3		
	27	②	2		
	28	③	2		
	29	③	3	／16	／16

年度	解答番号	正解	配点	第1回目得点	第2回目得点
R 3 (本試) ④	24	①	2	日付 /	日付 /
	25	⑤	2		
	26	②	3		
	27	②	3		
	28	②	3		
	29	④	3	／16	／16
H30 (新課程2回) ④	21	②	3	日付 /	日付 /
	22	①	3		
	23	②,③	4*¹		
	24	②	3*		
	25	④			
	26	②	3	／16	／16
H29 (新課程1回) ④	20	③	3	日付 /	日付 /
	21	③	3		
	22	③	3		
	23	④	3		
	24	③	3	／15	／15
R 2 ④A	33	④	5	日付 /	日付 /
	34	④	5		
	35	②	5		
	36	④	5	／20	／20
H31 ④A	33	②	5	日付 /	日付 /
	34	④	5		
	35	②	5		
	36	③	5	／20	／20
H30 ④A	33	②	5	日付 /	日付 /
	34	③	5		
	35	②	5		
	46	④	5	／20	／20
H29 ④A	35	③	5	日付 /	日付 /
	36	①	5		
	37	④	5		
	38	②	5	／20	／20
H28 ④A	35	②	5	日付 /	日付 /
	36	①	5		
	37	③	5		
	38	②	5	／20	／20
H27 ④A	35	④	5	日付 /	日付 /
	36	①	5		
	37	②	5		
	38	②	5	／20	／20
H26 ④A	35	④	5	日付 /	日付 /
	36	②	5		
	37	①	5		
	38	①	5	／20	／20

年度	解答番号	正解	配点	第1回目得点	第2回目得点
H25 ④A	35	②	6	日付 /	日付 /
	36	③	6		
	37	④	6	／18	／18

〈ヒストリー〉

年度	解答番号	正解	配点	第1回目得点	第2回目得点
R 4 ⑤	30	①	3	日付 /	日付 /
	31－32	④－⑤	3*		
	33	②	3*		
	34	⑤			
	35	④			
	36	①			
	37	③	3		
	38	③	3	／15	／15
R 3 (追試) ⑤	30	①	3	日付 /	日付 /
	31－32	①－④	3*		
	33	③	3*		
	34	④			
	35	④			
	36	②			
	37	①	3		
	38	④	3	／15	／15
R 3 (本試) ⑤	30	③	3	日付 /	日付 /
	31	④	3		
	32	④	3*		
	33	③			
	34	⑤			
	35	①			
	36－37	①－③	3*		
	38	①	3	／15	／15
H30 (新課程2回) ⑤	27	③	5*	日付 /	日付 /
	28	②			
	29	⑤			
	30	④			
	31	①			
	32	②,③,⑥	5*¹		
	33	③	5		
	34	①,③,⑥	5*¹	／20	／20
H29 (新課程1回) ⑤A	25	④	3	日付 /	日付 /
	26	④	3		
	27	④	3		
H29 (新課程1回) ⑤B	28	④*²	3		
	29	①*²	3		
	30	②*²	3		
	31	②,④ *³	4		
	32	③,⑤,⑥ *³	4		
	33	④	4	／30	／30

年度	解答番号	正　解	配点	第1回目得点	第2回目得点
R 2 ⑥A	46	①	6	日付　／	日付　／
	47	③	6		
	48	②	6		
	49	④	6		
	50	②	6		
R 2 ⑥B	51	②			
	52	④	6*		
	53	③			
	54	①		／36	／36
H28 ⑥A	47	①	6	日付　／	日付　／
	48	③	6		
	49	①	6		
	50	③	6		
	51	③	6		
H28 ⑥B	52	③			
	53	①	6*		
	54	④			
	55	②		／36	／36
H25 ⑥A	46	④	6	日付　／	日付　／
	47	①	6		
	48	③	6		
	49	①	6		
	50	①	6		
H25 ⑥B	51	①			
	52	⑤			
	53	④	6*		
	54	②			
	55	③		／36	／36

〈物語・手紙・メール・日記〉

年度	解答番号	正　解	配点	第1回目得点	第2回目得点
H30 ⑤	41	③	6	日付　／	日付　／
	42	②	6		
	43	②	6		
	44	①	6		
	45	③	6	／30	／30
H29 ⑤	42	①	6	日付　／	日付　／
	43	②	6		
	44	④	6		
	45	①	6		
	46	②	6	／30	／30
H28 ⑤	42	②	6	日付　／	日付　／
	43	③	6		
	44	②	6		
	45	③	6		
	46	②	6	／30	／30

年度	解答番号	正　解	配点	第1回目得点	第2回目得点
H27 ⑤	42	③	6	日付　／	日付　／
	43	③	6		
	44	④	6		
	45	④	6		
	46	④	6	／30	／30
H26 ⑤	42	①	6	日付　／	日付　／
	43	③	6		
	44	②	6		
	45	②	6		
	46	①	6	／30	／30

〈論理的文章〉

年度	解答番号	正　解	配点	第1回目得点	第2回目得点
R 4 ⑥A	39	③	3	日付　／	日付　／
	40	③	3		
	41	①	3		
	42	⑥	3*		
	43	③			
R 4 ⑥B	44	②	3		
	45	②	3		
	46	①	3		
	47−48	③−④	3*	／24	／24
R 3 (追試) ⑥A	39	②	3	日付　／	日付　／
	40	③	3		
	41	③	3		
	42	④	3		
R 3 (追試) ⑥B	43	④	3		
	44	③	3		
	45	④	3		
	46−47	③−⑤	3*	／24	／24
R 3 (本試) ⑥A	39	④	3	日付　／	日付　／
	40	③	3		
	41	④	3		
	42	②	3		
R 3 (本試) ⑥B	43	③	3		
	44	③	3		
	45−46	③−⑤	3*		
	47	④	3	／24	／24

年度	解答番号	正　解	配点	第1回目得点	第2回目得点
H30 (新課程2回) 6A	35	④	3	日付 ／	日付 ／
	36	②	3		
	37	①	3		
	38	①	3		
H30 (新課程2回) 6B	39	③	3		
	40	②	3		
	41－42	③－④	3*		
	43	②	3	／24	／24
H29 (新課程1回) 6	34	③*2	3	日付 ／	日付 ／
	35	①*2	3		
	36	①	3		
	37	①	3		
	38	③	3	／15	／15
H31 6A	46	②	6	日付 ／	日付 ／
	47	③	6		
	48	④	6		
	49	①	6		
	50	④	6		
H31 6B	51	①	6*		
	52	④			
	53	②			
	54	③		／36	／36
H30 6A	46	④	6	日付 ／	日付 ／
	47	②	6		
	48	①	6		
	49	①	6		
	50	②	6		
H30 6B	51	④	6*		
	52	②			
	53	③			
	54	①		／36	／36
H29 6A	47	④	6	日付 ／	日付 ／
	48	②	6		
	49	④	6		
	50	④	6		
	51	①	6		
H29 6B	52	④	6*		
	53	②			
	54	③			
	55	①		／36	／36

年度	解答番号	正　解	配点	第1回目得点	第2回目得点
H27 6A	47	④	6	日付 ／	日付 ／
	48	②	6		
	49	②	6		
	50	②	6		
	51	①	6		
H27 6B	52	③	6*		
	53	①			
	54	②			
	55	④		／36	／36
H26 6A	47	④	6	日付 ／	日付 ／
	48	①	6		
	49	①	6		
	50	③	6		
	51	③	6		
H26 6B	52	①	6*		
	53	④			
	54	②			
	55	③		／36	／36

［文法－頻出問題編］
〈文法・語法〉

年度	解答番号	正解	配点	第1回目得点	第2回目得点
H22 ②A	8	④	2	日付 ／	日付 ／
	9	③	2		
	10	④	2		
	11	③	2		
	12	④	2		
	13	④	2		
	14	④	2		
	15	③	2		
	16	①	2		
	17	①	2	／20	／20
H23 ②A	8	①	2	日付 ／	日付 ／
	9	③	2		
	10	①	2		
	11	①	2		
	12	②	2		
	13	①	2		
	14	②	2		
	15	④	2		
	16	③	2		
	17	②	2	／20	／20
H24 ②A	8	③	2	日付 ／	日付 ／
	9	①	2		
	10	①	2		
	11	②	2		
	12	④	2		
	13	①	2		
	14	②	2		
	15	①	2		
	16	①	2		
	17	④	2	／20	／20
H25 ②A	8	④	2	日付 ／	日付 ／
	9	④	2		
	10	①	2		
	11	③	2		
	12	①	2		
	13	①	2		
	14	①	2		
	15	④	2		
	16	①	2		
	17	②	2	／20	／20

年度	解答番号	正解	配点	第1回目得点	第2回目得点
H26 ②A	8	②	2	日付 ／	日付 ／
	9	③	2		
	10	③	2		
	11	①	2		
	12	②	2		
	13	④	2		
	14	④	2		
	15	②	2		
	16	③	2		
	17	④	2	／20	／20
H27 ②A	8	①	2	日付 ／	日付 ／
	9	③	2		
	10	③	2		
	11	②	2		
	12	①	2		
	13	③	2		
	14	①	2		
	15	④	2		
	16	②	2		
	17	④	2	／20	／20
H28 ②A	8	①	2	日付 ／	日付 ／
	9	①	2		
	10	②	2		
	11	④	2		
	12	②	2		
	13	①	2		
	14	①	2		
	15	③	2		
	16	①	2		
	17	④	2	／20	／20
H29 ②A	8	①	2	日付 ／	日付 ／
	9	②	2		
	10	④	2		
	11	①	2		
	12	②	2		
	13	③	2		
	14	④	2		
	15	①	2		
	16	③	2		
	17	①	2	／20	／20

解
答

年度	解答番号	正 解	配点	第1回目得点	第2回目得点
H30 ②A	8	③	2	日付 ／	日付 ／
	9	②	2		
	10	①	2		
	11	④	2		
	12	①	2		
	13	③	2		
	14	①	2		
	15	③	2		
	16	③	2		
	17	③	2	／20	／20
H31 ②A	8	②	2	日付 ／	日付 ／
	9	③	2		
	10	①	2		
	11	②	2		
	12	④	2		
	13	③	2		
	14	③	2		
	15	②	2		
	16	④	2		
	17	④	2	／20	／20
R 2 ②A	8	③	2	日付 ／	日付 ／
	9	①	2		
	10	③	2		
	11	③	2		
	12	①	2		
	13	①	2		
	14	①	2		
	15	④	2		
	16	②	2		
	17	①	2	／20	／20

〈語句整序〉

年度	解答番号	正 解	配点	第1回目得点	第2回目得点
H22 ②C	21	②	4*	日付 ／	日付 ／
	22	⑥			
	23	②	4*		
	24	①			
	25	②	4*		
	26	⑤		／12	／12
H23 ②C	21	③	4*	日付 ／	日付 ／
	22	②			
	23	②	4*		
	24	⑤			
	25	③	4*		
	26	⑥		／12	／12

年度	解答番号	正 解	配点	第1回目得点	第2回目得点
H24 ②C	21	②	4*	日付 ／	日付 ／
	22	⑤			
	23	⑤	4*		
	24	③			
	25	⑤	4*		
	26	③		／12	／12
H25 ②C	21	②	4*	日付 ／	日付 ／
	22	④			
	23	⑤	4*		
	24	①			
	25	④	4*		
	26	⑤		／12	／12
H26 ②C	21	④	4*	日付 ／	日付 ／
	22	⑤			
	23	③	4*		
	24	⑥			
	25	①	4*		
	26			／12	／12
H27 ②B	18	⑤	4*	日付 ／	日付 ／
	19	⑥			
	20	⑤	4*		
	21	①			
	22	④	4*		
	23	⑤		／12	／12
H28 ②B	18	⑤	4*	日付 ／	日付 ／
	19	①			
	20	③	4*		
	21	⑤			
	22	④	4*		
	23	⑥		／12	／12
H29 ②B	18	②	4*	日付 ／	日付 ／
	19	⑥			
	20	⑤	4*		
	21	①			
	22	⑥	4*		
	23	②		／12	／12
H30 ②B	18	③	4*	日付 ／	日付 ／
	19	②			
	20	④	4*		
	21	②			
	22	③	4*		
	23	②		／12	／12

年度	解答番号	正　解	配点	第1回目得点	第2回目得点
H31 ②B	18	②	4*	日付　／	日付　／
	19	⑤			
	20	⑥	4*		
	21	②			
	22	②	4*		
	23	⑥		／12	／12
R2 ②B	18	④	4*	日付　／	日付　／
	19	②			
	20	④	4*		
	21	③			
	22	⑤	4*		
	23	②		／12	／12

① 〈ビジュアル〉　　　問題 2p〜

R4　①A

あなたは高校のインターナショナルクラブでブラジルについて勉強しています。あなたの先生はブラジルの食べ物について調査するようあなたに言いました。あなたはブラジルの料理本を見つけ、デザートを作るのに使われる果物について読んでいます。

人気のあるブラジルの果物

 **クプアス**	 **ジャボチカバ**
・チョコレートのような香りと味。 ・ケーキのようなデザートやヨーグルトにあわせるのにもってこい。 ・ブラジル人はこの果物のチョコレート風味のジュースが好き。	・ブドウのような見た目。 ・摘み取ってから3日以内に食べると甘い風味がする。 ・酸味が出た後はジャム、ゼリー、ケーキを作るのに使う。
 ピタンガ	**ブリチ**
・赤と緑の2種類がある。 ・甘い赤はケーキを作るのに使う。 ・酸味のある緑はジャムやゼリーだけにしか使えない。	・内側はオレンジ色で桃やマンゴーに似ている。 ・とても甘い味で、口の中でとろける。 ・アイスクリーム、ケーキ、ジャムに最適。

問1 クプアスとブリチは両方とも ☐ 1 を作るのに使うことが出来る。

① ケーキ　　　　　② チョコレート
③ アイスクリーム　④ ヨーグルト

表のクプアスの説明2つ目にケーキのようなデザートやヨーグルトにあわせるのにもってこいとあり、ブリチの説明3つ目にアイスクリーム、ケーキ、ジャムに最適とあり、共通するのはケーキである。よって正解は①。

問2 酸味があるケーキを作りたい場合、使うのに最適な果物は ☐ 2 である。

① ブリチ　　　　② クプアス
③ ジャボチカバ　④ ピタンガ

表によると酸味があるのは緑のピタンガとジャボチカバである。ジャボチカバの説明3つ目に酸味が出た後はジャム、ゼリー、ケーキを作るのに使うとあるが、ピタンガの説明3つ目にジャムやゼリーだけにしか使えないとあり、ピタンガはケーキを作るのには使えないことがわかる。よって正解は③。

R4　①B

あなたはカナダのトロントにある市立動物園のウェブサイトを見ています、そして面白いコンテストのお知らせを見つけます。あなたはコンテストに参加しようと考えています。

コンテスト！
キリンの赤ちゃんに名前をつけよう
市立動物園の新しい動物を歓迎しよう！

5月26日に市立動物園で元気なキリンの赤ちゃんが産まれました。
彼はすでに歩き回ったり走り回ったりしています！
体重は66kg、身長は180cmです。
あなたの任務は、彼の両親、ビリーとノエルが赤ちゃんの名前を選ぶのを手伝うことです。

応募方法
◆名前を投稿するにはこのリンクをクリックし、指示に従ってください。 　　　　　　　　　　　　　　**→ここから入ってください** ◆名前は6月1日午前12時から6月7日の午後11時59分まで受け付けます。 ◆ライブウェブカメラでキリンの赤ちゃんを見ましょう、アイデアを出すのに役立ちます。 　　　　　　　　　　　　　　**→ライブウェブカメラ** ◆1回の投稿ごとに5ドル必要です。お金はすべて育ち盛りのキリンの赤ちゃんのエサに使われます。

コンテストの日程	
6月8日	動物園の職員が全ての候補の中から5つの最終候補を選びます。 最終候補の名前は午後5時までに動物園のウェブサイトに掲示されます。
6月9日	両親はどうやって優勝の名前を決めるでしょうか？ 結果を確認するには午前11時から午後12時までの間にライブ配信のリンクをクリックしてください！　　**→ライブ配信** 優勝した名前は午後12時以降に動物園のウェブサイトで確認してください。

商品
最終候補は5名全員、7月末まで有効な動物園一日無料券を手に入れることができます。 優勝した名前を投稿した方は、キリンの赤ちゃんとその家族の特別な写真と、プライベートナイトサファリツアーも手に入れることができます。

問1 コンテストには ☐ 3 の間参加することができる。

① 5月26日から5月31日
② 6月1日から6月7日
③ 6月8日から6月9日
④ 6月10日から7月31日

応募方法の2番目に6月1日午前12時から6月7日の午後11時59分とあるので、②が正解。

問2 キリンの赤ちゃんの名前のアイデアを投稿するとき ☐ 4 必要がある。

① 1日パスを買う
② 参加費を支払う
③ 市立動物園で5ドル使う
④ ウェブサイトでキリンを見る

応募方法の4番目に投稿1回ごとに5ドル必要とあり、5ドルの参加費を支払わなければならないことがわかる。5ドルは参加費であり、動物園で使うとする③は不適。また、応募方法の3つ目にウェブカメラを見るよう指示があるが、これは参加に必ず必要なものではない。よって、参加費を支払うという②が正解。

問3 応募した名前が5つの最終候補に選ばれた場合 5 することができる。

① 動物園に1日無料で入場する
② ライブのウェブサイトに無料でアクセスする
③ キリンの赤ちゃんに会い、餌をあげる
④ キリンの家族と一緒に写真を撮る

賞品の説明第1文に最終候補は5名全員、7月末まで有効な動物園一日無料券を手に入れることができます。とあるので、①が正解。選択肢の「free entry the zoo for a day」は本文の「free one-day zoo passes：動物園の1日無料券」の書き換え。

R3（追試） 1A

あなたは友達のシェリーを、家族との一泊のキャンプ旅行に参加するよう招待しています。彼女はあなたの携帯電話にいくつかの質問をするメッセージを送りました。

> こんにちは！私は明日のために自分のかばんに荷造りをしています、そしていくつかのことを確認したいです。夜にテントの中は寒くなりますか？毛布を持っていく必要はありますか？あなたが先週私に言ったのは知っていますが、念のため、どこで何時に待ち合わせていますか？

> シェリー、私はみんなのために温かい寝袋を持っていくつもりですが、自分のダウンジャケットを持ってくるべきです。次の日にカナヤマを歩いて登る予定なので、履き心地の良い靴を持ってきてください。私たちは午前6時にあなたの家の外に迎えに行きます。もし、あなたが家の外にいなければ、あなたに電話するつもりです。朝にお会いしましょう。

> ありがとう！私は待ちきれません！私は自分のジャケットとハイキングブーツを持っていくつもりです。準備します！☺

問1 シェリーは 1 を持っていく必要があるかどうか尋ねている。

① 毛布　　② ジャケット
③ 寝袋　　④ ウォーキングシューズ

シェリーの発言1第4文で毛布は必要か聞いている。

問2 あなたはシェリーが明日の朝、 2 ことを期待している。

① 彼女が準備でき次第電話する
② 会うためにキャンプ場に行く
③ あなたの家の外であなたを拾う
④ 彼女の家の外であなたを待つ

あなたの発言1第3文に朝6時にシェリーの家の外に迎えに行くとある。

R3（追試） 1B

あなたは英語のスピーチコンテストのチラシを先生から受け取り、申し込みたいと考えています。

第7回　ユースリーダースピーチコンテスト

ユースリーダー協会は毎年恒例のスピーチコンテストを開催する予定です。私たちの目標は日本の若者のコミュニケーションスキルとリーダーシップの技能の向上を手助けすることです。

今年の大会は3つのステージがあります。私たちの審査員はそれぞれのステージでの勝者を選びます。グランドファイナルに出場するためには、3つのステージ全てを見事に通過する必要があります。

グランドファイナル	優勝賞品
場　所：百周年ホール 日　時：2022年1月8日 テーマ：今日の若者、明日のリーダー	優勝者は、2022年3月にニュージーランドのウェリントンで行われるリーダーシップワークショップに出席することができます。

コンテストの情報

ステージ	アップロードするもの	詳細	2021の期限と日付
ステージ1	概要	語数：150－200語	8月2日の午後5時まで
ステージ2	あなたがスピーチを行っているビデオ	時間：7－8分	9月19日の午後5時まで
ステージ3		地方予選：優勝者が発表されグランドファイナルに進む。	11月21日に開催

グランドファイナルの採点情報

内容	ジェスチャーとパフォーマンス	声とアイコンタクト	スライド	審査員からの質問に対する回答
50%	5%	5%	10%	30%

➤ あなたは資料をオンラインでアップロードしなければなりません。日時は全て日本の標準時（ＪＳＴ）です。
➤ ステージ1と2の結果はそれぞれのステージの提出期限の5日後にウェブサイトで確認することができます。

詳細と申込フォームは、<u>こちら</u>をクリックしてください。

問1 第1ステージに参加するために、あなたは 3 をアップロードすべきである。

① 完成したスピーチの台本
② スピーチのためのスライド一式
③ スピーチの要約
④ あなた自身が話しているビデオ

選択肢の「summary：要約」が「a brief outline：概要」の書き換え。

問2 あなたが第2ステージの結果を確認できるのはいつからか？ 4

① 9月14日　　② 9月19日
③ 9月24日　　④ 9月29日

ステージ1と2の結果が確認できるのは締め切りから5日後からであるから、締め切りの9月19日の5日後である9月24日から。

問3　グランドファイナルで高得点をとるために、あなたが
最も注意を払うべきなのは内容と　5　である。
　　①表現やジェスチャー　　②審査員への応答
　　③視覚資料　　　　　　　④声の調節
グランドファイナルの表から最も配点が高いのは50%の内
容、次いで審査員からの質問に対する回答30%である。選
択肢の「responses to the judges：審査員への応答」が
「Answering Question from Judges：質問に対する回答」の
書き換え。

R3（本試）　①A

寮のルームメイトであるジュリーが、あなたの携帯電話
に依頼の書かれたメールを送っています。

助けて!!!
昨夜、私は歴史の宿題をUSBメモリースティックに保存しました。
今日の午後、大学の図書館でそれを印刷するつもりだったのですが、
USBを持ってくることを忘れてしまいました。今日の午後4時ま
でに先生にコピーを渡さなければなりません。図書館に私のUSBを
持ってきてもらえませんか？私の机にある歴史の教科書の上にある
と思います。教科書は必要ありません、USBだけが必要です♡

ごめんなさい、ジュリー、みつけられなかった。歴史の教科書は
ありましたが、USBメモリースティックはありませんでした。私は
部屋中探しました、机の下でさえも。本当に持っていませんか？念
のため、あなたのノートパソコンを持っていきます。

あなたが正しかった！確かに私が持っていました。鞄の底にあり
ました。ああ、ほっとした！とにかくありがとう☺

問1　ジュリーのお願いは何でしたか？　1
　　①彼女のUSBメモリースティックを持ってくること
　　②彼女の歴史の教科書を提出すること
　　③USBメモリースティックを彼女に貸すこと
　　④彼女の歴史の宿題を印刷すること
ジュリーの1番目のメッセージに、図書館に私のUSBを
持ってきてもらえませんか？とあるので、正解は①。
問2　ジュリーの2番目のメッセージにあなたはどのように
返信しますか？　2
　　①心配しないで。みつかるわ。
　　②それを聞いて本当にうれしいわ。
　　③あなたの鞄の中をもう一度見てみて。
　　④あなたはがっかりするに違いない。
ジュリーの2番目のメッセージに鞄の底にあったとあるの
で、みつかっていない①・②・④は不適。みつかったこと
を聞いて喜んでいる②が正解。

R3（本試）　①B

あなたのお気に入りのミュージシャンが日本でコンサー
トツアーを行うことになり、あなたはファンクラブに入る
ことを考えています。あなたは公式ファンクラブのウェブ
サイトを訪れました。

タイラークイックファンクラブ
　タイラークイック（TQ）のファンクラブ会員になることはとて
も楽しいです！あなたは常に最新のニュースを受け取ったり、たく
さんのわくわくさせるようなファンクラブ会員イベントに参加した
りすることができます。すべての新規会員は新規会員パックを受け
取ります。それには、会員カード、無料のサイン入りポスター、**TQ**
の3rdアルバム*Speeding Up*のコピーが入っています。新規会員
パックはあなたの自宅に配達され、あなたがファンクラブに入会し
た後、一週間程度で届きます。
　TQは世界中で愛されています。どの国からも入会は可能で、会
員証は1年間使えます。**TQ**ファンクラブには、Pacer、Speeder、
Zoomerという3種類の会員資格があります。

　下記の会員資格からお選びください。

得られるもの（♫）	会員オプション		
	Pacer（20ドル）	Speeder（40ドル）	Zoomer（60ドル）
定期Eメールとオンラインマガジンのパスワード	♫	♫	♫
コンサートツアーの日程の早期案内	♫	♫	♫
TQの毎週のビデオメッセージ	♫	♫	♫
毎月の写真のポストカード		♫	♫
TQファンクラブカレンダー		♫	♫
特別サイン会イベントへの招待			♫
コンサートチケットの20%割引			♫

確かめよう！
◇　5月10日までの入会で会費の10ドル割引を受けることができま
　す。
◇　すべての新規会員パックは4ドルの送料がかかります。
◇　入会1年目の終わりに、50%割引で更新、またはアップグレー
　ドができます。
　Pacer、Speeder、Zoomerのいずれであっても、**TQ**ファンクラブ
の会員であることを気に入るでしょう。詳しい情報や入会するに
は、<u>ここ</u>をクリックしてください。

問1　新規会員パックは　3　。
　　①TQの1stアルバムを含む
　　②5月10日に届けられる
　　③10ドルの送料が必要となる
　　④到着までに7日間かかる
①は1stではなく3rdなので不適。②は5月10日までに申
し込めば割引があり、届けられる日ではなく不適。③は10
ドルではなく4ドルで不適。④は「takes about seven days
to arrive：到着に約7日間かかる」が「arrive a week or so：
1週間ほどかかる」の書き換えで、正解は④。
問2　新規Pacer会員になった場合、何が手に入るか。
　　4
　　①コンサートチケットの割引とカレンダー
　　②定期Eメールとサイン会への招待
　　③ツアー情報と毎月のポストカード
　　④ビデオメッセージとオンラインマガジンのアクセス権
表より、Pacer会員の特典は、定期的なEメールとオンラ
インマガジンのパスワード、ツアー情報、毎週のビデオ

メッセージであり、Speeder会員及びZoomer会員の特典を含む①・②・③は不適。④の「access to online magazine：オンラインマガジンへのアクセス権」は、表の「online magazine password：オンラインマガジンのパスワード」の書き換えで、正解は④。

問3　ファンクラブ会員になってから1年後、あなたは　5　ことができる。

①50ドルでZoomer会員になる

②4ドルで新規会員パックを手に入れる

③半額で会員資格を更新する

④無料で会員資格をアップグレードする

Check it out！の1つ目より、会費の10ドル割引は5月10日までの早期加入割引なので①は不適。Check it out！の2つ目より、4ドルなのは新規会員パックの料金ではなく配送料なので②は不適。Check it out！の3つ目より、会員資格の更新とアップグレードが50％割引とされており、無料とする④は不適、「at half price：半額」は「at a 50% discount：50％割引」の書き換えで、正解は③。

H30（試行調査2回）　1A

あなたは英語クラブのメンバーです。あなたはクラブの1人である、マレーシア出身のヤスミンのお別れ会をしようと思っています。あなたはALTでクラブのアドバイザーであるアメリアからノートを受け取りました。

> 英語クラブのメンバーへ
> ヤスミンのための英語クラブお別れ会を、いつ行うか決めなければいけない時期です。彼女は12月15日に日本を去る予定なので、クラブのメンバーは来週いつか会うべきです。ヤスミンにその会に来るのに、いつが都合良いかを聞いて、私に知らせてくれませんか？その日を調整すれば、いくつかサプライズを計画してあなたを手伝いましょう。また、他の生徒を招待しても大丈夫ですか？これまでの6ヶ月以上の間彼女とテニスをして実に楽しい時間を過ごしたのでその会に参加したい、というテニス部の生徒を私は知っています。
>
> それでは。
> アメリア

問1　先生はあなたにヤスミンに　1　と尋ねてほしい。

①彼女がその会で何を食べたいのか

②彼女がいつその会に参加するのか

③彼女がその会をどこでしたいのか

④彼女がその会に誰を招待したいのか

アメリアからの手紙の5行目に、ヤスミンに都合のいい日を尋ねるように頼んでいる箇所がある。

問2　先生は　2　も招待したいと思っている。

①英語クラブに所属していない数人の生徒

②英語クラブとテニスチームのメンバー全員

③ヤスミンの他の英語の先生

④マレーシアで英語を勉強したいと思っている生徒

先生が招待しようとしているのは、ヤスミンとテニスをしたことのある数人のテニス部の生徒である。

H30（試行調査2回）　1B

あなたは街の英語のウェブサイトを訪れ、面白いお知らせを見つけました。

参加者募集：姉妹都市の若者会議
「共住について学ぶこと」

ドイツ、セネガル、メキシコにある私たちの街の3つの姉妹都市が、今度の3月に私たちの街に15歳から18歳までの若者10人をそれぞれ送ってきます。「共住について学ぶこと」と呼ばれる8日間に及ぶ若者の会議があります。それは私たちのゲストの日本への最初の訪問になります。

私たちは、参加者を探しています。私たちの街の高校から30人の生徒によるホストチーム、訪問する若者のための30軒のホストファミリー、そのイベントを執り行う20人のスタッフを必要としています。

スケジュール

3月20日	オリエンテーション、歓迎パーティー
3月21日	4カ国合同の小グループで観光
3月22日	伝統舞踊についての2つの発表： (1)セネガルの生徒、(2)日本の生徒
3月23日	伝統料理についての2つの発表： (1)メキシコの生徒、(2)日本の生徒
3月24日	伝統的な衣服についての2つの発表： (1)ドイツの生徒、(2)日本の生徒
3月25日	4カ国合同の小グループで観光
3月26日	ホストファミリーとの自由時間
3月27日	お別れパーティー

・パーティーと発表はコミュニティセンターで行われます。

・会議中の言語は英語になります。訪問者は英語のネイティブスピーカーではありませんが、彼らには基本的な英語技術があります。

登録には、12月20日の午後5時までに**ここ**をクリックしてください。

▶▶市役所国際課

問1　このお知らせの目的は、　3　ためにホストタウンから人々を見つけることです

①活動のスケジュールを決める

②イベントに参加する

③すべての姉妹都市を訪れる

④会議に関する報告書を書く

お知らせの最初に、参加者募集とあるので、②が正解。

問2　その会議の間、生徒は　4　。

①国際的な問題についての話し合いをします

②彼ら自身の文化の発表をします

③ほとんどの時間を観光に費やします

④言語を教えるために地元の高校を訪れます

スケジュールを見ると、日本の生徒が舞踊・料理・衣服について発表しているため、②が正解。

問3　すべての生徒が　5　ので、その会議はコミュニケーションの良い機会となるでしょう。

①異なる年齢のグループに分けられる

②日本語と英語の授業がある

③英語でいろんな人と話をする

④3つの姉妹都市からの家族と過ごす

スケジュールの下にある内容から会議が英語で行われるこ

とと、姉妹都市の生徒が基本的な英語技術を持っていることがわかるので、③が正解。

H29（試行調査1回）１A

あなたは香港にあるアミューズメントパークに行こうとしています。あなたはそのウェブサイトを見ています。

ブルーストーン
香港

ブルーストーン
アミューズメントパーク

トップ>混雑カレンダー

このウェブサイトはブルーストーンアミューズメントパークを訪れるのに最適な日にちを見つけるのに役立つでしょう。

お知らせ

「海賊の冒険」というタイトルの新しいショーが11月13日に始まります。

混雑カレンダー

下の表で、あなたは開園時間と閉園時間、混雑の程度を見ることができます。各欄の割合は、園内にいると予想される人数の推定です。最高は100%で、顔のアイコンで示されています。その割合は、前売り券と過去のデータに基づき自動的に計算されています。

顔のアイコンがついている日には、パークへの入場が困難になります。前売り券を持たない来場者は入場口で長時間待たなければいけないかもしれません。前売り券は1週間前までにオンラインでのみ入手可能です。

カレンダーの各日にちをクリックすることで、各アトラクションの平均待ち時間についての詳細な情報を見ることができます。

11月の混雑カレンダー （情報は毎日更新されます）						
月	火	水	木	金	土	日
5	6	7	8	9	10	11
55%	65%	70%	70%	85%	90%	(-.-;)
9:00-	9:00-	9:00-	9:00-	9:00-	9:00-	9:00-
17:00	19:00	19:00	19:00	21:00	21:00	21:00
12	13	14	15	16	17	18
55%	(-.-;)	(-.-;)	90%	85%	(-.-;)	90%
9:00-	9:00-	9:00-	9:00-	9:00-	9:00-	9:00-
16:00	21:00	21:00	21:00	21:00	21:00	21:00

問1 もしあなたが11月13日に前売り券なしでパークに行くのであれば、入場口でおそらく ☐ 1 ☐ でしょう。

①そのまま入れる

②55%だけさらに払わなければいけない

③駐車券を見せなければならない

④長い列にならんで立つ

第2段落によると、前売り券なしでは長時間入場口で待たなければいけないと書かれている。よって、正解は④。

問2 カレンダーの日にちをクリックすると、あなたは ☐ 2 ☐ についての情報を見つけることができます。

①来場者がどのくらいアトラクションで待たなければいけないのか

②アトラクションの前売り券の値段

③様々なパークレストランの食べ物や飲み物

④来場者はブルーストーンのどこに車を停めればよいか

第3段落によると、アトラクションの平均待ち時間について知ることができることがわかる。よって、正解は①。

H29（試行調査1回）１B

あなたは、ある日本の大学のオープンキャンパスの期間に、その大学を訪れています。あなたは面白いイベントについてのあるポスターを見つけました。

休日予定研究クラブ

HPRC

オープンキャンパス
イベント

高校生のためのHPRC
ミーティング

HPRCとは何か？

大学生活の最も素晴らしい部分の1つは、とても長い休日にあります。休日予定研究クラブ（HPRC）は、日本人と海外の学生によって運営されています。私たちのクラブは、全学年どの学部の生徒も歓迎しています。私たちの目的は、面白い休みの予定をお互いに作る手伝いをすることにあります。

日程：10月27日土曜日　午後2時から3時半

場所：個別学習センター

イベント：4人の生徒が、最近休暇中に経験したことについて話します。

概要と発表が記してある下の表を見てください。

話し手	内容	場所
1. メアリー・マクドナルド 農学部	＊田んぼや野菜畑で一生懸命に働いた ＊ホストファミリーと自給自足の生活	石川県の農家
2. シミズ・フミヒロ 文学部	＊国語の先生と授業教材の準備 ＊飛行機代と保険料は自費	カンボジアの小学校
3. ニシウラ・リサ 観光科	＊外国人のシェフを料理と翻訳で援助 ＊高給与	東京のスペイン料理レストラン
4. コバヤシ・ヒロキ 教育学部	＊柔道を教えた ＊飛行機代と部屋代は無料	ブルガリアのジュニアオリンピックトレーニングキャンプ

大学生へのメッセージ　**12月のHPRCミーティングで話し手として私たちと一緒に楽しみましょう！**

あなたには合計12分間の時間があります。あなたの話は、英語では、約8分間が良いでしょう。画像を載せたスライドを準備してください。それぞれの話の後には、4分間の質疑応答の時間があり、聞き手がいつもたくさんの質問をします。私たちのウェブサイトでもっとたくさんの情報を得ることができます。(http://www.hprc-student.net/)

問1 HPRCは ☐ 3 ☐ によって組織され運営されています。

①NGOのスタッフ　　②学生

③教師　　　　　　　④大学のスタッフ

「What is the HPRC」の2行目に、「日本人と海外の学生によって運営されています」とある。よって、正解は②。

問2 4人の話し手それぞれから ☐ 4 ☐ について知ることができます。

①大学の異なる学部の興味深い学科
②世界中の他の国々への低コストの旅行
③大学の休暇中の授業外での経験
④発展途上国の子供たちとのボランティアワーク

表の「場所」を見ると、4人の活動は学校外で行われている。よって、正解は③。

問3 12月のミーティングで、HPRCの話し手は ┃ 5 ┃ べきです。
①質問に答える準備をする
②ウェブサイトにスピーチ原稿を載せる
③英語と日本語で話す
④約20分で話す

12分間のスピーチの話の中で、4分間の質疑応答の時間が与えられている。よって、正解は①。

R2 ④B

問1 ┃ 37 ┃ ①

フランは手作りの宝石をどちらの日程でも売るつもりである。彼女はちょっとした空間を必要としている。それには、いくらかかるか。

①14ドル ②16ドル ③18ドル ④20ドル

フランは、2×2メートルの空間を選べば良いため、8ドル＋10ドル＝18ドルかかる。しかし、2つ目の▷によると、「両方に応募するのであれば、いずれの日も2ドル引き」になるので、18ドル－4ドル＝14ドルとなる。よって、正解は①。

問2 ┃ 38 ┃ ①

パットは冷蔵庫を含む、大きな家具をいくつか売りたいと思っているので、屋外の空間を必要としている。彼女はどの提案を利用することができるか。

①テントを作ってくれる無料のアシスタント
②キャンセルによる払い戻し
③空間の選択
④無料で大型トラックを利用すること

説明文5行目によると、「屋外の空間では、主催者が追加料金なしでテントを建てるのを手伝います」とある。よって、正解は①。

問3 ┃ 39 ┃ ②

マークは草木の石鹸とろうそくを作る。彼は屋内の空間を選んだ。以下の行為のなかで、どれが許されるか。

①水を簡単に手に入れるために流しに近い空間を選ぶ
②客が彼の石鹸を試すためボウルいっぱいの水を得る
③彼のブースでペットのハムスターをかごに入れて飼うこと
④彼の客にお試し用のキャンドルに火をつけさせる

1つ目の▷印によると、「水は屋内で利用可能」と分かる。よって、正解は②。

問4 ┃ 40 ┃ ④

以下のうち、このフリーマーケットに関して正しいものはどれか。

①人々は彼らが創った商品を売ることに落胆している
②人々は同じゴミ箱に何でも捨てて良い
③主催者はどちらの日程にも応募する応募者を選ぶ
④主催者はスケジュールの更新に関する情報を提供する

注意事項の2．によると、時間の変更に関しては「2日前にお知らせします」とある。よって、正解は④。

緑色の秋のフリーマーケット

私たちは今、グリーンリースポーツセンターでの秋のフリーマーケットの応募者を受け付けています。あなたが使った、あるいは手作りの商品を持ってきてください。私たちには、限られた数の空間があり、先着順に応募者を受け入れているので、早く応募用紙を送ってください。私たちは、ペット同伴可のマーケットですが、もしペットを連れてくる予定であれば、屋外の空間に応募しなければなりません。屋外の空間では、主催者が追加料金なしでテントを建てるのを手伝います。商品を運ぶのに必要であれば、トラックも追加費用で利用可能です。

	10月第3土曜日 （13：00～17：00）	10月第4日曜日 （10：00～15：00）
屋内（2×2メートル）	8ドル	10ドル
屋外（4×4メートル）	9ドル	11ドル

▷水は屋内で利用可能です。
▷もし土曜日と日曜日の両方に応募するのであれば、いずれの日も2ドル引きになります。

注意事項
1．空間の場所は主催者により決められます。相談も変更も不可です。
2．開始と終了時間の変更は、前もって2日前にお知らせします。
3．もし応募をキャンセルする場合は、全費用の80％を支払っていただきます。
4．ゴミは分別し、その日の終わりに適切なゴミ箱に捨ててください。
5．火気厳禁です。

H31 ④B

問1 ┃ 37 ┃ ③

4つの城の共通の特徴はなにか？
①損害の量
②絵画と武器の展示
③500年以上の歴史
④建設の目的

クレストベイル城は13世紀、ホルムステッド城は12世紀、王の城は11世紀、ローズバッハ城は15世紀なので、いずれも500年以上前に建てられている。

問2 ┃ 38 ┃ ②

グランドルフォーク大学のギタークラブの部員3人は、4月のある日の午後にコンサートをしたいと思っている。どの城を彼らは選ぼうとするか？
①クレストベイル城
②ホルムステッド城
③王の城
④ローズバッハ城

ホルムステッド城の説明に演奏に使える広場があることが書かれている。

問3　39　②

ある学校の先生らが生徒らを5月のある土曜日にグランドルフォークへ連れていきたいと思っている。その目的は、城を訪れその城のスタッフの説明を聞くことで、生徒のその地域の歴史に関する知識を広げることにある。先生らはどの城を2つ選ぶか。

　　①クレストベイル城とホルムステッド城
　　②クレストベイル城と王の城
　　③ローズバッハ城とホルムステッド城
　　④ローズバッハ城と王の城

城にスタッフがいるのは、クレストベイル城と王の城の2つである。

問4　40　②

お母さん・お父さん・4歳と8歳の子供2人は9月のある日にグランドルフォークにある城のうち1つを訪れようとしていて、良い芸術作品を見たいと思っている。いくらかかるか。

　　①14ユーロ
　　②17ユーロ
　　③20ユーロ
　　④25ユーロ

5歳以下の子供は無料なので、大人2人・子供1人の値段だけを考える。したがって、7×2＋3＝17ユーロになる。

グランドルフォークの城

クレストベイル城

この荒廃した13世紀の城は、グランドルフォークの北方の国境を守るために建てられ、現在研究者たちによって研究されている。日曜日を除く開城時期の間は、ガイドの人が、その研究が地元の歴史について何を明らかにするのかを説明する。

ホルムステッド城

ホルムステッド城は、12世紀に南方の国境地帯を守るために建てられ、16世紀に廃墟となった。入り口は標識によりその歴史がわかる。この城の広場は演奏にぴったりである。

王の城

11世紀にまで遡るが、王の城はその国の中では最も壮大な城の一つである。その多くの絵画と家具の収集品はその地域の景観を提供している。ガイドは毎日利用できる。

ローズバッハ城

城と呼ばれるが、これは完璧に保存された、純粋に家族の家として建設された15世紀の建造物である。月曜から金曜まで、ガイドが家族の歴史についての話をし、現代の彫刻の収集品を説明する。その部屋のいくつかは公共の催し物に利用できる。

	開城時間		入城料	
	月	時間	大人	子供（5〜16歳）＊
クレストベイル城	4月-8月	10：00-16：00	3ユーロ	1ユーロ
ホルムステッド城	4月-9月	10：00-17：00	5ユーロ	2ユーロ
王の城	4月-11月	10：00-18：00	7ユーロ	3ユーロ
ローズバッハ城	4月-7月	9：00-12：00	10ユーロ	5ユーロ

＊5歳以下の児童は入城料無料

H30　4 B

問1　37　④

ラルフ・ベアリソンは何に奮起させられてパパベアー料理教室をはじめましたか。

　　①彼は家族や友人が彼の料理の技術に嫉妬しているのを知っていた。
　　②彼は父親たちが料理にあまり興味を持っていないことを知っていた。
　　③彼は父親たちにプロの料理家になるための機会を与えたかった。
　　④彼は父親たちに素早く、美味しく、健康的な食事を調理することを教えたかった。

本文第3文を参照する。

問2　38　②

トニーはフランス料理コースに参加し値引き券を使うつもりである。また彼はエプロンとタオルのセットを学校から購入するつもりである。彼は総額いくら支払うか。

　　①270ドル　　②275ドル　　③285ドル　　④300ドル

フランス料理コースは250ドル。コース料理は値引き券により10％安くなり225ドル。エプロンセットは購入すると50ドルなので、総額は225＋50＝275ドル。

問3　39　③

エドは家族のために作れる料理の幅を広げたいと思っている。彼は週末と朝は自由な時間がない。どのコースを取る可能性が高いか。

　　①中華料理　　②イタリア料理
　　③日本料理　　④日曜日の家族朝食

①と④は週末に実施されるコースなので不可。②は午前中のコースなので朝に時間のとれないエドには向かない。したがって、③。

問4　40　④

パパベアー料理教室：お父さんのための料理コース

パパベアー料理教室はラルフ・ベアリソンにより1992年に設立されました。たくさんの父親が料理をすることを好んでいるにもかかわらず食事を準備する時間が充分にはもてないことがしばしばあると彼は認識していました。彼は美味しくて家族の健康に良い料理を短時間で作るという興味を分かち合いたいと思っています。パパベアー料理教室では、プロの料理人の指導の下で様々な料理を創作することができ、家族や友人から羨望の眼差しを受けることができます。以下の料理コースを5月第1週より開始します。

料理コース	曜日	時間	コース料金
イタリア料理	火曜	10時から12時	150ドル
フランス料理	水曜	9時から12時	250ドル
日本料理	木曜	15時から18時	250ドル
中華料理	土曜	17時から19時	200ドル
日曜日の家族朝食	日曜	8時から10時	150ドル

＊10歳から15歳のお子様はお一人様100ドルでお父様と日曜日の家族朝食コースにご参加いただけます。

▷全てのコースが10週間です。
▷料金は全ての材料を含んでいます。
▷包丁、フォークやスプーン、皿のような銀食器は学校がご準備いたします。

持参していただくもの
▷エプロンとタオル
　（毎週6ドルでエプロンとタオルのセットをレンタルいただくか、当方の店にて50ドルで新品のセットを購入いただくこともできます。）
▷お腹をすかせてくること！

設備や他の料理コースについての詳細はパパベアー料理教室のウェブサイトを御覧ください。

コース料金10％オフ　パパベアー料理教室

広告は ☐40 といっている。

①12歳の子供は日曜日のコースに無料で参加できる

②お父さんのための料理コースは3ヶ月以上続く予定である

③パパベアー料理教室は生徒に対して授業に材料を持参するように要求している

④パパベアー料理教室の生徒は作った料理を食べることができる

注意書きより子供一人の参加に付き100ドルかかるので①は誤り。全てのコースは10週間なので、②も誤り。また、材料は料金に含んでいるので③も誤り。

H29 ④B

問1 ☐39 ④

IAYPビデオ制作コンテストの目的は ☐39 を提供することである。

①同年代の新しい友人に出会う場所

②ビデオを制作するためのオーストラリアへの飛行機チケット

③パソコンでビデオを制作するための訓練

④若い人々の作品を展示する機会

書き出しの2文目に注目する。

問2 ☐40 ②

高校の野球チームのメンバーが海外の姉妹校からの選手との絆についての4分のビデオクリップを提出するつもりである。どのカテゴリーでエントリーをするべきか。

①カテゴリーA　　②カテゴリーB

③カテゴリーC　　④カテゴリーD

野球という点で考えるとA、絆つまり友情という点で考えるとBになる。4分のビデオなので5分以内のBとなる。

問3 ☐41 ④

以下のどれがこのコンテストの提出条件を満たしているか。

①若い日本人探偵主演の9分のミステリードラマ

②ラグビーの試合に向けて練習する生徒を取り上げた6分のビデオクリップ

③地方の映画祭で3位になった3分のビデオクリップ

④2017年10月30日にこのウェブサイトにアップロードされた3分のビデオクリップ

①はカテゴリーDだが7分を超えているので不可。②はカテゴリーAにあたるが、3分を超えているので不可。③は応募条件の3番めの初めての応募に反するので不可。

ビデオクリップコンテスト、エントリー募集

国際青年演出家協会（IAYP）は今年も毎年恒例のビデオ制作コンテストを開催することになりました。これは幅広い視聴者にあなたの作品を見ていただく素晴らしい機会です。25歳以下であればどなたでも参加できます。IAYPでは以下の4つのカテゴリーでご応募をお待ちしております。

	テーマ	最大時間
カテゴリーA	チームスポーツに関する題材	3分
カテゴリーB	友情に関連した題材	5分
カテゴリーC	真実に基づいた社会問題	5分
カテゴリーD	ドラマチックなエンディングのミステリー	7分

締切は2017年10月31日11：59（日本時間）。それぞれのカテゴリー上位3本が著名なビデオクリエイターによる委員会によって選ばれ、12月にこのウェブサイトに公開されます。総合優勝の一本には次回オーストラリアシドニーで開催されるIAYP協議会への招待チケットがあたえられます。この機会を逃さないで！ビデオカメラを引っ張り出して撮影を始めよう！

以下の手順を踏んでください。

▷ビデオを撮影し、あなたが選んだカテゴリーの適切な長さに合わせてパソコンで編集して下さい。

▷ ココ をクリックしてあなたについての詳細を記入しビデオをアップロードしてください。

ルール・条件

▷一人あるいは一団体につき一つのカテゴリーだけが選択できます。

▷締め切り前に送られたビデオのみが受け付けられます。

▷ビデオはオリジナルのもので初めて競技に提出されるものでなくてはなりません。

H28 ④B

問1 ☐39 ②

19歳のショップ店員のカズコは、美術館の活動に参加したいと思っているが、平日夜しか空いていない。どの活動を彼女は最も選ぶ可能性があるか。

①総合ツアー　　　　　②絵画教室

③写真ワークショップ　④ショートツアー

19歳なので【Adult】の欄をチェックしていく。平日で夜、つまり【pm】の遅い時間開催のものを探す。

問2 ☐40 ③

退職した夫婦と6歳の孫が週末午後の活動に一緒に参加したいと考えている。どの活動を彼らは選ぶ可能性が高く、全部でいくら払わなくてはいけないか。

①総合ツアー、20ドル　　②総合ツアー、40ドル

③ショートツアー、20ドル　④ショートツアー、28ドル

週末午後開催というところから①②は不適当。退職した夫婦は【Adult】なので一人10ドル、6歳の孫は【Child】に当たり【free】「無料」である。

問3 | **41** | ①

オクタゴン美術館

オクタゴン美術館（OMA）は絵画、彫刻、写真などの現代芸術の展示や企画を行っております。1972年にオクタゴン財団により設立されて以来、膨大な所蔵品を有すると同時に多くの常設展、また特別展、プロの芸術家や批評家による特別講義、学童を対象とした講義、専門家によるツアーガイドも開催しております。

入場料：5ドル/名（6歳以下のお子様－無料）

プログラム料金

ショートツアー (90分)	大人 (18歳以上)	10ドル	日に2回開催 午前9時 と 午後2時
	学生 (7歳から17歳)	8ドル	
	子供 (6歳以下)	無料	
包括ツアー (3時間)	大人 (18歳以上)	10ドル	火曜と土曜 午前10時
	学生 (7歳から17歳)	15ドル	
	子供 (6歳以下)	無料	
絵画教室 (90分)	大人 (18歳以上)	15ドル	月曜午後7時
	学生 (7歳から17歳)	8ドル	日曜午後7時
	子供 (6歳以下)	無料	水曜午前10時
写真 ワークショップ	大人 (18歳以上)	17ドル	日曜午後7時
	学生 (7歳から17歳)	12ドル	日曜午前10時

注

－ツアー、教室、ワークショップの料金には入場料金を含んでおります。
－ツアー、教室、ワークショップには少なくとも1週間前には事前に こちら よりご登録ください。
－隔週土曜日にOMAホールにおきましてゲストの講演者をお招きすると同時に大人の成人のお客様を対象に「アート・トーク」も開催しております。ご予約も追加料金も不要です。今月の予定につきましては、こちら をクリック。

ウェブサイトによると以下のうち、正しいものはどれ。

①「アート・トーク」に事前の予約は不要である。
②総合ツアーは毎日開催されている。
③入場料金はツアー料金に含まれていない。
④アマチュアの芸術家による講義がある。

注意事項の3番目第2文に予約も追加料金も不要とあるので①が正解。総合ツアーは火・土曜開催なので②は不適。注意事項の1番目に入場料金は含まれているとあるので③も不適当。④は最初の説明文の第2文に【lectures by professional artists and critics】とあるので、アマチュアの芸術家ではないので不適当。

グリーン国立公園キャンプ場ガイド

グリーン国立公園のキャンプ場は4月1日から11月30日まで開いています。

アプリコットキャンプ場

このキャンプ場から散歩道はグリーン山の頂上に続いています。頂上からの素晴らしい景色を楽しんでください。森の中にある自転車用道路でサイクリングを楽しむこともできます。

メープルキャンプ場

メープルキャンプ場はグリーン川に直接つながっています。魚釣りやボート、水泳のような活動をして楽しんでください。川のそばでキャンプファイヤーを楽しむこともできます。

オレンジキャンプ場

このキャンプ場はオレンジ湖のところにあり、快適なアウトドア体験を提供します。湖では水上スキーが人気です。他にも魚釣りや水泳、バードウォッチングなどの活動もあります。

ストーンヒルキャンプ場

松林がストーンヒルキャンプ場を囲んでいます。巨大な松の木が印象的です。森の中を自転車に乗ったりハイキングしたりすると、たくさんの野生動物を見ることができます。

キャンプ場情報

キャンプ場	タイプ	料金（1泊）	最大人数	最長泊数	施設案内	制限事項
アプリコット	テント(15)	$20	4	15泊	BG	－
メープル	テント(20)	$24	5	12泊	BG PG	－
オレンジ	特別客室(5)	$96	7	7泊	K E HS	ペット禁止
ストーンヒル	普通客室(10)	$32	8	14泊	E HS	花火禁止

料金＝1ヶ所あたりの料金（最大人数まで）；Max.＝最大

K キッチン, E 電気, BG バーベキューグリル HS 温水シャワー PG 運動場

問1 | **39** | ②

水上・水中活動が好きな人がウェブサイトを見ている。彼が最も興味を持ちそうなキャンプ場はどれか？

①アプリコットとメープルキャンプ場
②メープルとオレンジキャンプ場
③オレンジとストーンヒルキャンプ場
④ストーンヒルとアプリコットキャンプ場

川や湖での活動が楽しめるのはメープルとオレンジなので②が正しい。

問2 | **40** | ③

2人がグリーン国立公園で9泊する計画を立てている。彼らは自然を楽しみたいが、コンピュータを使うために電源が必要である。彼らが選びそうな場所に払わなければならない料金は1泊あたりいくらか？

①20ドル 　　②24ドル
③32ドル 　　④96ドル

電気が使用可能で、9泊できるのはストーンヒルのみなので③が正しい。

問3 | **41** | ①

4人家族がイヌを連れて4日のキャンプを計画している。彼らのキャンプ場への予算は3泊で100ドル以内である。彼らの旅行での一番の関心は国立公園でのバーベキューと自転車に乗ることである。この家族が最も選びそうなのは

どのキャンプ場か？
①アプリコット　　②メープル
③オレンジ　　　　④ストーンヒル

バーベキューとサイクリングを両方楽しめるのはアプリコットのみなので①が正しい。

H26　4 B

問1　39　②

<u>申し込みについて正しくないのは，次のうちどれか？</u>
①８月の間に申し込まなければならない。
②申し込みの時に，少なくとも16歳でなければならない。
③インターネットを通じて申し込まなければならない。
④申し込みは１回だけしかしてはいけない。

16歳以上でなければならないのは，申し込み時ではなくレース当日なので，②が間違い。

問2　40　①

<u>第26回のマラソンに参加し，レイクビルに住んでいる70歳の女性は，参加するのに　40　を支払わなければならない。</u>

　まず，レイクビルに住んでいるので，申し込み費はいらない。70歳は高齢者のカテゴリーなので，参加費は15ドル。ただし，前々回の第26回のマラソンに参加しているので，５ドル割引されるので，合計は15－5＝10ドル。

問3　41　④

<u>ウェブサイトによると，次のうちどれが正しいか？</u>
①申し込み費と参加費を現金で払うことができる。
②全ての問い合わせは，電話でしなければならない。
③受け入れられたかどうかは，オンラインで確認しなければならない。
④レースが終わるまでには，８時間ある。

支払いはクレジット決済のみなので，①は不適。下の方に，問い合わせのメールアドレスが載せられているので，②は不適。参加の可否は郵便で届くので，③は不適。レースは８時から16時までの８時間なので，④が正しい。

第28回　レイクビルマラソン
2015年２月26日

お申し込み
➤期限：2014年８月１日〜８月31日（期限を過ぎたものは，お受付けできません。）
➤レース当日に16歳以上であれば，どなたでもエントリーできます。
➤オンラインによる申し込みのみです。
➤お一人様につき，一回の申し込みしかできません。複数申し込まれた場合は，自動的に拒否されます。
➤虚偽の個人情報を記載したことが判明しますと，申し込みを取り消させていただきます。

選抜
➤申し訳ありませんが，レイクビル運動競技場の大きさの関係上，全ての方の申し込みをお受けすることはできません。
➤抽選で，15000人の走者に決定させていただきます。
➤申し込みされた方には，10月中旬ごろ，郵便で参加の可否をお知らせいたします。

お支払
➤オンラインによるクレジット決済のみです。
➤申し込み費はお返しできません。例外はございません。
➤参加費は抽選によって選ばれた方のみ必要です。

カテゴリー	申し込み費	参加費
未成年（16〜17歳）	15ドル	25ドル
成年（18〜64歳）	15ドル	50ドル
高齢者（65歳以上）	15ドル	15ドル

＊レイクビルに住んでいる方は，申し込み費が無料です！
＊＊直近２回のレイクビルマラソンのどちらかに参加された方は，５ドル割引します！

レースの日
➤受付：７時開始です。当日，全ての参加者は，写真付きの身分証明（例えば，免許証やパスポート）と参加通知書を提示してください。
➤レースのスケジュール：８時開始/16時終了（決められた時刻までにゴールできなかった走者は，走るのを止めなければなりません。）

お問い合わせは，marathondesk@lkve.com
申し込みはここをクリック

H25　4 B

問1　38　④

<u>スタジオのサービスについて正しいものはどれか。</u>
①客は撮影の１時間前に来店しなければならない。
②フレームは３色ある。
③写真は３営業日以内に送られる。
④スタッフが，客が素敵に見えるように手伝うこともある。

「当社のサービス（our service）」の１つ目に「スタイリストが髪セットとお化粧をお手伝いします」とあるので，④が適当。①の「１時間」は撮影にかかる時間であるので，①は不適。３種類あるのはフレームではなく写真のサイズであるので②も不適。また，「当社のサービス（our service）」の４つ目に写真は持ち帰りとあるので③も不適。

問2 　39　　③

会員ではない者が，同じ写真を個々に買うのではなく，Fantastic Package Planを利用するといくら安くなるか。

Fantastic Package Planは200ドルであり，この項目に，「大1枚，中2枚，財布サイズ8枚，2枚の複数写真シート，大用フレーム1つ」とある。また，大は1枚40ドル，中は1枚20ドル，財布サイズは1枚5ドル，複数写真シートは1枚50ドルであるので，Fantastic Package Planの内容を個々に買うと，$40 \times 1 + 20 \times 2 + 5 \times 8 + 50 \times 2 + 20 = 240$ドル。したがって$240 - 200 = 40$ドル安くなる。

問3 　40　　①

以下の記述のうち，正しいものはどれか。

①複数写真シートには5枚の写真を含めることができる。

②会員は年間費を40ドル払う必要がある。

③客は12月31日まで20周年記念割引を受けることができる。

④無料ギフトをもらうためには，Fantastic Club会員にならなければならない。

広告の表中に複数写真シートは「2枚から5枚の組み合わせ」とあるので，①は正しい。Fantastic Club会員の欄を見ると，40ドルは年会費ではなく入会費であるとわかるので②は不適。20周年記念は割引ではなく無料ギフトなので③も不適。④のように「会員にならなければならない」とはどこにもない。

Fantastic Photo Studio

家族写真専門

洗練された伝統的な写真も，より現代的な様式も気に入っていただけるでしょう。

当社のサービス

・スタイリストが髪セットとお化粧をお手伝いします。素敵に写りますよ！

・フルカラー，白黒，セピアの中から写真の様式をお選びいただけます。

・写真撮影はちょうど1時間です。

・お写真は3営業日以内に必ずお持ち帰りのご用意ができます。

本日ご予約のお電話を，555-456-0721へ。

基本写真タイプ（フレーム：各20ドル）

単一写真シート			複数写真シート
40ドル	20ドル	5ドル	50ドル
大	中	写真サイズ	2枚から5枚の組み合わせ

特典

200ドルのFantastic Package Planに含まれるもの

・大1枚，中2枚，財布サイズ8枚の単一写真シート

・お好きな複数写真シート2枚

・単一写真シート大用のフレームお1つ

Fantastic Club会員

たった40ドルで入会されると，Fantastic Package Planを含む，当社の全ての製品とサービスが2年間20パーセント割引となります。

記念祭スペシャル

Fantastic Photo Studio20周年記念をお手伝いください！12月31日までに撮影していただくと，無料ギフトを差し上げます。

② 〈事実・意見〉　　　問題 20p～

R4 　②A

あなたは未来のリーダー養成のサマープログラムに参加していて，イギリスの大学のキャンパスで行われています。あなたはコースの課題ができるように図書館に関する情報を読んでいます。

アバーマウス大学図書館
開館時間　午前8時から午後9時まで
2022年配布資料

図書館カード：学生証は，図書館利用カードとコピー機利用カードを兼ねています。ウェルカムパックに入っています。

本を借りる
本は一度に最大8冊を7日間借りることができます。本を借りるには受付に行ってください，2階にあります。本が期限までに返却されなかった場合，本が返却された日から3日間は図書館の本を借りることができません。

コンピューターを使う
インターネットに接続されたコンピューターは2階の正面玄関のそばにあるコンピューターワークステーションにあります。学生は自分のノートパソコンやタブレットを図書館に持ち込むことができますが，3階の学習室でのみ使用することができます。学生は静かに学習し，また，友人のために席を確保しないようにしてください。

図書館オリエンテーション
毎週火曜の午前10時に，4階の閲覧室で20分間の図書館オリエンテーションが開催されます。詳細は受付の職員までお問い合わせください。

過去の学生からのコメント
・図書館オリエンテーションがとても良かったです。資料も素晴らしかったです！
・学習室はとても混みあうことがあります。席を確保するためにできるだけ早く行きましょう！
・図書館内のWi-Fiはとても遅いですが，隣のコーヒーショップのWi-Fiはよいです。ちなみに，図書館の中にはいかなる飲み物も持ち込むことは出来ません。
・受付の職員は私の質問にすべて答えてくれました。何か助けが必要であれば行ってみてください！
・1階には図書館のビデオを見るためのテレビがあります。ビデオを見るときは，自分のイヤホンやヘッドホンを使う必要があります。テレビの隣にはコピー機があります。

※イギリスの大学の話なのでイギリス英語が使われていることに注意。

「プログラム」英：programme　　⇔米：program

「1階，2階」英：ground floor, first floor⇔米：first floor, second floor

問1　図書館でできることは　6　の2つです。

　A　コーヒーショップからコーヒーを持ってくること

　B　学習室で他の人のために席を確保すること

　C　3階にあるコピー機を使うこと

　D　コピーをするために学生証を使うこと

　E　学習室で自分のノートパソコンを使うこと

　①AとB　　②AとC　　③BとE

　④CとD　　⑤DとE

過去の学生からのコメントの3つ目に図書館の中にはいかなる飲み物も持ち込むことは出来ませんとあり，コーヒーの持ち込みはできず，Aは不適。コンピューターを使う第3文に「reserve seats for friends：友人のために席を確保する」ことが禁止事項となっており，選択肢の「save seats for others：他人のために席を確保する」はこの書き換えであるから，Bは不適。コピー機の場所についての記載はなくCは不適。図書館利用カードの説明に学生証が図書館利用カードとコピー機利用カードを兼ねていると書かれてお

り、Dは適切。パソコンを使うことについての第2文に学生は自分のノートパソコンやタブレットを図書館に持ち込むことができますが、3階の学習室でのみ使用することができます。とあるのでこれがEと一致する。よって、正解は⑤。

問2　あなたは図書館の正面玄関にいて、図書館オリエンテーションに行きたい。あなたは　7　必要がある。
　①1つ下の階に降りる　　②1つ上の階に上がる
　③2つ上の階に上がる　　④同じ階にいる

図書館オリエンテーションの第1文に図書館オリエンテーションは4階の閲覧室で行われるとあり、コンピューターを使う第1文に2階正面玄関とあるので、正面玄関は2階にあることがわかる。2階から4階に行くためには2つ上の階に上がらなければならないので、正解は③。

問3　図書館の正面玄関の近くに　8　。
　①コンピューターワークステーションはある
　②閲覧室はある
　③学習室はある
　④テレビはある

コンピューターを使う第1文に「2階の正面玄関のそばにあるコンピューターワークステーション」とあり、選択肢では「by：～のそばに」を「near：～の近くに」と言い換えている。よって、①が適切。

問4　8月2日に3冊の本を借りて、8月10日に返したとすると、あなたは　9　。
　①8月10日にさらに8冊の本を借りることができた
　②8月10日にさらに7冊の本を借りることができた
　③8月13日より前に本を借りることができなかった
　④8月17日より前に本を借りることができなかった

本を借りることの説明 第1文より、1度に8冊の本を7日間借りることができ、第3文より期限までに返さなかったときは返した日から3日間は本を借りられないことがわかる。8月2日に3冊の本を借りて、7日以上経過した8月10日に本を返しているので、8月10日から3日間、すなわち8月12日まで本を借りることができない。beforeはその日を含まないため、③は8月13日よりも前、すなわち8月12日まで本を借りることができないことになる。よって、正解は③。

問5　卒業生が述べた**事実**は　10　である。
　①ビデオを見るときはヘッドホンかイヤホンが必要である
　②図書館は午後9時まであいている
　③図書館のオリエンテーションの配布資料は素晴らしい
　④学習室はしばしば空いている

過去の学生のコメントの5つ目にビデオを見るときは、自分のイヤホンやヘッドホンを使う必要があります。とあるので、①が正解。

R4　2B

あなたは学校の英語新聞の編集者です。イギリスから来た交換留学生であるデビッドが、その新聞に記事を書きました。

あなたは動物が好きですか？イギリスは動物好きな国として知られており、イギリスの家庭の5軒に2軒がペットを飼っています。これは半分以上の家庭がペットを飼っているアメリカよりも低い数字です。しかし、オーストラリアが最もペットを飼っている家庭の割合が高いのです！

なぜそうなのでしょうか？オーストラリアで行われた調査結果が私たちにいくつかの解答を与えてくれます。

> ペットの飼い主は、ペットと暮らす利点として以下のものを挙げています。
> → ペットがくれる愛情、幸福、友情（90％）
> → もう一人家族がいるような感覚（犬や猫の飼い主の60％以上）
> → ペットがもたらす幸せな時間。ほとんどの飼い主が毎日3時間から4時間を「毛皮のある赤ちゃん」と一緒に過ごし、犬や猫の飼い主の半数以上は彼らと一緒に眠ります！
> 一つの欠点は、ペットは飼い主の外出中は世話をされなければならないことです。彼らの世話をしてくれる人を調達するのは飼い主にとって難しいかもしれません、ですから、25％の飼い主が休日や旅行にペットを連れていきます。

これらの結果はペットを飼うことは良いことであると示しています。一方、日本に来てから、私は空間、時間、費用といった別の問題を見てきました。ただ、私は狭いアパートにペットと暮らすことに満足している人がいることも知っています。最近、小さな豚がペットとして人気になっているということを聞きました。散歩に連れて行く人もいて、それは楽しいに違いありません、しかし、家の中で豚を飼うことは簡単なことなのだろうかと疑問に思います。

※デビッドはイギリスからの留学生なのでイギリス英語が使われていることに注意。
「調達する」英：organise⇔米：organize
「アパート」英：flat　　⇔米：apartment

問1　ペットを飼っている家庭の割合について、順位の**高い方から低い方に**示しているものはどれか。　11
　①オーストラリア ― イギリス ― アメリカ
　②オーストラリア ― アメリカ ― イギリス
　③イギリス ― オーストラリア ― アメリカ
　④イギリス ― アメリカ ― オーストラリア
　⑤アメリカ ― オーストラリア ― イギリス
　⑥アメリカ ― イギリス ― オーストラリア

第1段落第2文にイギリスは5軒に2軒とあり、同第3文でイギリスはアメリカより少ないこと、同第3文でオーストラリアが最も多いことがわかる。よって、②が正解。

問2　デビッドの報告によれば、ペットを飼うことのメリットの1つは　12　ということである。
　①お金を節約できる　　②長い間眠れる
　③人気者になれる　　④生活がより楽しくなる

オーストラリアの調査結果から愛情や幸せな時間などを得られることがわかるので正解は④。

問3　この調査からわかることを最もよく反映している発言は $\boxed{13}$ である。

①私は猫と一緒にテレビを見るとき居心地がよくない。
②私は毎日約３時間ペットと過ごしている。
③たいていのペットは車で旅行するのが好きだ。
④ペットは自分の部屋を必要としている。

オーストラリアの調査結果のペットを飼う利点の３つ目にほとんどの飼い主が毎日３時間から４時間を「fur babies：毛皮のある赤ちゃん」と一緒に過ごすとあり、これはペットのことであるから、正解は②。

問4　デビッドの日本でペットを飼うことについての意見をもっともよくまとめたものはどれか。 $\boxed{14}$

①日本でペットを飼うことは面倒ではない。
②人々はペットを飼うことをやめるかもしれない。
③ペットの飼い主はより多くの家族がいる。
④家の中で喜んでペットを飼う人もいる。

本文の第３段落第３文に狭いアパートでペットと暮らすことに満足している人がいるとあり、選択肢の「happy to keep pets inside their homes」は「are content living in small flats with pets：狭いアパートでペットと暮らすことに満足している人」の書き換え。よって、正解は④。

問5　この記事のタイトルとして最も適切なものはどれか。 $\boxed{15}$

①あなたのペットはあなたのベッドで寝ますか。
②ペットを飼うことは我々に何を与えてくれますか。
③あなたはどんなペットを飼っていますか。
④ペットの豚を飼ってみませんか？

記事の第１段落ではペットを飼っている家庭の割合、第２段落の調査ではペットを飼うことによる利点、第３段落では日本におけるペットをめぐる現状について書いてあり、第２段落について書かれている②が正解。

R3（追試）２A

あなたはイギリスでの環境キャンペーンの一環としてクラスメートが答えた使い捨てのボトルと再利用可能なボトルについての調査結果を読んでいます。

質問1：週にどれくらいの使い切りボトルの飲み物を買いますか？

ボトルの数	生徒数	週間小計
0	2	0
1	2	2
2	2	4
3	3	9
4	4	16
5	9	45
6	0	0
7	7	49
合計	29	125

質問2：あなたは自分の再利用可能なボトルを持っていますか？

回答要旨	生徒数	生徒の割合
はい、持っています。	3	10.3
はい、ですが使っていません。	14	48.3
いいえ、持っていません。	12	41.4
合計	29	100.0

質問3：もし、再利用可能なボトルを使っていないとしたら、理由は何ですか？

回答要旨	生徒の数
再利用可能ボトルを洗うのに時間がかかりすぎる。	24
使い捨てボトルの方が便利である。	17
多くの香り付きの飲み物が使い捨てボトルで飲むことができる。	14
使い捨てボトルを買うのにそれほどお金がかからない。	10
学校の自動販売機で飲み物を買うことができる。	7
再生利用可能ボトルは重すぎると感じる。	4
自宅に沢山の使い捨てボトルがある。	3
使い捨てボトルの水は未開封で長期保存が可能である。	2
（その他の理由）	4

問1　質問1の結果は $\boxed{6}$ を示している。

①生徒はそれぞれ平均して週に４本より少ない使い捨てボトルを買っている
②多くの生徒は週に２本より少ないボトルしか買わない
③半分以上の生徒が週に少なくとも５本のボトルを買っている
④生徒は週に125本より多くのボトルを買っている

質問1の表より、週に５本のボトルを買っているのは９＋７＝16人で生徒数の29人の半分よりも多い。よって、正解は③。

問2　質問2の結果は半分より多くの生徒が $\boxed{7}$ ことを示している。

①自分の再利用可能ボトルを持っていない
②自分の再生利用可能ボトルを持っている
③自分の再生利用可能ボトルを持っているが使っていない
④自分の再生利用ボトルを使っている

質問2の表より、再生利用可能ボトルを持っているのは３＋14＝17人で生徒数の半分より多い。よって、正解は②。

問3　質問3でクラスメートが述べている意見は、 $\boxed{8}$ である。

①家に使い捨てのボトルの備蓄を持っている生徒もいる
②学校に飲み物を買うための自動販売機がある
③再利用可能ボトルを洗うのに時間がかかる
④未開封の使い捨てボトルの水は長持ちする

質問3の表より、①②④は事実であり、意見にあたるのは③のみ。よって、正解は③。

問4　質問3でクラスメートが述べている事実は、使い捨てボトルは $\boxed{9}$ ということだ。

①学校で買うことができる

②使うのに便利

③持ち歩くのに十分に軽い

④買うのはそれほど高くない

質問3の表より、②③④は意見であり、事実にあたるのは①のみ。よって、正解は①。

問5 あなたのクラスメートが再利用可能ボトルを買わない理由で最も可能性が高いものはどれか？ 10

　①家に保管されている使い捨てボトルの飲み物がたくさんある。

　②利用できる飲み物の種類が少ない。

　③クラスメートにとって高価である。

　④それらは取り扱いが面倒である。

質問3の表より、回答で最も多いのは「It takes too much time to wash reusable bottles. : 再生利用ボトルを洗うのに時間がかかりすぎる。」であり、選択肢では「troublesome to deal with : 取り扱いが面倒である」と書き換えられている。よって、正解は④。

R3（追試） 2 B

あなたはイギリスで行われるどのサマープログラムに参加するか決める必要があり、そのため、講座情報と講座に関する以前の生徒のコメントを読んでいます。

コミュニケーションと異文化間学

クリストファー・ベネット博士　　　2021年8月3日から31日

bennet.christpher@ire-u.ac.uk　　火曜日と金曜日

電話：020-9876-1234　　　　　　午後1時から午後2時30分

オフィスアワー：予約のみ　　　　9回授業－1単位

講座の説明： 私たちは異文化を学び、異文化を持つ人々とのコミュニケーションの取り方を学びます。このコースでは、学生は異文化間の問題への対処方法の考えを発表する必要があります。

目標： この講座の修了後あなたは次のことができるようになるはずです

－異文化間の人間関係について理解

－異文化間の問題の解決方法を発表

－議論や発表を通してあなたの意見を表現

教科書： スミス．S（2019）．異文化学　ニューヨーク：DNC社．

評価： 合格するには全部で60％が必要

－2度の発表：90％（それぞれ45％）

－出席：10％

コースの受講者の評価（87の評価）　★★★★★（平均：4.89）

コメント

☺この授業を受講しましょう！クリスは素晴らしい先生です。彼はとても賢明で、親切です。この講座は少し努力を必要としますが、合格するには十分簡単です。あなたは文化の違いについて多くのことを学ぶでしょう。私のアドバイスは毎回の授業に参加することでしょう。よい発表をするのを本当に助けになりました。

問1 この講座であなたは何をするつもりですか？ 11

　①文化についての様々なテーマについて話し合う。

　②多くの異なる国を訪問する。

　③人間の関係についての映画を見る。

④文化についての最終レポートを書く。

目標の3つ目に議論や発表を通して意見を表現できるようにするとあるので、授業で議論を行うことがわかる。よって、正解は①。

問2 この授業は 12 生徒を対象としている。

　①異文化間の問題に興味がある

　②良い発表ができる

　③イギリスを観光するのが好きな

　④英語を話すことを学ぶ必要がある

講座の説明第2文に異文化間の問題への対処方法の考えを発表する必要がありますとある。よって、正解は①。

問3 ベネット博士に関する**事実**は 13 である。

　①彼は優れた教える技術を持っている

　②彼はよい指導者である

　③彼はこの講座の担当である

　④彼がこの講座を努力が必要なものにしている

①②④は意見であり、③のみが事実である。よって、正解は③。

問4 この講座に関して表現された**意見**は 14 である。

　①単位をとるのはそれほど難しくない

　②多くの生徒がこの講座に満足している

　③出席が最終的な成績に含まれる

　④生徒は週に2回授業がある

②③④は事実であり、①のみが以前の選択肢の「not so difficult to get a credit : 単位をとるのはそれほど難しくない」が受講生のコメントの「easy enough to pass : 合格するには十分簡単」の書き換え。②は評価を伴うものなので意見のように見えるが、以前の受講生の評価をみると5段階評価で平均が4.89となっており、多くの生徒がこの講座に満足していることは事実と言える。

問5 この講座に合格するためにあなたは何をしなければなりませんか？ 15

　①毎回の授業に来て議論に参加する。

　②異文化間の問題を探し、解決方法について議論する。

　③異文化間の問題に関するよい発表を行う。

　④ベネット博士のオフィスアワーの予約をする。

評価を見ると60％で合格とあり、評価の90％が2度の発表とある。よって、正解は③。

R3（本試）2A

あなたはあるイギリスの学園祭のバンド大会を運営する生徒として、順位を理解し説明するために、3人の審査員の点数とコメントをすべて調べています。

審査員の最終的な平均点

バンド名＼評価	演奏 (5.0)	歌唱 (5.0)	曲のオリジ ナリティ (5.0)	合計 (15.0)
グリーン・フォレスト	3.9	4.6	5.0	13.5
サイレント・ヒル	4.9	4.4	4.2	13.5
マウンテン・ペア	3.9	4.9	4.7	13.5
サウザンド・アンツ	(演奏せず)			

審査員の個別のコメント

ホッブズ氏	サイレント・ヒルは素晴らしい演奏者で、彼らは本当に聴衆とつながっているように見えました。マウンテン・ペアの歌唱は素晴らしかったです。私はグリーン・フォレストのオリジナル曲が好きです。見事でした！
リー氏	サイレント・ヒルは素晴らしい演奏を聴かせてくれました。彼らの音楽に対する聴衆の反応は驚くものでした。サイレント・ヒルは人気が出ると心から思います！マウンテン・ペアは素晴らしい声を持っていますが、ステージでの彼らはわくわくするものではありませんでした。グリーン・フォレストは素敵な新曲を演奏してくれましたが、彼らにはもっと練習が必要だと思います。
ウェルズ氏	グリーン・フォレストは新曲です。私はとても気に入りました！大ヒットする可能性があると思います！

審査員の共通の評価 (ホッブズ氏による要約)

それぞれのバンドの合計得点は同じですが、それぞれのバンドは大きく異なっています。リー氏と私にとって最も重要な要素は演奏だということで意見が一致しています。ウェルズ氏もまた同意見でした。それゆえに、1位は簡単に決定することができます。
2位と3位を決定するために、ウェルズ氏は歌唱力よりも曲のオリジナリティが重要であるべきだと提案しました。リー氏と私はこの意見に賛成しました。

問1 審査員の最終的な平均点によると、どのバンドが最もうまく歌ったか。 [6]
①グリーン・フォレスト　　②マウンテン・ペア
③サイレント・ヒル　　　　④サウザンド・アンツ

「sang the best：最もうまく歌った」のは「Singing：歌唱」の点数が最も高いマウンテン・ペアなので、正解は②。

問2 肯定的なコメントと批判的なコメントの両方をしたのはどの審査員か。 [7]
①ホッブズ氏　　②リー氏
③ウェルズ氏　　④誰もいない

表によると、ホッブズ氏とウェルズ氏は肯定的なコメントのみだが、リー氏はマウンテン・ペアに対して素晴らしい声を持っているが、ステージはわくわくしなかった、グリーン・フォレストに対して素敵な新曲だが、もっと練習が必要だと、肯定的なコメントと批判的なコメントを両方しているので、正解は②。

問3 審査員の個別のコメントからわかるひとつの**事実**は [8] である。
①すべての審査員がグリーン・フォレストの曲をほめた
②グリーン・フォレストはもっと練習が必要である
③マウンテン・ペアはとても上手に歌うことができる
④サイレント・ヒルは将来有望である

表より、②・③・④はリー氏やホッブズ氏の意見で、**事実**は全員がグリーンフォレストの曲をほめているという①のみなので、正解は①。

問4 審査員のコメントや共通の評価からわかるひとつの**意見**は [9] である。
①評価されたそれぞれのバンドは同じ合計得点をつけられた
②ウェルズ氏のオリジナリティに関する提案は賛成された
③サイレント・ヒルは本当に聴衆とつながっていた
④審査員のコメントが順位を決めた

表より、①・②・④はいずれも事実で、**意見**はホッブズ氏の意見が書かれた③のみなので、正解は③。

問5 審査員の共通の評価に基づいた最終順位は以下のうち、どれか。 [10]

	1位	2位	3位
①	グリーン・フォレスト	マウンテン・ペア	サイレント・ヒル
②	グリーン・フォレスト	サイレント・ヒル	マウンテン・ペア
③	マウンテン・ペア	グリーン・フォレスト	サイレント・ヒル
④	マウンテン・ペア	サイレント・ヒル	グリーン・フォレスト
⑤	サイレント・ヒル	グリーン・フォレスト	マウンテン・ペア
⑥	サイレント・ヒル	マウンテン・ペア	グリーン・フォレスト

共通の評価によると、「それぞれのバンドの合計点数は同じである」が、「演奏がバンドで最も重要な要素である」、「歌唱力よりも曲のオリジナリティが重要とすべき」との意見の一致がなされている。よって、1位は演奏の点数が最も高いサイレント・ヒル。次に、残りの2バンドのうち、より曲のオリジナリティの点数が高いグリーン・フォレストが2位、残るマウンテン・ペアが3位となる。よって正解は⑤。

R3（本試）②B

あなたは現在交換留学生として学んでいるイギリスの学校で、学校方針の変更について耳にしました。あなたはオンライン掲示板で方針についての議論を読んでいます。

新しい学校方針＜2020年9月21日投稿＞
宛先：P.E.ベルガー
差出人：K.ロバーツ

ベルガー先生へ

　全校生徒を代表して、セント・マークス校へようこそ。あなたは企業出身の初の校長と聞いておりますので、あなたの経験が学校の役に立つことを期待しています。

　あなたが提案している放課後の活動スケジュールの変更について1つの懸念をお伝えしたいと思います。節電が重要であることは理解していますし、これから暗くなるのが早くなるでしょう。これがスケジュールを1時間半短くした理由でしょうか？セント・マークス校の生徒は勉強と放課後の活動の両方に真剣に取り組んでいます。多くの生徒がこれまで通り午後6時まで学校にいたいと私に言ってきています。それゆえに、突然の方針変更についてもう一度考え直してほしいと思っています。

敬具
ケン・ロバーツ
生徒会長

返信：新しい学校方針＜2020年9月22日投稿＞
宛先：K.ロバーツ
差出人：P.E.ベルガー

ケンへ

　親切な投稿に深く感謝します。あなたはいくつかの重要な懸念、特に光熱費と学校活動に関する生徒の意見について述べました。

　新しい方針は節電とは何の関係もありません。この決定は2019年の警察の報告に基づいてなされました。その報告によれば、重大犯罪が5％増加し、私たちの街の治安が悪くなっています。私は生徒たちを守りたいので、暗くなる前に家に帰ってほしいのです。

敬具
P.E.ベルガー
校長

問1　ケンは新しい方針は　11　と思っている。
　①生徒たちにもっと勉強させることができる
　②学校の安全性を改善できるかもしれない
　③すぐに導入されるべきだ
　④放課後の活動の時間を減らすだろう

ケンの投稿の2段落に「あなたが提案している放課後の活動スケジュールの変更」、「スケジュールを1時間半短くした」とあり、④と一致する。よって、正解は④。

問2　ケンの掲示板への投稿に記載されているひとつの**事実**は　12　。
　①方針についてもっと議論が必要である
　②校長の経歴は学校を改善している
　③学校は生徒の活動について考えるべきだ
　④新しい方針を歓迎しない生徒がいる

ケンの投稿の2段落に「多くの生徒がこれまで通り午後6時まで学校にいたいと私に言ってきています」とあり、これは④と一致する**事実**である。よって正解は④。

問3　この方針の狙いが節電だと考えているのは誰か。　13
　①ベルガー先生　　②ケン　　③市　　④警察

ケンの投稿2段落に「節電が重要であることは理解しています」、「これがスケジュールを1時間半短くした理由でしょうか？」とあるので、節電が狙いだと考えているのはケン。よって正解は②。

問4　ベルガー先生は　14　という**事実**を新しい方針の根拠としている。
　①早く家に帰ることは重要である
　②街の安全性は低下している
　③学校は電気を節約しなければならない
　④生徒は保護を必要としている

①・④はベルガー先生の意見なので不適。ベルガー先生の投稿の2段落に「この決定は2019年の警察の報告に基づいて」おり、「重大犯罪が5％増加し、私たちの街の治安が悪くなっています」とあり、警察の報告に基づく**事実**である。よって正解は②。

問5　ケンが新しい方針に反対することを助けるために何を調査すべきか？　15
　①犯罪発生率と特定の地域との関連性
　②学校のエネルギーの予算と電気代
　③学校活動の長さに対する予算
　④放課後活動をしている生徒の勉強時間

問4にあるように治安の悪化が方針変更の理由であり、これに対する反論をする必要があるので、犯罪発生率と特定の地域との関連性を調べるべきであり、正解は①。

H30（試行調査２回）　②A

　あなたは学校の料理クラブのメンバーで、なにか異なるものを作りたいと思っています。ウェブサイトで、あなたは良さそうな料理のレシピを見つけました。

簡単なオーブンレシピ
ウェブサイトで評価されたオーブンで焼く料理トップ10のうちの１つを紹介します。あなたはこの料理がヘルシーで満足の行くものだとわかるでしょう。
肉とじゃがいものパイ
材料（４人前）
A　玉ねぎ１玉　人参２本　牛ミンチ500g
　　小麦粉大さじ２　トマトペースト大さじ１
　　ウスターソース大さじ１　サラダ油大さじ１
　　出汁大さじ２　塩コショウ

B　茹でたじゃがいも３つ　バター40g

C　スライスチーズ
手順
ステップ１：Aを作る
１．野菜を小さく切り、油を熱し５分炒める。
２．肉を入れ色が変わるまで炒める。
３．小麦粉を入れ２分かき混ぜる。
４．出汁、ウスターソース、トマトペーストを入れる。約30分炒める。
５．塩コショウで味をつける。

ステップ２：Bを作る
１．その間、じゃがいもを薄切りにする。
２．フライパンを熱し、バターを溶かす。じゃがいもを入れ３分炒める。

ステップ３：A、B、Cを混ぜ合わせ、焼く。
１．オーブンを200℃まで熱する。
２．Aをオーブン皿にいれ、Bで覆い、Cを一番上に置く。
３．10分焼く。熱い状態で出す。

～～～～～～～～～～～～～～～～

レビューとコメント
cooking@master　2018年１月15日15：14
これは本当に美味しいです！雪の日にはぴったりです。
Seaside Kitchen　2018年２月３日10：03
私の子供たちはこの料理が大好きです。作るのは全く難しくなく、私は子どもたちに何度も作りました。

問１　もしあなたが　6　と思うなら、このレシピは良いでしょう。
　①お昼ごはんにチキンを料理したい
　②甘いものが食べたい
　③寒い日に温かい料理を楽しみたい
　④熱を使わず素早い料理を準備したい
コメントに「雪の日にぴったり」とあるので、③が正解。

問２　手順に従うと、その料理は約　7　以内で食べる準備ができるはずです。
　①30分　　②１時間　　③20分　　④２～３時間
Aには５＋２＋30＝37分、Bには３分、Cには10分かかるので50分かかります。よって②が正解。

問３　生の人参が嫌いな人は　8　ので、この料理を食べるかもしれません。
　①人参が使われていない
　②たくさんの種類のスパイスが使われている
　③人参が調理されている
　④人参がとても新鮮なので

Aで人参が炒められているため、③が正解。

問４　ウェブサイトによると、このレシピに関する１つの**事実**（意見ではなく）は　9　だということです。
　①ウェブサイト上では高く評価されている
　②作るのが簡単である
　③パーティーに持っていくのに完璧である
　④とてもおいしい
「事実」とあるので、レビューにある意見は選ばないように。よって、正解は①。

問５　ウェブサイトによると、このレシピに関する１つの**意見**（事実ではなく）は　10　ということです。
　①親が何回もこの料理を作ってくれた
　②作るのが簡単
　③友達と料理することは楽しい
　④レシピは有名な料理人によってつくられた
「意見」はレビューを参考にすればよい。よって、正解は②。

H30（試行調査２回）　②B

　あなたの英語の先生が、来週の授業でのディベートの準備の役に立つ記事をくれました。コメントが１つ載っているこの記事の一部分が下に示されています。

フランスの学校には携帯がない
パリ、トレイシー・ウォルフによる記事
2017年12月11日午後４：07

フランス政府は2018年９月より、学生が学校で携帯を使用することを禁止するつもりである。学生は、携帯を学校に持ってくるのは許可されるが、学校にいる間は特別な許可がなければどんなときでもそれらを使うことは許可されないようである。この規則は、その国の初等学校と中等学校にいる全生徒に適応されるであろう。

ジーンミシェル・ブランカーは、フランスの文部大臣であるが、「近頃、学生が休憩時間にあまり遊ばなくなった。彼らはスマートフォンの前にただいるだけであり、教育的な視点から見て、それは問題である」と発言した。彼はまた「携帯は緊急時に必要とされるかもしれないが、彼らの使い方は、いくぶんか制御されなければならない」とも言った。

しかしながら、すべての親がこの規則に喜んでいるわけではない。何人かの親は「人は時代とともに生きなければいけない。子どもたちに、昔の子どもたちのときと同じようにさせようと強いるのは意味がない」と言った。さらには、他の親は「誰がその携帯を集めて、それをどこに保管しておくのか。持ち主にどうやって返すのか。もしすべての学校が、子どもたちが携帯を保管するためのロッカーを提供したら、巨額のお金が必要となるだろう」と付け加えた。

21のコメント

最新
ダニエル・マッカーシー　19歳
2017年12月19日午後６：11
フランスよくやった！学校は生徒たちに、計算の仕方を学ばせようとしていません。学校で学ぶべきことは他にたくさんあります。若い人々は、他の人とどうやって付き合っていくかというような社会的能力を育んでいく必要があります。

問１　記事で説明されている規則によると、フランスの初等中等学校の学生は　11　ことは許可されていない。
　①親に携帯代を払ってくれるように頼む
　②携帯を学校に持ってくる

③卒業後まで携帯を持つ

④特別な場合を除いて、学校で携帯を使う

本文3行目に、「特別な許可がなければどんなときでもそれらを使うことは許可されない」とあるので、正解は④。

問2　あなたの班は「学校での携帯の使用は制限されるべきである」という議題に賛成するでしょう。その記事の中で、あなたの班の役に立つ1つの意見（事実ではなく）は　12　ということでしょう。

①学生が授業中に勉強に集中することが必要である

②学生は授業と授業の間に友達と遊ぶべきである

③政府は学校での携帯の使用に関する新しい規則を施行するだろう

④長時間携帯を使うことは学生の目に害を与えるかもしれない

本文6行目に「近頃、学生が休憩時間にあまり遊ばなくなった」とあるので、正解は②。

問3　他の班はその議題に反対するでしょう。その記事の中で、その班の役に立つ1つの意見（事実ではなく）は　13　ということでしょう。

①携帯の使用をどのように制御するかを学生に教えることがより良い

②学生は日々の会話のために携帯を使うべきである

③学生の携帯を保管するための費用はとても高くなるだろう

④その規則はその国の初等中等学校の生徒全員に適応されるであろう

本文15行目に、「子どもたちが携帯を保管するためのロッカーを提供したら、巨額のお金が必要となるだろう」とあるので、正解は③。

問4　その記事の第3段落にある「人は時代とともに生きなければいけない」とは、人々が　14　べきだと言うことを意味します。

①いつ生きているかによって生活様式は変わる

②人気の傾向にかかわらず自分自身のやり方で生きる

③子供時代の記憶を思い出す

④学校に遅れないようにする

この段落では、昔は学校で携帯を使うことが珍しかったが、今では携帯は日常生活では必要なものであるので、学校も携帯を使えるようにすることは当たり前だ、ということが言いたいのであろう。よって、正解は①。

問5　彼のコメントによると、ダニエル・マッカーシーはその記事で述べられている規則に　15　。

①関する特別な危険は持っていない

②部分的に賛成している

③非常に賛成している

④非常に反対している

最後のコメントのところに、「よくやった！」とある。よって、正解は③。

H29（試行調査2回）　2 A

あなたは外国を旅行し、インターネットで食べる場所を見つけようとしています。以下にあるのは、レストランを訪れたことのある人々によって書かれたレビューです。

シロウのラーメン　★★★★☆　　ブーツ（3週間前）
イチオシ：チャーシュー麺。安いし、混んでいて、とてもうるさい。とてもカジュアルです。食べている間は急いでいるように感じました。開店時間は午後5時から午前6時。

アニーのキッチン　★★★☆☆　　キャリー（2週間前）
様々な雰囲気の中にいて、アニーのキッチンは失望させませんでした。メニューは世界中の料理が載っていて、13ページにわたる驚くほど長いものでした。正直、メニューを読むだけで25分かかりました。不幸なことに、料理が出てくるのはとても遅かったです。シェフのその日の料理は素晴らしかったのですが、値段はカジュアルスタイルのレストランにしては少し高かったです。

ジョニーのハット　★★★☆☆　　メイソン（2日前）
たくさん食べたいときにモッテコイです。でも、ちょっとの間待つ必要があるかもしれません。
★★★★★　　ルーズベルト（5日前）
ステーキファンにとって、ここは最高です！シェフがどの客の好みにも合わせてステーキ料理を準備してくれます。私のお気に入りは、カウボーイプレートで、完璧です！
★☆☆☆☆　　ケンちゃん（2週間前）
悲しいことに、平均以下なので、もう一度行こうとは思いません。ステーキは調理するのが長すぎる！魚料理にもがっかりしました。

問1　もしあなたが　6　ときなら、シロウのラーメンを訪れるだろうと思います。

①会話するのに静かな場所を探している

②夜中に空腹である

③フォーマルな食事をする必要がある

④カジュアルなランチを食べたい

開店時間が午後5時から午前6時なので、夜中に空腹であれば食事をすることができる。よって、正解は②。

問2　もしあなたが　7　ときなら、アニーのキッチンを訪れるだろうと思います。

①外で食事をしたい

②暇な時間がたくさんあるなら

③早く朝食を済ませなければならない

④安い料理を食べたい

メニューを読むのに25分もかかるというコメントがある。よって、正解は②。

問3　ジョニーのハットについての意見は、全員　8　でした。

①異なるもの　　　　②好意的

③否定的　　　④中立的

1つ目は、量と時間について。2つ目は、ステーキメニューについて。3つ目は、メニューと時間に対しての否定的な意見。3人の意見は全て異なる。よって、正解は①。

問4 レビューによると、以下のうちどれが個人的な意見ではなく、事実であるか。（複数回答可）　9
　①アニーのキッチンはたくさんの国々の料理を提供している。
　②ジョニーのハットはシロウのラーメンよりも静かではない。
　③ジョニーのハットは魚料理も提供している。
　④ジョニーのハットのシェフは仕事が得意である。
　⑤アニーのキッチンでのシェフの今日の料理は、最高である。
　⑥アニーのキッチンのメニューは素晴らしい。

①：正しい。メニューには世界中の料理が載っているとある。②：間違い。シロウのラーメンはとてもうるさいと書いてあり、またジョニーのハットは形式的なお店であることがレビューから判断できる。③：正しい。3つ目のレビューに魚料理に関する記述がある。④：そのようなことは書かれていない。⑤：間違い。レビューには、素晴らしいと書いてあるが少し高いとも書いてある。否定的な意見が書いてあるので最高とは言い難い。⑥：間違い。メニュー自体に関する意見は、「驚くほど長い」であり「素晴らしい」とは言えない。

H29（試行調査2回）　2 B

あなたは、学生がアルバイトをすることについてのディベートを行うつもりです。ディベートの準備のために、あなたの班は下にある記事を読んでいます。

学生とアルバイト

最近の研究によると、日本の高校生と大学生の約70%がアルバイトをしています。その研究は、学生たちは友達と出かけたり、服を買ったり、経済的に家族を助けたりするためにお金が必要なので、アルバイトをしていると報告しています。そのような共通の理由があるのであれば、私たちは次の疑問を考慮するべきであろう。学生がアルバイトをすることはいいのか悪いのか、という疑問を。

学生がアルバイトから様々なことを学ぶことができると考える人もいる。かれらはお金の価値と同等の、仕事の重要性や難しさを理解するようになる。さらには、彼らは人々とうまく付き合っていく方法を学ぶ。学生はコミュニケーション能力を向上させ、自信を得るのである。

学生がアルバイトをすることに関して否定的な点があると考える人もいる。1つ目に、勉学に害をもたらすかもしれない。一生懸命に働く学生は、授業中に疲れすぎて学校で悪い成績をとってしまうかもしれない。2つ目に、学生が仕事と学業のバランスをとるのは難しいと思われる。これがストレスとなりうる。3つ目に、学生は働きすぎることで仕事自体の否定的な見方を助長してしまうかもしれない。彼らは、卒業後、懸命に働く意欲を失ってしまうかもしれない。

あなたはどう思うだろうか。私の意見では、アルバイトは学生にとっては必ずしも悪いとは言えない。私の観点は、学生はアルバイトをしすぎないようにすべきであるということである。研究によると、もし学生が1週間に20時間以上アルバイトをするとしたら、おそらく先述の悲観的な経験をすることになるだろう、と示唆されている。

問1 記事にある研究の中で、学生は「　10　」と尋ねられている。
　①あなたは海外でアルバイトをしたことがありますか。
　②あなたは1週間でどのくらいの金額を稼ぎましたか。
　③どんなアルバイトがあなたに合っていると思いますか。
　④なぜあなたはアルバイトをするのですか。

第1段落3行目によると、アルバイトをしている理由を答えている。よって、正解は④。

問2 あなたの班は、学生がアルバイトをすることを支持する意見を集めたい。記事にあるそのような意見の1つは、学生が　11　ということである。
　①良い会話主になることができる。
　②ほとんどアルバイトをする
　③正社員となるためのより良い機会を持つ
　④適切に服を着る方法を学ぶ

第2段落4行目によると、「学生はコミュニュケーション能力を向上させ」とある。よって、正解は①。

問3 あなたの班は、学生がアルバイトをすることに反対する意見を集めたい。記事にあるそのような意見の1つは、学生が　12　ということである。
　①職場で役に立つはずがない
　②授業で良くない成績をとるかもしれない
　③家族とより多くの時間を過ごす
　④欲しい物を買うためにアルバイトをする

第3段落2行目に、「授業中に疲れすぎて学校で悪い成績をとってしまうかもしれない」とある。よって、正解は②。

問4 もし学生が1週間に20時間以上働くとしたら、彼らは　13　かもしれない。
　①高給与な仕事が必要だと感じ始める
　②アルバイトで懸命に働き続ける
　③学校を去った後、一生懸命に働くことに興味を失うかもしれない
　④家族から独り立ちしたい

第4段落3行目によると、「おそらく先述の悲観的な経験をすることになるだろう」とある。「先述の悲観的な経験」とは、第3段落の内容である。3つ目に「懸命に働く意欲を失う」とある。よって、正解は③。

問5 この記事の筆者は、学生がアルバイトをすることに　14　。
　①特別な意見は全く持っていない
　②概ね賛成である
　③強く賛成している
　④強く反対している

第4段落1行目によると、「アルバイトは学生にとっては必ずしも悪いとは言えない」とある。よって、正解は②。

H25　5

「トモとアキ」(2005) 日本
サトコ　日本　大阪
評価：★★★★☆

　私はついに，コダマユキオ著の有名な本が原作の受賞映画「トモとアキ」のDVDを見ました。私はこの本が大好きで，何度も読みました。コダマの日本の田舎生活の詳細な描写は驚くべきもので，物語はおもしろく感動的です。トモとアキは，都会の若い夫婦で，田舎の村に引っ越してきたのですが奇妙な新生活に苦しみます。原作ほど良いことはあり得ないと思っていたため，私はこの映画を長い間避けていました。ある意味では私は正しかった一方で，この映画はそれでも見てとても楽しめるものでした。

　映画の中の小さな村は現実的でしたが，コダマの文章を読んでいるときのように私がそこにいるようには感じられませんでした。原作では内気で平凡な人物のトモを演じている俳優は，その役にしてはあまりにも自信に満ちていて顔立ちがよく見えました。一方で，アキを演じている女優はとても真に迫っており，喜びや失望，悲しみといった感情を完璧に表わしています。アキは引越しを本当に後悔しています。映画の前半を通して，彼女はよく村でハイヒールを履き，完璧な化粧をしていることで都会での生活スタイルの少なくとも一部を維持しようとします。映画の力強い結末で，彼女は双子を産み，そのおかげで彼女は過去から完全に解き放たれ，村での生活に本当に満足するようになるのです。1つのおもしろい点は，当時まだ15歳のダイチジュンの登場で，近くの村出身の少年として脇役を演じていることです。私はこの俳優の大ファンで，彼は後の作品で有名になったのですが，彼の演技の才能はすでにこの小さな部分で現れています。

　私は原作をとてもよく知っていましたが，映画を見ることで原作に対する評価がさらに高くなりました。原作が大好きな人は誰でもこの映画をさらに楽しむことができ，映画が気に入った人は，本も読んでみてください！

ジョー　アメリカ　ニューヨーク州　バッファロー
評価★★★★★

　昨日，私の日本人の友達が「トモとアキ」を見るためにアジア映画祭に連れて行ってくれました。同時に字幕を読み，シーンに注目することが私には難しいので，いつもは外国語の映画を避けています。しかし，この映画は非常に魅力的で楽しいものであったので，私はすぐにせりふを読んでいたことを忘れました。この物語は，都会での忙しい生活から逃れようとする夫とともに，田舎に引っ越す若い女性を描いています。この映画の最もよいところは，日本の田舎の興味深くユニークな生活をいかに表現しているかです。カメラワークとサウンドトラックもこの経験に加わって，映画の明るい雰囲気によく合っています。私は2時間ずっと魅了され，楽しみました。

　冒頭の，主人公の女性のアキの目の前に大きなカエルが飛び出し，彼女の悲鳴が周囲の山々にこだまする場面に，私はすぐに引きつけられました。実のところ，彼女がファッションストア店員から農家の成功者へと変貌していく彼女の演技にとても感動しました。その女優は，特に虫や暴風雨，大量の泥と闘いながら菜園を経営していこうとしている場面では，才能あるコメディアンでもあります。

　いつも若者を奇妙な目で見ている多くの村の老人の中には，本当におもしろく変わった人物がいます。私のお気に入りは，村では伝説の，最後にはその夫婦のよい友達になるおばあさんです。映画の終盤での印象的な場面では，そのおばあさんがアキに野生きのこの調理法を教えながら，村の奇妙な民話を伝えます。

　全体的に，私は本当にこの映画が好きです。この物語はおもしろく，演技は素晴らしいのですが，とりわけ，映画の中で日本の文化の異なった側面を本当に見ることができることがよいです。この映画を強く勧めます！

問1　41　③
　この映画を見た後，サトコは　41　と思った。
　　①コダマユキコの人生を正確に表現している
　　②村にいるような気分になる
　　③いっそう原作が好きになった
　　④原作のファンは見るべきでない
サトコのレビューの第3段落第1文目に，「映画を見ることで原作に対する評価がさらに高くなりました」とあるので，③が適当。第2段落第1文目より②は不適。第3段落最終文より④は不適。①のようなことは書かれていない。

問2　42　④
　この映画を見る前，ジョーは　42　だろうと期待していた。
　　①貴重な文化経験
　　②原作とは異なる
　　③有名なので素晴らしい
　　④物語についていくことが難しい
ジョーのレビューの第1段落第2文目の「同時に字幕を読み，シーンに注目することが私には難しいので，いつもは外国語の映画を避けています」より，④が適当。

問3　43　②
　サトコとジョーは共に　43　を称賛している。
　　①主演男優の演技　　　　②主演女優の演技
　　③カメラワークの質　　　④原作の質
サトコのレビューの第2段落第3文目の「アキを演じている女優はとても真に迫っており」ジョーのレビューの第2段落第2文目の「彼女の演技にとても感動しました」より，②が最も適当。サトコは主演男優をほめていないので①は不適。カメラワークをほめているのはジョーだけなので③は不適。原作をほめているのはサトコだけなので④は不適。

解
説

問4 | 44 | ①

レビューによると，物語のテーマとしては | 44 | が最もふさわしい。

　　①新生活への適応
　　②昔の村の生活の歴史的に正確な描写
　　③現代社会における変化していく女性の役割
　　④伝統文化を共有することの重要性

レビューから，この物語は都会から引っ越してきた女性が，田舎での生活に悪戦苦闘しながらも，最終的には田舎の生活に適応していくものだとわかる。したがって①が最も適当。

問5 | 45 | ④

以下のうち，映画に出てくる場面の順番を表わしているものはどれか。

ジョーのレビューの第2段落第1文目から（D）は映画の冒頭であるとわかる。サトコのレビューの第2段落第5文目から（B）は映画の前半部分であるとわかる。ジョーのレビューの第3段落第3文目から（A）は映画の終盤であるとわかる。サトコのレビューの第2段落第6文目から（C）は映画の結末であるとわかる。したがって最も適当なものは④。

| 3 | 〈体験〉 | 問題 35p〜 |

R4 | 3 | A

　あなたは日本文化がほかの国々でどのように表現されているか興味がある。

　あなたはイギリスの若いブロガーの投稿を読んでいる。

エミリー　サンプソン
7月5日　月曜日　午後8時00分

　毎年7月の第1・第2日曜日に、ウィンズフィールドで「一切れの日本」と呼ばれる異文化交流イベントが行われます。私は昨日そこへ行く機会がありました。これは間違いなく訪れる価値があります！「ヤタイ（屋台）」と呼ばれる伝統的な出店がたくさんあり、参加体験や素晴らしい実演もありました。「ヤタイ」では、緑茶アイスクリームや「タコヤキ（たこ焼き）」、「ヤキトリ（焼き鳥）」がふるまわれました。「タコヤキ」は特に美味しかったです。みなさんも食べてみてください！

　私は3つの実演を見ました。1つは英語で行われた「ラクゴ（落語）」という喜劇です。笑っている人もいましたが、私はどういうわけか面白さが分かりませんでした。もしかすると私が日本文化についてあまり知らないからかもしれません。わたしにとって、他の2つ、「タイコ（太鼓）」と「コト（琴）」が最もよかったです。「タイコ」は迫力があり、「コト」は気持ちを落ち着かせてくれるものでした。

　私はワークショップと文化体験に参加をしました、それは面白かったです。ワークショップでは、「オニギリ（おにぎり）」の作り方を学びました。私が作ったものは少し形が変でしたが、美味しかったです。「ナガシ－ソウメン（流しそうめん）」体験は本当に面白かったです。調理された麺が竹製のウォータースライダーを滑り降りてくるのでそれを箸で掴もうとするものでした。麺を掴むのはとても難しかったです。

　一切れの日本を体験してみたいなら、このお祭りはあなたにぴったりです。私はチラシの写真を撮りました。見てみてください。

※エミリーはイギリス人のブロガーなのでイギリス英語が使われていることに注意。

「学ぶ：learnの過去分詞」英：learnt⇔米：learnd

一切れの日本
文化公園、ウィンズフィールド
7月第1・2日曜日開催（午前9時から午後4時まで）

食品販売する露店	体験型アクティビティ	伝統芸能の実演
緑茶アイスクリーム	ナガシ－ソウメン（麺）体験	コト（ハープ）
タコヤキ（タコの軽食）		タイコ（ドラム）
ヤキトリ（鶏肉の串焼き）	オニギリ（おにぎり）ワークショップ	ラクゴ（喜劇の語り聞かせ）

問1　エミリーのブログから、彼女が | 16 | ことがわかる。

　　①日本の伝統音楽を楽しんだ
　　②日本のドラムのたたき方を学んだ
　　③竹からウォータースライダーを作った
　　④屋台の食べ物を全て食べてみることができた

第2段落第1文で3つの実演を見たとあり、同第2文で1

つが落語、残りの２つが日本の伝統音楽である太鼓と琴で、最もよかったとあることから、日本の伝統音楽を楽しんだことがわかるので正解は①。

問2 落語を聞いている時、エミリーはおそらく ┃ 17 ┃ 。

①混乱していた　　②納得していた
③興奮していた　　④落ち着いていた

第２段落第３・４文より周りは笑っているのに自分は何が面白いのかわからなかったのであるから、エミリーは混乱していたと考えられる。よって、正解は①。

R4 ③B

あなたはアウトドアスポーツを楽しんでおり、登山雑誌で面白い話をみつけました。

スリーピークスチャレンジへの挑戦
ジョンハイランド

昨年の９月、登山者10名とミニバス運転手２名からなる私たち12名のチームは、「スリーピークスチャレンジ」に参加した、これはイギリスの登山者の間ではその難しさでよく知られている。ゴールはスコットランド（ベン・ネヴィス）、イングランド（スカフェル・パイク）、ウェールズ（スノードン）というそれぞれの最高峰に、およそ10時間の山と山との間の車で移動を含めて24時間以内に登る事である。これに備えるため、我々は数カ月間断続的にトレーニングを続け、入念にルートを計画した。私たちの挑戦はベン・ネヴィスの麓で始まり、スノードンの麓で終わることになる。

美しい秋の朝６時、私たちは最初の登山を始めた。トレーニングのおかげで、私たちは３時間弱で山頂に到達した。ところが、下山途中に私は携帯電話を落としたことに気が付いた。幸運なことに、チームの協力でみつかったが、私たちは15分を無駄にしてしまった。

その日の夕方早く、私たちは次の目的地であるスカフェルパイクに到着した。ミニバスの中での６時間の休憩の後、私たちは元気いっぱいで２番目の登山を開始した。しかしながら、暗くなるにつれて、私たちはペースを落とさなければならなかった。スカフェルパイクに登頂しきるのに４時間半かかった。再び、計画よりも長く時間がかかった、そして時間はなくなりつつあった。しかし、交通量が少なかったため、最後の登山を始めるときには予定通りの時間になっていた。私たちは時間内にチャレンジを達成させるより強い自信が出てきた。

不運なことに、私たちが最後の登山を始めてすぐに、激しい雨が降り始め、再びペースを落とさなければならなかった。滑りやすく、前を見るのはとても難しかった。午前４時30分、私たちはもはや24時間以内に終わらせることは出来ないことを悟った。それでもなお、私たちはまだ最後の山に登ることを固く決意していた。雨はますます激しくなり、２名のメンバーがミニバスに戻ることを決めた。疲れ果て、惨めな気持ちで、私たち残りのメンバーもまた下山する準備を始めた、しかし、そのとき空は晴れ、私たちは頂上のすぐ近くにいた。急に私たちの疲れも吹き飛んでしまった。時間チャレンジには成功しなかったが、登頂チャレンジには成功したのである。私たちはやり遂げた。なんていい気分だっただろう！

※イギリスの山に登る話なのでイギリス英語が使われていることに注意。
「気づく」英：realise⇔米：realize

問1 ①から④の以下の出来事を起こった順に並べ替えなさい。

┃ 18 ┃ → ┃ 19 ┃ → ┃ 20 ┃ → ┃ 21 ┃

①全てのメンバーがスコットランド最高峰の頂上に到達した。
②何人かのメンバーはスノードンに登ることをあきらめた。
③グループはウェールズにミニバスで移動した。
④チームメンバーは筆者の電話を探すのを手伝った。

第１段落第４文より、山に登る順番はスコットランドのベ

ン・ネヴィス、イングランドのスカフェルパイク、ウェールズのスノーデンの順。また、第２段落第３文より、筆者が電話を落としたのはベン・ネヴィスの下山中であることがわかる。よって、できごとが起こった順に並べ替えると、①→④→③→②となる。

問2 スカフェルパイクを制覇したときに予定より遅れていた理由は何か。 ┃ 22 ┃

①ベン・ネヴィスの山頂に到達するのに計画よりも長く時間がかかった。
②暗闇でうまく前に進むことが難しかった。
③登山者が体力を温存するために休憩をとった。
④チームは天候がよくなるまで待たなければならなかった。

第３段落第３文に「As it got darker…we had to slow down. 暗くなるにつれて…ペースを落とさなければならなかった」とあり、選択肢の「It was difficult to make good progress in the dark」がこれの書き換え。よって、正解は②。

問3 この話から筆者は ┃ 23 ┃ ということがわかる。

①満足感を感じなかった
②３つの山全ての頂上に到達した
③タイムチャレンジに成功した
④ミニバスの２番目の運転手だった

第４段落第８文より、時間には間に合わなかったものの、３つの山全ての頂上に登ったことがわかる。よって、正解は②。

R3（追試） ③A

あなたのイギリスの友人、ジャンが、新しい遊園地を訪れ、彼女の経験についてブログを投稿しました。

サニーマウンテンパーク：訪れるのに素晴らしい場所
ジャンによる投稿　2020年　９月15日　午後9時37分　ジャンの投稿

先月、ついにサニーマウンテンパークが開園しました。巨大ジェットコースターを含むたくさんのワクワクするアトラクションがある大きな遊園地です（地図を見てください）。私は先週、そこで友人と素敵な時間を過ごしました。

私たちはジェットコースターに挑戦するのを待ちきれませんでした、しかし、まず、私たちは配置を把握するため列車で園を一周しました。列車から、私たちはピクニックゾーンを見ました、そして昼食をとるのにいい場所だと思いました。しかし、ピクニックゾーンは既にとても混雑していました、そこで、私たちは代わりにフードコートに行くことに決めました。昼食の前に、私たちはディスカバリーゾーンに行きました。そこで科学アトラクションを体験するために待つ価値はありました。午後は、私たちはマウンテンステーションの近くのいくつかの乗り物を楽しみました。もちろん、私たちはジェットコースターも試しました、私たちの期待を裏切りませんでした。さらにアトラクションを楽しむためにディスカバリーゾーンへの帰る途中、私たちは休憩所で少し休憩をとりました。そこでは、湖越しの城という素敵な景色を眺めることができました。最後は、ショッピングゾーンに行き、そこで友人や家族にお土産を買いました。

サニーマウンテンパークはすごいです！私たちの最初の訪問は確実に最後にはならないでしょう。

（地図略）

問1　ジャンの投稿によると、　16　がわかります。
　　①ジャンは贈り物のためのショッピングゾーンを飛ばし
　　　ました。
　　②ジャンは科学アトラクションを楽しむためにしばらく
　　　待ちました。
　　③フードコートはピクニックゾーンよりも混雑していま
　　　した。
　　④ジェットコースターはジャンの期待に沿うものではな
　　　かった。
　　第2段落第5文に科学アトラクションを待つ価値はあった
　　と言っていることから科学アトラクションを楽しむために
　　待ったことがわかる。よって、正解は②。
問2　ジャンと彼女の友人が午後に休憩ととった場所はどこ
　　ですか？　17
　　①休憩所A　　②休憩所B
　　③休憩所C　　④休憩所D
　　湖越しに城が見えたとあることから休憩所－湖－城となっ
　　ている場所を選べばよい。よって正解は休憩所B。

R3（追試）　3 B

　　イギリスにいるあなたの友人が彼女のお気に入りの
　　ミュージシャンをあなたに紹介しています。もっとよく知
　　ろうと思ったとき、あなたは音楽雑誌の中で以下の記事を
　　みつけました。

デイブ・スター、生きる伝説

　かつて、ブラックスワンはイギリスで最も大きなロックバンドで
あった、そして彼らの精力的なリーダー、デイブ・スターが彼らの偉
業に大きな役割を果たしました。いまだ、ソロシンガーとして演奏し、
デイブの驚くべき才能は若いミュージシャンの世代に刺激を与えてき
た。

　彼が小さな少年の時、デイブはいつも歌ったり、おもちゃの楽器を
演奏したりしていました。彼はおもちゃのドラムをたたいている時よ
りも幸せなことはありませんでした。7歳の時、彼は最初の本物のドラ
ムセットを与えられ、そして、10歳までには、彼は上手に演奏する
ことができました。14歳までには、彼はギターもマスターしていま
した。彼がまだ高校生の時、彼はブルーバーズのメンバーになり、リズ
ムギターを演奏していました。経験を積むために、ブルーバーズは学
校のイベントやコミュニティセンターで無料で演奏しました。バンド
は、熱狂的なファンの小さな輪を築き上げました。

　デイブの大ブレイクは、彼の18歳の誕生日に、ブラックスワンのドラ
マーになるよう頼まれたときに起こりました。わずか2年で、バン
ドの公演は大きなコンサートホールで売り切れになっていました。そ
れゆえに、リードボーカルが家族とより多くの時間を過ごすために脱
退した時は衝撃でした。しかし、それがもはや彼のお気に入りの楽器
を演奏することができないことを意味するにもかかわらず、彼はリー
ドシンガーとして引き継ぐチャンスに飛びつきました。

　その後数年で、ブラックスワンはますます成功し、音楽チャートの
頂点に登り、さらに多くのファンを獲得しました。デイブは主要な作
詞家になり、バンドへの貢献を誇りに思っていました。しかし、キー
ボードプレイヤーの追加により、音楽は徐々に方向性を変えました。
デイブは不満を募らせていきました、そして、彼とリードギタリスト
はバンドを離れ、新しいグループを始めることを決めました。不幸な
ことに、デイブの新しいバンドはブラックスワンのレベルまで成功す
ることはできず、たった18ヶ月しか一緒にいませんでした。

問1　下記の出来事を起こった順番に並べなさい。
　　　18　→　19　→　20　→　21
　　①デイブはソロアーティストになった
　　②デイブはドラムを演奏することをあきらめた
　　③デイブがバンドにギタリストとして加入した
　　④デイブはキャリアのピークに達した
　　まず、第2段落第4文にデイブがまだ高校生の時にブルー
　　バーズのメンバーになり、リズムギターを演奏したとある。
　　a band=the Bluebirdsである。
　　次に、第3段落第1文でデイブは18歳の誕生日にドラマー
　　としてブラックスワンに加入した時に大ブレイクが訪れた
　　とある。
　　第3段落第2文でデイブのブラックスワン加入後2年で
　　ボーカリストがやめ、ドラムをあきらめてリードシンガーに
　　なっている。
　　第4段落1行目にデイブがブラックスワンのボーカルに
　　なったその後数年でブラックスワンが音楽チャートの頂点
　　に登ったとあり、同第5文にデイブのソロ活動はブラック
　　スワンのレベルまで成功することはできずとあるから、こ
　　れがデイブのキャリアのピークと言え、キャリアのピーク
　　→ソロ活動の順になる。よって、3→2→4→1の順とな
　　る。
問2　デイブはブラックスワンのリードシンガーになった、
　　なぜなら　22　から。
　　①彼がドラムを演奏するよりも歌うことを好んだ
　　②彼はバンドの音楽の方向性を変えたかった
　　③他のバンドメンバーがより成功したと思った
　　④前のメンバーが個人的な理由で脱退した
　　第3段落第3文「to spend more time with his family：家族
　　とより多くの時間を過ごすため」が選択肢の「personal
　　reasons：個人的な理由」にあたる。
問3　この話から、あなたは　23　ということがわかる。
　　①ブラックスワンはロック音楽の方向性を変えることに
　　　貢献した
　　②ブラックスワンのグッズはコンサートホールでよく売
　　　れた
　　③デイブは幼いころから音楽の才能を発揮していた
　　④デイブはリードギタリストに不満を募らせたためソロ
　　　になった
　　第2段落第3文で、10歳までにドラムを上手に演奏できる
　　ようになり、14歳までにギターもマスターしたとあるから、
　　幼いころから音楽の才能を発揮していると言える。

R3（本試）　③A

あなたはイギリスのホテルに宿泊することを計画している。あなたはある旅行アドバイスウェブサイトのQ＆Aで役に立つ情報をみつけた。

> 私は2021年3月にキャッスルトンにあるホーリーツリーホテルに滞在しようと考えています。このホテルはおすすめですか、また、バクストン空港からの移動は簡単ですか？　　（リズ）
> ― ― ― ― ― ― ― ― ― ― ― ― ― ―
> 回答
> 　はい、ホーリーツリーホテルを強くすすめます。私はそこに2回宿泊したことがあります。値段は高くないのに、サービスはとても素晴らしいです！　無料の朝食も素晴らしいです。（アクセス情報は<u>ここ</u>をクリックしてください。）
>
> 　そこへ行った私の経験を話させてください。
>
> 　初めて訪れたときは、地下鉄を利用しました、これは安くて便利です。列車は5分ごとに走っています。空港からは、モスフィールドまでレッド線に乗りました。ビクトリア行きのオレンジ線に乗り換えるのに通常7分程度かかるのですが、道順がよくわからなかったため5分余計にかかりました。ビクトリアからは、ホテルまでバスで10分でした。
>
> 　2回目は、ビクトリアまで高速バスに乗ったので、乗り換えについて心配をする必要はありませんでした。ビクトリアで、2021年夏まで道路工事をするという看板を見かけました。バスは10分ごとに走っていますが、今はホテルに行くのに通常の3倍時間がかかります。歩くことも可能ですが、天気が悪かったのでバスに乗りました。
>
> 　宿泊を楽しんでください！　　　　（アレックス）

ホーリーツリーホテルへのアクセス

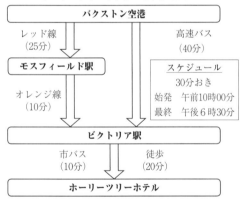

問1　アレックスの回答から、あなたはアレックスが [16] ことを学んだ。

① ホテルが便利な立地にあることを評価している
② キャッスルトンへ初めて訪れたとき、ビクトリア駅で道に迷った
③ このホテルは値段に見合う価値がある
④ 2回とも空港から同じ経路を使った

アレックスの回答の3段落で便利さを評価しているのは地下鉄についてなので①は不適。アレックスの回答の4段落より、道に迷ったのはモスフィールド駅であり、②は不適。アレックスは1回目は地下鉄と市バスを、2回目は高速バスと徒歩を使っているので同じ経路ではなく④は不適。アレックスの回答の1段落より「値段は高くないのに、サービスはとても素晴らしいです」とあるのでこれが「このホテルには値段に見合う価値がある」と一致する。よって正解は③。

問2　あなたは2021年3月15日の午後2時に空港から公共の交通機関で出発する。ホテルに最も早く到着する方法はどれか。 [17]

① 高速バスと市バス　　②高速バスと徒歩
③ 地下鉄と市バス　　　④地下鉄と徒歩

バクストン空港からビクトリア駅までは、高速バスなら30分おきしか走っていないが、ちょうど午後2時出発のバスがあるので、午後2時40分にビクトリア駅に到着する。地下鉄なら、5分おきに走っており、レッド線でモスフィールド駅まで25分、乗り換えに7分かかり、モスフィールド駅からビクトリア駅まで10分、最低でも合計42分と最大5分の電車の待ち時間がかかるので、最も早くて午後2時42分に到着する。よって、バクストン空港からビクトリア駅までは高速バスのほうが早い。

ビクトリア駅からホテルまでは市バスで通常10分で到着するが、2021年の夏まで道路工事のため普段の3倍かかるとのことなので30分かかる。徒歩であれば20分かかる。よって、ビクトリア駅からホテルまでは、徒歩のほうが早い。以上のことから、バクストン空港からビクトリア駅までは高速バス、ビクトリア駅からホーリーツリーホテルまでは徒歩が最も早く到着する方法、よって正解は②。

R3（本試）　③B

あなたのクラスメートがイギリスからの交換留学生によって書かれた以下のメッセージが学校通信に載っているのを見せてくれました。

> **ボランティア募集！**
> 　みなさんこんにちは！私はセーラ・キング、ロンドンから来た交換留学生です。今日は大切なことをみなさんに共有したいと思います。
> 　みなさんはさくら国際センターについて聞いたことがあるかもしれません。ここは、日本人と外国に住む人々とがお互いに知り合うことに役立つ機会を提供しています。料理教室やカラオケ大会のような人気のあるイベントが毎月開催されています。しかしながら、深刻な問題があります。建物が老朽化しているため、高額な補修が必要です。センターを存続させる資金調達を支援するため、多くのボランティアが必要とされています。
> 　私はその問題を数か月前に知りました。街で買い物をしているときに、募金活動に参加している人々を見ました。私は状況を説明していた活動のリーダー、ケイティに話しかけました。私がお金を寄付すると、彼女は私に感謝しました。彼女は町長に資金援助を申し出たが拒絶されたと私に言いました。彼らは募金活動を始めるほかなかったのです。
> 　先月、私はセンターで芸術に関する講義に参加しました。そこでも、私は募金活動を行っている人を見かけ、手伝うことを決めました。彼らが通りがかりの人へ寄付をお願いしているのに私が加わると、彼らは喜んでいました。私たちは懸命に寄付を求めようとしましたが、多くのお金を集めるには私たちの人数は少なすぎました。ケイティは涙を浮かべ、この建物はもうあまり長くは使えないだろうと言いました。私はもっと何か他にやる必要があると感じました。そのとき、快く手伝ってくれる生徒が他にもいるかもしれないという考えが浮かびました。ケイティはそれを聞いて喜びました。
> 　さて、私はみなさんに、私と一緒にさくら国際センターを支援するための募金活動をしてくださるようお願いしています。今日、私にメールを送ってください！交換留学生なので、私が日本にいることができる時間は限られています。しかし、私はその時間を最大限よいものにしたいです。一緒に活動することで、私たちは大きな変化を生じさせることができると思います。
>
> クラス3A
> セーラ・キング（sarahk@sakura-h.ed.jp）

問1　下記の出来事を起こった順に並べなさい。

$$\boxed{18} \rightarrow \boxed{19} \rightarrow \boxed{20} \rightarrow \boxed{21}$$

①セーラはセンターのイベントに参加した。

②セーラはセンターに寄付をした。

③セーラはケイティにある提案をした。

④募金活動員は町長に援助を求めた。

3段落後半、セーラがお金を寄付したときに、募金活動員は町長に資金援助を申し出たが断られたことを聞いており、④→②の順となる。3段落初めよりこれが2、3か月前。4段落初め、先月、センターで芸術に関する講義に出席したとあり、①は②よりも後となる。4段落後半、快く手伝ってくれる生徒が他にもいるかもしれないという提案をケイティに提案しているので③は①よりさらに後。よって正解は④→②→①→③となる。

問2　セーラのメッセージから、さくら国際センターは $\boxed{22}$ とわかる。

①経済的援助を世界中の人々に与えている

②友情を深める機会を提供している

③地域社会へニュースレターを発行している

④イギリスに交換留学生を送っている

2段落前半「日本人と外国に住む人々とがお互いに知り合うことに役立つ機会を提供しています」とあり、正解は②。

問3　セーラのメッセージを読んだ後、あなたは活動を手伝うことを決心しました。あなたはまず何をすべきですか。 $\boxed{23}$

①センターのイベントを宣伝する。

②詳しい情報を聞くためにセーラに連絡する。

③学校でのボランティア活動を計画する。

④新たな募金活動を開始する。

5段落初めより、セーラは「私と一緒にさくら国際センターを支援するための募金活動をしてくださるようお願い」しており、センターのイベントの宣伝、ボランティア活動の計画、新たな募金活動を依頼してはおらず、①・③・④は不適。5段落半ばに「今日私にメールをしてください」とあるので、最初にすべきはセーラに連絡することなので、正解は②。

H30（試行調査2回）　③A

あなたは学校の女性交換留学生によって書かれたブログにある、以下の話を見つけました。

> **文化祭**
> 9月15日　日曜日
> 　私は友達のタクヤと彼の高校の文化祭に行きました。私はそれまで日本の文化祭には行ったことがありませんでした。私たちは、最初はお化け屋敷に挑戦しました。それはよくつくられており、プロジェクターと良い音響機材を使って恐ろしい雰囲気を創り出していました。
> 　それから私たちは生徒たちによるダンスショーを見ました。彼らはかっこよくて踊りも上手でした。天気が悪かったのが残念でした。もし晴れていたら、彼らは外でダンスをしていたでしょう。お昼時になり、私たちは模擬店でハワイアンパンケーキとタイカレー、メキシカンタコスを食べました。それらは全部美味しかったのですが、私たちがイタリアンピザの店を見つけた頃には、それはすでに売り切れていました。
> 　午後は、私たちは2人とも歌を歌うのが大好きだったので、一緒にカラオケ大会に参加しました。驚くべきことに、私たちはもう少しで優勝するところでしたが、その大会には20人がエントリーしていたのでそれは驚くべきことでした。私たちは、たくさんの人々が私たちのパフォーマンスを気に入ってくれて本当に幸せでした。私たちはまた、生徒たちが作ったデジタル描画や短編映画を楽しみました。
> 　私は生徒たちが彼ら自身でこの大きな催し物を組織し準備したことが信じられませんでした。文化祭はかなり印象的でした。

問1　文化祭では、 $\boxed{16}$ 。

①お昼時までに模擬店の食べ物はほとんど売り切れてしまった。

②ダンスショーは悪天候のため室内で行われた

③お化け屋敷は電気機器を使わずに行われていた

④カラオケ大会は朝に開催された

本文6行目に「もし晴れていたら、彼らは外でダンスをしていたでしょう」とあるので、ダンスは室内で行われていたことがわかる。よって、正解は②。

問2　あなたはこのブログの筆者が $\boxed{17}$ ということがわかった。

①お化け屋敷やダンスショー、先生の絵画を楽しんだ

②カラオケ大会で歌い3位になった

③異なる料理を食べ、カラオケ大会で2位になった

④彼女のダンスと文化祭に関する短編映画を気に入った

ブログの作者は、交換留学生の女の子であり、本文中の表彰台の絵からカラオケ大会で2位となったことがわかる。また本文7行目に様々な国の料理を食べていることがわかる。よって、正解は③。

あなたは、ある留学の雑誌にあった以下の話を見つけた。

> **花とそれらに隠された意味**
> マエヤマ　ナオコ（ティーチング・アシスタント）
>
> 　花をあげることは、絶対的に良い行いです。しかしながら、海外にいるときは、文化の違いに気をつけるべきでしょう。
> 　デボラは、３週間の言語プログラムのため日本の私たちの学校にいたのですが、最初は彼女の故郷であるカナダ出身の生徒がいなかったので、緊張していました。しかし、彼女はすぐにたくさん友達を作り、教室の外でも中でも楽しい時間を過ごしていました。ある日、彼女の日本語の先生である林先生が駅の階段で転げ落ちて入院してしまったことをききました。彼女は本当に驚き動揺し、できるだけ早く彼に会いたいと思いました。デボラはクラスメイトと病院に行くことにし、先生を幸せにするために花瓶に赤いベゴニアの花を一輪挿して持っていきました。彼らが病室に入ったとき、彼は大きな笑顔で彼らを迎え入れました。しかしながら、デボラが彼にその赤い花を渡したとき、彼の表情が突然変わりました。デボラは、少し困惑しましたが彼女は彼に迷惑をかけたくなかったためその理由は聞きませんでした。
> 　後ほど、彼女の初歩的な日本語と辞書の助けもあり、デボラは私に彼女が病院へ行ったこと、彼女の日本語の先生の表情がベゴニアの花を渡したときにどのように変わったのかを話してくれました。デボラは、「赤は情熱の色なので、それは私のお気に入りの花です。私は、先生も、いつも指導について情熱的なのですが、もちろんそれが好きだろうと考えたのです」と言いました。
> 　不幸にして、花瓶の中の花の成長は、私たちが日本の病院に持っていくべきではないものでした。こういうわけで、花瓶の中の植物は根を持っているため、簡単には動かせません。日本の文化では、これらの事実を病院に居続けることと関連付ける人もいます。デボラは、花瓶に挿されたベゴニアの隠された意味を聞いてすぐ、彼女は林先生に謝りに行きました。

問１　その話によると、デボラの感情は次の順番で変わりました。　18
　①緊張→困惑→幸せ→驚き→申し訳ない
　②緊張→困惑→申し訳ない→驚き→幸せ
　③緊張→幸せ→驚き→困惑→申し訳ない
　④緊張→幸せ→申し訳ない→驚き→困惑
　⑤緊張→驚き→幸せ→申し訳ない→困惑
　⑥緊張→申し訳ない→困惑→幸せ→驚き

本文解説中にある下線部がデボラの感情の変化になります。よって、正解は③。

問２　デボラが選んだ贈り物は、　19　ということを示唆するかもしれないので、日本では適切ではありませんでした。
　①長期入院　②退院　③怒りの助長　④生への情熱

本文第４段落３行目に「これらの事実を病院に居続けることと関連付ける人もいます」とあるので、①が正解。

問３　この話から、あなたはデボラが　20　ということがわかりました。
　①彼女は授業でいくつかの花の意味がわかったので、先生のためにベゴニアを選んだ
　②ベゴニアによって、日本語を練習するだけでなく日本の文化について学んだ
　③先生に会いにティーチング・アシスタントと病院を訪れ、話を楽しんだ
　④林先生によりベゴニアの説明をされて、その隠された

意味を学んだ

本文第４段落にて、デボラは日本の文化における花に隠された意味を知り、また本文を通してデボラが日本語を勉強していることがわかっているため、②が正解。

H29（試行調査１回）　③A

あなたはベジトニアと呼ばれる国を訪れたいと思い、以下のブログを見つけました。

> **トマトリー島での春休み**
> ３月23日　日曜日
>
> 　私は家族とトマトリー島を訪れるためにベジトニアという名前の国に行きましたが、そこはベジトニア本島の南西に位置しています。トマトリーに行く最速の方法は、ポテノから飛行機に乗ることですが、それに比べフェリーが非常に安かったのでフェリーに乗りました。その島についたとき雨が降り始めたので、私たちは美術館とある城を訪れました。それから、私たちは温水浴を楽しみました。午後、夕食は美味しかったです。全てがとても新鮮でした。
> 　幸運なことに、翌日の朝は晴れました。私たちは自転車を借りて、海岸沿いを楽しく漕ぎました。その後、海辺に釣りをしに行きましたが、何も獲れませんでした。まあいいや、次は釣れるでしょう！午後には、美しい夕日を見て、その後たくさんの星を見ました。
> 　最終日、個人用のタクシーツアーに参加し、運転手はその島中の面白い場所にたくさん連れて行ってくれました。彼女はまた、その島の自然と文化についてもたくさん教えてくれました。私たちは、素晴らしい休日を過ごし、結果として、小さな島の美しさと文化により興味を持つようになりました。

問１　家族は　15　トマトリー島に行きました。
　①メイゴンから空路で
　②メイゴンから海路で
　③ポテノから空路で
　④ポテノから海路で

第１段落３行目によると、フェリーのほうが安かったためフェリーを利用したことがわかる。よって、正解は②。

問２　このブログから、あなたは　16　ということが分かります。
　①あまり混んでいないので、トマトリー島を訪れるのに最適な月は３月である
　②たとえ天気が悪くても、その島で楽しむことができるものがまだいくつかある
　③手頃な値段で様々なアウトドア活動と地元の食べ物を楽しむことができる
　④その島の自然と文化を説明してくれる、島を回るバスツアーを楽しむことができる

第１段落４行目によると、この家族は雨が降ったので美術館とある城を訪れたことがわかる。よって、正解は②。

解
説

H29（試行調査1回）　3 B

あなたは新聞に載っているセールスマンにより書かれた以下の話を見つけました。

機械の進行

ニック・ライトフィールド

トロントにある大学を卒業した後、私は貿易会社で働き始めた。私が様々な街で働き生活しなければならないということを意味する。私の最初の配属先はニューヨークで、そこはオフィスビルや店舗、夜遊びで有名だ。私は自由時間に、あちこち歩き周り面白い品々を売っている店を探すのが大好きだった。夜になっても、私は店から店へ歩き回ろうとした。

それから2日後、私は東京へ異動した。東京の第一印象は、ニューヨークと非常に似ている忙しい街ということだった。しかしながら、新宿の通りを夜歩いていた初日、私はある違いに気付いた。労働者や店員の群れている中に、私はキャンディのような色の照明を放っている明々とした自動販売機の列を見つけた。ニューヨークでは、ほとんどの自動販売機がオフィスビルや地下鉄の駅にある。しかし、私はほぼ全ての通りに兵士のように立っている、1日24時間コーヒーやジュース、カップ麺でさえ売っている、自動販売機の列を一度も想像したことはない。

新宿に立っていると、私はバンクーバーについて考えた。私はそこで生まれ育ったのだ。私にはそこは素晴らしい街だが、ニューヨークと東京での生活を経験すると、私はバンクーバーでは、どれほど私が何も知らなかったか認めなければならない。私が自分の人生についてずっと考えているとき、雨が降り出しました。私は傘の自動販売機に気付き、コンビニエンスストアに走ろうとした。助かった！それから私は、ことによると技術が進歩すれば、全てのものを機械から買うことができるだろうと考えた。自動販売機はコンビニエンスストアに取って代わるのだろうか。機械は私のようなセールスマンに取って代わるのだろうか。私はその夜あまり眠れなかった。それは時差ボケか何かだったのか。

問1　筆者は以下の順序で、あちこち異動していました：　17

① トロント→ニューヨーク→東京→バンクーバー
② トロント→バンクーバー→ニューヨーク→東京
③ バンクーバー→ニューヨーク→東京→トロント
④ バンクーバー→トロント→ニューヨーク→東京

筆者はバンクーバーで生まれ（第3段落1行目）、トロントにある大学を卒業し（第1段落1行目）、貿易会社に就職したあとニューヨークに最初配属され（第1段落5行目）、その後東京へ異動になった（第2段落1行目）。よって、正解は④。

問2　筆者は　18　と言っています。

① ニューヨークでの生活は東京での生活よりも快適である
② 東京での生活はニューヨークでの生活よりも面白くない
③ ニューヨークと東京の自動販売機の配置場所は異なる
④ 同じ商品が、ニューヨークと東京にある自動販売機で売られている

第2段落11行目によると、ニューヨークでは「ほとんどの自動販売機がオフィスビルや地下鉄の駅にある」とあるが、東京では「ほぼ全ての通りに」ある。よって、正解は③。

問3　筆者が東京にいる間、彼は　19　。

① 自動販売機を販売することについて考え始めた
② 彼の故郷なので、バンクーバーがより良いと気付いた
③ 街から街へ異動したことを後悔し始めた
④ 将来の彼の仕事について突然心配になった

第3段落最後の4行によると、「機械は私のようなセールスマンに取って代わるのだろうか」とある。よって、正解は④。

R2　5

数週間前、私はある山に私の飼っている犬と一緒に登山をしていたが、予想外のことが起こり私は彼を見失ってしまった。私は、探しに探したが彼を見つけることができなかった。彼は長い間私と一緒にいたので、心の一部を失ってしまったかのようだった。

その日から、私は奇妙な感情を抱いていた。それは悲しみとは異なり、極めて理解できない感情で、まるで何かが私を山に引き戻そうとしているかのようだった。だから、私は機会があるごとに、その山が安心感を私に与えてくれるかどうか確かめるため、バックパックを掴んだのであった。

ある晴れた日、私は山の麓に立った。この日はなにか違った感じがした。「私を許してくれ」と私は大声で言った。「きっと見つけるから！」私は深呼吸をし、この奇妙な引力がだんだん強くなりながら、旅を始めた。私がよく知っていると思う道に沿って進んでいった後、私は何だかよく知らない場所にいることに気付いた。私は少しパニックになり、足を踏み外し、こけてしまった。どこからともなく、1人の老人が私に向かって走ってきて、助けてくれた。

彼の優しく微笑んでいる顔を見て、私は安堵感を感じた。その老人は、山頂までの道を探していると言ったので、私たちは一緒に山を登ることに決めた。

すぐにその道は再び馴染みのあるものに感じ始めた。私たちは、私は犬のことも含めて、たくさんのことについて話した。私は彼に、私の犬はシェパードだと言った。彼が若いときは、警察犬としてしばらく働いていたが、怪我によりやめなければならなかった。その男は、少しの間警察官であったがやめたんだ、と言って笑い声を上げた。彼は、なぜかは言わなかった。その後、彼は警備員として長い間過ごした。彼もまたドイツ出身だった。私たちはこれらの類似点に笑いあった。

私たちはそれを知る前は、大きく開けた場所に到着し、休憩をとった。私はその男に、私の犬に何が起こったかを話した。「彼は、クマを追い払うために首に小さなベルをつけていた。私たちはまさにこの場所に来て、クマを見た。それは私たちの後ろで見ていた。私は、危険を感じ、クマを後ろから追いかけたので、犬を抱えるべきだった。私はそれから彼を見つけられなかった。もっと注意していればよかった」

私がその話を話していると、その男の表情が変わった。「それはあなたのせいではない。あなたの犬は、ただあなたを安全にしたかった」と彼は言った。「私は、トモはきっとあなたにこのことを話したかったのだと思う。そしてまた、諦めないでくれてありがとう」

トモは私の犬の名前である。私は彼にこれを伝えただろうか。その老人の言葉は、空に鳴り響いた。

私がなにかたずねる前に、その男は山頂へ急いで行こうと提案した。私は数週間前に犬と、これを行う予定だった。2時間以上の登山の後、私たちは頂上に到着した。私はバックパックを置き、私たちは素晴らしい景色を見ながら座った。その老人は私を見て言った「森が本当に神秘的な体験をさせてくれた」と。

私は休む場所を探してあたりを見た。私はすぐに寝てしまったので、かなり疲れたのだと思った。起きたとき、私はその老人がいなくなっていたことに気付いた。私は待ったが、彼は二度と戻らなかった。

突然、陽の光の中で、何かが私の目を捕らえた。私は、向こうまで歩き、小さい金属の名札をバックパックの後ろに見た。それは、私の両親が元々私の犬にくれた銀色の名札と同じものだった。トモと書いてあった。

私が、後ろで馴染みのある音を聞いたのはそのときだった。小さなベルの響きだった。私は振り向いた。私が見たものによって、とてもたくさんの感情が私を襲った。

山頂でしばらくして、私は旧友への名札に惹きつけられ、山の贈り物を身につけて慎重に家に帰った。私の心は非常に満たされたのだった。

問1 41 ①

41 ので、筆者は繰り返し山に戻った。

① 彼女は表現することのできない衝動を感じた
② 彼女は老人に会う予定だった
③ 彼女は魔法を練習することができると思っていた
④ 彼女はクマについて事実を知りたかった

第2段落によると、「極めて理解できない感情で、まるで何かが私を山に引き戻そうとしている」とある。よって、正解は①。

問2 42 ④

筆者の最近の旅で、最初に起こったのは、以下のうちどれか。

① 彼女は大きく開けた場所に着いた
② 彼女は山頂まで登った
③ 彼女はクマが走り去るのを見た
④ 彼女はある老人により助けられた

第3段落6行目によると、「どこからともなく、1人の老人が私に向かって走ってきて、助けてくれた」とある。よって、正解は④。

問3 43 ④

筆者の犬とその老人のどんな類似点が話されているか

① 彼らは職場で怪我をした
② 彼らは最近近親者の友人を失った
③ 彼らは筆者の知人であった
④ 彼らは大衆を保護する手助けをするために働いた

第5段落によると、筆者の犬は警察犬として働いた経歴があり、老人は警察官として働いた経歴がある。どちらも大

衆（一般市民）を護る役職である。よって、正解は④。

問4 44 ②

下線部のrang in the airが文章中で使われている意味に最も近いのは以下のうちどれか。

① 幸福を運んできた
② 痕跡を残した
③ 大きな音を立てた
④ 攻撃的なようだった

下線部は直訳すると「空中で鳴った」となる。筆者はこのとき、老人の言ったトモという名前を自分が言ったかどうか、反芻している。老人の言葉が耳に残っているのである。よって、正解は②。

問5 45 ②

筆者の感情は、最後の登山での経験を通してどのように変わったか。

① 彼女は落ち込み、それからより悲しくなった
② 彼女は決意し、それから安堵した
③ 彼女は希望に溢れていたが、ホームシックになった
④ 彼女は惨めだったが、楽しくなった

筆者は犬を見失った後、山の麓で老人と出会い、山に登ることを決意した。山頂までの体験の後、名札を見つけそれを身につけて家に帰り、心が満たされた。よって、正解は②。

H31 5

「クリスティーン、庭の手伝いに来てくれ。今日中に種を全部植えたいんだ。」父が私を呼んでいた。「忙しいの」と私は言った。父は自分の庭が大好きだが、当時私は土くれの中で働くことがどうして父をそこまで興奮させるのかわからなかった。

4月の終わりまで、彼の植物たちはきちんと列をなして育っていて、いずれの列にも野菜の名前をつけた木の杭を差していた。不幸なことに、5月の初め、父は事故で重傷を負った。彼は約2ヶ月の間入院しており、その間彼は自分の庭のことについてよく私に尋ねた。彼は家に帰ってきた後でさえ、しばらくベッドに寝ていなければならなかった。私の母は出張があったため、庭の世話をすることはできなかった。私は父に庭の心配をしてほしくなかったので、頼まれることなく怪我が治るまで私が庭の世話をするよと言った。私は小さな植物なら水をあげれば成長し続けると思い込んでいて、幸運なことにかなりの雨が降っていたから庭のことについてはあまり深く考えなかった。

7月のある土曜日の朝、父は私に言った「クリスティーン、野菜がそろそろ収穫できる時期のはずだ。今日はサラダにしよう！」と。私はボウルを持って庭に出た。私はリーフレタスを見て、葉の多くが半分食べられているのを見て動揺した。何匹もの虫が全部についていたのだ！私はそれらを取り去ろうとしたが、多すぎて取り切れなかった。次にニンジンを見たが元気そうには見えな

かった。私はニンジンを引き抜いたが、細くて、なにかが噛み付いたように見えた。

私は一瞬パニックになったが、いい考えを思いついた。私は財布を取り、急いでドアを出てから、なにか野菜を買うために最寄りの店まで自転車に乗っていった。家に帰って、父にサラダを作るため野菜を切りあげた。

私が父にサラダをあげたとき彼は言った。「おぉクリスティーン、なんて美しいサラダなんだ！私はニンジンがもうこんなに大きいなんて信じられないよ。レタスは歯ごたえがあって美味しい。お前は私の庭をとても良く世話してくれたんだね。」父はとてもうれしそうだったが、私は少し罪悪感を抱いた。

私はキッチンに戻り掃除していると母が最近行っていた出張から帰ってきた。母は、スーパーの袋を見た。私は、母に見られたとき、恥ずかしかった。だから、私は困惑して「父さんがサラダを食べたかったんだけど、庭がめちゃくちゃで。私は父さんにがっかりしてほしくなかったから、お店に行ったの。」母は笑ったけれども、私に庭の手伝いをする時間を作ること約束させ、私たちは次の数週間一生懸命に働いた。生の唐辛子を細かく切り刻み混ぜた水を作り、野菜に吹きかけた。私は、これはすごい考えだと思った。なぜならそのスプレーは人にも動物にも虫にすら害がないからだ。虫は、ただ単に辛い水が好きではないのである。虫なしの野菜はすぐに育ち、ついに収穫できた。

私は注意深く、サラダを作り父に渡した。彼は少し笑ってそれを見た。「クリスティーン、そのニンジンはこのサラダに入っているやつよりは小さいね、だけどそれよりも美味しそうだ。」私は、父が、私がお店に行ったことを全て知っていたのだと気づいた。私は微笑み返した。

今、私は、どんなに小さかろうと、たくさんの努力を何かを世話することに当てることが、その結果により感謝することにどんなに手助けとなりうるかをより理解している。おそらくこれが、父が庭を愛する理由の1つであろう。

数日のうちに父は庭に戻って来るだろう。私は父のすぐ側で、私ができるやり方で、父を助けよう。

問1 | 41 | ①

クリスティーンはもともと、| 41 | からガーデニングをすると言っていた。

①それが彼女の父親には大事なことであると知っていた
②彼女のガーデニング技術を向上させたかった
③父親にそれをするように頼まれていた
④野菜を育てることに興味があった

1，2段落で、父親が庭を大好きであることと、父親に頼まれることなくガーデニングをしていることが書かれている。

問2 | 42 | ②

庭での問題は次のうちどれか。

①動物がよく庭に穴を掘る
②昆虫がレタスやニンジンを食べた
③植物が水を与えられすぎた
④野菜に間違った印をつけた

3段落の後半に、虫がリーフレタスの葉を食べていることやニンジンに噛まれた跡があることが書かれている。

問3 | 43 | ①

クリスティーンは | 43 | なので、店で買った野菜でサラダを密かに作った。

①彼女の父親は庭の進捗を見ることができなかった。
②彼女の父親はそのとき入院していた。
③彼女の父親は彼女が野菜を買うのを手伝った。
④彼女の父親は彼女がスプレーを作るのを手伝った。

3段落前半で、父親はベッドで横になっているため、庭で育てている野菜を収穫するようクリスティーンに頼んだのである。つまり父親は、庭の様子を見ることができていない。

問4 | 44 | ③

下線部bug-freeにもっとも近い意味を次の中から選びなさい。

①全ての虫が死んだ
②虫は好きなことができる
③虫が全く見当たらない
④虫は全くお金がかからない

6段落の後半に、「なぜならそのスプレーは人にも動物にも虫にすら害がないからだ。虫は、ただ単に辛い水が好きではないのである。」とあるので、殺虫作用はないが近寄らなくなったことがわかる。

問5 | 45 | ③

クリスティーンはガーデニングの経験を通して何を学んだか。

①いつも雨の日の準備をする
②虫にがっかりしないようにする
③きつい仕事は価値がありうる
④1人で働くことが結果を生む

8段落の訳を参照。

R4　④

あなたはアメリカにあるロビンソン大学の新入生です。あなたはアパートに必要なものがどこで買えるか知るために、レンとシンディという2人の学生のブログを読んでいます。

ロビンソン大学の新入生ですか？
レンによる投稿　2021年8月4日午後4時51分

　大学入学のための準備はしていますか？家庭用品や家電製品が必要だけど、あまりお金をかけたくはないと考えていますか？大学の近くにセカンドハンドという素晴らしいお店があります。その店ではテレビ、掃除機、電子レンジなどの中古品を売っています。この店で売ったり買ったりすることが好きな学生がたくさんいます。こちらが現在販売中の商品です。多くの商品にとても手頃な価格がついていますが、在庫は限られています、お急ぎください！

セカンドハンド　新入生向けセール！			
テレビ	250ドル	2016年モデル	50インチ
電子レンジ	85ドル	2019年モデル	1.1立方フィート　900ワット
掃除機	30ドル	2017年モデル	幅9インチ×奥行14インチ×高さ12インチ
炊飯器	40ドル	2018年モデル	幅11インチ×奥行14インチ×高さ8インチ
湯沸かし	5ドル	2018年モデル	1ℓ

https://secondhand.web

　中古品の購入は環境に優しいです。それに加えて、セカンドハンドから買うことで、地元のビジネスをサポートしていることになります。じつはセカンドハンドのオーナーはロビンソン大学の卒業生なのです！

ロビンソン大学へようこそ！
シンディによる投稿　2021年8月5日午前11時21分

　もうすぐロビンソン大学での生活が始まりますか？あなたは家庭用品や家電製品を準備しているところかもしれません。
　あなたは4年間ここにいることになるでしょう、ですから、新品を買いましょう！私は1年生の時、新品よりも安かったので全ての家庭用品を大学の近くにある中古店で買いました。しかし、たった1ヶ月程度で動かなくなったものもあり、保証もありませんでした。私はすぐに買い替えなければならず、お店を見て回ることができませんでした、ですから私は全てのものを大規模チェーン店で買いました。2か所以上のお店で値段の比較ができたらよかったと思います。
　save4unistu.comというウェブサイトは、買い物に行く前に店ごとの値段を比較するのに便利です。以下の表は3つの大型店で最も人気のある新品の価格を比較したものです。

商品	カットプライス	グレートバイ	バリューセイバー
炊飯器 （幅11インチ×奥行14インチ×高さ8インチ）	115ドル	120ドル	125ドル
テレビ （50インチ）	300ドル	295ドル	305ドル
湯沸かし （1ℓ）	15ドル	18ドル	20ドル
電子レンジ （1.1立方フィート）	88ドル	90ドル	95ドル
掃除機 （幅9インチ×長さ14インチ×高さ12インチ）	33ドル	35ドル	38ドル

https://save4unistu.com

　全ての商品で保証が使えることに注目してください。ですから、もし何か動かなくなったとしても、簡単に交換することができます。バリューセイバーはすべての家庭用品に無料で1年の保証を付けています。商品が300ドル以上の場合、保証は4年間延長されます。グレートバイは全ての家庭用品に1年の保証を付けており、学生は在籍証明で上の表の価格から10％の割引を受けることができます。カットプライスは無料で保証を付けていません。5年保証のために商品ごとに10ドル支払わなければなりません。

　物事はあっという間です！待ってはいけません、さもないと買い損ねてしまうでしょう！

問1　レンが中古品の購入をすすめているのは ⎡24⎤ からである。
①大学を助けることになる
②多くの商品が環境に優しい
③学生にとって手頃な価格だ
④急いで必要なものを見つけることができる

「あまりお金をかけたくはないと考えていますか？」と呼び掛けており、選択肢の「affordable for students」は「priced very reasonably：とても手頃な価格がついている」の書き換え。よって、正解は③。

問2　シンディは ⎡25⎤ 買うことを提案している。
①時間の節約になるので、1つの大きなチェーン店で
②最安値を提示するので、ウェブサイトで
③交換保証がある新品を
④新品よりずっと安いので中古品を

新品を買いましょうと呼び掛けたあと、中古品を買って保証がなかったため新品を買わなければならなかったという失敗談を話しているのであるから、正解は③。

問3　レンとシンディはどちらも ⎡26⎤ するようすすめている。
①大学の近くの店で買う
②できるだけ早く家庭用品を買う
③学生割引を提供している店を選ぶ
④商品に保証のついている店を選ぶ

レンは「so hurry！：急いで！」、シンディは「Don't wait or you'll miss out！：待ってはいけません、さもないと買い損ねてしまうでしょう！」と言っている。よって、正解は②。

問4　もし、新品の家庭用品を最も安く買いたければ、あなたは ⎡27⎤ すべきです。
①シンディが投稿したURLにアクセス
②レンが投稿したURLにアクセス
③大型のチェーン店に行く
④大学に近い店に行く

シンディが投稿したURLにアクセスすると新品の商品の価格の比較ができるのであるから、新品の家庭用品を安く買うことができる。よって、正解は①。

問5　あなたは最も安いという理由で電子レンジを ⎡28⎤ で買うことに決めた。また、5年間の保証付きで最も安いという理由で、あなたはテレビを ⎡29⎤ で買うことに決めた。
①カットプライス　　　②グレートバイ
③セカンドハンド　　　④バリューセイバー

電子レンジの値段を比べるとセカンドハンドは85ドル、カットプライスは88ドル、グレートバイは90ドルの10％引きで82ドル、カットプライスは95ドルで、グレートバイが最も安い。よって正解は②。
テレビの値段を比べると5年間の保証付きでなければならないので、保証を受けられないセカンドハンドや、1年保証しかつけることができないカットプライスは条件が合わない。バリューセイバーは商品代金が300ドルを超えてい

るため 5 年保証付きで305ドル、カットプライスは 5 年保証にするには10ドル払う必要があるので300ドル+10ドルで310ドルとなり、バリューセイバーが最も安い。よって正解は④。

R3（追試） 4

あなたは、日本の観光についての発表の準備をしています。あなたは2018年日本を訪れた観光客のデータをクラスメートであるハンナとリックにメールで送りました。彼らの返信を元に、あなたは発表の概要を作成します。

データ：
（図表略）

あなたのメールへの返信：

こんにちは。

メールありがとう！それはとても興味深いデータですね。以前より、日本への観光客が増えているのは知っていますが、彼らの滞在期間に注意を払ったことはありませんでした。私はアジアからの観光客が短い滞在期間で来るのは、彼らが行き来が簡単にできるからだと考えています。

また、この表はアジア人観光客は、全体的に、ヨーロッパやオーストラリアからの観光客と比較して買い物に時間を費やす傾向にあることを示しています。これは、贈り物を贈ることがアジアの文化においてとても重要であり、家族や友人に贈り物を買いたいと思っているからだと推測しています。例えば、私は銀座、原宿、秋葉原の周辺で買い物をしている多くのアジア人観光客を見たことがあります。おそらく、彼らは宿泊にそれほど多くのお金を使う必要がなく、買い物により多くのお金を使うことができるのです。私はこのことについて話したいです。

しかし、私はアジアからの観光客は今や買い物の代わりに他の違う事をすることに興味を持つようになって来ていると聞いています。近い将来この種のデータにいくつか変化を見るかもしれません。

よろしくお願いします。
ハンナ
追伸　このメッセージはリックにも送っています。

こんにちは。

データを送ってくれてありがとう！これは私たちが発表の準備をするのに役に立つと思います！

私がデータを見て気付いたのは、オーストラリア人観光客が娯楽に最もお金を使っていることです。私はこれを示すつもりです。
また、先日、日本のテレビで、北海道でウィンタースポーツを楽しんでいるオーストラリア人に関する番組を見ました。私は、彼らはお金をいくらくらい使っているのだろうかと思います。詳細な情報を探すつもりです。もしあなたが何か見つけたら、どうか私に教えてください。これは将来の研究に役に立つでしょう。

それに加えて、私は観光客がどの国や地域から来たのかによって滞在期間において大きな違いがあるようだというハンナの意見に賛成します。

あなたはどうですか？消費性向に関してハンナが見つけたことについて話したいと思いますか？私はこれはとても興味深いと思います。

よろしくお願い致します。
リック
追伸　このメッセージはハンナにも送っています。

発表の草稿：

発表の表題：　_____ 24 _____

発表者　　　　　　話題

ハンナ：　　　 25

リック：　　　 26

私：　　　　滞在期間の関係

　　　比較例：

27 から来た人々は 28 から来た人々と比較して日本への滞在時間は半分と少しであるが、娯楽に使う金額はわずかにより多く使っている。

将来の研究テーマ：　　 29

問1 24 に適切なものはどれか？
①北海道で冬の休日に使われるお金
②東京での海外からの旅行者の買い物の予算
③日本での海外からの観光客の消費性向
④日本での娯楽への支出の増加
ハンナのメール第 2 段落でアジア人の、リックのメール第 2 段落でオーストラリア人の消費性向の特徴について発表したいと言っている。よって正解は③。

問2 25 に適切なものはどれか？
①日本でのオーストラリア人観光客の活動
②日本でのアジア人観光客の食費
③ヨーロッパ文化における贈り物の習慣
④アジアからの観光客による消費のパターン
ハンナのメール第 2 段落にはアジア人観光客がヨーロッパやオーストラリアからの観光客と比べて買い物に多くのお金を使うとあり、第 2 段落第 5 文にこれについて話したいとある。よって正解は④。

問3 26 に適切なものはどれか？
①オーストラリア人旅行者の娯楽への興味
②中国人の東京での消費性向
③オーストラリア人の北海道に関するテレビ番組
④アジアン人が日本で楽しむ様々な経験
リックのメール 2 段落にオーストラリア人観光客は娯楽に使う金額が最も多く、それについて発表したいとある。よって、正解は①。

問4 あなたはリックの提案に賛成し、データを見ている。
27 と 28 に最も適切なものを選びなさい。
①オーストラリア　②中国　③フランス　④台湾
発表の草稿の比較例に書かれている、滞在時間が半分と少し、娯楽に使っているお金がわずかに多いという 2 つの国を探せばよい。滞在日数は中国が9.7日、フランスが18.4日でフランスの半分9.2日より少し長いと言える。また、娯楽に一人当たりが使う金額を見ると中国が7,998円、フランスが7,358円と、わずかに中国が多い。よって、正解は②，③。

問5 29 に最も適切な組み合わせはどれか？
A：日本のウィンタースポーツのためのオーストラリア人の予算

B：東京への海外からの観光客の数の将来の変化
C：北海道への海外からの観光客に人気の食べ物
D：将来、日本でアジア人観光客が何にお金を使うか

①A，B　　②A，C　　③A，D
④B，C　　⑤B，D　　⑥C，D

ハンナのメール第3段落で買い物に最も多くの金額を使うアジア人観光客が買い物以外の何かに興味を持ち始めており、近い将来この種のデータにいくつか変化を見るかもしれないとある。また、リックのメール第3段落でオーストラリア人が北海道でウィンタースポーツにどれくらいお金を使っているかについて詳細に調べてみること、将来の課題に研究にも役に立つとある。よって、正解はAとD。

R3（本試）　4

あなたの英語の先生であるエマ先生が、あなたとクラスメートのなつきに、姉妹校からの生徒を迎える日のスケジュールの計画を手伝うよう頼んでいます。あなたはスケジュールのたたき台を作成できるよう、なつきとエマ先生のメールのやりとりを読んでいます。

こんにちは、エマ

　来月の12人のゲストとの1日のスケジュールについて、いくつかの考えと質問があります。あなたが私たちに言ったように、両校の生徒は午前10時から我が校の講堂でプレゼンテーションを行うことになっています。そこで、わたしは添付された予定表を見ています。彼らはあずま駅に午前9時39分に到着して、学校までタクシーに乗る予定ですか？

　私たちは午後の活動についても話し合っています。科学に関係する何かを観に行くのはどうでしょうか？2つの案があります、しかし、もし3つ目が必要であればお知らせください。

　来月、ウェストサイド水族館で行われる特別展示について耳にしましたか？海のプランクトンから作られた新しい栄養補助食品についてのものです。私たちはよい選択だと思います。人気があるので、もっとも混雑していない時間帯に訪れるのが一番いいでしょう。水族館のホームページで見つけたグラフを添付しています。

　イーストサイド植物園は、地元の大学と共同して植物から電気を作り出す興味深い方法を開発しています。運のいいことに、担当の教授がその日の午後早い時間に少し話をしてくれるそうです！行きませんか？

　みんなお土産を買いたいですよね？私はひばり駅の隣のウェストモールが一番いいと思いますが、おみやげを一日中持って歩き回りたくはありません。

　最後に、あずまの訪問者は全員、町の象徴である、我が校の隣にあるあずま記念公園にある像を見るべきだと思いますが、うまい予定を組むことができません。また、昼食の予定について教えてもらえませんか？

それでは
なつき

こんにちは、なつき

　メールありがとう！一生懸命やっていますね。あなたの質問に対する答えとしては、彼らは午前9時20分に駅に到着し、スクールバスに乗ります。

　水族館と植物園という午後のメインの2か所はいい考えだと思います、なぜなら、両校とも科学教育に力を入れており、このプログラムの目的が生徒たちの科学的な知識を向上させることだからです。しかし、念のため3つ目の提案があるほうが賢明でしょう。

　一日の終わりにお土産を買いましょう。午後5時にモールにつくバスに乗ることができます。ホテルはかえで駅から徒歩でほんの数分なので、こうすれば買い物におよそ1時間充てることができ、ホテルに午後6時30分までに戻ることができます。

　昼食については、学校の食堂がお弁当を提供する予定です。あなたが言っていた像の下で食べることができます。もし雨が降っていれば屋内で食べましょう。

　提案をありがとう。あなたたち二人でスケジュール案をつくってくれませんか？

よろしくお願いいたします
エマ

添付の時刻表

電車の時刻表

かえで―ひばり―あずま

駅	電車番号			
	108	109	110	111
かえで	8：28	8：43	9：02	9：16
ひばり	8：50	9：05	9：24	9：38
あずま	9：05	9：20	9：39	9：53

駅	電車番号			
	238	239	240	241
あずま	17：25	17：45	18：00	18：15
ひばり	17：40	18：00	18：15	18：30
かえで	18：02	18：22	18：37	18：52

添付のグラフ

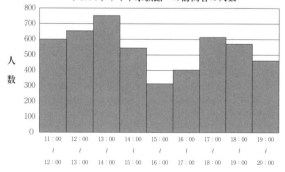

問1　姉妹校からのゲストは 24 番の電車で到着し、
　　　 25 番の電車でホテルに戻ります。

①109　　②110　　③111　　④238　　⑤239　　⑥240

エマ先生のメール1段落に、「午前9時20分に駅に到着し

てスクールバスに乗る」とあり、電車の時刻表のあずま駅の到着時刻を見ると109番の電車が9時20分着となっているので、24の正解は①。

また、その日の最後の予定であるウェストモールはひばり駅の隣にあり、午後5時から約1時間買い物をして、かえで駅から徒歩数分のホテルに午後6時30分までに戻れるとあるので、午後6時前後にひばり駅を出発し、午後6時20分過ぎにかえで駅に到着する電車を探せばよく、条件を満たすのは239番の電車であり、25の正解は⑤。

問2 スケジュール案の条件を完全に満たすのはどれか？ **26**

A：水族館　　B：植物園　　C：モール　　D：学校
姉妹校からの訪問のスケジュール案

→	→	→	→
9：30	13：30	15：30	17：00

①D→A→B→C　　②D→B→A→C
③D→B→C→A　　④D→C→A→B

なつきのメール1段落に、午前10時から講堂でプレゼンテーションをする予定になっているとあるので、1番目はD。次に、午後早くに、イーストサイド植物園の植物を使った発電方法の開発担当の教授が午後早くに話をしてくれるとあるので、午後1時半にスタートする2番目がB。なつきのメール3段落に水族館は最も人の少ない時刻が一番良いとされており、添付のグラフによると午後3時から午後4時が最も人が少ないので、3番目はA。エマ先生のメール3段落にお土産は一日の終わりに、バスで午後5時到着することができるとされているので、4番目はC、よって正解はD→B→A→Cとなっている②。

問3 雨が降らない限り、ゲストは昼食を **27** で食べる。
①植物園　②学校の隣の公園　③駅の隣の公園　④校庭
エマ先生のメール4段落に食堂でお弁当が提供され、学校の隣にあるあずま記念公園にある像の下で食べることができる、雨の場合は屋内で食べるとあり、正解は②。

問4 ゲストはその日 **28** 移動**しない**。
①バスで　②タクシーで　③電車で　④徒歩で
エマ先生のメール1段落にゲストは駅に到着し、スクールバスに乗るとしており、なつきのメール1段落4～5行目のタクシーに乗るのかという質問を否定している。エマ先生のメール3段落でホテルまで徒歩で数分とあり、徒歩でも移動する。よって正解は②。

問5 3つ目の意見として、プログラムに最適なのはどれか？ **29**
①ひばり遊園地　　②ひばり美術館
③ひばり城　　　　④ひばり宇宙センター
エマ先生のメール2段落、プログラムの目的は科学的知識の向上とあるので、科学に関係のあるものを選ぶ。科学に関係があるのはひばり宇宙センターであるから、正解は④。

H30（試行調査2回） **4**

あなたは生徒の読書習慣について研究しています。あなたは2つの記事を見つけました。

生徒たちの読書習慣　　　　　デビッド・ムーアによる
2010年7月

楽しんで読書をするということは、学校の宿題か仕事のためというよりもむしろ、ただ楽しさのために読書をしていることである。楽しんで読書をすることと教育的な結果とを結びつける強力な証拠がある。研究は楽しんで日々読書をする学生がそうでない学生よりもテストでいい点数をとったと示していた。研究者たちは、楽しんで読書をする人は、毎日ではないにしろ、勉強や情報を集めるための読書にたくさんの時間をかけているだけよりも、確かにより有益であるということも見つけた。さらには、頻繁に楽しんで読書をすることは、紙面あるいはデジタルの本を読むかどうかに関わらず、読み書きの能力の向上に強く関係している。

国際的な研究によると、2009年、15歳の学生の3分の2が日常的に楽しんで本を読んでいる。グラフは、6カ国の各学生のうち、楽しんで本を読んでいる学生の割合を示している。読書習慣は国ごとに異なり、いくつかの国では読書に著しい性差があった。

多くの国で、日々楽しんで本を読んでいる学生の割合は、2000年に行われた以前の研究のときから減少している。2000年に戻ると、平均して77％の女子と60％の男子が楽しんで本を読んでいた。2009年までに、これらの割合は74％と54％にそれぞれ落ちている。

私の意見では、今日の多くの学生がどんな本を読むべきなのか知らない。彼らにはお気に入りのジャンルやシリーズがないのだと言います。そういうわけで、日々喜んで読書をしている生徒の割合が減少しています。親や先生は、楽しんで読書をすることを日課にするために、学生が興味深い本を見つけるのを助けてあげるべきです。

「生徒たちの読書習慣」への意見　　　T.Yさんによる
2010年8月

学校の司書として、私はたくさんの国で働いてきました。私は、以前よりも日々楽しんで読書をしている生徒が、世界中でより少なくなっているということを知り少し悲しく思いました。デビッド・ムーア氏の記事によると、私の故郷の女学生のうち約60％が楽しんで読書をしていると報告していて、性差は約20％です。私はこれにがっかりしています。

より多くの生徒が読書の恩恵を知る必要があると思います。デビッド・ムーア氏が発言するように、喜んで読書をすることは学生の学問的能力に良い影響を与えます。定期的にたくさんの本を読む学生は、読解、数学、論理的問題解決においてより良い点数をとっています。また、楽しんで読書をすることは、学生の精神的な健康状態にいい影響を与えます。研究により、定期的に楽しんで読書をすることとストレスや抑うつのレベルが低いことには強い関係性があるということがわかりました。

これらの恩恵があるにも関わらず、学生は一般的にあまり十分な時間を読書に費やそうとはしません。私たちの日常生活は今や画面主体の環境で満たされています。学生はたくさんの時間を、ビデオゲームをしたりソーシャルメディアを使ったりテレビを見たりすることに費やします。私は、学生は画面の前にいる時間を減らすべきであり、短い時間でもいいので毎日本を読むべきだと思います。子供の頃に読書習慣を形作っておくことが、後の読書の習熟度に関係すると言われています。学校図書は、学生が数多くの資源を見つけるための良い場所なのです。

問1　デビッド・ムーア氏と司書の2人とも 21 とは述べていない。

①読書習慣の性差
②電子書籍を読むことに関係した問題
③学生間における読書習慣の変化
④子供時代の定期的な読書の重要性

デビッド・ムーア氏の第1段落の最後に「紙面あるいはデジタルの本を読むかどうかに関わらず、読み書きの能力の向上に強く関係している」とあり、利点については説明しているが、問題については述べられていないため、正解は②。

問2　司書は 22 出身である。

①オーストラリア　②フィンランド　③日本　④韓国

女子の割合が60％で性差が20％であるのはグラフよりオーストラリアである。よって、正解は①。

問3　記事によると、喜んで読書することは学生の 23 に良い影響を与える。（1つ以上選べる）

①キャリアの選択　　　②教育上の成功
③精神の健康　　　　　④ソーシャルメディアの見方

司書の発言の第2段落に、「学問的」と「精神」の2つに良い影響があると述べられている。よって、正解は②と③。

問4　デビッド・ムーア氏は学生が 24 と述べており、司書は 25 と述べている。（各空欄に異なる選択肢を選べ）

①それまでより忙しい
②どんな本を読むべきか決めることができない
③親と同じような本を選ぶ
④電子機器で遊ぶのを楽しむ
⑤テレビから有益な情報を得る

デビッド・ムーア氏の発言の第4段落1文目に、「今日の多くの学生がどんな本を読むべきなのか知らない」とあるので、 24 は②が正解。司書の発言の第3段落を通して、学生が画面に向かっている時間が長いということを述べているので、 25 は④が正解。

問5　両方の記事から得られる情報に基づいて、あなたは宿題のレポートを書こうとしています。あなたのレポートのタイトルとして最も良いのは「 26 」だろう。

①それを好きか否か、古典を読むことが重要である
②楽しんで読書することをあなたの日常生活の一部に
③楽しい読書が違う国で人気になりつつある
④学校図書：学校計画を行うための大きな資源

本文訳に何度も出てきましたが「楽しんで読書すること」が重要であることがわかります。よって、正解は②。

H29（試行調査2回）4

授業で、皆で下にある2つのグラフに基づいてレポートを書きました。あなたはアミとグレッグにより書かれたレポートを今読もうとしています。

ある研究が13歳から29歳までの人に対して行われました。表2にある質問に答えるために、参加者は1つ以上の理由を選ぶことができました。

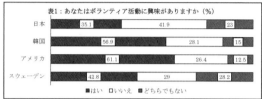

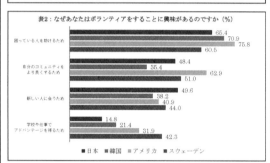

キタムラ・アミ

　私が予想していたよりも、ボランティアに興味を持っている日本人参加者の割合が高かったので、グラフ1を見たとき私は驚きました。私の知っている限り、私の友達の誰もボランティア活動をしている人はいません。だから、私たちは日本の学生にもっとボランティアをするように促して行くべきだと私は思います。

　それをするためには、ボランティアの仕事をするメリットを考えることが重要です。グラフ2によると、日本人参加者の65.4％が、困っている人を助けたいのでボランティアに興味があります、と言っています。また、「新しい人と会うため」を選択した日本人参加者の割合が4カ国の中で1番高かったです。

　私はもっと多くの日本人学生がボランティアの利点について学ぶべきだと思います。このように、文化祭のために私は「困っている人を助けることも新しい人と会うことも同時にできます！」と書いてあるポスターを作ろうと計画しています。私はたくさんの学生がそれを見て、ボランティアの仕事にもっと興味をもつようになればいいと願っています。

グレッグ・テイラー

　アメリカでは、ボランティアは一般的なので、私はボランティアに興味を持っている人々の割合が最も高いことには、驚きませんでした。グラフ2によると、たくさんのアメリカ人参加者が、困っている人を助けたいのでボランティアの仕事に興味があります、と答えています。私はこの理由が、学生が人々を助けることで達成感を得るため重要であると思います。

　しかしながら私は、日本人参加者の35.1％しかボランティアの仕事に興味があると答えていないことを見て驚いています。私は日本では、それはもっと一般的だと思っていました。グラフ2の情報によると、日本人参加者の数人しか、学校と仕事のアドバンテージを認識していないようです。私は最近、日本の大学生や企業が以前よりもボランティア経験により価値を置いていると聞きました。もし、もっと多くの学生がこれらのアドバンテージを理解したなら、ボランティアに対する彼らの関心が増加すると思います。

　学生は以下の2つの理由でボランティアの仕事をするべきだと思います。1つ目は、困っている人を助けることは学生に達成感を与えます。2つ目に、ボランティアは彼らに将来の経歴にもアドバンテージを提供するでしょう。それゆえ、私はボランティアの仕事を行う2つの利点について回報を書き、学校の生徒に配りたいと思います。

問1 | 20 |は、ボランティアの仕事に興味を持っている
日本人参加者の割合が予想より低いと感じた。
①アミ
②アミとグレッグの両方
③グレッグ
④アミとグレッグの両方とも（感じなかった）
アミは、第1段落1行目によると「予想していたよりも高
かった」と感じている。グレッグは、第2段落1行目によ
ると「驚くほど」低かったと感じている。よって、正解は
③。

問2 アミとグレッグの両方とも、日本の学生は | 21 |べ
きだと言う。
①他国の学生とボランティアの仕事をする利点について
話し合う
②卒業後にボランティアの仕事をすることを勉強し、そ
して考えることに焦点を置く
③ボランティアの仕事をすることがそれをする人に良い
影響を与えると知る
④ボランティアの仕事は他の国で有名になっていく
アミは、第3段落1行目によると「ボランティアの利点に
ついて学ぶべき」、グレッグは、第3段落3行目によると「将
来の経歴にもアドバンテージを提供する」と考えている。
よって、正解は③。

問3 アミもグレッグもレポート内では「| 22 |」につい
て言及してはいない。
①学校と仕事へのアドバンテージを得るため
②困っている人を助けるため
③自分のコミュニティをより良くするため
④新しい人と会うため
アミは、②（第2段落3行目）、④（第3段落4行目）につ
いて記している。グレッグは、①（第2段落3行目）、②（第
1段落3行目）について記している。よって、正解は③。

問4 彼らのレポートの中で、アミは［ a ］と言い、グ
レッグは［ b ］と言う。| 23 |
① a．調査をする b．スピーチをする
② a．調査をする b．回報を書く
③ a．ポスターを作る b．スピーチをする
④ a．ポスターを作る b．回報を書く
アミは、第3段落2行目によると「ポスターを作ろうと計
画しています」、グレッグは、第3段落4行目によると「2
つの利点について回報を書き、学校の生徒に配りたいと思
います」とある。よって、正解は④。

問5 あなたはインターネットで4つの記事を見つけた。
以下のタイトルに基づいて、アミとグレッグの双方の計
画にもっとも有用な記事は「| 24 |」だろう。
①ボランティアの仕事とコミュニティサービスとの違い
②海外でボランティアをしていく中でどのように友達を
作るか
③ボランティアの仕事を通して、困っている人を支援す
ること

④ボランティアの経験と将来の経歴
アミとグレッグの両方が共通して言及しているのは、問3
の解説にあるように、「困っている人を助けるため」につい
てである。よって、正解は③。

R2 | 4 |A

スポーツの指導者や選手は、パフォーマンスを向上さ
せるために、どのようにトレーニング計画を調整するか
に関心がある。練習の順序は、練習量を増やすことなく
得られる結果を知ることを容易にする可能性がある。あ
る研究が、異なるトレーニング計画が投球パフォーマン
スにどのように影響するかを調べるために、行われた。

この研究で、小学生が床に置かれた的にテニスボール
を投げた。彼らは的から3．4．5メートル離れた3箇所
からボールを投げた。その的は、中心（20センチ大）と
9つの外側の円からなっていた。彼らは投球の正確さを
示すためのゾーンとして役立った。もしボールが的の中
心に落ちれば、100点が与えられる。もしボールが外側
のゾーンの1つに落ちてしまった場合は、順に
90，80，70，60，50，40，30，20，10点が与えられる。もしボー
ルが的の外側に落ちた場合は、得点は与えられない。も
しボールが2つのゾーンを仕切る線上に落ちた場合は、
より高い方の得点が与えられる。

学生らは、ブロック・ランダム・コンバインドの3つ
の練習グループのうち1つが割り当てられた。全ての学
生が、ボールを使い的の中心に当てようとするために、
上投げで投げるように指示された。研究の初日、彼らは
それぞれ合計81回の投球を終えた。ブロックグループの
学生たちは、3箇所の投球場所のうち1箇所から27回投
げ、次の場所から27回投げ、最後の場所から27回投げて
練習を終えた。ランダムグループの学生たちはどの学生
も研究者が明示した投球場所の順番で81回ボールを投げ
た。このグループと同じ場所から2回だけ連続した投球
が許された。コンバインドグループでは、ブロックグ
ループの計画で始まり、徐々にランダムグループに変え
ていった。次の日、全ての学生が、12回の投球のパフォー
マンステストを終えた。

81回の投球練習の間に、ブロックグループは他の2つ
のグループよりもパフォーマンスが悪いという結果に終
わった。パフォーマンステストの得点もまた分析され
た。コンバインドグループは、3つのグループの中で最
もパフォーマンスが良く、次にランダムグループ、その
次にブロックグループであった。同様の結果が、ボウリ
ングや野球、バスケットボールで見られるような他の投
球動作のトレーニング計画で、大人でも得られるかどう
かは、未だ確かではない。これは次のセクションで取り
扱う。

問1 | 33 | ④
この図の5回の投球で達成された合計得点は何点か。
①200 ②210 ③220 ④230

中心から近い順に得点を見ていく。1球目：80と70を仕切る線上にあるため、80点。2球目：50点、3球目：50と40を仕切る線上にあるため、50点、4球目：30点、5球目：20と10を仕切る線上にあるため、20点、の合計230点。よって、正解は④。

問2　34　④

以下の記述のうち、実験に関して正しいものはどれか。

①ブロックグループでは、最初の投球位置と同じ場所から81回の投球がなされている。

②コンバインドグループの実験期間全体で、的からの距離は変化しないままだった。

③同じ位置からの一連の投球には、コンバインドグループの様々な投球方法が含まれている。

④同じ位置から一列に並んで3回以上投げることは、ランダムグループのルールに反する。

第3段落9行目によると、「2回だけ連続した投球が許された」ことがわかる。よって正解は④。

問3　35　②

以下の記述のうち、実験に関して正しいものはどれか。

①ブロックグループは、練習でもパフォーマンステストでも成績が最もよかった。

②ブロックグループは、パフォーマンステストでは3つのグループの中で成績は最低だった。

③コンバインドグループは、パフォーマンステストでのランダムグループよりも正確性が低かった。

④ランダムグループは、練習でもパフォーマンステストでも正確性が最低だった。

第4段落1行目によると、「ブロックグループは他の2つのグループよりもパフォーマンスが悪い」ことがわかる。よって、正解は②。

問4　36　④

この報告では、次に議論される可能性が最も高いのはどれか。

①下投げのイメージトレーニング

②若い学生の動作の観察

③目を閉じた状態での上投げ

④様々な種類の投球動作

第4段落5行目以降によると、他の投球動作に関して次のセクションで取り扱うことがわかる。よって、正解は④。

H31　4 A

芸術は人々の生き方を反映することもある。研究者たちは芸術がどのように衣装や社会的環境を描写するのか議論してきた。ある研究では、この考えが、家庭の食事を特徴づけている絵画にまで拡大できるかどうかを決定する、と伝えられた。この研究の結果は数種類の食べ物がなぜ描かれるのかを説明するのに役立つかもしれない。

研究者らは、1500年から2000年にかけて描かれた140点の家庭食の絵画を調査した。これらは、アメリカ合衆国・フランス・ドイツ・イタリア・オランダの5つの国のものである。研究者らは0はなし、1はあるとして、91種の食べ物の存在のためにそれらの絵画を調査した。例えば1個あるいはそれ以上の玉葱が絵画の中に描かれているとき、1として登録する。そして、それぞれの食べ物を含む、それらの国々から集められた絵画の割合を計算した。

表1には、選択された食べ物のある絵画の割合が示されている。研究者らはいくつかの発見について議論した。第一に、それらの国々の絵画のなかには、研究者らが予想していた食べ物を含むものがあった。貝はオランダの絵画に最も共通しており、それは国境の半分近くが海に接しているからと予想された。第二に、研究者らが予想した食べ物を含んでいない絵画もあった。アメリカ合衆国・フランス・イタリアは国境の大部分が大洋や海であるけれども、それらの国々の絵画のうち12%以下にしか貝と魚が見られなかった。鶏肉は一般的な食べ物であるが絵画の中にはめったに現れなかった。第三に、研究者らが予想していなかった食べ物を含む絵画もあった。例えば、ドイツの絵画の中には、国の6%しか海に面していないけれども、20%が貝を含んでいた。また、自然には育っていないけれども、オランダの絵画にはレモンが最も共通して見られた。

表1
絵画に見られる選ばれた食べ物の頻度を割合で示したもの

品	アメリカ合衆国	フランス	ドイツ	イタリア	オランダ
リンゴ	41.67	35.29	25.00	36.00	8.11
パン	29.17	29.41	40.00	40.00	62.16
チーズ	12.50	5.88	5.00	24.00	13.51
鶏肉	0.00	0.00	0.00	4.00	2.70
魚	0.00	11.76	10.00	4.00	13.51
レモン	29.17	20.59	30.00	16.00	51.35
玉葱	0.00	0.00	5.00	20.00	0.00
貝	4.17	11.11	20.00	4.00	56.76

これらの結果と以前の研究を比較して、研究者らは食べ物の絵は必ずしも正確な生活を描写しているわけではない、と結論づけた。研究者らは、このことについていくつか説明を提供している。一つは、芸術家がより大きな世界に対する興味を表現するためにいくつかの食べ物を描いているということである。他には、より挑戦的な食べ物を描くことで技術を見せたかったということである。例えば、特にオランダの画家の間では、レモンの表面とその内側の複雑さが、その人気を表すこともある。他の解釈が可能なら、異なる見方で絵画を調べてみる必要がある。それは、絵画が完成された時期と、食べ物の文化的な関係性である。両方の問題は次の章で取り上げよう。

問1　33　②

この研究におけるカテゴリー「リンゴ」では、2つの完全なリンゴと1つの半分に切ったリンゴのある絵画は、33として示されている

① 0
② 1
③ 2
④ 3

リンゴの個数にかかわらず、絵画の中にリンゴがあれば「1」、なければ「0」なので、1である。

問2 | 34 | ④

表1によると | 34 | からの絵画は
① フランス（の絵画）はドイツの絵画よりも低い割合でリンゴを含んでいる。
② フランス（の絵画）はオランダの絵画よりも高い割合でチーズを含んでいる。
③ イタリア（の絵画）はアメリカの絵画よりも低い割合でパンを含んでいる。
④ イタリア（の絵画）はドイツの絵画よりも高い割合で玉葱を含んでいる。

表1を見ると、リンゴは、フランス35.29％＞ドイツ25.00％
チーズは、フランス5.88％＜オランダ13.51％
パンは、イタリア40.00％＞アメリカ29.17％
玉葱は、イタリア20.00％＞ドイツ5.00％
したがって、④が正解である。

問3 | 35 | ②

本文と表1によると、 | 35 | 。
① アメリカの人々は鶏肉をよく食べるので、アメリカの絵画には鶏肉が頻繁に現れる。
② イタリアのほとんどが海の近くにあるにもかかわらず、イタリアの絵画の10分の1以下にしか魚は現れない。
③ レモンはオランダ人にとって自国のものなのでオランダの絵画の半分以上でレモンが現れる。
④ 5カ国それぞれは海に接しているため、その絵画の半分には貝が現れる。

イタリアの絵画に魚が描かれている割合は、表1より4％である。

問4 | 36 | ③

本文によると、これらの絵画の中の食べ物は | 36 | 。
① 画家の歴史の知識を説明する。
② 自国に滞在したいという画家の欲求を示す。
③ 画家の芸術技術と能力を示す。
④ 画家の地元の食材に対する愛情を反映する。

4段落の真ん中ほどに、「より挑戦的な食物を描くことで技術を見せたかったということ」とある。

H30 | 4 | A

　　色は消費者が様々なものを購入する際の重要なものである。マーケティング会社は小売店において購買意欲や望ましい雰囲気を作ることができる色を見極める必要がある。しかし、どの色がそれぞれの商品にとって評判が良くなるかを評価することは簡単ではない。なぜなら消費者は製品のタイプによって好みが異なるからである。

　　ここにある研究論文を通して、我々は色が消費者に与える影響についての理解を深めることが可能である。

　　この研究では研究者達は、参加者が買い物の際に色が重要だと考えているか、様々なものを買う時にどの程度色に影響を受けるか、そしていかなる感情や連想が様々な色と関連しているのかといった情報を得るためにドイツ人の消費者を調査した。まず、研究者たちはデータを調査し、参加者の68％が商品を購入時に色が決め手になったと述べたことから買い物をする際に色が実際に重要であると発見した。

　　次に、研究者は購入した商品によって消費者が色を重要視する程度が変化するかを調べた。図1は6つの日用品と参加者がそれらの商品を購入する時、色に重要と考えている割合を示している。上位2つの商品は両方とも参加者によって身につけられるものであり、下位3つは全て電化製品である。合計36.4％の参加者が携帯電話の色を重要と考えている。これは電化製品の中で最も高い割合だが、カバンの割合の半分をほんの少し超えるに過ぎず、カバンは1つ上位に位置している。

　　第3に、研究者たちは参加者の色に対する感覚や関係性を観察した。結果は赤は愛、危険、怒り、力など様々な意味があることを示した。緑は自然との関係や幸運、健康などをもたらす。更に、白はバランス、健康、落ち着きと関連している。それぞれの色がいくつか異なった意味を持っていることが結果として判明した。

　　上記で要約された発見はどのように色がドイツの消費者に影響しているかを示している。しかし、この影響は国々によって変化するかもしれない。このグローバル社会において、国際的に商品を売ることは部分的には増加するインターネットの使用のために簡単になってきた。それゆえ、商品選択の際に世界の他の場所の消費者が色を重要と考えているかを考えることが必要である。次の段落ではこの話題について説明を加えていこうと思う。

問1 | 33 | ②

この文には | 33 | という理由でどの色がより消費者に好まれるかを理解するのは難しいと述べている。
① 色の好みは世代によって違うから
② 消費者のお気に入りの色は異なる商品によって変わるから
③ 商品開発者は最も人気のある色を選択するから
④ 買い物する時に様々な商品が消費者により購入されるから

第1段落第3文参照。【anticipate】「予想する」

問2 | 34 | ③

図1では、（A）（B）（C）（D）はどれか。
第3段落第3文前半から（A）は身につけるものと判断できる。また同文後半から（C）、（D）が電化製品であることもわかる。第3段落最終文からバッグのひとつ下が携帯電話とわかるので解答は③となる。

問3 | 35 | ②

この文章によると以下の記述のうち正しいものはどれか。

①ドイツのビジネスは緑を消費者に対して情熱を示すものだと考えている。

②ドイツ人消費者は1つの色が複数の意味を含んでいると認識している。

③ドイツ人は赤い衣類よりも緑の衣類を好むようである。

④ドイツのメーカーは売り上げを観察して製品に対して1つの色を選んでいる。

4段落に注目する。①は赤色についての内容。③④はどこにも言及されていない。

問4 　36　 ④

最後の段落に続く可能性が最も高い話題はどれか。

①国際的なビジネスにおけるグローバル化が色の選択に与える影響

②他国における電子機器販売の重要性

③国際的なビジネスにおける商品選択へのインターネットの影響

④他国における消費者にとっての色の重要性

最後から2つ目の文に注目する。

H29 　4 A

スポーツをすることや運動するといった子供時代の身体的活動は年を取った時にとても健康のためになりうる。それゆえ、健康のために子供時代の身体的活動を促進することは重要である。校庭は子どもたちや青少年が身体的活動に参加するように促すことができる場所の一つである。したがって、校庭が生徒たちによってどう使われているかを知ることは彼らの身体的活動を促進するにあたって私たちに役立つ考えを提供してくれるかもしれない。

どういったタイプの校庭が使われているか、生徒たちはそれらの場所で活発であったか不活発であったかについて調査するためにデンマークの4つの学校である研究が行われた。その研究において、校庭は主要な特徴に応じて分類され定義付けされた。「グラス」は運動場や自然の芝生地帯で、しばしばサッカーのために使われているが、ラインやゴールが設置されていないものを言う。「マルチコート」はテニスやその他の球技のために設計された人工芝やゴムなどの様々な表面をしたフェンスで囲まれたエリアを示していた。「ナチュラル」は例えば藪や木々、自然の石などがあるエリアを指していた。「プレイグラウンド」は砂地のような安全な路面上のブランコや滑り台のような遊具のあるエリアを表していた。「ソリッドサーフィス」はコンクリートのような最も硬い表面のエリアを指していた。これらのエリアは平たいひらけた空間によって区切られていたが、しばしば試合のためにたくさんの印がペンキで塗られ、様々な場所にベンチが置かれていた。

GPS装置と他の器具を使って、研究者たちは生徒たち

の身体的活動の程度と同様に様々な校庭で過ごす生徒の時間の長さを測定した。図1は全生徒のそれぞれのエリアでの一日に過ごす時間の平均量及び子ども（12歳以下）と青少年（13歳以上）のそれらの平均を示したものである。ソリッドサーフィスは全生徒が最も時間を多く過ごしているエリアだということが明らかで、そしてそれにマルチコート、それからグラスが続いた。ナチュラルとプレイグラウンドは全生徒が類似した平均値を示したが、プレイグラウンドでの全生徒の平均はちょうど2分を超えていた。

さらに、この研究により子供と青少年の校庭で過ごす時間の平均量の違いも明らかになった。青少年と比較して、子供はナチュラルを除くすべての校庭でより多くの時間を過ごしていた。子供が費やす時間がより多いということは4つの学校の規則にある、子どもたちは昼食時に校庭を離れることができないが、青少年はそうしたい時に離れることができるという事実によって説明できるかもしれない。

身体的活動の程度を見てみると、研究者は校庭のエリア間の違いを発見した。グラスとプレイグラウンドにおいて生徒たちは最も活発であった。一方で、ソリッドサーフィスでは生徒たちはかなりおとなしかった、特に青少年はそこで過ごした時間のわずか7%の間だけ身体的に活発であった。

この研究による発見はさまざまな校庭の環境や特色のもつ潜在能力を調査する重要性を示している。生徒の健康を促進するために、子供と青少年のゲームの種類がどのように身体活動に参加するのに費やす時間の長さに影響を与えるかを観察することも利益になる。ではこれらの関係性について今から見てみよう。

問1 　35　 ③

この文によると、「マルチコート」と「ソリッドサーフィス」の違いは何ですか。

①マルチコートと違って、ソリッドサーフィスはより幼い生徒が遊ぶための人工的な芝を含んでいる。

②マルチコートと違って、ソリッドサーフィスは生徒の試合のためにつけられた境界線を含まない。

③ソリッドサーフィスと違って、マルチコートは様々な素材でできた比較的柔らかい表面をしている。

④ソリッドサーフィスと違って、マルチコートは何にも囲まれておらず、簡単にアクセスできるようになっている。

第2段落の第4文から第7文を比較する。①人工芝を含むのはマルチコートの方である。②境界線がないのはグラスである。④マルチコートはフェンスによって囲まれているので不適。

問2 　36　 ①

図1では、（A）（B）（C）（D）はどれか。

第3段落第3文より（B）がマルチコート、（A）がグラスとわかる。第4文の最後の記述からプレイグラウンドは平均して

２分を超えるとあるので、明らかに平均が２分に届かない(C)がナチュラルと判断できる。

問3 | 37 | ④

この文章の主題は | 37 | である。

①子ども時代の学校での身体的に活発であることの利点について議論すること

②身体的に活発な青少年の数を増やすために助言を与えること

③芝生のエリアで生徒が遊ぶように促している学校を紹介すること

④生徒の振る舞いに影響を与える校庭のタイプを示すこと

①は利点があるとは述べられているが内容について議論はされていない。②具体的な助言はないので不適。③全く言及されていない。

問4 | 38 | ②

最後の段落に続く可能性が最も高い話題はどれか。

①異なる活動の様々な学校環境を研究することの利点

②ゲームの種類と活発である時間の長さとの関係性

③青少年の身体的活動に校庭の環境が及ぼす影響

④校庭の表面が身体的活動を行う時間に及ぼす影響の方法

本文最後にある【relationships】≒【connections】とわかれば判断できる。

H28 ４A

①アメリカの消費者は特に1990年台から輸入される新鮮な果物の増加している量や種類から恩恵を受けている。現在の食料品店の青果部門は一年を通じて様々な新鮮な果物を陳列しているし、それらは国産の果物に付加するものとして世界中から持ち込まれている。

②青果輸入の急速な伸びはアメリカの青果市場に多くの影響を及ぼしている。例えば、アメリカではオレンジが国産の果物で最も多い一方で、アメリカの作物が凍るように冷たい天候を経験した際には時折突然増加することもありはするが、アメリカにおけるオレンジの輸入量は1990年代から一定の割合で増えている。（グラフ１参照）

③アメリカの国内市場は様々な国や地域からオレンジを輸入している。主な供給先の中では、メキシコは長い間供給先である。しかしながら、年間を通じてアメリカは新鮮なオレンジに対する需要があるために、特に国内のネーブルオレンジが利用できない夏の間は南半球の国々もまた主要な供給国となってきた。オーストラリアはそのような最初の国であり、1990年代前半にアメリカ政府からネーブルオレンジの許可を得て輸出を開始した。1990年代後半には南アフリカが、ごく最近ではチリがオーストラリアに続いた。

④アメリカでは、主に２種類のオレンジが国内で生産されている。「ネーブルオレンジ」と「バレンシアオレンジ」である。ネーブルオレンジ――ほとんど種がなく、

果肉は簡単にはがせる上に、みずみずしいというよりも引き締まっている――は生で食べるには最も人気のオレンジである。ネーブルオレンジは2010年から2012年までの間アメリカの新鮮なオレンジ市場の76％を占めていた。これに対して、バレンシアオレンジ――皮は薄く、まれに種を含み、みずみずしく甘い果肉である――は同期間で24％を占めていた。アメリカ一の青果市場のオレンジの供給元として、カリフォルニアは青果市場のネーブルオレンジの87％をバレンシアオレンジの81％以上を生産していた。

⑤国内の青果市場のオレンジの主な収穫期は11月から5月にかけてであり、その時期はカリフォルニアのネーブルオレンジの最盛期である。しかしながら、オレンジの生産量及び国内出荷量は６月から10月にかけて著しく減少する。新鮮なオレンジの輸入が国内消費量のまだごく一部を占めるに過ぎなかったごく初期においては、ネーブルオレンジが旬でない間はバレンシアオレンジが人気の品種だった。しかし図２に見られるように、南半球から輸入されるネーブルオレンジは夏の間はアメリカを席巻するようになった。

⑥季節ごとの生産周期のために、メキシコ産のオレンジの大部分はアメリカ市場に12月から6月にかけて到着するが、この時期はアメリカの国内供給量は比較的高い。対して、南半球の国々からの輸入は主に7月から10月にかけてであり、この時期アメリカの国内供給量は比較的低い。この傾向は他の多くの果物にも見られるものと同様である。

問1 | 35 | ②

図1では、（A）（B）（C）（D）は次のどれか。

主に第三段落を中心に判断する。第三段落第二文からメキシコが輸入先として長期間登場していることがわかる。よってグラフの最初から登場している（B）がメキシコと判断できる。また、同段落第四文から1990年台前半にオーストラリアが輸出を開始するとあるので（A）がオーストラリアと判断する。

問2 | 36 | ①

この文によると、以下のどれがネーブルオレンジとバレンシアオレンジの差異の一つを正確に説明しているか。

①ネーブルオレンジはバレンシアオレンジより種が少ない。

②ネーブルオレンジはバレンシアオレンジよりも果汁をたくさん含んでいる。

③冬にはバレンシアオレンジはネーブルオレンジよりも人気がある。

④バレンシアオレンジはネーブルオレンジよりも生で食べるのに適している。

第4段落第2文、第3文、第4文で答えを絞り込んでいく。

問3 | 37 | ③

この文の主題は何か。

①アメリカのオレンジ生産の季節ごとの変化の説明

②ネーブルオレンジとバレンシアオレンジの違いの説明

③アメリカのオレンジ生産とオレンジ輸入の関係

④アメリカ産のネーブルオレンジの質の改善

①は第5段落、第6段落に述べられているが文全体の主題とまでは言えない。②は第4段落で述べられているだけであるので主題とはいえない。④はこの文においては言及されていない。

問4 | 38 | ②

何の話題が最終段落に続く可能性が最も高いか。

①アメリカから南半球への他の果物の輸出割合

②他の果物の輸入における季節ごとの変化の統計

③南半球からのネーブルオレンジの船による輸送方法

④アメリカとメキシコにおける一般的に栽培されている果物の種類

第6段落の最後の文に注目する。

H27 ④A

ソーシャルネットワークサービス（SNS）は、ユーザーが他人と情報交換できるオンラインサービスであるが、ますます多くの若者が友人や家族と連絡を取り合うために使われている。しかしながら、若者によるSNS使用の増加によって、保護者や教師による不安も増加している。彼らは、プライバシーの問題や不愉快な接触を含む、若者たちがSNSを使うことがもたらすリスクへの備えができているかについて心配しているのだ。

2011年の調査では、オーストラリアの保護者、生徒、そして教師に、SNSを使用するときのリスク度への認識について、特に「安全」、「少し危険」、「とても危険」、「危険だが皆が使っていること」の中でどれにあてはまるかをたずねた。図1は、「安全」を選んだ生徒、言い換えれば「SNSの使用にリスクがないと感じている」生徒が4分の1以上いることを示している。さらに生徒の19.6%は、危険性は知っているけれど「皆が使っているもの」だから今もSNSを使っていた。生徒の回答とは対照的に、保護者と教師はSNSの使用に伴うリスクのことをより警戒しており、中でも教師の方がわずかに高リスクだと認識しているようだ。

興味深いことに、全ての生徒が同じリスク認識を持っていたわけではない。図2は学年ごとに生徒間を比較したものであり、「第7学年」は中学1年生を、「第10学年」は高校1年生を指している。SNS使用は「安全」だと答えた生徒の割合が学年に関わらずほとんど同じ一方で、「少し危険」を選んだ生徒の割合は学年が上がるごとに減少し、「リスクはあるが皆が使っているもの」の割合は増加していた。

さらに、その研究では情報セキュリティについて生徒に尋ねていた。第7学年から第10学年の生徒は、プライバシーについて次第に注意深くなり、誰が個人情報をオンラインで見ることができるかについて学年が上がるごとに注意深くなるということがわかった。第7学年の生徒は情報セキュリティに対する注意が最も足りないうえに、SNSの使用を「安全」か「少し危険」なものとしてしか判断していない傾向にある

ので、彼らは最も危険であると考えられていた。

それからその研究では、大人が若者とSNSのリスクについて話し合っているかどうかを分析した。ところがその結果はここでは明らかになっていなかった。その研究では保護者の91%以上と教師の68%がSNSの問題について生徒と話し合ったと回答したのがわかった一方で、生徒の半数近く（46.1%）が両親と話し合っていないと答え、4分の3近くの生徒（74.6%）が教師と話し合っていないと答えた。このズレについて考えられる説明がいくつかある。

問1 | 35 | ④

図1において、（A）、（B）、（C）は次のどれを指しているか。

第2段落第2文に「4分の1以上の生徒が「安全」を選んでいる」とあるので、（A）は生徒であることがわかる。また、同段落第4文に「保護者と教師はSNSの使用に伴うリスクのことをより警戒しており、中でも教師の方がわずかに高リスクだと認識しているようだ。」とあるので、「とても危険」の割合がわずかに高い（B）が教師だとわかる。

問2 | 36 | ①

第7学年の生徒が最もリスクが高いと考えられている理由の一つとして述べられているものは次のうちどれか。

①彼らはSNSを使うときにセキュリティについての注意深さが最も低い。

②彼らはSNSが「安全」だと考える可能性が最も低い。

③彼らはSNSが「とても危険」だと考える可能性が最も高い。

④彼らは友達と連絡を取るためにSNSを使う可能性が最も高い。

第4段落第3文に「第7学年の生徒は情報セキュリティに対する注意が最も足りないうえに、SNSの使用を「安全」か「少し危険」なものとしてしか判断していない傾向にあるので、彼らは最も危険であると考えられていた。」とあるので、①が正しい。

問3 | 37 | ②

この一節の主な目的は | 37 | ことである。

①SNSの使用による様々なリスクを説明する

②SNSのリスク認知における違いについて話し合う

③SNSを使用している生徒が増加している理由を説明する

④SNSに関する問題への解決策を提案する

①、③、④については本文で述べられていない。この一節で述べられているのは、生徒、教師、保護者などの属性や、生徒の学年によってリスクに対する認識が異なるということなので、②が正しい。

問4 | 38 | ②

最後の段落に続く話題は何がくると考えられるか。

①生徒がSNSの使用によって直面する様々なリスクの例

②生徒と保護者からの回答が異なっている理由

③生徒や保護者がインターネットをどの程度使っているかの傾向

④SNSを使用するより若い生徒達の数を減らすための方法
一番最後の文に「このズレについて考えられる説明がいくつかある。」とあるので，「このズレ」，つまり保護者や教師の回答と生徒の回答のズレについての説明が述べられると考えられる。よって②が正しい。

H26　④A
磁石と粘着：アメリカにおける州から州への移住についての研究

　自分が生まれた場所の近くに一生住む人がいる一方，どこか他へ移動する人もいる。ピューリサーチセンターによってなされた研究は，アメリカ人が州から州へ移動するパターンを調査した。研究では，それぞれの州を調査し，何人の成人市民が他の州からそこに移動してきたのかを測定した。このような居住者の割合が高い州は，「磁石」州とその報告書の中では呼ばれている。また，その研究は，それぞれの州で生まれた何パーセントの成人がまだそこに住んでいるのかを調査した。この数値が高い州を，「粘着」州と呼ぶ。その研究において，磁石でも粘着でもある州が存在する一方，どちらでもない州もあることがわかった。また，磁石か粘着かどちらかだけの州もあった。

　1と2のグラフは，磁石と粘着の基準で，州がそれぞれどのランクになるのかを示している。フロリダは，両方とも高いランクにある州の良い例である。現在の成人人口の70％が他の州で生まれ，かつフロリダで生まれた成人の66％がまだそこに住んでいる。一方，ウエストバージニアは特別，磁石でも（たった27％）粘着でもない（49％）。言い換えると，新しく来る者もほとんどおらず，ウエストバージニアで生まれた人は比較的あまりそこに住んでいない。ミシガンは，粘着が高いが，とても磁石が低い州の典型例である。反対に，アラスカは，磁石の基準で最上位近くにランク付けされ，全ての州の中でもっとも粘着が低い。

　また，グラフ1と2において，他に3つの極端な例が見られる。まず，ネバダは他の州で生まれた居住者の割合が高いが，このためネバダはアメリカの磁石のトップに位置している。ニューヨークは，他の国からの移民にとっては魅力的ではあるが，磁石の基準では反対側にある。3つ目の極端な例は，粘着の基準でアラスカの反対側にあるテキサスだ。テキサスは磁石がかなり弱いが，アメリカで最も粘着である。

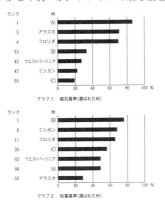

グラフ1. 磁石基準（選ばれた州）

グラフ2. 粘着基準（選ばれた州）

　その研究は，「移住者」が自分の故郷を離れ，「滞在者」が残る理由を解明するために続けられた。移住者にとって，他の州に移動しようと決めたことに影響を与える唯一の要因はない。彼らが挙げる移住の共通の理由は，仕事やビジネスの機会を求めてである。他にも，家族の絆，子どものために良い地域社会に住みたいという願望，退職といった個人的な理由もある。

問1　| 35 |　④
　もし，州が磁石であれば，| 35 |。
　　①そこで生まれた成人は，ほとんど残っていない。
　　②そこに住んでいる成人のなかには，どこか他の場所で生まれた者はほとんどいない。
　　③そこで生まれた多くの成人が残っている。
　　④そこに住んでいる多くの成人は，どこか他の場所で生まれた。
　第一段落に，磁石の定義が書かれている。磁石とは，他の州から移住してきた居住者の割合が高い州のことである。

問2　| 36 |　②
　グラフ1と2において，(A)，(B)，(C)を表している3つの州はどれか？
　まず，第三段落の第二文に，ネバダは磁石のトップに位置するとあるので，(A)。また，第三段落の最終文に，テキサスは最も粘着だとあるので，(B)。したがって，残った(C)がニューヨーク。

問3　| 37 |　①
　この文の趣旨は，| 37 |ことである。
　　①アメリカの移住の様々なパターンについて言及する
　　②なぜ，いくつかの州が他よりも有名ではないのか説明する
　　③そこで生まれた成人の割合が高い州を並べる
　　④ピューリサーチセンターがどのようにデータを集めたのか報告する
　この文の趣旨は，はっきりとした記載はないものの，第一段落の第二文があえて根拠となる①が答え。他の選択肢は記載がないか，趣旨とはなり得ないかのどちらかである。

問4　| 38 |　①
　どの話題が最終段落に続くかもしれないか？
　　①自分の故郷の州に残るアメリカ人もいる理由
　　②他の国からの移民を引きつける州
　　③他の州で移住者が求める職種
　　④磁石の州の地域社会において子どもを育てる方法
最終段落において，移住者が移住を決めた理由について述べられているので，その後，反対に，残る理由が続くのは自然な流れである。よって，①が答え。

H25　④A
　世界保健機構（WHO）は，世界中の人的保健資源の有効性と分布に関しての報告書を発表した。「世界保健報告2006」では，各国の医療環境に影響する要因を分析している。収集されたデータは，様々な状況を示し，各国で提供されている

医療改善のための長期活動計画をWHOが提案するのに役立っている。

国の医療状況に関係している大きな要因は，その国の医療従事者の数である。報告書には，世界中でこの専門家が驚くべきことに430万人も不足しているとある。さらに，医療従事者の不足は最貧国，特にサハラ砂漠以南に位置し，高い疾病率に直面している国々で最も深刻であることも指摘されている。表1が示しているように，例えばセネガルとガーナは1万人あたりの医師と看護師の数が非常に少なくなっている。

おそらく驚くべきことだろうが，ロシアやキューバといった国は，実のところ，より裕福な国よりも医療専門職の割合が高いことがあるのである。医療従事者の資格取得制度は国によって異なる。しかし，この2国は十分な専門職の数を確保することに，明らかに重点を置いている。

もう1つの重要な要因は国の医療費であり，表1に国内総生産（GDP），つまり全ての財やサービスの総額に対する割合が示されている。医師の割合が低いにも関わらず，アメリカやスウェーデン，フランスといった国々は，GDP比と実額の両方で，ロシアとキューバよりもはるかに医療に費やしている。

これらの要因とその他の条件を考慮して，WHOは世界的な医療従事者不足の解決策を提案してきた。特に懸念される地域には，ソマリアやアフガニスタンのような紛争国が含まれる。様々な国や機関が過去に経済援助を行ってきた。しかし，寄付金は必ずしも医療費増大にはつながらないので，報告書では，国々が継続可能な研修制度を確立する手助けとなる10ヵ年計画を勧めている。国際協力はWHOの提案に欠かせないものである。つまり危機にさらされている国々は，いろいろな国際パートナーの支援に頼ることができなければならないのだ。日本やイギリス，そして他の国々は医療知識も含めた援助をすることを期待されている。おそらくWHOの「医療の普遍的利用」という構想は現実的なものとなるだろう。

表1
各国の医療指標

国名	1万人あたり医師数	1万人あたり看護師数	医療費	
			GDP比	1人あたり実額（米ドル）
セネガル	0.6	3.2	5.1	29
（A）	1.5	9.2	4.5	16
アフガニスタン	1.9	2.2	6.5	11
日本	19.8	77.9	7.9	2662
（B）	25.6	93.7	15.2	5711
スウェーデン	32.8	102.4	9.4	3149
フランス	33.7	72.4	10.1	2981
（C）	42.5	80.5	5.6	167
キューバ	59.1	74.4	7.3	211

問1 　35　 ②

表1の（A）（B）（C）の3カ国を表わす組み合わせは以下のうちどれか。

第2段落の最終文に「ガーナは1万人あたりの医師と看護師の数が非常に少なくなっている。」とあるので，（A）はガーナだとわかる。また，第4段落の最終文に「医師の割合が低いにも関わらず，アメリカは，GDP比と実額の両方で，ロシアとキューバよりもはるかに医療に費やしている。」とあるので，（B）はアメリカだとわかる。さらに，第3段落の第1文目に「ロシアはより裕福な国よりも医療専門職の割合が高いことがあるのである。」とあるので，（C）はロシアだとわかる。したがって②が適当。

問2 　36　 ③

報告書によると，国の医療状況に最も影響を与える2つの側面はどれか。
①持続可能な研修制度と医療費。
②持続可能な研修制度と寄付金。
③医療従事者の数と医療費。
④医療従事者の数と寄付金。

第2段落の冒頭に「その国の医療従事者の数」，第4段落の冒頭に「国の医療費」が国の医療状況に関する重要な要因であると述べられているので，③が適当。

問3 　37　 ④

次の記述のうち正しくないものはどれか。
①世界的な医療従事者の不足は430万人であると報告されている。
②医師と看護師の割合は日本よりスウェーデンの方が高くなっている。
③WHOの報告には医療制度の乏しい国への援助活動計画も含まれている。
④WHOの報告では，比較的貧しい国々への医師，看護師のより多くの派遣を提案している。

①は第2段落の第2文，③は第5段落の第4文に一致する。また，表より②が正しいこともわかるので，正解は④。④のような記述は本文中のどこにもない。

⑤〈ヒストリー〉　　　　問題 78p〜

R4 ⑤

英語の授業で、あなたは偉大な発明家について発表を行うことになっている。あなたは以下の記事をみつけ、発表のためのメモを準備した。

誰がテレビを発明したか？簡単に答えられる質問ではない。20世紀初頭、機械式テレビシステムと呼ばれるものが存在したが、成功ではなかった。発明家たちはまた、電子式テレビシステムの開発を競い合った、そしてこれが後に今日私たちが持っているものの基礎となった。アメリカでは、電子式テレビシステムの特許を巡る争いがあり、人々の関心を集めた、なぜなら、ある若者と巨大企業との争いであったからである。この特許は発明家にこのシステムの開発、使用、販売ができる唯一の人となることができる公的な権利を与えるものであった。

フィロ・テイラー・ファーンズワースは、1906年にユタ州の丸太小屋で生まれた。彼の家庭には彼が12歳になるまで電気が通っていなかったため、彼は新しい家に引っ越した時、発電機（電気を作り出す機械）を見つけて興奮した。彼は機械技術や電気技術にとても興味を持っており、それに関する情報で見つけられるものは何でも読み漁った。彼はよく古い発電機を修理し、母親が使っていた手動式の洗濯機を電動式に変えさえしたものだった。

ある日、彼が父親のジャガイモ畑で働いていたときに、振り返り、自分が作った畝が全てまっすぐ平行に並んでいるのを見た。突然、ちょうど地面に並んだ畝のように、平行な線を使って画面に電子画像を作ることができるのではないかという考えが彼の頭に浮かんだ。1922年、高校1年の春学期に、彼の化学の教師であるジャスティン・トールマンにこの考えを示し、電子式テレビの構想についてアドバイスを求めた。黒板のスケッチや図式を使って、彼は教師にどのようにして完成させるかを見せると、トールマンはその考えを発展させるよう彼に勧めた。

1927年9月7日、ファーンズワースは初めて電子画像を送ることに成功した。その後数年で彼はライブ映像を放送することができるようさらにシステムを改良した。アメリカ政府は1930年にこのシステムに特許を与えた。

しかし、このようなシステムに取り組んでいたのはファーンズワース一人だけではなかった。RCA社（Radio Corporation of America）という巨大企業もまた、テレビに輝かしい未来を見出し、その機会を逃すまいとしていた。RCA社はウラジミール・ツヴォルキンを採用した。彼はすでに電子式テレビシステムに取り組んでおり、早くも1923年に特許を取得していた。しかし、1931年、彼らはファーンズワースのシステムの方がツヴォルキンのシステムよりも優れていたため、ファーンズワースに特許を売ってくれるよう大金を提供した。彼はこの申し出を拒否し、ファーンズワースとRCA社との特許争いが始まった。

RCA社は、ツヴォルキンが機能するシステムを作っていなかったとしても、1923年に取得したツヴォルキンの特許が優先されると主張して、ファーンズワースに対して訴訟を起こした。ファーンズワースは最初の2度の裁判では敗訴した。しかし、最後の裁判で、ファーンズワースが黒板に書いたものを書き写した教師が、ツヴォルキンの特許が出される少なくとも1年前にファーンズワースが電子式テレビシステムのアイデアを間違いなく持っていたという証拠を提出した。1934年、高校時代の恩師であるトールマンによって作られた手書きのメモの力で、裁判官はファーンズワースの特許を認めた。

ファーンズワースは1971年に64歳で亡くなった。彼はラジオやテレビを中心に約300のアメリカや外国の特許を持ち、そして1999年には、タイム誌は「タイム100：今世紀最も重要な人物の一人」にファーンズワースを選んだ。彼の死後のインタビューで、ファーンズワースの妻のペムはニール・アームストロングの月面着陸が放送されていたときのことを思い出した。彼女と一緒にテレビを見ながら、ファーンズワースは「ペム、これですべてが報われたよ。」と言った。彼の物語は動画を空中を通って送るという10代の頃の夢と、高校で黒板に書いたものが常に結びつけられていくだろう。

フィロ・テイラー・ファーンズワース（1906-1971）
— 30 —

若い頃
— 電気の通っていない丸太小屋で生まれた
— 31
— 32

重要な出来事の順序
- 33
- 34
- ファーンズワースが最初の画像を送ることに成功した。
- 35
- 36
- RCAがファーンズワースを裁判に訴えた。

結果
— ファーンズワースは 37 のおかげでRCA社との特許争いに勝った。

業績と評価
— ファーンズワースは約300個の特許を持っていた。
— タイム誌が今世紀最も重要な人物の一人に挙げた。
— 38

問1 発表に最適な副題はどれか。 30
①巨大企業に反抗する若き発明家
②高校教師から成功した発明家へ
③発電への果てしない情熱
④電子式テレビの未来

本文の第1段落第4文と具体的内容が書かれた第5段落、第6段落から「a young man：若い男＝ファーンズワース」、「a giant corporation：巨大企業＝RCA社」の間の特許を巡る争いについての記事であることがわかる。選択肢でそれぞれ「A Young Inventor」、「a Giant Company」と書き換えられている。よって、正解は①。

問2 若い頃を完成させるために 31 ・ 32 に入る最適な選択肢を2つ選べ。（順序は問わない）
①家庭に電気を供給するために発電機を買った
②父親の助けで電気の通った丸太小屋を建てた
③学校であらゆるテーマの本を読むことを楽しんだ
④彼の家庭の住宅設備を修理したり改良したりした
⑤農作業中に電子式テレビシステムのアイデアを思いついた

本文の第2段落第4文に古い発電機を修理し、手動式の洗濯機を電動式に変えさえしたとある。④は適している。また、本文の第3段落第1・2文より父親のジャガイモ畑で働いている時に平行線を使ってスクリーンに電子画像を映し出せるかもしれないと思いついたとあるので⑤も適している。よって、④と⑤が正解。

問3 5つの出来事（①〜⑤）の中から**4つ選び**、それらが起こった順に並べて主要な出来事の順序を完成させよ。
33 → 34 → 35 → 36

①ファーンズワースはRCA社の申し出を断った。

②ファーンズワースは自分のアイデアを高校の教師と共有した。

③RCA社は争いの最初の段階で勝利した。

④アメリカ政府はファーンズワースに特許を与えた。

⑤ツヴォルキンは彼のテレビシステムの特許を認められた。

主要な出来事の3つ目は第4段落第1文で、1927年9月7日に最初の電子画像の送信に成功したとあるのでこれを境に前半・後半に分けて考える。

前半、まず、第3段落第3・4文に、1922年の春学期にファーンズワースが科学教師のトールマンに自身の電子的テレビシステムのアイデアを示したとある。次に、第5段落第3文にツヴォルキンが1923年に電子式テレビシステムの特許を得ているとある。よって、 33 は②、 34 は⑤である。

後半、まず、第4段落第3文に、1930年にアメリカ政府がファーンズワースの電子式テレビシステムに特許を与えたとある。次に、1931年に第5段落第4・5文にRCA社がファーンズワースに特許を売るように申し出たがファーンズワースはこれを断ったとある。RCA社が最初の裁判に勝ったのは、重要な出来事の順序の最後にあるRCA社がファーンズワースに対する訴訟を起こした、よりも後であるから、③はいずれにも入らない。よって、 35 は④、 36 は①である。

問4　結果を完成させるのに 37 に最適な選択肢を選べ。

①ライバルの技術的劣位の受容

②トールマンによる経済的援助

③彼の教師が長年保存していたスケッチ

④RCA社の争いからの撤退

第6段落第4文に「handwritten notes made by his old high school teacher：高校時代の恩師の手書きのメモ」の力で裁判官はファーンズワースの特許を認めたとある。選択肢の「the sketches his teacher had kept for many years」はこの書き換え。よって正解は③。

問5　実績と評価を完成させるのに 38 に最適な選択肢を選べ。

①彼と妻はRCA社との研究で表彰を受けた。

②アームストロングの最初の月面着陸が放送されたとき、彼はテレビに出演した。

③彼の発明は歴史的な出来事をライブで見ることができるようにした。

④多くのティーンエイジャーが彼をテレビで見た後に自分自身の夢を追った。

第4段落第2文で彼はライブ映像を放送することができるようさらにシステムを改良したとあり、また第7段落第3段落でファーンズワースの妻ペムがアームストロングの月面着陸という歴史的な出来事を実際にテレビで見たことを思い出している。よって、正解は③。

R3（追試）　5

あなたはもし生きていればインタビューをしたい人物についてに話をします。あなたが選んだ人物についての次の文を読んで、あなたのノートを完成させなさい。

ヴィヴィアン・マイヤー

これは死ぬまで写真を撮る情熱を秘密にし続けた、あるアメリカのストリートの写真家の話です。彼女は介護士として生活していて、もしオークション会社で彼女の財産が売りに出されなければ、彼女の驚くべき作品は決して発見されなかったかもしれません。

2007年のことです。シカゴのオークション会社がヴィヴィアン・マイヤーという年老いた女性の財産を売りに出していました。彼女は保管料の支払いをしていなかったので、会社は彼女の物を売ることに決めました。彼女の財産は、主に古い写真やネガでしたがマルーフ、スラットレイ、プロウという3人の買い手に売られました。

スラットレイは2008年の7月に写真共有のウェブサイトでヴィヴィアンの写真を出版していたので、彼女の作品が面白いと思っていました。その写真は全く注目を浴びていませんでした。そして、10月にマルーフは選んだヴィヴィアンの写真を彼のブログにリンクを貼ると、すぐに何千人もの人々がその写真を見ていました。マルーフはヴィヴィアン・マイヤーの名前をその印刷物から見つけましたが、彼女について何も発見することができませんでした。そして、インターネットの検索によって彼女の死についての2009年の新聞記事に彼は辿り着きました。マルーフはヴィヴィアンの生涯についてもっと発見するためにこの情報を使い、みんなの注意を掴んだのが、ヴィヴィアンの不思議な生涯の話と彼女の写真の組み合わせでした。

ヴィヴィアンの生涯の詳細は2つの理由から限られています。第一に、彼女が生きている間誰も彼女にインタビューしなかったので、彼女がこんなにたくさんの写真を撮ったわけは誰も知らないのです。第二に、ヴィヴィアンが介護していた家族のインタビューから、彼女はとても非社交的な人だということが明らかです。彼女は友人がほとんどいませんでした。そのうえ、彼女は自分の趣味を秘密にし続けていたのです。

ヴィヴィアンは1926年にアメリカでオーストリア人の父とフランス人の母の間に生まれました。その結婚生活は幸せなものではなく、彼女の母と父は数年間離れて住んでいました。ヴィヴィアンは幼少期に頻繁にアメリカとフランスの間を移動して、時々フランスに住み、時々アメリカに住んでいました。しばらくして、ヴィヴィアンと彼女の母は成功した写真家であるジェーン・ベルトランと一緒にニューヨークで生活しました。ヴィヴィアンは若い時に写真に興味を持ったので、彼女の初めての写真はとても簡易なカメラを使って1940年代後半にフランスで撮られました。彼女は1951年にニューヨークにもどり、1956年にゲン

スバーグ家の介護士として働くためにシカゴに引っ越しました。この仕事のおかげで、彼女は写真を撮るためのより多くの時間を手に入れました。

1952年、26歳の時に彼女は初めて6×6判のカメラを購入し、シカゴの路上での生活の写真のほとんどがこのカメラによって撮られました。30年以上に渡って、彼女は子どもやお年寄り、お金持ち、貧しい人たちの写真を撮りました。写真を撮られたと気付かない人たちさえいました。彼女はまたたくさんの自画像を撮りました。そのいくつかは店のウインドウに自分自身を映したものでした。他は彼女自身の影を映したものでした。ヴィヴィアンは1970年初期までずっと、シカゴの生活を記録し続け、その頃に彼女の写真は新しいスタイルへと変化しました。

国際的な賞を受賞した「Finding Vivian Maier」と呼ばれるドキュメンタリー映画が、より多くの観客に対して、彼女の作品への興味をもたらしました。その映画のおかげで、ヨーロッパとアメリカで展示会が行われました。最も彼女のスタイルを表している写真を選ぶために、展示会を担当している人々は、「ヴィヴィアン・マイヤーなら何を現像しただろうか？」という質問に答えようとしています。この質問に答えようとするために、彼らは彼女のノートや、彼女が実際に現像した写真、ゲンスバーグによって報告された彼女の好みについての情報を用いました。ヴィヴィアンは成果よりもむしろとらえる瞬間にずっと興味がありました。だから、ヴィヴィアンの作品の背後にある不思議さにはおおいに「未熟な」部分が残っていると人は言うことができたのです。

発表ノート：
ヴィヴィアン・マイヤー
写真家ヴィヴィアン
☆彼女は介護士として働いている間にたくさんの写真を撮った。
☆彼女が生きている間誰もインタビューしなかったので、私たちは彼女についてあまり知らない。
☆ 30

ヴィヴィアンの作品
☆主な被写体：
・若い、年老いた、お金持ちの、貧しい人
・ 31
・ 32

彼女の作品はどうやって認識されるようになったのか
☆ヴィヴィアンの保管料が支払われてなかった。
☆ 33
☆ 34
☆ 35
☆ 36
☆彼女の生涯と作品についての情報の結合が、人々の興味を増大させた。

彼女の作品はどのように世界的に知られるようになったのか
☆賞を受賞した彼女の生涯と作品についてのドキュメンタリー映画は、新しい観客を獲得するのを助けた。
☆ 37

「大きな」答えられていない質問：ㅤ 38

問1　 30 　に入る最も適当な文を選びなさい。
①彼女の作品はオークションで売れるまでずっと発見されないままだった。
②彼女は30代の時に写真に引きつけられたと考えられている。
③彼女は行くところはどこでもカメラを持って行き、他人に自分の写真を見せた。
④彼女の写真の大多数はニューヨークで撮られた。

第1段落に「if it had not been～never have been discovered.」とあるので、①が答え。

問2　 31 　と 32 　に入る最も適当な語句を2つ選びなさい（順不同）。
①ドキュメンタリー形式の写真
②工業的な風景
③自然の風景
④彼女自身の写真
⑤店のウインドウ

第6段落に「She also took a number of self-portraits.」とあるので④が答え。
また、その後に「Vivian continued document Chicago life」とあるので①が答え。

問3　次の出来事を起こった順に並べなさい。
33 ～ 36
①買い手は自分のブログにいくつかの彼女の写真のリンクを貼った。
②彼女の死の報告が新聞に掲載された。
③オークション会社は彼女の古い写真とネガを売り始めた。
④彼女の作品はインターネット上に公開された。

第2段落より、③は2007年。
第3段落より、④は2008年7月、①は2008年10月、②は2009年。

問4　 37 　に最も適当な文を入れなさい。
①彼女の作品の展示会は、世界の様々な場所で開催されている。
②道の景色を特集した彼女の写真集は賞を受賞した。
③彼女は自分の写真をどのように取り扱ってほしいか詳細な指示を残した。
④ヴィヴィアンの従業員の子どもたちは、自分の写真を与えた。

最終段落に「The film led to exhibitions in Europe and the US.」とあるので①が答え。

問5　 38 　に入る最も適当な質問を選びなさい。
①「彼女は写真を撮るのにどんなタイプのカメラを使ったか？」
②「彼女はネガと写真をどこに保存していたか？」
③「彼女はなぜ介護士になるためにニューヨークを去ったのか？」
④「彼女はなぜ誰にも見せることなくそんなにたくさんの写真を撮ったのか？」

第 4 段落の「no one knew why she took so many photographs.」とあるので④が答え。

R3（本試） ⑤

　ある国際的なニュース記事を使って、あなたは英語の口頭発表のコンテストに参加しようと思っています。発表の準備として、以下のフランスからのニュース記事を読みなさい。

　5年前、サビーヌ・ルアス夫人は馬を失った。彼女はその馬が老衰で死ぬまで、20年の間一緒に過ごしていた。その時、彼女は二度と別の馬を飼うことはできないと感じた。寂しさから、彼女は近くの牧場の牛を観るのに何時間も費やした。そして、ある日、彼女は牧場主に牛の世話をさせてもらえないかと頼んだ。

　牧場主は承諾し、サビーヌは働き始めた。彼女はすぐに1頭の牛と友情を深めた。その牛が妊娠していたので、彼女は他の牛よりも多くの時間を過ごした。牛の赤ちゃんが生まれた後、赤ちゃん牛はサビーヌの周りをついてまわり始めた。不幸なことに、牧場主は雄牛を酪農牧場で飼い続けることに興味がなかった。牧場主は309と呼ぶ赤ちゃん牛を精肉市場に売ることを計画した。サビーヌはそのようなことにならないようにすることを決心し、牧場主に赤ちゃん牛と母牛を買わせてもらえないか尋ねた。牧場主は承諾し、彼女は彼らを買った。それから、サビーヌは309を街まで散歩させ始めた。およそ9か月後、彼女はついに動物を移動させる許可を得て、サビーヌの農場に牛たちを移動させた。

　そのすぐあと、サビーヌはポニーの提供の申し出を受けた。最初は、彼女はポニーをほしいのか確信がなかったが、彼女の馬の思い出はもはやつらいものではなかった、そこで彼女はポニーを受け入れ、彼をレオンと名付けた。それから、彼女は昔の趣味に戻ることを決心し、彼に障害飛越の訓練を始めた。彼女が名前をアストンと変えた309はレオンと多くの時間を過ごし、2頭は本当に仲良くなった。しかし、サビーヌはレオンとの日々のトレーニングにアストンが細心の注意を払うことも、アストンが技を覚えることも期待していなかった。若い雄牛は命令に応じて、常歩、襲歩、停止、後退、回転することをすぐに習得した。彼はサビーヌの声に馬のように反応した。そして、1300kgもの体重にもかかわらず、サビーヌを背中に乗せて1mの馬用障害物を跳ぶことをたった18か月で習得した。アストンはレオンを見続けることなしではこれらの技を習得することはなかったかもしれない。さらに、アストンは距離を理解し、ジャンプの前に歩幅を調整することができた。彼はまた、自分の間違いに気付き、何らサビーヌの助けを借りることなく修正をすることができた。それはまさに、オリンピックレベルの馬にしかできないことである。

　今では、サビーヌとアストンはヨーロッパ中の週末の市や馬のショーに行き、技術を披露している。サビーヌは「良い反応を得ました。たいてい、人々は本当に驚き、そして最初は彼が大きい、馬よりずっと大きいので、少し怖いかもしれません。多くの人々は角のある雄牛に近づきたがりません。しかし、一度彼の本性を見て、彼の実演を見ると、「あ、彼は本当にとても美しい」と言うことが多いです。」と言う。

　「見て！」とサビーヌはスマートフォンの中のアストンの写真を見せます。彼女は続けて「アストンがとても小さいとき、リードをつけて犬のように、人に慣れるように散歩に行ったものです。もしかすると、それが彼が人を気にしない理由かもしれません。彼はとても穏やかなので、特に子どもは、アストンを見ることや彼に近づく機会を得ることが本当に好きです。」

　数年にわたり、障害飛越をする巨大な雄牛のニュースは急速に広まり、いまや、アストンはオンライン上のフォロワー数を増やす主要な呼び物である。アストンとサビーヌはときに家から200から300kmも離れたところに移動する必要があり、それは宿泊しなければならないことを意味する。アストンは馬の運搬車で寝なければならないが、アストンにとって十分な大きさではない。

　「アストンは馬の運搬車が好きではありません。私は馬の運搬車で一緒に寝なければなりません。」サビーヌは言います。「でもね、彼が起きて体を動かすときは、私をつぶさないように気をつけてくれます。彼はとても紳士的です。彼は時々さびしくなり、レオンとあまりに長く離れることを嫌がりますが、それ以外はとても幸せです。」

あなたの発表のスライド

```
  30
中央高校英語発表大会
```

```
誰が誰か？（人物紹介）
主役　（　　　）,（　　　）,（　　　）⎫
                                    ⎬   31
脇役　（　　　）,（　　　）          ⎭
```

```
有名になるまでの物語
サビーヌの馬が死ぬ。→ 32 → 33 → 34 → 35 →
アストンとサビーヌがショーに行き始める。
```

```
アストンの能力
アストンは：
・レオンのトレーニングを見るだけで身に着けることができる。
・常歩、襲歩、停止をサビーヌが言えばすることができる。
・距離を理解し、歩幅を調節することができる。
・ 36
・ 37
```

```
アストンの現在
今日のアストン：
・障害飛越をする牛である。
・祭りやイベントにサビーヌとともに行く。
・ 38
```

問1　あなたの発表に最も適したタイトルはなんですか？
　　　 30
　　①動物を愛する人がポニーの命を救う
　　②アストンの夏の障害飛越ツアー
　　③馬のようにふるまう雄牛、アストンとの出会い
　　④ある牧場主と牛との関係

2段落後半で精肉市場に牧場主が売ろうとしたところをサビーヌが救ったのはポニーではなく牛の命であり、①は不適。4段落初めや6段落にアストンがサビーヌとヨーロッパ各地の市や馬のショーに行って技を披露したことが書かれているが、夏に限った話ではなく、②も不適。文全体で書かれているのは、牧場主と牛のアストンではなく、サビーヌと牛のアストンとの関係なので④は不適。アストンは馬のように技を行うことができるので、正解は③。

問2　「誰が誰か？」のスライドの最も適した組み合わせはどれですか？ 31

	主役	脇役
①	309、アストン、牧場主	サビーヌ、ポニー
②	アストン、アストンの母、サビーヌ	309、牧場主
③	アストン、レオン、牧場主	アストンの母、サビーヌ
④	アストン、サビーヌ、ポニー	アストンの母、牧場主

この話の主人公はスライドの1ページに描かれ、スライドに繰り返し名前の出てくる、馬のようにふるまう雄牛、アストン（＝309）と、その飼い主サビーヌ、アストンとともに育てられたポニーのレオンである。よって、正解は④。

問3　有名になるまでの物語を完成するために、起こった順に4つの出来事を並べなさい。

サビーヌの馬が死ぬ→

32 → 33 → 34 → 35

→アストンとサビーヌがショーに行き始める。

①アストンがジャンプを覚える
②サビーヌとアストンが一緒に何百キロも旅をする
③サビーヌが309とその母親を買う
④サビーヌが近所の牧場に働きに行く
⑤サビーヌが309を散歩に連れて行く

1段落初めでサビーヌの馬が死ぬ。2段落初めでサビーヌは近所の牧場で働き始め、2段落後半で309とその母親を買い、309を街に散歩に連れて行き始めた。3段落半ばで18か月でジャンプを覚えたとあり、4段落初めでアストンとサビーヌがショーに行き始めたとある。7段落にサビーヌとアストンが一緒に何百キロも旅をする様子が描かれているが、これはアストンがサビーヌとショーに行き始めるよりも後の話である。よって、正解は④→③→⑤→①。

問4　アストンの能力のスライドに2つの最も適切な項目を選びなさい。（順不同）　36 ・ 37

①間違いを自分で正すことができる。
②ポニーと並んでジャンプすることができる。
③騎手を背中に乗せてジャンプすることができる。
④馬よりも早く芸を身に着けることができる。
⑤写真のためにポーズをとることができる。

3段落後半に「自分の間違いに気付き、何らサビーヌの助けを借りることなく修正をすることができた」とあり、①と一致する。また、3段落後半に「サビーヌを背中に乗せて1mの高さの馬用障害物を跳ぶことをたった18か月で習得した」とあるので③と一致する。また、④は馬よりも早くとは書かれておらず、②と⑤については書かれていない。よって、正解は①と③。

問5　最も適切な項目でスライド、アストンの現在を完成させなさい。　38

①ファンの数が増加している
②サビーヌをとても裕福にしてきた
③とても有名なので、最早人間を恐れさせない
④1年のほとんどの夜を馬の運搬車で過ごしている

6段落初め、ジャンプする牛のニュースは急速に拡がり、いまや、アストンはオンライン上のフォロワー数を増やす主要な呼び物であると一致するから正解は①。

あなたの班は下にある雑誌の記事の情報を使って「アメリカのジャーナリズムに革命を起こした人物」と題されたポスターのプレゼンテーションの準備をしています。

ベンジャミン・デイは、ニューイングランドの印刷業者であるが、ニューヨークシティの新聞「ザ・サン」を刊行し、アメリカのジャーナリズムを永久的に変えた。ベンジャミン・デイは、1810年4月10日にマサチューセッツ州のスプリングフィールドで生まれた。彼は10代のときに印刷会社で働き、20歳のときにニューヨークにある印刷所と新聞社で働き始めた。1831年に、十分な金額のお金を貯蓄した頃、彼は自分自身の印刷業を始めたが、それは翌年街がコレラエピデミックに襲われたとき、困難になり始めた。彼の事業が失敗するのを防ぐ試みで、デイは新聞を始めることを決意したのである。

1833年、アメリカには650の週報新聞と65の日報新聞があり、平均売上は約1200部であった。アメリカの他の地域には安い新聞もあったが、ニューヨークでは通常6セントもかかるものであった。デイは多くの労働階級の人々が新聞を読むことができるが、興味を向けないことと非常に高価であることから、それらを買わないことを選んだのである。1833年9月3日、デイは印刷費用を1セントに抑えた「ザ・サン」を刊行した。「ペニー・プレス」の導入は、安い新聞として知られるようになったので、アメリカのジャーナリズムの歴史において重大な偉業であった。

デイの新聞記事は当時の他の新聞会社のそれとは異なっていた。政治に関する報道や書物や映画の批評の代わりに、「ザ・サン」は人々の日々の生活に焦点を当てていた。それは個人的な出来事や事件を報道する初の新聞だった。それはアメリカのジャーナリズムに転換を引き起こし、新聞がコミュニティと読み手の人生の重要な一部となっていったのである。デイは他の斬新な考えを思いついた。それは、街角で新聞を売る新聞売りである。人々は、新聞を買うために店に入る必要すらもなくなるだろうと思われた。

簡単に手に入るほど安い新聞の組み合わせは成功で、すぐにデイは「ザ・サン」で良い収入を得ていた。6ヶ月以内に、ザ・サンの発行部数は5000部に到達し、1年後、10000部にまで上がった。1835年までに、ザ・サンの売上は19000部に到達し、当時の他のどの新聞よりも多かったのである。その後の数年で、約12の新たなペニーペーパーが発行し、新たな新聞競争の時代が始まった。ザ・サンの成功は、他のジャーナリストがより低い値段で新聞を発行するように促したのである。市民戦争の時代までに、ニューヨーク市の新聞の平均的な値段はちょうど2セントにまで下がった。

彼は成功したにも関わらず、ザ・サンを経営してから約5年後、デイは新聞を発行する日々の仕事に興味を失ってしまった。1838年に、彼はザ・サンを義理の兄であるモーゼス・エール・ビーチに40000ドルで売り渡し、長年に渡り発行し続けた。新聞社を売り渡した後、デイは雑誌の発行を含めて、他の事業域に異動したが、1860年代までに彼は根本的には退職したのである。彼は1889年12月21日に没するまで静かに暮らした。比較的短期間アメリカの新聞事業に携わったけれども、デイは新聞が大衆に訴えるということを示す革命的な象徴として思い出されるのである。

アメリカのジャーナリズムに革命を起こした人物
■ベンジャミン・デイの生涯

期間	出来事
1810年代	スプリングフィールドで幼少期を過ごす
1820年代	27
1830年代以降	28 ↓ 29 ↓ 30 ↓ 31

■ザ・サンについて

▶1833年9月3日にザ・サンを刊行する
▶この新聞は次の理由により大いに成功した： 32

■アメリカのジャーナリズムにおける転換：新しい体系

▶ザ・サンのモットーは「 33 」であった。
▶ザ・サンはアメリカのジャーナリズムと社会を多くの方法で変えた： 34

問1 あなたの班のメンバーはデイの生涯における重要な出来事を表にしました。出来事を 27 ～ 31 の空欄にそれらが起こった順番に入れなさい。

①他の発行物を作り上げた
②印刷会社を設立した
③地元の印刷者としての経験を得た
④新聞事業を始めた
⑤事業が致命的な病気により脅かされた

27 ：第1段落3行目以降によると、デイは1810年に生まれ、10代のときに印刷会社で働いていることから、1820年代には印刷業を経験していることがわかる。よって、正解は③。 28 ：第1段落5行目以降によると、1831年に自身による印刷事業を始めたので、正解は②。 29 ：第1段落7行目以降によると、コレラが大流行したことがわかる。よって。正解は⑤。 30 ：第1段落8行目によると、新聞事業を始めたのがわかる。よって、正解は④。 31 ：第5段落4行目によると、デイは新聞社を売った後、雑誌の刊行をしようとしていたことがわかる。よって、正解は①。

問2 ポスターを完成させるのに最適な文を選びなさい。
（複数回答可） 32

①デイは労働階級の言語水準を向上させることに焦点を置いた。
②デイは新聞を流通させる新たな方法を導入した。
③デイは入手できる新聞の潜在的な要求に気付いていた。

④デイは簡単に理解することができるやり方で政治的な問題を報道した。
⑤デイは非常にたくさんの新聞をすべての家庭に供給した。
⑥デイはどんな種類の記事が読み手を惹きつけるかを理解した。

①：間違い。第2段落によると、デイは新聞の価格を下げることに焦点を置いている。
②：正しい。第3段落によると、デイは新聞の売り子や内容を日常的なものにすることで流通させた。
③：正しい。第2段落によると、デイは新聞の内容が興味を引くものでなく、価格も高すぎるという問題点に気づきそれを訂正したのである。
④：間違い。第3段落によると、政治的な問題ではなく、日常的な内容を新聞の記事にしたのである。
⑤：間違い。そのようなことは書かれていない。
⑥：正しい。②、③と同様の理由である。

問3 ザ・サンのモットーに最も近いものは次のうちどれか。 33

①政治より貴重なものなどない
②アメリカンドリームの日記
③ザ・サン：それは全てを照らす
④頂上の人々が太陽を手に入れる

デイは全ての人々に新聞を手にとってほしいと思い、新聞の価格や内容を考えていたのである。よって、正解は③。

問4 ポスターを完成させるのに最適な文を選びなさい。
（複数回答可） 34

①情報が普通の人にも広く知られるようになった
②ジャーナリストは政治的な関心をより意識するようになった
③ジャーナリストは社会に興味を与える話題をより多く書き始めた
④新聞は中流階級の読み手にはそれほど人気がなくなった
⑤新聞は読み書き教育を提供することで学校に置き換わった
⑥新聞の役割は以前よりもかなり重要になった

①：正しい。第2段落によると、新聞の価格が下がり内容が日常的なものになったので、様々な人が新聞を買えるようになったことがわかる。
②：間違い。①と同様。
③：正しい。①と同様。
④：間違い。第4段落によると、人気が出てきたので発行部数が伸びたことがわかる。
⑤：間違い。そのようなことは書かれていない。
⑥：正しい。第3段落によると、新聞はより社会に必要なものとなったことがわかる。

H29（試行調査1回） 5 A

あなたは学校新聞の編集者です。あなたはメアリーという名前のアメリカ人の学生によって書かれた折り紙についての記事にコメントを載せるよう頼まれました。

折り紙

[1] 日本にいるたくさんの人々が、折り紙という子供時代の記憶をもっているでしょうし、正方形の紙が動物や花のような美しい形に変えられていくわけです。折り紙は数世紀に渡って全ての年代の人々に広く楽しまれてきました。

[2] 最近のある出来事により、私たちは折り紙が海外では日本の伝統的な芸術形式であるとみなされていることが思い出されます。バラク・オバマ大統領が2016年に広島を訪れた際、彼は4匹の折り鶴を綺麗に作りました。彼はそのとき、広島市にそれらを贈呈しました。これは2カ国の友情と世界平和の約束の象徴とみなされています。

[3] 折り紙の2つの良い影響が、老人の治療とリハビリテーションに見られます。折り紙は紙を特定の形に折ることに非常に集中するのと同様に、指の正確な連動を必要とします。それは、アルツハイマー病のような精神的な問題に関連する、記憶消失の進行を遅らせると考えられています。また、折り紙は運動能力を維持し、脳の活動を活発にするのに役立つと考えられており、人が怪我から回復するのを助けるので、これらの理由から、日本の内側でも外側でも、折り紙が使用されるような、数多くの老人の治療とリハビリテーション計画があります。

[4] 子供たちもまた、折り紙から恩恵を受けています。彼らが楽しめている間に、折り紙は創造力と芸術的感性を育成します。これが、折り紙大会や展覧会のような幼い子どもたちのための催し物を定期的に開催する、非常に多くの関係性－国内と国外の両方の－という結果を生んだのです。これらの分野において活発であるたくさんの組織が海外で見られることは驚きでしょうか。

[5] A 。さらには、折り紙の紙を折る技術は薬への応用が見込まれています。 B 。2016年に、ある国際的な研究チームが、医療に使われうる小さな、紙の薄さのロボットを開発しました。そのロボットは、豚の材料で作られていますが、折り紙の紙のように折りたたまれ氷で作られたカプセルで覆われています。そのカプセルが患者により飲み込まれ、胃に到達すると、カプセルが溶け、周囲から水分を吸収しそのロボットが開きます。 C 。この後、そのロボットは、務めを行うために体外から操作されます。手技が完了すると、そのロボットは自然に体外に排出されます。 D 。

[6] 上記に示した例のように、折り紙はもはや、単に私たちの多くが子供時代に余暇活動として経験した、伝統的な日本の芸術形式ではないのです。実際、それは世界中の全世代の生活に良い変化を与えうる、強大な力です。その美しさの評価が、これからの世代を継続的に来させそうですが、最近では、折り紙が私たちの生活の他の様々な側面に影響するようになっています。

問1 メアリーの記事は主に 25 について議論している。

　①他の分野よりも、薬における折り紙の重要性
　②海外の多くの国々における新たな折り紙の開発
　③折り紙が世界平和と協力において果たす主要な役割
　④文化的、医学的、教育的目的のための折り紙の利用

[1] 段落で文化的、[3][5] 段落で医学的、[4] 段落で教育的な目的の例が挙げられている。よって、正解は④。

問2 [3][4] 段落におけるメアリーの意図はおそらく 26 ことです。

　①国外での、折り紙の発展の歴史を記述する
　②病気を治療するために折り紙を使う難しさを議論する
　③リハビリテーションと老人の治療、教育のために折り紙を使うことについての懸念を表現する
　④異なる年齢の人々の生活にとっての、折り紙の貢献を説明する

③が悩ましいが、メアリーは懸念（心配）しているのでは

なく、折り紙を使用することの良さを紹介しているため、老人と子どもたちにとっての折り紙の貢献度と考える。よって、正解は④。

問3 あなたはこの話題に関連した追加の情報を見つけ、メアリーが以下の文章を彼女の記事に追加するよう提案したいと思いました。[5] 段落の A 、 B 、 C 、 D と印がついた4箇所の中で、その文章が最も合うのはどれですか。 27

　　ロボットの開発者はこの技術が、例えば、誤ってそれを飲み込んだ子供の胃の中から、小さな電池を取り除くために使われうるだろう、と言います。

　①A 　②B 　③C 　④D

ロボットの技術に関する内容のうち、体外に出ることが述べられているのは、[5] 段落の最後の2行。上記の文章には「この技術が」と書かれているため、最後の2行よりも後に入れるべき文章だと考えられる。よって、正解は④。

H29（試行調査1回） 5 B

あなたは香辛料の特徴に関する発表の準備をしています。黒胡椒と白胡椒に関する以下の記事を見つけました。あなたはその記事を読みノートを取ろうとしています。

黒胡椒と白胡椒

[Part 1] いくつかの最近の研究により、私たちがより長く生きるのに役立つ香辛料の役割についての、私たちの理解は高まった。世界中には様々な種類の香辛料があり、おそらくあなた方はそれらのうちの2つ、黒胡椒と白胡椒についてよく知っているだろう。黒胡椒と白胡椒の両者は、同じコショウ属の植物の実からできる。しかしながら、それらは異なる経過をたどる。黒胡椒はコショウ属の、完全に熟す前の実から作られる。実のいずれの1粒も、ちょうど直径3ミリから6ミリの小さな緑色のボールのように見える。収穫された実は、天日干しされると黒くなる。干された実のどちらの1粒もペッパーコーンと呼ばれる。粉末にされた黒胡椒の色は、ペッパーコーンの皮の色からきている。一方で、白胡椒を得るには、そのコショウの実がさくらんぼ色のときに収穫する。その実の皮は、天日干しする前に取り除かれる。そのコショウの実の内側にある種の色は白色である。このようにして、白いペッパーコーンが処理される。その皮はとても薄いので、黒胡椒と白胡椒の大きさは同じくらいである。白胡椒は、それを処理する過程がより多いので、通常は、黒胡椒よりも高い。

[Part 2] 胡椒の風味はどこからきているのか。その鋭いスパイシーな味は、ピペリンと呼ばれる天然の物質により引き出される。ペッパーコーンの種だけでなく外側の殻にも、たくさんのピペリンが含まれる。それゆえに、黒胡椒の方が白胡椒より味が辛いという人もいる。黒胡椒もその風味をより複雑にする他の多くの物質を含んでいる。その複合した物質により生み出される黒胡椒の独特な風味は、多くの種類の料理に合う。白胡椒の風味は黒胡椒のそれよりも上品だとみなされることが多いが、その風味が弱すぎてステーキのような肉料理の味を引き出せない。その色のおかげで、白胡椒は、明るい色の料理によく使われる。マッシュポテトやホワイトソース、白魚が白胡椒で香り付けされるとより見栄えがいいのかもしれない。

[Part 3] 歴史上、人々は胡椒を民間薬として使用してきた。例えば、咳や風邪には有名な治療法だった。胡椒の健康に与える影響は、ピペリンにより起こされるものもある。ビタミンCのように、ピペリンには抗酸化作用がある。これは、この物質を含む食べ物を食べることで、私たちは有害な化学反応を防ぐかもしれない、ということを意味する。さらには、最近の研究により、胡椒はいくつかの病気の影響を軽減する、ということが分かった。ピペリンを含む全ての香辛料には、人体に対するこの効果があります。黒胡椒と白胡椒には、同様の健康に与える恩恵がある。

28 から 33 を埋めてノートを完成させよ。

ノート

概要：

Part 1： [28]

Part 2： [29]

Part 3： [30]

表：黒胡椒と白胡椒の比較

共通点	相違点
31	32

要点： [33]

問1 パート1，2，3の見出しとして最適なのは、それぞれ [28]、[29]、[30] である。（1つの選択肢は1度のみ使ってよい）

①香辛料としての胡椒の特徴

②健康に与える胡椒の効果

③黒胡椒と白胡椒の原産地

④黒胡椒と白胡椒の製法

[28]：パート1の4行目以降では、黒胡椒と白胡椒がコショウ属の植物からできることや、それらの処理の仕方について述べられている。よって、正解は④。[29]：パート2の1行目に、「胡椒の風味はどこからきているのか」とある。また、その後も胡椒の風味の素となる物質や、どの料理にどちらの胡椒が合うのかについて述べられている。よって、正解は①。[30]：パート3の1〜3行目で、胡椒が薬として使われていたことや、健康に与える影響について述べられている。よって、正解は②。

問2 以下の中で、記事の中で述べられている共通点と相違点は、それぞれ [31]、[32] である。（それぞれの欄には複数選択してよい）

①ビタミンC の量　　②病気に与える影響

③風味　　　　　　　④植物

⑤値段　　　　　　　⑥皮の除去

それぞれの選択肢について、共通ならばB=W、違うならばB≠W、どちらでも述べられてなければ×（Bは黒胡椒、Wは白胡椒を表す）と示す。①：パート2の2行目によると、胡椒の皮にも種にもピペリン（ビタミンCと同様の作用）は含まれているが、どちらもビタミンC自体は含まれていないため、×。②：パート2の6行目によると、「ピペリンを含む全ての香辛料には、人体に対するこの効果（抗酸化作用）があります」とあるので、B=W。③：パート2の3行目によると、「黒胡椒の方が白胡椒よりも味が辛いという人もいる」や「（白胡椒の方が）風味が弱すぎる」とある

ので、B≠W。④：パート1の4行目によると、「同じコショウ属の植物の実からできる」とあるので、B=W。⑤：パート1の最後の2行によると、「（白胡椒は）黒胡椒よりも高い」とあるので、B≠W。⑥：パート1の7〜11行目によると、黒胡椒は皮を剥かず天日干しをし、白胡椒は天日干しする前に皮を剥くことが分かるので、B≠W。よって、正解は [31]：②、④。[32]：③、⑤、⑥。

問3 この記事は主に [33] について議論している。

①ほかの香辛料と比較した、黒胡椒と白胡椒の利点と欠点

②人々が黒胡椒と白胡椒を作り始めた理由と、それらが有名でなくなった理由

③白胡椒が黒胡椒よりも良い理由と、それが私たちとって良い理由

④黒胡椒と白胡椒との共通点と相違点、また両者の健康に与える恩恵

問1、問2でも解説したが、Part 1とPart 2を通して、黒胡椒と白胡椒の共通点と相違点について述べられており、Part 3は健康に与える影響について述べられている。よって、正解は④。

R2　6

(1)自動販売機は日本では非常に一般的なので、あなたが行く先々でそれを見つけることができる。中には、電車の切符や食券を売っているものもあれば、お菓子や飲み物を売っているものもある。それらは、素早く快適に何かを買いたい人にとっては特に便利である。

(2)自動販売機は今日至るところで見つけられるが、それらは元々日本で開発されたのではない。最初の自動販売機は約2,200年前ギリシャの数学の先生によりつくられたと一般的に信じられている。この機械は、寺院の祈りで使われた特別な水を売っていた。水を購入したい人は、硬貨を入れ、それはバネに接続されている金属のレバーに当たる。そして、その硬貨の重さにより、硬貨が落ちるまである特定の量の水が注がれるのである。これは、その特別な水の量と等しいお金を人々が受け取っていたことを保証した。

(3)約1,000年前、鉛筆を売る自動販売機が中国で開発された。その後、1700年代には、硬貨操作のタバコボックスがイギリスのバーに現れた。人々はこれらのボックスの1つで売られている商品がほしいとき、硬貨を入れレバーを回す。商品は、客が拾い上げられるように落ちてくる。しかしながら、1880年代になって初めて、自動販売機が世界中に広まった。1883年に、あるイギリスの開発者がはがきと新聞を売る自動販売機を創った。これは人気となり、すぐにたくさんの国で、新聞や印鑑、他の品物を売る自動販売機が現れた。1904年に、自動販売機は日本で運用されるようになった。1926年、技術が進歩し、自動販売機は異なる金額で商品を売るように設定された。その後、より多くの種類の商品が売られた。こうなると、自動販売機産業は急速に広まったのである。

(4)その拡大のなかで、世界中の自動販売機産業が直面した最大の問題は、硬貨の使用ではなく、紙幣の使用であった。不正を行う人にとって、機械を騙すことができるお金を作ることが容易であると証明したので、これは挑戦だった。これにより自動販売機産業はより良い検出方法を確立し、これが、国々が偽造するのが困難なお金を開発する手段をとった１つの理由である。今や、現金の問題を防ぐだけでなく、クレジットカードや最近の電子払いの形態を導入するため、自動販売機は技術的に進歩した。

(5)自動販売機が最も人気になったのは、日本だった。現在は、日本には420万台以上の自動販売機があり、それらのうち約55％が紅茶やコーヒー、ジュースのような飲料を売っている。日本が世界の自動販売機の中心地となった主な理由の１つが、日本の全域的な安全水準である。自動販売機が窃盗を防ぐために録画をしなければならないような多くの場所と異なり、それらは日本のどこででも実質的には配置されうる。この並外れたほどの公共安全が、入手可能な商品の幅と同じくらい、観光客には驚愕に思われている。旅行客はしばしばバナナや生卵、米の袋のような予想外の商品を売っている自動販売機の写真を撮っている。観光客はそれらを日本文化に特有な面だとみなしていると理解できる。

(6)自動販売機の人気と便利さを考えると、近い将来それらが消えてなくなることはなさそうである。それらは、様々な品物が販売員の必要なく売ることのできる場所を提供する。次にあなたが寒い日に温かい飲み物を購入したいと思うときは、日本では少なくともそれを思い出し、次の曲がり角のあたりで自動販売機がおそらくあるだろう。

A

問1　46　①

第(2)段落によると、最初の自動販売機では何をすることができたか。

① 人々が、それから一定の量の液体を入手するのを許可すること

② 古代ギリシャの数学教師の本を提供すること

③ 観光客が祈りたいときに寺院に入るのを許可すること

④ それを創った人に安定した収入を与えること

第(2)段落４行目以降によると、「この機械は、寺院の祈りで使われた特別な水を売っていた」とある。よって、正解は①。

問2　47　③

第(3)段落によると、自動販売機に関する以下の記述のうち正しいのはどれか。

① イギリスの開発者の自動販売機は、様々な値段で品物を売っていた。

② 自動販売機による売上は高額な硬貨が現れたとき上昇した。

③ 自動販売機の技術は何世紀も前にアジアで発見された。

④ 自動販売機は18世紀までに世界中で一般的だった。

第(3)段落１行目によると、「約1,000年前、鉛筆を売る自動販売機が中国で開発された」とある。よって、正解は③

問3　48　②

第(4)段落にある、下線部の単語counterfeitの意味に最も近いものは以下のうちどれか。

① 違法な交換を受け入れること

② 認定されていない模造品を創ること

③ 認められていない技術を制限すること

④ 不必要な援助を引き受けること

第(4)段落では、自動販売機に紙幣を使おうとすること、その紙幣を偽造しようとする人がいること、偽造された紙幣を検出する方法を各国が開発していること、が書かれている。よって、正解は②。

問4　49　④

第(5)段落によると、日本の自動販売機に関して正しいものはどれか。

① 海外の旅行者は、それから購入するのをためらう

② それらのうち４分の３以上が様々な飲み物を売っている

③ そこで売られているかなり安全な商品が客を惹きつける

④ 様々な品物が、世界中においてそれらを独特なものにしている

第(5)段落８行目によると、「予想外の商品を売っている」「観光客はそれらを日本文化に特有な面だとみなしている」とある。よって、正解は④。

問5　50　②

この文章に最適なタイトルは何か。

① 日本社会における自動販売機の文化的恩恵

② 歴史的な観点から見た自動販売機の発展

③ 国際的な比較による自動販売機の経済的影響

④ 現代技術を通した自動販売機の国際化

文章全体を通して記述されていることをもとに判断する。第(2)(3)(4)段落では、自動販売機の過去からの変遷を、第(6)段落では自動販売機の未来に言及している。よって、正解は②。

B

| 51 | ② | 52 | ④ | 53 | ③ | 54 | ① |

段　落	内　容
(1)	導入
(2)	51
(3)	52
(4)	53
(5)	54
(6)	結論

① 自動販売機が１つの国で広範囲に存在することを可能にする特定の要因

②１つの自動販売機の創作とどのようにその機械が使われているのかの描写

③異なる形態のお金を導入した後で、自動販売機を建てる困難

④過去に異なる場所で売られていた自動販売機の品物の種類

51 ：第(2)段落では、自動販売機の例の１つとして、水を売っていたものが紹介されており、その仕組みについて記述されていることが分かる。よって、正解は②。

52 ：第(3)段落では、中国とイギリスにおける自動販売機が紹介されている。中国は約1000年前、イギリスは1700年代の内容である。よって、正解は④。 **53** ：第(4)段落では、自動販売機に使われるお金の変化（硬貨と紙幣）と、紙幣を導入した結果起こった、偽造紙幣の開発に関して記述されている。よって、正解は③。 **54** ：第(5)段落では、日本の自動販売機に関して記述されている。自動販売機が最も広まっているのは日本であり、それは自動販売機の中の品物が、珍しいものであるからだと書かれている。よって、正解は①。

H28 6

(1)オペラは表現の最高レベルにある人間の声を賛美する芸術である。特に偉大な歌手により演じられる際には、オペラのように興奮を生み、人々を感動させる芸術は他にない。そういった歌手たちは人間の声のためにこれまでに作曲されてきた最も偉大で最も困難な音楽を表現するために訓練されている。

(2)オペラは西洋古典伝統音楽の重要な一部である。オペラは人生に劇的な物語をもたらすために音楽、言葉、そして動作を用いる。オペラは16世紀終わりにイタリアで始まりその後ヨーロッパ中で人気になった。長い年月をかけてオペラは世界中の様々な音楽的演劇的な発展に反応してきたし今後もそうし続ける。最近数十年では最新のレコーディング技術を通じてより幅広い聴衆がオペラへといざなわれている。ラジオやテレビ、映画での演技のおかげで有名人になったオペラ歌手もいる。

(3)しかし、ここ数年、オペラは深刻な試練に直面している。これらのいくつかの原因は御し難いものである。近年のオペラの試練の一つは経済的なことである。近年の世界経済の減速は文化的な施設や芸術家のために利用できるお金が減っていることを意味している。この金銭の不足がオペラ歌手やその他の芸術家を支援するためにいくら支払われるべきなのかというより広範な問題を引き起こしている。社会は企業経営者に支払われる巨額の給料やスポーツアスリートと結ぶ数億円の契約は受け入れているようである。しかしオペラ歌手はどうだろう。どういうわけだか、芸術家は貧しい環境で苦しんでいる時だけ創造性を発揮できると考えている人もいるようだが、それは現実的ではない。もし、オペラ歌手を含む芸術家が必要な支援を欠いたとしたら貴重な才能が無駄になってしまう。

(4)金銭の不足だけでなくオペラの世界でのお金の使いみちも困難をまねいている。主なオペラ歌手は一般的には一つのショーを演じ終わって出演料が支払われる。彼らはショーが始まる前の数週間のリハーサルの間は通常何も受け取らない。役を演じる準備のために、彼らはレッスン料や授業料を支払わなければならない。もし彼らが病気になったり公演をキャンセルした場合、彼らは出演料を失うことになる。このシステムの不安定さがオペラの未来を危険に晒している。

(5)オペラが直面する他の問題が人気の娯楽によって影響を受けた聴衆の欲求をいかに満たすかということである。ポップ歌手は彼らがどんな音楽を奏でるかということと同じくらい彼らがどんな外見であるかということに基づいてしばしば判断される。それゆえオペラ歌手は、このポップカルチャーの影響を受けた聴衆に向けて演じる際は、今や「歌うモデル」であることが期待されている。これらの欲求は非現実的で有害でさえ有るかもしれない。もしオペラ歌手の体重があまりに軽すぎると彼らは大劇場やコンサートホールの隅々までマイク無しに充分な音を響かせることが出来ない。歌唱能力以上に身体的風貌を強調することは聴衆が最高の状態にある人間の声を聞き逃すことにつながってしまうかもしれない。

(6)オペラの問題点に対する簡単な解決法はないし、オペラの価値については様々な意見がある。しかし、毎年多くの若者がこの特殊な芸術形態においてその才能を伸ばそうと夢と希望をいだいて音楽科に登録する。オペラが多くの障害を切り抜け若い世代を魅了し続けているという事実はオペラが未だに非常に価値があり尊重されている芸術形態であるということを示している。

A

問1 **47** ①

第(2)段落によると正しいものは以下の文のうちどれか。

①オペラは新しい状況に適応することで発展をする。

②オペラファンは公演について有名人たちに感謝している。

③オペラ歌手はテレビや映画で歌うことを避けている。

④オペラ歌手の人生はドラマチックである。

第(2)段落最終文よりオペラ歌手がテレビ、ラジオ、映画に出演していることが分かる。したがって③は不適当であり、①が適当と判断できる。【thanks to〜】「〜のおかげで」という意味なので②を選ばないこと。④は言及されていない。

問2 **48** ③

第(3)段落において、「しかしオペラ歌手はどうであろう？」という質問を別の聞き方にするとどうなるか。

①オペラ歌手はどう準備をするか。

②我々はオペラ歌手をいかに利用すべきか。

③オペラ歌手にはどれほどの価値が有るか。

④オペラ歌手は総額どれくらい支払うか。

傍線部の直前の文から企業経営者やスポーツ選手が多額の給与をもらっていることが分かる。また、第(3)段落には【economic】、【shortage of money】、【salaries】、【poverty】などのお金に関係した単語が多いことから①や②は不適当であるということは判断できる。オペラ歌手は給与を支払われる側なので④は不適当である。

問3 | 49 | ①

(3)、(4)段落によると、どれが正しい文か。
①オペラ歌手は経済的に不安定である。
②オペラ歌手が出席を頼むのは富裕層だけである。
③オペラ歌手は公演前に出演料を支払われる。
④オペラ歌手は貧乏な方が上手く演じることができる。

第(4)段落の第5文、第6文からオペラ歌手は病気などにより公演キャンセルをするとお金がもらえないため収入が安定しないことがわかるので①が適当。②のような内容は記述がない。第(4)段落の第2、3文より出演料は公演後に支払われるとわかるので③は不適。第(3)段落第8文に「artists can be creative only if they suffer in poverty」とあるが、直後に「but this is unrealistic」「しかしこれは非現実的である」と言っているので④は不適当。

問4 | 50 | ③

どの文が(5)段落における筆者の意見を最も良くあらわしているか。
①オペラはどう演じられるべきか観客が最も良く知っている。
②オペラがもっと楽しいものになるためにマイクを使われるべきである。
③オペラ歌手の声は彼らの風貌よりも重要なものであるべきである。
④大衆文化はオペラにいい影響を及ぼしてきた。

第(5)段落第6文の内容から筆者がオペラ歌手の風貌よりも声に重きをおいていることが分かる。聴衆は第3文のように「models who sing」を望んでいるのであり①と矛盾する。②のような記述はない。④は第4文と矛盾する。

問5 | 51 | ③

この文章の最も良い題名は何か。
①オペラでのお金の稼ぎ方
②ポップカルチャーの一部としてのオペラ
③オペラの直面する課題
④オペラの歴史的背景

①は全く言及されていない。②、④は確かに該当するように感じる箇所もあるが、文全体を捉えるとそうではない。第3段落第1文の「opera has been facing serious challenges.」や第4段落第1文の「Not only the shortage of money ,but also the way money is managed in the opera world has led to hardships.」や第5段落第1文「Another problem faced by opera」などから文全体としてオペラの課題について記述されていることが分かる。

B

| 52 | ③ | | 53 | ① | | 54 | ④ | | 55 | ② |

段落	内容
（1）	オペラの紹介
（2）	52
（3）	53
（4）	54
（5）	55
（6）	オペラの将来

①世界経済のオペラに与える影響
②大衆文化のオペラへの影響
③オペラの過去から現在
④資金運用の問題

第(2)段落は2文目の「Opera started～」という文においてオペラの成り立ち、第4文の「In recent decades, ～」という文では最近のオペラについて述べられている。このことから、③が適当とわかる。

第(3)段落は3文目の「One current challenge to opera is economic」という文章から①か④が適当と判断できる。4文目の「The current world economic slowdown～」という箇所と、第(4)段落との関係から①が適当であると判断する。

第(4)段落は第1文の「the way money is managed in the opera」から判断すると、④が適当である。

第(5)段落は第1文の「audiences who influenced by popular entertainment」、第3文の「audiences influenced by this popular culture」などから②と判断できる。

H25 | 6 |

(1)ダンスは最も古い芸術の形式の1つであり，どの文化でも見られるもので，さまざまな目的で行われる。現代社会では，ダンスはエンターテイメントの一種として広く認識されている。多くの人が楽しみのためにダンスをし，舞台やスクリーンでのお気に入りのアーティストのダンスを見て楽しむ。ダンスはスポーツの一種でもある。各種のダンスコンテストがある。しかしこれらの明らかな働きに加えて，ダンスが社会で果たすことのできるより複雑な役割が他にある。

(2)ダンスは時に，地域社会の若者に社会の規則を教える手助けになる。メヌエットと呼ばれる種類のダンスはよい例だ。メヌエットの起源はフランスであり，18世紀にはヨーロッパの上流階級の間で普及した。イギリスでは，初舞台を踏む女性，つまり初めての舞踏会に出席することで大人社会へ仲間入りをする上流階級の女性は，初めてのメヌエットに向けて厳しい練習をした。彼女たちは，大抵，じっくりと動作や振る舞いを観察することになる人々の前でメヌエットを踊った。このダンスで彼女たちは，上流階級の一員のように振る舞う方法を学んだ。ある作家は，実際，メヌエットはこれまでに考案された最高の礼節の学校の1つであると考えた。

(3)ダンスは大人が地域社会の規則に確実に従うようにも使われてきた。1900年半ばに行われた，中央アフリカの一部に住む民族集団，ムブティ・ピグミー族が狩りの後に行うダンスに関する調査に，一例がある。狩りで何かがうまくいかなかったとしよう。例えば，動物を狩人の方へ追いやるために地面をたたく役割を怠ったことで，動物を捕らえる機会を逃してしまった場合だ。後で，誤った行為を示し，ひょっとするとその者に恥をかかせるために，ダンサーがその場面を演じたのである。このことが，今後の狩りを台無しにし得る行為の妨げになったことは容易に想像できる。

(4)ある文化では，ダンスは力を誇示する方法になり得る。例えば，1900年代半ばの別の報告に，ニューギニアのマーリング族が，軍事力を誇示し，起こりうる戦闘に備えて同盟軍を採用するためにダンスを行う様子を説明しているものがある。このダンスの後に戦闘がよく起こったのだが，このダンスは敵集団との平和的解決に貢献することもあったとも言われている。ダンスを通して，集団の規模と強大さは敵となる可能性のあるものにとって明らかとなり，このことが戦闘回避の助けになったのである。

(5)ダンスを通して，集団は伝統を示すことができ，それ故，集団の権威を高めることもできるのである。この一例が，かつてヨーロッパの植民地であったカリブ海の島国の，トリニダード・トバゴで行われる世界的に有名なトリニダードカーニバルである。このカーニバルの起源は，ヨーロッパの入植者がカーニバルを開催し，凝った衣装でダンスをしていた1700年代後半に遡る。アフリカ出身の人々は，多くは奴隷としてこの島にやってきており，大半はカーニバルから排除されていた。1838年に奴隷制が廃止された後，彼らはすっかりカーニバルに参加し始め，カーニバルの性格を変えた。彼らはダンスの中で，奴隷時代のシーンを演じ，彼ら自身の伝統を示した。彼らの演技は過去の不当な行為を示し，彼らの慣習を認めてもらう手段であった。

(6)伝統を維持し，集団の強さや文化の豊かさを示すといった，ここで論じたダンスの役割には，1つの共通する効果がある。それは集団の一員を団結させることである。ダンスはただの芸術的な表現だけではなく，集団が共有しているアイデンティティを強めるための方法でもある。明白ではないかもしれないが，この効果は私たちにもあてはまるかもしれない。例えば，私たちが参加している地方特有のダンスがあるかもしれない。私たちはなぜそのような活動に参加し，これらのダンスの起源はどのようなものであろうか。私たちの生活の中のダンスの役割を考えることで，私たち自身の社会の歴史や価値観についての興味深い発見につながることがある。

A

問1 46 ④

第(2)段落において，デビューする女性の話題は，46 の例を示すために取り入れられている。

①若者がメヌエットを学ぶためにどれくらい時間がかかったか

②ヨーロッパの上流階級が通った学校の種類

③メヌエットを踊っているときの女性の演じている役割

④適切な振る舞い方を学ぶ若者

第(2)段落の第1文目に「ダンスは時に，地域社会の若者に社会の規則を教える手助けになる」とあり，その直後に「メヌエットはよい例だ」とあるので，最も適当なものは④。

問2 47 ①

第(3)段落によると，ムブティ・ピグミー族は 47 。

①ダンスを通して不注意な狩人を罰した

②ダンスを通して慣習と伝統を伝えた

③1日の狩りの後，怠けた者にダンスをさせた

④ダンスで文化的に望ましい振る舞いを演じた

第(3)段落の第4，5文目に，「狩りで誤った行為があった場合に，狩りの後ダンスでその誤った行為を指摘し，当事者に恥をかかせる」といった記述があるので，①が適当。

問3 48 ③

第(4)段落は，マーリング族の間でダンスは 48 を阻止することもあったということを示唆している。

①兵士の採用　　②和平

③身体的闘争　　④力の誇示

第(4)段落最終文に「ダンスを通して～このことが戦闘回避の助けになったのである。」とあるので，③が適当。

問4 49 ①

第(5)段落では 49 が述べられている。

①トリニダードカーニバルがどのように変わったか

②カリブ海の地域が初めて植民地になったのはいつか

③アフリカのダンスの伝統が始まったのはどこか

④ヨーロッパ人がトリニダードカーニバルを始めたのはなぜか

第(5)段落の第5～7文目に「カーニバルは性格を変え，過去の不当な行為を示し，慣習を認めてもらう手段となった」といった記述があるので，適当なものは①。

問5 50 ①

この文章の本題は 50 ということである。

①ダンスは私たちを団結させ，また社会を理解するのに役立つことがある

②ダンスは上流階級の教育に重大な役割を果たす

③ダンスの主要な目的は楽しみと運動である

④ダンスの歴史を理解することは大切だ

文章の結論となる第(6)段落の第1文目に「伝統を維持し，集団の強さや文化の豊かさを示すといった，ここで論じたダンスの役割には，1つの共通する効果がある。それは集団の一員を団結させることである」，最終文に「私たちの生活の中のダンスの役割を考えることで，私たち自身の社会の歴史や価値観についての興味深い発見につながることがある。」とあるので，適当なものは①。

B

| 51 | ① | 52 | ⑤ | 53 | ④ | 54 | ② | 55 | ③ |

段落	内容
（1）	今日におけるダンスの典型的な役割
（2）	51
（3）	52
（4）	53
（5）	54
（6）	55

①適切な文化的行動を伝えるダンス

②ダンスがいかに集団の地位を改善するか

③ダンスに共通する機能と重要性

④ダンスを通した集団の力の誇示

⑤好ましくない行動を指摘するためにダンスを使うこと

第(2)段落は，メヌエットというダンスの例を用いて，ダンスが社会の規則を教える手助けになることを示している。したがって 51 に入るものは①。

第(3)段落ではムブティ・ピグミー族が誤った行動を指摘するのにダンスを使用した，との例が示されているので，52 に入るものは⑤。

第(4)段落の第1文目に「ある文化では，ダンスは力を誇示する方法になり得る」とあり，この段落ではこの例が示されている。したがって 53 に入るものは④。

第(5)段落の第1文目に「ダンスを通して～集団の権威を高めることもできるのである。」とあり，この段落ではこの例が示されている。したがって 54 に入るものは②。

残った③が 55 に入るのだが，第(6)段落には，第1，2文目に「ダンスの役割には1つの共通する効果がある。それは～」とあり，さらに段落全体でダンスの重要性について述べている。

H30　5

惑星Xの探査日誌よりの抜粋

<u>1日目</u>　我々の科学的発見のミッションは続いている。そして報告すべき胸躍ることがある。我々は生命を維持することが可能な惑星を遂に発見したかもしれない。近隣の星々は生命を維持するには暑すぎたり乾燥しすぎたりしていたが，この星は違うようだ。緑と茶色の部分が点在しているが表面は大半が青い液体で，惑星の周りをある種の白い物質が動いているようだ。

<u>4日目</u>　今我々は惑星軌道上を回っている。我々の仮説は正しかったようだ！いくつか惑星を周回する機械装置が存在しており，それらのデザインはかなり複雑である。それらは間違いなくある種の知的生命体によって作られたものだ。これらの機械は監視システムの一部だろうか。我々の接近を既に知らせているだろうか。なんら脅威が見当たらないので，装置を無視してさらに惑星に接近することを決めた。これらの発明家が友好的であれば良いのだが。

<u>8日目</u>　我々の生命を維持する貴重な液体で全てが覆われた我々の惑星と違い，この星の緑と茶色の部分はあまりにも乾燥しており我々は生存することができない。青い部分はほとんどが液体状態のH_2Oである。液体であるにもかかわらず，我々の星のそれとはかなり異なっている。それでも，我々はここで生命を見つけることができるかもしれない。少なくとも，我々の装備によると，その下には何か生物が存在しているようである。直接観察を始める準備をしてすぐに潜水するつもりだ。とても興奮していて今夜は眠れそうにない！

<u>9日目</u>　我々はこの未探査の液体に安全に侵入することに成功した。我々の周りの風景は柔らかい植物が穏やかに前後に揺れており，我々の星の風景にとても良く似ている。我々は様々な薄っぺらな泳ぐ生物も発見した。なんてことだ！この星で生物を発見した！しかし，発展した文明を産み出す能力をもった生物は全く発見できない。腕がなければ，これらの泳ぐ生物はたとえ賢くとも複雑な機械を組み立てることはできないであろう。この星の指導者は我々から隠れているのだろうか。我々と会うことに心配があるのだろうか。だから彼らは宇宙を調べるためにそれらの飛行物体を使用しているのだろうか。

うまくいけば，我々はいくつかの答えを見つけることができるだろう。

<u>12日目</u>　我々は底に横たわる大きな物体を発見した。その長い本体はどこか我々の宇宙船と似ている。それは

とても古く傷ついて見える状態で静かに横たわっていた。一見したところ、もはや使われてはいないようだ。おそらくこの惑星の古代文明の残骸の一部だろう。

19日目　潜水を始めて以来、我々はたくさんの普通ではない生物を目撃してきた。特に我々によく似た生物を発見してとても驚いた。その身体の上部は丸く軟らかかった。下部には2つの大きな目と長い腕が何本かあった。それはもくもくした黒い物質を置き去りながら、素早く逃げていった。それがこの惑星における最も知的な生命体かどうかは不明だが、我々の新発見への期待は膨らみ続けている。

39日目　今回の調査はすぐに終わりを迎えるだろう。我々はさらなる遺物と先に発見していたのとよく似た廃棄された物体を発見した。しかしそれらを作った生物の痕跡は見当たらなかった。おそらくこの惑星の指導者は死に絶えてしまったのだろう。とにかく、我々はこの惑星で生命を見つけだし、それはとても大きな発見だ。我々はもうこの惑星を出発しなくてはならないが、調査を続けるためにいつかきっと戻ってくるだろう。我々は素晴らしい報告とともに帰還する。

40日目　我々は静かに表層に浮上しそれから空中へと飛んだ。我々が惑星を離れるちょうどその時、乾燥したエリアに我々はたくさんの奇妙な生物を目撃した。なんということだ！我々のように液体の中で生活する生物は、彼らのような生物がいるなど思いもしなかった！船の液体の中で安全に漂いながら、我々は我々にとっての常識が誤った結論に我々を導くこともあるということを悟った。

問1　41　③
調査隊の旅の目的は何だったか。
①惑星の知的生命体を援助すること
②惑星を侵略し植民地を広げること
③母星の外で知的生命体を探すこと
④新しい宇宙船の性能を試すこと
1日目の日記の第2文に注目する。

問2　42　②
調査隊が宇宙から惑星を観察していた時に、彼らはその星の知的生命体は　42　と想像した。
①他者に対して攻撃的である
②進んだ技術を持っている
③宇宙に興味がない
④もはや生きていない
宇宙から観察している4日目の文章、第4文に注目する。

問3　43　②
9日目の文で使われているreservationsという単語は　43　の意味に最も近い。
①appointments（予約）　②concerns（心配）

③expectations（予想）　④protections（保護）
【reservation】「予約」に飛びつかないこと。文脈から①でないのは明らかである。

問4　44　①
以下のいずれが日記の筆者を最もよく描写しているか。
①タコに似た形をした生物
②他の惑星を探検している人間の科学者
③人間に似た宇宙生物
④腕のない知的で平べったい動物
19日目の第2文から、そこに描写されている生物が筆者に似ていることがわかる。

問5　45　③
探索者は全ての知的生命体は　45　と誤解していた。
①彼らの種族よりも創造的でない
②進化して陸に上がっていった
③何らかの液体に住んでいる
④彼らの言葉を理解する
40日目の日記に注目。

H29　5

あ〜〜〜〜。

大きなあくびをして私は目が覚めた。なんて素敵な朝だ！私はとてもスッキリしていた、いやいつもよりずっとスッキリしていた。今まで以上によりはっきりと鳥たちのさえずりを聞くことができた。私は階下からたちのぼるコーヒーの香りに気付いた。自分の前に腕を伸ばして背筋を伸ばした。とても気持ちよかった。まっすぐに座って、手をなめ、そしてそれで顔を洗い始めた…ん？…何かおかしい。なぜ私は手を舌で舐めていたんだ？なぜ私の体は毛に覆われていたのだ？私は何かを言おうとしたが、私の口から発せられた音は…「みゃお〜。」

私がいるのは確かに私の寝室だった。私が座っているのは確かに私のベッドだった。私が違った生物に変わってしまっているようだということ…それ以外は全ていつも通りだった。私は驚きの余り動けなかった。何もできなかった。私はとまどった…私は残りの人生を動物として過ごさなければならないのだろうか？私は怖くなってきた…しかしすぐにそういった感情は消えてしまった。そして、尻尾をふりながら、周囲を探検し始めた。猫の気持ちはこの様に変わりやすいと言われている。

階段を降りるに連れて、コーヒーの香りが強くなり何が朝食か判断できるようになった。おそらく猫の感覚は人間のそれよりも鋭い。台所に到着した時、私が見たものに心臓が止まりそうになった。それは「私」だった！人間の「私」がダイニングテーブルに座っていた。私は「私自身」から目が離せなかった。

人間の「私」はスマートフォンに夢中で、おそらく友達のメッセージに返事を書いているのかオンラインゲームをやっているのだろう。「私」はスマートフォンに向けて頭を下げて、肩を丸くし、背中を曲げて座っていた。

「私」はとても不愉快そうに見えた。

　「私」は時々少しトーストをかじったが、口の中の味に全く気付いていないようであった。実際に、私の記憶にあるトーストの味はぼんやりしていた。私は他に何が最近朝食として供されていたかも思い出すことができなかった。人間の「私」は電話を触っているあいだ皿の上にあるものならなんでも無関心に口の中に押し込んでいただけだった。「私」はメールやゲームにとても集中していたので「私」のまわりで何が起こっているのかということにはほとんど興味を持っていなかった。実際に、「私」の顔には全く表情がなかった。

　「ユウジ、あなた最近全く勉強してないでしょ。期末テストの準備はできてるの？少し心配だわ。」ママは言った。

　「んー」「私」は言った。「私」は一瞬不満そうな顔をしたが、すぐに消えた。「私」の顔はそれまでと同様の無表情にまた戻った。

　「こいつは好きじゃない」私は思った。しかしこの男は私だった。それを否定することはできなかった。初めて、他の人に本当は自分がどう見えているかを私は悟った。

　すると、「私」がテーブルから去ろうとし始めた時、私たちの目があった。「わっ、ママ、見て。台所に猫がいる。」

　なぜかはわからないけれど、私は走っていた。逃げなくてはいけないと思った。階段を駆け上がって、部屋の窓があいていることに気付いた。私はとんだ。奇妙な感覚がした。世界が突然変わってしまったようだった。私は身体が落ちるのを感じてそして…

　バン！

　私は目を覚ますと、自分の部屋の床に横になっていた。ゆっくりと身体をおこし、あたりを見渡した。全てがいつもどおりのようだった。私は自分の手を見た。もう毛に覆われていないことを見てホッとした。あくびをしながら立ち上がって、背中を伸ばすために腕を頭の上の方に伸ばした。無意識に、朝のいつもの習慣で、私はスマートフォンが完全に充電してある机の方に歩いていって…私は立ち止まった。

　一瞬立ち止まって、私はきびすを返して朝食のために階段を降りていった。

問1　`42`　①

ユウジが自分が猫に変わってしまっていると気付いた時、彼は最初　`42`　。

①驚いた　②戸惑った　③興奮した　④満足した

第3段落の第4文、【I was so surprised that …】とある。

問2　`43`　②

ユウジの母が彼に話しかけた時、彼は　`43`　のでイライラした。

①彼は彼女を喜ばせたかった

②彼女の言葉が彼を邪魔した

③彼の口は食べ物でいっぱいだった

④彼女が彼の勉強の邪魔をした

第6段落からユウジはスマートフォンに熱中していることがわかる。

問3　`44`　④

猫は「こいつは好きじゃない」と思った、なぜならユウジは　`44`　。

①彼が朝ごはんに食べた物の味を思い出せなかったから

②最後のテストのための勉強の努力を隠そうとした

③彼の母が彼の将来を心配していることをからかった

④彼のまわりの人や物への敬意を示さなかった

①②はどこにも言及ない。③も第8段落から母の心配に反応していないことがわかる。

問4　`45`　①

物語の終わりに、ユウジはスマートフォンを手に取らなかった、なぜなら　`45`　。

①態度を改める時だと決めたから

②まだ完全には充電されていないと悟ったから

③彼の以前の優先事項にこだわりたかったから

④母に叱られるのが恐かったから

第13段落最後の文からスマートフォンは充電されているので②は誤りとわかる。③は以前の優先事項がスマートフォンを触ることなので誤り。④は全く言及がない。

問5　`46`　②

この物語の主題はなんですか？

①猫は人間よりもずっと優れた感覚を持っている。

②自分自身を観察することは自己変革へとつながる。

③スマートフォンを使う人々は奇妙に見える。

④夢の中では信じられないことが起こる。

①は第3、4段落にしか言及がないので主題とはいえない。③は第9段落などに言及はあるが、あくまでスマートフォンを使う「私」が奇妙なので不適。第13、14段落で「私」がとった行動を踏まえると②が最適とわかる。

H28　`5`

①「誰もぼくがこんなに上手になるなんて思わなかっただろ。」ジョンおじさんは台所に立って賞をとった4品のコース料理をいかにしてまとめあげるかを私に見せながら言った。私はちょうど大学を卒業したてで、このディナーは彼からの私への贈り物だった。有名なシェフが私のために料理してくれるということはとても気分が良かった。その上、この数日中に彼は全国的な料理コンテストのビッグタイムクックオフに参加する予定だったので、私は興奮していた。

②ジョンおじさんが若かったとき、彼の家族は田舎に住んでいた。彼の母親は地方の学校で教師をしていたが、ジョンが10歳の時に、彼女は彼女の年老いた母親の面倒を見るために仕事をやめなくてはいけなかった。その時まで、彼の父親は優しく、ジョンと二人の妹と遊んでくれる十分な時間があった。しかし、請求書が積み上がるにつれて、家族は苦境に陥っていった。

ジョンの父はとうとうはるか遠くの都会で仕事につかなくてはならなくなり、週末しか帰宅できなくなってしまった。

③仕事のスケジュールが多忙なために、徐々にジョンの父は帰宅した時にはいつも疲れた顔を見せ始めるようになった。本当のことを言えば、彼は上機嫌な人からいつも機嫌が悪い人に変わっていた。彼は家にいる時は、休みたがるだけだった。彼は些細なことで度々ジョンを叱った。父に認められたくて、ジョンは最善を尽くしたが、充分だと感じることは決してなかった。遂に、彼は父を避け始めた。彼は友人とショッピングモールをぶらついたり、時には授業をサボったりし始めた。次第にジョンの成績は悪くなっていった。両親と先生は彼の将来を心配していた。

④ある日曜日の朝、ジョンの母が彼女の母の世話のために外出している間、父はテレビ部屋で昼寝をしていた。ジョンの妹達はお腹をすかせていて、ジョンは彼らのために何か料理を作り始めた。彼は料理の仕方はよく知らなかったが父をわずらわせたくなかった。

⑤突然、台所のドアがあくと、父がそこに立っていた。「父さん、もし起こしちゃったならごめんなさい。チェルシーとジェシカがお腹をすかせていて、彼らに卵を使って料理しようと思って。」父はしばらく彼を真剣に見つめていた。「卵?卵は今日みたいに素敵な日曜日のランチに相応しくない。庭でステーキを焼こう。」「本当に?疲れているでしょ。」「大丈夫。料理は好きなんだ。コックとしてアルバイトしていた学生時代の自分を思い出すよ。旨いステーキの下ごしらえの仕方を教えてやろう。」

⑥ジョンが驚いたことに、料理を始めると父はいきいきとしだした。彼はジョンを脇に立たせて彼に事細かに料理はある意味で科学プロジェクトのようなものだと説明しだした。「材料を正確に測ること、そして何が相性が良いかを知っておくことが必要だ。もしこのことをマスターすれば、沢山の人に喜びを提供できるぞ。」ジョンはここ最近では初めて父に親しみを感じた。それから、ジョンはより多くの時間を家で過ごすようになった。彼は定期的に家族に、それから後には大学の友人のためにも料理を振る舞うようになった。ジョンは料理をする時にいつも幸せを感じていたし、この幸せが彼の人生の他の部分にもあふれ流れ込んでいた。

⑦ジョンおじさんは大学を通じてレストランでアルバイトをして、結局彼は有名レストランのシェフになった。彼は本当にその職業が好きで、特殊技術を磨きながら一生懸命働いた。彼はついに自分自身の独自のスタイルの料理を提供するレストランを開店させることができた。彼はいくつもの賞を勝ち取り、お金持ちや有名人のために料理するようになった。

⑧ここで話をコンテストに戻そう。ジョンおじさんと私は彼が選ばれたことに興奮していた。しかし、彼は台

所で私と本当に感動的な何かを共有していた。「マイク」ジョンおじさんが言った、「私はビッグタイムクックオフの一部でテレビに出ることができることに興奮している。でも、一番うれしいことは私が最も気にかけている人々の一人である君とここに立っていること、そして話すことだ、ただ君と私でね。何年も前の夏のある晴れた日に父が私にしてくれたこととよく似ている。そして、それが私の人生に大きな影響を及ぼしたんだ。」

問1 | 42 | ②
　物語の始めでは、ジョンおじさんは | 42 | 。
　①ビッグタイムクックオフのために料理をしていた
　②マイクのために特別な食事を作っていた
　③コンテストに向けマイクを鍛えていた
　④レシピを改善しようとしていた
　第1段落第2文がヒントになる。

問2 | 43 | ③
　ジョンおじさんの父は | 43 | から都会で働き始めた。
　①彼は田舎暮らしに飽きてしまった
　②家族との時間を過ごすのがより簡単だった
　③家族は生活のためにお金が必要だった
　④ジョンおじさんの母は病気になってしまった
　第2段落第4文、第5文で判断する。④はジョンおじさんの祖母のことである。

問3 | 44 | ②
　なぜジョンおじさんの両親と先生は彼の将来を心配したのか。
　①彼はただ家で休みたかった。
　②彼は勉強への興味を失ってしまった。
　③彼は父を避けることをやめた。
　④彼はもはや上機嫌な人ではなかった。
　第3段落の最終文から判断する。①、④は彼の父についてのことなので誤り。③は逆である。

問4 | 45 | ③
　ジョンおじさんの人生を最も変える助けとなったものは何か。
　①賞をとったディナーを友人と食べたこと
　②ビッグタイムクックオフのような料理コンテストに出場したこと
　③料理を通じて父と絆をもったこと
　④台所でマイクと話すことに時間を費やしたこと
　第6段落の後半内容、第8段落の最終文をみれば明らか。

問5 | 46 | ②
　ジョンおじさんは何が最も価値があると気づいたか。
　①有名人のために独自の4品のディナーコースを考えること
　②親しい人々と意義のある関係を持つこと
　③テレビ番組での料理を通じて人々を幸せにすること
　④彼のレストランでたくさんの人に美味しい食事を提供すること
　第8段落第5文を見ると「what makes me the happiest is～」とあるのでその内容に注目する。

差出人：Jeff Whitmore <JeffW@×××××.com>
宛先：Kenji Okamoto <okamoto@×××××.com>
日付：2015年1月10日
件名：アドバイスの依頼

岡本先生へ

　私の名前はジェフ＝ウィットモアで，娘のアンナはあなたの生徒の一人です。ご存じのように，私たちは3年間シカゴで暮らした後，6ヶ月前に日本に戻ってきました。アンナはシカゴに行く前に日本の学校に在籍しており，当時は中学1年生でした。妻と私は娘のことで少し心配しているので，アドバイスの依頼を了承していただけることを願っています。

　彼女は成績も良く，授業と先生のことが好きです。特に，数字を好む傾向があり，数学の授業を愛しています。あなたの楽しい英語の授業のこともよく話してくれます。しかし約半年たっても，友達が一人もいないようです。先週，授業の間の休み時間に他の女の子たちはブラブラしたり雑談したりしているけれども，彼女はたった一人で読書をしている，と言いました。アンナは毎日一人で学校に歩いて登校するとも言っていました。これはアメリカにいた時とはとても違っています。

　新しい学校で友達をつくるには時間がかかるということは理解していますが，それでも娘は少し孤立しているのかもしれないと心配しています。できるだけ早く良い友達グループを作っていければいいと思います。一人でもいいので親しい友達ができれば，良い第一段階となるでしょう。私は今まで一度も娘のクラス担任の一人に連絡したことはなく，あなたを悩ませたくありません。私はただ，学校での娘の生活について先生の方がご存知かと思います。どうすれば娘がもっと個人的な関係をつくることができるかについて考えがあれば，教えていただけると嬉しいです。

敬具
ジェフ＝ウィットモア

差出人：Kenji Okamoto <okamoto@×××××.com>
宛先：Jeff Whitmore <JeffW@×××××.com>
日付：2015年1月10日
件名：Re：アドバイスの依頼

ウィットモアさんへ

　自分の生徒の一人の保護者の方から連絡をいただけるのはいつも嬉しいことであり，私はできるだけあなたの助けになればと思います。私はアンナと何回か一対一で話をしたことがあり，彼女が自信に満ち，人懐こい素晴らしい人間であることはわかっています。実際に，クラスの他の生徒とうまくやっているようなので，私はあなたの心配を聞いて驚きました。おそらく彼女はすぐに親友ができると思いますが，彼女の助けになるかもしれないと考えているアイデアがあります。

　一つは，私たちの学校には友情を築くのに良い環境を提供してくれる，たくさんの様々なクラブがあります。彼女は音楽を楽しむので，たぶんコーラス部に入りたいかもしれません。もし彼女がスポーツの方を好むなら，バレーボール部やサッカー部，そして空手部まであります。私も現在，新しく英語部を作っているところです。そこでは週に一回，英語で話をしたり音楽や映画を楽しんだりします。もしアンナが入部し，指導的な役割も受けてくれれば，英語という共通の趣味をもつ他の生徒と関係を築くことができます。ニュージーランドで過ごした経験を持つ，他クラスのある日本人生徒が，活動に参加しようと計画を立てています。彼らには共通点がたくさん見つかるかもしれません。

　もう一つの方法は，彼女が注目の的になる社会的な状況をつくることです。アンナはアメリカではよく庭でバーベキューパーティーをしていたと私に話してくれました。もし可能であれば，アメリカ式のバーベキューパーティーを開き，クラスの生徒を何人か招待してください。きっと彼らにとってわくわくする経験になるでしょう。もしかするとアンナが気楽にすごしていれば，生徒も彼女のことをもっと知るようになるでしょう。

　私の経験から言えば，正直なところ，あなたが心配するようなことはなく，遅かれ早かれ彼女は自分で友好関係を築くだろうと確信しています。しかし，もし私の考えが助けになると感じたら，私に知らせてください，その時は次の段階を一緒に考えましょう。

敬具
岡本ケンジ

問1　42　③

アンナはおそらくシカゴの学校ではどんな感じだったか？
　①彼女は教室に一人でいることが好きだった。
　②彼女は日本語の能力を見せびらかしていた。
　③彼女は多くの時間を友人と過ごした。
　④彼女は他の生徒をうらやんでいた。

1通目のメール本文第2段落第4文に，「彼女には友達が一人もいないようだ」とあり，第7文には「これはアメリカにいた時とはとても違っている」とあるので，アメリカにいた時はアンナには友達がたくさんいたと考えられる。よって③が正しい。

問2　43　③

ウィットモアのEメールの第2段落にある「～をひどく好む」という言葉は　43　の意味に最も近い。
　①～を集めている　　②～を交換する
　③～を好む　　　　　④～に不安である

この直後に「彼女は数学の授業を愛していた」とあるので，数字が「好き」だと推測できる。よって③が正しい。

問3　44　④

Eメールの情報によると，次の記述のうち，正しいのはどれか。
　①アンナは家で両親と学校生活について話していない。
　②アンナは英語の授業よりも日本語の授業の方が好きだ。
　③ウィットモア氏はアンナの学校の成績を心配している。
　④これはウィットモア氏が岡本先生に送った最初のEメールである。

1通目のメール本文第4文に「私は今まで一度も娘のクラス担任の一人に連絡したことはない」とあるので，④が正しい。

問4　45　④

ウィットモア氏とは違い，岡本先生はアンナが　45　と考えている。
　①クラスで他の生徒から孤立している
　②学校で多くの時間を読書に費やしている
　③良い成績をとるのに苦労するだろう
　④特別な支援がなくても友達はできるだろう

2通目のメール本文第1段落第4文に「おそらく彼女はすぐに親友ができると思います」とあるので，④が正しい。

問5　46　④

次の文のうち，岡本先生のウィットモア氏への提案でないものはどれか。
　①アンナに運動部か音楽部に入らせる
　②アンナのクラスメイトをイベントに招待する
　③アンナを英語部に参加させてあげる
　④アンナをニュージーランド旅行に連れて行く

2通目のメール本文第2段落第2，3文でコーラス部かスポーツのクラブに入ることを，第6文で英語部に参加することを勧めているので①と③ではない。第3段落第3文で

バーベキューパーティーを提案しているので②ではない。
④はどこにも書かれていないので④が正しい。

H26 ⑤

サルバドールの日記
2012年3月30日

　最後のレッスンは災難だった。チトセと私は大喧嘩をしてしまったのだ。彼女はアトリエに笑いながらやって来て，「見て，おじいちゃん。あなたの似顔絵を書いてきたわ。」と言った。その似顔絵の男は，髪がふさふさで，まっすぐに立っていて，若々しく見え，笑っていた。彼女はフランスの大学に入れるくらいの才能があるのかもしれないが，芸術家として大きな弱点がある。彼女が人物を描く際，しょっちゅう実際の人物よりもむしろ理想のイメージを描いてしまうのだ。私は，このことを数週間に渡り彼女に説明してきたが，彼女は全く聞こうとしなかった。私は少し怒って，「これは私ではないよ，お前は本当の芸術家ではない。」と彼女に言った。彼女も怒って，「もう先生は必要ないから，私に構わないで。」と言った。それから，私は，別れのプレゼントとして私が描いた似顔絵を彼女に見せ，「これが本当のお前だ！」と言った。彼女は，それを手に取り見ると「いいえ，そうじゃないわ！」と言い，出て行ってしまった。

　私は，彼女の両親ならわかってくれるだろうと思い，彼らにチトセの似顔絵をあげた。チトセが自分の容姿を変え始める2ヶ月前に，その似顔絵を描いたのだった。そして，それには私が2年間教えた高校生が描かれていると思う。私がそれを描いていた時，彼女はまだ天然パーマで，ストレートパーマをかけていなかった。彼女は，お気に入りの輪の形をしたイヤリングを含めて，今持っているアクセサリーを全くつけていなかった。また，そのときは化粧も全くしていなかった。これは，自分がまだアマチュアの芸術家だということを知っている，素晴らしい将来を持ったチトセだ。彼女が，歳を重ねるにつれ，どんどん大人のように行動し，見せたがっていることを，私は理解している。しかしながら，彼女は，大人になるということは他人の言うことに耳を傾けないことだと思っているようだ。もし，彼女が学ぶことをやめれば，偉大な芸術家になることは決してないだろう。

サルバドールへの手紙
2013年3月25日

　こんにちは，おじいちゃん。
　遅いのはわかっているのですが，最後に会ったときに怒ったことについて謝りたいです。最後のレッスンで，あなたがまだ私のことを子どもとして見ていると思ったので，私はあなたの言うことに耳を傾けなかったのです。あなたが似顔絵の中で私をどのように描いているかを見て，これが私の気持ちを強めました。私はとても傷付いたので，あなたのプレゼ

ントも受け取らずに立ち去ったのです。

　あなたはこのことを知らないと思いますが，私がフランスに向けて発つ時に，お母さんが私のスーツケースのひとつに，こっそりその似顔絵を入れたのです。私はそれを見つけた時，まだイライラしていたので，クローゼットの中に隠しました。私はしばらく似顔絵について考えたくなかったのですが，2ヵ月前に偶然，見つけてしまったのです。それを見た時，私は自分の絵を磨くために，人の言うことに喜んで耳を傾けているチトセに出会いました。私は，なってしまったチトセとは違うことに気付きました。彼女は，自分が大人であることをみんなに証明したかったので，他人の言うことに耳を傾けなくなったのです。それまで，私は美術の授業で本当にもがき苦しんでいたのですが，自分の弱点に気付いた後は，再び学び始め，私の絵はどんどん良くなりました。おじいちゃん，あなたはずっと私の先生ですよ。

　私は，自分が最後の授業であなたに見せた似顔絵を覚えています。あなたは，それを気に入らずに，見るがままにあなたを描きなさいと言いましたね。あなたがその日に教えてくれたことは，今の私には理解できます。私はあるがままに物事を描くべきで，そうすればそれらの真の美しさが輝くのですね。

　私は，私たちの似顔絵を描いたので，その写真を送ります。実は，それは私の街で行われた若手の芸術家のコンクールで，一等賞に輝いたのです。見てわかるとおり，私は自分をあなたが描いてくれたように描きました。それは，たくさんの可能性を持っているチトセとしてです。また，実際に見るがままのあなたを描きました。あなたのしわは，知恵の証拠です。杖は，自分の肉体的な問題を克服しようとする，あなたの意志を表しています。あなたの曲がった背中は，あなたがもっとも愛しているもの，つまり芸術と私に，あなたの強さをすべて注いでいることを表しています。

愛しています。
おじいちゃん。

問1 ▢42▢ ①
サルバドールはチトセに ▢42▢ ことをして欲しかった。
①物事をあるがままに正しく評価する
②芸術家のようにもっと着飾る
③他の芸術の先生を見つける
④若く見える人々を描く
日記の1段目に，実際の人物よりも理想のイメージを描いてしまうことがチトセの弱点だと書かれている。そして，手紙の3段目より，あるがままに物事を描くことの大切さをチトセが理解できたことがわかるので，①が適当。

問2 ▢43▢ ③
最後のレッスンで，チトセは自分の ▢43▢ と信じていた

ので，その似顔絵を受け取らなかった。

　　①家族は，彼女よりも正しく評価するだろう
　　②家族は，彼女の容姿を好まないだろう
　　③祖父は，彼女を大人として尊重しない
　　④祖父は，とても素晴らしい芸術家ではない
手紙の1段落に，祖父がチトセのことを子どもとして見ていることで，チトセが傷付いたことが書かれている。したがって，③が適当。

問3　44　②

次の中でどれが正しいか？

　　①チトセは，サルバドールが描いた似顔絵を両親にあげた。
　　②チトセは，手紙を書く前に新しい似顔絵を描いた。
　　③サルバドールは，チトセの似顔絵を描くのに2年かかった。
　　④サルバドールは，チトセが容姿を変えた後に似顔絵を描いた。
手紙の4段落より，チトセが描いた似顔絵がコンクールで一等になり，その写真を手紙と一緒に送ったことがわかるので，似顔絵は手紙を書く前に描かれている。したがって，②が適当。チトセの両親にあげたのは，サルバドールなので①は不適。2年はチトセを教えていた期間なので，③は不適。サルバドールは，以前の天然パーマで，アクセサリーや化粧もしていないチトセを描いたのであるから，④は不適。

問4　45　②

チトセの絵が良くなった最もふさわしい理由は何か？

　　①彼女は，コンクールに参加することでたくさんのことを学んだ。
　　②彼女は，再び他人の考えを受け入れるようになった。
　　③彼女は，化粧やイヤリングをつけることをやめた。
　　④彼女は，他の大人の意見に影響を与えようとした。
手紙の2段落に，チトセが人の話に耳を傾けないという弱点に気付き，再び学び始めたことで，絵が良くなったとあるので，②が適当。

問5　46　①

チトセが祖父に送った写真の似顔絵に最もふさわしいのは，次のうちどれか？

　　（i）祖父・・・日記の1段落より，「髪がふさふさで，まっすぐに立っていて，若々しく見え，笑っていた」のは，サルバドールが否定した最初の似顔絵の特徴だということがわかるので，写真の似顔絵はそうではないはずである。さらに，手紙の4段落より，しわがあり，杖をつき，背中が曲がっていることがわかる。
　　（ii）チトセ・・・手紙の4段落より，高校生の時のチトセが描かれていることがわかる。したがって，天然パーマで，化粧やアクセサリーをしていないはずである。
（i），（ii）を満たすのは①。

7　〈論理的文章〉　問題107p〜

R4　6 A

　あなたの研究グループは「1日の時間が人々にどのような影響を与えるか」について研究している。あなたは共有したいある記事をみつけた。次のミーティングまでに要約を完成させよ。

あなたにとって1日が始まるのはいつ？

　「あなたは朝型の人間ですか？」と問われたとき，「いいえ，私は夜のフクロウです。」と答える人がいます。このような人々は夜に集中したり，創造的なことをしたりすることができます。正反対の時間として「早起きの鳥は虫を捕まえる（＝早起きは三文の徳）。」というよく知られたことわざがある。これは早起きをすることが，食べ物を得たり，賞品を勝ち取ったり，目標に到達したりする方法であることを意味します。ヒバリは朝鳴く鳥です，ですから，フクロウと反対の早起きの鳥はヒバリです。日中活動的な生き物は「昼行性」，夜に現れる生き物は「夜行性」です。

　もうひとつのことわざに「早寝早起きは人間を健康に，豊かに，賢くする。」とある。ヒバリはベッドから飛び起きてしっかりした朝食とともに朝を迎えるかもしれない，一方，フクロウはスヌーズボタンを押し，ぎりぎりの時間に準備をし，たいてい朝食抜きである。彼らは食事の回数が少ないかもしれないが，遅い時間に食事をとる。食後の運動をしなければ，体重の増加を引き起こすかもしれない。おそらく，ヒバリの方がより健康である。フクロウはヒバリのスケジュールで仕事や勉強をしなければいけない。ほとんどの学校教育は午後4時までに行われるので，若いヒバリはある特定の仕事をより上手に行うことができるかもしれない。一日の早い時間に行われる商取引はヒバリをより豊かにするかもしれない。

　何が人間をヒバリやフクロウにするのか？ある説によると，昼か夜かの好みは生まれた時間と関係がある。2010年，クリーブランド州立大学の研究者たちは，人間の体内時計は生まれた瞬間に動き始めるだけではなく，夜に生まれた人間は生涯を日中のパフォーマンスに問題を抱えるかもしれないという証拠を発見した。たいてい，彼らの世界の経験は暗闇とともに始まっている。伝統的な授業や仕事は日中行われるから，私たちは一日が朝始まることを当然と思っている。寝ている人々は先頭に立てず，機会を逃すかもしれない。

　誰もが朝に一日が始まるシステムに従うだろうか？およそ6000年の歴史を持つ宗教的なグループであるユダヤ教の人々は，1日は日没から次の日没まで，夕方から夕方までで計測されると考えている。キリスト教徒はクリスマスイブでこの伝統を続けている。中国人は十二支の制度を使って，年を刻むだけでなく1日を2時間ごとに分割している。その最初の時間である子の刻は午後11時から午前1時までである。中国の文化もまた，1日は夜始まるのである。言いかえると，古来の風習はフクロウの時間の見方を支持している。

　研究は，フクロウはより賢く，より創造的であると示している。だから，もしかするといつもヒバリの方が賢いとは限らないのである！すなわち，ヒバリは「健康」，時に「裕福さ」で勝るが，「賢さ」では負けるかもしれない。初期の報告では，リチャード・D・ロバーツと，パトリック・C・カイロネンがフクロウの方がより知的である傾向があると述べている。後に，ロバーツが共著者の一人を務めたフランツ・ブレッケルによる広範囲の研究においても同様の結論に至っている。しかし，フクロウにとって良いニュースばかりではない。学業が困難になる可能性があるだけでなく，日中の職業の機会を逃し，ヒバリが寝ている間に遊ぶ，「夜遊び」の悪い習慣を楽しむ可能性が高い。夜遊びはお金がかかりがちである。バルセロナ大学の研究によると，ヒバリは几帳面で完璧を求め，ストレスをあまり感じない。フクロウは新しい冒険やわくわくさせるようなレジャー活動を求めるが，リラックスすることに困難を抱えていることが多い。

　人は変わることができるのだろうか？全ての結果が出ているわけではないが，若年層に関する研究によると，いいえ，容易には変えることができないものである，とのことのようである。そのため，若者は成長するにつれ，より自由を手に入れると，最終的にはヒバリかフクロウの性質に戻る。しかしながら，この分類は全ての人に当てはまるとは限らないのではないかという懸念が生じる。生まれた時が指標になる可能性があることに加えて，ネイチャーコミュニケーション誌に掲載された論文はDNAも時間に関する習慣に影響を与える可能性があるとしている。他の研究では，加齢や病気によって変化が起こる人もいることに焦点を当てるものもある。この分野では新たな研究が常に現れている。ロシアの大学生を対象とした研究は，6つのタイプがあることを示唆している，だから，フクロウとヒバリだけが周りにいる鳥ではないかもしれない！

あなたの要約メモ：

```
     あなたにとって1日が始まるのはいつですか？

語彙
  昼行性の定義： 39
    ⇔対義語：夜行性

主要な点
・私たちの全員が一般的な日中のスケジュールに簡単に適応できるわ
  けではないが、特に子どもの頃、それに従うよう強制されている。
・私たちそれぞれのもっとも活動的な時間は私たちの性質の一部であ
  ることを示す研究もある。
・基本的に、 40 。
・新たな研究とともに、考え方は変わり続けている。

興味深い詳細
・ユダヤ教とキリスト教は、中国の時間の区分と同じように、 41
  のために記事の中で言及されている。
・ 42 は人間の体内時計をセットし、知能と 43 における違い
  を説明するかもしれないとする研究もある。
```

問1 39 に適する選択肢を選べ。
　①目標をすばやく達成する
　②ペットの鳥を飼うのが好きである
　③日中活動的である
　④食べ物をみつけるのがうまい

第1段落第4文に「active during the day：日中活動的な」
生き物は「昼行性」とあるので、この書き換えの「lively in
the day time」の③が正解。

問2 40 に適する選択肢を選べ。
　①将来的には、より柔軟な時間や活動スケジュールが発
　　達するだろう
　②年を取るにつれ、午前中に社会活動を楽しむことがよ
　　り重要になる
　③私たちにとって一日で最も活動的な時間帯を変えるこ
　　とは難しいかもしれない。
　④フクロウのスケジュールで生きることは、最終的には
　　社会的・経済的利益につながるだろう。

第6段落第1～3文で人は変われるかという問いに対して
結果が完全に出ているわけではないが、若年層への調査に
よるといえ、人間は変わりにくいとあり、最終的にヒバ
リかフクロウの性質に戻るとあるので、これは昼行性と夜
行性を変えることができるかという話であることがわか
る。これは選択肢の「What time of day we perform best」
と一致する。よって、正解は③。

問3 41 に適する選択肢を選べ。
　①特定の社会では、長い間、一日は夜始まると考えられ
　　てきたことを説明する
　②過去においては、夜行性の人間はより信仰心が強かっ
　　たことを示す
　③朝の怠惰のせいでチャンスを逃すと長い間考えられて
　　きたことを言う

④フクロウはヒバリのスケジュールで仕事や学校に行か
　なければならないという考えを支持する

ユダヤ教とキリスト教、中国の時間区分によって何を説
明しているのかを考える。第4段落第2文でユダヤ教の
人々は1日が日没から次の日没まで、夕方から夕方までで
計測されると考えているとあり、同第3文にキリスト教徒
はクリスマスイブで伝統を継承しているとある。また、同
第6文で中国文化もまた1日が夜から始まるとしている。
続けて第7文で「言い換えれば、古代の習慣はフクロウの
時間の見方を支持している」とあるので、この3つの例は
1日が夜始まるという考え方「how owls view time＝a day
begins at night」を説明するためであることがわかる。よっ
て正解は①。

問4 42 と 43 に適する選択肢を選べ。
　①睡眠の量　　　②外見　　　　　③行動
　④文化的背景　　⑤宗教上の信条　⑥生まれた時刻

第3段落第2文に、ある説によると、「preference for day
or night：昼か夜かの好み」は「生まれた時間：time of birth」
と関係があると書かれており、興味深い詳細の2つ目の
「person's internal clock：人の体内時計」はこの書き換え。
よって、 42 に入るのは⑥。

第3段落第3文に、人間の体内時計は生まれた瞬間に動き
始めるだけではなく、夜に生まれた人間は生涯日中のパ
フォーマンスに問題を抱えるかもしれないという証拠を発
見したとあり、第5段落に知能や行動の違いについて具体
的な内容が書かれている。よって、 43 に入るのは③。

　あなたは「環境を守るために私たちが知っておくべきこと」というテーマの科学発表コンテストのためのポスターを準備している学生グループに入っています。あなたはポスターを作るために以下の文章を使っています。

プラスチックの再利用
—知っておくべきこと—

　世界は様々な種類のプラスチックであふれている。周りを見ると、何十ものプラスチックの商品を目にするだろう。より近くで見るとそれらにリサイクルマークがついていることに気づくだろう。日本では、あなたは下記の図1の1番目のようなマークを見たことがあるかもしれないが、しかし、アメリカやヨーロッパでは、より詳細な分類がされている。これらのリサイクルマークは、追いかけっこをしている矢印の三角形のように見え、ときに単純な三角形の中に1から7までの番号が書かれていることもある。このシステムは1988年に米国プラスチック産業協会によって始められたが、2008年からは国際標準化団体のひとつであるASTM（米国試験材料協会）インターナショナルによって管理されている。リサイクルマークは、使われているプラスチックの化学組成やリサイクル性についての重要なデータを提供している。しかし、物についているプラスチックのリサイクルマークは必ずしもその商品がリサイクルできることを意味するわけではない。どのような種類のプラスチックでできているか、そのプラスチックがリサイクルできる可能性があるかを示しているだけである。

図1　プラスチックのリサイクルマーク

PETE　HDPE　PVC　LDPE　PP　PS　その他
(PET)

　では、これらの数字は何を意味しているか。一方のグループ（番号が2，4，5）は人体に安全と考えられており、もう一方のグループ（番号が1，3，6，7）は、特定の状況では問題となる可能性がある。まず、安全性が高いグループから見ていこう。

　高密度のポリエチレンはリサイクルタイプ2のプラスチックで、通常HDPEと呼ばれる。毒性はなく、人体では心臓の弁や人工関節に使用されることがある。強度があり、−40℃の低温から100℃の高温まで使用することができる。HDPEはなんら害なく再利用することができ、ビール瓶のケース、ミルク入れ、いす、おもちゃにも適している。タイプ2の製品は数回のリサイクルが可能である。タイプ4の製品は低密度のポリエチレン（LDPE）でできている。使うのに安全であり、柔軟性がある。LDPEは絞り出し容器やパンの包装に使われる。現在、タイプ4のプラスチックはほとんどリサイクルされていない。ポリプロピレン（PP）はタイプ5の材料で、世界で2番目に広く生産されているプラスチックである。軽量で、伸縮性がなく、高い耐衝撃性、耐熱性、耐冷性を持っている。家具、食品の容器、オーストラリアドルのようなポリマー性の紙幣に使っている。タイプ5のプラスチックはたった3％しかリサイクルされていない。

　次に、2番目のグループ、タイプ1，3，6，7について見てみよう。これらは、それらが含んでいる化学物質やリサイクルの難しさからより課題がある。リサイクルタイプ1のプラスチックは通常PETE（ポリエチレンテレフタラート）として知られ、主に食品や飲み物の容器に使用される。PETEの容器、日本ではしばしばPETと表記される、は完全にきれいにすることが難しいので1度だけの使用にとどめるべきである。また、容器の中には軟化して変形を引き起こすものもあるため、70℃以上に加熱すべきではない。汚染されていないPETEはリサイクルが簡単で、新たな容器、衣類、カーペットにすることができるが、PETEがポリ塩化ビニル（PVC）で汚染されると、リサイクルできなくなる可能性がある。タイプ3のPVCは知られているプラスチックのうち、最もリサイクル性の低いプラスチックの1つと考えられている。専門家によってのみ廃棄されるべきであり、家や庭でけっして燃やしてはいけない。タイプ3のプラスチックはシャワーカーテンやパイプやフローリング材に見られる。タイプ6のポリスチレン（PS）、しばしばスタイロフォーム（発泡スチロール）と呼ばれるが、リサイクルは難しく、簡単に火がつく。しかし、安価に作ることができ、軽量である。使い捨ての飲料容器、即席麺の容器、そのほかの食品の包装に使用されている。タイプ7のプラスチック（アクリル、ナイロン、ポリカーボネート）はリサイクルが難しい。タイプ7のプラスチックはシート、ダッシュボード、バンパーなどのような自動車部品の製造によく使われる。

　現在、約20％のプラスチックしかリサイクルされておらず、およそ55％が最終的には埋め立て処理されている。それゆえに、異なる種類のプラスチックに関する知識は、廃棄物の削減や環境への意識の向上に役立つ可能性がある。

あなたの発表のポスター案：

> プラスチックのリサイクルマークを知っていますか？

> プラスチックのリサイクルマークとは何か？

> 　44

> プラスチックの種類とリサイクル情報

種類	マーク	説明	製品
1	PETE (PET)	このタイプのプラスチックは、一般的で通常リサイクルが容易である。	飲み物のボトル、食品容器など
2	HDPE	このタイプのプラスチックは、容易にリサイクルされ、　45　。	心臓の弁、人工関節、いす、おもちゃなど
3	PVC	このタイプのプラスチックは、　46　。	シャワーカーテン、パイプ、フローリング材など
4	4		

> 共通の特性をもつプラスチック

> 　47
> 　48

問1　ポスターの最初の項目の下で、あなたのグループは文章で説明されているように、プラスチックのリサイクルマークを紹介したい。下記のうち最も適しているものはどれか。　44

①それらはプラスチックのリサイクル性とその他関連する問題をランク付けした記号である。

②それらは化学組成やプラスチックのリサイクルの選択肢を提供している。

③それらはどの標準団体が一般的な使用のための認証をしたかを利用者に示す。

④それらはASTMによって導入され、プラスチック産業協会によって発展した。

第1段落第7文に、リサイクルマークは、使われているプラスチックの「chemical composition：化学組成」や「recyclability：リサイクル性」についての重要なデータを提供しているとある。選択肢の「chemical make-up」「recycling options」はこれらの書き換え。よって、正解は②。

問2　あなたは、タイプ2とタイプ3のプラスチックについての説明を書くよう頼まれている。　45　と　46　に最適な選択肢を選べ。

タイプ2　45

①そして、一度しか使用できないプラスチックとして知られている

②そして、広範囲の温度で使用されている

③しかし、人体に有害である

④しかし、飲み物の容器に適していない

第3段落第3文に強度があり、−40℃の低温から100℃の高温まで使用することができるとあり、正解は②。

タイプ3　[46]

①リサイクルが困難で、庭で焼却すべきではない

②燃えやすいが、柔らかく製造コストが安い

③無害な製品であることが知られている

④容易にリサイクルできることでよく知られている

第4段落第7文に知られているプラスチックのうち、最もリサイクル性の低いプラスチックの1つと考えられていること、第8文に専門家によってのみ廃棄されるべきであり、家や庭でけっして燃やしてはいけないことが書かれている。よって、正解は①。

問3　あなたは共通の特性を持ついくつかのプラスチックに関して発言している。この記事によると、下記のうちどの2つがふさわしいか。（順序は問わない）

[47]・[48]

①熱湯（100℃）はタイプ1とタイプ6のプラスチック容器に入れることができる。

②タイプ1，2，3のロゴがある製品はリサイクルが容易である。

③1，2，4，5，6のマークがある製品は食品や飲料に適している。

④タイプ5とタイプ6のマークがある製品は軽量である。

⑤タイプ4と5のプラスチックは耐熱性があり、広くリサイクルされている。

⑥タイプ6と7のプラスチックはリサイクルが容易で環境に優しい。

第4段落第3文にタイプ1のプラスチックはPETとして知られ、主に食品や飲料の容器に使われているとある。また、第2段落第2文にグループ（番号が2，4，5）は人体に安全と考えられているとあり、第3段落第2文に毒性はなく人体に使われていること、同第4文にHDPEはなんら害なく再利用することができミルク入れに適しているとある。さらに第4段落第11文にタイプ6のプラスチックは使い捨ての飲料容器、即席麺の容器、そのほかの食品の包装に使用されているとあるから、タイプ1，2，4，5，6のプラスチックは食品や飲料に適していると言える。よって、③は正しい。

第3段落第10・11文にタイプ5のプラスチックは軽量とあり、第4段落第10・11文にタイプ6のプラスチックも軽量と書かれている。よって、④も正しい。

よって、正解は③と④。

R3（追試）　[6]A

あなたはアメリカの交換留学生で、学校の演劇部に所属しています。あなたは、部を良くする手助けをしようとアイデアを得るためにあるアメリカのオンラインの芸術雑誌を読んでいるところです。

ロイヤル・シェイクスピア・カンパニーにおける最近の変化

ジョン・スミスによる

2020年2月20日

　私たちはみんな違う。世界が多くの種類の人々から成り立っていることをほとんどの人々が認識している一方、多様性、つまり私たちの差異を見せたり受け入れたりすることは、しばしば舞台芸術団体の中に反映していない。よって、障がいがある人々だけでなく、様々な背景からの人々をより良く表現するための映画や演劇に対する需要が増えてきている。イギリス芸術評議会は、この需要に答えて、すべての公的資金を受ける芸術団体に対してこの分野で改善を行うことを促している。積極的に反応しているある映画会社が、ロイヤル・シェイクスピア・カンパニー（RSC）であるが、その会社は世界で最も影響力のある映画会社のひとつである。

　イギリスのストラットフォード・アポン・エボンを拠点として、RSCはウィリアム・シェイクスピアや他のたくさんの役者による演劇を制作している。近年、RSCはイギリスの社会すべてを正確に表現するための試みとして多様性に焦点を当てている。採用する際は演者とスタッフ両方の民族的・社会的背景や、社会的性差、身体的能力のバランスを取るように一生懸命取り組んでいる。

　2019年の夏の間、RSCは、「お気に召すまま」、「じゃじゃ馬ならし」、「尺には尺を」という3つのシェイクスピアの喜劇を上演した。世界中の国の役者が雇われ、27人のキャストを形成し、今日のイギリスの多様性のある民族的、地理的、そして組織的な人口を反映していた。シーズン全体において社会的性差のバランスを達成するために、すべての役の半分は男性の役者に、半分は女性の役者に与えられた。キャストは障がいをもった3人（最近では「異なる能力をもつ」役者として参照されている）を含んでおり、ひとりは視覚障がい者、ひとりは聴覚障がい者、ひとりは車椅子を使用する人だった。

　変化は採用方針に留まらなかった。RSCは実際に観客が男女の力関係について考えてもらうことを促すために、劇の一部を書き換えた。例えば、女性と男性の役を入れ替えた。「じゃじゃ馬ならし」において、原作の「娘」の役が「息子」に変わり、男性の役者によって演じられた。同じ劇中で、男性の召使いの役が女性の召使いに書き換えられた。その役はエイミー・トリッグという車椅子を使う女性の役者によって演じられた。トリッグはその役を演じることにわくわくし、RSCの変化が他の芸術団体に大きな衝撃を与えるだろうと信じていた。RSCの他のメンバーはすべての多様性に興奮したので、同じ希望を表明した。それは、さらに多くの芸術団体がRSCの足跡をたどるのを促すことであろう。

　2019年夏の多様性を反映するRSCの決定は、自分の組織を包含的にしたいと思っている芸術団体のための新しいモデルであると見なすことができる。古典演劇の中の多様性を受け入れることを嫌がる人がいる一方、手を広げて歓迎する人もいる。ある課題は残っているが、RSCは進歩の顔としてその評価を受けている。

問1　記事によると、2019年の夏にRSCは[39]

①有名な俳優のために仕事の機会を与えた。

②異なった能力をもつ3人の演者を雇った。

③27人の人物を含む劇を探した。

④シェイクスピアと他の作家による劇を上演した。

第3段落の最終文に注目すると、④が答えとなる。

問2　この記事の著者は、エイミー・トリッグが[40]ので、彼女について述べている可能性が高い。

①RSCによって上演された劇のひとつの中で上手に演じた

②RSCのメンバーとして選ばれるために奮闘した

③包含的になるためのRSCの努力の良い例だった

④RSCのメンバーにとってロール・モデルだった

エイミー・トリッグについて述べられている第4段落より、③が答え。

問3　あなたは他の部員のためにこの記事を要約している。次のどの意見があなたの要約を完成させるのに最も適しているか。

［要約］

イギリスのRSCはその作品におけるイギリス社会の人口を反映させようと努力をしている。これを達成するために、多様な背景や能力を持った男女の役者とスタッフのバランスをとり始めている。それはまた演劇にも変化を加えた。結果的に、RSCは　41

①世界中から多くの才能のある役者を引き付けた

②何の反対もなく2019年のシーズンを完了した

③社会の期待と行動を一致させるのに寄与した

④保守的な映画会社としての評判を得た

第1段落に注目すると、③が答えとなる。

問4　あなたの演劇部はRSCの考えに賛成している。これらの考えによると、あなたの演劇部は　42　かもしれない。

①新しい国際的な作家によって書かれた劇を演じる

②原作通りに古典劇を上演する

③地元の人々のために車椅子を購入する基金を立ち上げる

④公演から社会的性差の固定観念を取り除く

第3、4段落において男性と女性の役を入れ替えることについて述べられているので、④が答え。

R3（追試）　6 B

あなたは市役所の健康フェアのためにポスターの発表を作っている生徒のグループのひとりです。あなたのグループのタイトルは「地域においてより良い口内衛生を促進すること」です。あなたはそのポスターを制作するために次の文章を使用しています。

口内衛生：鏡を見ること

近年、世界中の政府は口内衛生についての意識を向上するために取り組んでいる。多くの人々は一日に数回歯磨きをすることが良い習慣であると聞いている一方、おそらくこれが大事であるすべての理由を考慮しているわけではない。簡単に言うと、歯は重要である。歯は言葉を正確に発音するのに必要である。事実、口内衛生を怠ると実際に話すことが困難になり得る。さらにより良い基本的な必要性は、よく噛むことができるようになることである。噛むことは食物を潰し、体がそれを消化するのを容易にする。適切に噛むことはまた食の楽しみに関連している。平均的な人間は歯科で治療を受けた後片方で噛むことができないという欲求不満を経験したことがある。歯が弱い人は、いつもこの失望を経験しているかもしれない。言い換えると、口内衛生は人々の生活の質に影響を与えるのだ。

歯の基本的な機能は明らかである一方、多くの人は口が体にとっての鏡を提供していることに気付いていない。研究によると、良い口内衛生は良い一般的な健康の明らかなサインであるということである。口内衛生を怠っている人々は深刻な病気を発症する可能性がより高い。奨励されている日々の口内衛生の日課を無視することは、すでに病気で苦しんでいる人々に悪影響を与え得る。反対に、良い口内衛生を実践することは病気を防ぐことさえできるかもしれない。強く健康的な体はしばしば清潔でよく手入れのされた歯の反映である。

良い口内衛生を保つことは、人生通じての課題だ。フィンランドとアメリカの政府は、赤ちゃんが1歳を迎える前に両親は乳児を歯科医に連れて行くことを推奨している。フィンランドは実際に両親に通知をしている。ニュージーランドでは、18歳までの全員に無料の歯の治療を提供している。日本政府は8020キャンペーンを推進している。人々は歳を重ねるにつれて、様々な理由により歯を失う可能性がある。キャンペーンの目標は、80歳の誕生日にまだ少なくとも20本の歯が口の中にあることです。

日本を詳しく見てみると、厚生労働省は長年、高齢者の残っている歯の数についての調査データを分析している。ある研究者は、最年長の参加者をA（70〜74歳）、B（75歳〜79歳）、C（80歳〜84歳）、D（85歳以上）の4つの年代に分けた。それぞれの調査では、1993年を除いて、少なくとも20本の歯がある人々の割合は高い方からA、B、C、Dの順だった。しかしながら、1993年から1999年の間で、Aグループはたった6％しか改善しなかった一方、Bの増加が少しだけ高かった。1993年、Aグループの25.5％は少なくとも20本の歯があったが、2016年までにDグループの割合はAグループの最初の数より実際に0.2％高かった。Bグループは初め着実に増加したが、2005年から2011年の間に劇的に上がった。より十分な意識のおかげで、すべてのグループは長年にわたり十分に改善した。

歯科医は食事の後に歯を磨くことを長く奨励してきた。最善の口内衛生を積極的に求める人々は一日に数回歯磨きをするかもしれない。ほとんどの人は寝る前に歯を磨き、そしてそれから次の朝のある時間に再び歯を磨く。歯科医はまた、歯の間から物を取り除くために特別な種類のひもを使って毎日フロスをすることが重要だとも信じている。もうひとつの予防法は歯科医が歯の表面の周りで硬化し損傷を防ぐプラスチック製のジェル（シーラント）を使用し歯を覆うことだ。シーラントは特に子どもの使用に人気を得ている。これは一回のコーティングで、驚くべきことに80％の通常の問題を防ぐ。

歯科医を毎年、あるいはもっと頻繁に訪れることは重要だ。歯の治療は時々痛みを伴うので、積極的に歯科医に見てもらうことを避ける人がいる。しかしながら、人々は自分の歯科医を一生、文字通り自分を笑顔にしてくれる重要な人物だと見なし始めることが大切だ。

問1　初めのポスターの見出しの下に、あなたのグループは文中で説明されているように歯の重要さを表現したい。みんなはある１つの提案は適していないことに賛成している。あなたは次のうちどれを含めるべきではないか。
　　　43
　①A適切に話すことが重要
　②B食べ物を噛み砕く必要性
　③C食事を楽しむのに役立つ
　④D良い印象を作る必要がある
　⑤E生活の質を良くするのに必要不可欠

Dについては本文中に全く書かれていないので、④が答え。

問2　あなたはポスターの２番目の見出しを書くように頼まれている。次のうちどれが最も適当か。　44
　①若者を対象とした国の8020プログラム
　②より良い歯の治療のための国の広告
　③口内ケアを推奨する国の取り組み
　④幼児を歯科医に招待する国の仕組み

２番目の見出しの下を見ると、「フィンランド・アメリカ：１歳になる前の治療の推奨、ニュージーランド：若者向けの無料の治療、日本：8020キャンペーン」とあるので、③が答え。

問3　あなたは日本の研究者の調査結果を見せたい。次のうちどのグラフが、あなたのポスターに最も適しているか。　45

第４段落に注目する。　A、B、C、Dの順番になるのは、1993年だけは例外なので①が不適。
「2016年までにDグループの割合はAグループの最初の数より実際に0.2％高かった。」とあるので、②は不適。
「Bグループは初め着実に増加したが、2005年から2011年の間に劇的に上がった」とあるので、③不適。
したがって、④が答え。

問4　ポスターの最後の見出しの下に、あなたは本文に基づいて特別な助言を加えたい。次の記述のうちどの２つをあなたは使用すべきか。（順不同）　46　・　47
　①朝食を食べる前に歯を磨きなさい
　②毎日鏡で歯を確認しなさい
　③１年に少なくとも１回は歯科医に診てもらいなさい
　④プラスチックジェルを頻繁に歯に塗りなさい
　⑤毎日歯の間にデンタルフロスを使いなさい

最終段落に「歯科医を毎年、あるいはもっと頻繁に訪れることは重要だ。」とあるので、③は正解。
第５段落に「歯科医はまた、歯の間から物を取り除くために特別な種類のひもを使って毎日フロスをすることが重要だとも信じている。」とあるので、⑤は正解。

R３（本試）　6 A

　あなたはスポーツの安全性についての課題に取り組んでおり、下記の記事を見つけました。あなたはこれを読んで、わかったことをクラスメートに提供するためのポスターを作っています。

アイスホッケーをより安全にすること

　アイスホッケーは世界中で多種多様な人々に楽しまれているチームスポーツである。このスポーツの目的はパックと呼ばれる硬いゴム製のディスクをホッケースティックで相手チームのネットに入れることである。それぞれ選手６名の２チームが硬くて滑りやすいアイスリンクの上でこのペースの速いスポーツを行う。選手は時速30キロに達して空中にパックを放つこともある。このスピードでは、選手とパックの両方が深刻な危険を引き起こす原因となり得る。

　このスポーツのスピードと滑りやすいアイスリンクの表面のため、選手たちが倒れたり、お互いにぶつかったりしやすく、結果として様々な怪我を引き起こす。選手を守るための試みとして、ヘルメットやグローブ、肩、肘、脚のパッドといった装備が長年にわたって取り入れられてきた。これらの努力にかかわらず、アイスホッケーは脳震盪を起こす確率が高い。

　脳震盪は脳への損傷であり、機能の仕方に影響を与える。それは、頭、顔、首、その他の部位への直接、間接的な衝撃によって引き起こされ、ときに一時的な意識喪失を引き起こすこともある。それほど深刻でない例では、短時間、選手はまっすぐ歩けなかったり、はっきりと物が見えなかったり、耳鳴りを経験することもある。軽い頭痛だと思って脳が損傷を受けたとはわからない人もいる。

　怪我の深刻さがわからないことに加えて、選手はコーチがどう思うかを心配しがちである。過去、コーチたちは痛みにかかわらずプレーする丈夫な選手を好んだ。言い換えると、けがをして以後はプレーを辞めることが論理的であるように見えても、多くの選手はそうしなかったのである。しかし、近年、脳震盪は一生続く深刻な影響を持つ可能性があることがわかってきた。脳震盪歴がある人は集中力や睡眠にトラブルを抱える可能性がある。さらに、うつ病や気持ちの変化などの精神的な問題に苦しむ可能性がある。いくつかの例では、嗅覚障害や味覚障害を生じる可能性もある。

　カナダとアメリカのチームで構成されるナショナルホッケーリーグ（NHL）は、脳震盪に対処するため、より厳格なルールやガイドラインを作ってきている。例えば、2001年には、NHLは顔を守るためにヘルメットに取り付けられる透明なプラスチックのバイザーの装着を導入した。最初は、バイザーの装着は任意で、多くの選手たちは装着しないことを選んだ。しかし、2013年からは装着は義務となった。それに加えて、2004年に、NHLは他のプレイヤーの頭部を故意に殴った選手に対して、出場停止や罰金などの厳格なペナルティを科し始めた。

　また、NHLは2015年に脳震盪の監視員システムを導入した。このシステムでは、生中継とビデオリプレイへのアクセス権を持つNHLの競技役員が各試合中、目に見える脳震盪の兆候を監視する。まず、医学的な訓練を受けていない２人の脳震盪監視員が屋内競技場で試合を監視した。翌年には、医学的な訓練を受けている１から４人の脳震盪監視員が追加された。彼らはニューヨークのNHLの本部から試合を監視した。もし、選手が脳震盪になったと監視員が判断した場合、その選手は試合から排除され、医師による検査のための「静かな部屋」に連れて行かれる。排除された選手は医師の許可が出るまで試合に戻ることは許されない。

　NHLはアイスホッケーをより安全なスポーツにすることについてより一層の進歩を遂げてきた。脳震盪の原因と影響について多くのことが学ばれるにつれて、NHLは選手の安全をより確実にするためにさらなる対策を必ず講じるだろう。安全性の向上はアイスホッケーの選手とファンの人数の増加につながるかもしれない。

アイスホッケーをより安全にすること

アイスホッケーとは何か？
・選手たちは相手チームのネットに「パック」を入れることで得点する
・各チーム６名
・氷の上で高速で行われるスポーツ

主な問題：脳震盪の確率の高さ

脳震盪の定義
脳の機能の仕方に影響を与える脳への損傷

影響	
短期	**長期**
・意識喪失	・集中力の問題
・まっすぐ歩くことの困難性	・ 40
・ 39	・精神的な問題
・耳鳴り	・嗅覚及び味覚障害

解決策

ナショナル・ホッケー・リーグ（NHL）
・バイザー付きヘルメットの義務
・危険な選手への厳格なペナルティ
・脳震盪監視員の 41 への導入

要旨
アイスホッケー選手は脳震盪を起こす危険性が高い。
それゆえに、NHLは 42 。

問１　ポスターの 39 に最も適切な選択肢を選びなさい。
　①攻撃的なふるまい　　②思考困難
　③性格の変化　　　　　④不明瞭な視野

脳震盪の短期間の影響の例が入る。３段落後半「はっきり見ることができなくなるかもしれない」とあり、これが④と一致し、正解は④。

問２　ポスターの 40 に最も適切な選択肢を選びなさい。
　①視野の喪失　　②記憶の問題
　③睡眠障害　　　④不安定な歩行

脳震盪の長期間の影響の例が入る。４段落後半「脳震盪歴のある人は睡眠に問題を抱えるかもしれない」とあるので、これが③と一致し、正解は③。

問３　ポスターの 41 に最も適切な選択肢を選びなさい。
　①選手が試合に戻ることを許す
　②脳震盪になった選手を検査する
　③脳震盪を起こす選手に罰金を科す
　④脳震盪の兆候を示す選手を発見する

ポスターの解決策の欄に、NHL 41 するために脳震盪監視員を導入したとあり、６段落半ばに「試合中脳震盪の兆候を監視する」とあり、これが④と一致するので正解は④。

問４　ポスターの 42 に最も適切な選択肢を選びなさい。
　①選手がより強くなることを期待してきた

　②新たなルールやガイドラインを実行してきた
　③コーチたちに医学的な訓練を提供してきた
　④バイザーの装着を任意にしてきた

アイスホッケーを安全にするための要約が入る。アイスホッケーの選手は脳震盪になる危険性が高い。それゆえに 42 となる。５段落初めに「NHLは脳震盪に対応するためにより厳しいルールやガイドラインを作ってきている」とあるので、これが②と一致し、正解は②。

R３（本試）　6 B

あなたは保健の授業で栄養学を勉強しています。あなたはさまざまな甘味料についてさらに学ぶために教科書にある以下の文章を読むつもりです。

ケーキ、キャンディ、ソフトドリンク、私たちの多くは甘いものが大好きである。事実、若者は英語で何かが「良い」という意味で「甘い！」と言う。我々が甘いものについて考えるとき、サトウキビやテンサイから作られた普通の白砂糖を想像する。しかしながら、科学的発見は甘味料の世界を変化させてきた。今や、我々は多くの他の植物から砂糖を抽出することができる。最もわかりやすい例としてトウモロコシがある。トウモロコシは豊富にあり、安価で、加工が容易である。果糖ブドウ糖液糖（HFCS）は通常の砂糖よりも1.2倍甘いが、とてもカロリーが高い。科学者たちは科学を一歩前進させて、過去70年間にわたり、広く様々な人工甘味料を開発してきた。

最近の「米国健康栄養調査」では、アメリカ人の摂取エネルギーのうち平均して14.6％が食べ物そのものから由来するものではない「添加糖分」により摂取されたものであると結論付けている。例えば、バナナはホールフード（加工や精製を行わない食べ物）であるが、クッキーは添加糖分を含んでいる。添加糖分のカロリーの半分以上が甘くされた飲み物やデザート由来のものである。添加糖分の多くは、我々の体に極端な体重増加やその他の健康問題を含む、悪影響を与える。そのため、多くの人が飲み物、スナック、デザートにカロリーの低い代替品を選んでいる。

自然由来の白砂糖の代替的甘味料には、黒砂糖、はちみつ、メープルシロップが含まれるが、これらもまた、カロリーが高い傾向にある。したがって、代替的な「低カロリー甘味料」（LCSs）、ほとんどが人工化合物であるが、人気となってきた。今日、最も一般的なLCSsはアスパルテーム、Ace-K、ステビア、スクラロースである。全てのLCSsが人工的なものではなく、ステビアは植物の葉から作られる。

代替甘味料は料理に使うのは難しいかもしれない、なぜならば加熱できないものもあり、そのほとんどが白砂糖よりはるかに甘いからである。アスパルテームとAce-Kは砂糖の200倍甘い。ステビアは300倍甘く、スクラロースはステビアの２倍甘い。新たな甘味料の中にはさらに強烈なものもある。日本の会社が最近「アドバンテーム」を開発したが、砂糖の20,000倍甘い。何かを甘くするためにこの物質はほんの少量しか必要としない。

甘味料を選ぶときは、健康について考えることは重要である。たとえば、白砂糖を多く使ってデザートを作ることは、結果として体重の増加につながる可能性のある、高カロリーな食事となる。まさにこの理由からLCSsをより好む人もいる。カロリーはさておき、いくつかの研究では人工的なLCSsの消費は様々な健康についての懸念と関連付けている。LCSsの中には発がん性が疑われる強い化学物質が含まれているものや、記憶力や脳の発達への影響が見られるものがある、それゆえ、特に幼い子供、妊婦、老人にとって危険な可能性がある。キシリトールやソルビトールと言った関連性の少ない低カロリーの自然由来の代替甘味料はある。しかし、不運なことにこれらの甘味料は体内を極めてゆっくり進むので、大量に摂取すると胃に問題を引き起こす可能性がある。

何か甘いものが欲しいとき、これらの情報すべてを考慮しても、砂糖のような高カロリーの甘味料を選ぶか、LCSsを使うか決めるのは難しい。今日、多くの種類のガムやキャンディは１つかそれ以上の人工甘味料を含んでいる、それにもかかわらず、人工甘味料を温かい飲み物に入れようとしない人はいまだにこのようなものを買うかもしれない。各個人は選択肢を考え、必要性や環境に最も適した甘味料を選ぶ必要がある。

問1　あなたは　43　によって現代科学が甘味料の世界を
　　　変えたことを学ぶ。
　　　①新しい、より甘い白砂糖の種類を発見すること
　　　②アメリカ人のエネルギー摂取量を計測すること
　　　③新たな様々な選択肢を提供すること
　　　④多くの環境から新たに開発された植物を使うこと
　　1段落終わりに、「scientists have developed a wide variety
　of artificial sweeteners：科学者は広く様々な人工甘味料を
　開発してきた」が「providing a variety of new options：様々
　な新たな選択肢を提供すること」にあたる。よって、正解
　は③。

問2　あなたは今学んだことを要約しています。どのように
　　　表を埋めるべきですか？　44

甘さ	甘味料
高い	アドバンテーム
	（A）
	（B）
	（C）
低い	（D）

　　①（A）ステビア　　　　　（B）スクラロース
　　　（C）Ace-K、アスパルテーム　（D）HFCS
　　②（A）ステビア　（B）スクラロース
　　　（C）HFCS　　　（D）Ace-K、アスパルテーム
　　③（A）スクラロース　　　（B）ステビア
　　　（C）Ace-K、アスパルテーム　（D）HFCS
　　④（A）スクラロース　（B）ステビア
　　　（C）HFCS　　　　　　（D）Ace-K、アスパルテーム
　白砂糖と比較しての甘さは、1段落後半よりHFCSは1.2
　倍、4段落によれば、アスパルテームとAce-Kは200倍、
　ステビアは300倍、スクラロースはステビアの2倍なので
　600倍、アドバンテームは20,000倍となっており、甘い順に
　並べるとアドバンテーム、スクラロース、ステビア、アス
　パルテームとAce-K、HFCSとなる。よって、正解は③。

問3　あなたが読んだ記事によると下記のうち正しいものは
　　　どれか。（2つ選べ。順不同。）　45　・　46
　　　①代替的甘味料が体重の増加の原因になることが証明さ
　　　　れてきた。
　　　②アメリカ人の摂取エネルギーの14.6%を代替的甘味料
　　　　から得ている。
　　　③植物から代替的甘味料を得ることができる。
　　　④多くの人工甘味料は料理に使いやすい。
　　　⑤キシリトールやソルビトールのような甘味料はすぐに
　　　　は消化されない。
　　3段落より体重の増加の原因となるのは自然の代替的甘味
　料HFCSであり、人工的な代替的甘味料のうちLCSsと呼ば
　れるものはカロリーが低いので①は不適。2段落初めよ
　り、摂取エネルギーの14.6%を代替的甘味料ではなく、添
　加糖分により得ているので②は不適。3段落終わりより、
　ステビアは植物の葉から作られるので③は正しい。4段落
　初めより代替的甘味料は料理に使うのが難しいとされてお

り、代替的甘味料に人工甘味料も含まれるから④は不適。
　5段落後半「these move through the body extremely
slowly：体内を移動するのが非常に遅い」とあり、これが
⑤の「are not digested quickly：すぐに消化されない」と一
致する。よって、正解は③・⑤。

問4　筆者の立場を記述するのに最も適しているものはどれ
　　　か。　47
　　　①筆者は人工甘味料を飲み物やデザートに使うことに反
　　　　対している。
　　　②筆者は人工甘味料が従来の甘味料に取って代わること
　　　　に成功したと考えている。
　　　③筆者は将来の使用のためはるかに甘い製品を発明する
　　　　ことが重要だと述べている。
　　　④筆者は人々にとって賢明な選択をすることを重視すべ
　　　　きであると提案している。
　　6段落終わりに、「選択肢を考え、必要性と環境に最も適し
　た甘味料を選ぶ必要がある」とあり、④と一致する。よっ
　て、正解は④。

H30（試行調査2回）　6 A
　　あなたは性差と経歴の発展に関するクラスでのグループ
　発表のための準備をしています。あなたは下にある記事を
　見つけました。

**女性のパイロットはアジアの
パイロット危機を解決しうるか**

[1]　アジアにおける急速な航空旅行の成長とともに、パイロット不足が深刻な関心を呼ぶ問題になりつつある。統計によると、アジアを航空する観光客の数は現在1年間に約1億人にまで増加した。もしこの傾向が続けば、これから20年に渡りこの地域で226,000人の新たなパイロットが必要となるだろう。これらの仕事を全て補填するために、航空会社は、より多くの女性を雇う必要があるだろうが、女性は現在世界中の全パイロットののを3％を占めており、日本やシンガポールのようなアジアの国々においてはたったの1％しか占めていないのである。多くの新たなパイロットを見つけるために、そのように少ない女性パイロットを説明するような要因が調べられなければならないし、可能な解決策が探られなければならない。

[2]　女性がパイロットになる1つの潜在的な障害としては、多くの社会で長く存在している固定観念である。女性はこの仕事にはあまり向いていないという考えがあるのかもしれない。これは、男子は機械に強い傾向があり身体的に女子よりも強いという観念からある程度出てきたように思われる。最近の研究によると、若い女性は成功する見込みの薄い職業を避ける傾向があるらしい。それ故に、この性に関する固定観念により女性は挑戦することさえもしようとしないのかもしれない。マレーシア飛行アカデミーでは、例えば、なぜ登録した全訓練生の10%しか女性が占めていないということがよくあるのかを説明することになるのだろう。

[3]　しかしもう1つの問題は安全性を孕んでいる。人々は女性パイロットにより飛ばされる機体の安全性を心配してしまうかもしれないが、その心配はデータにより示されているわけではない。例えば、アメリカ合衆国で施行された膨大なパイロットのデータベースの分析により、男性と女性のパイロットの間で事故率に優位な差はないことが示された。代わりに、その研究によりパイロットの年齢や飛行経験といった他の要因が、その人が事故に巻き込まれやすいかどうかをより予測できる、と判明した。

[4]　女性パイロットの方がより良い飛行技術を持っていると予想されるにも関わらず、男性と女性のパイロットは、その仕事において異なる長所を与える技術を持っている。一方で、女性パイロットの方が飛び方を学ぶのが早いことが多い。操縦室での操縦は大きい人にとっては届きやすく使いやすいことが多いのである。男性は平均的に女性より大きい傾向がある。実際、女性よりも男性の方がほとんどの国の最小身長要求に合う傾向がある。また一方で、日本人の女性機長がいるように、女性パイロットは従業員間での会話を促すのがより得意なようである。

[5]　若い旅客が、女性が彼らの飛行機を飛ばしているのを見たら、彼らは女性パイロットを自然な現象として受け入れるようになる。今日の女性パイロットは家族と家で過ごす必要があるというような、固定観念的な見方や伝統的な習慣を壊す良い模範である。柔軟な仕事調整を提供することが、ベトナム航空によりすでに行われているように、女性パイロットの数を増やし、彼女らをその職業に留まらせる手助けとなる。

[6]　男性と女性は航空パイロットとして等しく働くことができると思われる。航空パイロットは男性であるべきであるという根拠のない信念を消し去るために、この点に関して、ある強いメッセージが若い世代に送られなければならない。

問1 文章によると、筆者はアジアにおける現在の状況を危機と呼んでいます。なぜなら、 35 からです。
① さらに多くの男性航空パイロットが以前よりも仕事を辞めている
② 事故率は男性と女性のパイロットの両方で増えている
③ 女性パイロットの数はこの数十年間変化していない
④ 将来必要とされるパイロットの数は現在よりもかなり多い
[1]の4行目によると、「226,000人の新たなパイロットが必要となる」とある。よって、正解は④。

問2 文章によると 36 において、男性と女性の間における違いはほとんどありません。
① どれほど簡単に飛行機の操縦を学習するのか
② どれほど事故に巻き込まれやすいか
③ どれほど多くの時間を仕事に費やしているのか
④ どのようにして人々がその仕事に合っているかを認識するのか
[3]の3行目によると、「男性と女性のパイロットの間で事故率に優位な差はない」とある。よって、正解は②。

問3 [4]段落において、筆者は 37 の例を挙げるために日本人の女性機長について言及するようです。
① 女性パイロットが職場に生むことができる貢献
② 飛行機を飛ばすための卓越した技術を持つ女性パイロット
③ 航空パイロットを訓練するための現在のシステムにおける問題
④ 珍しい達成事をした航空会社の雇用主
[4]の最終文によると、「女性パイロットは従業員間での会話を促すのがより得意なようである」とある。よって、正解は①。

問4 以下の文の中で、最も文章のまとめに適するものはどれですか。 38
① 女性パイロットに対する否定的な見方にもかかわらず、彼女らは男性パイロットと同じくらい成功しうる。
② 経済的な問題のために、アジアのパイロット学校の女生徒の割合はかなり小さい。
③ 将来、世界中の多くの国がアジアの国々のようにより多くの女性パイロットを雇い始めなければならないかもしれない。
④ 女性パイロットに対する主な障害は排除されたので、将来の女性パイロットの数を増やすことに関する懸念はほとんどない。
[6]によると、「男性と女性は航空パイロットとして等しく働くことができると思われる」とある。よって、正解は①。

H30（試行調査2回） 6 B

あなたは世界の生態系の問題に関する研究をしています。イエローストーン国立公園で何が起こったのかを理解するために、以下の記事を読もうとしています。

イエローストーン国立公園は、アメリカ合衆国の北部に位置しており、1872年に世界初の国立公園となった。この220万エーカーの公園の主なアトラクションの1つは、非常に多種多様な動物たちである。イエローストーンはオオカミを見るためには世界中で最適な場所である、と言う人々もいる。2016年12月時点では、公園内には最低でも180匹のオオカミと11の群れ（社会的な家族）がいた。1940年代までには、しかしながら、オオカミはイエローストーン国立公園からほとんどいなくなってしまった。今日では、これらのオオカミは戻ってきてうまくやっている。なぜ、彼らは戻ってきたのだろうか。

オオカミの数は狩りによって1920年代までに減少したが、それは政府によって規制された。ウシとウマとヒツジを育てる大牧場の牧場主たちは、彼らの動物を殺してしまうのでオオカミが好きではなかった。オオカミが狩りによって絶滅させられそうな時点で、他の問題が出てきた。ヘラジカの群れが増えてきたのである。ヘラジカは、シカの多くの種類であるが、冬にはオオカミの主な食料源である。ヘラジカの個体数が非常に増えたので、多くの植物を食べてその地域の生態系のバランスを乱してしまった。人々はヘラジカを見るのが好きなのかもしれないが、科学者は異常に増えてしまった個体数により引き起こされる損害を心配していた。

この問題を解決するために、アメリカ政府は、カナダから連れてきた若いオオカミを放つという彼らの意向を発表した。そのオオカミはヘラジカを狩り、個体数を減らす手助けとなることが望まれた。しかしながら、多くの牧場主がオオカミを連れ戻すことに反対したので、政府と牧場主が計画に合意するのに20年かかった。1974年に、オオカミの再導入を監督するために、あるチームが任命された。政府は1982年と1985年、最後に1987年に公式の修復計画を発行した。長期間の研究の後、公式の環境影響声明が発表され、31匹のオオカミが1995年から1996年の間にイエローストーンに放たれた。

ヘラジカの数を減らすためのこの計画は大きく成功した。2006年まで、イエローストーン国立公園のオオカミの推定個体数は、100匹以上であった。さらには、観察者は、導入後最初の10年の間に20000匹近くから10000匹以下にまでヘラジカの個体数が減少した要因が、オオカミであると信じた。結果として、たくさんの植物が成長し直し始めた。オオカミが牧場主の動物に与える危険性のため、オオカミの狩りさえも再び許可された。オオカミが脅威だと認識されるので、オオカミを狩ることが明白な解決策のように思えるかもしれないが、それは新たな問題を引き起こすかもしれない。2014年に発表された研究が提唱したが、オオカミを狩ることにより、オオカミが牧場主の動物を殺す頻度を増やしたのかもしれない。もしオオカミの群れのリーダーが殺されれば、その群れは崩壊するかもしれない。より小さい群れ、あるいは個別のオオカミが牧場主の動物を攻撃するかもしれない。それゆえ、現在はどれほど多くのオオカミを狩ることができるかに、制限がある。そのような手段が、オオカミの個体数の長期間の調整には重要なのである。

問1 1900年代早期のイエローストーン国立公園にいるオオカミの減少は、結果として 39 。
① 狩猟家の数の減少となったが、それはオオカミにとっては良かった。
② 牧場主の数の減少となったが、それは人口を減らした。
③ エラジカの数の増加となったが、それは生態系に害を与えた。
④ 樹木と植物の数の増加となったが、それはヘラジカが

隠れるのに役立った。

第2段落6行目によると、「ヘラジカの個体数が非常に増えたので、多くの植物を食べてその地域の生態系のバランスを乱してしまった」とある。よって、正解は③。

問2　以下の4つのグラフの中のどれがその状況を最も良く表しているか。　40

第3段落によると、1987年にはオオカミはほぼ絶滅の状態であった。ヘラジカの個体数が減少し始めたのは、1995年から1996年の間にオオカミが再導入されてからである。よって、正解は②。

問3　記事によると、以下のうち、どの2つが公園の現在の状況を伝えてくれるものはどれか。（**2つ選びなさい。**順序は問わない）　41 ・ 42

①30年以上前より多くの旅行客が公園を訪れている。
②一方の種が生き残り、もう一方は代わりに絶滅した。
③人々は再びこの場所のまわりでオオカミを狩り始めた。
④その公園にはオオカミとヘラジカの両方が、豊富な草木と同じくらいいる。
⑤公園にいるヘラジカの個体数を減らすための新しい規則がある。

第4段落6行目によると、「オオカミの狩りさえも再び許可された」とある。また、同段落5行目に「たくさんの植物が成長し直し始めた」、問2のグラフよりヘラジカとオオカミの両方が公園内にいることがわかる。よって、正解は③、④。

問4　この記事のタイトルとして最も適切なものは、　43 である。
①牧場主の動物の数の減少
②自然のバランスの問題を処理すること
③世界中の自然保全
④国立公園にヘラジカを放つこと

全体を通して書かれているのは、オオカミ・ヘラジカ・植物の個体数の増減についてです。これらの増減は、自然の生態系に関わるということが、第2段落に述べられています。よって、正解は②。

H29（試行調査1回）　6

あなたは授業で「オスカルのキャニオンキャンプ体験」という話の感想を書いています。

オスカルのキャニオンキャンプ体験

12歳のオスカルはキャニオンキャンプでの素晴らしい1週間を終えた。彼は、友達を作ったり、新しい技術を身に付けたり、他の多くの物の中でも科学への愛を発見したりして過ごした。そして、オスカルはある重要な教訓を学んだ。それは、ときに難しい局面に立ち合ったとき、ただそのままにしておくことが最善であることもある、というものである。彼は、物事はいつも見たままであるとは限らないということも学んだ。

キャニオンキャンプは、8歳から16歳までの男女のためのサマーキャンプである。アメリカでは、たくさんの種類のキャンプがある。しばしば、子どもたちは特別な技術に集中するか、宗教的な本や伝統の価値観を学ぶ。けれども、キャニオンキャンプは違う。その主たる目的は、子どもたちがコミュニケーションと相互の視点に基づいた考えを使い、困難な状況への対処の仕方を自分たちで発見することである。そのキャンプ期間に、泳ぐのを楽しみ、ゲームをし、体験型自然科学計画を行いながら、子どもたちは判断力と正誤の感覚を伸ばすのである。

これは、オスカルのキャニオンキャンプでの2度目の夏のことであるが、彼は喜んで、新しく来た人に周りを紹介した。初日、彼は、初めてキャンプに参加した同年代の少年であるディランに自己紹介をした。オスカルは、ディランが新しい状況に慣れるのを手助けするためにたくさんの時間を費やし、彼らはすぐに親友になった。彼らは2人ともテレビゲームと木登りをするのを楽しみ、キャンプではドッジボールのようなガガボールが2人とも大好きだった。他の子どもたちとボールを投げたり大声で笑ったりしながら、オスカルとディランは疲れ切るまでガガボールをした。その後、彼らは寝台に座れば、数時間自分たちの家や学校生活、キャニオンキャンプでどれだけ楽しんでいるかについて話した。

他のキャンプに入る人の中の1人に、クリストファーという名前の少年がいた。最初は、クリストファーは行儀の良い、楽しむことが好きな少年のようだと思われた。オスカルは、彼と友達になりたくて仕方なかった。しかしながら、クリストファーの振る舞いが変わるのはそれからまもなくだった。彼は、わざと布団を敷かなかった。彼はゲームや他の所持品を床のあちこちにほったらかしにした。彼は思慮深さに欠け自己中心的だった。そして、彼は意地悪で、オスカルとディランはすぐにそれが分かったのである。

「ディランは歯磨きをしていない。そして、臭い！彼は今日シャワーを浴びてないんだ」と、他の子どもたち全員がしっかり聞こえるように、朝食のときにクリストファーは叫んだ。

オスカルとディランはクリストファーの言葉を聞いて驚いた。オスカルはいつも一生懸命にみんなを楽しませようとしていた。クリストファーは他の2人の少年を動揺させるようなことを言ってとても楽しんでいるようだった。みんながお昼ごはんに並んでいるときに、彼はオスカルを前に押しさえもした。彼はオスカルが怒って抗議しているときにただ笑っていた。

オスカルはクリストファーの問題点についてキャンプのカウンセラーに相談した。彼女はクリストファーに強く警告したが、何かあれば彼の振る舞いはどんどん悪くなった。他の子どもたちは、キャンプでの楽しい活動を台無しにさせないように決め、ただ彼の邪魔をしないようにした。

これらの活動の中の1つには、科学の先生との話し合いがあった。オスカルは学校では科学に少しも興味を示さなかったけれども、これはキャンプで彼が本当に楽しんだものだった。彼らが発見した新しい科学的な事実のいずれにも、どん

どん興奮しながら、子どもたちはその先生と話した。オスカルは、反射光と特定の色をどのようにして見ているかについて学ぶことに、特に心を掴まれた。例えば、赤い物体は虹の全ての色を吸収するが、赤い色だけを私たちの目に反射しているのである。

「だから、」オスカルはディランに息もつかず報告した、「赤い物体は赤以外のすべての色で、それらは吸収されるんだ！すごくないか？僕は只々科学が大好きだ！」と。物事はいつも見たままであるとは限らないということに気づくようになった。

キャンプにいる人たちもまた、倫理学や一緒に経験するにつれてグループにとって最善であろう規則について話し合った。反対意見があればいつでも、それぞれの状況に関して何が正しく何が間違っているか、を考慮するために中断した、このようにして、彼らは協調性のあるグループとして一緒に機能することを学んだ。

これらの話し合いを通して、オスカルはある問題に対する明確な解決策は常には存在しないということを学んだ。ときには、クリストファーの悪いふるまいの場合のように、答えが、ただほったらかすことであることもある。オスカルは、動揺することが何かを変えることにはならないということ、劇的でなくその状況を解決する最善の方法がそれから逃れることであるということに気付いた。彼とディランは落ち着き、クリストファーの無礼な振る舞いに反応するのをやめた。これは上手くいったようだった。すぐに、クリストファーは少年たちに迷惑をかけることの興味を失った。その週の終わりが、オスカルにとってはとても早く来てしまった。彼のキャンプの思い出は、家に帰って数日経ってクリストファーのはがきを受けとったときも、未だに鮮明だった。

オスカルへ
　私はキャンプでの自分の振る舞い方をとても申し訳なく思っています。あなたとディランは本当にとても楽しそうに思えました。私はあまり運動が得意ではなかったので、独りぼっちのように感じました。その後、あなたが私の悪いふるまいに注意を払うのをやめたとき、私はいかに自分がバカだったのかに気づきました。私はそのとき謝りたかったのですが、とても恥ずかしかったのです。来年もまたキャンプに来るつもりですか？私はそこに行きます。そして、友達になれることを願っています！
じゃあね
クリストファー

そうです、彼のサプライズからもとに戻り、オスカルは、ほったらかしにすることが正しかったのだと思った。ポストカードを投函し、彼はキャンプで学んだことを思い出した。ときに、物事は見たままではないのだと。

| 34 | から | 38 | を埋めて感想を完成させなさい。 |

話の感想	タイトル： オスカルの キャニオンキャンプ体験

概要

序盤	中盤	終盤
新しく来た人を歓迎しながら、オスカルの2度目のキャニオンキャンプ体験が始まった。	34 → 35	オスカルは、キャンプで学んだことを、その問題への解決策を見つけたことに応用した。

主要人物

- オスカルは活動的で社交性がある
- クリストファーは友好的ではないように思えるかもしれないが、実際は 36 である。

あなたの意見

私は、オスカルがどのようにその問題に対処するかを本当は知らなかったと思います。彼が行ったことは全て 37 です。クリストファーの悪いふるまいが、さらに悪くならなくて彼は幸運でした。

この話が最も惹きつけそうなのは…

38 という読者

問1　(a)　34

① キャンプの参加者全員がすぐに仲の良い友達になれた

② キャンプにいる人のほとんどが楽しい活動を楽しむのをやめた

③ キャンプにいる人の中の1人が驚くほど態度を変えた

④ キャンプのカウンセラーがどうにかして深刻な問題を解決しようとした

第4段落によると、クリストファーがはじめと打って変わって、非常に行儀の悪い少年となったことがわかる。よって、正解は③。

問1　(b)　35

① クリストファーはとても悪くふるまうことを続けた

② ディランはどのように光が反射するかを理解することができた

③ オスカルはグループディスカッションで率先した役割を担っている

④ カウンセラーは自分の観点を再考した

第4段落から第7段落にかけて、クリストファーは行儀が悪いままであることがわかる。よって、正解は①。

問2　36

① 全ての活動に参加することができたわけではなかったので、ただ幸せではなかった

② はじめて家を離れて過ごしていたので、おそらく緊張した

③ 正直な意見を隠そうとしたので、キャンプにいるほとんどの人たちよりも頭が良い

④ 自分の友達と共有するためにゲームを持ってくるほど

十分に思いやりがあった

クリストファーがオスカルに宛てた手紙によると、クリストファーは運動があまり得意ではなかったため、疎外感を感じていたことがわかる。よって、正解は①。

問3　37
①困難な状況を避ける
②倫理と規則を話し合う
③他者を辱める
④とても仲良くなろうとする

第11段落によると、オスカルはクリストファーの振る舞いをほったらかしにしようという意図が見られる。具体的な解決策を思いついたわけではない。よって、正解は①。

問4　38
①夏の野外活動についての詳細な情報を得る
②様々なスポーツにおける子どもたちの成功についての感動的な話を読む
③子供時代の友達との経験を思い出す
④子供と大人との関係を理解する

全体の文章を通じて、オスカルとディランの友情の深め方、オスカルとクリストファーの確執と手紙によってその確執を明らかにする展開、が書かれている。よって、正解は③。

H31　6

(1)森の河川のそばの静かな小道から街を走るせわしい道路まで、人々は異なる場所に様々な形の道を創り上げてきた。これらは今私たちの周りのいたるところに存在し、それらを使うことは社会にとって重要である。これらの道は、人々の移動・物の運搬・次から次に素早くかつ安全に情報を送信することを可能にしてきた。歴史を通して、それらは私たちの日常生活の中で重要になってきたのだ。

(2)初期の道は、しばしば自然と地上に造られた。人々がその道を、歩いてあるいは馬の背に乗って旅した間に、長い期間を経て徐々にそれらは発展した。古代に、歴史上最初の車輪のついた台車が現れると注目すべき転機が訪れた。いったんこのことが起こると、人々は良く整備された道の重要性に気づいた。それゆえ、町・市街地・そして国全体が、栄えるためにそれらを改善させた。その結果、生活はより便利になり、地域社会は成長し、経済は発展し、文化は広がった。特に自動車が出現した後は、地上の道の重要性は更に増した。

(3)人々は水上の道も建設してきた。河川と運河は、人々があちこち移動するため、また物を運ぶための効果的な道として働いた。例えば、江戸時代の古き日本では、水の道は市街地の生活や経済を支える、農作物・海産物・木材の運搬のために使われた。人々はまた海を渡る道も拓いた。海路は、風・波・水深・海岸線の地形に基づいて発展したが、船の誘導には重要で、特に主に風力だけで移動するような日のときにはそうだった。これらの海路を使うことで、人々は非常に遠く離れたところまで旅することができ、それまでは辿り着くことのできなかったような場所にまで

行くことができた。数多くの重要な海路が現れ、それが自然資源や製品、思考の交換につながった。このことが、市街地や町を次々に繁栄させることになった。

(4)人々は同様に、空に道を拓き続けている。航空機が発明されてから、これらの空路により人々は簡単に長い距離を旅することが可能になった。風と空気の流れといった状況を考慮することにより最善の空路を発見した。結局のところ、人々は空中の高いところを安全かつ快適に旅することができるようになり、また莫大な距離を移動することに、ほんの少しの時間しかかからなくなった。実際、人々は、以前は船で日本からヨーロッパへ旅するのに1ヶ月以上必要だったが、一方で、今日航空機で1日あればいいのである。これら空路の確立のおかげで、何人もの人々が今や、観光したり友人を訪れたり仕事をするために世界中を旅している。

(5)今日、私たちには、新たな道の形であるインターネットがある。それは情報の電子的な交換に特化している。この世界規模の道を使うことにより、人々はかつて本や対人による会話で主に入手できていた情報を簡単に得ることができる。それは一度に大多数の人々全員に瞬時にメッセージを送ることができる。ある研究によると、35億人以上の人々が、これは全世界人口の約半分にあたるが、今日この電子的な道にアクセスしている。科学技術が進歩するにつれて、ますます多くの人々が情報を集めるため、また会話をするためにこの道を利用するだろう。

(6)人々がいる限り、彼らを繋げる道があり続けてきた。これらは、人々・物・情報の移動だけでなく、地域社会・経済・文化の発展にも貢献している。経路は人類の発展と繁栄において重要な役割を担ってきた。現在知られていない道が、将来さらに遠くへと私たちを連れて行ってくれるであろうことは間違いない。

A

問1　46　②
第1段落の下線部imperativeの意味に最も近いものを次から選びなさい。
①偶然的な
②重要な
③産業的な
④伝統的な

問2　47　③
第2段落によると、次の文章のうちどれが正しいか。
①初期の道は車輪のついた台車で旅した人々により創られた。
②人々の最初の道路は町や市街地の成長につながった。
③道路の発展は社会の多くの地域の進捗を招いた。
④道の改善は結果として自動車の発明につながった。

第2段落の真ん中以降の訳を参照。

問3　48　④
なぜ第3段落では江戸の例が紹介されたか。

①水上に道を創ることの難しさを描写するため

②そこが重要な町であるという事実を強調するため

③海岸線に沿って移動するための水路の使用を説明するため

④市街地にとっての水路の重要な役割を説明するため

第3段落のはじめに江戸についての記述があり、ここで水路の使用方法について書かれている。

問4 　49　 ①

第5段落は道について、私たちに何を伝えているか。

①道は世界中で目に見えない形で存在していると考えられうる。

②情報を動かす道は、危険であるとみなされることもある。

③道の根本的な機能は低下している。

④異なる種類の道の重要性は同じである。

第5段落では、インターネットと情報、その利用について書かれているため、これは目に見えない形でも道が存在していることの例である。

問5 　50　 ④

この記事の本題はなにか。

①人類は最初に様々な形式の快適な道路を創り上げた。

②輸送の改善には多額の費用がかかった。

③科学技術は世界中における道の開通に干渉した。

④人類の進歩は道の発達により助けられた。

文章を通して様々な道により人類の生活が豊かになったことが書かれている。また第6段落に「道は人類の発展と繁栄において重要な役割を担ってきた」とある。

B

| 51 | ① | 52 | ④ | 53 | ② | 54 | ③ |

段　落	内　　容
(1)	導入
(2)	51
(3)	52
(4)	53
(5)	54
(6)	結論

①人々や動物、車によって使われる道路の創造

②人々があちこちへ飛ぶための方法の発展

③情報伝達のための世界規模の道の設立

④船で旅したり物を運搬するための航路の開通

第2段落では、人々が歩いたり車が走ったりするための道路に関する記述がある。また最初に創られた道路の話をしているため、に入るものは①。第3段落では、江戸の話の後に海路について「人々はまた海を渡る道も拓いた」と書かれている。よってに入るものは④。第4段落では、最初に「人々は同様に、空に道を拓き続けている」とあるので航空機に関する段落であることがわかる。よって　53　に入るものは②。第5段落では、インター

ネットと情報の収集に関する内容が書かれているので　54　に入るものは③。

H30　6

(1)我々が世界をどう理解するかを、技術と関連した発見が大きく変えてきたことを歴史は我々に教えてくれる。多くの技術装置は、五感のような我々の自然容量の範囲を加えたり力を与えたりしてくれる。これらの装置の間では、多くの装置が我々は裸眼では見えないものを見えるようにしてくれる。この不可視から可視への変化は、我々の世界の理解に莫大な成果をもたらし我々の思考に強い影響を与えてきた。

(2)17世紀、ある科学者が2つのレンズをある方法によって一緒に用いることで物体が大きく見えるようになることに気付いた。彼はこの技術を最初の単純な望遠鏡を作るために使った。これらの古い望遠鏡を使って、初期の科学者は月の表面を詳細に描いたり木星が少なくとも月のような衛星を4つ持つことを見たりすることが可能だった。当時から人々は我々の視野を広げる様々な装置を開発してきた。例えば、地球のはるか上空にひろがる宇宙についての真実を暴いてきた。望遠鏡はすぐに手に届かない物に関して新しい視点を我々に与え続けている。

(3)その後、望遠鏡と似た原理を用いて顕微鏡が発達した。顕微鏡のおかげで我々はとても小さすぎて通常では見ることができない物を研究することができる。顕微鏡を通じて見ることは科学者に全く新しい世界を開いてくれた。顕微鏡の発明以前は、科学者は人間の組織や動植物の細胞の構造を見ることができなかった。彼らがこれらのものを見た時、まとまっていて分けることができないと考えていたものが実際にはより小さい構成要素によって構成されているものもあることに気付くようになった。これらは、顕微鏡の助けがあって初めて見ることができた。今日、電子顕微鏡のおかげで我々は分子のようなより小さなものでさえ調査することができる。このような進歩は、世界の物事の構成に関する我々の概念を変えてしまった。

(4)カメラの発明もまた見えない世界を見えるものにした。世界中ですべてのものは変化している。我々が見ることができるよりも速く変わるものもある。カメラは我々に異なった時点での変化を凍結する力を与えてくれる道具である。連続写真は鳥がどのように飛び立つのか、あるいはアスリートがどのように走るのかを明らかにしてきた。カメラのおかげでとてもゆっくりすぎて我々がたいてい気付かない変化をも見ることができる。例えば、何ヶ月、何年も隔てて撮られた同じ風景の写真を見比べることで、我々はどのように社会が変化するのかについて洞察を得ることができる。これらに加えて、カメラが我々の世界の認識を変えてきた他の方法がたくさんある。

(5)19世紀後半になって、新たに発見されたX線を使った機械が、我々が物を見る方法を進化させた。物事の表面だけを見ることよりもむしろ、我々は物の中や物を通して見る能

力を得て、多くの物の中身を視界に入れた。この能力は職場では実用的で、実験室や博物館では便利で、大学では教育的であることを証明した。その最も重要な活用は医学においてであった。医者はしばしば病気を診断したり体の中の問題を見付けてきたりすることが困難だった。X線のおかげで、患者の中身を見たり問題がある箇所を特定したり、それらを治療することができるようになった。このようなX線の使い方は、診断や治療のための新しい理解や方法をもたらした。

(6)様々な科学技術装置が裸眼で見ることができなかったものを観察することができるのを可能にしてきた。これは我々の周辺の世界についての我々の理解を劇的に変えてきた。それぞれの科学技術の進歩は予期していなかった方法で我々を変え、それぞれの発見は世界についての我々の知識を増やしてくれる。前に述べた装置と同様に、新たな装置が将来、我々の生活に影響を与え我々の考え方を変え続けていくであろう。

A

問1 | 46 | ④

段落(2)において使われているarchaicの意味は以下のどれに最も近いか。

①進歩した　　②現代の
③普通の、並の　　④原始的な

直前の一文がfirst simple telescopeについて述べていることに注目する。

問2 | 47 | ②

段落(3)によると、顕微鏡を使うことによって人々は何を学んだか。

①細胞はあまりに小さく顕微鏡ではみえない。
②物質は更に小さなもので構成されている。
③分子は最小の構成要素である。
④レンズのセットは物体の大きさを小さくする。

①はnotはないが否定の意味を含んでいることに注意。③、④は文章中では言及されていない。

問3 | 48 | ①

段落(4)によると、カメラは私たちに何をすることを可能にしたか。

①時間の中の瞬間を正確にとらえること
②急速な社会の変化を比較すること
③見えないものがより早く動けるようにすること
④何が起こるか予想すること

第4文に注目する。

問4 | 49 | ①

段落(5)によると、X線はどのように使われているか。

①身体の問題がある場所を見つけるため
②物体の表面の視野を改善するため
③絵画がいつ作られたかを学ぶため
④化学合成物の質を試すため

後ろから2文目に注目する。

問5 | 50 | ②

この文の要旨は何か。

①2つのレンズを使うことは人間の視野を改善することができる。
②技術の発展は我々の考え方に影響を与える。
③技術の危険性を人々は認識する必要がある。
④五感を変えていく際に技術はきわめて重要な役割を果たす。

第6段落に注目する。

B

| 51 | ④ | 52 | ② | 53 | ③ | 54 | ① |

段落	内　容
(1)	導入
(2)	51
(3)	52
(4)	53
(5)	54
(6)	結論

①物質の内部を調査すること
②小さなものの世界を探検すること
③一連の変化の間の瞬間を見ること
④宇宙を見るためのレンズを利用すること

第2段落はMoonなど天体の話が述べられていることから望遠鏡、第3段落は第2文のsmallなどの単語から顕微鏡、第4段落第4文からカメラ、第5段落はX-raysといった単語からレントゲンとそれぞれ推測できるのでそれぞれに適した選択肢を選ぶ。

H29 | 6 |

(1)たいていの人々にとって、友情は彼ら自身の価値ある重要な一部である。心理学者たちは揺るぎない友情はより良い自己理解につながると指摘してきた。我々は知人だけではなく親友とすらもいざこざに直面することがあるかもしれないが、そのことによって終わってしまう友情もありうるということも彼らは述べている。幸運にも、そのようないざこざが起こったときでさえ、友情を維持し保つ方法を見つけることは可能である。

(2)困難な状態に陥った友情を保つための一つの方法は連絡をとることである。友人が我々の感情を傷つけるような何かをしてしまったと考える時、我々の最初の反応は連絡を断つことだろう。しかし、プライドを捨て、そうしてしまうことを避けるほうがより良いだろう。例えば、メアリーは友人のスーザンが夜間学校を修了し卒業するまで毎週スーザンの子ども達の面倒を見ていた。しかし、その後数ヶ月間スーザンからメアリーには連絡がなかった。だから、スーザンは単に彼女を利用していただけだとメアリーは感じた。メアリーはスーザンとはもう話さないと決めた。しかし、結局メアリーは無理に自分自身の感情を無視して、

スーザンに彼女の落胆を伝えた。スーザンはすぐに謝り、勉強を修了したあとにいろいろなことに追いつこうとしていただけだったと言った。もしメアリーがそう言わなかったら、スーザンは問題があることを知らなかったであろう。怒っているかも知れない時でも、接触を断たないことは良い関係性を保つためにはとても重要である。

(3)友情の役に立つ他の方法は友人の観点から物事を見ることである。例えば、マークは自分が入院している時に彼女が御見舞に来なかったことから非常に腹を立てていた。後に、ケイトは幼少期に深刻な病気で入院して以来病院が怖いということをケイトの友人から彼は知った。マークはその時、ケイトが来なかった理由を悟り、怒るのではなく、彼女に共感した。

(4)友情と対処する重要な要素の一つは友情が我々のニーズや生活様式が展開するに従って変化しうるということを認識し受け入れるということである。例えば、高校の時に親友がいるかもしれないが、ひとたび卒業したり、就職や入学のため違う町に引っ越しをしたり、または結婚したりして、その友人とあまり頻繁に会わなくなったり、気持ちが変化するかもしれない。言い換えるならば、親密な友情も自然と変化するかもしれないのである。我々はまだ友人ではあるが以前と同じ状態ではないということもあるということを心にとめておかなくてはならない。

(5)どのように人々は友情を長く保っているのか。ある研究では、その秘密を明らかにするために長期間にわたり友人同士であった多くの人々に研究者がインタビューを行った。彼らは友情を終わらせかねない些細な誤解を大きな問題に発展しないようにしていると判明した。友人の観点に立つこと、そして正直な感情を表現することを恐れないことによって、インタビューを受けた人々は些細な問題が大きな問題にならないように保つことができていた。

(6)私たちはみんな友情は貴重であると知っている、しかし友情はいつも安定しているわけではないということも知っている。友情を維持する際の問題はあらゆる関係性において起こりうる良い時にも悪い時にも繋がりを強く保つということである。物事がうまくいっている時は、友情を楽しむ。もし物事が悪い方向にいけば、前述した点を思い出そう。時には我々は関係をもとに戻すこともできるだろうが、時には関係が変わりうることを受け入れ認めなくてはならないこともある。しかし友情の状態がどうであれ、友情は我々の人生の重要な一部であり続けるであろう。

A

問1 | 47 | ④

段落(1)によると、心理学者は友情についてなんと言っているか。

①友情はしばしば他人の所有物と比較される。

②不安定になると友情は修復することができない。

③友情は知人とのいさかいに我々を導く。

④友情は自分を知ることの助けとなるが問題も起こりうる。

第2文、第3文に注目。

問2 | 48 | ②

段落(2)の「swallow our pride」の意味に最も近いのは以下のうちどれか。

①誰かに感謝する

②感情をおさえる

③問題が起こることを認識する

④誰かに会うのをやめる

下線部の文頭に【however】と逆接の接続詞があることに注目する。直前の文に書いてあることが④の内容なのでそれと逆の内容を選ぶ。

問3 | 49 | ④

段落(5)によると、調査により | 49 | が重要だと判明した。

①本当の気持ちを表現するのをためらうこと

②誤解や争いを無視すること

③できるときはいつでも問題を我慢すること

④問題がささいなうちに解決すること

第3文に注目する。small,largeとminor,majorという対比表現もヒントになる。

問4 | 50 | ④

段落(6)によると、友情を維持するには何が難しいのか。

①新しい面白い友人を見つけること

②関係をいつ変えるべきか知ること

③友人が問題を抱えているかどうか確かめること

④良くない時期も親密でいること

第2文に注目する。challengeという単語をヒントに考える。

問5 | 51 | ①

この文のタイトルとして最適なものはどれか。

①長く続く友情のためのアドバイス

②自分自身と友人の守り方

③友情への鍵となる力

④友情の変化する性質

②、③は言及がない。④は第4段落で主に主張されているが、主題とまでは言えない。

B

| 52 | ④ | 53 | ② | 54 | ③ | 55 | ① |

段　落	内　　容
(1)	友情は大切であるという気付き
(2)	52
(3)	53
(4)	54
(5)	55
(6)	心にとどめておくべき大切なこと

①長期にわたる友情についての研究結果についての報告

②友人の視点から状況をみることの重要性

③友情が変質するということを理解することの意義

④友人と連絡を取り続けふれ合うことの価値

H27 ⑥

ハチを捕まえ，魚を数えること：どのように「市民科学」が働いているのか

(1)テキサスの晴れた午後の日，私の妻のバーバラはもう一度公園でオオカバマダラが産んだ卵の数を数えて記録している。データを集めた後，彼女はそれを，彼女を採用したプロの科学者と共有するだろう。別の州では，私たちの友人のアントニオが1年に4回，12ヶ所の異なる場所を訪れてカエルの声を聞く。彼は今，ほぼ20年間，科学者に自分の発見を提出し続けている。そして国の反対側では，私たちの姪のエミリーがその土地のハチを捕まえ，小さなタグを付け，地方大学の生物学科に週間報告を渡している。バーバラ，アントニオ，エミリーの成果に報酬を払っている人はいないが，3人とも皆，自分が市民科学者であることを幸運だと考えている。

(2)このような活動にボランティアがアシスタントとして参加するとき，彼らは市民科学という，市民を情報収集の支援へと招く，価値のある研究技術に従事している。その中には理科教師や学生もいるが，ほとんどは，単に自然の中で時間をすごして楽しんでいる素人である。彼らも科学者の手伝いをして，間接的に環境保護の支援をすることに誇りを持っている。彼らが参加する動きは，目新しいものではない。実際に，その起源は100年以上前に遡る。このタイプの計画で最も早いものの一つは，1900年に米国オーデュボン協会によって始められた，クリスマス・バード・カウントである。ところが，市民科学の計画は今まで以上に急増しており，その中の60以上の計画がつい最近のアメリカ生態学会で報告された。

(3)正式な研究において，専門の科学者や他の専門家には最高級の基準を維持する必要がある。調査が有効なものとして受け入れられるためには，それが綿密であるだけでなく，客観的かつ正確でなければならない。市民科学者は詳細にまで必要な注意力を維持することができないとか，素人は情報を集めて体系化するときに，調査の背景を誤解して間違えるだろうと反対する人もいるかもしれない。つまり，

市民科学は本当に信頼できると考えてもよいのだろうか。

(4)最近の2つの研究がそのことを示している。1つは，ボランティアの知識と技術に注目したものである。この研究の中で，科学者はアメリカ西海岸にいるカニのタイプを識別できるかボランティアに尋ねた。ほとんどすべての成人のボランティアがその課題を遂行することができ，小学3年生でさえ80パーセントの成功率だった。2つ目の研究では，専門家とそうでない人の手法を比較した。厳しく伝統的な手続きを受け，12人のスキューバダイビングのダイバーのグループがカリブ海にいる106種の魚を識別した。ボランティアがもっとリラックスして楽しめるように専門家によって考案された手続きを使って12人のダイバーによる第2グループが同じ海で同じ時間を費やした。驚くべきことに2番目の手法の方が成功した。このグループは合計で137種も識別したのだ。これらの結果は，素人が手伝った調査は，科学者が計画したものであれば信頼できるということを示唆している。

(5)最良の市民科学の計画というのは，お互いに有利な状況になるものである。一方では，科学団体は他よりも少ない費用ではるかに多くのデータを入手する。他方では，市民科学は一般社会にとって良いことである。つまり，それによって人々は自然の世界の中に出て行くことができ，科学的方法と関わることができる。さらに，知識を使い，データを集め，発見を共有するための訓練を採り入れてうまく設計された研究に参加するとき，人々は新しい考えや技術を学ぶことで満足が得られるのである。

(6)市民科学を使った科学研究のリストが急速に長くなっていることは，励みになると私は思う。それでも，私たちは市民科学の可能性にちょうど気付き始めたばかりなのだ。どれほど多くのボランティアが専門的な調査に貢献できるかを，もっと多くの科学者が気付く必要がある。私の考えでは，そろそろ「人々のための科学」という古く保守的な見識を広げ，「人々による科学」という大衆の見識を採り入れる時なのだ。

A

問1 47 ④

第(1)段落によると，段落において，市民科学者は 47 。

①他のボランティアのデータと自分たちのデータを比較する

②自分たちの集めた情報の対価としていくらかのお金を稼ぐ

③研究室で虫のライフサイクルを観察する

④専門家に自分たちの結果や活動を報告する

第(1)段落第2文の「share it with the professional scientist」，第4文の「submitting his finding to scientists」，第5文の「handing in weekly reports」から，この段落で述べられている3人は，専門家に結果報告をしているから④が正しい。

問2 48 ②

第(2)段落の「急成長している」という単語は， 48 とい

う意味に最も近い。

①口論の原因になっている　②急速に増加している

③人気を失っている　　　　④受賞している

第(2)段落第4文に「彼らが参加する動きは，目新しいものではない。」とあり，そのあとに第7文【However】「ところが」と接続の接続詞を使い，「60以上の計画がつい最近のアメリカ生態学会で報告された。」とあるので，計画は増加していると推測できる。よって②が正しい。

問3 　49　　②

第(4)段落において著者はなぜ80％の成功率を強調するのか。

①大人の成功率と否定的に対比するため

②全体の結果の質が高いことを証明するため

③どれくらいのタイプのカニがいるかを強調するため

④小学生の技術不足を明らかにするため

小学3年生「でさえ」(even) 80パーセントの成功率だと述べられていることから①，④のように否定的な表現ではない。③のカニのタイプは関係ないので，②が正しい。

問4 　50　　②

第(6)段落において個人の見識はなんと表現されているか。

①結局は，科学的な知識は主に素人からくるだろう。

②市民科学の長所を評価している科学者はまだ十分にはいない。

③ボランティアのデータを信頼することへの最近の転換は期待外れである。

④市民科学を使っているあまりにも多くの実験が，現在行われている。

第(6)段落第3文に「どれほど多くのボランティアが専門的な調査に貢献できるかを，もっと多くの科学者が気付く必要がある。」とあるので，同じ内容を述べている②が正しい。

問5 　51　　①

この記事における著者の主なメッセージは何か。

①市民科学はボランティアと専門家と社会の利益になる。

②科学調査は専門家の管理下のままにしておくべきだ。

③ボランティアによる魚の種類の識別には長い歴史がある。

④伝統的な科学は市民科学に取って代わっている。

第(5)段落に，「お互いに有利になる状況」とあり，そのあとに「一般社会にとって良いことである」とあるので，①が正しい。文章全体から著者が市民科学に賛成していることが読み取れるので，②は誤り。③のような内容はどこにも書かれていない。④は一見正しいように見えるが，第(6)段落第4文の「『人々のための科学』という古く保守的な見識を広げ，『人々による科学』という大衆の見識を採り入れる時なのだ」という著者の意見から，まだ「取って代わった」というところまで進んでいないことがわかるので誤り。

B

　52　　③　　　53　　①　　　54　　②　　　55　　④

段落	内容
（1）	導入：著者の個人的な例
（2）	52
（3）	53
（4）	54
（5）	55
（6）	結論：著者の将来への希望

①懸念：ボランティアの技術と知識

②証拠：ボランティアの努力による成功

③説明：定義と歴史

④意見：皆が関わることによる利点

第(2)段落は，市民科学という活動についての話とその起源や現状について書かれているので③が適当である。

第(3)段落は，市民科学という素人が行った調査が信頼できるものなのかという疑問について書かれているので①が適当である。

第(4)段落は，素人が行った調査でも成功した2つの研究について書かれているので②が適当である。

第(5)段落は，著者の意見がまとめられているので④が適当である。

H26　　6

聴くことの便利さと音質：他に重要なことはあるのか？

(1)1877年，トーマス・エジソンが蓄音機を発明した。それは，音を録音し，再生することができる新しい機器だった。初めて人々は，便利なことに自分の家でフルオーケストラの演奏を聴くことができたのだ。数年後，ベル研究所はもっと良い音質を提供する新しい蓄音機を開発した。それは，声や楽器の音がより鮮明で，真に迫ったものだった。これらの初期の製品は，音響技術の発展において2つの主要な視点を示している。それは，聴くことを簡単にすることと，私たちが聞く音楽の音質を改善することである。長年にわたる進歩は，両方の領域において重要な意義があったが，音楽そのものを技術だけに没頭させないようにすることが重要である。

(2)蓄音機は，音楽を聴くことをずっと便利にしたが，それは始まりにすぎなかった。1920年代におけるカーラジオの登場により，道路でも音楽が楽しめるようになった。外を歩きながらでも，ヘッドホンを通じて音楽を楽しむことを可能にした個人用音楽機器が開発されるにつれて，1980年代において携帯型音響機器に対する興味が，本当に高まり始めた。最近では，私たちは，小さなデジタルプレイヤーに何百枚ものアルバムを携帯し，とても小さなイヤホンでそれらを聴くことができる。

(3)私たちの音楽の楽しみに影響を及ぼすもうひとつの要因は，その音質である。1950年代において，ハイフィデリティ，略してハイファイという言葉が，最高級の音響再生

を提供する録音装置や音響機器を宣伝するために，企業によって一般的に使われるようになった。フィデリティとは，真実性という意味で，もともとの演奏に限りなく近い音楽を録音し，再生することを指す。もし，私たちが目を閉じて録音された交響曲を聴けば，まるでコンサートホールにいるかのように感じるというのが，理想である。1950年代からの技術の進歩によって，フィデリティが目標とするものにとても近づけるような最新の録音技術や再生機器を残す結果となった。

(4)今日，電器屋の中を歩いてみると，買い物客は，驚くほど多様な音響機器に直面する。携帯用の装置を探している人は，色や形，大きさがある中から，何百もの異なるイヤホンやヘッドホン，デジタルプレイヤーを選ぶことができる。オーディオファン，つまりハイフィデリティを重要視する音楽ファンのために，店のそれぞれの売り場が，ＣＤプレイヤーやアンプといった，しばしば高額となる大きなスピーカーや重量のコンポを目玉商品にしている。すべてのこの技術ととてもたくさんの選択肢を目の当たりにすると，音楽ファンはしばしば，彼らの聴くことへの要望にまさに合致する機器を探し，選ぶのに膨大な時間を費やしてしまう。

(5)機器を買った後でさえ，音響技術の進化は，時々，消費者の注意を音楽そのものからそらし続ける。携帯型装置の便利さのおかげで，人々は公園でのジョギングや通勤といった何かをしている間に，音楽を聴くことができる。このような状況においては，音楽は部分的に外の騒音の中に消え，そのせいで人は音楽を集中して聴くことが困難になる。あるいは，オーディオファンは，最高品質のフィデリティを手に入れるために，試行錯誤して自分のコンポを組み合わせることに，かなりの時間と労力を費やすかもしれない。

(6)とても多くの技術が手に入るので，実際に音楽を聴くことは，時々，二次的な問題のように感じるかもしれない。私たちは幸運にも，通勤電車にお気に入りの録音機器を持ち込むことができるが，もし，注意を他に向けたまま音楽を聴くと，大半の音楽の力を逃してしまう。同様に，高品質の機器を利用するのは良いことだが，もし，私たちが完璧なフィデリティを手に入れようと余計な心配をしてしまうと，私たちと音楽の間に，技術そのものがやって来てしまう。音楽は，すばらしく力強い芸術の形で，そしておそらく最も重要なことは，座って，聞いているものを正しく理解する時間を作ることである。エジソンや他の発明家の才能のおかげで，音楽の美しさは，今や以前よりも身近なものになっている。立ち止まって，心から聴くか聴かないかは，私たち次第だ。

A
問1 47 ④
第(1)段落によると，ベル研究所の蓄音機は，トーマス・エジソンのよりも 47 ことができた。
　①速く，安く作る
　②簡単に操作する

③多くの楽器を演奏する
④本物らしく音を再生する
第(1)段落の第３文に，ベル研究所が新しく開発した蓄音機は，「声や楽器の音がより鮮明で，真に迫ったものだった」とあるので，④が適当。

問2 48 ①
第(3)段落において，筆者は，今日の最高の音響機器は， 48 と述べている。
　①生のコンサートの音質をほとんど再現する
　②最高のコンサートホールにおいて生の音楽を演奏するのに使われる
　③もともとの演奏よりも，録音した音を良くする
　④１９５０年代のすばらしい演奏を再現する
第(3)段落の第２文に，最高級の音響再生装置たるハイファイは，「もともとの演奏に限りなく近い音楽を録音し，再生する」とあるので，①が適当。

問3 49 ①
第(4)段落によると，オーディオファンとは， 49 人々である。
　①音楽再生の質をとても気にする
　②よいコンサートホールで交響曲を演奏する
　③録音された演奏よりも，生のコンサートを好む
　④最高の音響機器を売る店で働く
第(4)段落の第３文に，オーディオファンとは，「ハイフィデリティを重要視する音楽ファン」だと書かれているので，①が適当。

問4 50 ③
第(5)段落をもとにすると，次のうち正しいのはどれか？
　①後ろの雑音のおかげで，人々はしばしば音楽に集中できる。
　②携帯音楽機器は，後ろの雑音を生み出しがちだ。
　③ハイファイシステムを組み立てることは，多大な努力を要することがある。
　④人々は忙しくなればなるほど，音楽を正しく理解するようになる。
第(5)段落の最終文に注目すればよい。

問5 51 ③
第(6)段落で筆者が言いたいのは， 51 ということである。
　①オーディオファンは，携帯機器で音楽を聴くのを楽しむ傾向にある
　②音響機器を買う時は，便利さが重要な要素である
　③技術にかかわらず，音楽は第一の考慮事項である
　④携帯機器は，おそらくハイフィデリティ機器に取って代わるだろう
第(6)段落で，筆者は音楽と技術を比べ，音楽を二次的とすることに否定的な立場であることが読み取れるので，③が適当。

B

| 52 | ① | 53 | ④ | 54 | ② | 55 | ③ |

段落	内容
（1）	音響技術の２つの目標
（2）	52
（3）	ハイフィデリティの考え
（4）	53
（5）	54
（6）	55

　①音楽を聴く利便性の進歩

　②音楽を聴く人の焦点についての関心

　③音楽に注意をすべて注ぐことの価値

　④販売されている音響機器の広い選択肢

第(2)段落は、蓄音機→カーラジオ→デジタルプレイヤーといった音響機器の進歩について書かれているので、①が適当。

第(4)段落は、電器屋には多様な音響機器が並び、その中から消費者が選ぶことできることが書かれているので、④が適当。

第(6)段落には、音楽を集中して聴くことの意義について書かれているので、③が適当。

残った②を、第(5)段落に入れる。

[文法－頻出問題編]

1 〈文法・語法〉 　　　　　　問題 138p～

H22 2 A

問1 | 8 | ④ 　　単語
「英語の課題は提出しましたか。」
「いいえ、でも半分は**終えています**。」
【be through】…「～を終える」

問2 | 9 | ③ 　　単語
明日、定期券の**期限が切れる**ので、更新しなければならない。
①activates …「～を活性化する」
②conceives …「(物事をまったく新しく)思いつく・考える」
③expires …「(契約などが)満期になる・(切符などの)期限が切れる」
④interferes …「邪魔をする」

問3 | 10 | ④ 　　前置詞
今日の会議を次の水曜日まで延期することはできますか。
①by …「…までに」
②in …「…のうちに・…のときに」
③on …「(曜日・日付)…に」
④until…「～まで」

問4 | 11 | ③ 　　イディオム
私は姉から大きな車を買わないように説得されました。
【talk A out of ～ing】…「Aに～しないように説得する。」
今回は受動態になっており、Aの部分が主語になっている。

問5 | 12 | ④ 　　仮定法
先月、ハンナと別れていなければ、私は彼女と二年間付き合っていることになっていたでしょう。
文脈より、過去の事実に反する仮定法過去完了であることがわかる。
仮定法過去完了の主節は、【would have 過去分詞】で表す。

問6 | 13 | ④ 　　態
救助センターにいた子犬は、その小さな女の子に**選ばれて**嬉しそうでした。
受動態を用いるべきであるから、【choose】の過去分詞形である【chosen】を選ぶ。

問7 | 14 | ④ 　　自動詞・他動詞
「なぜ、ジャックは仕事を辞めたのですか。」
「彼は、自分のカフェを開店するという**夢を実現**したかったのです。」
①come true …「(夢などが)実現する」自動詞
②increase …「増す」文脈より不適。
③make sure …「確かめる」文脈より不適。
④realize …「(希望・目的・夢などを)実現する」他動詞

問8 | 15 | ③ 　　単語
私の学校では、常任の先生が欠勤した時は、別の先生が代わりに授業をします。
①common …「一般的な・ありふれた」
②different …「違う」
③regular …「常任の・いつもの」
④retired …「退職した・引退した」

問9 | 16 | ① 　　単語
「私のコンピュータ画面の明るさを調整する手順をすべて踏むのは本当にイライラします。」
「それなら、簡単な方法でやったらどうですか。このキーを押すだけですよ。**ショートカット**です。」
①shortcut …「(コンピュータ)ショートカット・近道」名詞
②shortened …「短くする」動詞
③shorthand …「速記」名詞
④shortsighted …「近視の」形容詞
【That's the ～】とあることから、空欄には名詞が入ることがわかる。また、文脈よりコンピュータの話をしているので、①が適切である。

問10 | 17 | ① 　　接続詞
何年もの戦争の後、その国は多くの力を失ってしまいました。たとえそうだとしても、その影響は過小評価されるべきではありません。
①Even so …「たとえそうだとしても」
②Even though …「たとえ～するにしても」
③So …「だから」
④Thus …「したがって・だから」
文脈より、逆接を表す①または②が適当であるが、【Even though】の後はカンマを置かずに、直接、主語＋述語がくる。

H23 2 A

問1 | 8 | ① 　　動詞の用法、自動詞・他動詞
パパ、もし今学期末までに私の成績が上がったら、おこづかいをあげてくれないかしら。
【mind】は動名詞を目的語にとる動詞である。また、【my allowance】を目的語にとる動詞は他動詞の【raise】「あげる」であり自動詞の【rise】「あがる」は不適。したがって①が正解。

問2 | 9 | ③ 　　イディオム
「最近体重が増えているんだ。」
「もっと運動をしてしっかり健康に良い食事をするべきだよ。」
①carrying…【carry on ～】「～を続ける」
②increasing…【increase】「増える」
③putting…【put on】「増す」
④reducing…【reduce】「減る」
2人目の発言から、1人目は体重の増加を気にしていると判断できる。| 9 | の直後に【on】があることから適当なものは③だとわかる。

問3 　10　 ① 　　仮定法
ケンジはロンドンへの旅行はすばらしかったと私に話した。私もあの計画に**参加すればよかった**と思う。
【I wish＋仮定法過去完了】で、過去の事実に反する願望（〜すればよかったのに）を表す。したがって正解は①。
【participate】「参加する」
（参考）【I wish＋仮定法過去】は、現在の事実に反する願望（〜すればよいのに）を表す。

問4 　11　 ① 　　イディオム
飛行中に飛行機の窓の外を眺めると、家がダンボール箱の列のように見える。
①flight…飛行
②flowing…【flow】「流れる」の現在分詞
③flown…【fly】「飛ぶ」の過去分詞
④flyer…パイロット
【in flight】で「飛行中に」という意味をとる。

問5 　12　 ② 　　イディオム
ファンたちは映画スターを一目見ることができる**ことを期待して**、ドアの外で待った。
【in the hope of 〜ing】「〜を期待して」なので、正解は②
（参考）【catch sight of 〜】「〜を見かける、見つける」

問6 　13　 ① 　　単語
地元の診療所では、医師は**予約**したときのみ診察する。
①appointment…「予約」　②approval…「承認」
③reputation…「評判」　④resolution…「決心」

問7 　14　 ② 　　構文
不況時にでさえ、携帯電話料金を節約する**ことが難しいと思う**人もいる。
【find it〜to…】「…することが〜と思う」

問8 　15　 ④ 　　イディオム
申込書を書き終えました。誰に**提出しなければならない**でしょうか。
①announced…【announce】「公表する」の過去形
②applied…【apply】「申し込む」の過去形
③pointed…【point】「示す」の過去形
④supposed…【suppose】「思う」の過去形
【be supposed to〜】「〜しなければならない」

問9 　16　 ③ 　　単語
その家族の子どもはみんな正月休みに**集まる**でしょう。
①crowd…「群がる」　②form…「形成する」
③gather…「集まる」　④set…「定める」

問10 　17　 ② 　　イディオム
私の弟は野球がとても好きです。弟は優れた才能がある**とはいわないまでも**、熱心な選手です。
【if not 〜】「〜がないにしても、とはいわないまでも」

H24 ②A
問1 　8　 ③ 　　単語
公式な社内言語として英語を使う新しい方針を**採用して**いる会社がある。

①【absorb】「吸収する」
②【accompany】「ついていく」
③【adopt】「採用する」
④【appoint】「指名する」

問2 　9　 ① 　　イディオム
だれが電話を掛けたかによって、携帯電話の呼び出し音を変える方法を教えてくれませんか。
①【depend on】「〜によって決まる・〜次第で」
②【in spite of】「〜にもかかわらず」
③【on behalf of】「〜の代わりに」
④【rely on】「〜を頼りにする」

問3 　10　 ① 　　節
ベルさんは交通渋滞に巻き込まれています。重要な会議は**彼女が到着するまでに**終わっているでしょう。
時・条件の副詞節では、未来の表現は現在時制を用いる。
【be stuck in (a) traffic (jam(s))】「渋滞に巻き込まれる」

問4 　11　 ② 　　単語
電子レンジとトースターと暖房を同時につけていたら、ブレーカーが落ちました。
【on】「（機器などが）作動している」

問5 　12　 ④ 　　単語
ブラウンさんは崖をのぞきこみ、彼は**垂直な**崖の端に立っているとわかった。
①【circular】「円形の・丸い」　②【cubic】「立体の」
③【horizontal】「水平な」　④【vertical】「垂直な」

問6 　13　 ① 　　イディオム
自分の先生からの推薦状を持っている**ならば**、この海外プログラムに申し込むことができる。
【on the condition that〜】「〜という条件で・もし〜ならば」

問7 　14　 ② 　　単語
「ダイキの姉妹は双子だと聞きました。彼女たちに会ったことはありますか。」
「いいえ、私はまだ**どちらにも**会ったことはありません。」
【not〜either of—】「—のどちらも〜ない」（＝〜neither of—）

問8 　15　 ① 　　使役
個人的な感情が、そのような重要な決定をすることの**妨げにならない**ようにすべきだ。
【let〜［原形不定詞（—）］】「〜を（に）—させる」
【stand in the way】「邪魔になる・妨げになる」

問9 　16　 ① 　　関係代名詞
「シオリはどの子ですか。」
「少し前に**私が話していた**子です。」
　16　以下の文で【The one】を修飾している。oneと　16　の間には関係代名詞が省略してある。

問10 　17　 ④ 　　イディオム
彼が旅行代理店に入った後、より効率的に仕事を行うために、彼は英語力を向上しようと熱心に取り組みました。
【carry out】「実行する」

H25 ②A

問1 | 8 | ④　イディオム

本校の生徒の<u>ほとんど</u>は，学費を払うために夜にアルバイ<u>トをしていることを私は理解している。</u>

【most of〜】「〜のほとんど」

【almost】は「もう少し」という意味の副詞であり，「ほとんど」という意味を表す場合，【almost all of】の形を用いる。②は肯定文中なので，【any of】ではなく【some of】になるべきである。【anyone】は単数扱いなので③は不可。

問2 | 9 | ④　単語

今ここにいる７人のうち，１人は中国，３人はアメリカ，<u>その他の人はフランス出身だ。</u>

「ここにいる７人のうち」とあり，他の人は特定されているため，定冠詞の【the】が付くものを選ぶ。また，③は「もう１つ（人）の」という意味になるため不可。

問3 | 10 | ①　イディオム

私の兄弟は高校生のとき，非常に人気者であったに<u>違いない</u>。彼はまだ昔のクラスメイトからたくさんの年賀状をもらっている。

【must have ＋過去分詞】「〜だったに違いない」

【should（ought to）have ＋過去分詞】「〜すべきだった」

問4 | 11 | ③　時制

エリックの友達のミノルとサチコは，今夜７時にここに来る。彼はそのときまでに宿題を<u>終わらせているだろう。</u>

時制は未来であり，【by then】「そのときまでに」とあるので，未来完了形を用いる。

問5 | 12 | ①　構文

<u>かかりつけの医者が息子に人間ドックを毎年受けることを勧めた。</u>

suggestの後のthat節内は【主語＋（should＋）動詞の原形】となる。

【complete medical checkup】「人間ドック」

問6 | 13 | ①　イディオム

日本は４つの大きな島と多くの小さな島から<u>成っている。</u>

【consist of〜】「〜から成る」

問7 | 14 | ①　単語

<u>冬休みの間に祖父に会う機会はありましたか。</u>

①・④共に「〜の間」という意味を表すが，【during】は後に句，【while】は後に節（主語＋動詞）が続くので，①【during】が適当。

問8 | 15 | ④　イディオム

私は東京に行っても楽しくない。あの人ごみに<u>耐える</u>のは私にはつらい。

① 【put away】「片付ける」

② 【put on】「着る・太る」

④ 【put up with】「〜に耐える」

問9 | 16 | ①　イディオム

弟と私が子どもだった頃，母はよく私に弟から<u>目を離さな</u>いように頼んだので，弟は迷子にならなかったのだろう。

① 【keep an eye on】「〜から目を離さない」

② 【keep away from】「〜に近付かない」

問10 | 17 | ②　イディオム

私は高収入でよい地位を提案されたが，家族の近くにいたかったので<u>断る</u>ことを決めた。

【turn〜down】「〜を断る」

H26 ②A

問1 | 8 | ②　分詞

昨夜，私が窓の外を見た時，私の隣の庭でこそこそ動いている猫を見た。

| 8 | 以下が直前の【a cat】を修飾する。

問2 | 9 | ③　時制

パットとパムは初めて運動会で会って以来ずっと，お互い電子メールでやりとりしている。

【since】があるので，現在完了形（現在完了進行形）が適当である。

問3 | 10 | ③　節

私の母は，昼食を食べに外に出掛けるのか，家で食べるのか私に尋ねた。

【ask】の後の，【whether（if）〜】は「〜かどうか」という意味の節を作る。

問4 | 11 | ①　使役

私の妻は，息子に夕食を作らせたかったが，私は代わりにピザを注文した。

【have ＋人＋原形不定詞】で「人に〜させる」という「使役」の意味をなす。

問5 | 12 | ②　イディオム

私は，私たちが土曜日に学校の体育館を自由に使えるのは当然のことだと思っていた。

【take it for granted that〜】「〜を当然のことと思う」

問6 | 13 | ④　動詞の用法

誰がダンの誕生会を計画しているのか教えてくれませんか。

このような場合の「教える」は【teach】ではなく【tell】を使う。

問7 | 14 | ④　イディオム

レジの人が勘定を計算すると，合計が２００００円だったので，私たちは衝撃を受けた。

【add up】「計算する」

問8 | 15 | ②

健康保険に加入している人にとって，病院の治療費はずっと低い。

A：【cost】「値段，費用」，【fare】「運賃」

B：【those】は「those people」意味で使われ，後ろに関係代名詞【who】を伴う。

問9 | 16 | ③

私はかつてアメリカに２年住んでいたが，一度もグランドキャニオンに行ったことがない。たぶん，来年は行くだろう。

A：【spent】が現在完了形ではなく過去形なので，【ever】

は使えない。

B：【have been to〜】「〜に行ったことがある」。【visit】は他動詞なので，後ろに前置詞【to】は来ない。

問10　[17]　④

私の母は，とても一生懸命に生活をやりくりしようとしているので，私が不必要なものを買うのを決して許さない。

A：【make ends meet】「生活をやりくりする」

B：前後の文のつながりを考えると，順接の接続詞【so】が適当である。

H27　[2]A

問1　[8]　①　イディオム

君はまたおじいちゃんを怒らせたの？そんなばかなことはするべきじゃないよ。

【know better than〜】「〜ほど愚かではない」

問2　[9]　③　使役

スコットはコンピュータを盗まれたので警察署に行った。

【have＋A＋過去分詞】で「Aを〜される」という「使役」の意味をなす。

問3　[10]　③　接続詞

北日本ではほとんど雪が降らなかったという点で，昨冬はむしろ珍しかった。

【in that〜】「〜する点で」

問4　[11]　②　時制

私の孫娘は歌手としての道を歩み始めたが，将来さらに女優にもなって欲しいと思う。

【in the future】と未来の起こりうることについて話しているのでwish，hope，becameではなくwill becomeを選ぶ。

問5　[12]　①　時制

私は深く眠っていたので，今朝の午前2時に起こった自動車事故が聞こえなかった。

時制を考えると過去形になり，関係代名詞【that】の先行詞が【the car accident】であることから【happened】を選ぶ。

問6　[13]　③　分詞構文

私はいつも海の景色を楽しみながら，犬を散歩させて海辺を歩く。

付帯状況「〜しながら」を表す分詞構文。

問7　[14]　①　前置詞

富士山が青空を背景にして印象的に立っている。

【against】「〜を背景に」

問8　[15]　④　疑問詞

ごめんなさい。私たちはちょうど今，それについて話していましたが，最良の解決策は何と言いましたか？

【疑問詞＋did you say＋SV】という，疑問詞が文頭にきた間接疑問。

問9　[16]　②　接続詞

インターネットはとても強力な手段になったので，どこに住んでいる人々でも教育資源を利用することができる。

【so that構文】だけでなく，【so＋形容詞＋a＋名詞】という

語順にも気をつける。suchの場合は【such＋a＋形容詞＋名詞】となるので不適。

問10　[17]　④

その監督は，自分のチームがサッカーリーグを制覇するだろうと言っており，実際に次のシーズンで優勝した。

監督が言ったのは過去のことなので，【will】も過去形にする。

H28　[2]A

問1　[8]　①　過去完了

私がホームに着いた時、既に電車は到着していたので私は寒い中待つ必要がなかった。

「私」が到着する前（過去形）に「電車」は到着しているので、過去完了を使う。

問2　[9]　①　接続詞

東京は比較的小さな土地面積にもかかわらず、巨大な人口である。

②は前文を受けての逆接。③は前置詞なので節はとらない。④は副詞。

問3　[10]　②　受身の後置修飾

バイリンガルの両親に育てられた子供は自然に二つの言葉を学ぶだろう。

主語のChildrenに対応する動詞はlearnなので、後ろに動詞をそのままの形ではおけない。【bring up】で「育てる」。受動態なので過去分詞を置く。

問4　[11]　④　否定表現

私の姉は真面目な高校生ではなかったし、私もそうだった。

否定文で「〜もまたない」という表現の場合neitherを使う。【neither V S】SもまたVでない。語順に注意。

問5　[12]　②　イディオム

映画が始まる前に、携帯電話の電源が切られているかご確認下さい。

空欄の後ろに節を取りうるのは②のみ。

【make sure S V】「必ずSがVするよう確かめる。」

問6　[13]　①　イディオム

かなり進展することができたので計画より既に進んでいる。

【ahead of〜】「〜より進んで」

問7　[14]　①　形容詞

私の発表のあとの彼らの優しいコメントのおかげで、私はとても安心した。

②③④は副詞なので直後のcommentsを修飾できない。①は形容詞。

問8　[15]　③　接続詞

この必修授業を履修できないと、卒業できません。

意味を先に考えてから答えていく。前半も後半も否定の意味になるとわかれば③とわかる。

問9　[16]　①　助動詞・受動態

かつては木材が主な燃料として使用されていたが、今や化石燃料が広く使用されている。

【nowadays】「近頃は」この単語は通常現在形において用いるので②④は不適当。また、後半の文と前半の文が対比されていると考えられるので【used to V】「以前は〜したものだった」が入る。

問10　17　④　　人の性質を表す形容詞

毎日祖母の見舞いに行くとは彼はとても思いやりがある。
【it is 人の性質を表す形容詞　of 人 to V】人の性質の形容詞を用いる場合、for ではなく of を用いる。

H29　②A

問1　8　①　　前置詞

今日、科学の授業で塩水は0度では凍らないと学んだ。
値段、速度、程度を表す前置詞【at】「〜で」

問2　9　②　　形容詞

多くの専門家が若者のためにより多くの雇用機会を創出する必要があると考えている。
【the + 形容詞】＝【形容詞 + people】

問3　10　④　　イディオム

近所の葉が最近黄葉した。
【turn red（yellow）】⇒紅葉（黄葉）する

問4　11　①　　比較表現

私は家で食事をするほうがレストランで食事をするよりもずっと経済的なことが多いと思う。
比較級の強調では far, much, などが使える。very や too は使うことができない。

問5　12　②　　分詞構文

その映画の主演に選ばれてから、ラメシュはすぐにスターになった。
選択肢のどれも前半部に主語にあたるものがないので、分詞構文の問題とわかる。あとは、文脈から受動態の文と判断する。

問6　13　③　　複合関係形容詞

あなたが入手する情報は何であれ、できるだけすぐに私にお伝え下さい。
①②④をとった場合、information が主語となり、直後に名詞の you がくるのはおかしいので不可。

問7　14　④　　関係代名詞

台風は突如弱まった、そしてそのことはその村にとって良い知らせだった。
関係代名詞の非制限用法。よって①②は不可。which は前半の文そのものを指す。

問8　15　①　　使役

彼はラッシュアワーの電車に乗る際に、偶然傘がドアに挟まれた。

問9　16　③　　比較表現

このクラスにおいてアビーほど優しい人はいない。彼女はいつも困っている人々を助ける。

問10　17　①　　過去完了

アンジェリナは私にこの前の土曜日のお祭りを楽しんだかどうか尋ねてきた。

H30　②A

問1　8　③　　形容詞

ジェフは給料が低いためにその仕事の申し出を受け入れなかった。
expensive や cheap は物やサービスに対して使う。low や high は料金、経費、賃金などに使う。

問2　9　②　　副詞

ブレンダは何か飲むものを取りに下の階へ降りた。
【downstairs】で「階下へ、階下で」という意味の副詞。したがって、前置詞は不要である。

問3　10　①　　動名詞

ひじを怪我した後に、私は学校のバドミントンチームを辞めなくてはならなかった。
quit は目的語に to 不定詞ではなく動名詞をとる。同様に目的語に動名詞のみをとる動詞に avoid, mind, finish などがある。

問4　11　④　　イディオム

なぜ彼がそんなに古い車を買うことを決断したのか私には全く理解できない。
【beyond one's understanding】理解できない（理解を超えている）

問5　12　①　　時制

ニコルは全国的な小説コンテストで優勝した時、小説を書いて約7年になっていた。
過去形の won よりも更に過去の時点から小説を書き始めているので過去完了を使うことが明らか。

問6　13　③　　関係代名詞

我々の上司は病気のため自宅で寝込んでいた。だから、私たちは計画を終わらせるために必要だと思うことを行っていった。
先行詞がないので、先行詞を含む関係代名詞である what を選ぶ。

問7　14　①　　イディオム

はじめは気づかなかったが、風呂場には巨大なクモがいた。
【at first】「はじめは、はじめのうちは」

問8　15　③　　分詞

ラファエルは家の前の木にツバメのつがいが巣を作っているのを見た。
(B) 以下が直前を後置修飾している。

問9　16　③　　語法

まもなく桃の花が咲くだろう。きたる今週末にも咲くかもしれない。
【it will（should）not be long before 〜】「〜までもう間もなくだろう」

問10　17　③　　比較

メリッサは次の週末にスケートに行くぐらいならむしろスノーボードに行きたいと言った。
【would rather A than B】「B するよりもむしろ A したい」

H31　2A

問1　| 8 |　②　前置詞

空港行きのバスが予定より明らかに遅れているので、ケーシーは心配になってきた。

直後にschedule（名詞）が来ているので、前置詞が入る。したがって、③・④は不適。【after】は順番的に「〜の後」の意味。

問2　| 9 |　③　イディオム

もし急いでいるのであれば、いつもすぐに来てくれるダブルクイックタクシーを呼ぶべきです。

【in no time】「すぐに」

問3　| 10 |　①　副詞

高価なガラスの花瓶を落としそうになった後、ジェームズはその店にある他のどのものにも触らないと決めた。

【almost】は副詞だが、【most】は形容詞であることに注意。

問4　| 11 |　②　イディオム

私たちは時間を浪費しているため、早くその書類を変更するべきだ。

【run out of 〜】「〜を浪費する」

問5　| 12 |　④　動詞の語法

その新しい計画についてみんなの要求に合わせるのは不可能だった。

【meet】「〜に合う」

問6　| 13 |　③　副詞

キャンプ旅行に必要なもの全てのリストを書きなさい。さもないと、なにか買い忘れるかもしれない。

【otherwise】命令文の後で「さもないと」。

問7　| 14 |　③　名詞

文章は個人間での意思疎通の共通の手段となった。

【means】「手段、方法」単数でも複数でも同じ形である。

問8　| 15 |　②　分詞

私はその映画の完全に予想外の結末を見て驚いた。

【shock】「〜を驚かせる」【surprise】「〜を驚かせる」どちらも「人」に対しては「受動態」、「物」に対しては「能動態」と覚える。Aは人が主語なので受動態。Bは【ending】「結末」を分詞として修飾する。「（人を）驚かせるような結末」と考える。

問9　| 16 |　④　イディオム

休みの間、この高速での交通量の増加は避けられない。

【there is no doing】「〜することはできない」

問10　| 17 |　④　不定詞・副詞

その警察官は目撃者にその状況をできるだけ正確に描写するように頼んだ。

【ask 人 to 〜】「人に〜するように頼む」

【as 〜 as possible（one can）】「できるだけ〜」

（B）には【describe】を修飾する副詞が入る。

R2　2A

問1　| 8 |　③

「雨のため、試合での私たちのパフォーマンスは完璧とは程遠いものだった。」

far from A「Aとかけ離れた、Aとは程遠い」が正解。apart from A「A以外に、Aから離れて」、different from A「Aと異なる」、free from A「Aがない」は意味的に間違いであるが、いずれも重要イディオムであるので覚えておく。

問2　| 9 |　①

「非常ドアはこの廊下の両端に見受けられる。」

これらの選択肢の中で、後ろに名詞の複数形がつくのは、both「両方の」だけである。他の選択肢は、いずれも単数名詞が後ろにつく。

問3　| 10 |　③

「留学するという私の計画は、私が奨学金を受けることができるかどうかにかかっている。」

depend on A「Aに依存する、頼る」のAに当たる部分なので目的語、つまり名詞節を作る必要がある。空欄の後には完全な文がきているため、thatかwhetherが正解になるが、depend on that 〜という表現はないため、whetherを選ぶ。

問4　| 11 |　③

「ノリコはスワヒリ語を話すことができるし、マルコも話すことができる。」

so can S「Sも〜できる」と表せるので、soが正解。他の選択肢は、文法的に間違い。

問5　| 12 |　①

「毎日ジョギングをすると言うことと、それをすることとは別だ。」

A is one thing, and B is anotherとは「AとBは違う」「AとBは別だ」という意味である。one thing に対応して空欄に入れることができるのは、anotherしかない。

問6　| 13 |　①

「私たちの上司は熱心な労働者であるが、親しくなるのは難しいだろう」

get along with A「Aと仲よくやっていく」が正解。他は、get around to A「Aする機会ができる」、get away with A「Aを持ち逃げする」、get down to A「Aに下りる、Aに取り組む」という意味である。

問7　| 14 |　①

「アヤノが私の家に来たとき、たまたま誰も家にいなかった。」

it happens that SV「たまたまSがVする」が正解。happenは自動詞なので、動詞の後に直接目的語や節が来ることはない。よって、他の選択肢は間違い。

問8　| 15 |　④

「道路が空いてさえいれば、時間通りに家に帰ることができるだろう。」

条件・時を表すのはas long as A「Aしさえすれば」である。as far as A「Aの限りでは」は範囲・制限を表す。また、道路がblocked「通行止め」になっていれば遅れるはずである。

よってclear「きれいな」を選ぶ。

問9　16　②

「私は、あなたが体育祭に行くつもりがないと言っていたことを知っているが、それは重要なイベントだから、考え直してくれないか。」

give A a second thought「Aについて考え直す」が正解。takeはtake a second thought about A「Aについて考え直す」というイディオムで使われるため、この問題では間違い。

問10　17　①

「私は後ろの列に座っている2人以外は誰もわからない。」

not ～ any「全く（なにも）～ない」、except for A「A以外」が正解。eitherは（not ～）either of + 【2つを表す名詞】「どちらも～ない」、rather than A「Aよりむしろ」は内容的に間違い。

〈語句整序〉　　　　　　　　　　問題 149p～

H22　②C

問1　21・22　②・⑥

Something ～ saying：

Could you <u>tell me what made you</u> so upset with my email?

あなたがメールで書いたことがあなたの友人を怒らせました。何が彼女を怒らせたのか尋ねる際は、こう言うでしょう。

私のメールがどうしてあなたをそんなに怒らせたか教えてくれませんか。

　【tell A B】「AにBを伝える」
　【make A B】「AをBにする」

問2　23・24　②・①

You borrowed 800 ～ you could say：

This is <u>the 800 yen</u> I <u>owe you</u> for yesterday's lunch.

あなたは昨日友人から昼食代で800円借りました。お金を返す時、こう言うでしょう。

これは私があなたから昨日の昼食代で借りた800円です。

　【owe（人）for～】「～で（人）に借りがある」

私（I）があなた（you）に借りがあるので、I owe you for yesterday's lunchのかたまりができる。これはthe 800 yenのあとに続けると、the 800 yenを修飾することになり、意味も通る。

問3　25・26　②・⑤

"<u>When did you decide where you're going</u> for your vacation? I thought you weren't sure."

"I decided yesterday."

「休暇にどこに行くか、いつ決めたのですか。はっきりしていないと思ってました。」

「昨日決めました。」

【I decided yesterday】とあることから、空所は「いつ決めたのか」を尋ねる文章だとわかる。したがって文頭はwhen did you decidedと判断できる。残りは疑問詞、主語、動詞なので、容易に並べることができる。

H23　②C

問1　21・22　③・②

Thank you very much for <u>the great advice you gave me</u> when I bought my car.

私が車を買うときにすばらしい助言をくれて、ありがとうございます。

　【thank you for～】「～をありがとう」

この場合、forの後には名詞（節）が続くから、adviceが続く。さらに、adviceのあとに関係詞節（関係代名詞は省略）をもってきて、adviceを修飾する。

問2　23・24　②・⑤

"What's up with Jack? He seems so happy."

"He applied for a new job, and <u>the company called him in</u> for an interview."

246　共通テスト虎の巻【英語編】

「ジャックはどうしたの。とてもうれしそうよ。」

「新しい仕事に応募して、その会社が面接に彼を呼んだんだよ。」

【call 人 in for ～】「人を～に呼ぶ」

(参考)【apply for ～】「～に申し込む、応募する」

問3　25 ・ 26　③・⑥

Doing a homestay with a family in another country would help you develop your communication skills.

外国である家族のもとにホームステイすることは、コミュニケーション能力を向上させるのに役立つだろう。

【Doing ～ country】を主部と考え、【help＋目的語（～）＋原形不定詞（…）】「～が…するのを助ける」の形を組み立てる。

(参考) 原形不定詞＝toのつかない不定詞（動詞の原形のままの形）

H24　②C

問1　21 ・ 22　②・⑤

"Did you install that computer software you bought last week?"

"Yes. And I'm finding it easy to use."

「先週買ったコンピューターソフトウェアはインストールしましたか。」

「はい。使うのは簡単だとわかりました。」

【find it～】「～だとわかる」

問2　23 ・ 24　⑤・③

The entertainer was happily singing with her arms raised up in the air.

エンターテイナーは両手を挙げて楽しそうに歌っていました。

【with＋目的語（O）＋分詞（～）】「Oを～したまま」

問3　25 ・ 26　⑤・③

Because he came down with the flu, he was forced to stay at home for a week.

彼はインフルエンザにかかったので、1週間家にいなければならなかった。

【be forced to do】「～せざるを得ない」

H25　②C

問1　21 ・ 22　②・④

My friend, who can play basketball very well, practices three times as often as I do.

私の友達は、バスケットボールがとても上手で、私の3倍練習している。

【A times as～as…】「…のA倍～」

問2　23 ・ 24　⑤・①

Mary：What are some of reasons for your successful career?

Toshio：Mainly, I owe what I am to my uncle. He was the one who would always help me when I was in

trouble.

メアリー：あなたが出世した理由の一部は何ですか。

トシオ：主に、今の私があるのはおじのおかげです。彼は私が困っているときにいつも助けてくれる人でした。

【what A be】「今のA」

【owe～to…】「～に…を負う」

問3　25 ・ 26　④・⑤

Kevin：What's the legal driving age in your country?

Mie：In Japan, when people become eighteen, they are old enough to get a driver's license.

ケビン：あなたの国では、運転可能な法定年齢は何歳ですか。

ミエ：日本では、18歳になると、運転免許を取得するのに十分な年齢です。

【be…enough to～】「～するのに十分…」

H26　②C

問1　21 ・ 22　④・⑤

Dan：How did your health check go？

Mike：Not bad, but the doctor advised me to get regular exercise.

ダン：健康診断はどうだった？

マイク：悪くなかったよ、でも医者は定期的に運動しなさいと忠告したよ。

【advise＋人＋to～】「人に～しなさいと忠告する」

問2　23 ・ 24　③・⑥

Ken：Do you think your parents will let you study abroad？

Peg：I'm not sure, but I hope I can talk them into it.

ケン：あなたは両親が海外に留学することを許してくれると思う？

ペグ：わからないわ、でも私は彼らを説得したい。

【talk into】「説得する」

問3　25 ・ 26　①・④

Kazuki：Penny, I have to work late tonight, and I may not get back until 10 p.m.

Penny：It'll rain tonight. Don't get caught in the rain without an umbrella.

カズキ：ペニー、私は今夜遅くまで働かなければならないので、午後10時までに帰って来られないかもしれないよ。

ペニー：今夜は雨が降るよ。傘を持たずに、雨に遭わないようにしてね。

【get caught in the rain】「雨に遭う」

H27　②B

問1　18 ・ 19　⑤・⑥

Yuki：Have we met before？　You look very familiar to me.

Anne：I don't think so. If we had met, I would have recognized you for sure！

ユキ：私たち前に会ったことない？どこかであなたにお目

にかかったような気がするわ。

アンネ：そうは思わないわ。もし会っていたら，きっとあなたの顔を覚えているもの。

【for sure】「きっと」，仮定法過去完了【would have＋過去分詞】の順序に気をつける

問2　20 ・ 21 　⑤・①

Customer：Could I extend the rental period for the car ?

　　Agent：Yes, but <u>you will be charged an extra fee of</u> $50 for each additional day.

　　　客：車のレンタル期間を延長してもよろしいでしょうか。

　　業者：はい，しかし1日増すごとに50ドルの追加料金が請求されます。

選択肢に【be】があるので，【be charged】「請求される」と受動態の形にする。

問3　22 ・ 23 　④・⑤

　　Reiko：Shall we cook tonight, or order some Chinese food ?

　　Kyoko：Let's order Chinese <u>because I'm feeling too tired to start cooking</u>.

　レイコ：今夜一緒に料理する？それとも中華料理を注文する？

キョウコ：とても疲れていて料理を始める気になれないから中華料理を注文しましょう。

【feel tired】「疲れが出る」，【too～to…】「とても～すぎて…できない」

H28　②B

問1　18 ・ 19 　⑤・①

　Hotel clerk：Good evening, Mr. and Mrs. Gomez. How can I help?

Mrs. Gomez：Well, <u>we're wondering if you could tell</u> us how to get to the theater.

ホテル従業員：こんばんは、ゴメス様。いかがしましたか。

　ゴメス夫人：えぇと、どうやって劇場まで行ったらいいのか教えていただけるかしら。

【wonder if～】「～していただけないか」という依頼の婉曲表現。

問2　20 ・ 21 　③・⑤

　Student：Excuse me. I'd like to know what we will be discussing in next week's seminar.

Professor：I haven't decided yet, so <u>let me send you the details</u> by email.

　　生徒：すみません。来週のゼミでは何について議論するのか知りたいと思いまして。

　　教授：まだ、決めてないよ、だから詳細についてはeメールで知らせるよ。

【let me V】「私にVするのを許してください」

【send 人 物】「人に物を送る」（第4文型）の語順にも注意。

問3　22 ・ 23 　④・⑥

Interviewer：How did you change after becoming the head of such a large company?

　President：I <u>came to realize the need to manage</u> my time more effectively.

インタビュアー：このような大会社のトップになられた後、御自身はどう変わりましたか？

　　　社長：時間をより有効にうまく使う必要性を感じるようになりました。

【come to V】「Vするようになる」

theがあることから【need】を動詞ではなく名詞の「必要性」と考えるのがポイント。

H29　②B

問1　18 ・ 19 　②・⑥

　Keita：You have so many things in your room.

　Cindy：I know. Actually, <u>I find it difficult to keep</u> it neat and clean.

　ケイタ：部屋にものがとてもたくさんだね。

シンディ：わかってる。実は、きちんときれいにしておくことが難しいの。

このitは形式目的語。【find it C to do】の形は頻出なのでおさえておくこと。

問2　20 ・ 21 　⑤・①

　Ted：Professor Jones suggested that I rewrite this essay.

　Jack：Oh, well, <u>it may cost you a few hours</u>, but I'm sure you'll get a higher grade on it.

　テッド：ジョーンズ教授に論文を書き直すように言われたよ。

ジャック：うん、まあ、数時間はかかるかもしれないけど、きっともっと高い成績が取れるさ。

【cost 人 時間・労力】⇒「人に時間・労力を費やさせる。」

問3　22 ・ 23 　⑥・②

　Rita：Daniel and I have to go home now.

Father：Oh, <u>how come you are leaving earlier than</u> usual? I thought you were going to stay for dinner.

　リタ：ダニエルと私はもう家に帰らなくちゃ。

　　父：ええ、どうしていつもよりも早く帰るんだい？夕食までは居てくれると思ったよ。

【how come ～】⇒【why ～】

how come の場合、語順が【how come S V】となることに注意。

H30　②B

問1　18 ・ 19 　③・②

　Student：What are we going to do with the Australian students after they arrive?

Taecher：The first night, we'll have a barbecue by the river so that you all <u>can get to know each other</u>.

　　生徒：オーストラリアの留学生が到着した後に何をする予定ですか。

先生：最初の夜、皆がお互いに仲良くなれるように川の
　　　そばでバーベキューをするつもりです。

【get to ～】～するようになる

問2　| 20 |・| 21 |　④・②

　　Bridget：How was your basketball season last year?

　　Toshi：I <u>was the second highest scorer</u> on the team.

ブリジット：去年バスケットはどうだったの。

　　　トシ：チームで２番目の高得点者だったよ。

【the＋序数＋最上級】「～番目に…」

問3　| 22 |・| 23 |　③・②

　　Evan：I want to buy my first computer , but I don't know
　　　　　which one I should get.

　　Sam：Don't worry. Electronic stores always have experts
　　　　　available to give advice <u>to those who aren't familiar
　　　　　with</u> using computers.

エバン：初めてのコンピューターを買いたいと思っているの
　　　　だけど、どれを買ったらいいのかわからないよ。

　サム：心配いらないよ。電気屋にはいつもパソコンを使う
　　　　ことに不慣れな人にアドバイスをする人がいて利用
　　　　できるから。

【be familiar with ～】＝～に精通している、～をよく知っ
ている

H31　②B

問1　| 18 |・| 19 |　②・⑤

　　Yukio：Did you hear that a new entrance ID system will
　　　　　be introduced next month?

　　Lucas：Really? Do we need it? I <u>wonder how much it will
　　　　　cost</u> to replace the current system.

ユキオ：新しい入室IDシステムが来月導入されることは聞
　　　　いた？

ルーカス：本当に？僕たちそれ必要なの？現在のシステムと
　　　　　替えるためにどれだけの費用がかかるんだろう。

間接疑問文の並びは肯定文と同じであることに注意する。

【it costs 金額 to～】「～するのに（金額）がかかる」

問2　| 20 |・| 21 |　⑥・②

　　David：What's the plan for your trip to England?

　　Saki：I'll spend the first few days in London and then
　　　　　be in Cambridge <u>for the rest of my</u> stay.

デイビッド：イングランド旅行の計画はどんなだい？

　　　サキ：最初の数日はロンドンで過ごして、それから残
　　　　　　りの滞在日はケンブリッジにいるつもりよ。

【the rest of ～】「～の残り」

問3　| 22 |・| 23 |　②・⑥

　　Junko：The party we went to last night was very noisy.
　　　　　My throat is still sore from speaking loudly the
　　　　　whole time.

　　Ronald：Yeah. It can sometimes <u>be difficult to make
　　　　　yourself heard</u> in such a crowded place.

ジュンコ：昨夜私たちが行ったパーティーはとてもうるさ

かったね。ずっと大声で話していたから喉がいま
だに痛いよ。

ロナルド：うん。そんなに人が多い場所だったら声が聞こえ
　　　　　るようにするのが難しくなることもあるよね。

【make oneself heard】「自分の声が聞こえるようにする」

R2　②B

問1　| 18 |・| 19 |　④・②

　正：⑥would not ④have ①been ③completed ②by
　　　⑤the time

トニー：会場の装飾すばらしいですよね？私は時間通りに
　　　　終わらせられて嬉しいです。

　メイ：そうですね。本当にありがとうございます。あな
　　　　たの助けがなければ、今日の午後にゲストが全員
　　　　到着する時間までに、完成しなかったでしょう。

without A「Aがなかったならば」があるので、仮定法の文
章を作る必要がある。またthe time SV「SがVする時間」を
用いて後半の文章につなげる。by A「A（時間・期日）まで
に」。

問2　| 20 |・| 21 |　④・③

　正：⑥youngest ④of ⑤whom ②is studying ③music
　　　①in

イチロー：スミス氏には、今学校に２人の娘がいますね。

ナターシャ：正確には、彼には３人子供がいて、その中の
　　　　　　一番若い子はロンドンで音楽の勉強をしてい
　　　　　　るそうです。私はまだ彼女には会ってないと
　　　　　　思います。

the youngest of themとなるところを、関係代名詞whom（目
的格）を使ってthemの部分にいれることで、非制限用法の
関係代名詞節を作っている。

問3　| 22 |・| 23 |　⑤・②

　正：as planned or put it off

ピーター：今週末は雨が降るかもしれないので、私は公園
　　　　　でクラス会バーベキューをするべきかどうかま
　　　　　だわかりません。

　ヒカル：はい、計画通り行うか、延期するかを、来週ま
　　　　　でには決めなければなりません。私たちは雨の
　　　　　可能性について考えるべきでした。

as plannedはas（it is）plannedが元々の形である。asの後
のit isは省略されることが多いので覚えておく。put off A
（put A off）「Aを延期する」は、目的語が代名詞の場合は、
put A offの形になる。

令和5年

大学入学共通テスト

問題・解答解説

外 国 語 〔英 語(リーディング)〕 ［100点 80分］

無料質問ができる ‘とらサポ’

虎の巻の問題で「わからない」「質問したい」ときは、
“とらサポ” におまかせください！

【仮登録】→【本登録】→【会員番号発行】→質問開始！

左の QR コードが読み取れない方は、下記の URL へアクセスして下さい。

http://www.jukentaisaku.com/sup_free/

※ドメイン拒否設定をされている方は、〔本登録〕の URL が届きませんので解除して下さい。

（解答番号　1　〜　49　）

各大問の英文や図表を読み，解答番号　1　〜　49　にあてはまるものとして最も適当な選択肢を選びなさい。

第1問 (配点　10)

A　You are studying in the US, and as an afternoon activity you need to choose one of two performances to go and see. Your teacher gives you this handout.

Performances for Friday

Palace Theater *Together Wherever*	**Grand Theater** *The Guitar Queen*
A romantic play that will make you laugh and cry	A rock musical featuring colorful costumes
▶From 2:00 p.m. (no breaks and a running time of one hour and 45 minutes)	▶Starts at 1:00 p.m. (three hours long including two 15-minute breaks)
▶Actors available to talk in the lobby after the performance	▶Opportunity to greet the cast in their costumes before the show starts
▶No food or drinks available	▶Light refreshments (snacks & drinks), original T-shirts, and other goods sold in lobby
▶Free T-shirts for five lucky people	

Instructions: Which performance would you like to attend? Fill in the form below and hand it in to your teacher today.

✂ -

Choose (✓) one: *Together Wherever* ☐　　　*The Guitar Queen* ☐

Name: _____

問1　What are you told to do after reading the handout?　1

① Complete and hand in the bottom part.

② Find out more about the performances.

③ Talk to your teacher about your decision.

④ Write your name and explain your choice.

問2　Which is true about both performances?　2

① No drinks can be purchased before the show.

② Some T-shirts will be given as gifts.

③ They will finish at the same time.

④ You can meet perfomers at the theaters.

B You are a senior high school student interested in improving your English during the summer vacation. You find a website for an intensive English summer camp run by an international school.

GIS

Intensive English Summer Camp

Galley International School (GIS) has provided intensive English summer camps for senior high school students in Japan since 1989. Spend two weeks in an all-English environment!

Dates: August 1-14, 2023

Location: Lake Kawaguchi Youth Lodge, Yamanashi Prefecture

Cost: 120,000 yen, including food and accommodation (additional fees for optional activities such as kayaking and canoeing)

Courses Offered

◆**FOREST**: You'll master basic grammar structures, make short speeches on simple topics, and get pronunciation tips. Your instructors have taught English for over 20 years in several countries. On the final day of the camp, you'll take part in a speech contest while all the other campers listen.

◆**MOUNTAIN**: You'll work in a group to write and perform a skit in English. Instructors for this course have worked at theater schools in New York City, London, and Sydney. You'll perform your skit for all the campers to enjoy on August 14.

◆**SKY**: You'll learn debating skills and critical thinking in this course. Your instructors have been to many countries to coach debate teams and some have published best-selling textbooks on the subject. You'll do a short debate in front of all the other campers on the last day. (Note: Only those with an advanced level of English will be accepted.)

▲**Application**

Step 1: Fill in the online application **HERE** by May 20, 2023.

Step 2: We'll contact you to set up an interview to assess your English ability and ask about your course preference.

Step 3: You'll be assigned to a course.

問1 All GIS instructors have ☐ 3 ☐ .
   ① been in Japan since 1989   ② won international competitions
   ③ worked in other countries   ④ written some popular books

問2 On the last day of the camp, campers will ☐ 4 ☐ .
   ① assess each other's performances   ② compete to receive the best prize
   ③ make presentations about the future   ④ show what they learned at the camp

問3 What will happen after submitting your camp application? ☐ 5 ☐
   ① You will call the English instructors.   ② You will take a written English test.
   ③ Your English level will be checked.   ④ Your English speech topic will be sent.

第2問 (配点 20)

A　You want to buy a good pair of shoes as you walk a long way to school and often get sore feet. You are searching on a UK website and find this advertisement.

Navi 55 presents the new *Smart Support* shoe line

Smart Support shoes are strong, long-lasting, and reasonably priced. They are available in three colours and styles.

nano-chip

Special Features

Smart Support shoes have a nano-chip which analyses the shape of your feet when connected to the *iSupport* application. Download the app onto your smartphone, PC, tablet, and/or smartwatch. Then, while wearing the shoes, let the chip collect the data about your feet. The inside of the shoe will automatically adjust to give correct, personalised foot support. As with other Navi 55 products, the shoes have our popular Route Memory function.

Advantages

Better Balance: Adjusting how you stand, the personalised support helps keep feet, legs, and back free from pain.

Promotes Exercise: As they are so comfortable, you will be willing to walk regularly.

Route Memory: The chip records your daily route, distance, and pace as you walk.

Route Options: View your live location on your device, have the directions play automatically in your earphones, or use your smartwatch to read directions.

Customers' Comments

● I like the choices for getting directions, and prefer using audio guidance to visual guidance.

● I lost 2 kg in a month!

● I love my pair now, but it took me several days to get used to them.

● As they don't slip in the rain, I wear mine all year round.

● They are so light and comfortable I even wear them when cycling.

● Easy to get around! I don't need to worry about getting lost.

● They look great. The app's basic features are easy to use, but I wouldn't pay for the optional advanced ones.

問1　According to the maker's statements, which best describes the new shoes?　6

① Cheap summer shoes　　　　　② High-tech everyday shoes

③ Light comfortable sports shoes　④ Stylish colourful cycling shoes

問2　Which benefit offered by the shoes is most likely to appeal to you?　7

① Getting more regular exercise　　② Having personalised foot support

③ Knowing how fast you walk　　　④ Looking cool wearing them

問3　One **opinion** stated by a customer is that ┌ 8 ┐.

① the app encourages fast walking　② the app's free functions are user-friendly

③ the shoes are good value for money　④ the shoes increase your cycling speed

問4　One customer's comment mentions using audio devices.　Which benefit is this comment based on?　┌ 9 ┐

① Better Balance　② Promotes Exercise　③ Route Memory　④ Route Options

問5　According to one customer's opinion, ┌ 10 ┐ is recommended.

① allowing time to get accustomed to wearing the shoes

② buying a watch to help you lose weight

③ connecting to the app before putting the shoes on

④ paying for the *iSupport* advanced features

B　You are a member of the student council.　The members have been discussing a student project helping students to use their time efficiently.　To get ideas, you are reading a report about a school challenge.　It was written by an exchange student who studied in another school in Japan.

Commuting Challenge

　Most students come to my school by bus or train.　I often see a lot of students playing games on their phones or chatting.　However, they could also use this time for reading or doing homework.　We started this activity to help students use their commuting time more effectively.　Students had to complete a commuting activity chart from January 17th to February 17th.　A total of 300 students participated: More than two thirds of them were second-years; about a quarter were third-years; only 15 first-years participated.　How come so few first-years participated?　Based on the feedback (given below), there seems to be an answer to this question:

Feedback from participants

HS:　Thanks to this project, I got the highest score ever in an English vocabulary test.　It was easy to set small goals to complete on my way.

KF:　My friend was sad because she couldn't participate.　She lives nearby and walks to school.　There should have been other ways to take part.

SS:　My train is always crowded and I have to stand, so there is no space to open a book or a tablet.　I only used audio materials, but there were not nearly enough.

JH:　I kept a study log, which made me realise how I used my time.　For some reason most of my first-year classmates didn't seem to know about this challenge.

MN:　I spent most of the time on the bus watching videos, and it helped me to understand classes better.　I felt the time went very fast.

問1　The aim of the Commuting Challenge was to help students to ☐ 11 ☐ .

  ① commute more quickly

  ② improve their test scores

  ③ manage English classes better

  ④ use their time better

問2　One <u>fact</u> about the Commuting Challenge is that ☐ 12 ☐ .

  ① fewer than 10% of the participants were first-years

  ② it was held for two months during the winter

  ③ students had to use portable devices on buses

  ④ the majority of participants travelled by train

問3　From the feedback, ☐ 13 ☐ were activities reported by participants.

  A：keeping study records

  B：learning language

  C：making notes on tablets

  D：reading lesson notes on mobile phones

  ① A and B　　　② A and C　　　③ A and D

  ④ B and C　　　⑤ B and D　　　⑥ C and D

問4　One of the participants' opinions about the Commuting Challenge is that ☐ 14 ☐ .

  ① it could have included students who walk to school

  ② the train was a good place to read books

  ③ there were plenty of audio materials for studying

  ④ watching videos for fun helped time pass quickly

問5　The author's question is answered by ☐ 15 ☐ .

  ① HS　　　② JH　　　③ KF　　　④ MN　　　⑤ SS

第3問 (配点 15)

A You are studying at Camberford University, Sydney. You are going on a class camping trip and are reading the camping club's newsletter to prepare.

Going camping? Read me!!!

Hi, I'm Kaitlyn. I want to share two practical camping lessons from my recent club trip. The first thing is to divide your backpack into three main parts and put the heaviest items in the middle section to balance the backpack. Next, more frequently used daily necessities should be placed in the top section. That means putting your sleeping bag at the bottom; food, cookware and tent in the middle; and your clothes at the top. Most good backpacks come with a "brain" (an additional pouch) for small easy-to-reach items.

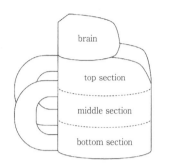

Last year, in the evening, we had fun cooking and eating outdoors. I had been sitting close to our campfire, but by the time I got back to the tent I was freezing. Although I put on extra layers of clothes before going to sleep, I was still cold. Then, my friend told me to take off my outer layers and stuff them into my sleeping bag to fill up some of the empty space. This stuffing method was new to me, and surprisingly kept me warm all night!

I hope my advice helps you stay warm and comfortable. Enjoy your camping trip!

問1 If you take Kaitlyn's advice, how should you fill your backpack? 　16

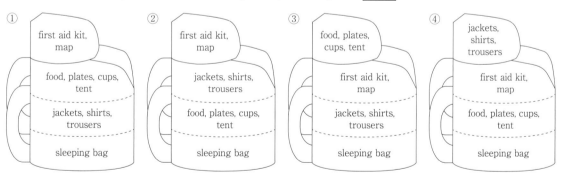

問2 According to Kaitlyn, 　17　 is the best method to stay warm all night.

① avoiding going out of your tent ② eating hot meals beside your campfire

③ filling the gaps in your sleeping bag ④ wearing all of your extra clothes

B Your English club will make an "adventure room" for the school festival. To get some ideas, you are reading a blog about a room a British man created.

Create Your Own "Home Adventure"

Last year, I took part in an "adventure room" experience. I really enjoyed it, so I created one for my children. Here are some tips on making your own.

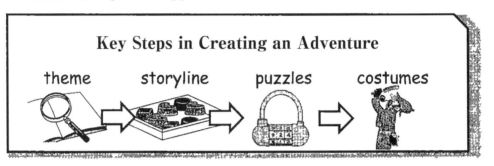

First, pick a theme. My sons are huge Sherlock Holmes fans, so I decided on a detective mystery. I rearranged the furniture in our family room, and added some old paintings and lamps I had to set the scene.

Next, create a storyline. Ours was *The Case of the Missing Chocolates*. My children would be "detectives" searching for clues to locate the missing sweets.

The third step is to design puzzles and challenges. A useful idea is to work backwards from the solution. If the task is to open a box locked with a three-digit padlock, think of ways to hide a three-digit code. Old books are fantastic for hiding messages in. I had tremendous fun underlining words on different pages to form mystery sentences. Remember that the puzzles should get progressively more difficult near the final goal. To get into the spirit, I then had the children wear costumes. My eldest son was excited when I handed him a magnifying glass, and immediately began acting like Sherlock Holmes. After that, the children started to search for the first clue.

This "adventure room" was designed specifically for my family, so I made some of the challenges personal. For the final task, I took a couple of small cups and put a plastic sticker in each one, then filled them with yogurt. The "detectives" had to eat their way to the bottom to reveal the clues. Neither of my kids would eat yogurt, so this truly was tough for them. During the adventure, my children were totally focused, and they enjoyed themselves so much that we will have another one next month.

問1 Put the following events (①~④) into the order in which they happened.

| 18 | → | 19 | → | 20 | → | 21 |

① The children ate food they are not fond of.

② The children started the search for the sweets.

③ The father decorated the living room in the house.

④ The father gave his sons some clothes to wear.

問2 If you follow the father's advice to create your own "adventure room," you should 　22　 .

① concentrate on three-letter words

② leave secret messages under the lamps

③ make the challenges gradually harder

④ practise acting like Sherlock Holmes

問3 From this story, you understand that the father 　23　 .

① became focused on searching for the sweets

② created an experience especially for his children

③ had some trouble preparing the adventure game

④ spent a lot of money decorating the room

第4問 (配点 16)

Your teacher has asked you to read two articles about effective ways to study. You will discuss what you learned in your next class.

How to Study Effectively: Contextual Learning!

Tim Oxford

Science Teacher, Stone City Junior High School

As a science teacher, I am always concerned about how to help students who struggle to learn. Recently, I found that their main way of learning was to study new information repeatedly until they could recall it all. For example, when they studied for a test, they would use a workbook like the example below and repeatedly say the terms that go in the blanks: "Obsidian is igneous, dark, and glassy. Obsidian is igneous, dark, and glassy...." These students would feel as if they had learned the information, but would quickly forget it and get low scores on the test. Also, this sort of repetitive learning is dull and demotivating.

To help them learn, I tried applying "contextual learning." In this kind of learning, new knowledge is constructed through students' own experiences. For my science class, students learned the properties of different kinds of rocks. Rather than having them memorize the terms from a workbook, I brought a big box of various rocks to the class. Students examined the rocks and identified their names based on the characteristics they observed.

Rock name	Obsidian
Rock type	igneous
Coloring	dark
Texture	glassy
Picture	

Thanks to this experience, I think these students will always be able to describe the properties of the rocks they studied. One issue, however, is that we don't always have the time to do contextual learning, so students will still study by doing drills. I don't think this is the best way. I'm still searching for ways to improve their learning.

How to Make Repetitive Learning Effective

Cheng Lee

Professor, Stone City University

Mr. Oxford's thoughts on contextual learning were insightful. I agree that it can be beneficial. Repetition, though, can also work well. However, the repetitive learning strategy he discussed, which is called "massed learning," is not effective. There is another kind of repetitive learning called "spaced learning," in which students memorize new information and then review it over longer intervals.

The interval between studying is the key difference. In Mr. Oxford's example, his students probably used their workbooks to study over a short period of time. In this case, they might have paid less attention to the content as they continued to review it. The reason for this is that the content was no longer new and could easily be ignored. In contrast, when the intervals, are longer, the students' memory of the content is weaker. Therefore, they pay more attention because they have to make a greater effort to recall what they had learned before. For example, if students study with their workbooks, wait three days, and then study again, they are likely to learn the material better.

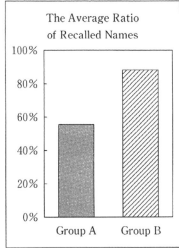

Previous research has provided evidence for the advantages of spaced learning. In one experiment, students in Groups A and B tried to memorize the names of 50 animals. Both groups studied four times, but Group A studied at one-day intervals while Group B studied at one-week intervals. As the figure to the right shows, 28 days after the last learning session, the average ratio of recalled names on a test was higher for the spaced learning group.

I understand that students often need to learn a lot of information in a short period of time, and long intervals between studying might not be practical. You should understand, though, that massed learning might not be good for long-term recall.

問1　Oxford believes that 24 .

① continuous drilling is boring　　② reading an explanation of terms is helpful

③ students are not interested in science　④ studying with a workbook leads to success

問2　In the study discussed by Lee, students took a test 25 after their final session.

① four weeks　② immediately　③ one day　④ one week

問3　Lee introduces spaced learning, which involves studying at 26 intervals, in order to overcome the disadvantages of 27 learning that Oxford discussed. (Choose the best one for each box from options ①～⑥.)

① contextual　② extended　③ fixed　④ irregular　⑤ massed　⑥ practical

問4　Both writes agree that 28 is helpful for remembering new information.

① experiential learning　　② having proper rest

③ long-term attention　　④ studying with workbooks

問5　Which additional information would be the best to support Lee's argument for spaced learning? 29

① The main factor that makes a science class attractive

② The most effective length of intervals for spaced learning

③ Whether students' workbooks include visuals or not

④ Why Oxford's students could not memorize information well

第5問 (配点 15)

Your English teacher has told everyone in your class to find an inspirational story and present it to a discussion group, using notes. You have found a story written by high school student in the UK.

Lessons from Table Tennis

Ben Carter

The ball flew at lightning speed to my backhand. It was completely unexpected and I had no time to react. I lost the point and the match. Defeat… Again! This is how it was in the first few months when I started playing table tennis. It was frustrating, but I now know that the sport taught me more than simply how to be a better athlete.

In middle school, I loved football. I was one of the top scorers, but I didn't get along with my teammates. The coach often said that I should be more of a team player. I knew I should work on the problem, but communication was just not my strong point.

I had to leave the football club when my family moved to a new town. I wasn't upset as I had decided to stop playing football anyway. My new school had a table tennis club, coached by the PE teacher, Mr Trent, and I joined that. To be honest, I chose table tennis because I thought it would be easier for me to play individually.

At first, I lost more games than I won. I was frustrated and often went straight home after practice, not speaking to anyone. One day, however, Mr Trent said to me, "You could be a good player, Ben, but you need to think more about your game. What do you think you need to do?" "I don't know," I replied, "focus on the ball more?" "Yes," Mr Trent continued, "but you also need to study your opponent's moves and adjust your play accordingly. Remember, your opponent is a person, not a ball." This made a deep impression on me.

I deliberately modified my style of play, paying closer attention to my opponent's moves. It was not easy, and took a lot of concentration. My efforts paid off, however, and my play improved. My confidence grew and I started staying behind more after practice. I was turning into a star player and my classmates tried to talk to me more than before. I thought that I was becoming popular, but our conversations seemed to end before they really got started. Although my play might have improved, my communication skills obviously hadn't.

My older brother Patrick was one of the few people I could communicate with well. One day, I tried to explain my problems with communication to him, but couldn't make him understand. We switched to talking about table tennis. "What do you actually enjoy about it?" he asked me curiously. I said I loved analysing my opponent's movements and making instant decisions about the next move. Patrick looked thoughtful. "That sounds like the kind of skill we use when we communicate," he said.

At that time, I didn't understand, but soon after our conversation, I won a silver medal in a table tennis tournament. My classmates seemed really pleased. One of them, George, came running over. "Hey, Ben!" he said, "Let's have a party to celebrate!" Without thinking, I replied, "I can't. I've got practice." He looked a bit hurt and walked off without saying anything else.

Why was he upset? I thought about this incident for a long time. Why did he suggest a party? Should I have said something different? A lot of questions came to my mind, but then I realized that he was just being kind. If I'd said, "Great idea. Thank you! Let me talk to Mr Trent and see if I can get some time off practice," then maybe the outcome would have been better. At that moment Patrick's words made sense. Without attempting to grasp someone's intention, I wouldn't know how to respond.

I'm still not the best communicator in the world, but I definitely feel more confident in my communication skills now than before. Next year, my friends and I are going to co-ordinate the table tennis league with other schools.

Your notes:

Lessons from Table Tennis

About the author (Ben Carter)

· Played football at middle school.

· Started playing table tennis at his new school because he ⟨ 30 ⟩ .

Other important people

· Mr Trent: Ben's table tennis coach, who helped him improve his play.

· Patrick: Ben's brother, who ⟨ 31 ⟩ .

· George: Ben's classmate, who wanted to celebrate his victory.

Influential events in Ben's journey to becoming a better communicator

Began playing table tennis → ⟨ 32 ⟩ → ⟨ 33 ⟩ → ⟨ 34 ⟩ → ⟨ 35 ⟩

What Ben realised after the conversation with George

He should have ⟨ 36 ⟩ .

What we can learn from this story

· ⟨ 37 ⟩   · ⟨ 38 ⟩

問1　Choose the best option for ⟨ 30 ⟩ .

  ① believed it would help him communicate　　② hoped to become popular at school

  ③ thought he could win games easily　　④ wanted to avoid playing a team sport

問2　Choose the best option for ⟨ 31 ⟩ .

  ① asked him what he enjoyed about communication

  ② encouraged him to be more confident

  ③ helped him learn the social skills he needed

  ④ told him what he should have said to his school friends

問3　Choose **four** out of the five options (①～⑤) and rearrange them in the order they happened.

  ⟨ 32 ⟩ → ⟨ 33 ⟩ → ⟨ 34 ⟩ → ⟨ 35 ⟩

  ① Became a table tennis champion　　② Discussed with his teacher how to play well

  ③ Refused a party in his honour　　④ Started to study his opponents

  ⑤ Talked to his brother about table tennis

問4　Choose the best option for ⟨ 36 ⟩ .

  ① asked his friend questions to find out more about his motivation

  ② invited Mr Trent and other classmates to party to show appreciation

  ③ tried to understand his friend's point of view to act appropriately

  ④ worked hard to be a better team player for successful communication

問5　Choose the best two options for ⟨ 37 ⟩ and ⟨ 38 ⟩ . (The order does not matter.)

  ① Advice from people around us can help us change.

  ② Confidence is important for being a good communicator.

  ③ It is important to make our intentions clear to our friends.

  ④ The support that teammates provide one another is helpful.

  ⑤ We can apply what we learn from one thing to another.

第6問 (配点 24)

A You are in a discussion group in school. You have been asked to summarize the following article. You will speak about it, using only notes.

Collecting

Collecting has existed at all levels of society, across cultures and age groups since early times. Museums are proof that things have been collected, saved, and passed down for future generations. There are various reasons for starting a collection. For example, Ms. A enjoys going to yard sales every Saturday morning with her children. At yard sales, people sell unwanted things in front of their houses. One day, while looking for antique dishes, an unusual painting caught her eye and she bought it for only a few dollars. Over time, she found similar pieces that left an impression on her, and she now has a modest collection of artwork, some of which may be worth more than she paid. One person's trash can be another person's treasure. Regardless of how someone's collection was started, it is human nature to collect things.

In 1988, researchers Brenda Danet and Tamar Katriel analyzed 80 years of studies on children under the age of 10, and found that about 90% collected something. This shows us that people like to gather things from an early age. Even after becoming adults, people continue collecting stuff. Researchers in the field generally agree that approximately one third of adults maintain this behavior. Why is this? The primary explanation is related to emotions. Some save greeting cards from friends and family, dried flowers from special events, seashells from a day at the beach, old photos, and so on. For others, their collection is a connection to their youth. They may have baseball cards, comic books, dolls, or miniature cars that they have kept since they were small. Others have an attachment to history; they seek and hold onto historical documents, signed letters and autographs from famous people, and so forth.

For some individuals there is a social reason. People collect things such as pins to share, show, and even trade, making new friends this way. Others, like some holders of Guinness World Records, appreciate the fame they achieve for their unique collection. Cards, stickers, stamps, coins, and toys have topped the "usual" collection list, but some collectors lean toward the more unexpected. In September 2014, Guinness World Records recognized Harry Sperl, of Germany, for having the largest hamburger-related collection in the world, with 3,724 items; from T-shirts to pillows to dog toys, Sperl's room is filled with all things "hamburger." Similarly, Liu Fuchang, of China, is a collector of playing cards. He has 11,087 different sets.

Perhaps the easiest motivation to understand is pleasure. Some people start collections for pure enjoyment. They may purchase and put up paintings just to gaze at frequently, or they may collect audio recordings and old-fashioned vinyl records to enjoy listening to their favorite music. This type of collector is unlikely to be very interested in the monetary value of their treasured music, while others collect objects specifically as an investment. While it is possible to download certain classic games for free, having the same game unopened in its original packaging, in "mint condition," can make the game worth a lot. Owning various valuable "collector's items" could ensure some financial security.

This behavior of collecting things will definitely continue into the distant future. Although the reasons why people keep things will likely remain the same, advances in technology will have an influence on collections. As technology can remove physical constraints, it is now possible for an individual to have vast digital libraries of music and art that would have been unimaginable 30 years ago. It is unclear, though, what other impacts technology will have on collections. Can you even imagine the form and scale that the next generation's collections will take?

Your notes:

Collecting

Introduction
- ◆ Collecting has long been part of the human experience.
- ◆ The yard sale story tells us that ⬚39⬚ .

Facts
- ◆ ⬚40⬚
- ◆ Guinness World Records
  - ◇ Sperl: 3,724 hamburger-related items
  - ◇ Liu: 11,087 sets of playing cards

Reasons for collecting
- ◆ Motivation for collecting can be emotional or social.
- ◆ Various reasons mentioned: ⬚41⬚ , ⬚42⬚ , interest in history, childhood excitement, becoming famous, sharing, etc.

Collections in the future
- ◆ ⬚43⬚

問1　Choose the best option for ⬚39⬚ .

①　a great place for people to sell things to collectors at a high price is a yard sale

②　people can evaluate items incorrectly and end up paying too much money for junk

③　something not important to one person may be value to someone else

④　things once collected and thrown in another person's yard may be valuable to others

問2　Choose the best option for ⬚40⬚ .

①　About two third of children do not collect ordinary things.

②　Almost one third of adults start collecting things for pleasure.

③　Approximately 10% of kids have collections similar to their friends.

④　Roughly 30% of people keep collecting into adulthood.

問3 Choose the best options for ⬚41⬚ and ⬚42⬚ . (The order does not matter.)

① desire to advance technology   ② fear of missing unexpected opportunities

③ filling a sense of emptiness   ④ reminder of precious events

⑤ reusing objects for the future   ⑥ seeking some sort of profit

問4 Choose the best option for ⬚43⬚ .

① Collections will likely continue to change in size and shape.

② Collectors of mint-condition games will have more digital copies of them.

③ People who have lost their passion for collecting will start again.

④ Reasons for collecting will change because of advances in technology.

B   You are in a student group preparing for an international science presentation contest. You are using the following passage to create your part of the presentation on extraordinary creatures.

Ask someone to name the world's toughest animal, and they might say the Bactrian camel as it can survive in temperatures as high as 50℃ , or the Arctic fox which can survive in temperatures lower than −58℃ . However, both answers would be wrong as it is widely believed that the tardigrade is the toughest creature on earth.

Tardigrades, also known as water bears, are microscopic creatures, which are between 0.1 mm to 1.5 mm in length. They live almost everywhere, from 6,000-meter-high mountains to 4,600 meters below the ocean's surface. They can even be found under thick ice and in hot springs. Most live in water, but some tardigrades can be found in some of the driest places on earth. One researcher reported finding tardigrades living under rocks in a desert without any recorded rainfall for 25 years. All they need are a few drops or a thin layer of water to live in. When the water dries up, so do they. They lose all but three percent of their body's water and their metabolism slows down to 0.01% of its normal speed. The dried-out tardigrade is now in a state called "tun," a kind of deep sleep. It will continue in this state until it is once again soaked in water. Then, like a sponge, it absorbs the water and springs back to life again as if nothing had happened. Whether the tardigrade is in tun for 1 week or 10 years does not really matter. The moment it is surrounded by water, it comes alive again. When tardigrades are in a state of tun, they are so tough that they can survive in temperatures as low as −272℃ and as high as 151℃ . Exactly how they achieve this is still not fully understood.

Perhaps even more amazing than their ability to survive on earth—they have been on earth for some 540 million years—is their ability to survive in space. In 2007, a team of European researchers sent a number of living tardigrades into space on the outside of a rocket for 10 days. On their return to earth, the researchers were surprised to see that 68% were still alive. This means that for 10 days most were able to survive X-rays and ultraviolet radiation 1,000 times more intense than here on earth. Later, in 2019, an Israeli spacecraft crashed onto the moon and thousands of tardigrades in a state of tun were spilled onto its surface. Whether these are still alive or not is unknown as no one has gone to collect them—which is a pity.

Tardigrades are shaped like a short cucumber. They have four short legs on each side of their bodies. Some species have sticky pads at the end of each leg, while others have claws. There are 16 known claw variations, which help identify those species with claws. All tardigrades have a place for eyes, but not all species have eyes. Their eyes are primitive, only having five cells in total—just one of which is light sensitive.

Basically, tardigrades can be divided into those that eat plant matter, and those that eat other creatures. Those that eat vegetation have a ventral mouth—a mouth located in the lower part of the head, like a shark. The type that eats other creatures has a terminal mouth, which means the mouth is at the very front of the head, like a tuna. The mouths of tardigrades do not have teeth. They do, however, have two sharp needles, called stylets, that they use to pierce plant cells or the bodies of smaller creatures so the contents can be sucked out.

Both types of tardigrade have rather simple digestive systems. The mouth leads to the pharynx (throat), where digestive juices and food are mixed. Located above the pharynx is a salivary gland. This produces the juices that flow into the mouth and help with digestion. After the pharynx, there is a tube which transports food toward the gut. This tube is called the esophagus. The middle gut, a simple stomach/intestine type of organ, digests the food and absorbs the nutrients. The leftovers then eventually move through to the anus.

Your presentation slides:

Tardigrades:
Earth's Ultimate Survivors

1. Basic Information
· 0.1 mm to 1.5 mm in length
· shaped like a short cucumber
·
· 44
·
·

2. Habitats
· live almost everywhere
· extreme environments such as...
  ✔ 6 km above sea level
  ✔ 4.6 km below sea level
  ✔ in deserts
  ✔ −272℃ to 151℃
  ✔ in space (possibly)

3. Secrets to Survival

"tun"   active
· 45
· 46

4. Digestive Systems 47

5. Final Statement
 48

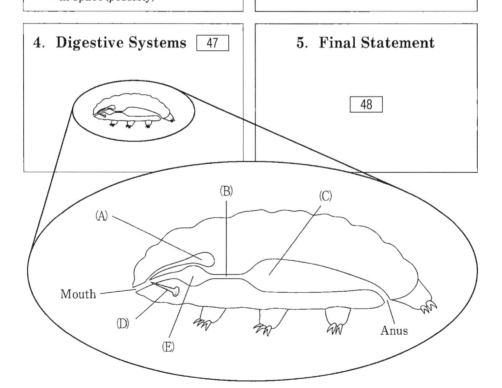

(A)   (B)   (C)

Mouth

(D)

(E)

Anus

問1　Which of the following should you **not** include for ⬛44⬛ ?

① eight short legs 　　　　　　　② either blind or sighted

③ plant-eating or creature-eating 　④ sixteen different types of feet

⑤ two stylets rather than teeth

問2　For the **Secrets to Survival** slide, select two features of the tardigrade which best help it survive.　(The order does not matter.)　⬛45⬛ ・ ⬛46⬛

① In dry conditions, their metabolism drops to less than one percent of normal.

② Tardigrades in a state of tun are able to survive in temperatures exceeding 151℃ .

③ The state of tun will cease when the water in a tardigrade's body is above 0.01%.

④ Their shark-like mouths allow them to more easily eat other creatures.

⑤ They have an ability to withstand extreme levels of radiation.

問3　Complete the missing labels on the illustration of a tardigrade for the **Digestive Systems** slide.　⬛47⬛

①	(A) Esophagus	(B) Pharynx	(C) Middle gut		
	(D) Stylets	(E) Salivary gland			
②	(A) Pharynx	(B) Stylets	(C) Salivary gland		
	(D) Esophagus	(E) Middle gut			
③	(A) Salivary gland	(B) Esophagus	(C) Middle gut		
	(D) Stylets	(E) Pharynx			
④	(A) Salivary gland	(B) Middle gut	(C) Stylets		
	(D) Esophagus	(E) Pharynx			
⑤	(A) Stylets	(B) Salivary gland	(C) Pharynx		
	(D) Middle gut	(E) Esophagus			

問4　Which is the best statement for the final slide?　⬛48⬛

① For thousands of years, tardigrades have survived some of the harshest conditions on earth and in space.　They will live longer than humankind.

② Tardigrades are from space and can live in temperatures exceeding the limits of the Arctic fox and Bactrian camel, so they are surely stronger than human beings.

③ Tardigrades are, without a doubt, the toughest creatures on earth.　They can survive on the top of mountains; at the bottom of the sea; in the waters of hot springs; and they can also thrive on the moon.

④ Tardigrades have survived some of the harshest conditions on earth, and at least one trip into space. This remarkable creature might outlive the human species.

問5　What can be inferred about sending tardigrades into space?　⬛49⬛

① Finding out whether the tardigrades can survive in space was never thought to be important.

② Tardigrades, along with other creatures that have been on earth for millions of years, can withstand X-rays and ultraviolet radiation.

③ The Israeli researchers did not expect so many tardigrades to survive the harsh environment of space.

④ The reason why no one has been to see if tardigrades can survive on the moon's surface attracted the author's attention.

	解答番号	正解	配当
R 5 ①A	1	①	2
	2	④	2
R 5 ①B	3	③	2
	4	④	2
	5	③	2
R 5 ②A	6	②	2
	7	②	2
	8	②	2
	9	④	2
	10	①	2
R 5 ②B	11	④	2
	12	①	2
	13	①	2
	14	①	2
	15	②	2
R 5 ③A	16	②	3
	17	③	3
R 5 ③B	18	③	3*
	19	④	
	20	②	
	21	①	
	22	③	3
	23	②	3
R 5 ④	24	①	3
	25	①	3
	26	②	2
	27	⑤	2
	28	①	3
	29	②	3
R 5 ⑤	30	④	3
	31	③	3
	32	②	3*
	33	④	
	34	⑤	
	35	③	
	36	③	3
	37－38	①－⑤	3*
R 5 ⑥A	39	③	3
	40	④	3
	41－42	④－⑥	3*
	43	①	3
R 5 ⑥B	44	④	2
	45－46	①－⑤	3*
	47	③	2
	48	④	2
	49	④	3

(注)　1　＊は，全部正解の場合のみ点を与える。
　　　2　－（ハイフン）でつながれた正解は，順序を問わない。

第1問

A あなたはアメリカで勉強していて、午後の活動として2つの公演のうちどちらか1つを選んで見に行く必要がある。先生はこのプリントをあなたに渡している。

金曜日の公演

パレス・シアター どこでも一緒	グランド・シアター ギターの女王
笑いあり涙ありの恋愛劇	カラフルな衣装が目玉のロックミュージカル
▶午後2時開演（休憩なし、上演時間1時間45分） ▶終演後、ロビーで俳優と話すことが出来る ▶飲食禁止 ▶無料Tシャツを幸運な5名にプレゼント	▶午後1時開演（15分休憩2回を含む上演時間3時間） ▶開演前、衣装を着た出演者にあいさつする機会がある ▶軽食（スナックと飲み物）、オリジナルTシャツその他のグッズがロビーにて販売される

指示：どちらの公演に参加したいですか？以下の書式に記入し、本日中に先生に提出しなさい。

✂- -

1つを選択(✓)：どこでも一緒 □　　ギターの女王 □

氏名：＿＿＿＿＿＿＿＿＿＿＿＿＿

問1 あなたはプリントを見た後何をするよう言われているか？　　**1**

①下部を完成させて提出しなさい。
②公演についてもっと調べなさい。
③あなたの決定を先生に伝えなさい。
④名前を書き、選択したものを説明しなさい。

　プリント下部にある指示に「以下の書式に記入し、本日中に先生に提出しなさい」とあり、正解は①。

問2 どちらの公演についても正しいことは何か。　　**2**

①開演前に飲み物を買うことはできない。
②プレゼントとしてTシャツがもらえる。
③同じ時間に終わる。
④劇場で出演者に会うことが出来る。

　『どこでも一緒』は「終演後、ロビーで俳優と話すことが出来る」、『ギターの女王』は「開演前、衣装を着た出演者にあいさつする機会がある」とあり、どちらの公演も劇場で出演者に会うことが出来る。よって、正解は④。

B あなたは夏休みの間に英語を上達させることに関心がある高校生である。あなたはあるインターナショナルスクールが運営する英語集中夏キャンプのウェブサイトを見つけた。

GIS 英語集中 夏キャンプ	ギャレー・インターナショナル・スクール（GIS）は1989年から日本の高校生向けに英語集中夏キャンプを提供しています。すべて英語の環境での2週間を過ごしましょう！

日程：2023年8月1日～14日
場所：山梨県、河口湖ユースロッジ
費用：120,000円、食費・宿泊費も含む（カヤックやカヌーなどのオプション活動は追加料金）

提供されるコース

◆**森**：基本的な文法構造を理解し、簡単な話題で短いスピーチを行い、発音のコツを学びます。講師たちは20年以上いくつかの国で教えてきた経験があります。合宿最終日には、他の参加者全員が聞く中、スピーチコンテストに参加します。

◆**山**：グループで英語の寸劇を作って演じます。このコースの講師たちはニューヨーク、ロンドン、シドニーの演劇学校で働いた経験があります。8月14日に参加者全員が楽しめるように寸劇を演じます。

◆**空**：このコースではディベートの技術とクリティカルシンキングについて学びます。講師たちはディベートのチームをコーチするために多くの国々へ行った経験があり、これがテーマのベストセラーの本を出版した者もいます。最終日に他の参加者全員の前で短いディベートを行います。（注：英語上級者のみ受け入れます。）

▲**申し込み**

ステップ1：2023年5月20日までに<u>こちらの</u>オンライン申込書に記入して下さい。

ステップ2：英語力を評価し、希望コースを確認する面接を設定するために、ご連絡いたします。

ステップ3：コースが割り当てられます。

問1 GISの講師は全員　　**3**　。

①1989年からずっと日本にいる
②国際大会で優勝している
③外国で働いたことがある
④人気のある本を書いたことがある

　森コース第2文に「20年以上いくつかの国で教えてきた経験があります」、山コース第2文に「ニューヨーク、ロンドン、シドニーの演劇学校で働いた経験があります」、空コース第2文に「講師たちはディベートのチームをコーチするために多くの国々へ行った経験があり」とあり、講師全員が外国で働いたことがあることがわかる。よって、正解は③。

問2 合宿最終日、参加者は　　**4**　。

①お互いのパフォーマンスを評価しあう
②最優秀賞をとるために競い合う。
③未来についての発表を行う。
④キャンプで学んだことを見せる。

　森コース第3文に「合宿最終日には、他の参加者全員が聞く中、スピーチコンテストに参加します」、山コース第3文に「8月14日に参加者全員が楽しめるように寸劇を演じます」、空コース第3文に「最終日に他の参加者全員の前で短いディベートを行います」とあり、どのコースの参加者も合宿最終日である8月14日にキャンプで学んだことを他の参加者の前で見せることがわかる。よって、正解は④。

問3 合宿の申し込みをした後はどうなるか？　　**5**

①英語の講師に電話をする。
②英語のライティングのテストを受ける。
③あなたの英語レベルが確認される。
④あなたの英語のスピーチのトピックが送られる。

　申し込みのステップ1で申し込みをした後の流れであるが、ステップ2で「英語力を評価し、希望コースを確認する面接を設定するために、ご連絡いたします」とある。電

話はGISからかかってくるので①は誤り。面接で英語力を評価するのであるから，ライティングのテストを受けるのではなく②は誤り。申し込みのステップには書かれていないので④は誤り。「英語力を評価する」＝「英語レベルが確認される」なので正解は③。

第2問

A　あなたは学校まで長距離を歩き，よく足が痛くなるのでよい靴を買いたい。あなたがイギリスのウェブサイトで検索していると，この広告を見つけた。

ナビ55から新しいスマートサポートシューズの紹介
スマートサポートシューズは丈夫，長持ち，手頃な価格です。
3つの色，スタイルが選べます。

特徴
スマートサポートシューズは，ⅰサポートアプリケーションに接続するとあなたの足の形を分析するナノチップが搭載されています。あなたのスマートフォン，パソコン，タブレット，スマートウォッチなどにダウンロードしてください。そして，靴を履いている間に，チップにあなたの足に関するデータを収集させます。靴の内側が適切にあなた個人に合わせた足のサポートを提供するために自動的に調整されます。他のナビ55製品と同じように人気のルートメモリー機能も搭載されています。

利点
よりよいバランス：あなたの立ち方を調整し，あなた個人に合わせたサポートによって，足，脚，背中が痛みから解放されます。
運動の促進：とても快適なので，定期的に歩こうという気持ちになります。
ルートメモリー：チップがあなたが歩いているときに日々のルート，距離，ペースを記録します。
ルートオプション：あなたの現在地をデバイスで見る，イヤホンで案内を自動再生する，スマートウォッチで案内を見るために使うことが出来ます。

顧客のコメント
● 私は案内の方法を選ぶことが出来ることが気に入っており，視覚案内よりも音声案内を使うほうが好きです。
● 私は1か月で2キロ痩せました！
● 今は気に入っていますが，靴に慣れるのに数日かかりました。
● 雨の中でも滑らないので，一年中履いています。
● とても軽くて快適なのでサイクリングのときも履いています。
● 移動するのが楽です！道に迷う心配をする必要がありません。
● 見た目がかっこいいです。アプリの基本的な機能は使いやすいですが，オプションの高度な機能にお金を払わないと思います。

問1　メーカーの説明によると，この新しい靴をもっともよく表しているものはどれか？　**6**
　①安い夏用の靴
　②先端技術の普段用の靴
　③軽くて快適なスポーツ用の靴
　④おしゃれでカラフルなサイクリング用の靴
　特徴の第1文に「あなたの足の形を分析するナノチップを搭載しています」第3文に「靴を履いている間に，チップにあなたの足に関するデータを収集させます」第4文に「靴の内側があなた個人にあわせた足のサポートを与える

よう自動的に調整されます」第5文に「ルートメモリー機能が搭載されています」など，先端技術が使われていることがわかる。また，利点の運動の促進に「定期的に歩こうという気持ちになります」とあるので普段履く靴であることがわかる。よって，正解は②。

問2　あなたにとってこの靴のどの利点が最も魅力的か？
　7
　①定期的な運動の量が増えること
　②個人に合わせた足のサポート
　③どれくらい早く歩いているかを知ること
　④履くとかっこよく見えること
　リード文に「あなたは学校まで長距離を歩き，よく足が痛くなるのでよい靴を買いたい」とあるので，足が痛くなることが靴を買う理由であることがわかる。また，利点のよりよいバランスに「あなたの立ち方を調整し，あなた個人に合わせたサポートによって，足，脚，背中が痛みから解放されます」とあり，足の痛みがなくなることがわかる。よって，正解は②。

問3　顧客が述べた一つの意見は **8** である。
　①アプリは早歩きを促す
　②アプリの無料機能は使いやすい
　③靴は値段に見合う価値がある
　④靴は自転車をこぐスピードを上げる
　顧客のコメントの7つ目に「アプリの基本的な機能は使いやすいですが，オプションの高度な機能にお金を払わないと思います」とあり，高度な機能は有料で基本的な機能は無料であることがわかる。無料である基本的な機能について使いやすいとあるので，正解は②。

問4　顧客のコメントの一つでオーディオ機器の使用について言及している。このコメントはどの利点に基づくものか？　**9**
　①よりよいバランス
　②運動の促進
　③ルートメモリー
　④ルートオプション
　顧客のコメントの1つ目に私は「案内の方法を選ぶことが出来ることが気に入っており，視覚案内よりも音声案内を使うほうが好きです」とあり，これは利点のルートオプションにある「あなたの現在地をデバイスで見る，イヤホンで案内を自動再生する，スマートウォッチで案内を見るために使うことが出来る」に基づいている。よって，正解は④。

問5　顧客の意見によると，**10** が推奨されている。
　①靴を履くのに慣れるために時間をかけること
　②体重を落とすのを助けるために時計を買うこと
　③靴を履く前にアプリに接続すること
　④ⅰサポートの高度な機能のためにお金を払うこと
　顧客のコメントの3つ目に「今は気に入っていますが，靴に慣れるのに数日かかりました」とあるため，靴に慣れるのに時間がかかることがわかる。よって，正解は①。

B　あなたは生徒会役員の一人です。生徒会役員は生徒たちが時間を有効に使うのを助けるための学生プロジェクトについて話し合っています。アイデアを得るために，あなたはある学校の挑戦についてのレポートを読んでいます。そのレポートは日本の別の学校で勉強している交換留学生によって書かれたものです。

通学チャレンジ

　私の学校では，ほとんどの生徒が学校に来るのにバスか電車を使っています。私は多くの生徒がスマートフォンでゲームをしたりおしゃべりしたりしているのをよく見ます。しかし，彼らはその時間を読書や宿題をするために使うことも出来ます。生徒たちが通学時間をより有効に使うことを助けるために，私たちはこの活動を始めました。生徒たちは1月17日から2月17日までの間，通学活動表を完成させなければなりませんでした。合計300人の生徒が参加しました。3分の2以上が2年生，約4分の1が3年生，1年生は15人だけしか参加しませんでした。1年生の参加者がなぜこんなに少ないのでしょうか。フィードバック（以下）にこの質問に対する答えがあるようです。

参加者からのフィードバック

HS：このプロジェクトのおかげで，私は英語の語彙力テストでこれまでで最高の点数を取ることが出来た。通学時に達成するための小さな目標を立てることは簡単だった。

KF：友達は参加できなくて悲しんでいた。彼女は学校のすぐ近くに住んでいて学校へ歩いて通学している。他の参加方法があった方がよかった。

SS：私が乗る電車はいつも混んでいて立たなくてはならない，だから本やタブレットを開くスペースはなく，私は音声教材のみ使ったが，とても足りなかった。

JH：私は勉強の記録をつけて，自分がどのように自分の時間を使っているか理解することができた。どういう訳か，大部分の1年生の同級生はこのチャレンジについて知らなかったようだ。

MN：私はバスの中の多くの時間を映像を見ることに使った，そしてそれが私が授業をよりよく理解することを助けてくれた。私は時間が過ぎるのがとても早く感じた。

問1　通学チャレンジの狙いは生徒が　11　するのを手助けすることである。
　①より早く通学する
　②テストの点数を改善する
　③英語の授業をよりうまくやっていく
　④彼らの時間をより上手に使う

　レポートの第4文に「生徒たちが通学時間をより有効に使うことを助けるために私たちはこの活動を始めました」とある。よって，正解は④。

問2　通学チャレンジに関するひとつの**事実**は　12　である。
　①1年生の参加者は10%以下だった
　②冬の間2か月行われた
　③生徒たちはバスではポータブル機器を使わなければならなかった
　④参加者の多数は電車で通学している

　レポートの第6文に参加者は300人，1年生の参加者は15人である。これは全体の5%，よって10%以下である。よって，正解は①。

問3　フィードバックによると，参加者によって報告された活動は　13　である。
　A：勉強の記録をつけること
　B：言語を学ぶこと
　C：タブレットでノートを取ること
　D：携帯電話で授業のノートを読むこと
　①AとB　　②AとC　　③AとD
　④BとC　　⑤BとD　　⑥CとD

　フィードバックでHSが「私は英語の語彙力テストでこれまでで最高の点数を取ることが出来た」とあり，言語の学習のBにあたる。また，JHが「私は勉強の記録をつけて」とあり，Aにあたる。よって正しいのはAとBであり，正解は①。

問4　通学チャレンジに関する参加者の意見の一つは　14　である。
　①徒歩で学校に通う生徒も参加できるようにすべきだった
　②電車は本を読むのによい場所だ
　③勉強するための音声教材はたくさんある
　④楽しさのためにビデオを見ることは時間が早く経つことを助ける

　フィードバックでKFが「友達は参加できなくて悲しんでいた。彼女は学校のすぐ近くに住んでいて学校へ歩いて通学している。他の参加方法があった方がよかった。」とあり，正解は①。

問5　筆者の疑問は　15　によって答えられた。
　①HS　　②JH　　③KF　　④MN　　⑤SS

　筆者の疑問とは「1年生の参加者がなぜこんなに少ないのでしょうか」であり，フィードバックでJHが「どういう訳か，大部分の1年生の同級生はこのチャレンジについて知らなかったようだ。」と述べており，これが1年生の参加者が少なかった理由である。よって，正解は②。

第3問

A　あなたはシドニーにあるカンバーフォード大学で勉強しています。あなたはクラスのキャンプ旅行に行く予定で，準備のためにキャンプクラブのニュースレターを読んでいます。

キャンプに行くのですか？私を読んでください！！！

　こんにちは，ケイトリンです。私は最近クラス旅行で得た2つの実践的なキャンプの知識を共有したいです。1つ目は，バックパックを3つの主要部に分け，最も重い物を中間部に置くことでバックパックのバランスをとることです。次に，より頻繁に使う日用品は上部に置くべきだということです。つまり，寝袋を底部に置き，食べ物，調理器具，テントを中間部に，そして服を上部に置くことを意味します。よいバックパックの多くは小さな取りやすい物のために「ブレイン」（追加のポーチ）が備わっています。

　昨年，私たちは夜に野外で料理して食べることを楽しみました。私はキャンプファイアの近くに座っていましたが，テントに戻るまでには凍るように寒くなっていました。寝る前にもう一枚上着を着ましたが，それでも寒かったです。その時，友達が私に寝袋の空間を埋めるために上着を脱いで詰め込むように言いました。この詰め込む方法は私にとって新しい方法でしたが，驚くことに一晩中暖かく過ごすことができました！

私のアドバイスがあなたがたが暖かく快適に過ごすことの助けになることを願っています。キャンプ旅行を楽しんでください！

問1 ケイトリンのアドバイスに従うと，バックパックにどのように詰めるべきですか？ 16
①救急セット，地図
食べ物，皿，カップ，テント
上着，肌着，ズボン
寝袋
②救急セット，地図
上着，肌着，ズボン
食べ物，皿，カップ，テント
寝袋
③食べ物，皿，カップ，テント
救急セット，地図
上着，肌着，ズボン
寝袋
④上着，肌着，ズボン
救急セット，地図
食べ物，皿，カップ，テント
寝袋
ケイトリンは最も重い物を中間部に，小さくてすぐ取れるものをブレインにと言っているので，正解は②。

問2 ケイトリンによると， 17 が一晩中暖かく過ごすための最も良い方法である。
①テントから出ないこと
②キャンプファイアのそばで暖かい食べ物を食べること
③寝袋の空間を埋めること
④余分な衣類をすべて着ること
第2段落第4文～第5文に「友達が私に寝袋の空間を埋めるために上着を脱いで詰め込むように言いました。この詰め込む方法は私にとって新しい方法でしたが，驚くことに一晩中暖かく過ごすことができました！」とあり，正解は③。

B あなたの英語クラブが文化祭で「アドベンチャールーム」を作る予定です。アイデアを得るために，イギリス人男性が作った部屋についてのブログを読んでいます。

あなただけの「ホームアドベンチャー」を作ろう
昨年，私は「アドベンチャールーム」体験に参加しました。私は本当に楽しかったので，子どものためにアドベンチャールームを作りました。あなただけのアドベンチャールームを作るコツがこちらです。

アドベンチャーを作るための重要なステップ
テーマ → 筋書き → 謎 → 衣装

まず，テーマを決めます。息子たちはかなりのシャーロックホームズファンだったので，私は探偵ミステリーにしました。私は家族部屋の家具を配置し直し，古い絵画やランプを加えて場を設定しなければなりませんでした。

次に，筋書きを作ります。私たちは「消えたチョコレート事件」にしました。子どもたちは探偵となり，消えたお菓子のありかを突き止めるため，手がかりを探します。

3つ目のステップは謎と課題を作ることです。解決策から逆算して作業するというのが役に立つ考え方です。もし，課題が3桁の暗証番号の錠前で施錠された箱を開けることであれば，3桁の暗証番号を隠す方法を考えます。古い本はメッセージを隠すのに最適です。謎の文章を作るために異なるページにある単語に線を引くのはとても楽しかったです。謎は最終目標に近付くにつれて難しくすべきことを覚えておいてください。気持ちを盛り上げるために，私は子どもたちに衣装を着せました。長男は私が虫眼鏡を渡したとき，すぐにシャーロックホームズのように振舞い始めました。それから，子どもたちは最初の手がかりを探し始めました。

この「アドベンチャールーム」は私の家族のために特別に設計したものなので，私は個人的な課題をいくつか作りました。最後の課題として，2つのカップを用意してプラスチックのステッカーを貼り，ヨーグルトで満たしました。「探偵たち」は手がかりを明らかにするために底まで食べなければなりませんでした。私の子どもたちは2人ともヨーグルトを食べないので，彼らにとって本当に大変でした。アドベンチャーの間，子どもたちはすっかり集中していてとても楽しそうだったので，来月も行う予定です。

問1 次の出来事（①～④）を起こった順に並べなさい。
18 → 19 → 20 → 21
①子どもたちは好きではない食べ物を食べた
②子どもたちはお菓子の捜索を始めた
③父親は家のリビングに飾りつけをした
④父親は息子たちに着るものを与えた
まず，第2段落第3文に「私は家族部屋の家具を配置し直し，古い絵画やランプを加えて場を設定しなければなりませんでした」とあり，これが③にあたる。次に，第4段落第7文に「気持ちを盛り上げるために，私は子どもたちに衣装を着せました」とあり，これが④にあたる。さらに，第4段落第9文に「子どもたちは最初の手がかりを探し始めました」とあり，これが②にあたる。最後に，第5段落第2文から第4文に「最後の課題として，2つのカップを用意してプラスチックのステッカーを貼り，ヨーグルトで満たしました。「探偵たち」は手がかりを明らかにするために底まで食べなければなりませんでした。私の子どもたちは2人ともヨーグルトを食べないので，彼らにとって本当に大変でした」とあり，これが①にあたる。よって，正解は③→④→②→①。

問2 父親のアドバイスに従ってあなただけの「アドベンチャールーム」を作るとしたら，あなたは 22 べきである。
①3文字の言葉に集中する
②ランプの下に秘密のメッセージを残す
③課題をだんだん難しくする
④シャーロックホームズのように振舞う練習をする
「謎は最終目標に近付くにつれて難しくすべきことを覚えておいてください」とある。よって，正解は③。

問3 この話から，あなたは父親は 23 ということがわかる。

①お菓子を探すことに集中するようになった
②子どもたちのために特別な経験を作った
③アドベンチャーゲームの準備にトラブルがあった
④部屋を飾り付けるのに多くのお金を使った
「この「アドベンチャールーム」は私の家族のために特別に設計した」とある。よって，正解は②。

第4問

あなたの先生はあなたに勉強の効果的な方法についての2つの記事を読むように言っている。あなたは次の授業で何を学ぶかについて議論する。

効果的に勉強する方法：文脈学習！

ティム・オックスフォード
ストーン市立中学校理科教師

理科の教師として，私は常々勉強に苦労している生徒を助ける方法について考えている。最近，私は彼らの主な勉強方法が新たな情報をすべて思い出せるようになるまで繰り返し勉強することだということがわかった。例えば，彼らがテストに向けて勉強していた時，彼らは下の例に示すようなワークブックを使い，空欄に入る用語を繰り返し言っていた「黒曜石は火成岩で，黒っぽくて，ガラス質。黒曜石は，火成岩で，黒っぽくて，ガラス質…」これらの生徒たちはその情報を勉強しているかのように感じているだろうが，すぐに忘れてテストで悪い点数を取る。また，この種の反復学習は退屈でやる気が出ない。

彼らの学習を助けるために，私は「文脈学習」を試しに取り入れてみた。この勉強方法では，新たな知識は生徒自身の経験を通して作り出される。私の理科の授業では，生徒は違う種類の岩の特性を学んだ。ワークブックから用語を覚えるのではなく，私は様々な種類の岩が入った箱を授業に持って行った。生徒たちは岩を調べ，彼らが観察した特徴をもとに名前を特定した。

この経験のおかげで，私は生徒たちは自分たちが学んだ岩の特性をいつでも説明することが出来るようになるだろうと思う。しかし，ひとつ問題なのは，いつも文脈学習をする時間があるとは限らないので，学生たちは今まで通り反復練習をして勉強することになる。私はこれが一番よい方法だとは思わない。私は今もなお彼らの学習を改善する方法を探している。

岩石の名前	黒曜石
岩石の種類	火成岩
色	黒っぽい
質感	ガラス質
写真	

反復学習を効果的にする方法

シェン・リー
ストーン市立大学教授

文脈学習に関するオックスフォード氏の考えは洞察力に富んでいた。私はそれが有益であり得ることには同意する。もっとも，反復もまたうまく機能し得る。しかしながら，彼が論じていた「集中学習」と呼ばれる反復学習の方法は効果的ではない。「分散学習」と呼ばれるもう一つの別の種類の反復学習があり，それは生徒たちが新しい情報を記憶し，より長い間隔をあけて復習する。

勉強の間隔は重要な違いである。オックスフォード氏の例では，彼の生徒たちはおそらく勉強するためにワークブックを使って勉強したのは短い間隔だったのだろう。このような場合，復習を続けるにつれて，内容に注意を払わなくなったのかもしれない。その理由はもはや内容が新しくなく，簡単に無視されることができたからである。対照的に，間隔がより長いと，生徒たちの内容の記憶は弱くなる。それゆえに，以前習った事を思い出すのに大きな努力をしなければならないため，彼らはより多くの注意を払う。例えば，生徒たちがワークブックを勉強するとき，3日待ってもう一度勉強すると，その教材をより理解することができる可能性が高い。

先行研究が分散学習の利点を証明している。ある実験では，AグループとBグループの生徒が50種類の動物の名前を覚えようとした。両グループともに4回学習したが，グループAは1日間隔で，グループBは1週間間隔で学習した。右の図が示すように，最後のセッションの28日後では，名前を記憶していた平均的な割合は分散学習をしたグループの方がより高かった。

私は生徒たちは短い間隔で多くの情報を学習する必要がある場合が多く，勉強の間隔を長くすることが実践的でないかもしれないということは理解している。ただし，集中学習が長期記憶にはよくないということは理解すべきである。

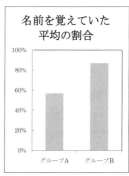

名前を覚えていた平均の割合

問1 オックスフォードは **24** と考えている。
①継続的反復練習は退屈である
②用語の説明を読むことは役に立つ
③生徒たちは理科に興味がない
④ワークブックを使った勉強は成功につながる
オックスフォードの記事の第1段落最後の文で「この種の反復学習は退屈でやる気が出ない。」としている。よって，正解は①。

問2 リーが論じた研究において，生徒は最後のセッションの **25** 後テストを受けた。

①4週間　　②すぐ　　③1日　　④1週間

28日後の最後の学習セッションとある。よって，正解は①。

問3　リーは，オックスフォードが論じた　27　学習の不利な点を克服するため　26　間隔で学習する分散学習を紹介している。（それぞれの空欄に最も適するものを選択肢①〜⑥から選べ。）

①文脈の　　②延長された　　③固定された
④不規則な　　⑤集中した　　⑥実践的な

オックスフォードが論じたのは反復学習のうち「集中学習」であり，その不利な点を学習の間隔を延長することによって克服したのがリーが第1段落第4文で述べている分散学習である。よって　26　に入るのは②，　27　に入るのは⑤。

問4　筆者のどちらも賛成しているのは　28　は新しい情報を覚えることに役に立つことである。

①経験学習　　　②適切な休息
③長期の注意　　④ワークブックで勉強すること

オックスフォードが有効性を主張している文脈学習は経験を通した学習であり，リーも記事の第1段落第1文・第2文で効果的でありうることには賛成している。よって，正解は①。

問5　リーの分散学習に関する主張を支えるのに最適な追加情報はどれか。　29

①理科の授業を魅力的にする要因
②分散学習に最も効果的な間隔の長さ
③生徒のワークブックが画像を含むかどうか
④なぜオックスフォードの生徒が情報をよく覚えられないか

リーの第3段落で，先行研究によれば1日間隔で勉強するよりも1週間間隔で勉強する方が，名前を覚えている割合の平均が高いことが証明されているが，最も効果的な間隔は明らかではないので，それが追加されればよりリーの分散学習の主張を支えることができる。よって，正解は②。

第5問

あなたの英語の先生がクラスのみんなに向けて印象的な物語を見つけ，メモを使ってディスカッショングループにそれを発表するように言った。あなたはイギリスの高校生によって書かれた物語を見つけた。

卓球から得た教訓
ベン・カーター

ボールが電光石火の速さで私のバックハンドに飛んできた。完全に予想外で，私に反応する時間はなかった。私はポイントを失い，試合に負けた。敗北だ…また！卓球を始めた最初の数か月はこのような感じであった。私は歯がゆい思いをしたが，今ではこのスポーツが単によりよい選手になる方法以上のことを私に教えてくれたのだとわかる。

中学校時代，私はサッカーが大好きだった。私は得点王の一人だったが，チームメイトとうまくいっていなかった。コーチはよく，むしろチームプレイヤーになるべきだと言った。私はその課題に取り組むべきだとはわかっていたがコミュニケーションは私の得意分野ではなかった。

私は家族が新しい街に引っ越す際，サッカークラブをやめなければ

ならなかった。私はいずれにせよサッカーをやめようと決めていたので気持ちが動転することはなかった。新しい学校には体育教師のトレント先生がコーチしている卓球部があり，私は卓球部に参加した。正直に言うと，私が卓球部を選んだのは個人競技のほうが私にとってやりやすいと思ったからだ。

最初は，私は勝つよりも負けるほうが多かった。私はイライラして，よく練習が終わった後は何も言わずにまっすぐ家に帰った。しかし，ある日，トレント先生が私に言った。「ベン，君は良い選手になるかもしれないが，自分の試合についてもっと考える必要がある。何をする必要があると思う？」「わかりません。」私は返事をした「もっとボールに集中するとか？」「そうだ。」「しかし君は，相手の動きについても学び，それに応じて君のプレイを対応させる必要がある。君の相手はボールではなく，人間であることを忘れてはいけない。」とトレント先生は続けた。このことは私に深い印象を与えた。

私は相手の動きにより注意を払い，意図的に自分のプレイスタイルを修正した。簡単ではなく，かなりの努力を使ったが，私の努力は報われ，私のプレイは改善した。私は自信を付け，練習の後居残りをするようになった。私はスタープレイヤーになり，クラスメイトは以前より私に話しかけようとした。私は，私が人気になったと思ったが，私たちの会話は盛り上がる前に終わっているようだった。私のプレイは改善したかもしれないが，私のコミュニケーション能力は明らかに改善していなかった。

兄のパトリックは私がうまくコミュニケーションをとれる数少ない人間の一人だった。ある日，私の問題について彼に説明しようとしたが，理解させることができなかった。私たちは話題を卓球のことに切り替えた。「実際，卓球の何が楽しいの？」彼は物珍しそうに聞いた。私は，「相手の動きを分析して瞬時に次の動きを決定するのが好きなんだ」と言った。パトリックは考え込んでいるようだった。「それって，コミュニケーションをとるときのスキルに似てるね」と言った。

その時，私は理解できなかったが，その会話のすぐ後に卓球のトーナメントで銀メダルを勝ち取った。私のクラスメイトは本当に嬉しそうだった。その一人のジョージが走ってきて「やぁ，ベン！」「お祝いパーティーをしよう！」と彼は言った。私は考えることなく「できないよ。練習がある。」と返事をした。彼は少し傷ついたようで，それ以上何も言わずに歩いて去って行った。

彼はなぜ怒ったのか？私はこの出来事について長い間考えていた。なぜ彼はパーティーを提案したのか？私が何か違うことを言うべきだったのか？たくさんの疑問が心に浮かんだが，その後，私は彼がただ親切だったことを理解した。もし私が「いい考えだね，ありがとう！トレント先生に話して，少し練習が休めないか確認してみるよ」と言っていたら，もしかすると良い結果になったかもしれない。その瞬間パトリックの言葉が理解できた。人の意図を理解しようとしない限り，私はどう反応したらよいか理解できないのだ。

私は今も世界で一番コミュニケーションをとるのが上手とは言えないが，確実に今は以前と比べてコミュニケーションスキルにより自信を感じている。来年，私は友達とほかの学校との卓球リーグを設定するつもりだ。

あなたのメモ

卓球から得た教訓

著者について（ベン・カーター）
・中学校ではサッカーをしていた。
・新しい学校で卓球を始めたのは　30　。

他の重要人物
・トレント先生：ベンの卓球のコーチで，彼のプレイを改善することを助けた。
・パトリック：ベンの兄で，　31　。
・ジョージ：ベンのクラスメイトで，彼の勝利を祝いたかった。

ベンがコミュニケーション上手になる旅での影響のあった出来事

卓球を始めた→　32　→　33　→　34　→　35

ベンはパトリックとの会話の後に何を理解したか

彼は □36 すべきだった。

この話から何を学ぶことが出来るか

・□37

・□38

問1 □30 に最適な選択肢を選べ。

①彼のコミュニケーションに役立つと考えたから

②学校で人気者になりたかったから

③簡単に勝てると考えたから

④チームスポーツを避けたかったから

第3段落第5文に「私が卓球部を選んだのは個人競技のほうが私にとってやりやすいと思ったからだ」とある。よって，正解は④。

問2 □31 に最適な選択肢を選べ。

①コミュニケーションをとることの何が楽しいか尋ねた

②もっと自信を持つように励ました

③彼が必要とするソーシャルスキルを学ぶことを助けた

④学校の友達に何を言うべきだったか教えた

第6段落最後の文でベンの卓球の楽しさについて「それって，コミュニケーションをとるときのスキルに似てるね」と発言しており，第8段落第7文第8文で「人の意図を理解しようとしない限り，私はどうやって反応したらよいか理解できないのだ」とパトリックの言葉の意味を理解し，他人とコミュニケーションを取る方法を考えるヒントとなっている。よって，正解は③。

問3 5つの選択肢（①〜⑤）から4つを選び，起こった順に並べ替えなさい。

□32 → □33 → □34 → □35

①卓球のチャンピオンになった

②先生と上手にプレイする方法について話し合った

③お祝いパーティーを断った

④相手について学び始めた

⑤兄と卓球について話した

まず，第4段落でトレント先生とよい選手になるにはどうしたらよいか話し合っているので，②にあたる。次に，第5段落でトレント先生からのアドバイスに従って，相手の動きについて考えているので，④にあたる。さらに，第6段落で兄のパトリックと卓球について話しており，⑤にあたる。最後に第7段落で銀メダルを取った時にクラスメイトのジョージからお祝いパーティーの誘いを受け断っているので③にあたる。ベンは銀メダルを取っているがチャンピオンにはなっていないので①は内容が誤っている。よって，②→④→⑤→③となる。

問4 □36 に最も適する選択肢を選びなさい。

①彼のやる気についてもっと知るために友達に質問すべきだった

②感謝を示すためにトレント先生や他のクラスメイトもパーティーに呼ぶべきだった

③適切な行動をとるために彼の友人の考え方を理解しようとすべきだった

④コミュニケーションを成功させるためチームプレイヤーになる努力をすべきだった

第8段落最後の文に「人の意図を理解しようとしない限り，私はどう反応したらよいか理解できないのだ」とあり，ジョージの意図を考えるべきであったことがわかる。よって，正解は③。

問5 □37 と □38 に入る最も適切な選択肢を選びなさい。（順不同。）

①周りの人間からのアドバイスは私たちが変化することを助ける。

②コミュニケーションが上手になるのに自信は重要だ。

③友達に気持ちを明らかにすることは重要だ。

④チームメイトがお互いにサポートし合うことは役に立つ。

⑤私たちはあることから学んだことを別のことに応用することができる。

まず，負けることの方が多かったベンが第4段落のトレント先生のアドバイスによって第5段落ではスタープレイヤーになっているのであるから，①は正しい。次に，第6段落でベンの「相手の動きを分析して瞬時に次の動きを決定するのが好きだ」という発言に対し，パトリックが「それって，コミュニケーションをとるときのスキルに似てるね」と言っており，第8段落最後の文でベンもこの言葉の意味を理解し，第9段落第1文で「今は以前と比べてコミュニケーションスキルにより自信を感じている」とあり，卓球での相手の動きを分析する能力をコミュニケーションに応用することができると言えるので⑤も正しい。よって，正解は①と⑤。

第6問

A あなたは学校のディスカッショングループに入っている。あなたは以下の記事を要約するように頼まれている。あなたはメモだけを使ってそのことについて話すつもりである。

収　集

　収集は文化や世代を超え，昔から社会のあらゆるレベルに存在してきた。博物館は物が収集され，保存され，伝承されてきたことの証拠である。収集を始める理由は様々なものが存在する。例えば，Ａさんは毎週土曜に子どもと一緒にヤードセールに行くことを楽しむ。ヤードセールでは，いらないものを自分の家の前で売る。ある日，アンティークのお皿を探しているうちに，ある珍しい絵に目を奪われ彼女はわずか数ドルで購入した。ゆっくり時間をかけて，彼女は印象に残った似た作品を見つけ，今では，彼女はささやかなコレクションを持っている。それらの中には彼女が支払ったよりも価値があるものもあるかもしれない。ある人にとってのごみが他の人にとっては宝物になり

得る。どのように収集が始まったかにかかわらず，物を集めることは人間本来の性質である。

　1988年，研究者であるブレンダ・ダネットとタマル・カトリエルが10歳未満の子どもについて80年間の研究を分析したところ，子どもの約90％が何かを集めていることがわかった。このことから，人は幼い段階から何かを集めるのが好きであることがわかる。大人になってからも，人は物を収集することを続ける。この分野の研究者は成人のおよそ３分の１がこの習性を維持しているということについておおむね賛成している。これはなぜか？主な説明では感情に関係しているとされている。友達や家族からのグリーティングカード，特別なイベントのドライフラワー，ある日砂浜で拾った貝殻，古い写真など，様々なものをとっておく人もいる。他の人にとっては，収集が自身の若いときにつながるものとなる場合もある。彼らは野球カード，漫画，人形，ミニカーなど小さな頃からずっと持っているかもしれない。歴史への愛着を持つ人もいて，彼らは歴史的な文書，有名な人物からの署名入りの書簡や直筆のサイン，などを探し求めて放さない。

　人それぞれに社会的な理由がある場合もある。人はピンバッジのようなものを集めて，共有したり，見せたり，交換さえしたりして，この方法で友達を作る。他にも，ギネスの世界記録保持者のように，独特な収集で名声を得るものもいる。カード，ステッカー，切手，コイン，そしておもちゃは「普通の」コレクションの頂点にあるが，もっと予想外のものに傾倒する収集家もいる。2014年９月，ギネス世界記録は，ドイツのハリー・シュペールを，Ｔシャツ，枕，犬のおもちゃに至るまで3724点の世界で最も多くのハンバーガーに関するコレクションを持っていると認定した。シュペールの部屋は全てハンバーガーに関するもので満たされている。同様に，中国のリウ・フーチャンはトランプの収集家で，11087組の違うトランプを持っている。

　おそらく，最もわかりやすい動機は喜びである。純粋に楽しみのために収集を始める人もいる。彼らはただ頻繁に眺めるためだけに絵画を購入して飾ったり，音源や古めかしいビニールで包まれたレコードを集めて，お気に入りの音楽を聴くことを楽しんだりするかもしれない。このタイプの収集家は自分たちの大切な音楽の金銭的な価値にそれほど興味がない傾向にあるが，一方，特に投資として集める人もいる。ある古典的なゲームは無料でダウンロードすることができるが，オリジナルのパッケージのまま開けずに持っていること，「ミントコンディション」で，ゲームの価値を大きくする。様々な価値のある「コレクターズアイテム」はある程度経済的な安全を確保することができる。

　この，物を収集するという行動は遠い未来まで確実に続くだろう。なぜ物を集めるかという理由が変わらず続いたとしても，技術の進歩はコレクションに影響を与えるだろう。技術は物理的な制約を取り除くことができるので，今では30年前には考えられなかった膨大な量の音楽や芸術作品のデジタルライブラリーを各自持つことができる。しか

し，技術がコレクションに与える他の影響は不明である。次世代のコレクションの形態や規模を想像することができるだろうか？

あなたのメモ

> **収集**
>
> 紹介
> ◆ 収集は長く人間の経験の一部となってきた。
> ◆ ヤードセールの話は 39 。
>
> 事実
> ◆ 40
> ◆ ギネス世界記録
> ◇ シュペール：3724点のハンバーガーに関連するもの
> ◇ リウ：11087組のトランプ
>
> 収集の理由
> ◆ 収集の動機は，感情によるものと社会的理由によるものがあり得る
> ◆ 様々な理由が言及されている 41 ， 42 ，歴史への興味，子ども時代の興奮，有名になること，共有，など
>
> 収集の未来
> ◆ 43

問１ 39 に最も適する選択肢を選びなさい。
①コレクターに高い金額で物を売るのに最適な場所はヤードセールである
②人々は商品に誤った評価をしてしまう可能性がある，結局がらくたにお金を払いすぎてしまう
③ある人にとって重要でないものが他の人にとって価値があることがある
④いったん収集し，他の人の庭に投げ込まれたものは他の人にとっては価値がある
　第１段落第８文に「ある人にとってのごみが他の人にとっては宝物になり得る」とあり，正解は③。

問２ 40 に最も適する選択肢を選びなさい。
①約３分の２の子どもが普通の物を集めていない
②約３分の１の大人が喜びのために収集を始めている
③約10％の子どもが友達と似たコレクションを持っている
④約30％の人が大人になっても収集を続けている
　第２段落第３文に「大人になってからも，人は物を収集することを続ける。」第４文に「この分野の研究者は成人のおよそ３分の１がこの習性を維持しているということについておおむね賛成している」とあり，正解は④。

問３ 41 と 42 に最も適する選択肢を選びなさい。
　（順不同。）
①先端技術への欲望
②予期せぬ機会損失への恐れ
③空白を埋める感覚
④大切な出来事を思い出させるもの
⑤未来のために物を再利用すること
⑥なんらかの利益を探すこと

第2段落第5文第6文に「これはなぜか？主な説明では感情に関係しているとされている」「友達や家族からのグリーティングカード，特別なイベントのドライフラワー，ある日砂浜で拾った貝殻，古い写真など，様々なものをとっておく人もいる」とありこれが④にあたり，第4段落第4文に「特に投資として集める人もいる」同第6文に「様々な価値のある「コレクターズアイテム」はある程度経済的安全を確保することができる。」とあり，これが⑥にあたる。

問4　43 に最も適する選択肢を選びなさい。
　　①収集は規模や形態が変わり続けていきそうである。
　　②ミントコンディションのゲームのコレクターはそれらのより多くのデジタルコピーを持つだろう。
　　③収集への情熱を失った人々が再び収集を始めるだろう。
　　④収集の理由は技術の進歩によって変わるだろう。
　　第5段落第4文第5文に「しかし，技術がコレクションに与える他の影響は不明である。次世代の収集の形態や規模を想像することができるだろうか？」とあり，収集の形態や規模が変化するであろうことが示唆されている。よって正解は①。

B　あなたは国際科学発表コンテストの準備をするグループに所属しています。あなたは驚くべき生き物についての発表のあなたの担当する部分を作るために以下の文章を使っています。

　世界で最も頑丈な動物の名前は何かと聞くと，摂氏50度もの高温まで耐えられるフタコブラクダか，マイナス58度以下の低温まで耐えられるホッキョクギツネと答えるかもしれません。しかし，どちらの答えも間違っている，クマムシが地球で最も頑丈な動物であると広く考えられているからである。

　クマムシは水のクマとして知られる微生物であり，その体長は0.1ミリメートルから1.5ミリメートルである。彼らは標高6,000メートルの山から海面下4,600メートルまで，大体どこでも生きることができる。クマムシは厚い氷の下や温泉の中でさえ見つけることができる。ほとんどのクマムシは水の中に生息しているが，地球で最も乾燥している場所でも見つけることができる。ある研究者は25年間雨が記録されていない砂漠の岩の下でクマムシを発見したと報告している。クマムシは何滴かの水か，薄い水の層がありさえすれば生きていくことができる。水が干上がると，クマムシも干上がる。彼らが3パーセント以外の水分を失うと，彼らの代謝は通常のスピードの0.01パーセントまで落ちる。干からびたクマムシは「樽」と呼ばれる一種の深い眠りの状態にある。この状態は再び水に浸かるまで続く。そのとき，スポンジのように水を吸収し，再び何事もなかったかのように息を吹き返す。クマムシは樽の状態が1週間であろうと10年間であろうとたいした問題ではない。水に囲まれた瞬間，クマムシは再びよみがえる。クマムシ

が樽の状態のとき，クマムシはマイナス272度から151度までの温度で生き延びられるほど頑丈である。クマムシがどうやってこれを達成しているかはいまだ完全には解明されていない。

　おそらく，5億4000万年以上存在しているというクマムシの地球上での生存能力よりもいっそう驚くべきは，宇宙空間での生存能力である。2007年，ヨーロッパの研究者たちがたくさんの生きたクマムシをロケットの外側に載せて宇宙空間に送り出した。地球に戻ってきたとき，クマムシの68パーセントがまだ生きていたのを見て研究者たちは驚いた。これは，10日間，ほとんどのクマムシが，地球上で浴びる1000倍以上の激しいX線や紫外線の放射の中生き延びたことを意味する。その後，2019年にイスラエルの宇宙船が月面に衝突し，何千万の樽の状態のクマムシが表面にばらまかれた。誰も収集しに行っていないので，これらのクマムシが生きているかどうかはわからない，これは残念だ。

　クマムシは，短いキュウリのような形をしている。クマムシは体の両側に4本ずつ短い脚がある。足の先端にはねばねばした足の裏を持つ種や，爪がある種もいる。16の爪のバリエーションが知られており，爪をもつ種の識別をするのに役立つ。すべてのクマムシは目のための場所はあるが，すべての種が目を持っているわけではない。クマムシの目は原始的で，全部で5つの細胞しかなく，それらのうちたった1つの細胞だけが光を感じることができる。

　基本的に，クマムシは植物を食べるものと，それ以外の動物を食べるものにわけることができる。植物を食べる種は腹口，すなわちサメのように顔の一番下にある口を持っている。他の動物を食べる種は端子口，すなわちマグロのように顔の真正面にある口を持っている。クマムシの口は歯がない。しかし，尖刺棘と呼ばれる2本の鋭いとげを持っており，植物の細胞や，より小さな動物の体を突き刺して内容物を吸い出す。

　どちらのタイプのクマムシも単純な消化器系を持っている。口は咽頭（のど）につながり，消化液と食べ物が混ぜ合わせられる。咽頭の上に位置するのが唾液腺である。これは口に注ぎ，消化を助ける液体を作る。咽頭の後は，食べ物を腸に運ぶ管がある。この管は食道と呼ばれる。中腸は胃と腸のような器官で，食べ物を消化し，栄養を吸収する。残されたものは最終的に肛門へと移動する。

あなたの発表のスライド

	1．基本的な情報
	・体長0.1ミリメートルから1.5ミリメートル
クマムシ：	・短いキュウリのような形
地球の究極の生存者	・
	44
	・
	・

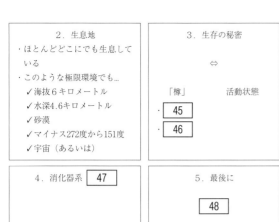

2．生息地	3．生存の秘密
・ほとんどどこにでも生息している ・このような極限環境でも… ✓海抜6キロメートル ✓水深4.6キロメートル ✓砂漠 ✓マイナス272度から151度 ✓宇宙（あるいは）	⇔ 「樽」　　　活動状態 ・　45 ・　46

4．消化器系　47	5．最後に 48

問1　 44 　に含めるべきでないものは以下のうちどれか？

① 8本の短い脚

② 目が見えるか見えないか

③ 植物を食べるか，動物を食べるか

④ 16種類の足

⑤ 歯ではなく2本の尖刺棘

　クマムシの基本的な情報に含めるべきでないものを選ぶ。第4段落第3文に「16の爪のバリエーションが知られており」とあり，16種類あるのは足ではなく爪なので④は誤り。よって，正解は④。

問2　生存の秘密のスライドのために，生存に最も役に立っているクマムシの2つの特徴を選びなさい。（順不同。）
45 ・ 46

① 乾燥状態では，彼らの代謝は通常時の1パーセント未満に落ちる。

② クマムシは樽状態で151度以上の温度まで生存することができる。

③ クマムシの体の水分が0.01パーセント以上になると，樽状態は終わる。

④ 彼らのサメのような口は他の動物を食べることを可能にする。

⑤ 彼らは極度の放射線に耐えることができる能力がある。

　第2段落第8文に「彼らが3パーセント以外の水分を失うと，彼らの代謝は通常のスピードの0.01パーセントまで落ちる」とあり，①は正しい。同第13文に「クマムシが樽の状態のとき，彼らはマイナス272度から151度までの温度で生き延びられるほど頑丈である」とあり，151度を超えても生存できる訳ではなく，②は誤り。同第10文に「この状態（＝樽状態）は再び水に浸かるまで続く」とあり，水分が0.01パーセント以上になると終わるわけではないので，③は誤り。第5段落第2文に「植物を食べる種は腹口，すなわちサメのように顔の一番下にある口を持っている」とあり，サメのような口は動物ではなく植物を食べるのに適しているので，④は誤り。第3段落第4文に「10日間，ほとんどのクマムシが，地球上で浴びる1000倍以上の激しいX線や紫外線の放射の中生き延びたことを意味する」とあり，⑤は正しい。よって，正解は①と⑤。

問3　消化器系スライドのクマムシのイラストの空欄を埋めなさい。 47

① (A) 食道　　(B) 咽頭　　(C) 中腸
　 (D) 尖刺棘　(E) 唾液腺

② (A) 咽頭　　(B) 尖刺棘　(C) 唾液腺
　 (D) 食道　　(E) 中腸

③ (A) 唾液腺　(B) 食道　　(C) 中腸
　 (D) 尖刺棘　(E) 咽頭

④ (A) 唾液腺　(B) 中腸　　(C) 尖刺棘
　 (D) 食道　　(E) 咽頭

⑤ (A) 尖刺棘　(B) 唾液腺　(C) 咽頭
　 (D) 中腸　　(E) 食道

　第5段落第4文・第5文に「クマムシの口は歯がない。しかし，尖刺棘と呼ばれる2本の鋭いとげを持っており」とあるので(D)は尖刺棘である。第6段落第2文・第3文に「口は咽頭（のど）につながり，…咽頭の上に位置するのが唾液腺である」とあるので(E)が咽頭，(A)が唾液腺である。第6段落第5文・第6文に「咽頭の後は，食べ物を腸に運ぶ管がある。この管は食道と呼ばれる」とあるので(B)は食道，(C)は中腸である。よって，正解は③。

問4　最後のスライドに最も適する記述を選びなさい。
48

① 何千年もの間，クマムシは地球や宇宙で厳しい環境を生き抜いてきた。彼らは人類よりも長く生存し続けるだろう。

② クマムシは宇宙から来て，ホッキョクギツネやフタコブラクダの限界を超えた温度で生存することができる。だから彼らは間違いなく人間よりも強い。

③ クマムシは，紛れもなく，地球上で最も頑丈な生き物である。彼らは山の頂上，海の底，温泉の水の中，月の上でも繁栄することができる。

④ クマムシは地球で最も厳しい環境で，そして，少なくとも1回宇宙への旅行を生き抜いた。この驚くべき生き物は人類よりも長生きするかもしれない。

　クマムシは何千年もの間宇宙を生き抜いてはいないので①は誤り，クマムシは宇宙から来ていないので②は誤り，第3段落第6文よりクマムシが月の上でも繁栄することができるかは確認できていないので③は誤り。第2段落第2文から第5文に「彼らは標高6,000メートルの山から海面下4,600メートルまで，大体どこでも生きることができる。クマムシは厚い氷の下や温泉の中でさえ見つけることができる。…地球で最も乾燥している場所でも見つけることができる。ある研究者は25年間雨が記録されていない砂漠の岩の下でクマムシを発見したと報告している」とあり，地球上の厳しい環境で生き抜いてきたことがわかる。また，第3段落第2文第3文に「2007年，ヨーロッパの研究者たちがたくさんの生きたクマムシをロケットの外側に載せて宇宙空間に送り出した。地球に戻ってきたとき，クマムシの68パーセントがまだ生きていたのを見て研究者たちは驚いた。」とあり，一度宇宙に行って生還している。

よって正解は④。

問 5 クマムシを宇宙に送ったことについて何が推測される
か？ 49

①クマムシが宇宙で生きることができるかどうかにつ
いてわかることは重要であると考えられていなかった。

②クマムシは，他の生き物と共に数百万年もの間存在
し，X線や紫外線に耐えることができる。

③イスラエルの研究者たちはここまで多くのクマムシが宇
宙の厳しい環境で生存できるとは予想していなかった。

④クマムシが月面で生きているかどうかを誰も確かめな
かった理由は筆者の興味をひいた。

　第3段落第2文に「2007年。ヨーロッパの研究者たちが
たくさんの生きたクマムシをロケットの外側に載せて宇宙
空間に送り出した。地球に戻ってきたとき，クマムシの68
パーセントがまだ生きていたのを見て研究者たちは驚い
た」とあり，研究者チームが宇宙でクマムシが生存できる
か確かめる実験を行ったことがわかるので，重要と考えて
いなかった訳ではない，よって①は誤り。「10日間，ほと
んどのクマムシが，地球上で浴びる1000倍以上の激しいX
線や紫外線の放射の中生き延びたことを意味する」のでク
マムシが強いX線や紫外線を浴びても生存することができ
ることはわかるが，地球でどうだったかはわからないので
②は誤り。「多くのクマムシが生存しているのを見て驚い
た（＝予想していなかった）」のはヨーロッパの研究チー
ムであるから，③は誤り。「イスラエルの宇宙船が月面に
衝突し，何千万の樽の状態のクマムシが表面にばらまかれ
た。誰も収集しに行っていないので，これらのクマムシが
生きているかどうかはわからない，これは残念だ。」とあ
り，筆者の興味を引いていることがわかる。

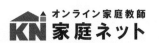

大学入学共通テスト

問題・解答解説

外　国　語　〔英　語(リーディング)〕　$\begin{bmatrix}100点\\80分\end{bmatrix}$

無料質問ができる　'とらサポ'

虎の巻の問題で「わからない」「質問したい」ときは、
"とらサポ" におまかせください！

【仮登録】→【本登録】→【会員番号発行】→質問開始！

左の QR コードが読み取れない方は、下記の URL へアクセスして下さい。

http://www.jukentaisaku.com/sup_free/

※ドメイン拒否設定をされている方は、〔本登録〕の URL が届きませんので解除して下さい。

（解答番号　1　～　49　）

各大問の英文や図表を読み，解答番号　1　～　49　にあてはまるものとして最も適当な選択肢を選びなさい。

第1問 （配点　10）

A　You are studying English at a language school in the US. The school is planning an event. You want to attend, so you are reading the flyer.

The Thorpe English Language School

International Night

Friday, May 24, 5 p.m.-8 p.m.

Entrance Fee: $5

The Thorpe English Language School (TELS) is organizing an international exchange event. TELS students don't need to pay the entrance fee. Please present your student ID at the reception desk in the Student Lobby.

● **Enjoy foods from various parts of the world**

　Have you ever tasted hummus from the Middle East? How about tacos from Mexico? Couscous from North Africa? Try them all!

● **Experience different languages and new ways to communicate**

　Write basic expressions such as "hello" and "thank you" in Arabic, Italian, Japanese, and Spanish. Learn how people from these cultures use facial expressions and their hands to communicate.

● **Watch dance performances**

　From 7 p.m. watch flamenco, hula, and samba dance shows on the stage! After each dance, performers will teach some basic steps. Please join in.

Lots of pictures, flags, maps, textiles, crafts, and games will be displayed in the hall. If you have some pictures or items from your home country which can be displayed at the event, let a school staff member know by May 17!

問1　To join the event free of charge, you must 　1　.

① bring pictures from your home country

② consult a staff member about the display

③ fill out a form in the Student Lobby

④ show proof that you are a TELS student

問2　At the event, you can 　2　.

① learn about gestures in various cultures

② participate in a dance competition

③ read short stories in foreign languages

④ try cooking international dishes

B You are an exchange student in the US and next week your class will go on a day trip. The teacher has provided some information.

Tours of Yentonville

The Yentonville Tourist Office offers three city tours.

The History Tour

The day will begin with a visit to St. Patrick's Church, which was built when the city was established in the mid-1800s. Opposite the church is the early-20th-century Mayor's House. There will be a tour of the house and its beautiful garden. Finally, cross the city by public bus and visit the Peace Park. Opened soon after World War II, it was the site of many demonstrations in the 1960s.

The Arts Tour

The morning will be spent in the Yentonville Arts District. We will begin in the Art Gallery where there are many paintings from Europe and the US. After lunch, enjoy a concert across the street at the Bruton Concert Hall before walking a short distance to the Artists' Avenue. This part of the district was developed several years ago when new artists' studios and the nearby Sculpture Park were created. Watch artists at work in their studios and afterwards wander around the park, finding sculptures among the trees.

The Sports Tour

First thing in the morning, you can watch the Yentonville Lions football team training at their open-air facility in the suburbs. In the afternoon, travel by subway to the Yentonville Hockey Arena, completed last fall. Spend some time in its exhibition hall to learn about the arena's unique design. Finally, enjoy a professional hockey game in the arena.

Yentonville Tourist Office, January, 2024

問1 Yentonville has 3 .

① a church built 250 years ago when the city was constructed

② a unique football training facility in the center of the town

③ an art studio where visitors can create original works of art

④ an arts area with both an art gallery and a concert hall

問2 On all three tours, you will 4 .

① learn about historic events in the city   ② see people demonstrate their skills

③ spend time both indoors and outdoors   ④ use public transportation to get around

問3 Which is the newest place in Yentonville you can visit on the tours? 5

① The Hockey Arena   ② The Mayor's House

③ The Peace Park   ④ The Sculpture Park

第2問 (配点 20)

A You are an exchange student at a high school in the UK and find this flyer.

 Invitation to the Strategy Game Club

Have you ever wanted to learn strategy games like chess, *shogi*, or *go*? They are actually more than just games. You can learn skills such as thinking logically and deeply without distractions. Plus, these games are really fun! This club is open to all students of our school. Regardless of skill level, you are welcome to join.

We play strategy games together and...

- learn basic moves from demonstrations by club members
- play online against club friends
- share tips on our club webpage
- learn the history and etiquette of each game
- analyse games using computer software
- participate in local and national tournaments

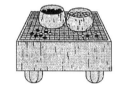

Regular meetings: Wednesday afternoons in Room 301, Student Centre

- -

Member Comments

- My mind is clearer, calmer, and more focused in class.
- It's cool to learn how some games have certain similarities.
- At tournaments, I like discussing strategies with other participants.
- Members share Internet videos that explain practical strategies for chess.
- It's nice to have friends who give good advice about *go*.
- I was a complete beginner when I joined, and I had no problem!

問1 According to the flyer, which is true about the club? [6]

① Absolute beginners are welcome.

② Members edit computer programs.

③ Professional players give formal demonstrations.

④ Students from other schools can join.

問2 Which of the following is **not** mentioned as a club activity? [7]

① Having games with non-club members ② Playing matches against computers

③ Sharing game-playing ideas on the Internet ④ Studying the backgrounds of strategy games

問3 One **opinion** stated by a member is that [8].

① comparing different games is interesting ② many videos about *go* are useful

③ members learn tips at competitions ④ regular meetings are held off campus

問4　The club invitation and a member's comment both mention that ⬚9⬚ .

　① new members must demonstrate experience

　② online support is necessary to be a good player

　③ *shogi* is a logical and stimulating game

　④ strategy games help improve one's concentration

問5　This club is most likely suitable for students who want to ⬚10⬚ .

　① create their own computer strategy games

　② improve their skill level of playing strategy games

　③ learn proper British etiquette through playing strategy games

　④ spend weekends playing strategy games in the club room

B　You are a college student going to study in the US and need travel insurance. You find this review of an insurance plan written by a female international student who studied in the US for six months.

There are many things to consider before traveling abroad: pack appropriate clothes, prepare your travel expenses, and don't forget medication (if necessary). Also, you should purchase travel insurance.

When I studied at Fairville University in California, I bought travel insurance from TravSafer International. I signed up online in less than 15 minutes and was immediately covered. They accept any form of payment, usually on a monthly basis. There were three plans. All plans include a one-time health check-up.

The Premium Plan is $100/month. The plan provides 24-hour medical support through a smartphone app and telephone service. Immediate financial support will be authorized if you need to stay in a hospital.

The Standard Plan worked best for me. It had the 24-hour telephone assistance and included a weekly email with tips for staying healthy in a foreign country. It wasn't cheap: $75/month. However, it was nice to get the optional 15% discount because I paid for six months of coverage in advance.

If your budget is limited, you can choose the Economy Plan, which is $25/month. It has the 24-hour telephone support like the other plans but only covers emergency care. Also, they can arrange a taxi to a hospital at a reduced cost if considered necessary by the support center.

I never got sick or hurt, so I thought it was a waste of money to get insurance. Then my friend from Brazil broke his leg while playing soccer and had to spend a few days in a hospital. He had chosen the Premium Plan and it covered everything! I realized how important insurance is—you know that you will be supported when you are in trouble.

問1　According to the review, which of the following is true?　[11]
① Day and night medical assistance is available with the most expensive plan.
② The cheapest plan includes free hospitalization for any reason.
③ The mid-level plan does not include the one-time health check-up.
④ The writer's plan cost her over $100 every month.

問2　Which is **not** included in the cheapest option?　[12]
① Email support
② Emergency treatment
③ Telephone help desk
④ Transport assistance

問3　Which is the best combination that describes TravSafer International?　[13]
A : They allow monthly payments.
B : They design scholarship plans for students.
C : They help you remember your medication.
D : They offer an Internet-based registration system.
E : They require a few days to process the application form.

① A and D　　　② A and E　　　③ B and D
④ B and E　　　⑤ C and D

問4　The writer's **opinion** of her chosen plan is that [14] .
① it prevented her from being health conscious
② she was not satisfied with the telephone assistance
③ the option for cost reduction was attractive
④ the treatment for her broken leg was covered

問5　Which of the following best describes the writer's attitude?　[15]
① She believes the smartphone app is useful.
② She considers travel preparation to be important.
③ She feels the US medical system is unique in the world.
④ She thinks a different hospital would have been better for her friend.

第3問 (配点 15)

A Susan, your English ALT's sister, visited your class last month. Now back in the UK, she wrote on her blog about an event she took part in.

Hi!

I participated in a photo rally for foreign tourists with my friends: See the rules on the right. As photo rally beginners, we decided to aim for only five of the checkpoints. In three minutes, we arrived at our first target, the city museum. In quick succession, we made the second, third, and fourth targets. Things were going smoothly! But, on the way to the last target, the statue of a famous samurai from the city, we got lost. Time was running out and my feet were hurting from walking for over two hours. We stopped a man with a pet monkey for help, but neither our Japanese nor his English were good enough. After he'd explained the way using gestures, we realised we wouldn't have enough time to get there and would have to give up. We took a photo with him and said goodbye. When we got back to Sakura City Hall, we were surprised to hear that the winning team had completed 19 checkpoints. One of our photos was selected to be on the event website (click here). It reminds me of the man's warmth and kindness: our own "gold medal."

Sakura City Photo Rally Rules

- Each group can only use the **camera** and **paper map**, both provided by us
- Take as many photos of **25 checkpoints** (designated sightseeing spots) as possible
- **3-hour** time limit
- Photos must include **all 3 team members**
- All members must move **together**
- **No** mobile phones
- **No** transport

問1 You click the link in the blog. Which picture appears? ☐ 16

①

②

③

④

問2 You are asked to comment on Susan's blog. Which would be an appropriate comment to her? ☐ 17

① I want to see a picture of you wearing the gold medal!

② You did your best. Come back to Japan and try again!

③ You reached 19 checkpoints in three hours? Really? Wow!!

④ Your photo is great! Did you upgrade you phone?

B You are going to participate in an English Day. As preparation, you are reading an article in the school newspaper written by Yuzu, who took part in it last year.

Virtual Field Trip to a South Sea Island

This year, for our English Day, we participated in a virtual science tour. The winter weather had been terrible, so we were excited to see the tropical scenery of the volcanic island projected on the screen.

First, we "took a road trip" to learn about the geography of the island, using navigation software to view the route. We "got into the car," which our teacher, Mr Leach, sometimes stopped so we could look out of the window and get a better sense of the rainforest. Afterwards, we asked Mr Leach about what we'd seen.

Later, we "dived into the ocean" and learnt about the diversity of marine creatures. We observed a coral reef via a live camera. Mr Leach asked us if we could count the number of creatures, but there were too many! Then he showed us an image of the ocean 10 years ago. The reef we'd seen on camera was dynamic, but in the photo it was even more full of life. It looked so different after only 10 years! Mr Leach told us human activity was affecting the ocean and it could be totally ruined if we didn't act now.

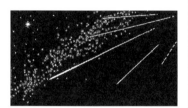

In the evening, we studied astronomy under a "perfect starry sky." We put up tents in the gymnasium and created a temporary planetarium on the ceiling using a projector. We were fascinated by the sky full of constellations, shooting stars, and the Milky Way. Someone pointed out one of the brightest lights and asked Mr Leach if it was Venus, a planet close to Earth. He nodded and explained that humans have created so much artificial light that hardly anything is visible in our city's night sky.

On my way home after school, the weather had improved and the sky was now cloudless. I looked up at the moonless sky and realised what Mr Leach had told us was true.

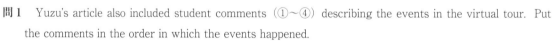

問1　Yuzu's article also included student comments (①~④) describing the events in the virtual tour. Put the comments in the order in which the events happened.

| 18 | → | 19 | → | 20 | → | 21 |

① I was wondering how dangerous the island was. I saw beautiful birds and a huge snake in the jungle.

② It was really shocking that there had been many more creatures before. We should protect our beautiful oceans!

③ Setting up a camping site in the gymnasium was kind of weird, but great fun! Better than outside, because we weren't bitten by bugs!

④ We were lost for words during the space show and realised we often don't notice things even though they're there.

問2　From the tour, Yuzu did **not** learn about the ⎵22⎵ of the south sea island.

① marine ecosystem　　② night-time sky　　③ seasonal weather　　④ trees and plants

問3　On the way home, Yuzu looked up and most likely saw ⎵23⎵ in the night sky.

① a shooting star　　② just a few stars　　③ the full moon　　④ the Milky Way

Your college English club's room has several problems and you want to redesign it. Based on the following article and the results of a questionnaire given to members, you make a handout for a group discussion.

What Makes a Good Classroom?
Diana Bashworth, writer at *Trends in Education*

As many schools work to improve their classrooms, it is important to have some ideas for making design decisions. SIN, which stands for *Stimulation, Individualization,* and *Naturalness,* is a framework that might be helpful to consider when designing classrooms.

The first, Stimulation, has two aspects: color and complexity. This has to do with the ceiling, floor, walls, and interior furnishings. For example, a classroom that lacks colors might be uninteresting. On the other hand, a classroom should not be too colorful. A bright color could be used on one wall, on the floor, window coverings, or furniture. In addition, it can be visually distracting to have too many things displayed on walls. It is suggested that 20 to 30 percent of wall space remain free.

The next item in the framework is Individualization, which includes two considerations: ownership and flexibility. Ownership refers to whether the classroom feels personalized. Examples of this include having chairs and desks that are suitable for student sizes and ages, and providing storage space and areas for displaying student works or projects. Flexibility is about having a classroom that allows for different kinds of activities.

Naturalness relates to the quality and quantity of light, both natural and artificial, and the temperature of the classroom. Too much natural light may make screens and boards difficult to see; students may have difficulty reading or writing if there is a lack of light. In addition, hot summer classrooms do not promote effective study. Schools should install systems allowing for the adjustment of both light and temperature.

While Naturalness is more familiar to us, and therefore often considered the priority, the other components are equally important. Hopefully, these ideas can guide your project to a successful end.

Results of the Questionnaire

Q1: Chose any items that match your use of the English club's room.

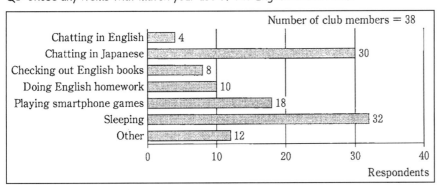

Number of club members = 38

Item	Respondents
Chatting in English	4
Chatting in Japanese	30
Checking out English books	8
Doing English homework	10
Playing smartphone games	18
Sleeping	32
Other	12

Q2: What do you think about the current English club's room?

Main comments:

Student 1 (S1): I can't see the projector screen and whiteboard well on a sunny day. Also, there's no way to control the temperature.

S2: By the windows, the sunlight makes it hard to read. The other side of the room doesn't get enough light. Also, the books are disorganized and the walls are covered with posters. It makes me feel uncomfortable.

S3: The chairs don't really fit me and the desks are hard to move when we work in small groups. Also, lots of members speak Japanese, even though it's an English club.

S4: The pictures of foreign countries on the walls make me want to speak English. Everyone likes the sofas — they are so comfortable that we often use the room for sleeping!

S5: The room is so far away, so I hardly ever go there! Aren't there other rooms available?

S6: There's so much gray in the room. I don't like it. But it's good that there are plenty of everyday English phrases on the walls!

Your discussion handout:

Room Improvement Project

■ **SIN Framework**
- What it is: ☐ 24 ☐
- SIN = Stimulation, Individualization, Naturalness

■ **Design Recommendations Based on SIN and Questionnaire Results**
- Stimulation:

  Cover the floor with a colorful rug and ☐ 25 ☐.

- Individualization:

  Replace room furniture.

  (tables with wheels → easy to move around)

- Naturalness:

  ☐ 26 ☐

  A. Install blinds on windows.   B. Make temperature control possible.

  C. Move projector screen away from windows.   D. Place sofas near walls.

  E. Put floor lamp in darker corner.

■ **Other Issues to Discuss**
- The majority of members ☐ 27 ☐ the room as ☐ 28 ☐ 's comment mentioned. How can we solve this?
- Based on both the graph and ☐ 29 ☐ 's comment, should we set a language rule in the room to motivate members to speak English more?
- S5 doesn't like the location, but we can't change the room, so let's think about how to encourage members to visit more often.

問1　Choose the best option for ☐ 24 ☐.

① A guide to show which colors are appropriate to use in classrooms

② A method to prioritize the needs of students and teachers in classrooms

③ A model to follow when planning classroom environments

④ A system to understand how classrooms influence students' performance

問2　Choose the best option for ☐ 25 ☐.

① move the screen to a better place   ② paint each wall a different color

③ put books on shelves   ④ reduce displayed items

問3　You are checking the handout. You notice an error in the recommendations under Naturalness. Which of the following should you **remove**?　26

①　A　　　②　B　　　③　C　　　④　D　　　⑤　E

問4　Choose the best options for　27　and　28　.

27

①　borrow books from　　　②　can't easily get to　　　③　don't use Japanese in

④　feel anxious in　　　⑤　take naps in

28

①　S1　　　②　S2　　　③　S3　　　④　S4　　　⑤　S5　　　⑥　S6

問5　Choose the best option for　29　.

①　S1　　　②　S2　　　③　S3　　　④　S4　　　⑤　S5　　　⑥　S6

You are in an English discussion group, and it is your turn to introduce a story. You have found a story in an English language magazine in Japan. You are preparing notes for your presentation.

Maki's Kitchen

"*Irasshai-mase*," said Maki as two customers entered her restaurant, Maki's Kitchen. Maki had joined her family business at the age of 19 when her father became ill. After he recovered, Maki decided to continue. Eventually, Maki's parents retired and she became the owner. Maki had many regular customers who came not only for the delicious food, but also to sit at the counter and talk to her. Although her business was doing very well, Maki occasionally daydreamed about doing something different.

"Can we sit at the counter?" she heard. It was her old friends, Takuya and Kasumi. A phone call a few weeks earlier from Kasumi to Takuya had given them the idea to visit Maki and surprise her.

Takuya's phone vibrated, and he saw a familiar name, Kasumi.

"Kasumi!"

"Hi Takuya, I saw you in the newspaper. Congratulations!"

"Thanks. Hey, you weren't at our 20th high school reunion last month."

"No, I couldn't make it. I can't believe it's been 20 years since we graduated. Actually, I was calling to ask if you've seen Maki recently."

Takuya's family had moved to Kawanaka Town shortly before he started high school. He joined the drama club, where he met Maki and Kasumi. The three became inseparable. After graduation, Takuya left Kawanaka to become an actor, while Maki and Kasumi remained. Maki had decided she wanted to study at university and enrolled in a preparatory school. Kasumi, on the other hand, started her career. Takuya tried out for various acting roles but was constantly rejected; eventually, he quit.

Exactly one year after graduation, Takuya returned to Kawanaka with his dreams destroyed. He called Maki, who offered her sympathy. He was surprised to learn that Maki had abandoned her plan to attend university because she had to manage her family's restaurant. Her first day of work had been the day he called. For some reason, Takuya could not resist giving Maki some advice.

"Maki, I've always thought your family's restaurant should change the coffee it serves. I think people in Kawanaka want a bolder flavor. I'd be happy to recommend a different brand," he said.

"Takuya, you really know your coffee. Hey, I was walking by Café Kawanaka and saw a help-wanted sign. You should apply!" Maki replied.

Takuya was hired by café Kawanaka and became fascinated by the science of coffee making. On the one-year anniversary of his employment, Takuya was talking to Maki at her restaurant.

"Maki," he said, "do you know what my dream is?"

"It must have something to do with coffee."

"That's right! It's to have my own coffee business."

"I can't imagine a better person for it. What are you waiting for?"

Maki's encouragement inspired Takuya. He quit his job, purchased a coffee bean roaster, and began roasting beans. Maki had a sign in her restaurant saying, "We proudly serve Takuya's Coffee," and this publicity helped the coffee gain popularity in Kawanaka. Takuya started making good money selling his beans. Eventually, he opened his own café and became a successful business owner.

Kasumi was reading the newspaper when she saw the headline: *TAKUYA'S CAFÉ ATTRACTING TOURISTS TO KAWANAKA TOWN*. "Who would have thought that Takuya would be so successful?" Kasumi thought to herself as she reflected on her past.

In the high school drama club, Kasumi's duty was to put make-up on the actors. No one could do it better than her. Maki noticed this and saw that a cosmetics company called Beautella was advertising for salespeople. She encouraged Kasumi to apply, and, after graduation, she became an employee of Beautella.

The work was tough; Kasumi went door to door selling cosmetics. On bad days, she would call Maki, who would lift her spirits. One day, Maki had an idea, "Doesn't Beautella do make-up workshops? I think you are more suited for that. You can show people how to use the make-up. They'll love the way they look and buy lots of cosmetics!"

Kasumi's company agreed to let her do workshops, and they were a hit! Kasumi's sales were so good that eight months out of high school, she had been promoted, moving to the big city of Ishijima. Since then, she had steadily climbed her way up the company ladder until she had been named vice-president of Beautella this year.

"I wouldn't be vice-president now without Maki," she thought, "she helped me when I was struggling, but I was too absorbed with my work in Ishijima to give her support when she had to quit her preparatory school." Glancing back to the article, she decided to call Takuya.

"Maki wasn't at the reunion. I haven't seen her in ages," said Takuya.

"Same here. It's a pity. Where would we be without her?" asked Kasumi.

The conversation became silent, as they wordlessly communicated their guilt. Then, Kasumi had an idea.

The three friends were talking and laughing when Maki asked, "By the way, I'm really happy to see you two, but what brings you here?"

"Payback," said Takuya.

"Have I done something wrong?" asked Maki.

"No. The opposite. You understand people incredibly well. You can identify others' strengths and show them how to make use of them. We're proof of this. You made us aware of our gifts," said Takuya.

"The irony is that you couldn't do the same for yourself," added Kasumi.

"I think Ishijima University would be ideal for you. It offers a degree program in counseling that's designed for people with jobs," said Takuya.

"You'd have to go there a few times a month, but you could stay with me. Also, Takuya can help you find staff for your restaurant," said Kasumi.

Maki closed her eyes and imagined Kawanaka having both "Maki's Kitchen" and "Maki's Counseling." She liked that idea.

Your notes:

Maki's Kitchen

Story outline

Maki, Takuya, and Kasumi graduate from high school.

↓
- [30]
- [31]
- [32]
- [33]

Maki begins to think about a second career.

About Maki
- Age: [34]
- Occupation: restaurant owner
- How she supported her friends:

  Provided Takuya with encouragement and [35].

  〃　　Kasumi　〃　　　〃　　and [36].

Interpretation of key moments
- Kasumi and Takuya experience an uncomfortable silence on the phone because they [37].
- In the final scene, Kasumi uses the word "irony" with Maki. The <u>irony</u> is that Maki does not [38].

問1　Choose **four** out of the five events (①〜⑤) and rearrange them in the order they happened.

[30] → [31] → [32] → [33]

① Kasumi becomes vice-president of her company.　② Kasumi gets in touch with Takuya.

③ Maki gets her university degree.　④ Maki starts working in her family business.

⑤ Takuya is inspired to start his own business.

問2　Choose the best option for [34].

① early 30s　② late 30s　③ early 40s　④ late 40s

問3　Choose the best options for [35] and [36].

① made the product known to people　② proposed a successful business idea

③ purchased equipment for the business　④ suggested moving to a bigger city

⑤ taught the necessary skills for success

問4　Choose the best option for [37].

① do not want to discuss their success　② have not spoken in a long time

③ regret not appreciating their friend more　④ think Maki was envious of their achievements

問5　Choose the best option for [38].

① like to try different things　② recognize her own talent

③ understand the ability she lacks　④ want to pursue her dreams

A Your English teacher has assigned this article to you. You need to prepare notes to give a short talk.

Perceptions of Time

When you hear the word "time," it is probably hours, minutes, and seconds that immediately come to mind. In the late 19th century, however, philosopher Henri Bergson described how people usually do not experience time as it is measured by clocks (**clock time**). Humans do not have a known biological mechanism to measure clock time, so they use mental processes instead. This is called **psychological time**, which everyone perceives differently.

If you were asked how long it had taken to finish your homework, you probably would not know exactly. You would think back and make an estimate. In a 1975 experiment, participants were shown either simple or complex shapes for a fixed amount of time and asked to memorize them. Afterwards, they were asked how long they had looked at the shapes. To answer, they used a mental process called **retrospective timing**, which is estimating time based on the information retrieved from memory. Participants who were shown the complex shapes felt the time was longer, while the people who saw the simple shapes experienced the opposite.

Another process to measure psychological time is called **prospective timing**. It is used when you are actively keeping track of time while doing something. Instead of using the amount of information recalled, the level of attention given to time while doing the activity is used. In several studies, the participants performed tasks while estimating the time needed to complete them. Time seemed shorter for the people doing more challenging mental activities which required them to place more focus on the task than on time. Time felt longer for the participants who did simpler tasks and the longest for those who were waiting or doing nothing.

Your emotional state can influence your awareness of time, too. For example, you can be enjoying a concert so much that you forget about time. Afterwards, you are shocked that hours have passed by in what seemed to be the blink of an eye. To explain this, we often say, "Time flies when you're having fun." The opposite occurs when you are bored. Instead of being focused on an activity, you notice the time. It seems to go very slowly as you cannot wait for your boredom to end. Fear also affects our perception of time. In a 2006 study, more than 60 people experienced skydiving for the first time. Participants with high levels of unpleasant emotions perceived the time spent skydiving to be much longer than it was in reality.

Psychological time also seems to move differently during life stages. Children constantly encounter new information and have new experiences, which makes each day memorable and seem longer when recalled. Also, time creeps by for them as they anticipate upcoming events such as birthdays and trips. For most adults, unknown information is rarely encountered and new experiences become less frequent, so less mental focus is required and each day becomes less memorable. However, this is not always the case. Daily routines are shaken up when drastic changes occur, such as changing jobs or relocating to a new city. In such cases, the passage of time for those people is similar to that for children. But generally speaking, time seems to accelerate as we mature.

Knowledge of psychological time can be helpful in our daily lives, as it may help us deal with boredom. Because time passes slowly when we are not mentally focused and thinking about time, changing to a more engaging activity, such as reading a book, will help ease our boredom and speed up the time. The next occasion that you hear "Time flies when you're having fun," you will be reminded of this.

Your notes:

```
                  Perceptions of Time
Outline by paragraph
  1.  [ 39 ]
  2.  Retrospective timing
  3.  Prospective timing
  4.  [ 40 ]
       ➤ Skydiving
  5.  Effects of age
       ➤ Time speeds up as we mature, but a [ 41 ].
  6.  Practical tips

My original examples to help the audience
  A.  Retrospective timing
      Example: [ 42 ]
  B.  Prospective timing
      Example: [ 43 ]
```

問1　Choose the best options for [39] and [40].

① Biological mechanisms　② Effects of our feelings　③ Kinds of memory

④ Life stages　　　　　　 ⑤ Ongoing research　　　 ⑥ Types of time

問2　Choose the best option for [41].

① major lifestyle change at any age will likely make time slow down

② major lifestyle change regardless of age will likely make time speed up

③ minor lifestyle change for adults will likely make time slow down

④ minor lifestyle change for children will likely make time speed up

問3　Choose the best option for [42].

① anticipating a message from a classmate

② memorizing your mother's cellphone number

③ reflecting on how many hours you worked today

④ remembering that you have a meeting tomorrow

問4　Choose the best option for [43].

① guessing how long you've been jogging so far

② making a schedule for the basketball team summer camp

③ running into your tennis coach at the railway station

④ thinking about your last family vacation to a hot spring

B You are preparing a presentation for your science club, using the following passage from a science website.

Chili Peppers: The Spice of Life

Tiny pieces of red spice in chili chicken add a nice touch of color, but biting into even a small piece can make a person's mouth burn as if it were on fire. While some people love this, others want to avoid the painful sensation. At the same time, though, they can eat sashimi with wasabi. This might lead one to wonder what spiciness actually is and to ask where the difference between chili and wasabi comes from.

Unlike sweetness, saltiness, and sourness, spiciness is not a taste. In fact, we do not actually taste heat, or spiciness, when we eat spicy foods. The bite we feel from eating chili peppers and wasabi is derived from different types of compounds. Chili peppers get their heat from a heavier,oil-like element called capsaicin. Capsaicin leaves a lingering, fire-like sensation in our mouths because it triggers a receptor called TRPV1. TRPV1 induces stress and tells us when something is burning our mouths. Interestingly, there is a wide range of heat across the different varieties of chili peppers, and the level depends on the amount of capsaicin they contain. This is measured using the Scoville Scale, which is also called Scoville Heat Units (SHU). SHUs range from the sweet and mild *shishito* pepper at 50-200 SHUs to the Carolina Reaper pepper, which can reach up to 2.2 million.

Wasabi is considered a root, not a pepper, and does not contain capsaicin. Thus, wasabi is not ranked on the Scoville Scale. However, people have compared the level of spice in it to chilis with around 1,000 SHUs, which is on the lower end of the scale. The reason some people cannot tolerate chili spice but can eat foods flavored with wasabi is that the spice compounds in it are low in density. The compounds in wasabi vaporize easily, delivering a blast of spiciness to our nose when we eat it.

Consuming chili peppers can have positive effects on our health, and much research has been conducted into the benefits of capsaicin. When capsaicin activates the TRPV1 receptor in a person's body, it is similar to what happens when they experience stress or pain from an injury. Strangely, capsaicin can also make pain go away. Scientists found that TRPV1 ceases to be turned on after long-term exposure to chili peppers, temporarily easing painful sensations. Thus, skin creams containing capsaicin might be useful for people who experience muscle aches.

Another benefit of eating chili peppers is that they accelerate the metabolism.   A group of researchers analyzed 90 studies on capsaicin and body weight and found that people had a reduced appetite when they ate spicy foods. This is because spicy foods increase the heart rate, send more energy to the muscles, and convert fat into energy. Recently, scientists at the University of Wyoming have created a weight-loss drug with capsaicin as a main ingredient.

It is also believed that chili peppers are connected with food safety, which might lead to a healthier life. When food is left outside of a refrigerated environment, microorganisms multiply on it, which may cause sickness if eaten. Studies have shown that capsaicin and other chemicals found in chili peppers have antibacterial properties that can slow down or even stop microorganism growth. As a result, food lasts longer and there are fewer food-borne illnesses. This may explain why people in hot climates have a tendency to use more chili peppers, and therefore, be more tolerant of spicier foods due to repeated exposure. Also, in the past, before there were refrigerators, they were less likely to have food poisoning than people in cooler climates.

Chili peppers seem to have health benefits, but can they also be bad for our health? Peppers that are high on the Scoville Scale can cause physical discomfort when eaten in large quantities. People who have eaten several of the world's hottest chilis in a short time have reported experiencing upset stomachs, diarrhea, numb hands, and symptoms similar to a heart attack. Ghost peppers, which contain one million SHUs, can even burn a person's skin if they are touched.

Luckily the discomfort some people feel after eating spicy foods tends to go away soon—usually within a few hours. Despite some negative side effects, spicy foods remain popular around the world and add a flavorful touch to the table. Remember, it is safe to consume spicy foods, but you might want to be careful about the amount of peppers you put in your dishes.

Presentation slides:

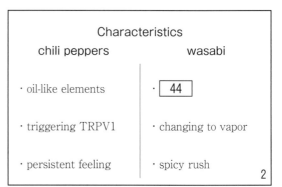

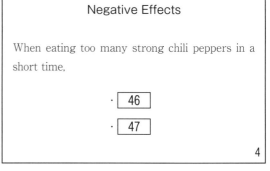

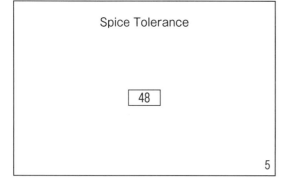

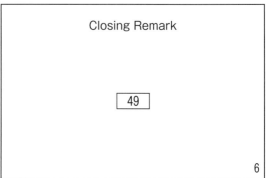

問1　What is the first characteristic of wasabi on Slide 2?　44

①　burning taste　　②　fire-like sensation　　③　lasting feeling　　④　light compounds

問2　Which is an **error** you found on Slide 3?　45

①　A　　②　B　　③　C　　④　D　　⑤　E

問3　Choose two options for Slide 4.　(The order does not matter.)　46　・　47

①　you might activate harmful bacteria.　　②　you might experience stomach pain.

③　you might lose feeling in your hands.　　④　your fingers might feel like they are on fire.

⑤　your nose might start hurting.

問4　What can be inferred about tolerance for spices for Slide 5?　48

①　People with a high tolerance to chili peppers pay attention to the spices used in their food.

②　People with a high tolerance to wasabi are scared of chili peppers' negative effects.

③　People with a low tolerance to chili peppers can get used to their heat.

④　People with a low tolerance to wasabi cannot endure high SHU levels.

問5　Choose the most appropriate remark for Slide 6.　49

①　Don't be afraid.　Eating spicy foods will boost your confidence.

②　Next time you eat chili chicken, remember its punch only stays for a second.

③　Personality plays a big role in our spice preference, so don't worry.

④　Unfortunately, there are no cures for a low wasabi tolerance.

⑤　When someone offers you some spicy food, remember it has some benefits.

筆記〈リーディング〉			
	解答番号	正　解	配　点
R6 ①A	1	④	2
	2	①	2
R6 ①B	3	④	2
	4	③	2
	5	①	2
R6 ②A	6	①	2
	7	②	2
	8	①	2
	9	④	2
	10	②	2
R6 ②B	11	①	2
	12	①	2
	13	①	2
	14	③	2
	15	②	2
R6 ③A	16	②	3
	17	②	3
R6 ③B	18	①	3*
	19	②	
	20	③	
	21	④	
	22	③	3
	23	②	3
R6 ④	24	③	3
	25	④	3
	26	④	3
	27	⑤	2
	28	④	2
	29	③	3
R6 ⑤	30	④	3*
	31	⑤	
	32	①	
	33	②	
	34	②	3
	35	①	3*
	36	②	
	37	③	3
	38	②	3
R6 ⑥A	39	⑥	3*
	40	②	
	41	①	3
	42	③	3
	43	①	3
R6 ⑥B	44	④	2
	45	④	2
	46－47	②－③	3*
	48	③	3
	49	⑤	2

（注）　1　＊は，全部正解の場合のみ点
を与える。
2　－（ハイフン）でつながれた
正解は，順序を問わない。

第1問

A あなたはアメリカにある言語学校で英語を学んでいます。その学校がイベントを計画しています。あなたは出席したいと考えており、チラシを読んでいます。

ソープ英語学校
インターナショナル・ナイト
5月24日金曜日　午後5時 – 午後8時
入場料：5ドル

ソープ英語学校（TELS）は国際交流イベントを開催します。TELSの生徒は入場料を支払う必要はありません。学生ロビーにある受付で学生証をご提示ください。

● **世界各地の食べ物を楽しみましょう**
中東のフムスを食べたことはありますか？メキシコのタコスはどうですか？北アフリカのクスクスは？全部試してみてください！

● **様々な言語や新しいコミュニケーション方法を体験しましょう**
「こんにちは」「ありがとう」などの基本的な表現をアラビア語、イタリア語、日本語、スペイン語で書きましょう。これらの文化を背景に持つ人々が意思を伝えるためにどのように表情や手を使うのか学びましょう。

● **ダンスを見ましょう**
午後7時からフラメンコ、フラ、サンバのステージを見ましょう。それぞれのダンスが終わった後、パフォーマーが基本のステップを教えます。どうぞご参加ください。

ホールでは、たくさんの写真、旗、布、工芸品、ゲームが展示されます。イベントで展示することができる母国の写真や品物をお持ちの方は5月17日までに学校スタッフまでお知らせください！

問1 イベントに無料で参加するためには、　**1**　必要がある。

1　母国の写真を持ってくる
2　展示についてスタッフに相談する
3　学生ロビーの申込用紙を書く
4　TELSの生徒であることの証明を見せる

本文第2文にTELSの生徒は入場料を払わなくてよいとあり、その条件として第3文に「学生証（＝TELSの学生であることの証明）を提示してください」とあるので、正解は4。

問2 イベントでは、　**2**　ことができる。

1　さまざまな文化でのジェスチャーについて学ぶ
2　ダンス大会に参加する
3　外国語で書かれた短編小説を読む
4　国際的な料理を作ることに挑戦する

本文2つ目の●第2文に「これらの文化を背景に持つ人々が意思を伝えるためにどのように表情や手を使うのか学びましょう」とあり、選択肢の「さまざまな文化でのジェスチャーについて学ぶ」がその書き換え。よって、正解は1。

B あなたはアメリカにいる交換留学生で、来週あなたのクラスは日帰り旅行に行く予定です。先生はいくつかの情報を提供しました。

イェントンビルのツアー
イェントンビル観光局は3つのツアーを提供します。

歴史ツアー
聖パトリック教会への訪問で一日は始まります。この教会は市が1800年代半ばに設立された時に建てられました。教会の反対側にあるのは20世紀初頭の市長の家です。家とその美しい庭のツアーも予定されています。最後に、公共のバスで市内を横断し、平和公園を訪れます。平和公園は第二次世界大戦後すぐに開園し、1960年代に多くのデモが行われた場所でした。

芸術ツアー
朝はイェントンビル芸術地区で過ごします。まずはヨーロッパやアメリカの多くの絵画があるギャラリーから始めます。昼食の後、通りの向かいにあるブルトン・コンサートホールでコンサートを楽しみましょう。その後、アーティスト通りまで少し歩きます。この地区は新しい芸術家のスタジオやその近くにある彫刻公園ができた年である数年前に開発されました。彼らのスタジオで芸術家の制作活動を鑑賞した後は、公園を散策し木々の中で彫刻を見つけましょう。

スポーツツアー
朝一番に、郊外にある屋外施設でフットボールチームであるイェントンビル・ライオンズのトレーニングを見ることができます。午後は、地下鉄で昨年の秋に完成したイェントンビル・ホッケーアリーナへ向かいましょう。展示ホールでしばらくこのアリーナのユニークなデザインについて学びましょう。最後はアリーナでプロホッケーの試合を楽しみましょう。

イェントンビル観光局、2024年1月

問1 イェントンビルには　**3**　がある。

1　市が作られた年である250年前に建てられた教会
2　市の中心部にあるユニークなフットボールのトレーニングセンター
3　訪問者がオリジナルの芸術作品を作ることができるアートスタジオ
4　ギャラリーとコンサートホールの両方がある芸術エリア

芸術ツアーの説明第2文に「ヨーロッパやアメリカの多くの絵画があるギャラリー」、第3文に「通りの向かいにあるブルトン・コンサートホール」とあるので正解は4。

問2 3つのツアー全てで、あなたは　**4**　だろう。

1　市の歴史的な出来事を学ぶ
2　人々が技術を実演するのを見る
3　屋内と屋外の両方で過ごす
4　移動に公共の交通機関を使う

歴史ツアーでは、説明の第3文に「家（＝屋内）とその美しい庭（＝屋外）のツアーも予定されています」とある。芸術ツアーでは、説明の第2文で「アートギャラリー（＝屋内）」、第3文で「コンサートホール（＝屋内）」、第4文で「芸術家のスタジオ（＝屋内）」、第5文で「彫刻公園（＝屋外）」に行くとある。スポーツツアーでは、説明の第1文で「屋外の施設（＝屋外）」、第3文に「展示ホール（＝屋内）」、第4文に「アリーナ（＝屋内）」に行くとあるので、3つ全てのツアーで屋内と屋外の両方で過ごすと言える。よって、正解は3。

問3　あなたがツアーで訪れることができる場所のうち最も新しいものはどれか？　5
　　1　ホッケーアリーナ
　　2　市長の家
　　3　平和公園
　　4　彫刻公園
　　ホッケーアリーナはスポーツツアーの説明の第2文に「昨年の秋に完成した」，市長の家は歴史ツアーの説明の第2文に「20世紀初頭の市長の家」とあり，平和公園は歴史ツアーの説明第5文に「第二次世界大戦後すぐ」，彫刻公園は芸術ツアー第4文より「彫刻公園ができた年である数年前」とある。よって，最も新しいのは昨年の秋に完成したホッケーアリーナであり，正解は1。

第2問

A　あなたはイギリスの高校で学んでいる交換留学生で，このチラシをみつけました。

戦術ゲームクラブへのご招待

チェス，将棋，碁のような戦略ゲームを学びたいと思ったことはありますか？それらは実はただのゲームではありません。あなたは気を散らすことなく，論理的に深く考える能力を学ぶことができます。それに加えて，これらのゲームは本当に面白いです！当クラブは本校の生徒全員が参加することができます。スキルレベルは問わず，参加を歓迎いたします。

私たちは戦術ゲームを一緒に遊び…
● クラブのメンバーの実演によって，基本的な動きを学びます。
● クラブの友達とオンラインで対戦します。
● クラブのウェブページでコツを共有します。
● それぞれのゲームの歴史と礼儀作法を学びます。
● コンピュータのソフトウェアを使ってゲームを分析します。
● 地方トーナメントや全国トーナメントに参加します。

定例会議：水曜の午後，学生センター301号室

- -

メンバーのコメント

– 思考がクリアに，穏やかに，そしてより授業に集中するようになった。
– いくつかのゲームには一定の類似性があることを学ぶのはすばらしい。
– トーナメントで，他の参加者と戦略について議論することが好きです。
– メンバーはチェスの実践的な戦略を説明するビデオを共有します。
– 碁についてよいアドバイスをくれる友達を持つことはいいことです。
– 私は参加した当初は全くの初心者だったのですが，問題はありませんでした！

問1　チラシによるとクラブについて正しいものはどれか。　6
　　1　全くの初心者も歓迎である。
　　2　メンバーはコンピュータプログラムを編集する。
　　3　プロのプレイヤーは正式な実演をしてくれる。
　　4　他の学校の生徒も参加できる。
　　チラシの本文第6文に「スキルレベルは問わず，参加を歓迎いたします。」とあり，選択肢の「全くの初心者も歓

迎である」はこの書き換え。よって，正解は1。

問2　クラブの活動として言及されて**いない**ものはどれか。　7
　　1　非クラブメンバーとゲームをすること
　　2　コンピュータと対戦すること
　　3　ゲームプレイのアイディアをインターネットで共有すること
　　4　戦術ゲームの背景を学ぶこと
　　チラシの6つ目の●に「地方トーナメントや全国トーナメントに参加します」とあり，非クラブメンバーとゲームをすることがわかる。また，チラシの3つ目の●に「クラブのウェブページでコツを共有します」とあり，選択肢の「ゲームプレイのアイディアをインターネット上で共有する」がこの書き換え。チラシの4つ目の●に「それぞれのゲームの歴史と礼儀作法について学ぶ」とあり，選択肢の「戦術ゲームの背景を学ぶ」がこの書き換え。選択肢2はチラシに書かれておらず，正解は2。

問3　メンバーによって述べられている**意見**は　8　である。
　　1　違うゲームを比較することは面白い
　　2　碁についての多くのビデオは役に立つ
　　3　メンバーは大会でコツを学ぶ
　　4　定例会議はキャンパス外で開かれる
　　メンバーのコメントの2つ目に「いくつかのゲームには一定の類似性があることを学ぶのはすばらしい」とあり，選択肢の「違うゲームを比較することは面白い」はこの書き換え。よって，正解は1。

問4　このクラブへの招待文とメンバーのコメントの両方で言及しているのは　9　である。
　　1　新しいメンバーは経験を示さなければならない
　　2　よいプレイヤーであるためにはオンラインサポートが必要である
　　3　将棋は論理的で刺激的なゲームである
　　4　戦略ゲームは集中力を改善することを助ける
　　招待文の第3文に「あなたは気を散らすことなく，論理的に深く考える能力を学ぶことができます」とあり，メンバーコメントの1つ目に「思考がクリアに，穏やかに，そしてより授業に集中するようになった」とあり，正解は4。

問5　このクラブは　10　たい生徒に最も向いている。
　　1　自分のパソコンで戦術ゲームを作り
　　2　戦術ゲームの技術のレベルを向上させ
　　3　戦術ゲームを通して適切なイギリスの礼儀作法を学び
　　4　週末をクラブの部屋で戦術ゲームをするのに使い
　　チラシの1つ目の●に「クラブのメンバーの実演によって，基本的な動きを学びます」，3つ目の●に「クラブのウェブページでコツを共有します」，5つ目の●に「コンピュータのソフトウェアを使ってゲームを分析します」とあり，初心者には基本的な動きを学び，中上級者にはコツの共有やゲームの分析によって戦術ゲームの技術を向上させようとしていることがわかる。よって，正解は2。

※イギリスの高校の交換留学生の話なのでイギリス英語が使われていることに注意。

招待文5つ目の●「分析する」

　英：analyse ⇔ 米：analyze

招待文最後の行「センター」

　英：centre ⇔ 米：center

B　あなたはアメリカに留学している大学生で旅行保険を必要としています。あなたはアメリカで6か月勉強している留学生の女性の保険プランのレビューをみつけました。

海外旅行する前に考えなければならないことがたくさんあります。つまり，適切な服を詰めること，旅行費用を準備すること，そして（必要があれば）薬を忘れないことです。また，旅行保険に加入すべきです。

私がカリフォルニアのフェアヴィル大学に留学していたとき，私はトラブセーファーインターナショナルの旅行保険に加入しました。オンラインで15分もかからず申し込むことができ，すぐに適用されました。どのような支払方法も可能で，たいていは月単位の支払です。3つのプランがあり，全てのプランは1回の健康診断を含んでいます。

プレミアムプランは月額100ドルです。このプランは24時間受付のスマートフォンのアプリと電話サービスを通した健康サポートを提供しています。病院に入院しなければならない場合は即時の金融サポートを受けることができます。

スタンダードプランは私に最も合っていました。このプランは24時間受付の電話アシスタントがあり，外国で健康に過ごすためのヒントが書かれたEメールが毎週届きます。月額75ドルは安くはありませんでした。しかし，6か月分の前払いをしたので15パーセント割引を受けることができてよかったです。

もし，予算が限られているのであれば，エコノミープランを選ぶことができ，このプランは月額25ドルです。このプランは他のプランと同じように24時間の電話受付サービスがありますが，救急医療にしか適用されません。また，サポートセンターが必要と判断した場合は病院までのタクシーを割引料金で手配してくれます。

私は病気になったり，けがをしたりすることはありませんでした，だから保険に加入することはお金の無駄だと思っていました。そんな時，ブラジルから来た友人がサッカーをしている時に足を骨折し，病院で2～3日入院することになりました。彼はプレミアムプランに加入していて，全てが補償されました。私は保険がいかに重要であるかを理解しました。保険は自分が困ったときに助けてくれるものなのです。

問1　レビューによると，以下のうち正しいものはどれか？
　　　11
　　1　最も高いプランでは昼夜問わずの医療サポートを受けることができる。
　　2　最も安いプランはいかなる理由でも適用される無料の入院保障がある。
　　3　中級レベルのプランは1回限りの健康診断を含まない。
　　4　レビューの筆者のプランは毎月100ドル以上かかる。
　　第3段落第2文に「24時間受付のスマートフォンのアプ

リと電話サービス」とあり，選択肢の「昼夜問わずの医療サポート」がこの書き換え。よって，正解は1。

問2　最も安いプランに含まれ**ない**ものはどれか？　12
　　1　Eメールサポート
　　2　救急治療
　　3　電話のヘルプデスク
　　4　輸送サポート
　　最も安いのは第5段落の月額25ドルのプランであり，その保障内容は同第2文の「24時間の電話受付サービス」「救急医療」，同第3文「病院までのタクシーを割引料金で手配」＝「輸送サポート」であり，1のEメールサポートのみが保障内容に含まれない。よって，正解は1。

問3　トラブセーファーインターナショナルについての記述で最も適切な組み合わせはどれか？　13
　　A：月払いが可能である。
　　B：学生のための奨学生プランを設計している。
　　C：薬について思い出させてくれる。
　　D：インターネットベースの登録システムを提供している。
　　E：申請書の処理に2～3日かかる。
　　1　AとD　　2　AとE　　3　BとD
　　4　BとE　　5　CとD
　　第2段落第3文に「どのような支払方法も可能で，たいていは月単位の支払です」とありAは正しい。第2段落第2文に「オンラインで15分もかからず申し込むことができ」とあり，Dは正しい。よって，正解は1。

問4　自分が選んだプランに関する筆者の**意見**は　14　。
　　1　そのプランのせいで健康を意識することができなかった
　　2　電話サポートに満足していない
　　3　割引のオプションは魅力的だ
　　4　彼女の足の骨折の治療費はカバーされた
　　第4段落第4文「15％割引を受けることができてよかった」とあり，選択肢の「割引のオプションは魅力的だ」はこの書き換え。よって，正解は3。

問5　筆者の態度をもっともよく説明しているのはどれか？
　　　15
　　1　スマートフォンのアプリは便利だと思っている。
　　2　旅行の準備は重要だと考えている。
　　3　アメリカの医療制度は世界では独特だと感じている。
　　4　友人には別の病院のほうがよかったと思っている。
　　第1段落第1文「海外旅行する前に考えなければならないことがたくさんある」とあり，その後に具体的な準備の内容が書かれているので，旅行の準備は重要だと考えていることがわかる。よって，正解は2。

第3問

A　あなたのALTの妹であるスーザンが先月あなたのクラスを訪れました。今はイギリスに戻っていて，彼女は自分が参加したあるイベントについてブログを書きました。

こんにちは！
私は外国人旅行者向けのフォトラリーに友人達と参加しました：右のルールをご覧ください。フォトラリーは初心者なので，私たちは５つのチェックポイントだけを目指すことを決めました。3分以内に私たちは最初の目標に到着しました。立て続けに2つ目，3つ目，4つ目の目標に到着しました。物事は順調に進んでいました！しかし，最後の目標である，この町出身の有名な侍の像に向かう途中，

さくら市フォトラリーのルール
・それぞれのグループは私たちから提供された**カメラと紙の地図**のみを使うことができます
・**25のチェックポイント**（指定された観光スポット）の写真をできるだけ多く撮ってください
・制限時間は**3時間**です
・写真は**チーム3人全員**が写っていなければなりません
・全てのメンバーは**一緒に移動**しなければなりません
・**携帯電話の使用禁止**
・**交通機関の使用禁止**

私たちは道に迷ってしまいました。時間は迫っていて，私の足は2時間歩きっぱなしで痛くなっていました。私たちは助けてもらうためにペットのサルと一緒の男性を呼び止めましたが，私たちの日本語力も彼の英語力も十分ではありませんでした。彼がジェスチャーを使って説明してくれた後，私たちは最後の目標に行くのに十分な時間はなく，あきらめなければならないことがわかりました。私たちは彼と一緒に写真を撮って別れを告げました。私たちがさくら市庁舎に戻ったとき，優勝チームは19個のチェックポイントをクリアしたと聞いて驚きました。私たちの写真の1枚がイベントのウェブサイトに掲載されることになりました（ここをクリック）。その写真は男性の暖かさや優しさを私に思い出させてくれ，そして，それが私たちの「金メダル」なのです。

問1 ブログのリンクをクリックするとどの写真が表示されますか？ 16

まず，写っている人物について，ブログの最後の文に写真がサルを連れた男性の暖かさや優しさを思い出させてくれるとあるので，サルを連れた男性が写っているものを選ぶ。

次に，写真の背景について，第11文・第12文に男性と写真を撮り，別れを告げてからさくら市庁舎に戻ったとあるので，背景はさくら市庁舎ではない。よって正解は2。

問2 あなたはスーザンのブログにコメントするよう頼まれています。彼女への適切なコメントはどれですか？ 17

1 私はあなたが金メダルをかけている写真が見たいです。

2 あなたは最善を尽くしました。日本に戻ってもう一度挑戦しましょう！

3 3時間で19箇所のチェックポイントを回ったのですか？本当？すごい！！

4 あなたの写真はすばらしい！携帯電話をアップグレードしたのですか？

ブログ第14文に男性の暖かさと優しさが金メダルであると書かれており，スーザンのチームは優勝して金メダルをもらったわけではないので1は誤り。第12文より19個のチェックポイントを回ったのはスーザンのチームではなく，優勝チームであり，3は誤り。フォトラリーのルールの6個目に携帯電話の使用禁止とあり，スーザンは携帯電話で写真を撮っていないので4は誤り。よって，正解は2。
※イギリス人の話なのでイギリス英語が使われていることに注意。

スーザンのブログ第10文目「気づく」

英：realise ⇔ 米：realize

フォトラリールール6個目「携帯電話」

英：mobile phone ⇔ 米：cell phone / cellular phone

B あなたはイングリッシュデイに参加する予定です。準備として，あなたはユズによって書かれた学級新聞の記事を読んでいます。ユズは昨年イングリッシュデイに参加しました。

南洋の島へのバーチャル遠足

今年のイングリッシュデイは，バーチャルサイエンスツアーに参加しました。冬は天気が悪かったので，スクリーンに投影された火山島の熱帯の景色に私たちは興奮しました。

まず，私たちは島の地形を学ぶためにルートを表示するナビゲーションソフトを使って「車での旅に出」ました。私たちは「車に乗り込み」，その車を担任のリーチ先生がときどき停車させたので，わたしたちは窓の外を見ることができ熱帯雨林についてよく理解することができました。その後，見たことについてリーチ先生に質問しました。

その後，私たちは「海に潜り」海洋生物の多様性について学びました。私たちはライブカメラを通してサンゴ礁を観察しました。リーチ先生は私たちに生物の数を数えられるかどうかを尋ねましたが，あまりに多くの生き物がいました！それから，先生は10年前の海の画像を見せました。私たちがカメラで見たサンゴ礁もダイナミックでしたが，写真の中のサンゴ礁はより生命力に満ちあふれていました。たった10年で全く違って見えました！リーチ先生は人間の活動が海に影響を及ぼしており，私たちが今動かなければ海は完全に駄目になってしまう可能性があると私たちに言いました。

夕方には，私たちは「満天の星空」の下で天文学について学びました。私たちは体育館にテントを張りプロジェクターを使って，天井に臨時のプラネタリウムを作りました。私たちは星座，流れ星，天の川でいっぱいの空に心を奪われました。誰かが最も明るい星の一つを指さしてリーチ先生にあれは地球に近い星である金星ですか？と聞きました。先生は頷いて，人間があまりに多くの人工的な光を作り出したために，私たちの都市の夜空にはほとんど何も見えないことを説明しました。

放課後，家に帰る途中，天気は良くなり今では空に雲ひとつありませんでした。私は月のない空を見上げ，リーチ先生が私たちに話したことが真実であることを理解しました。

問1 ユズの記事にはバーチャルツアーでの出来事について述べている生徒のコメント（1～4）も含まれています。コメントを出来事が起こった順に並べてください。 18 → 19 → 20 → 21

1	2
私はこの島はどれほど危険なんだろうと思いました。私はジャングルで美しい鳥と，巨大な蛇を見ました。	以前はもっと多くの生物がいたことはとても衝撃的でした。私たちは私たちの美しい海を守るべきです。

3	4
体育館にキャンプ場を作るのはある種奇妙でしたがとても楽しかったです！私たちは虫にかまれないので屋外よりもよかったです。	私は天体ショーの間言葉を失いました。そして，私たちはしばしばそれらがそこにあっても気付かないことを理解しました。

順序としては、第2段落第1文より「私たちは島の地形を学ぶためにルートを表示するナビゲーションソフトを使って「車での旅に出」ました」とあり、その過程で美しい鳥や巨大な蛇を見たことがわかる。次に、第3段落第1文より「私たちは「海に潜り」海洋生物の多様性について学びました。」とあり、その過程で同4文から第6文で10年前の写真を見ていることがわかる。第4段落第2文より、体育館にテントを張っている。第4段落第5文より人間が作り出した人工的な明かりによって星がほとんど見えないと説明している。よって、1→2→3→4の順である。

問2 ツアーから、ユズは南の海の島の [22] について学ばなかった。

1　海洋の生態系　　2　夜の空
3　季節の天気　　　4　木と植物

第2段落第2文で「熱帯雨林についてよく理解することができました」とあり、木や植物について学んだことがわかるので、4は正しい。第3段落第1文に「海洋生物の多様性について学びました」とあり、1は正しい。第4段落第1文に「天文学について学びました」とあり、2は正しい。3は本文に書かれていないので誤り。よって、正解は3。

問3 家に帰る途中、ユズは顔を上げ、おそらく夜空に [23] を見たに違いない。

1　流れ星　　　2　ほんのわずかな星
3　満月　　　　4　天の川

第5段落第2文に「私は月のない空を見上げ、リーチ先生が私たちに話したことが真実であることを理解しました」とあり、リーチ先生が話した内容とは第4段落第5文の「人間があまりに多くの人工的な光を作り出したために、私たちの都市の夜空にはほとんど何も見えない」である。「月のない空」とあるので3は誤り、「私たちの都市の夜空にはほとんど何も見えない」のであるから、1・4は誤り。よって、正解は2。

第5段落第2文「理解する」英：realise ⇔ 米：realize

第4問

あなたの大学の英語クラブの部屋はいくつか問題を抱えており、あなたはそれを再設計したいと考えています。下記の記事とクラブのメンバーに配られたアンケートの結果に基づいて、グループディスカッションのための資料を作ります。

何が良い教室を作るか？
ダイアナ　バッシュワース、「教育の動向」の筆者

多くの学校が教室を改善しようとするとき、デザインを決定するためにいくつかのアイディアを持つことは重要です。SIN、すなわち刺激、個別化、自然さという枠組みは教室の設計をするときに役立つかもしれません。

まず、刺激、には2つの側面があります：つまり、色と複雑さです。これは、天井、床、壁、そして室内家具に関係しています。例えば、色が乏しい教室はつまらないかもしれません。一方、教室はカラフル過ぎてもいけません。明るい色は、壁一面、床、窓のカバー、家具のどれかに使うことができます。それに加えて、壁にあまりに多く

のものを掲示することは視覚的に気が散るかもしれません。壁の20～30パーセントは空いた状態にしておくことが推奨されます。

次の枠組みの項目は個別化です。個別化は所有者意識と柔軟性という2つの考慮要素が含まれています。所有者意識とは教室が個人個人に合っていると感じることを指します。例として、生徒の体格や年齢にあった椅子や机を持つこと、収納スペースや生徒の作品やプロジェクトを展示するための場所を提供することなどがあげられます。柔軟性で重要なのは異なる種類の活動を許容する教室を持つことです。

自然さは自然光と人工光の両方の質と量、そして教室の温度に関連します。自然光が過剰だとスクリーンやホワイトボードが見えにくくなるかもしれませんし、光が不足すると生徒は読んだり書いたりすることが難しくなるかもしれません。それに加えて、暑い夏の教室は効率的な学習を促進しません。学校は自然光と人工光の両方と温度を調節することができるシステムを導入すべきです。

自然さは私たちにとって、より身近なものであり、それゆえに優先事項とみなされることが多いですが、その他の要素も同様に重要です。これらのアイディアがプロジェクトを成功に導く手助けになればよいと望みます。

アンケート結果

質問1：あなたの英語クラブの部屋の使い方に合うものを選べ。

部員の数＝38人

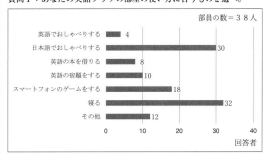

	回答者
英語でおしゃべりする	4
日本語でおしゃべりする	30
英語の本を借りる	8
英語の宿題をする	10
スマートフォンのゲームをする	18
寝る	32
その他	12

質問2：現在の英語クラブの部屋についてどう思うか？
主なコメント

生徒1（S1）：私はプロジェクターのスクリーンとホワイトボードが晴れた日はよく見えません。また、温度を調節する方法がありません。

S2：窓のそばでは、日光で文字が読みにくくなります。部屋の反対側だと十分な光が当たりません。また、本は整理されておらず、壁はポスターで覆われています。私は居心地が悪く感じます。

S3：椅子は私には合わず、小さなグループになって学習するときに机は動かしにくいです。また、英語クラブであるにもかかわらず、多くのメンバーが日本語を話しています。

S4：壁にある外国の絵が私に英語を話したいと思わせてくれます。みんなはソファが好きです。ソファはとても快適なので私たちはよくこの部屋を寝るために使います！

S5：部屋はとても遠いので、私はそこにほとんど行ったことがありません。ほかの部屋は使えませんか？

S6：部屋は灰色が多すぎます。私は好きではありません。しかし、たくさんの日常英語フレーズが壁に貼られているのはいいです！

あなたの話し合いのための資料

部室改善プロジェクト

■SINの枠組み

- SINとは何か　[24]
- SIN＝刺激、個別化、自然さ

■SINとアンケートの結果に基づく推奨デザイン

- 刺激：
  床をカラフルなラグで覆い、[25]。

－ 個別化：

　　家具を交換する。

　　　（車輪付きのテーブル→移動しやすい）

－ 自然さ：

　　26

　　A．窓にブラインドを導入する。

　　B．温度のコントロールを可能にする。

　　C．プロジェクターのスクリーンを窓から離す。

　　D．ソファを壁の近くに置く。

　　E．暗いコーナーにフロアランプを置く。

■話し合うべきほかの問題点

－ 28 のコメントが言及しているように，メンバーの多くは部屋を 27 。どのように解決すればよいか？

－ グラフと 29 のコメントに基づくと，私たちはメンバーが英語を話すモチベーションが上がるように部屋での言語のルールを作るべきか？

－ S5は場所が気に入らないが，部屋を変えることはできない。だからメンバーがもっと頻繁に部屋に来たくなるようにする方法について考えよう。

問1 24 に最も適する選択肢を選べ。

1 教室に適した色を見せるガイド

2 教室での生徒と先生のニーズの優先順位を決めるためのルール

3 私たちが教室の環境について計画するときにしたがうべきモデル

4 教室がどのようにして生徒のパフォーマンスに影響を与えるかのシステム

第1段落第2文に「SIN…という枠組みは教室の設計をするときに役立つかもしれません」とある。「教室の環境について計画する」＝「教室の設計」と考えると，3が適切。よって，正解は3。

問2 25 に最も適する選択肢を選べ。

1 スクリーンをよりよい場所に移動させる

2 それぞれの壁を違う色で塗る

3 棚に本を置く

4 展示しているアイテムを減らす

刺激について書かれた第2段落第6文から第7文に「壁にあまりに多くのものを掲示することは視覚的に気が散るかもしれません。壁の20～30パーセントは空いた状態にしておくことが推奨されます。」とあり，アンケート結果質問2に対するS2のコメントに「壁はポスターで覆われています。」とあるので，壁の掲示物を減らす必要がある。よって，正解は4。

問3 あなたは資料を確認している。あなたは自然さの下の推奨項目に間違いを見つけた。以下のどれを**取り除く**べきか？ 26

1 A　2 B　3 C　4 D　5 E

アンケート結果質問2に対するS4のコメントに「ソファはとても快適なので私たちはよくこの部屋を寝ること

に使います」とある。選択肢Dにあるようにソファを壁の近くに置いてもこの問題が解決できるわけではないし，光や温度の話でもないので自然さの項目に入れるのにもふさわしくない。よって，正解は4。

問4 27 と 28 に最も適する選択肢を選べ。

27

1 から本を借りる

2 簡単に行けない

3 では日本語を使ってはいけない

4 に不安を感じる

5 で昼寝をする

28

1 S1　2 S2　3 S3

4 S4　5 S5　6 S6

アンケートの結果から多くの生徒に当てはまる部屋の使い方は「日本語とおしゃべりする」と「寝る」であり，そのうちアンケート結果質問2のコメントで言及されているのはS4の「ソファはとても快適なので私たちはよくこの部屋を寝ることに使います！」である。よって，正解は 27 は5， 28 は4。

問5 29 に最も適する選択肢を選べ。

1 S1　2 S2　3 S3

4 S4　5 S5　6 S6

「グラフと 29 のコメントに基づくと，私たちはメンバーが英語を話すモチベーションが上がるように部屋での言語のルールを作るべきか？」とあるのでメンバーが英語を話すモチベーションが上がるように部屋での言語のルールを作るべきか考えなければならないような問題点があげられているコメントを選べばよい。アンケート結果質問2のS3のコメントに「英語クラブであるにもかかわらず，多くのメンバーが日本語を話しています」とあり，グラフにも時間の使い方として英語でのおしゃべりよりも日本語でのおしゃべりのほうが7倍以上いるということが示す問題点とも一致している。よって，正解は3。

第5問

あなたは英語のディスカッショングループに所属しており，あなたが話を紹介する番である。あなたは日本の英語雑誌である物語を見つけた。あなたは発表のためのメモを準備している。

マキのキッチン

「いらっしゃいませ」二人の客が彼女のレストラン，マキのキッチンに入ってきたのでマキは言った。マキは父親が病気になった19歳の時に家業に加わった。父親が回復した後，彼女は続けることに決めた。最終的には，マキの両親が引退し彼女がオーナーになった。マキにはおいしい食事をとるためだけではなく，カウンターに座り彼女と話をするために来る常連客が多くいた。彼女の仕事はとてもうまくいっていたが，マキは時折何か違うことをすることを空想していた。

「カウンターに座ってもいいですか？」という声が聞こえた。その声の主は彼女の古い友達のタクヤとカスミだった。カスミがタクヤに数週間前に電話し，マキに会いに行って驚かせるためのアイディアを

思いついていたのだ。

◆◆◆◆◆

タクヤの携帯電話が振動し，カスミという見慣れた名前が彼の目に入った。

「カスミ！」

「こんにちは，タクヤ，あなたを新聞で見たわ。おめでとう！」

「ありがとう。ねえ，先月の高校の20周年の同窓会にいなかったね。」

「そう，行けなかった。私たちが卒業してから20年経つなんて信じられない。実は，最近マキと会ったか聞くために電話をしたの。」

◆◆◆◆◆

タクヤの家族はタクヤが高校生になる少し前にカワナカ町に引っ越してきた。彼は演劇部に入部し，そしてそこでマキとカスミに出会った。3人は親友になった。卒業後，タクヤは俳優になるためにカワナカ町を離れ，一方カスミとマキは町に留まった。マキは大学で勉強したいと決心し，予備校に入学した。一方，カスミは仕事を始めた。タクヤは様々な役のオーディションを受けたが，不合格が続き，彼は辞めてしまった。

実は卒業して1年後，タクヤはカワナカ町に夢破れて帰ってきていた。彼はマキに電話し，そして彼女は彼に同情した。彼はマキが家族のレストランを経営するために大学に入学するという計画を断念したことを知って驚いた。彼が電話したのは彼女の仕事の第一日目だった。なぜか，タクヤはマキにアドバイスせずにはいられなかった。

「マキ，僕はいつも君の家族のレストランが出しているコーヒーを変えるべきだと思っていた。僕はカワナカ町の人々はもっと濃い味を好むと思う。他の銘柄を薦めさせてもらえると嬉しい。」と彼は言った。

「タクヤ，あなたは本当にコーヒーに詳しいのね。あ，私がカフェ・カワナカの横を通ったときに求人募集の看板を見たの。応募するべきだわ！」マキは答えた。

タクヤはカフェ・カワナカに雇われ，コーヒー作りの科学に魅了されていった。彼が働き始めて1周年記念の日に，タクヤはマキのレストランでマキと話をしていた。

「マキ。」彼は言った。「君は僕の夢を知っているかい？」

「コーヒーに関する何かのはずだわ。」

「その通り！自分でコーヒーに関する事業をすることだよ。」

「あなた以上にふさわしい人は想像できないわ。あなたは何を待っているの？」

マキの励ましはタクヤを鼓舞した。彼は仕事を辞め，コーヒー豆の焙煎機を買い，コーヒー豆の焙煎を始めた。マキはレストランに「私たちは自信をもってタクヤのコーヒーをお出しします。」という看板を掲げ，この宣伝はカワナカ町のコーヒーの人気が増加することに貢献した。タクヤはコーヒー豆を売ることで大金を稼ぐことができるようになった。最終的には，彼は自分自身のカフェをオープンし，成功したビジネスオーナーとなった。

◆◆◆◆◆

カスミは新聞を読んでいるとき「タクヤのカフェが観光客をカワナカ町へひきつける」という見出しを見つけた。「誰がタクヤがこんなに成功すると考えた？」カスミは昔のことを思い出しながら心の中でそう思った。

高校の演劇部で，俳優にメイクをするのがカスミの役割だった。彼女は誰よりも上手にメイクをすることができた。マキはこれに気付き，化粧品メーカーのビューテラが販売員を募集している広告を出しているのを見た。彼女はカスミに応募するようにすすめ，卒業後，彼女はビューテラの社員となった。

仕事は大変だった，カスミは一軒一軒化粧品を売りに行った。売れ行きがよくない日は，カスミはマキに電話し，マキはカスミを励ました。ある日，マキはあるアイディアを思いついた。「ビューテラはメイクアップのワークショップをやっているんじゃない？あなたはそっちの方が向いていると思う。あなたは人にメイクの仕方を教えることができるわ。みんなメイクの方法を気に入って，たくさん化粧品を買うわ。」

カスミの会社は彼女がワークショップを行うことを承諾し，ワークショップはヒットした。カスミの売り上げはとてもよく，高校を卒業してから8か月で，彼女は昇進し，イシジマ市という大きな都市に転

勤になった。それから，彼女は着実に出世し今年，ビューテラの副社長になった。

「私はマキがいなかったら副社長にはなれなかった。」彼女は思った。「彼女は私がもがいているときに助けてくれた，でも，私はイシジマ市での仕事に没頭しすぎていて，彼女が予備校を辞めなければならなかったとき，彼女を助けることができなかった。」記事をチラッと見返して，彼女はタクヤに電話することを決めた。

◆◆◆◆◆

「マキは同窓会にいなかった。僕は何年も彼女に会っていない。」タクヤは言った。

「私も同じ。残念だわ。私たちは彼女がいなかったらどうなっていただろう？」カスミは尋ねた。

彼らが罪の意識を伝えるにつれて，会話は静かになった。その後カスミがあるアイディアを思いついた。

◆◆◆◆◆

友人3人で談笑しているときにマキは尋ねた。「ところで，私は2人に会えてすごくうれしいんだけど，どうしてここに来たの？」

「お返しだよ。」タクヤが言った。

「私，何か悪いことした？」マキは尋ねた。

「いいや，反対だよ。君は信じられないくらい人をよく理解することができる。君は他人の強みを見極めて，どのように使えばいいかを教えてくれる。僕たちがその証拠だ。君は僕たちの才能に気付かせてくれた。」タクヤが言った。

「皮肉なのはあなたがあなた自身に同じことができないということ。」カスミが付け加えた。

「僕はイシジマ大学が君にとって理想的だと思う。イシジマ大学は働いている人向けのカウンセリング学位プログラムを提供している。」タクヤが言った。

「月に何回かは大学に行かなければならないけど，私の家に泊まることもできる。それに，タクヤはあなたのレストランのスタッフを見つけるのを助けてくれる。」カスミが言った。

マキは目を閉じてカワナカ町に「マキのキッチン」「マキのカウンセリング」の両方があることを想像した。彼女はそのアイディアが気に入った。

あなたのメモ：

マキのキッチン

あらすじ

マキ，タクヤ，カスミが高校を卒業する。

↓

30
31
32
33

マキがセカンドキャリアについて考え始める。

マキについて

・年齢： 34

・職業：レストランのオーナー

・彼女がどのようにして友人を支えたか：

　　タクヤを励まし，そして， 35 。

　　カスミを励まし，そして， 36 。

重要な場面の説明

・カスミとタクヤは電話で居心地の悪い沈黙を経験した，なぜなら彼らが 37 だからである。

・最後の場面で，カスミはマキについて「皮肉」という言葉を使っている。この皮肉とはマキが 38 ないということだ。

問1 　5つの出来事（1〜5）のなかから**4つ**選び，起こった順に並びかえよ。

$$\boxed{30} \rightarrow \boxed{31} \rightarrow \boxed{32} \rightarrow \boxed{33}$$

1　カスミが会社の副社長となる。
2　カスミがタクヤと連絡をとる。
3　マキが大学の学位をとる。
4　マキが家業を始める。
5　タクヤが彼自身で仕事を始めるよう励まされる。

カスミとタクヤとマキは同級生である。第4節第4段落第3文に「彼女は着実に出世し今年，ビューテラの副社長になった」とあり，同第5段落第2文「記事をチラッと見返して，彼女はタクヤに電話することを決めた」とあるので，カスミが会社の副社長となったのは今年であり，その後タクヤに電話することを決めたので，1→2である。カスミがタクヤに電話をしたのが卒業して20年後の同窓会の次の月である。

マキは最後に大学の学位を取るようすすめられているだけであり，まだ大学の学位をとってはいない。よって，3は誤り。

第1節第1段落第2文に「マキは父親が病気になった19歳の時に家業に加わった」とあり，タクヤが彼自身で仕事を始めるよう励まされたのは，タクヤがカフェ・カワナカで働き始めて1周年のときであり，タクヤがカフェ・カワナカで働き始めたのはマキが家業に加わるよりも後であるから，4→5である。

4・5は卒業後数年の出来事であるのに対し，1・2は卒業後20周年の同窓会が行われた今年の出来事である。よって，4→5→1→2の順になる。

問2 　$\boxed{34}$ に最も適する選択肢を選べ。

1　30代前半　　2　30代後半
3　40代前半　　4　40代後半

現在は20年後の同窓会の次の月であるから，マキの年齢は30代後半である。よって，正解は2。

問3 　$\boxed{35}$ と $\boxed{36}$ に最も適する選択肢を選べ。

1　製品を人々に紹介した
2　成功するビジネスアイディアを提案した
3　ビジネスのための設備を購入した
4　より大きな都市への移動を提案した
5　成功に必要なスキルを教えた

第3節最終段落第3文に「「私たちは自信をもってタクヤのコーヒーをお出しします。」という看板を掲げ，この宣伝はカワナカ町のコーヒーの人気が増加することに貢献した。」とあり，看板を通してタクヤのコーヒーを人々に紹介していることがわかる。よって，$\boxed{35}$ に入るのは1。

第4節第3段落マキの発言に「ビューテラはメイクアップのワークショップをやっているんじゃない？あなたはそっちの方が向いていると思う。あなたは人にメイクの仕方を教えることができるわ。みんなメイクの方法を気に入って，たくさん化粧品を買うわ。」第4節第4段落第1文に「カスミの会社はワークショップを行うことを承諾

し，ワークショップはヒットした。」とあり，マキがカスミにワークショップの提案をし，それが成功したということがわかる。よって，$\boxed{36}$ に入るのは2。

問4 　$\boxed{37}$ に最も適する選択肢を選べ。

1　成功について話し合いたくない
2　長い間話していない
3　友人をもっと理解しなかったことを後悔している
4　マキは彼らの成功に嫉妬していると思っている

第5節に「彼らが罪の意識を伝えるにつれて，会話は静かになった」とあり，第4節最後のカスミの発言「彼女は私がもがいているときに助けてくれた，でも，私はイシジマ市での仕事に没頭しすぎていて，彼女が予備校を辞めなければならなかったとき，彼女を助けることができなかった」がこの罪の内容である。マキが予備校を辞めなければならないときにそれを理解しなかったことに罪の意識を感じている。よって，正解は3。

問5 　$\boxed{38}$ に最も適する選択肢を選べ。

1　違うことに挑戦するのが好きで
2　彼女自身の才能に気づいて
3　彼女に欠けている能力を理解して
4　夢を追いかけたいと思って

第6節のタクヤの第2発言「君は信じられないくらい人をよく理解することができる。君は他人の強みを見極めて，どのように使えばいいかを教えてくれる。僕たちがその証拠だ。君は僕たちの才能に気付かせてくれた」カスミの第1発言「皮肉なのはあなたがあなた自身に同じことができないということ」から，他人の才能に気づかせることはできるが，自分の才能に気づくことができないということである。よって，正解は2。

第6問

A　あなたの英語の先生はこの記事をあなたに割り当てました。あなたは短い話をするためのメモを準備しなければなりません。

時間の認識

「時間」という言葉を聞いたとき，おそらく時間，分，秒がすぐに思い浮かぶだろう。しかし，19世紀後半，哲学者のアンリ・ベルクソンは普段人々がどのようにして，時計で計測された時間（**時計時間**）として時間を経験していないかについて説明した。人間は時計時間を計測するための既知の生物学的メカニズムを持っていない，だからその代わりに精神的なプロセスを使う。これは，**心理的時間**と呼ばれ，誰もが認識の仕方は異なる。

宿題を終わらせるのにどれくらいかかったか聞かれたとしたら，おそらく正確にはわからないだろう。あなたは思い返し，推測をするだろう。1975年の実験では，参加者は単純な形か複雑な形のどちらかを一定時間見せられ，記憶するよう指示された。その後，彼らはどれくらいの時間そ

の形を見ていたか尋ねられた。答えるために，彼らは**回顧的計時**と呼ばれる精神的プロセスを使った，それは，記憶から拾い集めた情報を基に時間を見積もるものである。複雑な図形を見せられた参加者は時間を長く感じ，単純な図形を見せられた参加者はその逆の経験をした。

　心理的時間を計測するもうひとつのプロセスは**予測的計時**と呼ばれるものである。それはあなたが何かをしながら積極的に時間を記録しようとするときに使われる。思い出された情報の量を使う代わりに，活動している間に時間に払われた注意のレベルが使われる。いくつかの研究によると，参加者は課題を完成させるのにどれくらいの時間が必要か推測しながら課題を行った。より課題に集中することが要求される精神的な活動をする人々は実際よりも時間が短く感じた。より単純な課題を行った参加者はより長く感じられ，待機している，あるいは何もしていない参加者は最も長く感じられた。

　感情の状態も時間の感覚に影響を与える。例えば，コンサートを楽しむあまり，時間を忘れることがある。そして後になって，瞬く間に何時間も過ぎてしまっていることに驚く。これを説明するために，しばしば「楽しい時間はあっという間に過ぎる」と言う。退屈な時には逆のことが起こる。活動に集中するよりも，時間に注目しているのだ。時間がとてもゆっくり過ぎるように感じるので，退屈が終わるのを待つことができない。恐怖もまた時間の認識に影響を与える。2006年の研究によると，60人以上の人々が初めてスカイダイビングを体験した。高いレベルで不快に感じている人々はスカイダイビングに費やした時間を実際にかかった時間よりもずっと長く感じた。

　心理的時間の流れ方もまたライフステージによって異なるようだ。こどもたちは絶えず新しい情報と出会い，新しい経験をする，そしてそのことがそれぞれの日を忘れられない日にし，思い出す時により長く感じさせる。また，誕生日や旅行のように予定されたイベントは，楽しみにして待っているので時間はゆっくりと過ぎる。多くの大人にとって，知らない情報にはめったに出会わず，新しい経験も頻繁ではない，だからそれほど精神的な集中が要求されず，それぞれの日はそれほど記憶に残らないようになる。しかし，このことはいつも当てはまるとは限らない。転職や引っ越しなどのような劇的な変化が起こると，日常は揺さぶられる。このような場合，人々の時間の経過はこどもの時間と同じように経過する。しかし，一般的に言うと，時間は私たちが成熟するにつれて加速していく。

　心理的時間の知識は，退屈への対処を助けるかもしれないので，私たちの日々の生活に役に立つ。私たちが精神的に集中せず，時間について考えているときは時間がゆっくりと経過するので，本を読むなどのより魅力的な活動に切り替えることで，退屈を和らげ，時間が速く経過することを助けることができる。「楽しい時間はあっという間に過ぎる」という言葉を次に聞いたとき，あなたはこれを思い出すだろう。

あなたのメモ．

時間の感覚

段落ごとの概要
1. 　39
2. 　回顧的計時
3. 　予測的計時
4. 　40
　➤スカイダイビング
5. 　年齢の影響
　➤成長するにつれて時の流れは速くなる，しかし　41　。
6. 　実践的なヒント

聴衆を助けるための私のオリジナルの例
A. 回顧的計時
　例：　42
B. 予測的計時
　例：　43

問1　39　と　40　に最も適する選択肢を選べ。

　1　生物学的メカニズム　　2　感情の影響
　3　記憶の種類　　　　　　4　ライフステージ
　5　進行中の研究　　　　　6　時間の類型

　段落単位の概要なので，第1段落及び第4段落に書かれている内容を選べばよい。

　まず，第1段落第2文に「時計時間」，第4文に「心理的時間」という時間の類型が書かれている。よって，39　に入るのは6。

　次に，第4段落のスカイダイビングについての記述を見ると，第4段落第10文に「高いレベルで不快に感じている人々はスカイダイビングに費やした時間を実際にかかった時間よりもずっと長く感じた」とあり，感情が時間の認識に影響を与えることが書かれている。よって，40　に入るのは2。

問2　41　に最も適する選択肢を選べ。

　1　どんな年齢であっても，生活の大きな変化は時間の経過を遅くしがちである
　2　年齢にかかわらず，生活の大きな変化は時間の速度を速くしがちである
　3　大人の生活の小さな変化は時間の経過を遅くしがちである
　4　こどもの生活の小さな変化は時間の速度を速くしがちである

　第5段落に年齢による影響について書かれている。第2文に「こどもたちは絶えず新しい情報と出会い，新しい経験をする，そしてそのことがそれぞれの日を忘れられない日にし，思い出す時により長く感じさせる。」とあり，第6文から第7文にかけて「転職や引っ越しなどのような劇的な変化が起こると，日常は揺さぶられる。このような場合，人々の時間の経過はこどもの時間と同じように経過する。」とある。よって，大きな変化「major lifestyle change

＝drastic change」によって，こどもの時の流れと同じように，すなわち，ゆっくりと経過することがわかる。よって，正解は1。

問3　[42]に最も適する選択肢を選べ。
　　1　クラスメートからのメッセージを予測すること
　　2　母親の電話番号を記憶すること
　　3　今日どれくらい働いたかを思い出すこと
　　4　明日会議があることを覚えていること
　「回顧的計時」の例として適当なものを選ぶ。回顧的計時とは第2段落第5文より，「記憶から拾い集めた情報を基に時間を見積もるものである」とあり，今日どれくらい働いたかを思い出すことは働いた記憶から拾い集めた情報を基に時間を見積もるものであり，回顧的計時と言える。よって，正解は3。

問4　[43]に最も適する選択肢を選べ。
　　1　これまでどれくらいジョギングを続けてきたかを推測すること
　　2　バスケットボールチームのサマーキャンプのスケジュールを組むこと
　　3　駅でテニスのコーチとばったり出くわすこと
　　4　最後に行った温泉への家族旅行について考えること
　「予測的計時」の例として適当なものを選ぶ。予測的計時とは，「何かをしながら積極的に時間を記録しようとするときに使われ」るものであり，ジョギングをしながらどれくらいの時間続けてきたかを推測することがこれにあたる。よって，正解は1。

B　あなたは以下の科学のウェブサイトの文章を使って，科学クラブのための発表の準備をしている。

唐辛子：人生のスパイス

　チリチキンに入っている赤いスパイスの小さなかけらは素敵な彩りを添えるが，ほんのすこしでもそれを噛むと口の中が火の中にいるようにピリピリすることがある。これを好む人もいれば，この痛みを避けたい人もいる。しかし，一方でワサビをつけた刺身を食べることができる場合もある。このことは，辛さの正体はなんなのか，そして，トウガラシとワサビの違いはどこから来るのか，という疑問を生じさせる。

　甘味，塩味，酸味とは異なり，辛さは味ではない。事実，私たちは辛い物を食べているとき，実際には熱さや辛さを味わってはいない。私たちがトウガラシとワサビを食べて感じる辛さは違う種類の化合物に由来している。トウガラシはカプサイシンという油のようなより重い分子から辛さを得ている。カプサイシンは口の中に焼けるような感覚を長く残す，なぜなら，カプサイシンがTRPV1と呼ばれる受容体を刺激するからだ。TRPV1はストレスを誘発し，私たちに何かが口の中をピリピリさせていることを伝える。興味深いことに，トウガラシの種類によって辛さの幅は広く，そのレベルは含まれているカプサイシンの量に

よって決まる。それはスコヴィル・スケールによって測定され，スコヴィル・ヒート・ユニット（SHU）とも呼ばれる。SHUは50-200SHUの甘くてマイルドなシシトウガラシから，最大2,200,000SHUに達するカロライナ・リーパーまでの幅がある。

　ワサビはトウガラシではなく根と考えられていて，カプサイシンを含んでいない。したがって，ワサビはスコヴィル・スケールでランク付けされていない。しかし，人々はワサビの辛さをスコヴィル・スケールの下限近くの1000SHU付近のトウガラシの辛さと同程度だとされている。トウガラシの辛さに耐えられないのにワサビ風味の食事を食べることができる人がいる理由は，ワサビに含まれる辛味成分の密度が小さいからである。ワサビに含まれている分子は簡単に蒸発し，私たちがそれを食べた時，辛さが鼻に抜ける。

　トウガラシを食べることが私たちの健康にいい影響を与えることがあり，カプサイシンの利点について多くの研究がされてきた。人の体の中でカプサイシンがTRPV1の受容体を活性化させる時，ケガからストレスや痛みを経験した時と同じようなことが起こる。奇妙なことに，カプサイシンは痛みを取り去ることもある。科学者はTRPV1がトウガラシに長時間さらされると活性を失い，一時的に痛みを和らげることを発見した。それゆえに，カプサイシンを含むスキンクリームは筋肉痛になった人に役立つかもしれない。

　トウガラシを食べるもう一つの利点は，代謝を促進することである。ある研究者グループがカプサイシンと体重に関する90の研究を分析し，辛い食べ物を食べるとき，人々は食欲が減退することを発見した。辛い食べ物は心拍数を増加させ，より多くのエネルギーを筋肉に送り，脂肪をエネルギーに変える。近年，ワイオミング大学の研究者たちがカプサイシンを主成分とする減量薬を作った。

　トウガラシは食品の安全にもつながると考えられており，それがより健康的な生活につながることがある。食品が冷蔵されていない環境に置かれたままにされると，微生物が増殖し，それを食べると病気を引き起こすかもしれない。研究によるとトウガラシに含まれているカプサイシンや他の化学物質は抗菌作用を持っており，微生物の成長を遅らせ，または止めることができる。その結果として，食べ物はより長持ちし，食中毒は少なくなった。これは，なぜ暑い気候に住む人々がより多くのトウガラシを使う傾向にあり，そしてそれゆえに，繰り返しさらされることで辛い食べ物へのより強い耐性がある傾向にあることを理由づけるかもしれない。また，過去，冷蔵庫が存在するよりも前には，彼らはより涼しい気候に住む人々よりも食中毒になりにくかったようである。

　トウガラシは健康面で利点があると考えられる，しかし，体への悪影響がある可能性もあるのではないか？高いスコヴィル・スケールのトウガラシは大量に食べると，身体的な不快感を引き起こすことがある。世界でもっとも辛いト

ウガラシを短時間でいくつか食べた人からは，胃のむかつき，下痢，手のしびれ，心臓発作に似た症状を経験したことが報告されている。1,000,000SHUのゴーストペッパーは，それに触れたら肌にやけどを負わせることさえある。

　辛いにも何人かの人々が辛い食べ物を食べた後に感じた不快感はすぐに，たいていは数時間で，消えてしまう傾向にある。いくつかのネガティブな副作用にもかかわらず，辛い食べ物は世界中の人々の間で人気なままであり，食卓に豊かな風味を添えている。覚えておいてほしいのは，辛い食べ物を食べることは安全だが，食事に入れるトウガラシの量について気を付けたほうがいいかもしれないということである。

発表のスライド：

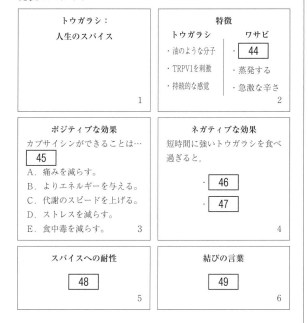

問1　スライド2のワサビの一番目の特徴は何か？　44
　　1　焼けるような味　　2　火のような感覚
　　3　持続する感覚　　4　軽い化合物
　　スライド2のトウガラシの特徴は「油のような分子」，本文第2段落第4文ではさらに詳しく「油のようなより重い分子」とされている。これに対し，ワサビは本文第3段落第4文に「辛味成分の密度が小さい（＝軽い）」とある。よって，正解は4。

問2　スライド3に見られる**誤り**はどれか？　45
　　1　A　　2　B　　3　C
　　4　D　　5　E
　　スライド3に書かれているのはカプサイシンのポジティブな効果である。まず，本文第4段落第3文に「カプサイシンは痛みを取り去ることもある」とあり，Aは正しい。次に，第5段落第1文に「トウガラシを食べるもう一つの利点は，代謝を促進することである」とあり，Cは正しく，同第3文「辛い食べ物は心拍数を増加させ，より多くのエネルギーを筋肉に送り，脂肪をエネルギーに変える」

とあり，Bも正しい。さらに，第6段落第3文～第4文に「トウガラシに含まれているカプサイシンや他の化学物質は抗菌作用を持っており…その結果として…食中毒は少なくなった」とあり，Eは正しい。
　よって，本文に書かれていないDが誤りである。よって，正解は4。

問3　スライド4に当てはまる選択肢を選べ。（順序は問わない）　46　・　47
　　1　有害な細菌を活性化するかもしれない。
　　2　胃痛を経験するかもしれない。
　　3　手の感覚がなくなるかもしれない。
　　4　指が燃えているように感じるかもしれない。
　　5　鼻が痛み出すかもしれない。
　　短時間に強いトウガラシを食べ過ぎるとどうなるのかを選ぶ問題。第7段落第3文に「胃のむかつき（＝胃痛）」「手のしびれ（＝手の感覚がなくなる）」とある。よって，正解は2と3。

問4　スライド5に入るスパイスへの耐性に関し推測できることは何か？　48
　　1　トウガラシへの耐性が高い人々は食事に使うスパイスに注意を払っている。
　　2　ワサビへの耐性が高い人々はトウガラシのネガティブな効果を恐れている。
　　3　トウガラシへの耐性が低い人々はそれらの辛さに慣れることができる。
　　4　ワサビへの耐性が低い人々は高いSHUレベルに耐えることができない。
　　第6段落第5文に「これは，なぜ暑い気候に住む人々がより多くのトウガラシを使う傾向にあり，そしてそれゆえに，繰り返しさらされることで辛い食べ物へのより強い耐性がある傾向にあることを理由づけるかもしれない」とあり，辛い食べ物に対する耐性が先天的なものではなく，辛い食べ物に繰り返しさらされることによって獲得されるものであることが推測される。よって，正解は3。

問5　スライド6に最も適切な言葉を選べ。　49
　　1　怖がらないで。辛い食べ物を食べることはあなたに自信をつけるだろう。
　　2　次にチリチキンを食べるときは，その辛さはほんの一瞬しか残らないことを思い出してほしい。
　　3　スパイスの好みは個性が大きな役割を果たしているので，心配しなくてよい。
　　4　不運なことに，ワサビへの耐性の低さを治癒する方法はない。
　　5　辛い食べ物を誰かが勧めてきたら，利益があることを思い出してほしい。
　　辛い食べ物と自信との関係についてはどこにも書かれておらず，1は誤り。第2段落第5文に「カプサイシンは口の中に焼けるような感覚を長く残す」とあるので，2は誤り。スパイスの好みと個性との関係についてはどこにも書かれておらず，3は誤り。ワサビの耐性の低さを治癒する

方法についてはどこにも書かれておらず，4は誤り。第7段落にトウガラシの利点について書かれており5は正しい。よって，正解は5。